Strategy for the Global Market

In the twenty-first century, the global community constantly strives to bring structure and order to the world through strategic means. From the highest levels of governments and militaries to multilateral institutions, NGOs, and corporations, a strategy for the future of a company, region, country, or even the world is tantamount to success. Yet few understand what strategy actually is and how it can be developed, planned, and implemented.

Strategy for the Global Market combines a fundamental study of the theory of strategy with its practical applications to provide a new approach to the global emerging market. Due to the technological transformations in communications and transportation, and the birth and development of both the global community and the global marketplace over the past twenty years, the world's population and corporations are in much closer contact with their counterparts across the globe than ever before. This has led to increasing competition and even rivalries. Understanding the strategic environment, as well as solving problems either through amicable means or conflict, requires the powerful instrument of strategy to remain efficient and to triumph.

Features of this book include:

- Methodology and practical recommendations for all stages of developing and implementing strategy.
- A comprehensive guide with explanations and descriptions, for the preparation and orderly compilation of all necessary strategy documents.
- Real-world examples taken from corporate, government, and military strategizing practices in emerging market countries and the global marketplace.

This book should be on the desk of every national, regional, and military leader, corporate executive, manager, and student of strategy.

Dr. Vladimir Kvint has been a professor of strategy, management systems and international economics at Fordham University, New York University's Stern School of Business, American and LaSalle Universities, and Babson College and serves as chair of the Financial Strategy Department in the Moscow School of Economics at Moscow State University, Russia. He is a member of the Bretton Woods Committee and the Russian Academy of Sciences, a US Fulbright Scholar, and a well-established strategic advisor.

Drawing on 45 years of experience in global markets, gained as a student, teacher, and active advisor across sectors and regions, Vladimir Kvint offers a wise and powerful theory of business strategy and provides a roadmap to practitioners which, if followed with discipline, will inform tactics and lead to long term success.

Sharon P. Smith, *President, University of Pittsburgh at Greensburg, USA*

This pathbreaking book studies the concept of strategy, surveying its development from ancient times to the present and showing how it is basic to both economic growth and the quality of life. Strategists, Kvint explains, work to find new perspectives and to project new scenarios into the future. This original, deep, and practical book is a must-read for all of us who want to understand modern economies.

Edmund S. Phelps, *the 2006 Nobel Laureate in Economics and Director, Center on Capitalism and Society, Columbia University, USA*

Kvint does a superb job of clearly explaining business strategy and the global market environment. The book is very timely and it is well suited for executives in strategic implementation as well graduate students in business, economics, finance or international affairs. Strategy practitioners and their firms will gain tremendous insights from this excellent explanation of the concepts.

Y. Joseph Ugras, *Dean of the College of Professional and Continuing Studies, LaSalle University, USA*

Strategy for the Global Market

Theory and Practical Applications

Vladimir Kvint

Routledge
Taylor & Francis Group
NEW YORK AND LONDON

First published 2016
by Routledge
711 Third Avenue, New York, NY 10017

and by Routledge
2 Park Square, Milton Park, Abingdon, Oxon OX14 4RN

Routledge is an imprint of the Taylor & Francis Group, an informa business

Library of Congress Cataloging in Publication Data
A catalog record for this book has been requested

ISBN: 978-1-138-89210-1 (hbk)
ISBN: 978-1-138-89212-5 (pbk)
ISBN: 978-1-315-70931-4 (ebk)

Typeset in Bembo
by Cenveo Publisher Services

To all strategists who have and will improve the world.

Remembering, not withstanding, that the true worth of a man is to be measured by the objects he pursues.

Marcus Aurelius Antonius Augustus, Stoic philosopher
and Roman Emperor (121–80 CE), *Meditations*.

How wonderful it is that nobody need wait a single moment before starting to improve the world.

Anne Frank, diarist whose life was ended in Bergen-Belsen
concentration camp at age 15 (1929–45), *The Diary of a Young Girl*.

Contents

List of Plates

Color plates are located between pp. 205 and 206.

List of Figures

List of Maps

List of Tables

About the Author

Dr. Kvint's 45 years of scholarly economic and strategic studies have been focused on the development and practical application of both the theory of strategy and the theory of the global emerging market.

Coupled with his experience solving real-world strategic problems, and his deep knowledge of the rules of strategic thinking, he brings a unique perspective to the important issues facing strategists around the world. Prior to his academic experience, he worked in the non-ferrous metals industry above the Arctic Circle in Norilsk—the world's most northern city. He received his mining-electrical engineering degree in Siberia and, later, a Ph.D. in Economics from the Plekhanov Moscow Institute of National Economy, as well as a Doctor of Science in Economics from the Institute of National Economy of the Russian Academy of Sciences. In 1988, he received a lifetime professorship of political economy and, while living in the United States, was elected to one of the world's most prestigious think tanks, the Russian Academy of Sciences, as a lifetime Foreign member. He is a member of the Bretton Woods Committee in Washington, DC, the World Academy of Art and Science, and he is a 2001 US Fulbright Scholar.

After teaching at the Vienna Economic University in Austria, Dr. Kvint was a professor of Management Systems and International Business at Fordham University in New York, where he taught for about 15 years. He served as a professor in International Economics at Babson College and American University in Washington, DC, and as an adjunct professor of strategy at NYU's Stern School of Business and, most recently, at LaSalle University. In 2007, he was elected as chair of the Financial Strategy Department of Moscow State University's Moscow School of Economics. He also teaches courses on the theory of strategy and quality of life at the North-West Institute of Management of the Russian Presidential Academy.

Dr. Kvint was a director of emerging markets at Arthur Andersen in New York and at Metromedia International Telecom, and served as a global head of emerging markets at one of the largest architectural and planning firms, RMJM, until December 2012. He was a consultant for several global companies, including General Electric and Transamerica, among other major corporations.

He has received honorary doctorates from several universities in the United States, Russia, Albania, Ukraine, Kazakhstan, and Kyrgyzstan. His published articles and books on economics, strategy, management systems, and the political economy of emerging markets are widely translated. His analysis of strategy has appeared on CNN and in *Forbes*, the *Harvard Business Review*, *Bloomberg Business*, the *New York Times*, the *Los Angeles Times*, *The Times* (London) and *The Independent* (London). He lectures on strategy and the global emerging market in Europe, including at the London School of Economics,

Imperial College (London), and the Universities of Edinburgh, Antwerp, Leuven, and Free Brussels, as well as major universities in Eastern Europe, Russia, Turkey, Brazil, Uruguay, and the United Arab Emirates. In the United States, he has presented his strategic studies at leading universities including Harvard, Columbia, Georgetown, George Washington University, the Wharton Business School, and the University of California, Los Angeles.

He has provided advice to governments of several developed and emerging market countries, including Russia, the US, Albania, Bahrain, Brazil, Bulgaria, Taiwan, Turkey, Ukraine, and the United Arab Emirates, among others.

Acknowledgments

It is always difficult to start and complete any manuscript. The author always needs, strategically speaking, a triggering event. The crucial starting point for me in embarking on and finalizing this book were the numerous conversations on strategy with Nobel Laureate Edmund Phelps and his wife Viviana during the summer of 2013, a dialogue that continued throughout the writing of this manuscript. I am very grateful to both of them. I am also very thankful to my friends Valery Makarov, Alexandr Nekipelov, Vladimir Shamakhov, Joseph Ugras, and Murad Alimuradov for encouraging me to write and finalize this book. I especially have to express my gratitude to two very talented young scholars, Sarah Davis and Greig Roselli, who spent most of their time with me polishing and putting the finishing touches on the manuscript, so that my very kind editors at Routledge, Sharon Golan and Jabari LeGendre, had no choice but to accept it. The perennial difficulty for the first reader of a manuscript is to peruse it while it is still raw, and for this I would like to give credit to Elizabeth Schmermund for her improvements and thoughtful suggestions, as well as Derek Lucarz, who gave a careful reading of the first chapter. This book contains the most up-to-date statistics, reflected in the numerous tables and figures, and for this I am very grateful for my research associates Murad Alimuradov, Andrey Beletsky, Victor Chendulaev, Daria Gavrilina, Ekaterina Ivanova, Alexey Karpov, and Maxim Savin.

Time flies by quickly—for a quarter of a century I have lived, worked, researched, and written books and articles in the United States. And throughout this time, absolutely all my publications have had the same first readers: my closest friends—my two talented daughters—Liza and Valeria.

To write a book over a long period of time requires not only a hard-working attitude and discipline, but also inspiration. And for inspiring me, I must thank my lovely and gifted friend Varia Rykova, who was more concerned about my approaching deadline than I. It would be wrong for me not to mention that throughout the time I have dedicated to writing on strategy, I have always felt the support of my mother, who passed away more than 30 years ago. Finally, without the unflagging support of all my friends who have accompanied me on my life's journey, I could not have accomplished the objectives I set out for myself. And for this—thank you to everyone I have not mentioned in this acknowledgement or accidentally may have missed.

Keynote Definitions

Strategy is the system of finding, formulating, and developing a doctrine that will ensure long-term success if followed faithfully.

Strategy is wisdom with a defined vector to success and with an assessment of resource limitations.

The **Strategist** is a wise, disciplined, and optimistic professional with a strategic mindset, a vision of the future, and intuition. He or she is armed with a strategizing methodology to utilize broad and deep knowledge of entities and a comprehensive understanding of the most influential objective trends.

A **Strategic Management System** is a managerial process of strategy formulation, implementation, and functioning aimed at establishing or improving and enlarging the strategizing object's priorities according to its fundamental values and interests.

Formal strategy is the final product of strategizing that takes into consideration previously updated forecasts, public values, and interests, and which consists of a defined mission statement, long-term vision (including priorities), objectives, and goals. This long-term strategy must also include a particular scenario to be implemented via the strategic plan and a strategic management system that monitors its implementation.

The **Global Marketplace (GMP)** is a strategic system of economic relationships between consumers, companies, governments, and multilateral institutions from around the world that allows real-time cooperation and competition regardless of location.

An **Emerging Market Country (EMC)** is a society transitioning from a dictatorship to a free market–oriented economy, with increasing economic freedom, gradual integration within the GMP and with other members of the global emerging market, an expanding middle class, improving standards of living, social stability, and tolerance, as well as an increase in cooperation with multilateral institutions.

The **Global Emerging Market (GEM)** is a new economic, strategic, and political phenomenon of the world economy and the global marketplace, encompassing emerging market countries and their regional blocs, which, despite varying geopolitical characteristics, are united by comparable levels of risk and developing free-market infrastructure. These factors of the GEM unify vectors of development of emerging market countries toward economic freedom and global integration, attracting international economic and business cooperation and competition.

The **Global Order** is a political and economic system of cooperation that emerges organically or as a result of the strategic influence of multilateral institutions, superpowers, and other nations, though not necessarily by cooperative means. The global order provides customary procedures, allowing the avoidance or mitigation of conflict while promoting stability and sustainable development by offering countries, regional blocs, and corporations a means to negotiate disputes among themselves and to develop mutually beneficial solutions to global challenges.

The **Global Business Order** is a subsystem of the global order that provides a relatively stable framework for cooperation between businesses with global, regional, and national institutions, allowing the predominantly evolutionary development of the global marketplace. It is a set of customs by which corporations compete and cooperate with other businesses in the global marketplace, exploiting opportunities offered by it without violating human rights, national interests, or regional and global standards and agreements.

Foreign Direct Investment (FDI): The roots of the economic strategy nature of FDI stem from competitive opportunities abroad: a workforce of appropriate quality, available capital, effective management systems, technology, and know-how—all of which lead to a high level of faster returns, with a manageable level of risk, as outlined by a comprehensive feasibility study and strategy.

Risk of Foreign Direct Investment is an innate characteristic of cross-border business related to the threat of predictable or unpredictable negative changes of the external environment or of a company's internal resources, with manageable and unmanageable consequences leading to potential losses.

List of Abbreviations

AAI	Arthur Andersen International
ADIA	Abu Dhabi Investment Authority
ADR	American depository receipts
AIG	American International Group
APEC	Asia-Pacific Economic Cooperation
ASEAN	Association of Southeast Asian Nations
BCE	Before the Common Era
BCIU	Business Council for International Understanding
BIS	Bank of International Settlements
BISIP	Bank of International Settlements Investment Pool
BOP	bottom of pyramid
BRIC	Brazil, Russia, India, and China
BRICS	Brazil, Russia, India, China, and South Africa
BTU	British thermal unit
CAFTA	Central American Free Trade Agreement
CARICOM	Caribbean Community
CBP	Customs and Border Protection Agency
CE	Common Era
CEO	chief executive officer
CESCE	Compañía Española de Seguros de Crédito a la Exportación
CIS	Commonwealth of Independent States
COMESA	Common Market for Eastern and Southern Africa
COO	chief operating officer
COSO	Committee of Sponsoring Organizations
CPI	consumer price index
C-TPAT	Customs-Trade Partnership against Terrorism
ECOWAS	Economic Community of West African States
EMC	emerging market country
EMTA	Emerging Markets Traders Association
EU	European Union
FATF	Financial Action Task Force
FDI	foreign direct investment
G7	Group of Seven
G8	Group of Eight
GDP	gross domestic product
GDR	global depository receipts

GE	General Electric
GECF	Gas Exporting Countries Forum
GEM	global emerging market
GMP	global marketplace
GNI	gross national income
GNP	gross national product
GUAM	Georgia, Ukraine, Azerbaijan, and Moldova
GWP	gross world product
HDI	Human Development Index
HIPC	heavily indebted poor country
IAEA	International Atomic Energy Agency
IBRD	International Bank for Reconstruction and Development
ICC	International Chamber of Commerce
ICE	Immigrant and Customs Enforcement
IDA	International Development Association
IDR	international depository receipts
IFC	International Finance Corporation
IJV	international joint venture
IMD	International Institute for Management
IMF	International Monetary Fund
IPO	initial public offering
IRS	Internal Revenue Service
ISO	International Organization for Standardization
IT	information technology
LOI	letter of intent
MBA	Master's in business administration
Mercosur	also known as: Mercosol; a regional bloc of countries from the Southern Cone of South America
MIGA	Multilateral Investment Guarantee Agency
MSCI	Morgan Stanley Capital International
MU	memorandum of understanding
NAFTA	North American Free Trade Agreement
NASDAQ	National Association of Securities Dealers Automated Quotations
NATO	North American Treaty Organization
NGO	non-governmental organizations
NYSE	New York Stock Exchange
OAA	Osaka Action Agenda
OECD	Organization for Economic Cooperation
OPEC	Organization of the Petroleum Exporting Countries
OPIC	Overseas Private Investment Corporation
OTCBB	Over The Counter Bulletin Board
OTSW	opportunities, threats, strengths, and weaknesses
P-EMC	pre-emerging market country
PERT	Program Evaluation and Review Technique
PPP	purchasing power parity
R&D	research and development
RBC	Royal Bank of Canada
S&P	Standard and Poor's

SAFTA	South Asia Free Trade Agreement
SAR	special administrative region
SDR	special drawing right
SWOT	strengths, weaknesses, opportunities, and threats
TCO	Tengizchevroil
TPES	Total Primary Energy Supply
UNCTAD	United Nations Conference on Trade and Development
UNIDO	United Nations Industrial Development Organization
USSS	United States Secret Service
USTR	Office of the United States Trade Representative
WBG	World Bank Group
WTO	World Trade Organization

Preface

After 45 years of studying and writing on the theory of strategy and the practical experience of strategizing corporate, regional, and national progress in several developed and emerging market countries, I decided it was time to summarize my knowledge and experience on the theory of strategy, the theory of the global emerging market, and its practical applications. It required effort to synthesize and comb through piles of notes and analytical work on these topics, but I had the opportunity to do it and finally present this book to readers due to the support of Routledge. This monograph is a continuation of my previous book, also published by Routledge: *The Global Emerging Market: Strategic Management and Economics*. The main difference between the two books is in their focus. The first one concentrated on the theory of the global emerging market and its strategic application. The book which you have now in your hands focuses mainly on strategy itself: its theory, methodology, and strategizing practice. In this work, I do my best to prove that the general theory and methodology of strategy can be applied to any strategizing object, including world, national, and regional economies, and corporations, and can be useful in strategizing the universe of the life of any individual. Strategy actually begins with an evaluation of how individual values are reflected in the interests and priorities of the strategizing object.

The fledgling ideas for both of these books were born in the permafrost above the Arctic Circle in Siberia, where I began my professional life. As a metal worker and underground mining electrical engineer, my mind seemed to constantly return to my very first professional conundrum—why do workers with radically different levels of productivity, integrity, and initiative receive the same compensation? Later in my career, when I was promoted to the deputy head of a large high-tech company, I was frequently discouraged from creating substantial differences in compensation for employees by distinguishing between those who worked hard and showed initiative and work ethic, and those who simply counted down the minutes for the work day to end.

My career began 15 years after Stalin's brutal dictatorship and 5 years after Khrushchev's "thaw," a period when Stalin's cult of personality had been largely dismantled and Soviet leaders were regularly visiting capitalist countries for the first time. One of the greatest benefits of this relatively less brutal period in Soviet history was the availability of several books on economics and business, translated from English, German, and Japanese, such as Paul Samuelson's *Foundations of Economic Analysis*, Jay Wright Forrester's *Industrial Dynamics*, and John H. Hutchinson's *Management Strategy and Tactics*. These books, together with the conversations of a few Russian economists like Nobel Laureates Wassily Leontief and Leonid Kantorovich, as well as Leonid Abalkin, Abel Aganbegyan, Alexandr Granberg, and Valery Makarov, were the most important intellectual role models of my early academic career. All of them, later in life, became my colleagues and friends.

One young economic-mathematician, Anatoli Alexeiev, helped to build in my mind a mathematical bridge between economics and technology. Despite the Soviet Union's backward economic system, its economic research capabilities were actually quite strong. In fact, Russian universities produced three Nobel Laureates in economics. With the aid of these books, and the insight gained from the experience of my surrounding social and business life and the preparation of my first Ph.D. dissertation, I began to analyze the success and failures of centralized economic systems. By the end of the 1970s, I found what seemed to be the fundamental flaw of any dictatorship: oppressive systems inevitably produce goods of lower quality than those of free countries due to a disregard for economic freedom. The Soviet dictatorship had an established system of planning and (often brutal) control, but lacked a means of positive motivation—one of the most important functions of any management system. This is the cause of the production of inferior goods, wide-scale environmental pollution, lower productivity, and the subsequent lower quality of life, poverty, and misery found in all totalitarian regimes.

Coincidently, after I came to this conclusion, I was invited to work at the Russian Academy of Sciences, the premier Russian think tank established by Peter the Great in the eighteenth century. For a number of reasons—chiefly the secretive voting system used by its members—the Academy remained practically the only free institution in the Soviet Union (a position it still holds even though ironically the capability of the Academy was substantially diminished in 2013 by a decision of the Russian government to remove research institutes from its organizational structure). At the Academy, I began to calculate when—not if—the Soviet empire would disappear. Enriching the trends through analyzing the unofficial—i.e., undoctored—economic statistics, I tried to figure out how long the Soviet Union could survive. This was impossible to do without analyzing the world economy and the international political environment. At the beginning of the 1980s, when Prime Minister Margaret Thatcher and President Ronald Reagan, two ardent anti-communist leaders, came to power, they increased pressure on the Soviet dictatorship, primarily by exponentially increasing military expenses. It was clear to me that the regime's centralized economy could no longer bear the military expenses needed to maintain the strategic balance with the western world that was so important to Soviet leaders. In 1982, when Chancellor Helmut Kohl came to power with the goal of unifying Germany and, concurrently, Poland, the Soviet Union's largest satellite, began to experience intense tension from an internal democratic movement, the future became clear to me. I predicted that "by 1992, there will be no country called the Soviet Union," which was the exact phrase later published in my op-ed piece in the *New York Times*.[1] For roughly two years prior to the publication of this piece, I tried to publish an article with the following blunt title: "Russia Should Quit the Soviet Union." I sent a draft of the article to several publications, all of which either thought it was a joke, something for the distant future, or could not even conceptualize the difference between the Soviet Union and Russia, which were generally used as synonyms in the West at that time. The publication of this article was further hindered by the fact that I was forbidden to travel outside the Soviet Union to the free capitalist world. With great difficulty, I was eventually able to skirt this issue. Thanks to great friends like Karl zu Schwarzenberg, at that time president of the International Helsinki Federation for Human Rights, I found myself in Vienna in December 1988, discussing with him the history and future of our world. It is interesting to look back on that time; we both made several predictions, but neither of us could have anticipated that he would one day become a citizen of the free, noncommunist country of the Czech Republic—a state that did not yet exist—and eventually a senator, minister of foreign affairs, and deputy prime minister.

It is often easier for people to foresee the future of countries than that of their own lives. Even Nostradamus, who saw centuries into the future, could not anticipate the death of his first wife and children. Finally, during my first trip to the United States, in 1989, I met with three great visionaries and journalists, a combination that is rather rare—Malcolm Forbes, Jim Michaels, and Laury Minard, the then leading editors of *Forbes Magazine*. They understood my perspective and, on February 5, 1990, my article entitled "Russia Should Quit the Soviet Union" appeared as a cover story in *Forbes*. At that time it was called a "revolutionary proposal." It is always the case for strategists and forecasters, when they propose their ideas, that the overwhelming majority says they are wrong and their predictions are not realistic. When they do indeed become reality, it is natural for people to forget their initial skepticism.

When in late December 1992 the Soviet Union did disappear, Jim Michaels wrote in the sideline of *Forbes*, "When few thought the Soviet empire could ever break up, Vladimir Kvint predicted and advocated the withdrawal of the Russian Republic from the U.S.S.R...Kvint's articles in *Forbes* on events in the Soviet Union have been close to prophetic."

The reason that I mention all of the above is to show not only how difficult it is for strategists to enrich the right vision and strategic scenario, but also how it is of equal importance to stick to one's own strategy. Only time can prove if a strategy is correct. I made this conclusion after almost four decades of experience not only as a professor, but as an executive and strategic advisor to companies from two worlds: developed and emerging market countries. Once a strategy is proven correct, do not look for applause from the crowd, but search out new strategies. The right strategy can be based on great intuition, but can seldom work without theory and deep knowledge of the issue at hand. And I hope that from this point of view, my book will be helpful for readers' strategic observations and essential for practical use.

Vladimir Kvint
February 5, 2015
New York City

Note

1 Kvint, V. (1990). "Opportunities in Soviet Disintegration." *New York Times*. October 28. Retrieved from www.nytimes.com/1990/10/28/business/forum-opportunities-in-soviet-disintegration.html

Part I

Strategy

Theory and Methodology

1 Uncovering Philosophical Roots for a Theory of Strategy

Practical wisdom secures us power over others.[1]

Aristotle (384–322 BCE)

In the world of knowledge the idea of the good appears last of all, and is seen only with an effort.[2]

Plato (427–347 BCE)

For to be in a state of meditation is to be finished, while to exist is to become.[3]

Søren Kierkegaard (1813–1855)

Interrelationship between Philosophical and Strategic Thoughts

The importance of true strategic thoughts and strategy itself is often neglected or ignored in the modern world. While de facto strategic thought has been used for hundreds and thousands of years in military and governmental capacities, the knowledge and concrete understanding of the phenomenon of strategy didn't exist. This is why the genealogy of strategy is explored later in the chapter. Strategy still remains surprisingly underestimated, misused, or misunderstood within certain powerful corporations, governments, and military bodies. Even successfully navigating one's personal life requires a strategic mindset and rules of strategy development and implementation. It is my argument and contention that aspects important to this strategic mindset and strategizing practice can be taught. This book aims to provide the philosophical roots and historical background to the theory of strategy, as well as important strategic considerations for modern entities, in order to bring strategy to the forefront of corporate, governmental, and military decisions—where it must remain in order to ensure success in the complex global community. Major failure in all of these spheres of humankind's activities can be attributed to the prevalent attention to tactical and operational decisions and routine, instead of focusing on the enrichment of long-term strategic solutions and vectors to success.

Beginning with the works of early strategists, such as Roman leader and author Frontinus and Emperor Maurice (539–602 CE), the theory of strategy has sporadically developed over the past 2,000 years in leaps and bounds; however, strategy is still very much a work in progress. In this book, I attempt to systematize the building blocks of classical, modern, and contemporary works to ground strategic theory and practice. Strategists and leaders must seriously study, analyze, and comprehend the different categories of strategic thought and their practical vision must be perfected during the processes of strategy development and implementation. In order to do this, it is necessary to incorporate major issues within ancient philosophical and classical analytic military works into our modern-day decision-making processes in any field of leadership. The theory of strategy, like any other theory, must be learned from the beginning. Modern and upcoming leaders can learn a great deal from these ancient works written during strategy's birth, and from a sustained inquiry into the genesis of strategy in the ancient world up to now.

While there are certain major distinctions between philosophical thought and strategic thought, the pair together forms a complementary whole. In order to explain the importance of philosophical study in successful strategy development, I must turn to my own experience, growing up and maturing under the influence of dialectical materialism, which was the basis of Marxism. At that time, my intellectual worldview was above all influenced by the works of Aristotle, Spinoza, along with other metaphysicians, but also by the philosophical idealism of Hegel and the ancient philosopher Philo of Alexandria. My intellectual development within these philosophical traditions, as well as my now 40 years of experience in strategy development and implementation—strategizing—led to my conclusion that a strategist's way of thinking should form a complete and undivided consciousness in substantial agreement with a philosophical worldview.

Strategists aim for a holistic and interconnected world perception; in this way, both a great depth of vision and an evaluation of environmental realities and facts unite both philosophers and strategists. However, philosophers are concerned with truthful statements that are verified by facts and, in this way, are somewhat distinct from strategists, who are more concerned with the future reality yet to be determined. For strategists, facts cannot be ignored, but they hold less importance than for philosophers. Of course, correctly understanding events through strategic thinking can, to a lesser extent, validate selected strategic perspectives and scenarios. Strategists can ignore current facts since they must ultimately look into the future, where current events can be forgotten, considered not related at all, or hold less influence on future "realities" than previously envisioned. Strategists work to establish new strategic perspectives, priorities, and scenarios where current facts do not exist and future facts will remain mostly mysterious, even to strategists with a long-term vision. Most future facts at the period of strategy development cannot be known; this is why strategists and philosophers differ in how they analyze and make conclusions regarding these facts, and in the way these facts are incorporated into their findings. Strategists need facts, which always belong to the past, for analysis, and not necessarily for inclusion in any formal strategic scenario.

Strategic and philosophical thoughts also originate from slightly different traditions and schools with various levels of maturity. No one science is as mature as philosophy. Strategy as a theory, in contrast to the majority of other sciences, has not yet gone far beyond its infancy. Philosophical ideas typically begin with abstraction and involve few, if any, practical examples, except for the field of ontology, which is much closer to strategy than any other philosophical analysis. The initial observation of Plato (427–347 BCE) that the world is not perfect is purely an ontological one, which for me is a statement of his interpretation of facts. In contrast to other philosophical schools, strategic thought is primarily rooted in concrete examples used to prove strategic accuracy. As Napoleon (1769–1821) said:[4]

> Tactics, evolutions, and duties may be learned in treatises, but the science of strategy is only to be acquired by experience, and by studying the lessons of the campaigns, of the great captains. These lessons have been to keep one's forces united; to leave no weak part unguarded; seize with rapidity on important points; and to inspire terror

> at the reputation of your arms, which will at once maintain fidelity and secure subjection.[5]

In this text, Napoleon explicitly recommends that leaders not only make conclusions through theory, but through their strategic experience, as well as through studying other leaders' campaigns. Unlike Napoleon, philosophers generally focus less attention on practice, often purposefully preferring theoretical thought over the practical application of their ideas. Confucius (551–479 BCE) wrote: "By three methods we may learn wisdom: first by reflection, which is noblest; second by imitation, which is easiest; and third by experience, which is the bitterest."[6]

At first glance, these two geniuses—Napoleon and Confucius—directly contradict each other. Confucius reflects on wisdom and how to obtain wisdom, while Napoleon speaks about strategy. A deeper analysis shows that, in fact, they are speaking about distinct characteristics of the same phenomenon. Both discuss different qualities of strategists and strategies, but address the same subject. By combining their two ideas, we can establish a soft definition of strategy:

***Strategy* is wisdom with a defined vector to success and with an assessment of resource limitations.**

From this point of view, a strategist's way of thinking and categorizing is closer to an ontologist, who studies fundamental rules and principles of reality, both economic and social. Strategy as a science, unlike philosophy, has developed less rules and categories in its terms, theories, methods, and methodology. My studies in strategy and philosophy have led me to conclude that some of the major categories of ontology, like time and space, are also predominant in strategy, both as a science and a practice. From this point of view, the philosophical roots of strategy can be found in the works of Plato (and his ideas inherited from Socrates), Aristotle, Parmenides, and, later, Descartes, Spinoza, Heidegger, and other metaphysicians working on rationalism, empiricism, and organicism. These roots are all anchored in ontology.

It is even more theoretically interesting and practically important to analyze the thoughts of great philosophers and strategists who lived in the same historical periods and in the same parts of the world. Some of the earliest recorded sources of this kind are the works of the masterful strategist Sun-Tzu (544–496 BCE) and the philosopher Confucius, who both lived in the sixth and fifth century BCE. Naturally, there is a danger in analyzing works that are over 2,500 years old and written in an ancient language. There is also the problem of the original text. Sun-Tzu's works were compiled and rewritten about 400 years after he lived by Sima Qian (145–86 BCE), known as the Grand Historian. Translations of ancient works also vary depending on the translator. For instance, in Sun-Tzu's *The Art of War*, Ralph D. Sawyer and Mei-Chun Lee Sawyer translate a line in Chapter 1 about the five major qualities of the commander during wartime: "The general encompasses wisdom, credibility, benevolence, courage, and strictness."[7] This same line was translated by John Minford in 2002 to read more poetically:

> Command is
> Wisdom,
> Integrity,
> Compassion,
> Courage,
> Severity.[8]

This example illustrates how difficult it is for scholars to find the correct meaning in the writings of great ancient philosophers and strategists. In the above quotes, one ancient word is translated in two different ways: "credibility" by Sawyer and "integrity" by Minford. These words are similar, but they do have different meanings, especially for strategists. Credibility is related to how people perceive others in terms of truthfulness, which is one of the most important rules and principles for strategists. Integrity represents internal qualities of virtue. Credibility comes with integrity. It is an error to conflate the two terms. If a strategist agrees to develop a strategy to produce weapons of mass destruction, there must be credibility in their work. If the strategy goes against the strategist's own moral code, he should not agree to develop such a strategy. If he does agree, he has to put aside the issue of moral integrity and work only towards credibly implementing the strategy. These are just some of the pitfalls facing strategists who study ancient texts in order to apply their words to contemporary understandings and practices. In Chapter 2 of this book, a discussion of Rule 8 will return us to this complex issue.

Nonetheless, this quote references what are known as the cardinal Confucian virtues: humanity (here as compassion), wisdom, and sincerity (here as integrity). Even from this short quotation, it is clear that deep strategic thoughts are always drawn in to the same categories that provide the basis of philosophical processes of thought and a deep understanding of reality. Moreover, it is even more interesting to note that Aristotle, who lived about 150 years after Sun-Tzu and Confucius in a very different part of the world, and who obviously did not know about them, mentions the same basic categories as well. Even with very different backgrounds and practice, they all identify ideas using the same categorical concepts. Their relationship to their states' and regions' military practices unifies all three of these geniuses. Many of Aristotle's thoughts that we consider strategic most probably originated from teaching Alexander the Great (356–323 BCE) and analyzing his victorious practice ("praxis"). Sun-Tzu, by comparison, analyzed using his military years as a commander. Confucius most likely also analyzed the rules and experiences of the principalities in which he lived. Confucius, who occupied different positions in government, lived during a time when several dynasties were simultaneously at war. These warring factions must have informed his strategic analysis. Thus, certain brilliant philosophers and de facto strategists understood the complex and important link between their two domains of thought.

Despite the fact that most philosophers do not make distinct recommendations for strategy, their ideas communicated through philosophical tractates, or treatises, can still enrich strategic practice. Modern strategists can improve their practical experiences and expertise through analyses of historical and contemporary leaders' work and achievements. If practitioners, statesman, military generals, and business executives study the experiences of famous successful military, political, and business leaders, then theoretical strategists will create methodological recommendations from both theoretical works and their practical applications. In addition to the above-mentioned *Art of War* translated by Ralph Sawyer and John Minford, I read an old Russian translation by the late Professor Nikolai Konrad, a member of the prestigious Russian Academy of Sciences. Konrad translated the title of Sun-Tzu's book as *A Tractate of Military Art,* alluding to the philosophical nature of the work. After reading all three of these translations, the title that makes the most practical sense to me would be *A Strategy of Power.* In today's world, the book is not often used in warfare, but is highly regarded in the business domain. The continuing legacy of Sun-Tzu's work comes from its application not only for business and military leaders, but also for anyone interested in strategic power. It is a useful text for any individual who wants to direct his or her personal path.

Outstanding leaders like Alexander the Great and Napoleon honed their distinguished ability by first studying theoretical works or listening to great teachers. Only after first studying did their military experience improve. The father of Alexander the Great, Phillip II of Macedon, could not find a better teacher for Alexander than the greatest philosophical mind of all time, Aristotle. Napoleon often remembered his teachers at the *Ecole Militaire* (Military Academy) with fondness.

To continue studying the epistemological roots of strategic thought and its appropriate translations from ancient languages, it is useful to address related issues in sacred texts. Even the most read texts in the world that in essence discuss the subject of strategy have multiple translations, some of which use the term *strategy* and some of which do not. For example, the Old Testament, a sacred text for both Jewish and Christian religions and a substantial text for Islam as well, describes strategic issues. In 2 Kings 18, Hezekiah, the legendary king of Judah, sends a representative to the king of Assyria with a message that emphasizes his "strategic" advantage. The Assyrian king is impressed and sends his field commander to ask, "You say you have strategy and military strength—but you speak only empty words. On whom are you depending, that you rebel against me?" (2 Kings 18:20).[9] Even then, a strong leader was considered equally important to military power and strategy! However, this sentence reads differently in the seventeenth-century King James English translation: "Thou sayest, (but they are but vain words,) I have counsel and strength for the war. Now on whom dost thou trust, that thou rebellest against me?"[10] One translator uses the word *strategy*, while the other uses "counsel." However, we can deduce that, at least in this instance, "counsel" represents sound strategic advice. Otherwise, there would be no reason for Hezekiah to mention it alongside—and even, in context, as more important than—military power. As modern readers, it is important to assess these translations to the best of our abilities while paying attention to the context in which related terms are used.

Theoretically speaking, Hezekiah was correct to put strategy (or strategic advice) ahead of direct military power. Sun-Tzu similarly said:

> Therefore, to gain a hundred victories in a hundred battles is not the highest excellence; to subjugate the enemy's army without doing battle is the highest of excellence.
>
> Therefore, the best warfare strategy is to attack the enemy's plans, next is to attack alliances, next is to attack the army, and the worst is to attack a walled city.[11]

Gaius Julius Caesar (100–44 BCE) said something resembling Sun-Tzu's idea (according to translator John Carter) almost 500 years later, and most probably without any knowledge of either his works or the words of Hezekiah:[12] "To win by strategy is no less the role of a general than to win by arms."[13] In 1869, W.A. McDevitte and W.S. Bohn translated this same work by Julius Caesar, using the word *tactic* and not *strategy*. The term *tactic* is often described as a component of the larger term *strategy* (although the two are very different in terms of time horizon and ways of thinking), which is a plan that can encompass many tactics, although these definitions once again become unstable when using translations of ancient texts. In fact, in Book I of *Civil Wars* (50 BCE), from which this quote is excerpted, there is no mention of "strategy" or "tactic" at all. Caesar wrote: "cur denique fortunam periclitaretur? Praesertim cum non minus esset imperatoris consilio superare quam gladio."[14] Caesar employs the word *consilio*, which represents a "victorious idea" (of a strategic or tactical nature), and not about the use of physical force by the commander. Furthermore, Caesar could not have even used the term *stratagem* because Sextus Julius Frontinus (40–103 CE) coined this term about 100 years later in the first century CE.[15]

Sun-Tzu, Hezekiah, and Caesar all came to the same conclusion: Great strategic ideas (derived from the term *counsel*) are more powerful than armies and more destructive than victories on the battlefield. Even in contemporary times, strategy is more powerful than basic economic factors in national economies with enormous natural resources. This is the result of talent, wise and educated leaders, and the use of professional strategists' recommendations. This idea is similarly found in several sacred texts: for example, in the Qu'ran, God gives advice to Mohammed to seek counsel from his companions, "O Mohammed, when you are going to do any work, or when you are confronted with an important matter, confer with your companions."[16] Sun-Tzu became the first known professional strategist and adviser (to his ruler), and was eventually appointed head of the army by the leader of his principality. Because of the successful implementation of his ideas, Sun-Tzu's text survives as a practical guide to strategy. Many others, like Hezekiah and Caesar, consistently relied on advice from others in making their own decisions.

This is in contrast to Stalin, who relied on his own sense and knowledge, which was obviously not enough to build a correct and winning strategy—at least at the beginning of the war. Stalin had no vision to predict Hitler's advances. The same problem of not taking counsel seriously also arose when Anna Ioannovna, the niece of Peter the Great who became empress of Russia in 1730, succeeded to the Russian throne. Upon her ascension, the nobility—through the Russian Privy Council—issued strict conditions for her to rule the country as a constitutional monarchy. These conditions stated that, in order to keep the country cohesive, whole, and prosperous, the empress had to rely on advice. She initially agreed, but immediately upon succession to the throne, she publicly ripped up the document and became a free-wheeling absolute monarch, driven by her own will and influenced by her lover. As a result, her ten-year reign was not very successful.

Any leader with a strategic mindset and a wealth of experience understands how to use strategic ideas, and not extensive use of weapons, capital, natural resources, or labor, to win battles or positions of power. Roman statesman and commander Sextus Julius Frontinus dedicated the first two chapters of his obscure book *Stratagems* to the power of the essentially strategic plan; in these chapters, he states that the most important component of strategy is keeping one's strategy concealed while finding out the opponent's plan. In order to understand the difference between strategy and "stratagems," it is best to go to the source of the latter term, Frontinus:

> Let them remember to discriminate between "strategy" and "stratagems", which are by nature extremely similar. For everything achieved by a commander, be it characterized by foresight, advantage, enterprise, or resolution, will belong under the head of "strategy," while those things which fall under some special type of these will be "stratagems." The essential characteristic of the later, resting, as it does, on skill and cleverness, is effective quite as much when the enemy is to be evaded as when he is to be crushed.[17]

The translation of this quotation from Frontinus into English is too liberal with its usage of the word *strategy*. The translator erroneously attributes the word *strategy* to Frontinus, which he never used directly. Frontinus did not know this term or at least did not use it in his writings.[18] Nonetheless, in 2013, Winged Hussar published *Stratagems* with the subtitle "The Roman Strategy at War."[19]

For the particular description of these two terms, listed above as "strategy" and "stratagems," Frontinus used the Greek στρατηγικῶν and στρατηγημάτων. A precise translation of these terms into English would be "generalship" and his own term *stratagems*. From my perspective, "generalship" has some elements of strategy within its definition. But it is mostly the high-level operational and tactical activity in the chain of command. Of course, the translator has some contextual basis for using this term *strategy*, but according to my findings, this term in its adjectival form was only born centuries later during the Byzantine era. It is one more example of how one should be wary of any translation that may take away from the author's original meaning and word choice.

Frontinus developed and systematized his own stratagems into twelve categories:

1. On concealing one's plans
2. On finding out the enemy's plans
3. On determining the character of war
4. On leading an army through places infested by the enemy
5. On escaping from difficult situations
6. On laying and meeting ambushes while on the march
7. How to conceal the absence of the things we lack to supply substitutes for them
8. On distracting the attention of the enemy
9. On quelling a mutiny of soldiers
10. How to check an unseasonable demand for battle
11. How to arouse an army's enthusiasm for battle
12. On dispelling the fears inspired in soldiers by adverse omens.[20]

The majority of these twelve categories are mandatory for any strategist and any strategic analysis. Nobody questions today that one's strategy must be kept confidential from enemies or competitors. It is clear from Frontinus (as from the earlier works of Sun-Tzu and Caesar) how important it is to know the plans of your adversaries, who hope to topple Stratagems 1 and 2. Any strategist also always tries to develop a strategic plan while avoiding difficult situations (Stuatagem 5). Strategic motivation is one of the three major strategic management functions (Stratagems 11 and 12). Or, as Stratagem 8 states, "distracting the attention of the enemy" or a competitor. Some of these stratagems, like numbers 9, 11, and 4 (to a degree), have more tactical characteristics than strategic. Nonetheless, Frontinus could not underline differences between strategy and stratagems because stratagems by essence belong to the core of strategy. On the other hand, *generalship*, the term he actually uses in the text rather than *strategy*, has little strategic meaning. This is why Frontinus discriminates between "generalship" and "stratagems," and why it is useless to distinguish between "strategy" and "stratagems."

After searching without success for the actual term *strategy* in the works of Caesar, Frontinus, and other early authors, I finally turned to Emperor Maurice, the Byzantine ruler from 582 to 602 CE, as one of my last hopes of finding any usage of the term in sources dated earlier than the nineteenth century. This proved to be difficult, as we do not know the original title that Maurice intended for his work, today known as *Strategikon*. The earliest known copy of this treatise was written in the tenth century about 300 years after Maurice's reign, and was commissioned by the Byzantine Emperor

Constantine VII without mentioning Maurice's title.[21] The original title in Ancient Greek was "Ούρβκίου τακτικά στρτηγικά," which contains the words *tactic* and *strategic*. The librarian of Cardinal Barberini created the first version of this work under the name *Strategikon* in 1664, more than 1,000 years after the death of Maurice. Once again I did not succeed in finding any earlier usage of the term *strategy* before Maurice used the term *strategic* as an adjective.

Though the etymology of the word is unknown,[22] descriptions and applications of strategy are present throughout *Strategikon*. Book II of this treatise, titled "The Calvary Battle Formation," contains the meaning of strategy (not the term itself) in a sentence that rightly connects the category of "strategy" to two of its major, predominant qualities: time and space.[23] Maurice states, "Strategy makes use of times and places, surprises and various tricks to outwit the enemy with the idea of achieving its objectives even without actual fighting. Strategy is essential to survival and is the true characteristic of an intelligent and courageous general."[24] At the beginning of Book VII, the author differentiates between "tactics" and "strategy," stating: "A ship cannot cross the sea without a helmsman, nor can one defeat an enemy without tactics and strategy."[25] Later in the same section, the translator uses the term *generalship* as a synonym for strategy, a practice I have noticed with other authors and translators as well.

The authorship of *Strategikon* is sometimes called into question. For me, the detailed attention given to economic resources as well as the maintenance of well-stocked and supplied troops help to prove that Maurice is the author. Many other notable contemporary authors mistakenly do not pay such close attention to these economic and organizational issues. This detail belongs more to a statesman than to military leaders. Maurice started his military career as a successful general at an early age, leading a victorious campaign against the Sassanid Persian Empire. After he became emperor, he continued his military triumphs against the Sasanians, as well as the Avars, Balkans, and other tribes found in modern Italy and North Africa. His great military battles, followed by many years of state rule, were the experiential basis for his treaty. More than one and a half millennia later, his book is still relevant. In the following example, Maurice combines his experience as a field commander and a statesman to provide useful advice for even modern-day military strategists. Before a direct confrontation with an enemy, Maurice recommends:

> To try simply to overpower the enemy in the open, hand to hand and face to face, even though you might appear to win, is an enterprise which is very risky and can result in serious harm. Apart from extreme emergency, it is ridiculous to try to gain a victory which is so costly and brings only empty glory.[26]

Throughout *Strategikon*, Maurice demonstrates that his strategic conclusions are drawn not only from his vast experience, but also from the achievements of many ancient strategic giants, such as Hannibal. In the way that he evaluates victories via strategy, Maurice is similar to Sun-Tzu, King Hezekiah, and Caesar.

Without a doubt, the works of Frontinus and Emperor Maurice belong to the fundamental beginnings of the theory of strategy's development, which is still, almost 2,000 years later, "under construction." Strategists and leaders have to seriously inquire into and comprehend the categories of "stratagem" and their historical precedents in order to perfect modern processes of strategizing. Strategists and leaders have to be prepared to be efficient strategizers, especially because of the new conditions developing and dominating the knowledge economy, the new phenomena of the twenty-first century—the global marketplace and the global community (which will be discussed later in the book and especially in Chapter 5). For any success, resources that are often in short supply are almost always needed, but resources are still less important than efficient strategy. In an integrated global marketplace (GMP), a modern phenomenon that will be defined in the next section, any artificial self-isolation—or autarchy—cannot increase the efficiency of an economy or a population's standards of living in any country. Effective strategy must always be oriented to the integration of nations within the global community and the cooperation of companies on the GMP. Moreover, in the process of this integration, the role and scale of natural resources is declining in comparison with the wide use of quickly updated technological improvements and innovations. This means strategic thought is more important than ever before, even if it is not as prevalent as it must be.

Development of Strategic Ideas into Theory and Methodology

As we have seen, strategy as an idea has been used for most of recorded history, and at least since Ancient Greece and China. However, the term *strategy* has gone through considerable changes in definition over the past 200 years and has outgrown its original connotations. If you ask a hundred people to define strategy, they will most likely respond in a common theme: it is about critical issues and it concerns the future. But the majority (including some military and business leaders and statesman) will also make strategy a synonym for many other concepts that either preceded or are derivatives of strategy, contain elements of strategy, or may not be related to the actual essence of strategy at all. Most people use the word *strategy* to define all operational or practical decisions and activities, and, often, subtle distinctions between operational, tactical, and strategic decisions are lost. Moreover, professionals in the theory and practice of the decision-making process, as well as in all fields of human activity, also quite often use the word *strategy* incorrectly. Many professionals incorrectly use terms like *forecast*, *prediction*, *strategic plan*, and *strategic vision* as synonyms for strategy.

The problem with the early writers on issues related to strategy—like Sun-Tzu, Thucydides, Frontinus, and other authors prior to Generals Carl von Clausewitz (1780–1831) and Baron Antoine-Henri Jomini (1779–1869)—is that translators too freely use the term *strategy* when the original authors did not use this term at all. The ancient books on strategy were certainly talking about the essence of strategy, but never used the term outright. Emperor Maurice used the word *strategic* in his writings, as demonstrated earlier in this chapter. In the work of another Byzantine emperor, Leo VI the Wise (866–912), who seems to have substantially borrowed ideas and other elements from Emperor Maurice's text, you can also find the word *tactic*, which he used to describe some strategic issues. This emperor had authorized 60 books, found today in Greek under the unified title *Basilika*. One of these books, *Tactica,* describes tactical policy, interspersed with strategic issues. This is more proof that tactic is a much older applied science (Thucydides's use of this term is discussed later in this chapter) than strategy. However, the concept of strategy can still be found, to some extent, in these early works, even if it is not accurately defined. Emperors Maurice and Leo the Wise used the word *strategikon* and, before them, Frontinus implemented the term *stratagems*. Both terms are better translated and understood as "generalship." This translation should relate very well to today's notion of "management," but

I would argue that the word *generalship* is not *strategy* in the fullest meaning of these two terms. This has been a long-standing "disagreement" among many different translators.

Originally, the term "strategy" was used to describe the actions of a military commander making serious military decisions. Later, the term began to be used to describe the decisions made by any high-ranking military officer, from a general decision in a long-term war to the reallocation of forces in a particular battle. During the twentieth century, strategy took on a new definition for business and corporate long-term decision-making processes.

In the middle of the twentieth century, business executives reignited a newfound interest in historical strategic books. The works of Sun-Tzu and Miyamoto Musashi (1584–1645), a seventeenth-century Japanese samurai, became particularly popular. Strategists started to develop two distinct and usually separate fields: business strategy and military strategy. By the end of the twentieth century, theory and strategic practices were divided into three main categories: military strategy, business strategy, and state strategy, often called "grand strategy." This last term primarily addresses the strategy of national and regional governments, outside of the military, who protect and help develop national values and state strategic interests. This is why newfound interest in the old concept of strategy brought modern readers to very old, and from time to time almost forgotten, books. In the nineteenth century, several military commanders and officers wrote memoirs that described large-scale decision-making methods and the development of a long-term vision and, in essence, strategy.

It is our loss that most of the ancient great military commanders did not leave behind written records of their vision or descriptions of their strategies. The materials we do have were mostly written generations after these leaders lived. For example, Quintus Curtius Rufus, who wrote extensively about Alexander the Great, completed his works over 400 years after Alexander. There are some notable exceptions, such as Gaius Julius Caesar. In the modern era, Napoleon Bonaparte also left behind his military legacy in his letters, memoirs, and in his *Military Maxims*, even though he did not write a systematic work on strategy.

The military historian Theodore Ayrault Dodge (1842–1909) once named Hannibal "the father of strategy."[27] This is somewhat inaccurate for two reasons. For one, the chronology is incorrect; both Sun-Tzu and the great historian Thucydides (460–395 BCE) wrote rules and recommendations that could be defined as strategic 150 to 250 years before Hannibal (247–between 181 and 183 BCE). Alexander the Great also demonstrated brilliant strategy roughly more than 100 years before Hannibal. Second, we do not have any writings by Hannibal himself.

There are several books from the middle to late nineteenth century that describe the methodology of strategy. The most profound of these books is *On War* by Carl von Clausewitz, which was published posthumously in 1832. General Antoni-Henri Jomini wrote another historic work dedicated to strategic issues around the same time as Clausewitz. In their written words, it is possible to observe the strategic vision of leaders who could implement their strategic knowledge into practice.

Baron Jomini was initially a Napoleonic general (and was awarded both of these titles—baron and general—by Napoleon himself) before becoming a Russian general in 1813. He was a well-regarded commander and teacher at the Academy of the General Staff of Russia. His second book, *Précis de l'art de la guerre: Des principales combinaisons de la stratégie, de la grande tactique et de la politique militaire,* was published in 1822 in French.

A Russian edition was released in 1840 and an English version came out in 1862 with an erroneously translated title, *The Art of War*.

In the 1840 Russian edition, Jomini defined strategy as "all thoughts combin[ing] the theater of war."[28] The definition includes thirteen factors:

1. Determining the particular location for the theater of war.
2. Selecting and establishing a permanent base of activity.
3. Defining a subject of activity, both for the offense and the defense.
4. Choosing a decisive location for the theater of war.
5. Establishing fronts of activity and the defensive lines.
6. Choosing the roots of activities, which lead to the front of activity.
7. Selecting the best strategic lines for a particular activity. This includes different maneuvers to unify all lines related to this activity.
8. Timing all activity and strategic reserves.
9. Correctly maneuvering the troops.
10. Storing supplies close to the armies' movements.
11. Considering fortresses as a strategic location for protection of an army, or as a barrier in defensive tactics.
12. Enforcing army camps and bridges to these camps.
13. Sabotaging separate army units.[29]

After defining these factors, Jomini differentiated between "strategy" and "tactic." Immediately following his definition of strategic elements, he wrote, "[T]he second branch of military art is tactic. It unifies the movement of the army on the day of a battle and the different configurations of military branches during offenses."[30] Jomini also separated a third component from both strategy and tactic: logistics, or the practical movement of an army.

Baron Jomini's division of strategy, tactics, and logistics was innovative for his time and has led to disputes and discussions among scholars and professionals familiar with his work. On the division of strategy, tactics, and logistics, Jomini wrote:

> [M]any pointless disputes took place regarding the limits of these three different branches. According to my definition, strategy is an art that allocates military activities over a geographical space but still keeps them united in a theater of war. Tactic is the art of fighting within that space while also having an escape route … this space is a territory of 12–15 km.[31]

This additional definition of strategy perfectly unifies all the essential elements of strategy, and clearly discriminates strategy from tactic and logistics.

Jomini is one of the first modern authors to use the term *strategy*—not *stratagem* like Frontinus, or *strategikon* like Emperor Maurice. After all my research, I have concluded that the term *strategy* should be credited together to Maurice and Napoleon and to Jomini and Clausewitz. Napoleon, Jomini, and Clausewitz wrote roughly during the same period and come from similar military backgrounds. The books of Jomini and Clausewitz can be considered alongside the legacies of leaders such as German Field Marshal Count Helmuth von Moltke (1800–1891) and Chancellor of the German Empire and Prussian Minister President Prince Otto von Bismarck (1815–1898), among others.

No one before Jomini so clearly delineated the meaning of strategy from tactics and logistics. This contribution is difficult to underestimate. Yet in modern strategic studies he is relatively unknown compared to Clausewitz or Helmuth von Moltke. It is my hope that this book will bring a little more recognition to this theorist and practitioner of strategy.

Due to increased interest in strategy during the twentieth and twenty-first centuries, scholars and writers began to use the works and writings of ancient historians in their strategic studies. In fact, these books are almost entirely dedicated to recording history with only indirect descriptions of strategic practices as they relate to various wars. While it is most certainly helpful to use ancient authors and historical texts to illustrate strategic ideas and thoughts, using such works as strategic textbooks will mislead readers. The best example of this kind of book is Thucydides' *History of the Peloponnesian Wars*. Reading carefully through this book, I could not find one sentence with the term *strategy* in it; obviously, this word was not in Thucydides' vocabulary. However, this outstanding historian of antiquity uses other terms like *tactic* and *policy*. From my point of view, the term *tactic* was used by Thucydides rarely but accurately to describe tactical issues, like the application of military forces during battle. The word *policy* was used more often but less precisely, and illustrated concepts strategic in character. However, the term *strategy* cannot be found.

The History of the Peloponnesian Wars has a connection to state and financial policies, but less so than Sun-Tzu's book *The Art of War*. Sun-Tzu makes it absolutely clear that strategy can address any public activity of state and regional governments and financial and supply practices, not just military activity. Thucydides' book, as well as Sun-Tzu's, is a good source for strategists to find examples of strategic decisions executed by ancient leaders.[32] This literary historical text also contains an analysis of the ruler Minos' leadership. Minos was "the first person known to us by tradition as having established a navy … He made himself master of what is now called the Hellenic sea, and ruled over the Cyclades, into most of which he sent the first colonies, expelling the Carians and appointing his own sons governors; and thus did his best to put down piracy in those waters, a necessary step to secure the revenues for his own use."[33] Minos implemented this idea, strategic by nature, for state purposes, collecting taxes and revenues, and to dominate regions around the Cretan islands by establishing a permanent fleet. He was the first known ruler to use his fleet and navy for this governmental routine purpose, and not just for military victories. Even though Thucydides, as already stated, never used the word *strategy*, it is evident from his work that Minos was a strategist. We can only share this view of Minos because Thucydides' description of this hero was strategic. Even if Minos did not exist, Thucydides himself underlined the importance of Minos' activity as a statesman, and not just a military commander, which was strategic in nature. According to Thucydides, Minos was also the first one who used a sea fleet as a means of communicational service and delivery: "[A]s soon as Minos had formed his navy, communication by sea became easier, as he colonized most of the islands, and thus expelled the malefactors."[34] Minos' strategic talent stretched far beyond war, and helped to improve and change daily life in Knossos years before Agamemnon came to power as commander during the Trojan War. Both Minos and Agamemnon enjoyed continued strategic success by encouraging neighboring leaders to join them on mutual expeditions that resulted in a communal fleet that could be used by all for shared benefits. This is clearly described by Thucydides, without using strategic terminology or correctly defining this particular talent of Minos. However, Thucydides did highlight that "through the possession of a fleet" Agamemnon did eventually increase his power.[35] Even more, from the way Thucydides described the activities of Minos, we can say he was also the first strategist to discover the idea of regional economic integration and to implement this concept of power by marshaling his fleet. This last quotation by Thucydides leads us to the conclusion that strategy is not an automatic and major characteristic of dictators and their regimes: "[W]herever there were tyrants, their habit of providing simply for themselves, of looking solely to their personal comfort and family aggrandizement, made safety the great aim of their policy, and prevented anything great proceeding from them; though they would each have their affairs with their immediate neighbors."[36]

The roots of strategy can also be found in sacred texts such as the Torah, the New Testament, and the Qu'ran, among few others. Leaders like Moses—whom all three monotheistic religions claim—had a strategy. At the start of his leadership, he received a "strategic mission" and objectives from God. After the exodus from Egypt and during the journey to the Promised Land, he developed his own strategic goals and scenarios. The successful strategy he developed to win several military battles allowed him to implement his appointed divine mission as well. Even for people who do not belong to one of the three monotheistic religions, or any religion at all, it is important to study these texts from a strategic point of view. The successful strategies of Moses, his successor Joshua, King David and King Solomon teach us valuable strategic lessons today.

Readers can and do challenge me for using the Torah and the New Testament as historical texts for use in strategic practice. However, archeological findings—including the caves in Qumran—continuously show that these religious texts should also be taken seriously as historical texts, as they include deep history from at least 2,000 years ago. Sun-Tzu represents the best Chinese military strategy of his time, though due to its later popularity in Japan and Korea, it can be more broadly considered a representation of East Asian military strategy. Strategic practices found in major religious manuscripts, as well as in the books of Sun-Tzu, can be considered the beginning of historical strategy and the original sources on the theory of strategy. Confucius lived during the same time as Sun-Tzu and several generations before Aristotle and Alexander the Great; these great men all belong to the history of strategy. The philosophical works of Aristotle and Confucius contain the seeds of theoretical ideas of strategy. Even Homer's epic poems the *Odyssey* and the *Iliad* hold deep thoughts that are strategic by nature and depict examples of efficient strategic decisions. It is obvious that sections of these epic poems are historically accurate and represent authentic uses of strategic elements by real strategists, whether or not they were successful.

Marcus Aurelius was another colossal figure of the ancient world who combined the roles of statesman, philosopher, and military leader. Unfortunately, his philosophical works have been greatly undermined in literature and his work in defining and developing strategic ideas have not been given enough credit. I consider his books to be extremely important when understanding several major strategic categories, including objectives, goals, and the quality of strategic leaders.

Even famous quotes from many great strategists and statesmen were often taken from secondhand sources, leading to some doubt about their authenticity. However, strategists should be grateful for the original material we do have in writings that were not specifically devoted to strategy. Napoleon, who dictated his memoirs, did not leave (as stated before) any thoughts behind that could be classified as a direct systematic concept of strategy. But we do get an understanding about his strategic mindset from points made in his writings and letters, be they to his compatriots, colleagues, or lovers. A few strategic points can even be found in his love letters to Empress Josephine!

Another very valuable source of strategic thought can be found in the work of the contemporaries of great strategists, though they are also rare. Most often we find the works of great strategists in written accounts that came centuries later. For instance, the work of first century writer and consul Quintus Curtius Rufus is a work of deep history, but it was still written at the considerable distance of four centuries from his source material. To give some context, it is the same chronological gap that exists between Steve Jobs and Peter the Great.

Lack and Necessity of Strategy in the Twenty-First Century

A population's well-being, and even a nation state's existence, necessitates a long-term strategy. Generally, a strategic horizon should be at least 10 to 20 years into the future, but can be projected as much as 50 to 100 years ahead. The closer to the present, the more detailed a strategy must be. The proper use of strategy could potentially prevent a state from suffering through tremendous turmoil or falling into total collapse. State and national strategy must contain viable scenarios for both peace and war, as well as for post-war recovery and changes in reserves and in the resources of basic economic factors. Scenarios should be based on predictions of possible revolutionary changes in technology due to upcoming scientific achievements or tenable forecasts that provide a visible understanding of upcoming future consequences. National strategy requires scenarios for the most difficult *force majeur* times: ecological catastrophes, drastic climate changes, declines in agricultural productivity, unexpected mass diseases, or defense preparation to face aggression from any country worldwide. In addition, both current politics and contemporary individuals in power constantly influence strategies. As Napoleon said, "The great difficulty with politics is, that there are no established principles."[37] Strategy must have principles, regardless of the politics. The development of strategy begins with an analysis of a population's values, which transform into national interests. Through understanding and redefining strategic principles and interests, values are enriched into major strategic priorities. This is why politics only complicate the process of strategic development. There is a huge difference between politics and strategy: strategy requires principles. A strategy without principles is a strategy that cannot be successful in the long run. If a politician interrupts the development, implementation, or enforcement of a strategy, this interruption must be economically prized.

In the middle of the nineteenth century, as described above, the theory of strategy as a specific subject of research and application initially appeared only in military theoretical and analytical studies. Generals Jomini and Clausewitz began to systematize previously existing fragments in mostly historical and military writings related to the core of strategy. While it was their manuscripts that first introduced and appropriated the term *strategy*, they still wrongly used the term to cover tactical and operational issues. For example, Field Marshal Moltke not only revitalized the works of Clausewitz, he implemented, improved, and deepened the understanding of his own military practice. If Moltke had not used and widely discussed the work of Clausewitz, these writings would have been substantially forgotten by the end of the nineteenth century. Because of Jomini's and Moltke's work, strategic theory began to be taught as its own separate subject in military academies during this time.

By the beginning—and up until the middle—of the twentieth century, the term *military strategy* had become de facto synonymous with the term *strategy* in general. But after World War II, the conceptualization of strategy went beyond the battlefield, and elements of strategic ideas found in military books, essays, and in academies were implemented across several different fields of human intellectual activity. New books on the practical application of strategy development and improvisation began to appear in the early 1970s. New translations of the ancient writings of Sun-Tzu, Thucydides, Caesar, and Emperor Maurice appeared, as well as the modern works of Carl von Clausewitz, Antoine-Henri Jomini, and later Napoleon and Bismarck. Individuals and entities began to use the strategies revealed by these military masterminds in corporate and state strategizing processes, as well as for individual strategies or those used in the wider global community. This is why some of their books became very popular outside military spheres, especially among business strategists.[38] The study of strategy had become a prerequisite for individuals working in the business world, in domestic corporate activities, and, most particularly, at the international level because of the accelerated development of multinational corporations. These tendencies resulted from the influence of several global trends, the most dominant trend at the time was that of internationalization. This was a period of business world development prior to the birth of globalization—an extremely powerful trend that will be discussed later in this book. The increasing competition between businesses in the domestic and international arenas made studying strategy a requirement for decision-makers of companies, its trusts, conglomerates, syndicates, and other various organizational forms of collaboration against competitors in the markets of raw materials and parts, as well as in the markets of distributions of final products and services (and even in labor markets where companies compete for scientists, high-quality professionals, and experienced blue-collar workers).

Corporate leaders started to understand keen competition with other companies as a kind of business and corporate war. As a result, they began to study and read books and articles, and commissioned proprietary practical strategic recommendations that had previously only been used by militaries. It was the dawn of corporate strategy development and a renewed widespread attention to books that had been gathering dust on the shelves of libraries. Demand grew in the corporate world and in business schools for books on strategy. Scholars and teachers at business schools started to develop practical and methodological recommendations specific to corporations. Courses on strategic decision-making became quite popular in the early 1970s and even earlier. This process of discovery resulted in a historical paradigm shift within strategy research. For the first time, the quality and quantity of business strategy research began to surpass the work done by professionals and scholars in military strategy.

The tendency towards the popularization of strategy had some negative consequences as well. The word *strategy* could be used without any real understanding of the term and was often misused and devalued. For example, the operational activity on stock exchanges, with a horizon of two or three hours, or at least a couple of weeks, was called stock-picking strategy or currency exchange strategy. Practitioners still found the majority of books on business and corporate strategies useful, although they were neither analytical nor theoretical. But good books are often born from the soil fertilized by the bad ones. These books were representative of "best practice" analysis and recommendations that illustrated only by example extreme business cases of top-level executives who brought either success or failure to their entities. However, teaching and writing on the subject of corporate and business strategies improved the quality of this theoretical work and strategic practice as well. The development of terminology and distinct categories of strategy separated the subject of corporate strategy from economic, financial, and military strategy. Because the practice of economic strategy development began much later, its methodology and theory are still under construction. National economic strategy can be practical only when enterprises—and corporations—that consist of national and regional economies develop and follow their own business or corporate strategies. It is important to note that an analysis of many national and regional economic strategies shows that they are much less developed, less practical, and have a less established theoretical base than the business strategies of corporations (and they lag behind military strategies as well).

At the beginning of the twenty-first century, due to the birth and development of the global marketplace and the initial stages of the global community, there was a projected new shortage for top-level strategic decision-makers. This also generated demand for theoretical, methodological, and practical strategic recommendations about how to compete and collaborate within the framework of the global marketplace and global community. Practically, this is a relevant issue for scholars in the fields of military and corporate strategies who are starting to move slowly to the global arena, generating demand in the GMP for strategic research and recommendations. Also, in a reversal of influence, military strategists began to use corporate strategists' theoretical works and to analyze their practice.

The birth and functioning of emerging market countries and, later, the formation of the global emerging market led not only to new opportunities and threats for corporate leaders but also hastened national leaders and heads of governments to order recommendations regarding state and regional strategies and advice about their development and implementation. The second decade of the twenty-first century showed that the global community is a reality that has already necessitated the development of theory and methodological strategic recommendations to solve different global issues related to ecological problems, mass diseases, migration, and drugs, prostitution, and weapons trafficking, among other issues. The subjects of these strategies are not only global multilateral institutions like the United Nations, the World Bank, and the World Trade Organization, but also some non-institutional organizations like the G7 and G20, which do not have executive bodies but nonetheless require unified strategies to be discussed and adopted at their annual meetings. Many societal organizations that operate on a global scale, such as migration organizations and different unions, need their own strategies. The development of multilateral regional unions and agencies with their own institutions, such as the European Union, Mercosur, ASEAN, ECOWAS, and approximately 100 others, means that they would like to have their own strategies as well. These practical requests for strategic methodology and recommendations have motivated scholars to study and develop the general theory of strategy with an overall aim for strategic implementation in any sphere of human activity, making adjustments according to the particular characteristics of the strategizing subject (e.g. military headquarters, corporate executives, national or regional governments, ministries with different sectorial responsibilities, etc.).[39]

Development of a System of Strategy

Very few countries in the world have state strategies encompassing all of their regions and industries. Among the largest nations in the world, only China has come close to developing a unified strategy; since 1978, under the leadership of Deng Xiaoping, China has developed and monitored strategy for a 100-year vision. In fact, most contemporary nations have different sectorial or special purpose strategies (like NASA's 200 year strategic plan), but do not have a unified national strategy as China does. When a nation has a particular strategy and follows it, the outcome is almost always successful if the strategy is honestly developed and if governments allocate the required resources for continuing its implementation.

When governments of states or regions declare their strategy, but do not allocate resources for this strategy, the strategy limps along for several months and is eventually removed from the national agenda quietly. In an attempt to avoid these problems, some governments present not a strategy, but a "concept" without a description of its required resources. All of these countries would never implement these "concepts" in practice; rather, they are only declarations combining what a government would like to say and what the nation would like to hear. This kind of "concept," or so-called "strategy without resources," is just a way to mislead the population. Very often countries without strategy, placed in extraordinary situations due to the lack of well-developed scenarios that could lead the nation like a beacon through difficult times of change, sink in an ocean of catastrophe.

The global marketplace and the global community also increased the demand for recommendations on strategy use and implementation, from that point forward, not only for military and corporate leaders, but also for heads of states and governments, and leaders of regional multilateral unions and global institutions like the UN, the World Bank, and the IMF, among others.

At the end of the twentieth century, after the failure of dictatorial regimes in an overwhelming majority of command economy countries, a new generation of leaders came to power as the heads of states and governments. These new national leaders mostly oriented themselves towards economic freedom, were more educated than their predecessors, and often had experience in corporate or military sectors and science. This new leadership increased the demand for strategic recommendations and strategies. Consequently, it became evident during the 1990s that there was a substantial lack of specially trained professionals who could work on the development of strategies and monitor their implementation in any entity, regardless of its specialization and profile.

Furthermore, a lack of resources, shortages in basic economic factors, and social needs in countries using new dimensions strategies oriented towards economic and business development (which later became known as emerging markets) gave birth to a new trend: competition between national governments and domestic companies in the global arena for foreign investments, raw materials, sustenance, and even for the appointments of highly trained top-level foreign professionals in various areas. To be successful in this competition, governments started to develop national strategies, and then regional governments and heads of sectorial ministries started to imitate national governments. This is the reason why not only national strategies began to be widely developed in the 1990s, but also why specific national, economic, financial, and later, ecological, scientific, and technological strategies were added to the agenda. Regions within national boundaries started to compete as well for resources and control of leadership. Global trends of regional integration, more and more transparent national borders, and increasing international cooperation on political, economic, and cultural issues had positive impacts, but also gave rise to terrorism, prostitution, and the trafficking of drugs and weapons. It forced national governments and occasionally regional ones to develop security strategies to increase the dynamics of governmental influence through national security strategies in the military and in industrial and ecological safety. The dynamism of all these trends increased and complicated competition in the corporate world in the domestic, international, and global arenas. Intense professional competition in different industries and regions, and among corporations, institutions, and governmental structures, motivated some individuals (especially those who sought professional careers) to develop their own strategies—strategies for their professional and even personal lives. But it seems that the majority of executives and managers who work for leading enterprises that already have strategies and who participate in the development and implementation of these new or updated strategies overwhelmingly do not have—and do not try to have—a strategy for their own lives and careers. Nonetheless, books focusing on practical recommendations (often without any rigorous theoretical base) appeared in the 2000s, filling the shortage for those who decided to strategize their own lives. Books issued at major publishing houses even targeted specific age groups: for example, one book promised to help teenagers develop a strategy to direct and guide their lives.[40] The majority of strategies developed during this period of "strategic boom" were useless due to the lower quality of self-declared "professional strategists." As a result, strategy development also became a sphere of corruption and imitation of real strategizing processes.

All of these tendencies led to various developed strategies that proliferated at the beginning of the twenty-first century and were named based on their own specific characteristics: national strategies, national security strategies, national economic and financial strategies, and regional strategies. These processes of strategy development required a methodological basis and practical recommendations for a variety of strategy types. The result of these tendencies generated a practical necessity for concepts that I prefer to call holistic strategy. An illustration of this kind of national holistic strategy concept is presented in Figure 1.1.

This is why the system of strategies (encompassing national strategy, scientific and innovative strategy, economic strategy, financial strategy, ecological strategy, national security strategy, regional strategies, sectorial strategies, military strategy, corporate strategy, strategy of global issues, and strategies of individuals) is very unstable: the incomparable levels of quality of development and inequality of theoretical bases across different elements of the system.

Due to the fact that state-owned corporations played and continue to play an important role in national economies, especially in countries with former command

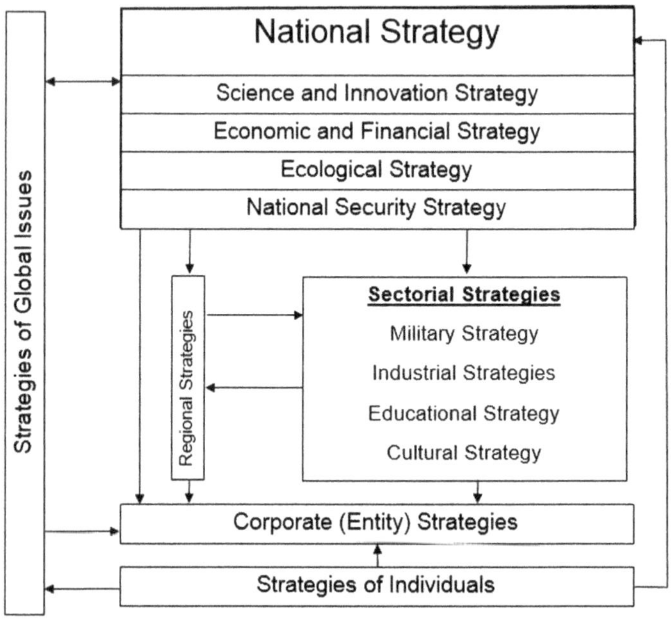

Figure 1.1 Concept of National Holistic Strategy

economies, sectorial ministries (e.g. ministries of energy, health, or heavy industry—to mention a few) generated increased demand for professional strategists who could develop strategies for their executive bodies. This is why sectorial strategies appear first strongly presented in the structure of holistic national strategies and then subsequently in regional ones. Under the influence of the processes of development of national, regional, and sectorial strategies, the role of corporate strategists was substantially complicated by the fact that corporate strategies tend to be influenced by all substrategies of holistic national strategies. Multinational corporations started to develop their own strategies focused on collaboration and operations with the national strategies of several countries in which their facilities were located or in countries where these corporations distributed a substantial part of their sales.

Any strategy—it does not matter for which object, institution, or entity it is developed—must have the same primary theoretical basis for the stages of strategy development regardless of the strategizing object (state, military power, region, business enterprise, or individual career). It is very important to note that the use of business strategy for the development of state and regional strategies was limited in providing practical recommendations for any of these strategies for several reasons: first, there was a substantial lack of studies and publications specifically dedicated to the theory of strategy; second, the lack of general methodological steps equally useful for any type of strategy despite the strategizing object; and third, in the overwhelming majority of cases, the most readily available books dedicated to military strategy or business strategy do not use a theoretical basis for their recommendations and exclusively rely on the authors' observations and practical experience. Even in books dedicated to business strategy for practical strategists, or any practitioners who work on strategy, it is very difficult to find clearly defined methodical guidance describing step-by-step strategy development, which elements these documents must include, how to begin implementation of the strategy in practice, and when and how to finish this work (including documents explaining an exit strategy). As a result, practically developed strategies very often fail without the inclusion of vitally important elements, such as the right order of implementation of these strategies and the correctly allocated resources required for strategic success. This is why it is easy to find missing strategic steps (e.g. entry strategy, exit strategy, adequately developed strategic management systems with required elements and functions, etc.) when reading these strategic documents.

In this book, I rely on my 40 years of strategic studies and participation in the development of strategies in Asia, Europe, and North and South America. Since I gained most of my experience from working in emerging market countries, the majority of examples in this book are taken from the EMC.

However, due to the nature of general strategic recommendations, these examples can be equally useful—as all general methodology is—for any strategizing object in any country. Obviously, more detailed practical recommendations require more specific elements and instructions related to the characteristics and priorities of the strategizing object. In a best-case scenario, any particular strategy has to be based on a theory of strategy, a general methodology of strategy development, and implementation. Finally, details and practical recommendations have to be specific to the strategizing object. Practically useful recommendations and instructions start from, as stated above, the study and enrichment of values, then the transformation of these values into interests, and the inclusion of both of these categories in the formation of strategic priorities. Throughout this book, I will use examples to prove that true strategic interests are concentrations of values.

Strategy as a phenomenon deserves its own theory. Strategy requires its own analytical methods and apparatus, including principles, priorities, hypotheses, and laws specific to trends, methods of development and practical use, defined systems for each element, and factors that can be analyzed and used regardless of the strategized object. The strategizing processes of a state, region, army, or corporation must adhere to the general rules of strategic thinking, strategy development, and implementation. Strategy as a theory should provide clear elemental content. Along these lines, a long-term strategic approach should start with the study of the theory and history of strategy, and conclude with the practice of strategic development and implementation. This order is relatively rigid. Starting with the history of strategy, for instance, is much less efficient because many historical works—even those by Herodotus, Homer, and Thucydides—do not define and structure the events they describe as a result of strategic thoughts and decisions. A student of history can define certain historical events as strategic only through an understanding of the theory of strategy.

Strategy requires a very different mindset than other subjects, not only in the day-to-day way of thinking culled from current events, but also from a meaningful analysis of the history of military battles, economic trends, cultural achievements, and societal prosperity. Strategy requires its own vision, philosophical schools of thought, different sets of rules, and analysis of particular elements in a precise order. Any strategist must begin with an understanding of the predominant values of a region's individuals, communities, and societies in order to select the salient value for following the process of strategizing.

My analysis shows that the ruling dominant law of strategy is different from the ruling laws of politics or economy. The major political law of any state is typically the constitution or common law of the land. The major economical law can be the law of values, the law of costs, or the law of supply and demand. In strategy, however, the major law is the law of time, as I will analyze and prove later in this book. A time-sensitive analysis of strategy is a criterion that must always be in place through the development and implementation of all elements of any strategy. The law of time is not the only rule of strategy; development and justification of the theory of strategy require discovering and developing other laws of strategy, monitoring major trends that influence strategy, and changing a society's priorities. Analysis of strategic practice proves Napoleon's point of view that the two most important criteria of the strategic decision-making process are time and space. On the basis of this postulate, we can conclude that strategy as a phenomenon has kinematical characteristics. Strategy and kinematics have the same two initial notions: time and space. These two major sciences also have nearly identical main goals: to predetermine the strategized object's (or, in kinematics, the studied object's) vector and speed of movement.

A classification of strategy is largely done (as was already mentioned) by the strategized object, e.g. a company, region, and state, or by sectorial areas of strategy, such as social, economic, financial, military, and athletic, among others. Strategy determines its classification, such as reactive or proactive and aggressive or defensive types of strategy. These terms of classification are mostly worthless, as any aggressive strategy can be considered from some point of view as defensive, or vice versa. Strategists misled by this way of thinking usually pay much more attention to proactive and aggressive strategies than reactive and defensive strategies because the latter require a much more difficult analysis of various scenarios among the competitor's goals, behavior, and movement. Defensive strategy also steers part of strategists' attention away from opportunities that almost always unexpectedly appear or become recognizable, and in this way, strategists can fail to take the road to great success at the right moment. From a theoretical and practical point of view, this often leads to rudimentary strategies. For example, prior to World War II, the Soviet Union did not even have a concept of defense, much less a full strategy, according to the most distinguished Red Army commander during World War II, Marshal Georgy Zhukov. Stalin's strategic idea was simple and wrong: he aimed to win any military conflict on the enemy's territory with "small blood," or minimal loss of life. As we know from history, this rudimentary defense strategy did not work, and Hitler's blitzkrieg operation rapidly swallowed up Russia's European territory up to the Volga River. This was only a temporary success for Hitler, however, due to the absence of any reasonable strategy in the Third Reich as well. The lack of a defense strategy cost the Soviets enormous losses, both in population and infrastructure. After World War II, Marshal Zhukov wrote a special memorandum to the joint chiefs of staff—the general headquarters of the Red Army—about the importance of having such a defensive strategy. Zhukov's reasoning drew heavily from Field Marshal Moltke, who wrote numerous works on this issue and dedicated particular attention to the defensive positioning of forces. Moltke focused on topographical differences of territories for the purpose of understanding both defensive and offensive strategies. He rightly noted that the conditions that make a defensive strategy work could easily become blockades for an aggressive, offensive strategy. In Moltke's words, "The same obstacle that supports the defense makes an advance difficult. An unobstructed front is strong enough for the defense and is the most advantageous for an immediate transition to the offense."[41]

Napoleon's own understanding of the strategic rules found in defensive battles grew from his studies of the outstanding strategic leader Frederick the Great, King of Prussia (1712–1786). Yet his conclusions were strictly Napoleonic, as evidenced in his famous statement that "the best means of defense is attack."[42] Napoleon used this defensive strategy only three times in his career: at Leipzig in 1813, and at La Rothière and Arcis the following year. All of these were in the twilight of his leadership. Throughout his career, as is clear from the above quotation, Napoleon looked for aggressive strategies, and his victorious legacy is substantially linked to this strategic way of thinking. Strategists should indeed follow Napoleon's strategy and search out aggressive strategic scenarios instead of relying on inferior defensive methods. In this way, strategists will become better at monitoring and seizing opportunities that appear unexpectedly and that will lead them, and the objects they strategize, to tremendous success.

The strategies mentioned throughout this chapter cannot be represented in a pyramid structure, but rather as substantial branches of strategies that continually influence each other. Many of these branches purposefully attempt to interact and even cooperate. The sheer number of entities in need of strategy generates an enormous demand for professional strategists in graduate schools around the world, especially in the domains of business, governmental affairs, and public services. But this process has not yet fully matured, and very few professional graduate schools have majors in Strategy (this subject will be covered in Chapter 4).

Philosophical Category of Good Life and Its Transformation to Quality of Life as the Essence of Strategy

Correlation between the Categories of Values and Quality of Life in Developed and Emerging Market Countries

As discussed above, an overwhelming majority of strategic ideas are rooted in philosophical (especially ontological) concepts. Strategy is a continuation and application of particular philosophical ideas to specific fields of human activity. Ideas, rules, and even categories of diverse philosophical schools have had different influences on the birth of strategy as a theory, on its development, and on its practical applications. After years of experience in strategy development and implementation, and after writing analytical works on this subject, I have come to the conclusion that, among all philosophical schools, metaphysics and its areas of ontology have had the most influence on the development of strategy.

One initial category of ontology interrogated by Socrates and Plato, and then substantially developed by Aristotle in his political philosophy, is the category of the good life. Through years of history and its adoption—or rejection—by leaders, this ontological category became the most influential to the theory of strategy and strategizing practice. The role of this category varies in the different political, economic, and social conditions of societies and depends on levels of their social and political maturity, as well as their economic development. The more society has developed, the more important the value and role of human life become in society; when human life becomes the center of societal morale and culture, it is then given more attention by society's leaders. The more importance placed on individuals in society, the more a practical role of the category of good life arises. But practical use of this ontological category requires its transformation to more measurable and manageable political and economic categories. And at this stage, the category of good life has become a deep core of the theory and practice of strategy.

Any strategy can be successful, and enthusiastically accepted by society, when it properly reflects the values of individuals and society as a whole. When strategy is initially formulated to focus on these values, enriching them as national interests to become the essence of national strategic priorities, this is characteristic of a properly established beginning of strategy development. The mission statement of any strategy, from an ontological point of view, is to transform individual and societal values through gratifying and enriching national interests to a formulated core of strategic priorities.

An individual's quality of life, well-being, and level of satisfaction are determined through values that are subjectively defined: how the individual's needs are met, for example, by the quality of goods and services. In the theory of good life analyzed by Plato's Socrates in the record of his trial (399 BCE) found in the *Apology*, and then further systematized by Aristotle in *Nicomachean Ethics* (350 BCE), happiness as a philosophical category also factors in the development of a person's well-being.[43] In modern times, the good life first appeared on the economic agenda at the end of the twentieth century, primarily in the status of individuals found in developed societies where the role and value of human life were much higher than in undeveloped and developing countries. In the twentieth century, psychologists like Sophia Lyubomirsky, Martin Seligmann, and the famous humanistic thinker Abraham Maslow began to study happiness. Maslow's work is the closest to economic theory before the appearance of Professor Daniel Kahneman. Kahneman offers a substantially profound analysis of happiness and well-being that focuses on an evaluation of self-satisfaction, mood, and happiness.[44] He pays attention to multidimensional measurements of happiness and well-being without fully accepting a theory of individual self-satisfaction. Nonetheless, in his book *Thinking Fast and Slow*, he dedicates two special chapters to the category of happiness: "Thinking About Life" and "Experienced Well-Being." Kahneman does not recommend directly applicable and exact indicators, which can be helpful for practitioners forming a simple evaluation and measurement of happiness. Rather, according to Kahneman, any economic category needs to be measured, as Descartes proposed.

According to the European Quality of Life Survey (EQLS), which was conducted in 2003, 2007–2008, and 2011, the characteristics of happiness among EU citizens of 27 countries were ranked in the following order of priority:

- 73 percent of people surveyed—health is the most important indicator of happiness;
- 44 percent—feeling of love;
- 37 percent—employment and satisfaction with work;
- 35 percent—peace;
- 32 percent—money;
- 27 percent—friendship and feeling of friendship;
- 24 percent—freedom.[45]

The remaining people surveyed placed characteristics of justice, education, pleasure, religious belief, tradition, order, and solidarity (in that order) towards the bottom of the list. These priorities of happiness represent the values of individuals in developed countries of western civilization, which include Europeans as well as Americans and Canadians. Similar results were reached in other studies, such as the World Happiness Report.[46]

However, the populations of emerging market countries (a term that will be presented later in this book along with related studies), even if they are already members of the European Union, emphasize a different order in their priorities of characteristics of happiness. This significant difference is due to faster population growth in emerging market countries as compared to in developed countries; thus, the age division on the priority of characteristics by happiness is more visible. In non-EU nations, which are integrating into the global community much more slowly, this gap between the younger and older generations is even wider. It is particularly evident in Russia (according to several publications),[47] where the population under 25 years old, all of whom grew up in the post-communist period, report that the major characteristics of happiness are money, followed by a tie for second place between freedom and human rights, with personal dignity coming in next. For people over the age of 55, who grew up during difficult years of tyranny and a communist dictatorship, the priorities in the definition of happiness are noticeably different. Labor and employment rank first, followed by human rights and satisfaction with one's work coming in second, then work ethic (being industrious), money, and freedom. Therefore satisfaction with quality of life is influenced by substantially different characteristics of value between the individuals of developed and emerging market countries. A higher level of economic freedom in society encourages stronger market competition and a wider range of quality and quantity in goods and services, which in turn lead to a higher level of consumer satisfaction, since consumers feel they can find goods and services that meet their expectations and reflect their values. Inversely, the values of people in developed countries are much more difficult to satisfy than people in emerging markets and lag behind developing countries because the expectations of the former are much higher than the latter.

In emerging market and developing countries, and especially in countries with a strict command system like North Korea, Cuba, Zimbabwe, and to some extent Belarus, the requirements are substantially lower and are based on the availability of goods and services due to shortages and/or to the low income of the majority of the population. This lack of freedom of choice forces consumers to purchase lower quality goods and services far below their requirements and expectations due to the fact that there are simply no other available goods and services on the market. In countries with a command economy, competition on the market is almost non-existent. Consumers do not have any freedom of choice and, because they buy goods and services of marked lower quality, the companies that produce these goods and services have no incentive to increase the quality of what they produce. There are no alternatives within the market, and their products are purchased regardless of quality. Command economies decrease the quality of products and destroy workers' motivation to produce higher quality goods and services. This negative situation grows because the workers' compensation almost never relates to the quality of the goods and services they produce. With the decrease in motivation for employees comes a decrease in the productivity of labor. This is why the productivity of labor in countries with a command economy is always lower than countries with a free market–oriented economy.

I agree with the Nobel Laureate in Economics Edmund Phelps when he comments, "We do not have to infer from data on productivity growth the presence (or absence) of dynamism—as physics inferred the existence of dark matter and dark energy."[48] When discussing labor quality and productivity, dynamism is a much wider and deeper category than just statistical analysis. It is related more to the modern values of society, a separation from traditional values that Professor Phelps correctly identifies in his 2013 book, where he relates dynamism to desire, capacity, and the scope of innovative activity. In dictatorial countries and command economies, the lack of motivation prevents a society's dynamism by curbing any creativity in employees, and especially in blue-collar workers.

In order to improve this situation in both developed and emerging market countries, strategic management systems in any civilian or military sector should pay special attention to their methods of encouraging creativity in all those who implement and practice strategy. Creativity is an essential factor in working strategy. No one strategy is perfect when it is developed, as strategists cannot fully ascertain social and economic conditions 5, 10, or 30 years after its development. Creative people will help to ensure the future success of a strategy. Here again I agree with Edmund Phelps's proposition that innovations are not just high-tech achievements. Even strategy that builds upon the most cutting-edge technology cannot be successful if the people who are implementing it do not demonstrate an innovative and creative working ethic. Corporatism during strategy implementation brings together the values of the people who are strategically involved and allows all basic economic factors (and in particular labor resources), financial capital, infrastructure, and technology to be shaped and changed for the better. As another Nobel Laureate in Economics, Friedrich Hayek, once wrote, "Society's course will be changed only by a change of ideas."[49]

With strategy development, it is important that new societal ideas are mirrored in the changes of values on the corporate,[50] regional, and national levels. These levels must be sensitive to these changes when developing strategy. Strategic monitoring then must result in a correction of strategy development and implementation according to changed social values and ideas.

The most negative situation in command economies appears in countries with an artificially detailed centralized planning system, which is created to predetermine what each enterprise in the country must produce and what the price will be for these goods and services, despite the cost of production, quality of employees, capacities of technological equipment, infrastructure, and the real requirements of the market. The situation is aggravated by employees' lack of financial motivation. This system mostly motivates people through punishment, not financial rewards. The population has much lower standards for their quality of life and satisfaction, which lead to a lack of happiness.

Under these economic conditions, usually of a dictatorship, social ills such as alcoholism, drugs, crime, and disillusionment with the government spread, while any imported goods and services from abroad became privileges that only the elite can afford ("nomenclature"). The domestic goods and services that are produced according to the centralized planning system are of such low quality that a substantial portion of these products (like the goods produced in the Soviet Union, for instance) are not bought by consumers and are sent directly from the market shelves back to be utilized and repurposed as raw materials to produce more goods of even lower quality. This cycle is negative, and eventually leads to the destruction of the command economic system itself; as people are forced to buy low quality goods and services, the production value also decreases and waste skyrockets, which negatively impacts the environment around the production facilities as well as in residential areas.

This is how the quality of life in developed countries grows at a faster rate in comparison to countries with a dictatorship. Ultimately, in command economy states, dissatisfaction with quality of life follows a lower level of freedom of choice and leads to social transformation and political processes often with revolutionary characteristics. The result of these processes is always the same: the creation of conditions for the beginning of a free market to develop, followed by an increased level of choice and satisfaction in goods and services. Eventually this leads to a stronger feeling of happiness and contentment with quality of life. And this is how ontological understandings of happiness and the category of the good life connect with the pure economic category of quality of goods and services. This connection between philosophical and economic analysis helps to determine and predict political and economic transformations in societies.

My economic studies began in the 1970s, and were mostly related to methodological and practical issues in studying economic efficiency of technological methods to improve the quality of goods and services when motivation was mostly prohibited as a means to improve quality because of the political and economic limitations of the Soviet Union. Specifically, my studies were related to the economic evaluation of technological preparation for the production of new goods and services. The implementation of unified standards of technological preparation of production leads to a higher predetermined quality of goods, a decrease of waste, a smaller negative impact on the environment, and ultimately a higher quality of life.[51]

It is important to note that studies of standardization to improve quality of life were used by several countries while forming different approaches to sustainable economical development, as well as by different national and international organizations in their practical studies on the quality of goods and the variety of values (see below for more details). Countries with newly developed market-oriented economies (especially emerging market countries which were accepted into the European Union during the 1990s and 2000s) demonstrated a shift in values closer to those found in developed European countries. However, it would be wrong to think that the transition of values is a one-sided movement, with predominantly developed countries influencing the values of Eastern European countries. The influence is actually more of a symbiotic relationship, where both sides are impacted by each other. It is easy to analyze this relationship by comparing the dynamics of populations from these two groups of countries through their priorities in the category of happiness.

As previously discussed, the survey conducted in 27 different countries in the European Union targeted two distinct populations: those of developed countries and those, according to my classification, of the global emerging market. The result of this study showed that the priorities of these different populations are essentially almost the same. When surveyed, people were asked to indicate the most important characteristic of happiness. Both groups answered health as their strongest indicator: 80 percent in emerging markets and 73 percent in developed countries. The value and importance of employment is ranked second, with 39 percent saying it is the most important indicator in emerging market countries, and 31 percent in developed countries; this difference of 8 percent is quite substantial. There are also discrepancies in how each population group views the link between money or wealth and happiness. In emerging markets, 38 percent said this was the most important characteristic of happiness. In developed countries, only 25 percent of those surveyed ranked wealth as the most important characteristic of happiness. This is a difference of 13 percent. The only happiness indicator that switched in importance between the two different population groups was justice. In developed countries, the justice characteristic was chosen by only 24 percent of those polled, placing after freedom, which polled at 32 percent. Among people in emerging market countries, justice as a leading indicator was chosen by 22 percent, and freedom by 19 percent of the population. This indicates that while justice is more important than freedom for people in emerging market economies, for the most part their priorities are similar to developed countries.

In the global arena, western values are more influenced by the values of populations in emerging market countries, which make up approximately 71 percent of the global population as of 2015. Under the influence of global trends such as globalization and regional economic integration (both of which will be analyzed later in Chapter 8), processes on the scale of the global marketplace have moved towards a conversion of values, and have resulted in the global community. The formation of the GMP and the contribution of its employees to a global community predetermine the collision of values of people in developed and emerging market countries. This process requires a more unified quality management system, including the management of quality in goods and services, and ultimately the management of quality of life.

For the political system of any country, the most important strategic concept must be oriented towards preferences and priorities that reflect the basic needs and choices of the majority of the population. Without understanding this strategic concept and its connection with guarantees of a population's freedom of choice, it is impossible to sustain market development and substantially improve quality of life. In the Soviet Union and Eastern European communist countries during the 1970s and 1980s, there were several attempts to create different systems to improve the quality of both military and civilian goods and services. In all of these countries, quality management systems were not focused on employees' motivation, both for workers and engineers, but on the development and strict implementation of state standards. These standards were implemented due to political limitations that forced out a system of motivation and made domestic companies use comprehensive systems of product quality management, which covered both industrial activities and state requirements. The main goal of these kinds of quality management was to improve product quality in order to meet the expectations of both domestic corporate and individual consumers and, to a lesser extent, of those who exported these countries' products.

In command economies, any further attempt to improve the quality of goods and services made the political system's limitations even more apparent. The complicated and inefficient centralized planning system used in many command economies could not factor in multiple companies producing the same particular type of product.

These systems simply were not created for people to have a choice among a variety of different options for one particular type of product. In the Soviet Union, for example, economists tried to find methods to increase the quality of goods and services despite lack of motivation. Dr. Okrepilov created the original quality management system used in Leningrad (now St. Petersburg). This system was implemented in 1976 and used for five years. During that time, it decreased the time needed to produce new products, reduced waste, improved product quality, allowed for faster progress to newer and better models, and was adaptable for use in any company. However, it did not improve the life expectancy or the aesthetics of the products; under the limitations of a command economy, it is next to impossible to improve these conditions. It soon became obvious that the only way to improve the quality of goods and services in cases of low motivation was to develop state standards for these characteristics. The improvement in quality of goods and services through the enforcement of state standards in these countries became unique, as the implemented standards supposedly had the same authority as any other law in the country. Yet even this system faced tremendous problems under a command economy. First, the existing standards for the highest quality of goods and services were unrealistic for the outdated and inefficient machinery parks located in most state-owned companies. This is why guidelines that outlined the recommended qualities of different goods and services were not written according to the requirements of corporate and individual consumers, but to the technological capability of most production companies; in other words, the majority of industry facilities' average production technological capabilities dictated the quality guidelines for these goods and services, which was not optimal. Second, even with the lower level of requirements and standards, no more than 60 percent of the guidelines were implemented and practiced. In general, there was no motivation for improving the quality of a product on the corporate level. Employees and companies were compensated the same amount regardless of what they produced, which resulted in many more inferior products. Consumers' freedom of choice was not met. The reluctance of communist bloc countries' leadership, including in the Soviet Union, led to an overall lack of motivation.

Following the failure of many command economies worldwide due to the collapse of the military dictatorships in Latin America and Turkey, the communist system in the Soviet Union and Yugoslavia, and dictatorial regimes in many Pacific Asian countries, new leaders who came to power in these countries began to build market-oriented economies. In order to gain public support, they were first motivated to decrease the gap in the quality of goods and services between their populations and the populations of developed countries.

This approach is especially important as an upcoming knowledge-based economy increases the role of intellectual property in comparison to the role of equipment and material ownership within companies. If any country would like to declare a national strategic mission to return to mass flourishing based on homegrown innovation (as Edmund Phelps strongly suggests), the system must place the individual at the center of economic development. The individual is the generator of new intellectual capital. The necessity of an individual's creative role makes it vitally important to increase standards of living as part of the principles of national strategy. This, in turn, necessitates a wider opening of the country's economic borders and economies to the global marketplace, a requirement for any country's membership in the World Trade Organization (WTO). A good economy is connected to success and personal development, including to individual education.

The good life can be described as a high quality of life and has to organically reflect democratic values, human rights, cultural and religious tolerance, and environmental improvement. This approach cannot be implemented in the majority of dictatorial states that have lower standards of living.

The continuing failure of dictatorships throughout the world, the widespread utilization of new technological achievements in infrastructural industries like transportation and telecommunication, alternative energy production, and the increasing liberalization of international trade and other cross-border economic relations (especially under the umbrella of the WTO) have all pointed to the continuous cooperation of almost all countries in the world economy's framework. The critical mass of international economic cooperation brought the business world to a new level of economic integration and a new phenomenon: the global marketplace and its subsystem, the global workplace. Even the development of a global order reflects the characteristics of the GMP and the global workplace, while simultaneously influencing them. Aforementioned dynamics that decrease both the gap in quality of life and in the quality of goods and services between global emerging markets and developed countries now make it more difficult for professional strategists, governmental leaders, and corporate executives when choosing where to invest; there are equally lucrative prospects in both domestic and foreign countries. It is only natural for investors not to venture into the unknown. This is why the converging values of populations in global emerging markets and developed countries push entrepreneurs in the global emerging market to a new strategic course of rapidly increasing the quality of industrial conditions and produced goods and services. Western values and the values of global emerging markets will substantially collide within the next 25 to 35 years, mostly in the interests of people in the global community. This process will lead to the development of a new global order that focuses on the good life in the global community.

Strategic Values and Priorities in Different Political-Economic Systems

While studying efficiency and strategy in the production of goods and services (especially production preparation) and analyzing the quality of goods in the Soviet Union and the countries of Eastern Europe and Mongolia, I observed a lower quality of goods and services, a huge waste in production, and much lower levels of efficiency and productivity, especially in comparison to Western European countries, the United States, and Japan. I concluded that the Soviet Union and other countries in the Communist and Economic Association (Comicom) would be unable to fulfill their populations' needs for goods and services due to the low quality of domestically produced goods and the inefficiency of production, as well as high levels of pollution. This is why I needed to research and find the root cause for such low-quality consumer goods in the political economy of the socialist system. As referenced above, this search eventually led me to analyze philosophical categories, focusing on the term "quality of life" and specifically on Aristotle's ideas of the "good life."[52]

Aristotle connected his ideas of the good life to an even more abstract and conceptual category known as *eudaimonia*, which originated from Socrates as well and describes the happiness and wellness of the individual. This category of eudaimonia—and I assume his teaching of Alexander—led Aristotle to form a political philosophy. But if eudaimonia mirrors the highest level of the good life, it is imperative to compare, measure, and distinguish the good life from the lower levels of life. From this point of view, I understood that, in order to develop appropriate strategic priorities and scenarios, it was necessary to analyze different aspects of the good life and all the components of quality that are integrated in the final account of quality of life. Without understanding the measurements of quality of life through different indicators, it is difficult to find ways to improve it. Strategy development in any region or country must be properly orientated; any strategy has to have a predominant orientation to improve quality of life and standards of living, decrease poverty, and, in the final account, to increase the happiness of the population. When strategists know how to increase quality of life on national and regional levels, they know which priority they must reach, how to establish these priorities, and what they have to do to motivate corporations and entrepreneurs to invest in the enrichment of these priorities. In order to put priorities on the practical agenda of nations, regional governments, and corporations, or in front of military power, strategists have to allocate sufficient competitive advantages for each priority. Otherwise, the implementation in practice of these priorities will just be fantastical or will cause nations, regions, or militaries to overspend required resources that nations, regional governments, and corporations (or military units) possess, or even that they do not have. As will be discussed later, no priority should be put on the practical agenda in a corporate system of planning without sufficient competitive advantages. Otherwise any products and services reached after the implementation of this priority could put corporations and regions in bankruptcy and set up nations for disaster.

The category quality of life—unlike the category of good life—is not nearly analyzed enough in philosophy, political economy, and even less in strategic studies—the field furthest behind in analyzing this issue. Yet the strategic development of society and its levels of maturity require a comprehensive system for measuring quality of life; whereas the category of good life cannot be measured from a philosophical point of view, it is mandatory to evaluate quality of life for strategic practice. An analysis of the differences in quality of life in multiple economic systems and countries have led to large-scale conclusions in the fields of politics, economics, strategic studies, and some technological sciences. In particular, the maturity and stability of a society can be measured by the proportional development of the role of its middle class. The predominance of middle-class values, especially in comparison to the extremes found in lower-class and upper-class values, contribute to a strategic development of society's dynamism (this is one of the most important categories for Edmund Phelps in his book *Mass Flourishing*).[53] These characteristics strategically describe the maturity of society, the level of prosperity of its population, and the stability of any country at large. The middle class in developed

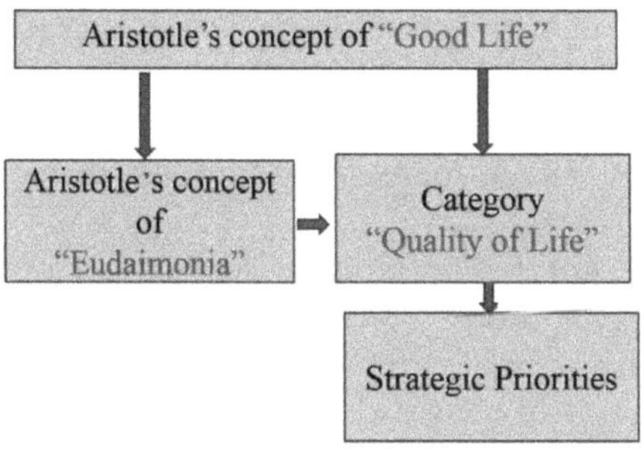

Figure 1.2 Quality of Life—Epistemology of Category
© Dr. Vladimir Kvint, 2012

countries has a higher level of lifestyle (which is a major characteristic of quality of life), a stronger level of strategic influence in society, and is closer to the quality of life of their country's upper class, especially in comparison with the role of the middle class in developing and emerging market countries. (The last economic category "emerging market countries"—and in particular "global emerging market"—was developed and defined from the beginning of the 1990s through my studies and publications, where the kinetic role of the middle class is strategically important in maturing these countries and differentiating them from the category of "developing countries."[54])

When studying the course of the middle class and its strategic role in society, I questioned: Why is labor productivity in countries with command economies always lower than in countries with market economies? It is easy to hypothesize that economic differences are caused by the character of the political system, but it is difficult to prove if high levels of freedom in societies are a precursor for a higher quality of life, which in this definition substantially represents the higher quality of goods and services as well as the prevention of pollution and an improved environment. The determination of political freedoms and their transformation into economic prosperity through free market relations, or, broadly stated, through higher levels of economic freedom, is made when a society predetermines a faster rate for labor productivity growth in comparison with increased volume of production and the growth rate of the country's population.

Though in this case, why do we often observe higher income per capita in countries with lower levels of political freedom (for example, in Qatar, Kuwait, Bahrain, or Brunei) than in countries with much more well-developed political freedoms and market relations? My studies show that this question is not related to the analysis of political freedom, but rather to economic and market-related freedoms colliding in the category of economic freedom, an indivisible part of which is freedom of choice. In particular, this is freedom of choice in the preference of goods, services, and location. Together, these characteristics predetermine the level of quality of life in different countries.

The study and evaluation of these characteristics separately—and then as integrated results—led to a practical measurement of freedom of choice, which can be seen at various levels of its maturity in different countries. The systematic influence on the development of different characteristics in these categories is essentially quality of life strategic management. On the one hand, this approach is related to the philosophy of existentialism, which states that individuals *always* possess a "permanent ownership" over their freedom of choice.[55] On the other hand, derivatives of political freedom within the category of freedom of choice (of goods, services, and location) can lead under dictatorial regimes to a complete lack of freedom of choice. These external factors—called "facticities" in existentialism—limit the freedom of choice for individuals and often change their system of values, which ultimately may damage the dictatorship itself due to that particular economic system's lower level of efficiency. In order to continue to prove this point, I would need to discuss Sartre's existential postulate in more depth; however, that should be the subject of another book.

I therefore analyzed the philosophical and political-economic bases of development within a sample of economic systems, looking for reasons that explain the different levels of quality of life under different political and economic systems, and developed ideas and proposals for the strategic management of quality of life based on these findings. Such an analysis gave me the opportunity to predict the disintegration of the Soviet Union, which I published at the end of the 1980s.[56] And, in 1990, it gave me the basis to develop methodological and practical strategic recommendations about the future of different political-economic systems that are predetermined by freedom of choice and quality of life and, in the best of cases, will emulate the characteristics of the good life.

By 2025, there will be a need for a **new strategic paradigm for the global order**. Further development of humankind will be impossible under current conditions of exponential population growth and the increasing deficit of resources essential to life without the development and implementation of creative strategies on the regional, national, and global level. The economic and social crises of the first decade of the twenty-first century demoralized the public psyche. Humankind is in need of a new strategic paradigm of success and hope. The imminent new global order has to take this into consideration as it creates a new strategy for survival and for sustainable growth.

Dynamics of Strategic Paradigms, Values, Interests, and Priorities

The analysis of strategies on national and regional levels has to start with a study of both the status quo and the dynamics of national and regional values. For strategic purposes, national values must mirror the majority of its people's values, both traditional and modern. It is also important to consider creative values as well, which according to Edmund Phelps will guarantee the proliferation of homegrown innovations that, in turn, drive a nation's dynamism.

The values of individuals are important to consider during the strategy-related development process of national interests, but can also be a hindrance, as some national interests cannot easily represent the values of just one individual. For example, a country's military values overlap with societal values and even, in a broader sense, state values, but must also be taken into account as their own category during the development of national interests for the following process of strategy formulation. The near constant possibility of war or increasing tensions and competition have always and will always continue to influence societal and individual morale, which has to be monitored and maintained in strategy adjustment.

Both individual and societal values provide accurate summaries of a nation's entire value system, which can be ranked for strategic purposes according to the level of support among individuals. On the basis of this ranking, among other influences, social values appear, which remain one of the main ontological sources when enriching and clarifying the formation of strategic national interests.

During strategy development, however, national interests should not only be limited to individual and societal values. They must also represent the nation's strategic interests in internal development as well as the nation's external positioning in the global arena,

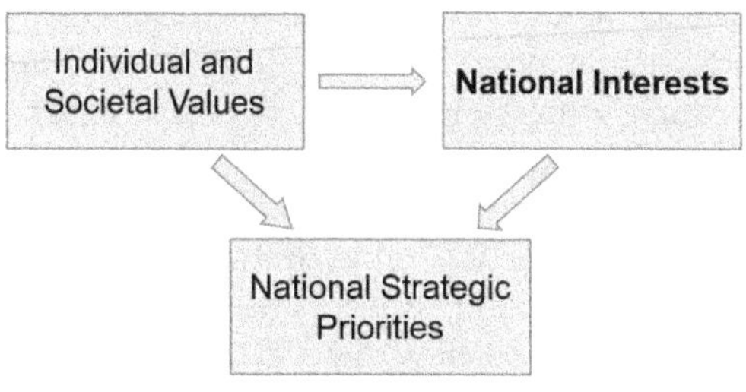

Figure 1.3 Vision of an Ontological Approach to National Strategy Development

regardless of the size of the country. Globalization and the disappearance of many of the barriers between global, regional, and local communities increase the importance of national interests. A national strategy must represent these interests, apply them in practice, and foster their growth. Only after the formulation of national interests will political, social, economic, and ecological strategists be prepared to adjust strategic principles and preferences and to create and/or improve a nation's strategic priorities. This stage of strategy development is very important, and should be treated as such when presented to the nation's leadership tasked with the responsibility of solidifying public support. Without the approval and support of national leadership, a designed strategy will never reach the next stages of practical strategic development.

At the same time, the role of strategists in formulating, selecting, and improving strategic principles, priorities, and scenarios must remain active. Strategists must initiate, conduct, and monitor the process of selecting every priority during the preparation of particular campaigns in order to ensure competitive advantages in the global arena or in the vitality of internal regional or sectorial strategic development. Hannibal ben Hamilcar Barca secured his victory on the Apennine Peninsula by selecting his own priorities to create a superior advantage that was only partially related to his competitive advantage—for example, his plan to march an entourage of elephants through the Alps to Rome. Roman soldiers had never before seen these huge creatures and, as such, fled in terror. Unfortunately, this competitive advantage only worked for a short period of time. When the Roman Republic soldiers later attacked Carthage on its own territory, the elephants no longer surprised them. The Roman soldiers realized that elephants are only dangerous when attacked from the front. They then avoided a frontal attack by the stomping elephants and, instead, flanked the elephants from the sides, thus slaughtering them and strategically taking over Carthage.

Typically, a strategist would use the approach outlined by Professor Michael Porter, who describes five competitive forces that shape strategy. But the problem with this approach is that Porter believes there is a direct correlation between power and profitability (according to him, "The strongest competitive force or forces determine the profitability of an industry and become the most important to strategy formulation"), which is not always a correct determination. Power does not influence profitability by competitive forces.[57] This theory does not allow for any strategic fields and issues where profitability is not a criterion. I am not referring to military fields only, but also to business, where strategy should be oriented towards a time-sensitive analysis of all priorities, not just profit. Quite often, it is more important to be the first to lay claim to a novel niche market even though this motivation can be unprofitable; however, in the long run it makes more strategic sense.

I do agree with Professor Porter when he writes "the most salient force, however, is not always the most obvious."[58] Even more so, the most profitable competitive advantages of strategy are silent components. Repeating someone's best practices may not be the main goal for strategists in the early part of strategy development. Instead, they are looking above the horizon for the entire strategic competitive advantages. However, when a strategy reaches full maturity, the best practices of the beginning of strategy development will already be forgotten or outdated. Repeating a competitor's best practices is a tricky endeavor, as it requires a thorough understanding of how the strategic elements that previously brought victories can change, and not necessarily for the better, in a new environment at a different time. In order to successfully implement and practice the teachings of a great strategist like Sun-Tzu or the Byzantine Emperor Maurice, the strategist must analyze and develop a sense of current and realistically obtainable strategic advantages, ones that will help the strategist to repeat the best practices of a competitor through an alternative method. With a proper strategic approach, the strategist will not spend a huge amount of resources just to simply try to overpower competitors or enemies. An alternative asymmetrical way always has the element of surprise and often is much cheaper and faster than direct competition through a symmetric answer.

If a particular priority does not meet the criteria set during the process of strategizing national interests, strategists and those in leadership have alternative steps they can take: the first of which is to create new competitive advantages that will become the new priority. Strategists can either improve outdated competitive advantages, so that they will once again be strong enough to support a particular priority, or remove the priority from the strategic agenda altogether. Usually in this situation a government can start to subsidize a new study to research and develop novel competitive advantages that use priorities not currently secured by competitive advantages, and eventually add them to the agenda during the next period of strategy updating.

Figure 1.4 and the preceding explanation about the correlation between values and national priorities should give any strategist pause about the study and ranking of national values. In any final account, a deeper understanding of the philosophical and practical roots of these values will make any strategy more practical, more efficient, and, quite often, will gain more support from the majority of people. This support is not needed during the process of strategy development, but is crucial for strategy implementation, especially on national and regional levels.

It is important to find the correlation between a nation's values and the values of other nations, while understanding how they influence each other. In the twenty-first century, however, this approach does not extend far enough because the majority of nations are now members of a new global community—a new reality born under the overpowering influence of the global marketplace. Both of these phenomena are a result of one of the major and most powerful global trends: globalization.

So far there has not been any strategy developed solely for the global marketplace because the GMP does not operate like a corporation or state (a fact I applaud, as I will

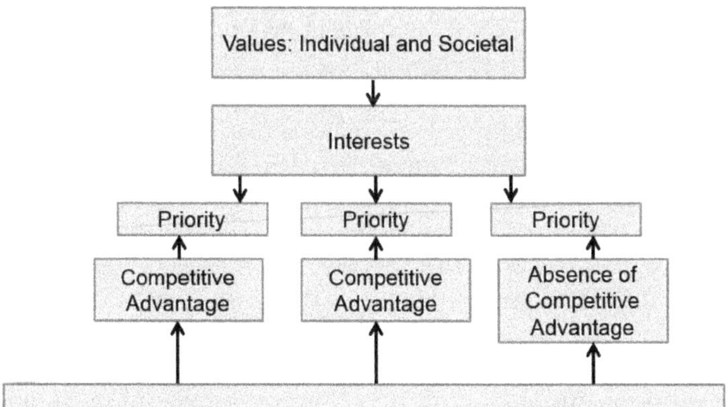

Figure 1.4 Correlations between Values, Interests, Priorities, and Competitive Advantages
© Dr. Vladimir Kvint, 2013

be the last person to support a global corporation or government on the scale of the GMP). Strategists developing the strategy of any nation or multinational corporation must incorporate the objective interests of the global community and consider how these interests are carried out in the GMP.

It is possible to analyze objective interests through the study of the integration of different global trends, such as social, economic, political, and technological trends. Because of the large scale of the global community, it is very important to identify its common values. Ontological and sociological studies give new practical meaning to surveys that aim to understand the mutual values of people from different nations and cultures. These mutual values found within the global community must be at the top of the agenda for global institutions like the United Nations, World Bank, IMF, WTO, etc. If not, the role of global institutions is undermined, as in the case of the International Organization for Standardization (ISO). International standards must first and foremost be oriented to global values, and only after that can they represent international and national values. Undoubtedly, a few small but efficient organizations will be created in order to improve the development of a global community and global marketplace.

There has been embarrassingly little research done on global strategy—the strategy of both the global community and the GMP. A global strategy will be put in practice through a global order, and must be oriented to the values and interests of all nations, and not just the powerful few. This is why the global order must be part of strategic studies and needs to receive more interest from strategists (and not only political scientists). Currently, those who are most interested in the global order are those who also support conspiracy theories. This is not the book for them, because so many conspiracy theorists already believe in a global order, albeit one made up of shadowy figures that pull the strings of all countries and are responsible for all major events in human history. I know from personal experience that it is impossible to change their minds.

When discussing strategy, we must focus more on the influence of freedom of choice—that is, the combined impact of economic and market-relation freedoms—than traditional political freedom alone. This is particularly true when studying freedom of choice in the market of goods, services, and location, as they predetermine the level of quality of life in a country. On the one hand, this approach is related to the philosophy of existentialism, which states that individuals always (!) possess "permanent ownership" over their freedom of choice. On the other hand, derivatives of political freedom will often lead to a complete lack of freedom of choice under the worst versions of dictatorial regimes.

What most amazed me during my time studying values is that economists typically pay little if any attention to the philosophy of existentialism. It is not used in their research. I bring up freedom of choice now because it is used on occasion, but as a common phrase and not as a category. However, I believe it should be a requirement when discussing values. One obvious example of a book that uses the term is *Free to Choose: A Personal Statement* by Milton and Rose Friedman.[59] However, they never mention freedom of choice as an existentialist category.

Early in my studies I found answers to my economic questions in books by Jean-Paul Sartre, who wrote much on the freedom of choice. However, I came to some different conclusions on a few issues, which led me to calculate and formulate the correct timing for the disintegration of the Soviet Union. Sartre believed that freedom of choice is an internal human characteristic found in all of us. Sartre implies that freedom is an indissoluble right that cannot be taken away, but perhaps he underestimated the brutality of dictators such as Stalin or even, in the first quarter of the twenty-first century, the oppressive regime of North Korea. Sartre did not experience the level of brutality orchestrated by these regimes. Otherwise he would have thought twice. Under factual analysis, I wholeheartedly agree with the thesis by Nobel Laureate in Economics Milton Friedman that the ability to choose is a significant privilege found in capitalism.

A major problem for business strategists and even for strategists who are involved in the development of governmental strategy is economic determinism. Quite often, strategists incorrectly put economics at the top of their priority list during the process of strategy development but mostly ignore social issues. From a strategic point of view, this is a serious mistake that can mislead all strategy on national and regional levels and, in many cases, in the strategy of corporations; when social issues are ignored, it can cause economic goals to become obsolete and lead to civilian disobedience or to a lack of employee motivation in corporations. In fact, before the theory of chaos was developed, French philosopher Hippolyte Taine (1828–1893) was already studying chaos from the point of view of society and social problems. This is why Taine's philosophy is essential for strategists, along with other philosophical schools. He dedicated a substantial section of his studies and writings to systemizing and understanding chaos.[60] Of course, Taine primarily studied the chaos of art, which he then connected to the changes needed in society and societal values. This is why his work is useful to strategists, who look to convert social values to social interests and, ultimately, to priorities in a particular strategic object, be it regional, state, corporate, or even global. It should be no surprise that, as a philosopher of art, Taine was one of the founders of the School of Political Science (L'École libre des sciences politiques) in Paris. Today he is largely forgotten, but those who study chaos theories and theorists must still analyze his work.

A deep understanding of the philosophical roots of strategy gives strategists the required knowledge to develop better methodology of strategy and to avoid many mistakes during the initial process of strategy development—the stages at which strategists have to connect national, social, and economic interests to enrich strategic priorities. A wrong strategic priority will usually mislead hundreds, thousands, or millions of people, use up resources, and waste misdirected time on activities.

Rehabilitation, Adoption, and Burgeoning of a Symbol for Strategy

Traditionally, from the time of Ancient Greece and Rome, all specific and important fields of human activities—especially societal and public ones—had a symbol that initially appeared in mythology as the gods and protectors of these activities. For example, Hermes for the Greeks—Mercury for the Romans—was the symbol of trade and has now become a contemporary symbol of mail and delivery, as well as commerce. For hunters, the goddess of hunting was Artemis for the Greeks—Diana for the Romans—and, for gatherers, Demeter for the Greeks—Ceres for the Romans—was the chosen beacon of hope. Almost everyone knows the symbol for medicine, the caduceus, which is two intertwined snakes enveloped by wings—the instrument held by Hermes (Mercury).

We can continue this discussion of deities and what they represent by asking ourselves, "Who is the god and symbol of strategy?" It is very distinct and different from the signs and practices the Greeks and Romans used. The symbol of strategy has to contain symbolic references to an understanding of the past and a deep vision towards the future.

The symbol should also illustrate an overwhelming attention to time because time, which I will discuss later on in this book, is a major and very influential category and predominant law of strategy. A symbol of strategy must focus substantially on space as well because strategy is always related to monitoring changes in the external and internal environments of any strategizing object.

For some time, it was very difficult for me to conceive of a unified symbol for strategy. But then I found the answer. I was visiting St. Michael's Castle, which was erected in 1797–1801 in St. Petersburg as a new royal residence by the Russian Emperor Paul I, the great-grandson of Peter the Great. I saw four different statues of Janus in the halls of the castle.[61] And, at first, I was surprised. Why would Paul give such attention to this symbol of a two-faced deity who is only associated with double-crossing and lying to different individuals and separate groups of people? Paul I, as far as I knew, was not the kind of person who lied much, so it could not be in his interest to have four statues of Janus in his own residential palace. I quickly went to study the mythology of Janus and found out that Janus was the figure who might have inspired Emperor Paul I to appreciate the heroic past of his great-grandfather and to help him, as he had hoped, see the right passage to the future. Paul would have enjoyed the ability to see, at the same time, both the past and the future. The past for him was no less important than the future because he was looking for power and influence modeled on the leadership of Peter the Great. Paul even erected a monument to Peter the Great in front of this castle with the sign, "To great-grandfather from great-grandson." And like the sufferers in Dante's *Inferno*, who can only see the future and the past but not know the present, strategists would want to have both abilities despite any impending obstacles in order to see the past and to carve out efficient routes to future opportunities.

In Roman mythology, Janus was the god of beginnings and transitions, and the keeper of gates, passages, and endings. But why, on most statues, does one of Janus's faces depict an old bearded man while the other shows a young man's "clean-shaven" face? The answer to this question makes Janus the most suitable symbol of strategy. Janus has two faces depicting different ages because the old man is looking to the past, while the young man is looking into the future. Due to Janus's ability to see both the past and the future, he is the god of gates and changes but also—and this is most important to strategists—he is the god of time![62] With this new understanding of the "role" of Janus, it immediately became apparent to me why Paul I had at least four statues of Janus in his castle.[63]

Taking all of the above into consideration, I have to conclude that to rehabilitate the image of the mythological hero Janus is to show that he is not a double-crossing liar. This popular image of him has to be sent to the garbage can of history. Some people might suggest other symbols of strategy: Athena, for example, is the goddess of wisdom, reason, justice, and law, and she has several other functions as well—she's already too busy. But her functions do not all fold into the field of strategy in the same way that Janus embodies all and only the functions of strategy.

Perhaps I must declare Janus as the symbol of strategy (both as a science and as a practice). From now on, he is not only the god of gates and doors, but also the guardian of strategy. I hope that scholars and practitioners of strategy will not challenge my suggestion. It would be eye-opening to see appropriate graphic representations of this rehabilitated and reincarnated Janus crafted by those who are gifted in art and design.

So now strategy has its symbol and its "god."

Notes

1 Aristotle. (2001). *Basic Works of Aristotle*. R. Mckeon (Ed.) and W.R. Roberts (Trans.). New York: Modern Library, p. 1371b.
2 Plato. (1892). *The Dialogues of Plato*. B. Jowett (Trans.). Oxford UK: Clarendon, p. 217.
3 Kierkegaard, S. (2002). *Concluding Unscientific Postscript*. A. Hannay (Trans.). Cambridge, UK: Cambridge University Press, p. 168.
4 In this particular quotation, Napoleon does not use the term *stratégie*, but rather the term *la grande tactique* to make the distinction between tactic and grand tactic. D'Aguilar translates it as "science of strategy," which seems an accurate translation to me. Earlier in the same book when Napoleon writes about "opérations de stratégie" and tactics he does use the term *strategy*. Nonetheless, as far as I know, no one has found the term *strategy* in Napoleon's personal writings. After the end of his campaigns, the term appeared in the writings of Generals Jomini and Clausewitz. Napoleon, at about the same time, incorporated the term *strategy* into his *Military Maxims*. I can conclude that in the second and third decades of the nineteenth century, the term appeared in the writings of a narrow circle of professionals. But Napoleon was the first giant military leader who used this term. I will discuss the origin of the term *strategy* later in this chapter.
5 Napoleon. (1987). *Military Maxims of Napoleon*. G. D'Aguilar (Trans.) and D. Changler (Ed.). Boston: Da Capo Press.
6 Cited by Lyons, N. (2010). *Handbook of Reflection and Reflective Inquiry: Mapping a Way of Knowing for Professional Reflective Inquiry*. New York: Springer, p. 87.
7 Sun-Tzu. (1994). *The Art of War*. R.D. Sawyer and M.L. Sawyer (Trans.). Boulder, CO: Westview Press, p. 167.
8 Sun-Tzu. (2002). *The Art of War*. J. Minford (Trans.). New York: Penguin Group, p. 4.
9 *New International Version*. (2011). Grand Rapids, MI: Zondervan.
10 *King James Version*. (2007). Naples, FL: Trident Reference Publishing.
11 Sun-Tzu. (1994). *The Art of War*. R.D. Sawyer and M.L. Sawyer (Trans.). Boulder, CO: Westview Press, p. 177.
12 We do not know of any sources stating that a translation of the Torah in Latin existed during Caesar's time. While he could have read the Torah in Ancient Greek, we have no evidence of this.
13 Gaius Julius Caesar. (1998). *The Civil War*. J. Carter (Trans.). New York: Oxford University Press, 1:72.
14 McDevitte, W.A., and Bohn, W.S. *The Works of Julius Caesar* (Parallel Latin/English) Civil Wars Book I (50 BCE), p. 1.72. Available at http://sacred-texts.com/cla/jcsr/index.htm
15 Study of Frontinus and his term *stratagem* will be introduced later in this chapter.
16 Cited by Niẓām, -M., and Darke, H. (2002). *The Book of Government or Rules for Kings* London: Curzon, p. 92.
17 Frontinus, S.J. (2012). *Strategemata*. C.E. Bennet (Trans.). Seattle, WA: Praetorian Press, p. 7.
18 Frontinus, S.J. *Strategemata*. Retrieved from http://penelope.uchicago.edu/Thayer/L/Roman/Texts/Frontinus/Strategemata/1*.html
19 Frontinus, S.J. *Strategemata*. Retrieved from http://penelope.uchicago.edu/Thayer/L/Roman/Texts/Frontinus/Strategemata/1*.html
20 Frontinus, S.J. (2012). *Strategemata*. C.E. Bennet (Trans.). Seattle, WA: Praetorian Press, p. 8.
21 Today this is housed in the Laurentian Library (Biblioteca Medicea Laurenziana) in Florence, Italy.
22 Even though it obviously has grown from the Ancient Greek word *strategy*, which was a military title without reference to the process of decision-making.
23 It seems to me that what Emperor Maurice meant when he used στρτηγικά can be approximately translated as "generally, with long-term importance" or "widely important."
24 Emperor Maurice (2002). *Maurice's Strategikon: Handbook of Byzantine Military Strategy*. Philadelphia, PA: University of Pennsylvania Press, p. 23.
25 Emperor Maurice (2002). *Maurice's Strategikon: Handbook of Byzantine Military Strategy*. Philadelphia, PA: University of Pennsylvania Press, p. 67.
26 Emperor Maurice (2002). *Maurice's Strategikon: Handbook of Byzantine Military Strategy*. Philadelphia, PA: University of Pennsylvania Press, p. 64.

27 Emperor Maurice (2002). *Maurice's Strategikon: Handbook of Byzantine Military Strategy*. Philadelphia, PA: University of Pennsylvania Press, p. 65.
28 Dodge, T. (1891). *Hannibal: A History of the Art of War among the Carthaginians and Romans down to the Battle of Pydna, 168 B.C., with a Detailed Account of the Second Punic War*. New York: Houghton, Miffin, & Co., p. 629.
29 The following translation of Jomini's text is mine.
30 Jomini, Baron de (1840). *Précis de l'art de la guerre: Des principales combinaisons de la stratégie, de la grande tactique et de la politique militaire*. Brussels: Meline, Cans et Copagnie (Russian edition), pp. 139–140.
31 Jomini, Baron de (1840). *Précis de l'art de la guerre: Des principales combinaisons de la stratégie, de la grande tactique et de la politique militaire*. Brussels: Meline, Cans et Copagnie (Russian edition), pp. 139–140.
32 Jomini, Baron de (1840). *Précis de l'art de la guerre: Des principales combinaisons de la stratégie, de la grande tactique et de la politique militaire*. Brussels: Meline, Cans et Copagnie (Russian edition), p. 141.
33 As an aside, it is also possible to describe the use of strategy from legendary or religious figures like Abraham, Moses, and King David, among others. However, there is dispute among scholars about using the Torah, the New Testament, and the Qu'ran as historical sources. While I personally see these texts as both historical and religious, I would like to start with the unquestioned historical text of Thucydides.
34 Thucydides. (2006). *The Peloponnesian War*. R. Crawley (Trans.). New York: Barnes & Noble Classics, pp. 10–11. Original work published between 431 and 400 BCE; translation originally published in 1876.
35 Thucydides. (2006). *The Peloponnesian War*. R. Crawley (Trans.). New York: Barnes & Noble Classics, p.16. Original work published between 431 and 400 BCE; translation originally published in 1876.
36 Thucydides. (2006). *The Peloponnesian War*. R. Crawley (Trans.). New York: Barnes & Noble Classics, p. 19. Original work published between 431 and 400 BCE; translation originally published in 1876.
37 Thucydides. (2006). *The Peloponnesian War*. R. Crawley (Trans.). New York: Barnes & Noble Classics, p. 31. Original work published between 431 and 400 BCE; translation originally published in 1876.
38 Napoleon. (1916). *Napoleon in His Own Words*. J. Bertaut, H.E. Law, and C.L. Rhodes (Trans.). Chicago: A. C. McClurg & Co.
39 Of course, for any newcomer to this field, translators can make finding and reading these authors' works more complicated since many of them do not know strategic terminology and do not bother to correctly translate even the titles of these works. The books of multiple writers, including Sun-Tzu, Clausewitz, Jomini, and some works of Moltke, all have the same English title: *Art of War*. This translation is far from the authors' original titles.
40 Liddel Hart, among other authors, uses the term *grand strategy* to describe and explain the strategic use of national—and mostly political—resources. In this book, I use *grand strategy* simply to describe national or state strategy; this can also be considered *high strategy* from the point of view of particular nations' pure interests. But globalization and integration, which will be analyzed later in this book, have led to the birth of the global community and global marketplace; these trends require their own strategy, which can also be called *higher strategy* in relation to the separate strategies of different national states. For all of the above reasons, I will not use the terms *grand strategy* and *higher strategy* in this book.
41 McGraw, J. and McGraw, P. (2000). *Life Strategies for Teens*. New York: Fireside (Simon & Schuster).
42 Moltke, H. (1995). *Moltke on the Art of War: Selected Writings*. D.J. Hughes (Ed.). Novato, CA: Presidio Press, p. 167.
43 Chandler, D.G. (1966). *The Campaigns of Napoleon*. New York: Macmillan, p. 180.
44 Plato significantly expands on Socrates's commitment to living a good life and develops a theory of political philosophy in *Republic* that is an extended treatment of what constitutes the good life.

45 Dr. Daniel Kahneman received the Nobel Prize in Economics in 2002 for his studies on integrated economic analysis with insights from cognitive psychology during decision-making processes under conditions of uncertainty. He studied mostly with Dr. Amos Tversky.

46 *European Quality of Life Survey*. (2012). Brussels: Eurofund.

47 *The World Happiness Report*. (2013). J. Helliwell, Richard Layard, and Jeffrey Sachs. New York, NY. Retrieved from http://unsdsn.org/wpcontent/uploads/2014/02/WorldHappinessReport2013_online.pdf

48 Pantin, V., and Lapkin, V. (1999). *Evolution of Values Orientation of Russians in the 1990s*. Retrieved from http://ecsocman.hse.ru/data/056/826/1231/v_lapkinx2cx20v_pantin_pro_99.doc

49 Phelps, E.S. (2013). *Mass Flourishing: How Grassroots Innovation Created Jobs, Challenge, and Change*. Princeton, NJ: Princeton University Press, p. 15.

50 Leeson, R. (2013). *Hayek: A Collaborative Biography*. Basingstoke, UK: Palgrave Macmillan, p. 55.

51 It doesn't matter if we are discussing any business or military unit, or economic subsystem.

52 My colleague Vladimir Okrepilov and I gave substantial attention to studies of quality of life improvement through standardization. This instrument—at least at first glance—did not seem to fully relate to the nature of political and economic systems in society, and, thus, we did not face much resistance from any level of the Soviet government. During this period, my studies mostly related to the changes of values in different societies over time, an analysis of different values of various populations in developing countries, and the influence these values had on both the political and economic transformation of societies. There was particular interest in how this could lead both to failures in different dictatorships and to the transformation of these countries to a new group of emerging market countries. This topic was also my main subject of study during the 1990s and 2000s. From the 1980s, Okrepilov's studies mostly related to the analysis of different characteristics of quality, their influence on changes in quality management systems, and the development of these systems. By bringing our findings together, we were able to conduct more detailed studies about the different systems that can be used for the management and measurement of quality of life.

53 Aristotle. (2000). *Nicomachean Ethics*. R. Crisp (Trans.). Cambridge, UK: Cambridge University Press.

54 Phelps, E.S. (2013). *Mass Flourishing: How Grassroots Innovation Created Jobs, Challenge, and Change*. Princeton, NJ: Princeton University Press.

55 Kvint, V. (2009). *The Global Emerging Market: Strategic Management and Economics*. New York: Routledge.

56 Sartre, J.-P. (1993). *Essays in Existentialism*. New York: Citadel Press.

57 Deep strategic analysis always can surprise a great scholar and visionary if he or she does not give special attention to particular issues. I remember well when, on January 3, 1990, I said to Dr. Henry Kissinger in his office that, according to my analysis, by 1992 the Soviet Union would disappear from the political map. He responded with the following advice: of course the Soviet Union would disappear, but it would not happen during our lifetime—the Communist Party, KGB, and the Red Army kept the Soviet Union together like this [he showed me his clenched fist as a symbol of the three dictatorial instruments' power]. He also told me that predicting with exact dates is always dangerous. Later that same year, the *New York Times* published my article practically with the exact same prediction—and, of course, the Soviet Union ceased to exist in late December of 1991. This example shows how powerful deep strategic analysis can be and how almost anyone can do it by following the rules of strategic thinking (see Chapter 2).

58 Porter, M. (2008). *The Five Competitive Forces that Shape Strategy*. Cambridge, MA: Harvard University Press, p. 40.

59 Porter, M. (2008). *The Five Competitive Forces that Shape Strategy*. Cambridge, MA: Harvard University Press, p. 40.

60 Friedman, M., and Friedman, R.D. (1980). *Free to Choose: A Personal Statement*. New York: Harcourt Brace Jovanovich.

61 Taine, H., and Durand, J. (1931). *The Origins of Contemporary France*. New York: P. Smith, volumes 2–4.

62 I hope and believe that the curators of St. Michael's Castle have since installed the four statues of Janus in one hall.

63 Ovid. (1933). *Ovid's Fasti.* J.G. Frazer (Trans.). London and Cambridge, MA: William Heinemann Ltd. and Harvard University Press, part I, pp. 133–140. Retrieved from the Perseus Project, http://catalog.perseus.org/catalog/urn:cts:latinLit:phi0959.phi007/

64 This is due to the fact that this emperor's mother, Catherine the Great, did not like him and even tried to skip over him in the line of succession and designate his son Alexander as her successor. (Alexander later participated in the coup d'état against his father Paul and then fought with Napoleon—but unlike Napoleon, he did not demonstrate strategic capability.) Unlike Emperor Alexander I, Paul I definitely had strategic vision and, during his very short reign, made several strategic moves and even took over the role of the grand master of the Order of Malta; due to this, Russia controlled a substantial part of the Mediterranean Sea, which never occurred again.

2 The Strategic Thought Process

> By three methods we may learn wisdom: First, by reflection, which is noblest; second, by imitation, which is easiest; and third, by experience, which is the bitterest.[1]
>
> Attributed to Confucius (551–479 BCE)

> Tactics, evolutions, and duties may be learned in treatises, but the science of strategy is only to be acquired by experience, and by studying the lessons of the campaigns, of the great captains. These lessons have been to keep one's forces united; to leave no weak part unguarded; seize with rapidity on important points; and to inspire terror at the reputation of your arms, which will at once maintain fidelity and secure subjection.[2]
>
> Napoleon (1769–1821)

Keynote Definitions

Strategy is the system of finding, formulating, and developing a doctrine that will ensure long-term success if followed faithfully.
Strategy is wisdom with a defined vector to success and with an assessment of resource limitations.[3]
The **Strategist** is a wise, disciplined, and optimistic professional with a strategic mindset, a vision of the future, and intuition. He or she is armed with a strategizing methodology to utilize broad and deep knowledge of entities and a comprehensive understanding of the most influential objective trends.

The Strategic Mindset in Strategy Development and Implementation

On the basis of Chapter 1, we can conclude that the theory of strategy and its definition originated with the analysis of the works of Frontinus, Maurice, Leo VI, Napoleon, Jomini, Clausewitz, and Moltke. The probability of events, the projection of current and upcoming objective trends in the future, and the analysis of the pattern of current situations around the strategizing object make it less difficult to conduct an analysis of trends on the canvas of dynamics of values and interests. This also increases the accuracy of the strategizing processes. In developing successful strategies and analyzing historical strategic success, I have yet to meet a bulletproof, 100 percent correct strategy for the future. In fact, I have yet to see a strategy designed that was more than 85 percent accurate. Inaccuracy in strategy is due to the uncertainty and chaos of the future, but also to interfering human factors that can influence strategy positively and negatively, and can change the object and subject of strategy, both during strategic development and its implementation.

Despite inevitable inaccuracies, strategists can still feasibly strategize with the use of predictions and forecasts to later devise a strategic plan. How then do strategists move forward, factoring in values and interests, and determining the influence of global, regional, and sectorial trends on the future of the strategized object? This largely depends on the capability of strategists, who are bolstered by algorithmic results of their knowledge, vision, and intuition. Experience, a strategic mindset, and a clear analysis of strategic factors and rules also contribute to the strategist's capability.

All such elements, which are desirable to strategists, can be taught and learned, and strategists often teach these strategic processes and categories. But some people are born with an innate strategic mindset, and this intellectual capacity for strategy gives them an immediate advantage. More often than not, these strategists have strong feelings of responsibility to use their advantage for the strategic good of all. The disadvantages of those who do not have any natural inclination towards strategy can be compensated for through studying the values and trends of winning strategies and experiencing the strategic mindset. This is also how a person with natural strategic talent can develop a genius-level strategic mindset. Therefore, the aphorism still holds true that practice makes perfect, and talent can and must be developed and polished through education and experience. Certainly differing opinions on this subject remain; the dispute between those who think strategic talent can be learned and those who think it is innate has been called by philosophers the "Learner's Paradox." But I believe that strategists, even those who do not have divine inspiration, can still achieve a high-quality strategic mindset through arduous study from disciplined teachers. Obviously, practitioners who disagree with me have Plato on their side, who, in his Socratic dialogue *Meno*, argues that the virtuous qualities of a leader cannot be taught or learned. The combination of natural abilities and the knack for achieving satisfactory results is a rare double trait that is "neither an inborn quality nor taught, but comes to those who possess it as a gift from the gods."[4]

Aristotle challenges Plato in his *Ethics*, which is a consolation for me, as he takes the more optimistic approach and argues that desirable traits in a strategist can develop over the course of a lifetime in the activity of *doing*.[5] For this to occur, in addition to their education, strategists must also be optimists, or at least develop an optimistic mentality. The word Aristotle uses in Ancient Greek is *phronesis*, which means more than just "wisdom" and can easily include "strategy" as well.[6] For Aristotle, the temperate leader cannot only be taught temperance in the classroom, but achieves it by acting justly and temperately. Virtues are the activities of the strategist used as a means to achieve the highest end. For example, Aristotle taught Alexander the Great and his other pupils to be brave, and he explained that bravery is a mean between cowardice and foolhardiness. Cowards are never optimistic, and fools are hardly strategists. So, despite all disagreements between Plato and Aristotle on the category of optimism, Aristotle taught Alexander to be optimistic when developing de facto strategy.[7]

Why is the majority almost always wrong when selecting the correct strategic course? It is primarily because no other people outside of strategists have dedicated their talents, time, knowledge, and even lives to developing victorious strategies. A well-thought-out strategy always faces tremendous criticism because it often runs against the opinion of the majority and seemingly against common sense. Regarding the opinion of the crowd, I agree with the findings of sociologists who argue that groupthink can be devastating for society since it tends to aim for unanimity among members of the group rather than genuinely seeking out rational, workable solutions to a problem.[8] When all groups consist of only strategists, groupthink can be minimized. A strategist, and above all a strategic leader, especially while preparing strategy implementation in practice, must campaign for his or her strategy; this involves developing arguments to protect it, delivering public speeches to support it, and addressing decision-makers to convince them of the validity of his or her strategy. As Napoleon said, "In our time no one has the conception of what is great. It is up to me to show them."[9]

Prior to an analysis of trends, values, and forecasts, it is important to study processes of strategic thinking and the development of power in a strategic mindset. This is because any person without a developed strategic vision and strategic comprehension will be unable to contribute to the formulation and description of global trends and values. From historical to contemporary strategists, the greatest strategizers continually develop their strategic thinking, challenge themselves with new ideas, and increase their strategic capacity.

A solid strategic mindset and carefully acquired wisdom can be similar qualities in an individual, regardless if she or he is a strategist or not. However, the strategic person is not necessarily wise, and the wise person may not be a strategist. Aristotle wrote at the beginning of his *Metaphysics* that "[a]ll people by nature desire to know,"[10] and this optimistic dictum most certainly explains why Aristotle taught Alexander the Great to be wise. Aristotle was a good teacher and used multiple methods, the best of which were fables. Both wise and strategically minded individuals can become strategists with additional well-honed strategy development and implementation training. The strategist's wisdom is mirrored in his critical attitude to his own strategic conclusions and recommendations. He or she has to keep this attitude, and not just during the process of strategy development and implementation; it has to be a non-stop approach even during all processes of strategy monitoring, while the strategy is still actual and in use. As Saint-Exupéry writes in *The Little Prince,* a novel written for children, which includes a passage on the power of wise, strategic judgment:

> "Then you shall judge yourself," the king answered. "That is the most difficult thing of all. It is much more difficult to judge oneself than to judge others. If you succeed in judging yourself rightly, then you are indeed a man of true wisdom."[11]

Strategic study of values and interests mostly result from inferring from existing reality with an analyzable environment of the strategizing object. When strategists work on enriching strategic priorities, they must start to plan for a not-so-distant future and then, on the basis of more or less known information, go forward into completely unknown territory, while taking into consideration, and preliminary evaluation of, the opinion of the majority (not for rigorous implementation) who are the generators of public values. Strategy should be taught through the study of its theory and the analysis of strategy implementation. Strategy implementation should be studied in order to learn to draw a strategic and practical roadmap for an unknown future. Good strategists are like a powerful army; however, this army does not have recruits, but only volunteers.

It is not surprising that great strategists consider strategy to be a more powerful weapon than any ammunition stored in a military garrison. As Napoleon writes, "There are but two powers in the world, the sword and the mind. In the long run the sword is always beaten by the mind."[12] Practically all the conventional weapons available in the twenty-first century were created or used during Napoleon's era in some variation. Napoleon was skilled in all the available weaponry known to him, but he still considered strategy to be more powerful than any other weapon. In this quote, the sword represents the most powerful physical weapon, which will always be less powerful than the brilliant strategy of minds.

In this chapter I present several examples of strategic ways of thinking, concluding with the 15 rules of strategic thinking. Prior to this section, I will outline simplified ways of strategic thinking. I always try to compare my way of strategic thinking with other modern-day professional strategists, such as William Cohen (1940–) and Donald Rumsfeld (1932–), who both teach strategic ways of thinking and are practitioners of strategy.

In my proposed 15 rules of strategic thinking, Rule 1 states that the majority is almost always wrong, because the majority primarily uses common sense and logic. Strategists can use logic, but it is not good enough. Strategy is not merely a discipline involving forms and laws but must also incorporate correct ways of thinking. It is more than a science about conditions, analyses, and conclusions (although these are all important aspects of strategic thinking). Strategy is about prediction and a vision of future prospects, uncertainties, and risks. Formal and informal logic are useful for existing conditions, but not for unknown prospects. Strategists must develop a more objective and abstract way of thinking in order to tackle these unknowns.

It is impossible to develop a strategic mindset through studying rules and books on strategy alone—it is a good tactic, but still not good enough. It is important to experience strategic development and implementation firsthand, and to analyze what occurs, but this is too costly without theoretically developed rules. Strategists must take what they are taught and compare it with actual implementation of strategy. Only then will they gain a better comprehension of strategy. As Hegel would say when criticizing Kant, "But to seek to know before we know is as absurd as the wise resolution of Scholasticus, not to venture into the water until he had learned to swim."[13] A very experienced statesman, Donald Rumsfeld, who has worked in the administrations of three American presidents (Richard Nixon, Gerald Ford, and George W. Bush), calls his rules "Leadership Lessons." These lessons were and still are applicable to business, politics, war, and life. He also named his book after his rules. Chapter 4 of his book is entitled "Thinking Strategically."

Strategy is the most philosophical, theoretical, and yet practical element of success. Strategic success can be the result of many years of experience and extensive knowledge or of a fresh young mind with an unconventional point of view and, most importantly, free of intellectual inertia. Sound strategy is a constant process of rethinking and reevaluating. Whether at work, at play, or at rest, the strategist is always strategizing. The development of strategy is the privilege of top-level decision-makers, as well as professionals who dedicate their efforts to formulating, monitoring, redesigning, and updating strategy. It is the apex of management. Strategy is an extremely powerful tool. A strategy based on an intensive theory and bulletproof analysis can lead an entity from failure to the top of its field. On the other hand, a strategy that is not tailored to the particular situation or that is theoretically flawed may lead a company at the top of its field to disorder and failure. The strategist may very well hold the future of a company, a military power, or a country in his or her hands, which yields an incredible amount of pressure and responsibility. However, dictatorial leaders usually do not possess a strategic mindset and often voluntarily take on this responsibility due (among other qualities) to a lack of vision and wisdom. The wrong strategy will bring about the collapse of the entire strategic framework, along with all that went into its development and implementation. The organizational structure and management systems previously implemented, personnel hired, resources allocated, and day-to-day operational activities all become irrelevant and obsolete when the strategy behind them fails.

In order to truly comprehend strategy—its very essence—one must develop a strategic mindset. It is not so easy to grasp the practical and theoretical significance of the keynote definitions presented at the beginning of this chapter if one's mind is not already strategically oriented. A successful strategy cannot be discovered, developed, or even fully understood with a traditional mindset. Daily needs and routines train the mind to be operational, short-term, non-prospective, and non-strategic. The success of practically every great leader or visionary is largely the result of a well-tuned strategic mindset. One of the best examples of such a leader is the great visionary Konrad Adenauer (1876–1967). Adenauer occupied high-ranking positions in pre–Nazi Germany and was among the very few German leaders who immediately and completely rejected Hitler's ideas of National Socialism. Adenauer's criticism ran contrary to the "common sense" notion of millions of his compatriots. He was exiled and later forced into a prison camp. His mindset conflicted with the shortsighted opinion of the majority(!) of Germans at the time. Thankfully, his vision and steadfastness were validated when he became the first chancellor of West Germany after World War II.[14]

Illustrating the importance of a well-developed strategic mindset, Adenauer said, "[W]e all live under the same sky, but we don't all have the same horizon."[15] His example demonstrates not only the challenges of formulating an accurate strategic vision of the future, but also the importance of sticking to this vision, regardless of the opposition one faces. Even in the face of imprisonment and death imposed by the power structure of his country, Konrad Adenauer refused to stray from his prospective vision. The seeds of a potential future leader are in his devotion to mission: as Napoleon stated, "Nothing is so rare as steadfast devotion" to strategy.[16] Strategists should aim to be steadfast in grasping objective trends and must devote considerable time to formulating priorities and then setting objectives and goals according to these priorities. Before one's competitors spot the same strategic opportunities, strategists must construct a beacon to guide the past to the future, while tirelessly devising the most efficient path to success.

US Air Force Col. John R. Boyd, the famous military strategist and fighter-plane designer, offers a practical understanding of the strategic mindset as "a mental tapestry of changing intentions for harmonizing and focusing our efforts as a basis for realizing some aim or purpose in an unfolding and often unforeseen world of many bewildering events and many contending interests."[17] Practically, the beginning of this description paraphrases the well-known idea that strategy is a science requiring an artist's touch. In this case the artist's touch is the strategic mindset, which interprets and connects facts in a way that those without this mindset cannot. A trained strategic mindset possesses the acoustic ability to listen, the intellect to understand, and the judgment to single out the best opinions and advice of other experts. Some (especially those in the military) believe that strategy is primarily reserved for the highest levels of military leadership. A colleague of Col. Boyd's and Professor of National Security Policy in the Department of National Security and Strategy at the US Army War College, Col. Harry Yagger, argues that

> [G]ood strategy development requires the military professional to step out of the planning mindset and adopt one more suited for strategic thinking. In the strategic mindset, the professional military strategist embraces the complexity and chaos of the strategic environment and envisions all its continuities and possibilities in seeking to create favorable strategic effects in support of national interests.[18]

In fact, in recent history, it was civilians who developed strategy according to national interests, which uniformed strategists then converted into military doctrine. In the twenty-first century, the overwhelming majority of strategists are civilians. However, very few of them were actually trained to be strategists. Keeping this in mind, Professor Yagger's position is understandable—strategic practice and theory are an important part of the curriculum in military colleges and universities. In business schools, however, strategy is only one of many courses and is not a major. This situation is beginning to change. At the beginning of the twenty-first century, several universities have started to provide strategy as its own curriculum of study, such as the University of Rochester, which created a major in economics and business strategies.[19]

Strategic Ways of Thinking

There are three basic approaches to strategic thinking. The first approach is New Dimensions Strategy (NDS). NDS requires an ability to think beyond an entity's current agenda in order to recognize and analyze radically innovative paths to success, even if they may fundamentally alter the entity's current activity. From practically infinite possibilities, the strategist must select a strategic objective, to which a substantial part of the entity's resources will then be dedicated. It would be wrong to say that all of the entity's resources are dedicated to the selected strategic priority and corresponding objectives, because when an established entity discovers a new approach, at least for the short term, it continues to use some resources for its existing operations.

Typically, new dimensions strategy is not designated as the primary approach in books on strategy. Most books steer the reader toward the improvement of current functions, and focus less on exploring radically new options. This book considers such an approach, which is referred to as an Improvement Strategy (IS), secondary to a new dimensions strategy. Unlike NDS, an improvement strategy is based primarily on the systematic analysis of the entity's subsystems, elements, and functions, as well as their interaction with one another.

In *The Mind of the Strategist: The Art of Japanese Business*, Kenichi Ohmae, former director of McKinsey & Company and a leading strategic analyst, gives the following description of strategic thinking, which specifically describes an improvement strategy:

> In strategic thinking, one first seeks a clear understanding of the particular character of each element of a situation and then makes the fullest possible use of human brainpower to restructure the elements in the most advantageous way. Phenomena and events in the real world do not always fit a linear model. Hence the most reliable means of dissecting a situation into its constituent parts and reassembling them in the desired pattern is not a step-by-step methodology such as systems analysis. Rather, it is that ultimate nonlinear thinking tool, the human brain. True strategic thinking thus contrasts sharply with the conventional mechanical systems approach based on linear thinking. But it also contrasts with the approach that stakes everything on intuition, reaching conclusions without any real breakdown or analysis.[20]

One of the best practical examples of a successful improvement strategy is found in the leadership of Jack Welch, chairman and chief executive of General Electric. In 1995, Welch adopted and then developed Six Sigma—a process to define and measure efficiency in manufacturing (initially introduced to the business community in 1986 by

Motorola). Six Sigma is "a highly disciplined process that helps us focus on developing and delivering near-perfect products and services."[21]

Practically, GE's version of Six Sigma provides a means to describe the standard deviation from constrained limits, which ideally is as small as possible. It is a strategic methodology of specific scope to find and analyze problems, and in doing so increase the efficiency of products in respect to customer needs. It is a pure improvement strategy that companies throughout the world have adopted. An efficient improvement strategy will lead to a new generation of products and services or to a substantial reduction in production costs via a more effective combination of basic economic factors. One of the drawbacks of this strategy is that it prevents a company from aggressively looking for strategies of revolutionary opportunities.

To summarize the first approach to strategic thinking, NDS focuses on finding and evaluating new spheres and new prospects of activity. While the second approach, the improvement strategy, focuses on optimizing existing functions.

The third approach is referred to as Combination Strategy (CS). A CS always requires more investment and time than either an NDS or an IS. This strategy is useful for business or military entities that must remain consistent with existing strategy (with some improvements), while at the same time investing in new and revolutionary ideas as well (which is the basis of NDS). Practically speaking, with CS entities trying to maintain previous strategy can continue to operate on the basis of old strategy with some improvement. These entities can start to invest in innovative NDS. However, NDS can be implemented very slowly in the conditions of the third approach because it requires extra time, investments, and practice. Entities lose their strategic advantage, which is to be first in practice due to their new strategy. What is good about CS is that entities never stop their current operations and, at the same time, try to proceed through totally new pathways.

In summary, the efficiency of this strategy depends on leadership entities and conditions, as well as the circumstances of their decisions and environmental operations. The following example demonstrates when a third approach would be appropriate: if a company produces a vital product for the state that is critical to national security, the company cannot just cease production. According to proven studies, new revolutionary products will be in demand, and the company must spend resources for the research and development of future new goods or services. CS enables an entity to achieve efficiency and profitability by improving existing operational systems and technologies while at the same time pursuing revolutionary new ideas on a parallel path.

Regardless of which one of the three strategic approaches is chosen, a strategist must remember that although detailed quantitative time-sensitive analysis is absolutely required, the crucial element in strategic thinking is always intuition.

Sustainable efficiency and/or profitability is a key criterion of the effective strategic approach and strategic management. One method that strategists can use to improve profitability is the application of natural laws (physics, chemistry, and other natural sciences) to improve the efficiency of large-scale business or military operations. For example, the ideas of Ilya Prigogine, who won the Nobel Prize for Chemistry in 1977 for his "contributions to non-equilibrium thermodynamics, particularly the theory of dissipative structures,"[22] have many practical strategic applications. A "dissipative structure" is basically one that is far from its equilibrium, such as a company with low profitability, a government with unbalanced accounts, or a military unit with improper ammunition and weapons for its objective. In all cases, these entities have to strategically reorient themselves

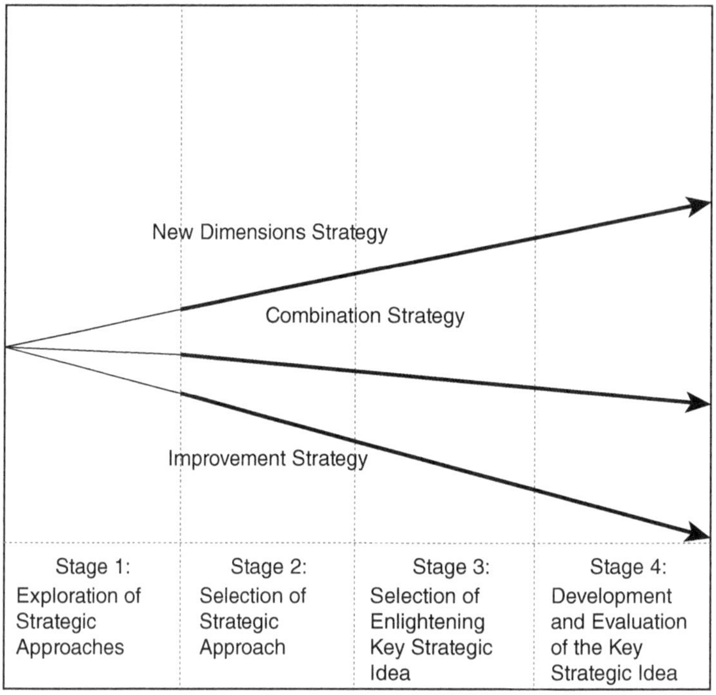

Figure 2.1 Dimensions and Stages of the Strategic Thought Process
© Dr.Vladimir Kvint, 2010

toward outside, domestic or international cooperation. An inefficient company, military unit, or country province has four basic strategic options: the first three options are dividing it, raising investment by selling partial ownership and using this income for subsequent reorganization, or downsizing. If none of these steps is taken, Prigogine's theory helps to predict that the company, military unit, or province will eventually cease to exist. In terms of thermodynamics, the inflow of investment can be understood as the energy needed to sustain the structure. The fourth option is a managerial one: the company can change its strategic leadership, improve its management system, and in doing so attain the energy required to sustain the company's, military unit's, or state's administrative region.

Stages of the Strategic Thought Process

The *exploration of the three strategic approaches* is the **first stage** of the strategic thought process. The **second stage** is the *selection* of one of them. The **third stage** of the strategic thought process, the *stage of enlightenment*, employs long-term vision and analytical skills to sift through the less important factors and focus exclusively on those of strategic significance. In other words, the main focus of this stage is to find the enlightening key idea of the potential strategy. At this stage, strategists need a mental spotlight that projects and focuses all intellectual capacity on the key prospective idea. The **fourth stage** is the *strategic evaluation and development* of the fundamental prospective idea selected in stage three. This is the stage where the "flesh and bones" of the strategic idea are formed.

Characteristics of the Strategic Mindset

Strategists have to be both *rigid* and *flexible*, depending on the analysis of the dynamics of external and internal factors. Strategists should always be *open to feedback* from users of their strategy and to the forecasts and strategic ideas of others. However, no idea from outside the strategist's mind can be rejected or accepted without a serious reevaluation—and always from a *long-term perspective*. With a strategic mindset, the strategist has to *assess the impact* of all relevant facts, studies, forecasts, and analyses from other experts and *refocus* his or her path accordingly. The *reevaluation of the past*, *extrapolation of known trends*, and *exploration of the future* are the daily activities of the strategist. At all stages of strategic development and implementation, the reexamination of accomplishments and facts is routine. This should also be done in order to prevent the repetition of previously diagnosed mistakes. However, routines are extremely dangerous for strategists; they are a practical manifestation of intellectual inertia. In an effort to counteract such forms of inertia, Eric Schmidt (1955–), the CEO of Google, one of the most successful companies of the first decade of the twenty-first century, formally required his employees to dedicate 20 percent of their activity to non-operational, innovative efforts. This has undoubtedly helped establish a strategic mindset in Google's employees and has been a significant factor in the company's consistently cutting-edge technological offerings. A strategic mindset has to constantly strive to look beyond daily routines in order to *connect the past directly to the future*, building a conceptual road from the visible and known to the invisible and unknown. This cannot be done without a blend of *analytical skills* and *artistic creativity*. The strategic mindset always has to be oriented toward the optimization of resources on the path to success—not the maximization of the result, which in some cases can actually be harmful. Optimization is the main path to success. The achievement of sustainable success is one of the most important elements of the strategic mindset. Leaders with a strategic mindset think of the ultimate victory not as the destruction of their competitors but as the prevention of competition by rendering their competitors obsolete; unnecessary competition is an inefficient use of an entity's resources.

Logically, the roots of strategy are in military applications. Over the past 200 years, strategy has become a theoretical and practical weapon in politics, the military, economics, business, and any activity that requires a long-term vision and the ability to find and allocate resources to achieve sustainable success. For strategists, sustainability of success is a crucial issue. Strategy is not about the temporary achievement of objectives and goals; it is about long-term, sustainable success. The definition of long and short term is relative—typically, strategy is not developed for a period shorter than three years. Five- and ten-year strategies are standard for national and regional governments, multinational corporations, or national military armies and fleets. If an entity tries to develop a strategy for a shorter period, the time of strategy development may be longer than the period of its use, making it outdated at the moment of its implementation. For this reason, the "current time" of strategy development is typically about six months ahead of real time for beginning strategy development. Strategists should envision the external and internal environment of the entity in six months and take these conditions as the starting moment for strategy development. In 1812, Napoleon captured Moscow at great expense. However, due to a lack of resources, he was not able to hold it. After only a few weeks he left the city. This is an example of one of the most brilliant strategic minds in history focusing only on victory instead of on long-term sustainable success. He won every battle on his way to Moscow but lost the war and almost his entire army. Like Napoleon's experience in Russia, the US's "shock and awe" strategy in Iraq in 2003 was initially very successful. Saddam Hussein's regime was promptly dismantled; however, it very quickly became apparent that the US did not have a strategy to sustain this success. The cost of this strategic miscalculation has been a tremendous amount of resources as well as the lives of thousands of US soldiers and Iraqi citizens. The same idea applies to business. As both the external and internal environment for any entity is constantly in flux, the starting platform for the development of a strategy must be a clear understanding and description of the expected conditions in six months. Without a strategy that focuses on long-term, sustainable success, finding and occupying a new niche in the marketplace or utilizing a new technology will achieve only a temporary victory.

In the words of Professors Thomas H. Davenport, Marius Leibold, and Sven Voelpel:

> [T]he key elements of a strategy mindset can also be described as a set of mental spaces occupying individuals' minds at any particular period of time. Fauconnier describes mental space as providing a medium in which cognitive activities can take place, i.e., the partial cognitive structures that emerge when we think and talk. And it is in these mental spaces that domains are defined, reasoned, changed, and merged for purposes of understanding and action. Furthermore, mental spaces are interconnected and can be modified as thought and discourse unfold.[23]

Once an individual develops a strategic mindset, it is a tool that will never be lost as long as it is in practical need and regularly used. Dr. Gilles Fauconnier, a professor of the University of California, San Diego, mentioned in the above text, is a leading authority in cognitive psychology and the study of the mindset. The mental spaces described by Dr. Fauconnier must be oriented in such a way as to be capable of distinguishing a company that is on the verge of falling apart from one that is going through an extremely challenging time but has a long-term future. To those without a strategic mindset, these two companies may appear to be in very similar situations. In reality, they are in fundamentally different situations in that one company has a strategy that will lead them out of a difficult period, and the other does not. An entity can operate only temporarily without a strategy. Such entities are like boats with a cracked hull—they may be able to stay afloat for a brief period, but it is only a matter of time before they sink to the bottom of the ocean. Companies enjoying success without a strategy are in a precarious situation. They allocate their resources to expanding the production of highly sought-after goods or services, unaware of technological advancements or crossovers from other industries that (combined with the right strategy) will create substitute products—and eventually their company's obsolescence. There are numerous examples of this type of short-sighted success. Think of all of the software companies that have moved into the hardware, mobile, or telephony business and then put the industry's dominant company out of business. Contrary to popular opinion, strategy is not needed only during times of crisis—when a country is at war or when a company encounters a threatening situation. This could not be further from the truth. One of the great challenges of success is resisting the drift toward complacency.

The Three Axes of Strategic Thought

Strategists always have to explore all three approaches to strategic thinking and decide if the situation facing an entity calls for a revolutionary strategic change or a reevaluation and revision of the strategic plan. Regardless of which strategy is chosen, all strategic thought occurs within the following three axes: *time*, *cost*, and *space*. The nature and dynamics of time and space are typically thought of as the realm of physics. Actually, this dilemma is a fundamental concept of strategy. Napoleon theorized that "strategy is the art of making use of time and space. I am less concerned about the latter than the former. Space we can recover, lost time never."[24] In 1905, almost a century after Napoleon, Albert Einstein developed a slightly more complex explanation, which eventually became known as the Special Theory of Relativity. In 1908, the mathematician Hermann Minkowski made a geometric illustration for Einstein's theory (see Figure 2.2 on p. 64), which developed the concept of "spacetime" by combining the three dimensions of space, with time as the fourth dimension.[25] Einstein's and Minkowski's work have very practical implications for strategists. However, contrary to the concepts of physics, time and space in political, economic, and business strategy can be intertwined beyond the concept of spacetime, to the point of these axes' becoming interchangeable. Strategists must understand time as the space for strategic development. Strategy is developed only in time, while space is where most resources are allocated. Strategists should understand space as more than just territory. Strategy is the product of the multiplication of time, cost, and space, where space may be understood through developed and implemented strategic ideas. Time is strategy's developmental space during the allocation of all resources in strategic non-physical space. Unlike in economics, resources in strategy are not necessarily physical; they can be intangible, like information or strategic ideas, paths, or methods to achieve success. Even the most practical self-made billionaire will describe the development of strategy (the fourth stage) as beginning with an idea and ending with an idea, although the evaluation may lead the strategist to a refined idea or a radically new one. From the perspective of information theory, ideas are just new information in various forms. Of course, the implementation of any strategic plan must be feasible given limited resources. For entrepreneurs, strategy is always about the idea coupled with the critical factor of time.

For the strategic mindset, it is impossible to overestimate the role of intuition. The prism of intuition clarifies strategic ideas, without which an evaluation of the three axes of strategic thought has limited utility. While quantitative analyses are paramount, intuition is a vital part of the strategic thought process. Intuition is the grandmother of all excellent strategies; without it, the development of a vision, the direction of quantitative analyses, and an efficient strategic management system are nearly impossible. Intuition will develop with experience and/or a conscious fine-tuning of the mind toward strategic analysis. Often, improvement strategies can bring long-term success on the basis of an effective quality management system. Improvement strategy is a success when first-class and operationally efficient practices maintain strategic leadership, especially production and national leadership, in the global arena during an extended period. The best example of this is the success of Japanese consumer electronic and car manufacturing industries during the last quarter of the twentieth century. Daily quality management and continuous improvement based on the ideas of Edward Deming brought Japan numerous strategic advantages. Corporate America responded with a strong asymmetric answer to the Japanese strategy of improvement. Several American companies—like IBM, Microsoft, and Apple—appeared on the global stage with revolutionary products and ideas. The Japanese continued to improve outdated products, but around the start of the new century, Japanese corporations and strategies started to lose direction.

Japanese corporations' loss of leadership is an example of how a long-term product line and services improvement strategy can lose its competitive edge to strategies involving new dimensions. The Japanese operational effectiveness of the 1970s and 1980s—which was a pioneering practice at the time—did not work in the new technological age of the twenty-first century. At that time, "Japanese companies rarely developed distinct strategic positions." Some continued success of "Sony, Canon, and Sega for example—were the exception rather than the rule."[26] But even these companies' successes were based on the lower cost and quality of existing products, and not on revolutionary products and ideas.

The Quality of a Strategist

Having presented the approaches, stages, and characteristics of the strategic thought process, the next logical step is to describe who the strategist is. The strategist is like an astronomer. An astronomer does not create stars, comets, or planets; he or she discovers them and interprets their significance in relation to the wider cosmos from the finite vantage point of planet Earth. In the same spirit, strategists explore and analyze the global world order or marketplace to discover and understand new trends and their impact on particular companies, countries, new markets, and the GMP—or even on the global order itself. The strategist acts as a navigator, guiding a company, military structures, government, or any legal entity from the present to a future destination: anticipating, avoiding, and reacting effectively to the unknowable obstacles of the future. Most strategists do not develop brand new military powers, new products, technologies, standards, etc.; rather, they are adept at honing in on practical applications and potential.

The first step to becoming a strategist is a deep reorientation, retuning, and reformatting of one's thought process, in order to eventually develop a strategic mindset. The benefits of doing this are enormous. Strategists should have a clear grasp of the most powerful objective trends, including global trends, and the ability to formulate priorities, in order to set objectives and goals according to these priorities. Professional strategists must devise the most efficient paths towards the beacons of their prospective visions, before their competitors spot the same strategic opportunities. The strategist is not involved in operational, day-to-day activity. Present-day activities are already the past for the strategist. Nonetheless, strategists should be in regular contact with operational managers and officers, in order to get feedback from them about challenges and requirements. Gleaned from their predictions and forecasts projected at least six months into the future, strategists can anticipate and forecast potential events by constructing a future-contained model of the "present." All forecasts and starting points for strategy development have to be made from this time-based platform. Keep in mind that this formulation of time does not apply to strategists who focus on stock and currency markets. In these markets of extreme uncertainty, strategy applies to everything beyond one month; an accurate prediction of an event in money management five months ahead of time would be a major feat. Strategists have to be as precise as possible with their predictions. This is what makes strategy so difficult— for the more precise a strategist's prediction, the more likely it will be wrong. One failed prediction is all that is necessary for a strategist to lose credibility. In this sense, the strategist is like a minesweeper; his first mistake is often his last. However, from another point of view, strategists must always study strategists', enemies', and competitors' past mistakes—as well as their own—for elements of new successful strategy under upcoming conditions, or the environment of another strategizing object. At the same time, I always recommend that strategists do not overspend time researching the environmental conditions of old strategies. It's a dead strategic landscape. A strategist will be successful only if he or she can see the moment of conception. In other words, success for a strategist is based on the ability to recognize the very beginning of a trend and predict its implications before enemies or competitors can. Strategists must have the ability of foresight and mental capacity to determine the political, economic, technological, and other conditions that will exist at the future moment—roughly six months ahead—when the process of implementing a new strategy will begin. A true strategist must condition him or herself to envision potential events and feel as though he or she lives in the conditions of the future more so than the current situation.

A strategist must be able to clearly recognize the most effective competitive advantages that, when aligned with the availability of resources, will enable the realization of key entity priorities. Even the most well-developed and thought-out strategies will inevitably collide with some unexpected threats. The strategist must be able to efficiently and effectively address the obstacles that arise. The strategist should aim to maneuver around foreseeable obstacles, but in situations where obstacles cannot be avoided, the strategist must develop methods for addressing the roadblocks and deal with their impact directly.

Strategists must possess the ability to expect the unexpected and to execute decisions that are unfathomable to their competitors. The Latin proverb attributed to Cicero, "Hannibal ante portus," translated as "Hannibal is at the gate," alludes to a prime example of foretelling the unexpected and of unconventional decision-making. When faced with the seemingly impossible task of transporting an army with elephants through treacherous mountainous terrain with no roads, Hannibal famously quipped, "I will either find a way, or make one." His unconventional route, where he brought dozens of elephants and an army of 10,000 men over the Alps, is his most famous campaign. Hannibal made a decision that his competitors did not foresee. The Romans felt they were secure and did not predict having to protect the Alps from invasion, yet Hannibal fought his way into northern Italy.

In the corporate world, charting an unconventional route begins with an examination of the strategic departments of major corporations. Unfortunately, not all corporations have a department dedicated specifically to strategy—even in the twenty-first century when strategy has become a proven instrument to success. Who are the employees in these departments, and what do they do? Strategic branches or strategic initiative departments (as they are sometimes known) in both multinational corporations and medium-size companies typically have two types of employees assigned to strategy. The first are very experienced, connected, and knowledgeable. In addition to being well-informed about the respective field, industry, and region, these strategists generally have a deep knowledge of geography, political science, political economy, economics, business, and technology, among many other fields. However, experience and knowledge are only half of the equation. Strategic departments are usually not capable of generating truly revolutionary ideas unless hiring managers acquire new talent. Freshly minted strategists have an understanding of the entity for which they work. Novices make up for their lack of experience with their ability to think outside of the box. In the spirit of Adenauer, they seek new horizons nestled under familiar skies. To disagree with their highly accomplished and respected colleagues takes chutzpah—and it is indeed this very bold and gutsy quality young strategists should possess. The most innovative and successful corporate strategies are usually the result of the collaborative efforts between experienced, seasoned individuals and the innovative ideas of newcomers (especially in the Global Emerging Market and other emerging fields) and there are also exceptional cases in which young or old strategists have some qualities of both types of strategists. For small and family-run businesses with limited resources, it is a significant challenge to find even two employees with the aforementioned qualities to develop and implement strategy.

Typically, in these companies, strategy is the work of the owner, top-level management, and possibly an accountant or engineer. Due to limited resources, strategy is updated only periodically, which puts such companies at a disadvantage to larger competitors that have the means to constantly reassess and reevaluate their strategy. A great strategic idea or revolutionary business concept can bring tremendous success to businesses that begin as small or family-run operations (e.g. Walmart, Microsoft, and Google). In order to operate efficiently and to achieve a high degree of success, strategists and strategic leaders must understand the essence, elements, methods, and forms of management systems as well as their main functions—planning, motivation and control—according to indicators of strategic efficiency.

The capabilities of a strategist are strongly connected to three intertwined lines of thought and analysis. First, he or she must be able to understand existing statistical and empirical data from a higher level of abstract thinking and visualization than his or her own. Second, the data must be assessed at the core level of detail. Third, his or her studies must be guided by an intuitive ability to distill noise and pluck out the key factors and drivers of a strategy. Strategists and leaders share many mutual characteristics, but not all. Regarding mutual categories, there is one that is very important. Victory for leaders or success from a full implementation of strategy requires patience. Even with critics' resistance to promoting a strategy, bringing it through years of resistance requires not only patience but also perseverance, which is patience through time. This requires a long time and lasts from a minimum of three years to a strategist's lifetime. During this period, detractors will tell you that the strategy is not working; however, it takes many years for the final nails and bullets of strategy to take effect. Or, in the example of China, much longer—the nation's strategy implementation has been a century-long process, and is still continuing. A successful and victorious end requires patience for all state and corporate leaders, military commanders, and strategists. For strategists, personal patience and sticking to their strategy is the form of perseverance needed to endure long-term competition and resistance from enemies, competitors, and critics. Patience and perseverance are instruments for achieving strategic victory and success. To prove my postulate about patience, I would like to bring to the attention of my readers one recorded sentence (but not proven) from the autobiography of Tamerlane (1336–1405). It was said that, while sleeping, he received word from the divine that "patience is the key to happiness." Don't forget that strategy is a long way to the implementation of happiness.[27] This is definitely a philosophically proven maxim.

Prophets and Strategists

Prophecy is an old concept. It was a trade and skill long before the prophecies recorded in both Jewish and Christian Scriptures. Even earlier in the Mesopotamian era, we find records about "professional" diviners who were mouthpieces for an invisible and unknown superpower or deity. In the history of monotheistic religions, being a messenger is perhaps the biggest function of a prophet; yet prophets are not only messengers, but also predictors and, from time to time, even leaders. In the stories of Abraham and Moses, recounted in Genesis and Exodus, as well as in the Qu'ran, prophets took on a proactive role, and can be considered prophet-leaders. Moses is particularly important for strategists as a model of the prophet-leader. The capacity of Moses was so enormous that the Torah states, "Never again did there arise in Israel a prophet like Moses" (Genesis 34:10). He started as a messenger and subsequently grew into a great leader—and in some ways a masterful strategist. His successor Joshua was not necessarily a prophet, but rather a leader and military strategist. Another famous prophet in Biblical history was Samuel. He began as a prophet and, like Moses, became a prominent leader and strategist during the war against the Philistines around 1040 BCE (the event and date, however, are not proven historical facts). According to the work of J. Hampton Keathley III in his article "The Major Prophets," the English Bible and Hebrew Bible have some differences in their description of prophets and in their importance. For example, Keathley remarks, "Daniel, usually viewed as one of the Major Prophets in the English Bible, actually appears in the third division of the Hebrew Canon called 'The Writings.'"[28] According to the Book of Samuel, some prophets have different functions. A prophet is someone who observes and understands, and who is also a seer. In another verse, Samuel describes the prophet as "Nabu," or someone who calls and announces (1 Samuel 9:9).

It seems to me that in many Christian traditions prophets are understood to be more passive, and are called by the divine rather than taking up the "profession" themselves. At any rate, we can conclude that both types of prophets are either used by a higher power that wants to make an announcement for a major event that will presumably happen in the future, or have the extra capacity to see the future and announce it to their audience. In these examples, a prophet is a visionary and a predictor, but not necessarily a leader.

In the majority of cases, delivered prophecies were so outside of the common person's understanding that prophets were not taken seriously by their contemporaries, like Cassandra the Trojan priestess, who foretold the fall of Troy, until the events came to pass. In the Torah, the word "Navi" connotes a prophet with a strong and accurate vision, like the figures of Moses and Samuel, while Navi'im' indicates "prophet" only, with no leadership characteristics.

It is not uncommon in the history of prophecy for a leader/strategist to present his strategic vision in such a way that it is considered a prophecy for a short time after it is implemented. While we can say that some strategists may be *close* to prophetic, they may not be considered a prophet. There are some predictors who can see far ahead (even through centuries) but they are neither prophets nor messengers. The most famous example of such an outstanding individual is Nostradamus (1503–1566). In about 1550, he started to publish his predictions, and in 1555 he collected them into the first edition of his book *Centuries*, which since then has often been translated as *The Complete Prophecies of Nostradamus*. Nostradamus himself considered his predictions prophecies. In his preface to the first edition of his book, he addressed his son Caesar, presenting himself as a prophet:[29] "Such alone as are inspired by the divine power can predict particular events in a spirit of prophecy."[30] Nonetheless, in the same preface, he writes:

> Now, my son, although I have inserted the name of prophet here, I will not attribute to myself so sublime a title; he who is called prophet now, once was called seer, and prophets are those properly, my son, that see things remote from the natural knowledge of mankind. Or, to put the case, the prophets, by the means of the perfect light of prophecy, may see divine things, as well as human (which cannot but be seeing the effects of future predictions) and do extend a great distance, for the secrets of God are incomprehensible, and their efficient power is far remote from the natural knowledge, taking their origin in the free will, causing those things to appear which otherwise could not be known, neither by human auguries nor by any hidden knowledge or secret virtue under Heaven. Only by the means of some indivisible eternal being, and by Herculean agitation the causes come to be known by the celestial motion.[31]

Reading the above text by Nostradamus, it seems possible that he attributed both powers to himself, as a prophet and a visionary (seer).[32] Though he attributes these powers, he also does not appear sure of whether he is prophet or seer, or if he has both capacities. He sometimes conflates and mixes the visionary power of prophet with the "professional" force of predictor (seer). For years, I have been impressed with the accuracy of his visions and his predictions, closed off from him by centuries of uncertainty. After fighting my own doubts, I concluded with reluctance and without any excitement that Nostradamus is a predictor (seer), but not a prophet. I cannot judge all of his quatrains, but with his prophetic precision many of his predictions have come true. Prophets demonstrate their ability over long periods of time, and make predictions about events much further in the future than a typical strategic plan or even strategic concept. Their wisdom and vision encompass centuries, like the visions of the prophet Daniel. For the contemporaries of prophets, it is difficult and sometimes impossible to believe what the prophet is saying, and often by the time it comes true, these contemporaries are long gone and forgotten.

Do not conclude from the above texts that every single leader mentioned in sacred texts was a prophet. The Biblical King David is an excellent example of a man who was not a prophet, but the greatest leader in Israelite history. While not exhibiting any prophetic qualities himself, David did surround himself with prophets, such as Nathan. At this point in Israelite history, the "professions" of prophets and leaders were already divided. Prophets are often also considered wise, though typically the first descriptive characteristics are "abnormal" or "crazy." In Hellenic history, the role of a wise person and diviner were split, and no serious philosopher would ever be considered a prophet as well, while neither would be considered a leader (although Plato argues in *Republic* that philosophers should be kings). It is logically possible that Alexander the Great consulted[33] with the oracle at Delphi for future predictions, as several historians have discussed.

For a strategist, the most important quality held by a prophet and not a philosopher is the prophet's correlation with time. Prophets almost always relate their vision on a time scale. Strategy and strategic scenarios are always related to time. Time is the first consideration, and the strongest influence on strategy and strategists. Despite the fact that some Marxian economists consider the first economic law to be the law of values or law of costs, while another school of economists consider the first law of economics to be "the greater the demand the higher the price," in strategy, both price and demand can be fundamentally changed by time. For this reason, *the first law of strategy is the law of economizing time* (law of time).

Professionals who offered strategic advice also existed during ancient times. This is an old institution; given what we know, we can say that the advisors of pharaohs in Ancient Egypt were strategists. The same can be said about the viziers who advised sultans in the Ottoman Empire in a predominantly Muslim world. What we don't know is the balance between myth, psychology, early beliefs, and true strategic knowledge.

What is the difference between a prophet and a strategist? In most historical or legendary cases, prophets foresee the future of a nation or individual, be it good or bad. Prophets do not plan, and do not present multiple scenarios based on their findings. They simply perceive the future without alternatives. A strategist by necessity will always have multiple scenarios. If a strategist is absolutely certain, it is possible to present just one scenario, but this is rare. Even a strategic genius will have more than one outcome after developing and planning a strategy, and predicting one absolute result is foolish. I always recommend having two or three objectively designed scenarios.

Prophets do not have alternates because they are not strategizing about the future; rather, they are predicting it. If I am a theoretical strategist and practitioner, and I believe in the ability of prophets to foresee the future without any strategic development or implementation, then I also believe that I have no capability to change the future predicted by a prophet, regardless of my strategic mindset. It will not matter what I do, because this is no longer strategy, it is *destiny*, and it brings humankind to a predicted end. In a future foretold by a prophet, the only response is to be ready to face it.

There are a few unique cases where I believe a strategist went beyond a strategy and predicted the future. In reading Napoleon's memoirs of his 1812 military campaign in Russia, he could foresee his devastating loss. Yet despite this loss, and the criticism that followed, he would still do it over again. He had no explanation for his action, but also no alternative. I have thought about Napoleon's attitude here often, and have concluded that while he knew what was going to happen, he could not change his course. He finished his war with empty and tied hands. He lost not only his campaign, but his army and thousands of lives on both sides and changed the course of France for the worse. He was abruptly vanquished at the relatively young age of 43 and at the height of his talent and success as a statesman and military leader. He made this statement about the irresistibility of attacking Russia because he honestly believed he had no other choice. I am convinced it was a prophecy. It is the only way to explain why a person with such a brilliant strategic mind can write that despite losing everything he would do it all over again.

A prophet is not a practical leader. A prophet is a spiritual leader, and is part of a nation's soul. This is why prophets who combine their abilities with leadership skills are so unique. In the majority of Christian theologies, three separate leadership roles are presented in the Old Testament: prophet, priest, and king. Sometimes these roles were combined. Aaron was the first priest, but Moses was the prophet and de facto leader. During the "Time of the Judges" before King Saul, the judges were leaders and priests. It is very rare to find a time when a prophet is also a practical leader, like Moses or Mohammad (570–632). However, Moses was never the official state leader of the Israelites, as he died before they settled into a nation.

Strategy as a profession has its roots in the military sphere. However, in our earliest written history, people with strong intuition, a deep knowledge, and a clear vision can be considered strategists. One such example was Marcus Aurelius. Few speak of this great philosopher, emperor, and strategic leader as a prophet, though throughout his life we do not see strong divisions between these different qualities of the emperor. Few true philosophers were also heads of state like Marcus Aurelius.

Fifteen Rules of Strategic Thinking

The following 15 rules were developed throughout my 40 years of difficult experience as an economist-turned-strategist in several countries, some of which were in conflict with each other on different continents. These rules can act as an aid and guideline for the further development and use of the strategic mindset. A practical set of rules can be especially helpful for strategists when they are in an environment with which they are not entirely familiar, like strategists from developed countries that deal with the Global Emerging Market. Emerging market countries are characterized by significantly more uncertainty in their markets than those of the developed world, where the rules of engagement are well established. The strategist's 15 rules can also be used as algorithmic tools to guide the discovery, formation, development, and implementation of strategy, especially in markets with high levels of uncertainty and risk.

- Rule 1: The Strategist Can Never Rely on Common Sense Alone
- Rule 2: The Majority Is Quite Often Strategically Wrong
- Rule 3: Strategically, the Present Is Already the Past
- Rule 4: The Strategist Must Learn from Past Successful Strategies
- Rule 5: No One Strategy Lasts Forever
- Rule 6: Inertia of the Mind Is the Strategist's Greatest Adversary
- Rule 7: The Strategist Should Not Fall into Predictable Patterns and Scenarios
- Rule 8: A Successful Strategy Cannot Be Dishonest
- Rule 9: The Strategist Must Be Able to Convert Future Chaos into Systems of Successful Prospects
- Rule 10: An Asymmetric Strategic Response Is More Efficient than a Symmetric One
- Rule 11: The Strategist Must Always Be an Optimist
- Rule 12: Always Overestimate the Competitor or Enemy and Appropriate Their Best Qualities
- Rule 13: Strategic Support and Orientation on Innovations Can Provide Huge Strategic Advantages
- Rule 14: The Strategist Should Optimize Limited Resources, Using Time as the Determining Factor
- Rule 15: The Strategist Must Figure Out the True Values, Interests, and Priorities of the Strategizing Object and Not What Leadership Demands

The strategic rules selected and described below may seem rigid and uncompromising, but they are presented in this fashion to give a clearer understanding of how to use them efficiently. The prerequisite for the use of all of these rules is wisdom—something that does not necessarily depend on one's age.

Rule 1: The Strategist Can Never Rely on Common Sense Alone

Common sense is a conclusion based on practical and daily evaluation of reality. It is knowledge based on sensory experience—what we can see with our eyes, taste with our tongues, hear with our ears, and touch with our fingers. Common sense derives from contact with the tangible, physical world; while it is necessary in day-to-day life, it is not useful when attempting to predict and strategize about the future. In fact, common sense is completely useless, because if we try to predict the future with it, we are only taking present fleeting observations and applying them to the future. Yet the present is nothing more than the past; it is only what we have seen and heard during previous moments. People are therefore trying to bring the past into the future, which always has different conditions and influences.

We can base some correct predictions upon an analysis of the past, but it is not advisable. Regardless, people still continue to base future predictions and strategizing processes on past occurrences because most of us do not have enough ability to foresee the future. Strategy is our best ability to predict and strategize through the future, and this ability can be natural and cultivated through training and education (granted, this latter option is more difficult, but it is possible). Often, strategists who were not born with this ability acquire it through hard work, a positive attitude, and training. But without strategy, the ability to secure future success with high probability is drained. As a great philosopher of the early Roman Empire, Philo of Alexandria (25 BCE–50 CE) said:

> We form our judgment of present events without paying any prudential attention to the future, being influenced by the erroneous guidance of our outward senses instead of the secret operations of the intellect; for the things which are openly conspicuous and before our hands so as to be taken up by them, are comprehended by our eyes, but our reasoning power outstrips them, hastening onwards to what is invisible and future; but nevertheless, we obscure the vision of our reason, though it is far more acute than those bodily powers of sight which are exercised by the eyes.[34]

Common sense generally obscures an accurate strategized scenario and insightful strategy. Conclusions based on common sense can be made by anyone, but they often ignore the very deep and complicated processes that lie beneath the surface of an issue. As the philosopher Hegel said, the quintessential—that is the pure, highly concentrated essence of a phenomenon—is not what lies on the surface. Strategy must go beyond what is obvious to everyone. Strategizing processes should be based on an intense, interdisciplinary analysis of environmental, political, economic, business, and technological systems and factors that determine possible outcomes. The conditions and functions of these systems are too complex to be understood, let alone predicted and strategized on the base of common sense. In fact, great strategic ideas are very often rejected by common sense, which is based on habitual knowledge manufactured to maintain the status quo. A great strategic idea rejects customary knowledge through the implementation of innovative methods of production or the introduction of a previously unknown good or service, military operation or governmental practice.

One of the best examples of a revolutionary strategy rejected by common sense is the vision of Bill Gates. In 1975, Gates founded Microsoft based on the idea that "the computer would be a valuable tool on every office desktop and in every home."[35] At the time, single-person computers were extremely expensive. Mainframe computers occupied entire rooms and were used exclusively by research institutions and the most advanced companies. According to the common knowledge of 1975, Gates's ideas were unrealistic. He experienced the pressure of common sense, and the subsequent lack of attention to his "impractical" ideas; he states, "During the PC industry's infancy, the mass media paid little attention to what was going on in the brand-new business. Those of us who were enthralled by computers and the possibilities they promised were unnoticed outside our own circles and definitely not considered trendy."[36] However, history and the immense wealth Gates has acquired have vindicated his revolutionary strategic vision.

Common sense does not only reject strategies based on unanticipated technological advancements and organizational innovations. There are many examples of very simple strategies that are initially rejected but prove lucrative and successful once implemented. For example, the mail-order-DVD business model of Netflix was initially proposed to and rejected by Blockbuster, which did not think that people would want to receive movies via mail. Practice proved otherwise, and in 2006 Netflix's quarterly profit more than doubled.[37] Ironically, in an attempt to compete with Netflix, Blockbuster tried to offer an almost identical service, but in a few years the company went bust due to a lack of ability to see the new strategic opportunities that their competitors did not miss. Understandably, the idea of disregarding common sense may seem strange, but it is crucial for the development of long-term successful strategy. Albert Einstein may have put it best when he said that "common sense is the collection of prejudices acquired by age eighteen."[38] To think strategically requires thinking that breaks through the hardened shell of common sense. Common sense usually directly contradicts accurate assessment and strategic vision. Strategy should extend deeper than what is known today as innovative or novel and reach beyond what may be obvious for everyone.

Rule 2: The Majority Is Quite Often Strategically Wrong

Much like the strategic rejection of common sense, a strategist must accept the seemingly counterintuitive notion that, when it comes to strategy, the majority is almost always wrong. Søren Kierkegaard (1813–1855), who is considered the father of existentialism, wrote about the destructive quality of public opinion when he stated "the crowd is untruth."[39] The German philosopher Martin Heidegger (1889–1976) in his book *Being and Time* also related the crowd to untruth.[40] When the authentic self is lost, independent choices get carried along by the crowd and prevent truth from emerging in important decision-making processes. Only by "specifically bring[ing] itself back to itself from its lostness in the 'they'" can the individual rise above the crowd, Heidegger argued.[41] In this way, the strategist is aware of the fickle, and sometimes uncritical, opinions of the majority; when contemplating the example of the personal life of Heidegger, one has to think twice before sharing the opinion of the majority. Conclusions based on comprehensive and intensive analysis almost always defy the popular opinions of society, which are based primarily on common sense. After all, the majority of society has not invested substantial time and energy, combining knowledge with intense analysis and research, in finding the solution to a particular challenge. The majority has collective knowledge but lacks the prospecting ability to extract the "diamonds," or truthful and far-sighted strategies for the future, from this mountain of empty ore. When strategists find such diamonds they must hold on to and embrace them without hesitation. It is the strategist's responsibility to convince skeptical decision-makers and the non-believing, amateur majority that a particular proposed strategy is the right one for the future of the strategizing object. Once a strategy is finally successfully implemented, the majority will inevitably forget about the opposition it mounted and the strategist who created it as well. They again will be weary of accepting unusual predictions, victorious scenarios, and revolutionary strategic ideas. The most innovative strategies almost always face derision from the majority. The general population lacks the specific knowledge, experience, and dedication of strategists, who usually have focused all their professional life on the resolution of a particular challenge. The majority does not refer only to mainstream society. Strategic decisions in corporate headquarters, military units, and governmental cabinets are often the result of collaboration between executives and the boards of directors, military commanders and their generals, and prime ministers and their cabinets, but are rarely endorsed by a consensus. Any truly revolutionary winning strategy will initially experience rejection from most people who did not invest their time in its development to achieve a deep understanding of the topic. The various parties involved will often hold divergent views on the strategic direction that ought to be pursued. Quite frequently, such disagreements lead to changes on the board of directors or general meetings of military headquarters.

The story of almost every successful entrepreneur or military leader fully endorses this rule. In 1963, for example, when Leslie Wexner came up with the idea to create a global business by selling women's clothing and underwear, many thought he was joking. More than 40 years later, the L Brands Corporation—which includes Victoria's Secret, Bath &

Body Works, Henri Bendel, among other brands—is thriving, and Leslie Wexner is one of the world's richest people. This is an indisputable confirmation of his strategic vision and his company's status as a premier global brand with a large and expanding presence in the GEM.

In fact, a reaction of shock and disbelief from the majority can often be an indication of a correct innovative strategy. The annals of history are filled with numerous example of this. The "Iron Chancellor" Prince Otto von Bismarck, the great strategist who unified Germany during the late nineteenth century, in a quote widely attributed to him, said, "a government must not waver once it has chosen its course. It must not look to the left or right but go forward."[42] The Biblical Moses is a good example of this. What would have happened if Moses had listened to the voice of the majority? He was a great leader because he believed deeply in and was committed to very unusual, yet perfectly apt advice. He brought his people through the wilderness, and his legacy has lasted for thousands of years. The modern strategist will most likely never have as reliable an advisor as Moses. Nevertheless, a strategist must be prepared to maintain faith in his strategy when it is widely rejected. According to Eric Schmidt, the CEO of Google, "the story of innovation has not changed. It has always been a small team of people who have a new idea, typically not understood by people around them and their executives."[43]

Rule 3: Strategically, the Present Is Already the Past

For the strategist, the present is already the past. A successful strategist's professional thinking—and vision—will always be at least three to five years ahead of everyone else's projections. As no one has invented a time machine, strategists must travel to the future using only their minds. The future cannot be understood only by an analysis of current and past events. Such an approach will result in outdated forecasts that are nothing more than the extrapolation of current trends. It takes sunlight eight minutes to travel to Earth; thus, images of the sun are always from the past. The same applies to business, economics, the military, and politics: without intensive systematic strategic study and contemplation updated on the basis of monitoring and vision, the past is all that can be observed.

One of the simplest ways to illustrate this rule is to return to the issue of "spacetime." A simple illustration of the mathematician Dr. Hermann Minkowski's light cone, which he developed to illustrate Einstein's Theory of Special Relativity, is a great way to visualize the position of the strategist (see Figure 2.2).

The lower cone represents past spacetime, while the upper cone represents future spacetime. At the moment when strategists give the "creative touch" to a new strategy, they are at the vertex of these two connected cones. New strategies are developed at the point where the past and the future meet. This conception of time is very useful for strategists.

Rule 4: The Strategist Must Learn from Past Successful Strategies

The position of the strategist in Minkowski's spacetime cone, between the future and the past, increases the importance of studying historical strategic stories and past successful strategies when strategizing future scenarios. While strategists should not merely extrapolate current or past trends, ignoring lessons from previous victorious strategies altogether is even worse. Some strategic ideas are extremely appealing but have been unsuccessfully attempted by many strategists throughout history. Using a concept that has failed in practice over and over is a foolish waste of resources. One inventor from Florida, John Kanzius, claims he has

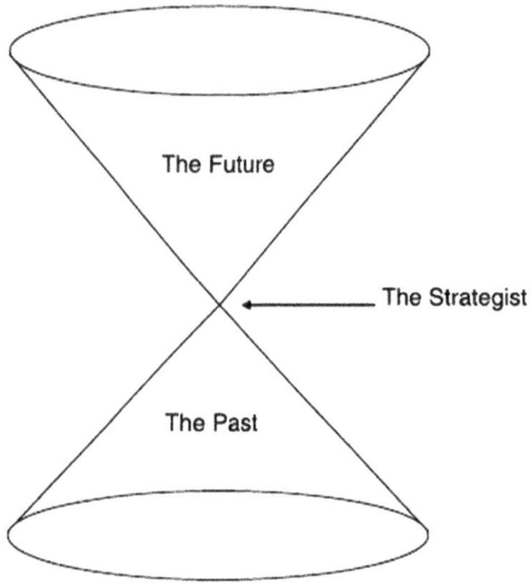

Figure 2.2 The Strategists' Position between the Past and the Future

figured out how to create enriched hydrogen from burned saltwater. This would essentially create a basis for a perpetual motion machine—an idea that has never been successfully implemented since its initial proposal in medieval times. However, the possibility always exists that what did not work in the past or was unsuited to wide-scale implementation may be efficient in new economic and technological conditions. Keeping this in mind, historical lessons—both ancient and modern—have to be revisited and analyzed intensively, within the context of emerging trends, technological developments, and innovations. What was impossible to do 10 to 15 years ago in countries like China due to low levels of education or purchasing power may be a contemporary requirement to stay in business or to occupy top-level military and governmental positions. Another example of this is the use of bioethanol as a fuel for cars. This idea was rejected even during the end of the twentieth century, but was reborn in the twenty-first century and is spreading throughout the world. It has already become a requirement to use a blend of gasoline and ethanol in the European Union, China, Japan and several US states. Many countries and other US states have encouraged the use of this ethanol-fuel blend (E85), which is far more environmentally friendly than regular gasoline. New technologies give the opportunity to farmers in remote rural areas to produce bioethanol as a fuel or biobutanol from communal agricultural waste or decaying forestry. Biofuel technologies that were once roundly rejected by the majority are now in great demand. Another example of this is how innovative fracking technologies allowed shale gas and oil fields to become more competitive and efficient.

Rule 5: No One Strategy Lasts Forever

The strategist's job is most difficult when an entity is presently enjoying success. In these cases, even when strategic analysis shows that conditions in three to five years will drastically change, most would prefer to maintain the status quo. This mentality is particularly prevalent among those responsible for operational activity. To these people, strategists represent a threat to their success and stature. They tend to have the "if it ain't broke, don't fix it" mentality. This is reminiscent of the opinion given by the ancient Chinese strategist and poet (a rare combination!) Du Mu, who lived in the ninth century CE and wrote, "there is no one constant supremacy."[44]

When strategic leaders of state or military power or entrepreneurs make strategic decisions about the future, they have to balance current advantages or profits (especially when profits are high and the company or military force occupies a winning or leading position) with a potential future for its efficiency or profits. All ministers, commanders, or executives report to their superior bodies and shareholders, and all entrepreneurs analyze their past quarter or year. These analyses are all based in the past. Nonetheless, executives, generals, and entrepreneurs cannot afford to make the mistake of assuming that success in the past will guarantee success in the future. Nothing lasts forever. For this reason it is necessary—though very difficult—for leaders, commanders, and executives, in spite of current success, to invest time, human capital, and money into future strategic scenarios. This is why smart leaders will cut R&D expenditures last. They must be willing to replace practices that have been successful in the past with new, unproven but innovative methods, ammunition, or equipment, as they anticipate changing conditions. It is generally easier for new companies or units, and those who are currently unsuccessful, to develop and accept strategies for the future. For example, when Google first appeared with its highly disruptive technology, it was not hard for its executives and strategists to envision the future; they did not have the baggage of past success to inhibit strategic decision-making. As of 2008, Google's share of the search engine market has grown to 65.1 percent,[45] more than nine times that of Microsoft, a company that was once synonymous with cutting-edge computer technology. Microsoft has been forced to come to terms with the fact that market dominance, like everything else, does not last forever (like Facebook—already on the way down!—complacency has replaced innovation as a result of success).

In the GEM, changes usually occur much more frequently than in developed economies. This even applies to issues that are relatively unchanging in the developed world, such as the national legal framework. In the GEM, legal systems are in almost constant flux. A major mistake that many executives and investors from the developed world have made in the GEM is to rely too heavily on political connections. In the volatile and uncertain environment of the GEM (compared with developed countries), established political connections can very suddenly become useless. Many foreign investors in Turkmenistan lost large sums of money when the dictator Turkmenbashi unexpectedly died and they realized that the only thing protecting their investments was his handshake. These investors learned—painfully—that in the long term, legal documents are more reliable than the handshake of a dictator.

As the Roman philosopher Marcus Fabius Quintilian (35–96 CE) observed, "[T]hus, if we say that the world had a beginning, we must admit that it is to have an ending; because everything that has had a beginning, must have an end."[46]

Rule 6: Inertia of the Mind Is the Strategist's Greatest Adversity

Inertia is a major obstacle for innovative strategic ideas. Once an entity becomes accustomed to day-to-day operations, it is extremely difficult to accept change. This is why chief operating officers (COOs) are typically very averse to radical ideas, especially when things are going well. The implementation of a new strategy could undermine a COO's successful career. This is a further illustration that employees who focus on operational issues are, by nature, opponents of strategists.

When an entity does not have a strategy, inertia inevitably sets in. The entity becomes accustomed to its activity and does not explore alternatives, even in the face of declining demand for its product, service, or function, or in another example, a military force's location. This is another case in which the laws of natural science have useful strategic applications. In terms of strategy, Isaac Newton's (1643–1727) first law of motion (the law of inertia) can be reinterpreted in the follow way: When the influence of all factors is balanced, it is almost impossible to increase economic efficiency. Equilibrium is the adversary of strategic improvement. Innovative strategic ideas are applicable to an entity only when it lacks balance or the status quo is changing. Newton's second law of motion can also be applied to strategic situations, but only in cases where the entity is unbalanced and strategists have to find the net influence of different forces acting upon the entity and the ratio between this and the entity's size. For example, in large companies, small changes in the balance of relevant political, social, and economic forces do not have much of an impact. Strategists have to figure out how forces can be changed and strengthened to redirect the entity toward its current or new strategic objectives and goals.

Strategic investments in an entity are successful only until the point at which the entity moves from balance to imbalance. In order to change the strategic direction of an entity at equilibrium, imbalance must be created via a strategic force, such as a revision of laws and under-law regulations, changes in investment inflows, the implementation of new technologies, etc. The larger the entity, the more difficult it is to overcome inertia. For this reason, it is easier for individual entrepreneurs, small business owners, and regional and municipal leaders to change their activity and implement new dimensions strategies. Small businesses and entrepreneurs from the developed world were the first to take advantage of the enormous opportunities in emerging market countries. In many cases, these were émigrés returning to their homelands, which were in the initial stages of establishing free markets. These émigrés, with their connections and knowledge of their motherland, were light years ahead of major corporations from developed countries, many of which were ignorant of the strategic opportunities in the GEM. In general, the first entrants to the GEM were less influenced by inertia both in their methods of thinking and in practice. Nevertheless, after overcoming the initial challenges of establishing a business in a new and foreign environment, many of these people found themselves in balanced entities and, thus, eventually under the influence of inertia.

For strategists there is a dialectical contradiction between balance and sustainability on the one hand and imbalance and improved efficiency on the other that plays an important role in the development, implementation, and monitoring of strategy. An imbalanced economic and business system is more dynamic than a balanced one, but not sustainable. For this reason strategists attempt to bring balance to entities through systematization. However, once balance is reached, the strategist has to anticipate imbalance and prepare the appropriate strategic update. This process is very challenging and often requires the use of mathematical methods, which is difficult because the dynamics of balance and imbalance are non-linear and thus not easily modeled.

Inertia can be seen as the enemy of any new idea because it can substantially alter or even ruin the current strategic scenario. Donald Rumsfeld offered an insightful perspective when he said, "New ideas often receive a negative reaction at the outset, regardless of their value."[47] This is especially true when the idea has a high value and requires substantial changes and investments.

Rule 7: The Strategist Should Not Fall into Predictable Patterns and Scenarios

To be predictable is very dangerous for a strategist, because it means an enemy or competitor can easily assess your future actions and strategize accordingly. Even if a strategist is repeating his or her own successful strategic approach, that is predictable. Napoleon lost his last battle at Waterloo mostly because he was trying to repeat early successful methods and means of victory. By that time his enemies had already evaluated most of his methods and strategic practices. Field Marshal Arthur Wellesley, the first Duke of Wellington (1769–1852), was one of them.[48] During pre-battle analysis, he accurately predicted the majority of Napoleon's moves. Napoleon did not have the time, ability, or drive to be as imaginative then as he was during Austerlitz—the battle he won at the pinnacle of his strategic genius. He forgot the dictum he had coined earlier in his military career, "Imagination rules the world."[49] I should also mention that some historians do attribute his failure at Waterloo to illness, which resulted in a lack of strategic preparedness on his part. At any rate, on that battlefield, the factor of time worked against Napoleon on several occasions.

The strategist should never be afraid to use an unconventional approach. In fact, such an approach is often the most effective paths toward success. Unfortunately, when an unconventional strategy brings success, competitors will then study, adapt, and implement it. Strategists must anticipate their opponents' adaptations. Napoleon was always an advocate of unconventional strategies. But his experience illustrates the dangers of falling into a predictable pattern. His strategies became widely known, and, eventually, his opponents used them against him.

Any strategy, even a previously successful one, should not be blindly repeated. The conditions needed to implement the strategy will be different than any previous conditions. Strategists may look to their own previous successes, but must be aware that their competitors or enemies will do the same, in order to use this information against them. A competitor or enemy can systematically destroy even the most efficient strategy under new conditions. Donald Rumsfeld accurately described this when he said, "This war isn't like the last war, this war isn't like the next war. This war is this war."[50] Each new strategic situation requires a new strategy, or at the very least an update of the most successful previous one. Strategists should always be aware of what their opponents are and are not expecting.

Rule 8: A Successful Strategy Cannot Be Dishonest

A strategist must always strive to uphold moral integrity. The consequences of a disingenuous strategy result in the dissemination of incorrect and erroneous messages in society, an increase in income-distribution inequality, and the distribution of low-quality goods and services. The strategist has to respect and feel responsible for those whom the strategy will affect. If, however, a strategist has decided to take on strategic development for an immoral product (e.g. weapons of mass destruction for national security reasons), he or she must approach it with honesty, credibility, and good faith, or not take it on at all. The means by which strategic objectives are achieved may be morally suspect, but should never be dishonest.

The same applies to strategists. The means by which strategic objectives are achieved can be immoral but not dishonest. Why don't corporations with innovative technologies share them with their competitors? Morally speaking, shouldn't life-saving technologies be as widely available as possible? Restricting the use of such technologies may be immoral, but it is not dishonest. Nevertheless, regardless of the moral quality of a strategy, or the type of entity for which it is being developed, without honesty and credibility the strategy will never be successful, at least in the long term. However, without a strong sense of morality, the strategy will likely wither and die long before implementation, or it will at least become less efficient. Typically, the morality of a strategy has to be addressed in that strategy's mission statement or vision. The consequences of strategies that lack morality include the wrong and untruthful message to society.

According to Dr. Nicole Immorlica, of Northwestern University, and Mohammad Mahdian, a researcher for Yahoo, "a strategy for a player is a function that outputs an announced preference list for any input preference list. Hence the truthful strategy is the identity function."[51] This statement supports the simple idea that the values and interests of the strategizing object should predetermine the entity's announced mission statement and vision, which should then be mirrored in its real strategic objectives and goals; otherwise, the entity will mislead both society and shareholders. The same idea applies to a governmental system of strategy: "economic policy cannot be independent from targets, which society advances."[52] However, it is not unusual for company leadership, military commanders, or even for heads of governments and states to ignore society, their own customers, and their shareholders, and focus only on misleading their competitors by a public announcement of a fake vision or made-up objectives. This may be controversial, but it is not an unusual practice and has even become "business as usual."

In the mid-1980s, two young European entrepreneurs went to Brazil looking for business opportunities. They found a serious think tank that was seeking to expand its consulting activity in Europe. The young entrepreneurs presented themselves as the owners of a major European consulting company. They signed an agreement with the Brazilian think tank, on behalf of a European company that existed only in their minds. Later, upon returning to their country, they legally established a consulting company. The Brazilian think tank eventually realized that these entrepreneurs were dishonest and found better partners. They also opened a legal case against the two Europeans because, at the moment when the agreement was signed, the European consulting company did not exist, and all information presented about it was fraudulent. The agreement was nullified and the two entrepreneurs did not get anything out of their efforts but a bad reputation and large debts for their travel and legal fees. They understood the opportunities that the GEM presented, but they did not anticipate the emergence of an age of complete accountability, whereby even companies lacking familiarity and connections with the international business community have the ability to access information that eventually brings all dishonesty to light. The great Russian military and spiritual leader of the thirteenth century, Grand Prince Alexander Nevsky the Great of Novgorod (1219–1263) said, "God is not in power, but in truth."[53] In strategy, power and truth are not mutually exclusive. The winning strategy has to be both powerful and truthful.

Rule 9: The Strategist Must Be Able to Convert Future Chaos into Systems of Successful Prospects

Strategists always deal with chaos, because the future is unknown and, thus, unsystematized. Depending on which of the three strategic approaches is selected, the strategist will deal with a level of uncertainty that varies substantially. New dimensions strategies involve absolute uncertainty and chaos. Everything is unclear; from total chaos, strategists have to find the best and wholly innovative strategic idea and develop the appropriate strategic management system for the application of this idea. Chaos is what separates the strategist from the idea upon which his strategy will be based. The second approach—an improvement strategy—involves substantially lower levels of uncertainty. Regardless of the selected approach, various levels of chaos and uncertainty are unavoidable. Strategists work on the edge of chaos, bridging the gap between existing systems of production or military power enforcement and unknown strategic opportunities of the future. According to Dr. Shona Brown, an executive at Google, and Dr. Kathleen Eisenhardt of Stanford University, "being at the edge of chaos means being only partially structured. The intuition behind the edge of chaos is that change occurs when strategies and their related organizations are sufficiently rigid so that change can be organized to happen but not so rigid that it cannot occur."[54] Strategists guide an entity through several stages of strategic improvement and development. When an entity first enters the ocean of chaos, driven by the sail of the new strategy, chaos becomes preliminarily systematized for the foreseeable future. It is at this point that strategists have to be flexible enough to correct or adjust certain characteristics of the strategy.

Strategists should not be influenced to choose improvement strategies over new dimensions strategies because of the lower amount of chaos. Chaos is unavoidable. Consequently, risk management is a major part of the strategizing process and of strategy itself. Even the smallest amount of uncertainty immediately and substantially increases risk. Strategists in the GMP cannot avoid risk and must be prepared to face it. This is especially true for all strategies that deal with the GEM, which is, relative to the developed world, less known, less predictable, and possesses a greater variation of characteristics among its economies. Risk management is largely about managing chaos by creating systems and recognizing patterns. Those who try and avoid risk altogether will never be victorious. To say the least, any strategy not oriented to address risk is not grounded in reality.

The strategist must tackle every issue with a systematic approach in order to find relationships and correlations between facts and events that appear to be unrelated. The strategist must create order from chaos, guiding a company from a murky present to bright future objectives. Analyzing issues within a systematic context is the most effective way of achieving this. Without a systematic approach and "without strategy to focus effort, chaos can ensue as people pull in a variety of directions."[55] Employees always need a leader who is able to choose a single direction from the multitude of options and lead the entity in the corresponding direction. Executives can do this through intuition, talent, and with the right strategy.

Strategists attempting to systematize chaos must be prepared for unpredictable challenges. No strategy is perfect and no one can predict all potential threats. At the same time, strategists cannot be so consumed with preparing for threats that they are unable to take advantage of unexpected opportunities. If strategists think their strategy is perfect, they are either completely out of touch with reality or naïve. Typically, strategic executives and strategists are better prepared to face threats than opportunities. As a result, they are often incapable of taking advantage of unexpected fortuitous situations because the windows of opportunity will open only for a brief period. When strategists fail to seize an opportunity, it is safe to assume that their competitors will not make the same mistake.

Rule 10: An Asymmetric Strategic Response Is More Efficient than a Symmetric One

A strategic response can be either symmetric or asymmetric. The most effective reactive strategy is almost always asymmetric. Symmetric reactions essentially take the same strategic approach as one's opponent, which is predictable and allows the competitor to stay at least one step ahead. In strategic thought, a typical false cliché states that "if a strategy worked for competitors, it will work for us." However, the strategy was successful for the competitor with distinct characteristics operating under different conditions, such as different weapons and unique technological resources, employees, raw materials, market segment, etc. Repeating a strategy that was efficient for a competitor or enemy will not achieve the same success, if any. This approach is an example of the bandwagon effect, where companies do not carefully analyze, strategize, or create their own strategy, but simply adopt strategies that have recently achieved success. For example, rising gasoline costs in the summer of 2008 led to a wave of companies, including General Motors, Hotels.com, and Callaway Golf Co., among many others, offering promotions like gas cards to their customers.[56] Some of these companies should have thought about different options: for instance, instead of providing a debit gas card, they could have simply reduced prices or offered cash back. The symmetric strategy basically repeats what competitors have done, which is rarely successful and never catches competitors off guard. Furthermore, it is difficult to redirect consumers by offering the same product as competitors. While it is crucial to understand a competitor's strategic thought, this alone will not produce a winning strategy. An asymmetric strategic response, on the other hand, puts competitors under pressure to reevaluate their strategy. An asymmetric response produces goods and services that will actually attract customers away from competitors or will open a new market niche. Successful asymmetric strategies eventually become the base for symmetric responses in the next iteration of competition.

In January 2002, Airbus surprised Boeing—its biggest competitor—when it announced that production of the A380 would begin. The A380 can fly 8,000 nautical miles and carry 500 to 800 passengers at a speed approaching Mach 0.9. Boeing executives felt very threatened, as they were far behind on a similar project (the symmetric response). Boeing strategists instead proposed an asymmetric response. They argued that the upcoming expansion of the European Union from 15 to 27 (or more) members would increase the frequency of European flights. They predicted that this would increase the demand for medium-range commuter planes rather than long-range, high-capacity planes. Boeing focused its resources on the production of the next-generation 737, a plane more suited for European travel. By 2004, Boeing delivered the 1,500th next-generation 737 to ATA Airlines, reaching this milestone faster than any other commercial airplane in history. This is a great example of a successful asymmetric response.

Another example of an asymmetric strategy is Linux Corporation's response to Microsoft's release of the Vista operating system in January 2007. Linux is a producer of operating systems for computers, comparable to Windows or Mac OS X.[57] Rather than try to develop a similar program, Linux chose to develop a revolutionary project to "shift the desktop's purpose from a 'file manager view' used to display a static set of icons to a dynamic, contextual project management tool."[58]

An asymmetric strategic response can be particularly effective for companies in emerging market countries when a major competitor mergers with or is bought by a multinational corporation. Many multinational corporations do not have a global strategy. In order to establish a presence in emerging markets, these companies often purchase a local company and make it a subsidiary. Such subsidiaries tend to be barely integrated with the multinational corporation. In general, executives of these corporations expect market conditions in their segment of the emerging market to remain the same. At the very least, they do not expect unusual steps from local existing competitors of their subsidiary. This provides other domestic companies with the opportunity to make an unexpected, asymmetric response. Strategists of multinational corporations should always anticipate such asymmetric responses from domestic competitors when establishing new subsidiaries by acquisition. In the GEM, multinational corporations should always use asymmetric entry strategies when possible. For example, when a company that produces home appliances acquires a subsidiary in an EMC that has successfully sold refrigerators in its national market, an asymmetric strategy would be to redirect the specialization of the subsidiary into a new niche market that still uses the existing production facilities, like the production of freezers. These products are not widely used in emerging markets, but demand for them is increasing. Because of worries about food shortages in many EMCs and developing countries, people are buying more food than they can consume at once; these supplies, of course, must be preserved.

Asymmetric strategy can be reactive but also aggressive, especially against a much stronger enemy or competitor. Robert the Bruce (1234–1329), the king of Scots, is an excellent example of this rule. He consistently had a smaller army and/or more limited resources than his enemies, but his asymmetric strategy was flawless. He deduced that when the enemy is stronger or bigger, it is better to cause smaller, more frequent, and more painful damages rather than starting out with an open large-scale attack. Attack what is most precious to the enemy, and the enemy will understand that each time they attempt to gain more ground, they will inflict damage on their own campaign. As Robert Greene rightly observes, Robert the Bruce compared this strategy to a wasp sitting on your skin.[59] Clever people know to not provoke a wasp when it is on your skin, even if they've never been bit before. A well-known proverb expresses a similar idea: "Let sleeping dogs lie." This example highlights that it takes time, energy, and resources to develop successful competitive strategic advantages, and that often a smaller spending of resources, and a quieter path to success, can do more harm to a competitor or enemy than a loud, flashy one. An asymmetric approach is always much less predictable by counterparts, and can cost much less in terms of human capital, other resources, and time. For greater flexibility during strategic maneuvers and more efficient manageability, the Biblical Gideon, the Ancient Greek king Leonidas I, Hannibal, and the Russian generalissimo Prince Alexander Suvorov in the eighteenth century all preferred to use smaller forces when facing their enemies. The Bible says that during one of Gideon's most important fights, he trained 300 soldiers; this number is familiar to us because of Leonidas I's victory in the battle of 480 BCE and its depiction in the movie *300* (2006). Many business executives have also gained great success with their very limited resources over much more powerful companies. During the 1990s and 2000s, many small start-ups with technological advantages and efficient strategies began to take over much larger corporations.

An asymmetric strategy is usually efficient when it requires fewer resources than the competitor's strategy, as well as less time consumed. Naturally, it becomes inefficient when the enemy's strategy produces harmful results. After losing battle after battle to Hannibal, the Roman army decided to implement an asymmetric strategy. Instead of continuing war on the Apennine Peninsula, they attacked his Carthage home, an attack for which Hannibal was not prepared. He lost the Punic Wars because of Rome's asymmetric strategy.

Rule 11: The Strategist Must Always Be an Optimist

The strategist has to be an optimist. When facing powerful competitors, strategists must realize that strength is always relative. Strategists must focus on finding stronger responses to powerful challenges. When the implementation of strategy does not go well or a competitor unexpectedly announces a very efficient strategy, the strategist must maintain optimism and patience in the face of these threats. Former heavyweight boxing champion Mike Tyson once said, "Everybody has a strategy until I hit them."[60] Strategists have to be able to endure the punches thrown at them by market forces, and especially from their competitors.

Pessimism is a major barrier to successful strategic decision-making. For strategists there is nothing worse than when a strategy that proves to be completely accurate over time was not implemented due to a lack of faith from executives or decision-makers. According to a proverb coined by Napoleon, "A leader is a dealer in hope."[61] It is easy for the strategist to become extremely pessimistic when this happens. When executives or a board of directors accept a strategy, they are hopeful and optimistic, but the strategist is fearful and overcome with responsibility and pressure. According to Dr. Svend Frolund,

> [T]here are two extreme implementation strategies for constraint evaluation. A *pessimistic* strategy will evaluate the constraints before dispatching a message. An *optimistic* strategy will concurrently dispatch a message and evaluate the constraints. If the constraints are not satisfied, an optimistic strategy 'rolls back' the message dispatch.[62]

However, there is one area in which strategists can benefit from pessimism: cost. In general, strategists should anticipate the unexpected costs of strategy implementation. Unfamiliar conditions in emerging market countries turn many strategists away prior to even a detailed evaluation of opportunities in these markets. Often, EMCs have very limited financial resources and issues with profit repatriation, which discourages many strategists before they evaluate the abundant natural resources and huge market potential for these countries.

Even in the face of tremendous challenges and uncertainty, Russian and American strategists remained optimistic about their space programs. As a result, in 1961, the Soviet Union sent the first man, Yuri Gagarin (1934–1968), into orbit, and in 1969 the US sent Neil Armstrong (1930–2012) to the moon. These achievements would not have been accomplished without the optimism of the Russian rocket scientist and Russian Academy of Science member Sergei Korolev (1907–1966) and President Kennedy (1917–1963). Strategists must maintain their optimism throughout all stages of development and particularly during implementation, when a great many more people are involved with the proposed strategy. They also have to be averse to implementing the many unnecessary changes that are often proposed when major strategies are put into practice.

Unlike executives, strategists do not directly unify employees, although they must think about the consolidation of people around the proposed strategy. Executives, boards of directors or the government manage the actual consolidation. Once they accept the strategy, it is their responsibility to unify stakeholders behind the strategic idea. A qualified majority of people will follow leaders during difficult times if the leader is steadfast and optimistic. In strategy, steadfastness is next of kin to victory.

Rule 12: Always Overestimate the Competitor or Enemy and Appropriate Their Best Qualities

Strategists should always overestimate the resources and abilities of their competitors. One will almost never know the exact resources available to competitors, or their strategy for optimizing those resources. More than that, *a weak competitor is not necessarily a defeated competitor*. As the very experienced military and civilian consultant Dr. Steve Osborne wrote, "a common mistake is to underestimate competitors and overestimate your own capability. When in doubt, give the advantage to your competitor. The consequences of overestimating a competitor are less than the consequences of underestimating."[63] Dr. Osborne highlights a wider understanding of the problem of self-estimation first noticed by Alfred Adler in the early twentieth century. Adler's *The Practice and Theory of Individual Psychology* is a must-read for anyone looking to develop his or her strategic thinking.

Overestimating will prevent being caught off guard as a result of either a miscalculation of resources or an unanticipated, extremely efficient, resource-optimizing strategy. Prior to the Battle of Alesia in 52 BCE, Julius Caesar found out that he possessed one-fifth of the warriors that the Gauls had. The leader of the Gauls, Vercingetorix (82–42 BCE), was a talented commander. Caesar allocated his very limited resources in an innovative and unusual way and developed such an unanticipated strategy that he won the battle decisively. As a result, present-day France became part of the Roman Empire for the next six centuries.

Suleiman the Magnificent (1494–1566) was a sultan of the Ottoman Empire in the sixteenth century. He won thirteen campaigns throughout Europe and Asia, and had one very important rule about strategic thinking: *never* underestimate your enemy. Even if your enemy is an ant, treat him like he is a lion. Never forget this rule, and victory will be yours. To understand your competitor, you must imagine him having the same strategic ability that you possess, putting yourself in the mind of the competitor and looking at your actions through his eyes. Simply put, you must put yourself in your competitor's shoes. It will give you a better understanding of the situation you are facing.

The great strategists of history not only analyzed their experiences and improved them for future success, but also studied the strongest characteristics of their competitors and enemies. When attempting to avoid capture by King Saul, King David left his kingdom to spend several years with the enemies of the Israeli state, studying their strengths and weaknesses. His first step, upon returning to Israel with his new "allies," was to win over Saul's leadership. Later, David used this knowledge of his enemies to win against them, using their own strongest methods of warring to attack their weakest positions. The same idea is emphasized in Book VIII of *Strategikon*: always study the methods and weapons of the enemy and use this knowledge for your success.[64] Maurice underlined that if the enemy is unfamiliar, even if this unfamiliar enemy looks weak, you should not attack immediately. First, send a few soldiers to bother your enemies to observe how they will react and what action they take.

Rule 13: Strategic Support and Orientation on Innovations Can Provide Huge Strategic Advantages

Strategists must always search for innovative ideas and figure out the best methods and organizational vehicles by which to implement them in their particular field. Innovation can come in many forms, such as advances in science and technology, management systems, etc. For example, Julius Caesar used innovative construction methods and advancements in munitions to achieve military success. Similarly, Napoleon exploited innovations in artillery to defeat his opponents, and Cornelius Vanderbilt (1794–1877) used technological achievements in railroad wheels and brakes to create a vast commercial empire. J.P. Morgan (1837–1913) amassed a huge fortune and revolutionized the financial system by developing modern investment banking practices.

Strategists read the same websites, newspapers, and magazines as millions of other people, but their focus is oriented toward the use of innovations as vehicles to success. Again, strategists must draw on knowledge from many fields. Typically, macroeconomics, microeconomics, and management systems are all taught as separate disciplines. The strategist must combine knowledge from all of these fields, among others. The development of a successful strategy requires an extremely eclectic mind. As a result, business education should be redesigned on a multidisciplinary basis, synthesizing macroeconomics, microeconomics, statistics, applied mathematics, political science, systems analysis, and managements systems with a strategic focus. Many academic programs that focus on strategy narrow its scope, focusing exclusively on "the relationship between politics and military power including the preparation, the threat and use of force, and its latent presence in international politics."[65] This is far from a complete description of the modern requirements of strategists. Regardless of the entity for which a strategy is being developed, geographical, political, social, military, economic, business, and technological issues all must be discussed in order to successfully choose the right strategic approach and scenario.

Rule 14: The Strategist Should Optimize Limited Resources, Using Time as the Determining Factor

Hannibal was the master of using limited resources successfully. In his battle near Cannes, he had 35,000 troops against Rome's 80,000. Yet he used his leadership, knowledge of the terrain, and Rome's own decisions for victory. For example, he arranged his troops in a line, with the smallest unit in the middle. He then positioned himself within the smallest unit. The Romans assumed that this small group was the weakest link and attacked them. As they moved in, other units flanked the Romans, with a hidden cavalry joining in the attack. The Carthage troops would eventually enclose and destroy them. Legend says that Hannibal had them locked in so tightly that the Romans could not even draw their swords. He was an innovator of strategic military formations.

While Rule 3 dealt primarily with the dialectic relationship between time and space, Rule 14 focuses on a dialectical issue that is always on the strategist's agenda. One of the fundamental dilemmas for strategists regarding the implementation phase is deciding between reducing time at the expense of resources and conserving resources at the expense of time. This basically comes down to the relationship between capital investment and the time required for a recovery of this investment. When facing this dilemma, time is the factor that determines the strategic cost effectiveness of any decision. By increasing capital investment, the implementation phase is shortened, and production—based on the newly implemented strategy—can begin sooner. Economizing time is the first law of strategy. This law can apply to the ratio of time and space (discussed in Rule 3) and the ratio of resources and time. It is especially applicable in the context of the unyielding onslaught of competition in the global marketplace. Saving time, even at the expense of extra resources, increases the likelihood of an entity forging ahead of its competitors in a new market niche, in their reaction to changing conditions, etc. Essentially, during the implementation phase, an entity should allocate extra resources to reduce the time of this phase if the company can produce goods and services (according to the new strategy) during this saved time that will cover the extra resources allocated or will position the company ahead of strategically important competitors. The mathematical approach and calculations of this issue are presented later in Chapter 3 in the section on strategy implementation. Strategists always have to remember that, unlike popular opinion, time is not on anyone's side. Strategists should always find methods by which they can make any competitor's time-related advantage obsolete. Ideally, strategists should find methods to use the resources of their competitors to optimize the expenditure of an entity's time and resources.

I hope it is clear from the above description of Rule 14 that any strategy will likely fail without a realistic evaluation of scale and potential for available resources. For strategists personally, there can be one more useful aspect to this rule: be realistic when promising that your strategy will be bulletproof and victorious. On this point, I would like to refer to the shared belief of two strategic geniuses: without realizing it, Frederick the Great repeated and supported the same strategic rule set forth by Tamerlane (Timur) several centuries before in his *Autobiography*: "I never promised anything which I was not in a capacity to implement and practice."[66]

Rule 15: The Strategist Must Figure Out the True Values, Interests and Priorities of the Strategizing Object and Not What Leadership Demands

Working under contract for a client is a very challenging undertaking. In many cases, the client will not understand the situation from a strategic perspective. After the strategist conducts an intense study of the client's situation, he may find that the client's vision is flawed, and what he wants is not what will provide long-term success for the client and its entity. The strategist must not be influenced by the client's way of thinking. A lack of imagination, from which some clients may suffer, can be contagious, and will prevent the development of a successful strategy.

The strategist must avoid the clip mentality—an attractive image of the strategy or its scenario not founded in substantive thought. When the strategy is sold, the client may realize that they are not receiving what they initially wanted or were promised. Nevertheless, when presenting a strategy to executives or clients, it should be as streamlined as possible, focusing only on ideas that are absolutely crucial to the implementation of the strategy, unless the client asks the strategist to elaborate on particular issues. It is not necessary to explain the intellectual development of the strategy or any other superfluous information to clients: unnecessary details take away from the core of the strategic scenario. Clients should always be presented with a short executive summary of the core ideas of the strategy, as well as the results of its implementation. The entire study should be available, but in many cases it would be uninteresting and overwhelming to clients, especially when the client is a board of directors. When trying to convince a client, it is important to get to the point. Any mathematical formulas used in the development of a strategy should be used only to convince decision-makers of the limitation of their resources and what they *cannot* do. It is generally not a good idea to use mathematics to prove what should be done. This is especially true in the executive summary. People tend to have an aversion to mathematical formulas. It is usually best to explain the concept in words and graphics.

Strategists must achieve a balance between clarity and complexity in the presentation of a strategy. The more complex and hard to understand a strategy, the more difficult it is for competitors to develop countermeasures. However, complexity also makes it more difficult to promote and gain support. The strategy must be well understood by those who are responsible for its implementation, but in order to gain widespread support, slogans are very useful. Slogans can convey a strategy's gist without going into detail. Slogans act as a popular version of the mission statement, with minimum information and maximum appeal. Strategists working internationally, especially within the GEM, have to factor language comprehension into their presentations. They should generally prepare presentations in at least two languages—the national language and English. Cultural issues are extremely important to take into consideration during the presentation of a strategy. Native speakers have to be consulted regarding the connotations and associations of every single symbol in the presentation. Once a strategy is approved and implemented, it no longer belongs to the strategist—it belongs to clients, executives, and the world.

In addition to the strategist's 15 rules, it is important to mention that a strategy's area of influence is usually wider than the targeted area. In the overwhelming majority of cases, strategy can be improved during the process of implementation by putting together a number of different details that were not visible during a strategy's stage of formation and development. Testing a strategy is like testing a nuclear bomb. In real conditions, it is tested the day it is dropped.

For a comparison of the strategist's 15 rules presented in this book, it may be of interest to the reader to examine other authors' rules of strategy. According to the "10 Essential Principles of Strategy" by Dr. William A. Cohen, a major general of the US Air Force:

1. The Fundamental Principle: Commit Fully to a Definite Objective
2. Seize the Initiative and Keep It
3. Economize to Mass Your Resources
4. Use Strategic Positioning
5. Do the Unexpected
6. Keep Things Simple
7. Prepare Multiple, Simultaneous Alternatives
8. Take the Indirect Route to Your Objective
9. Practice Timing and Sequencing
10. Exploit Your Success[67]

Some of General Cohen's rules are based on the same general principles as the 15 rules of strategy recommended in this book. However, some of them are not mentioned in this book and can be useful. The rules "Seize the Initiative and Keep It" and "Exploit Your Success" are particularly useful during the phase of strategy implementation. What General Cohen called principles of strategy, according to analysis of elements of strategy, are rules of strategic thinking, which like all rules of strategy are working principles of strategy.

I would be remiss to not conclude this chapter with General Clausewitz's remarks in *On War* about the prodigious strategic successes of practitioner Frederick the Great, King of Prussia: "What we rather admire above all is the sagacity of the King in this respect, that pursuing a great object with very limited means, he undertook nothing beyond his powers, and *just* enough to gain his object."[68] When Clausewitz highlights the qualities that gave Frederick the Great his nickname, he stresses that Frederick never set goals that were outside of his ability to implement and practice. I consider Clausewitz's summation of Frederick the Great one of the best descriptions of a strategist's outstanding qualities. Let us speak briefly about this two-line description of Frederick the Great's talents. First of all, although by European standards he was not a sovereign of a large country like France or Great Britain, he nonetheless proclaimed very ambitious and aggressive strategic objectives.[69] Second of all, due to the limited size and relative strength of Prussia compared to larger and more powerful states, it might seem that the title "Great" is not a realistic one. Frederick set objectives and goals that required the substantial resources that he needed to overpower Prussia's resourceful enemies and competitors. He concentrated all of his country's resources and power strictly with the aim of achieving these goals. He did not do anything outside of this strategic path to reach his target. He was not only a military leader, but also sovereign over a population that he could not impoverish. Frederick reached his goal by concentrating only the required amount of resources as well as the needed quality—just enough to reach his very ambitious objective. This was his magic key in winning the Seven Years' War and the War of the Bavarian Succession against much more powerful enemies. Due to his genius, he left behind a technologically updated and unified Prussia. Napoleon considered Frederick the Great not as a great strategist, but as the greatest tactical genius of all time—a commendation with which I disagree even though I admire Napoleon. [70] In 1807, when Napoleon visited the grave of Frederick the Great in Potsdam, he said, "If this man was still alive, I would not be here."[71] This is why Frederick II became Frederick the Great.

Notes

1 *Dictionary of Quotations* (1899). J. Wood (Ed.). London, New York: Frederick Warne & Co. Retrieved from www.bartleby.com/345/authors/110.html
2 Napoleon. (1987). *Military Maxims of Napoleon*. G. D'Aguilar (Trans.) and D. Changler (Ed.). Boston: Da Capo Press.
3 Strategy is a multi-layered concept and its core is so overwhelmed that no one definition can fully cover it. Due to this difficulty, I am giving the reader three choices. Each one is right, but no one of them contains all the meaning of this powerful term.
4 Plato, and Cooper, J.M. (2005). *Meno* in *Complete Works*. Indianapolis, IN: Hackett, p. 897 (99e).
5 Aristotle. *Nicomachean Ethics* (2000). R. Crisp (Trans.). Cambridge, UK: Cambridge University Press.
6 *Phronesis* can be translated as "practical wisdom."
7 Bose, P.S. (2004). *Alexander the Great's Art of Strategy: The Timeless Leadership Lessons of History's Greatest Empire Builder*. New York: Gotham Books, p. 31.
8 Mazzola, P., and Kellermanns, F.W. (2010). *Handbook of Research on Strategy Process*. Cheltenham, UK: Edward Elgar, p. 552.
9 Napoleon Bonaparte to Auguste Marmont, as quoted in Connelly, O. (2006). *Blundering to Glory: Napoleon's Military Campaigns*. Lanham, MD: Rowman & Littlefield Publishers, Inc., p. 29.
10 Aristotle. (2008). *Metaphysics: The Basic Works of Aristotle*. C.D.C. Reeve and R. McKeon (Trans.) New York. Modern Library (Book I, part I, line 1).
11 Saint-Exupéry, A. de (2004). *The Little Prince*. R. Howard (Trans.) Orlando, FL: Harcourt Publishing, p. 32.
12 Heinl, R. (1966). *Dictionary of Military and Naval Quotations*. Annapolis, MD: United States Naval Institute, p. 318.
13 Hegel, G.W. (1991). *Hegel's Phenomenology*. R. Norman (Trans.). Farnham, UK: Ashgate Publishing, p. 11.
14 Bell, J. (1963). *Life Magazine*. "'Old Wolf' Adenauer Sits at Bay." April 26. Retrieved from https://books.google.com/books?id=RkkEAAAAMBAJ
15 Cited by Agel, J., and Glanze, W.D. (1987). *Pearls of Wisdom*. New York: Perennial Library. p. 10.
16 Napoleon. (1916). *Napoleon in His Own Words*. J. Bertaut, H.E. Law, and C.L. Rhodes (Trans.). Chicago: A.C. McClurg & Co., p. 21.
17 Hammond, G.T. (2001) *The Mind of War: John Boyd and American Security*. Washington DC: Smithsonian Institution Press, p. 161.
18 Yagger, H. (2006). *Strategic Theory for the 21st Century: The Little Book on Big Strategy*. Darby, PA: Diane Publishing Co., p. 73. Retrieved from www.au.af.mil/au/awc/awcgate/ssi/strat_theory_21c_yarger.pdf
19 University of Rochester. Major in Economics and Business Strategies. Retrieved from www.econ.rochester.edu/UG/businesseconomics.html

20 Ohmae, K. (1982). *The Mind of the Strategist: The Art of Japanese Business.* N.p.: McGraw-Hill, p. 13.
21 General Electric (1999). *What Is Six Sigma? The Roadmap to Customer Impact.* Retrieved from www.ge.com/sixsigma/SixSigma.pdf
22 Nobel Foundation. (n.d.). The Nobel Prize in Chemistry 1977. Retrieved from http://nobelprize.org/nobel_prizes/chemistry/laureates/1977/
23 Davenport, T.H., Leibold, M., and Voelpel, S. (2006). *Strategic Management in the Innovation Economy: Strategy Approaches and Tools for Dynamic Innovation Capabilities.* Berlin: Wiley-VCH, p. 121.
24 Yorck, W.M. (1902). *Napoleon as a General.* London: K. Paul, Trench, Trübner & Co., p. 48.
25 Rosenkranz, Z. (1998). *The Einstein Scrapbook.* Baltimore, MD: The Johns Hopkins University Press, pp. 32–33.
26 Porter, M.E. (2011). "What Is Strategy?" in *On Strategy.* Boston: Harvard Business Review Press, p. 8.
27 Some sources attribute this sentence to Arab proverbs, but the majority attribute it to Tamerlane.
28 Keathley, J.H. III (n.d.). *The Major Prophets.* Retrieved from https://bible.org/seriespage/major-prophets
29 In Latin the text reads, "Soli numine divino afflati praesagiunt et spirit prophetico particularia."
30 Nostradamus. (1994). *The Complete Prophecies of Nostradamus.* H. C. Roberts (Trans. and Ed.). New revised edition, L.R. Amsterdam and H. Amsterdam (Eds.). London: Thorsons, p. xviii.
31 Nostradamus. (1994). *The Complete Prophecies of Nostradamus.* H. C. Roberts (Trans. and Ed.). New revised edition, L.R. Amsterdam and H. Amsterdam (Eds.). London: Thorsons, pp. xviiii–xix.
32 Propheta dicitur hodie, olim vocabatur videns.
33 Aristotle. (2014). *The Complete Works of Aristotle: The Revised Oxford Translation, One-Volume Digital Edition.* J. Barnes (Ed.). Princeton, NJ: Princeton University Press.
34 Philo. (2010). *Works of Philo, Volume 4.* C.D. Yonge (Trans.). N.p.: Digireads.com Publishing.
35 Microsoft. (n.d.). PressPass. Information for journalists—Bill Gates. Retrieved from www.microsoft.com/presspass/exec/billg/bio.mspx
36 Gates, B. (1995). *The Road Ahead.* New York: Viking Penguin, p. xii.
37 Reuters. (2007). *Netflix Profit Up, Revenue at Low End of Estimates.* Retrieved from www.reuters.com/article/companyNewsAndPR/idUSWEN65832007041
38 Einstein, A. (1996). *Bite-size Einstein: Quotations on Just about Everything from the Greatest Mind of the Twentieth Century.* J. Mayer and J.P. Holmes (Eds.). New York: St. Martin's Press, p. 25.
39 Kierkegaard, S. (1998). *The Point of View.* Princeton, NJ: Princeton University Press, p. 109.
40 As often happens with philosophers, sociologists, and scholars, Heidegger did not follow his own theory, and initially fell under the influence of German Nazism.
41 Heidegger, M. (1962). *Being and Time.* New York: Harper, p. 312.
42 Attributed to Bismarck.
43 Schmidt, E. (2008). *How Google Fuels Its Idea Factory. Bloomberg Business Week.* April 28. Retrieved from www.businessweek.com/stories/2008-04-28/how-google-fuels-its-idea-factory/
44 Sun-Tzu. (2002). *The Art of War.* J. Minford (Trans.). New York: Penguin, p. 138.
45 Helft, M. (2007). "Google's Market Share Grows and Grows and Grows." *New York Times.* December 28. Retrieved from http://bits.blogs.nytimes.com/2007/12/28/googles-market-share-grows-and-grows-and-grows/
46 Quintilian, M.F. (1805). *Quintilian's Institutes of Eloquence: or, The Art of Speaking in Public, in Every Character and Capacity.* Vol. I. London: Dewick and Clarke, p. 313
47 Rumsfeld, D. (2013). *Rumsfeld's Rules: Leadership Lessons in Business, Politics, War and Life.* New York: HarperCollins Publishers, p. 36.
48 At the end of his career, Wellesley became the prime minister of the United Kingdom.
49 Abbott, J.S.C. (1855). *The History of Napoleon Bonaparte: With Maps and Illustrations: In 2 Volumes.* London: Sampson Low, p. 318.
50 Rumsfeld, D. (2013). *Rumsfeld's Rules: Leadership Lessons in Business, Politics, War and Life.* New York: HarperCollins Publishers.
51 Immorlica, N., and Mahdian, M. (2005). "Marriage, Honesty, and Stability." In *Proceedings of the Sixteenth Annual ACM-SIAM Symposium on Discrete Algorithms.* Philadelphia, PA: Society for Industrial and Applied Mathematics, p. 56.

52 Nekipelov, A. (2004). "Public Preferences and Their Role in Shaping Russian Economic Development." *Distinguished Lecture Series n. 14.* Warsaw: Academy of Entrepreneurship and Management, p. 17.

53 Kvint, V. (2009). *The Global Emerging Market: Strategic Management and Economics.* New York and London: Routledge, p. 273.

54 Brown, S.L., and Eisenhardt, K.M. (1998). *Competing on the Edge: Strategy as Structured Chaos.* Watertown, MA: Harvard Business Press., pp. 11-12.

55 Mintzberg, H., Ahlstrand, B., and Lampel, J. (2005). *Strategy Safari: A Guided Tour through the Wilds of Strategic Management.* New York: Simon and Schuster, p. 15.

56 Ramde, D. (2008). "Companies Offering Free Gas to Attract Business." *Business Week.* June 8. Retrieved from www.businessweek.com/ap/financialnews/D91627380.htm

57 Linux. (2009). "What Is Linux? An Overview of the Linux Operating System." Retrieved from www.linux.com/whatislinux/119700

58 Sanders, N. (2007). "KDE's Plasma Is Heating Up." Retrieved from www.linux.com/feature/114560

59 Greene, R. (2007). *The 33 Strategies of War.* London: Profile Books, p. 139.

60 Zuckerman, M. (2008). "What They Should Have Said." *US News and World Report.* January 14, p. 68.

61 Napoleon. (1916). *Napoleon in His Own Words.* J. Bertaut, H.E. Law, and C.L. Rhodes (Trans.). Chicago: A.C. McClurg & Co., p. 52.

62 Frolund, S. (1996). *Coordinating Distributed Objects: An Actor-based Approach to Synchronization.* Cambridge, MA: MIT Press, p. 115.

63 Osborne, S.R. (2002). *Winning Government Business: Gaining the Competitive Advantage.* Vienna, VA: Management Concepts, p. 100.

64 Emperor Maurice (2002). *Maurice's Strategikon: Handbook of Byzantine Military Strategy.* Philadelphia: University of Pennsylvania Press, p. 23.

65 Strategic Studies. Johns Hopkins University. Retrieved from www.sais-jhu.edu/academics/functional-studies/strategic/

66 Timur. (2004). *Autobiography.* Sir H.M. Elliot (Trans.). Lahore: Sang-e-Meel Productions, 1:12.

67 Cohen, W.A. (2004). *The Art of the Strategist: 10 Essential Principles for Leading Your Company to Victory.* New York: AMACOM.

68 Clausewitz, C. (1908). *On War.* J.J. Graham and F.N. Maude (Trans.). London: Kegan Paul, Trench, Trübner & Co, p. 169.

69 A paraphrase of this idea, due to its efficiency, often appears in modern strategic books. I, for example, like the presentation of the same idea by Michael Porter, who wrote, "The essence of strategy is choosing what *not* to do." Porter, M. (2011). "What Is Strategy?" in *HBR's 10 Must Reads on Strategy.* Boston: Harvard Business Review Press, p. 20.

70 Koch, H.W. (1978). *A History of Prussia.* New York: Barnes and Noble Books, p. 126,

71 Clark, C. M. (2006). *Iron kingdom: The rise and downfall of Prussia, 1600–1947.* Cambridge, Mass: Belknap Press of Harvard University Press, p. 307.

Part II

Strategy in Practice

3 Developing and Implementing Strategy

The best laid plans of mice and men often go awry.[1]

Robert Burns, Scottish poet (1759–1796)

At first people refuse to believe that a strange new thing can be done, then they begin to hope it can be done, then they see it can be done—then it is done and all the world wonders why it was not done centuries ago.[2]

Frances Hodgson Burnett, English author (1849–1924)

Keynote Definitions

Formal strategy is the final product of strategizing that takes into consideration previously updated forecasts, public values, and interests, and which consists of a defined mission statement, long-term vision (including priorities), objectives, and goals. This long-term strategy must also include a particular scenario to be implemented via the strategic plan and a strategic management system that monitors its implementation.

System of Strategy

Hierarchy of Strategy

Strategy is a systematic phenomenon. By its very nature, it is multidisciplinary; by its influence, it is multidimensional, and by its structure, it is hierarchical. Before the twenty-first century, many companies focused entirely on national economic strategy, particularly sectorial strategies, and much less on regional, corporate (for other competitive companies), and unit strategies (see Figure 3.1). However, with the birth and development of the global marketplace and the global emerging market, the system of strategy has become more complex and incorporated more subordinate levels. Globalization has led corporate strategists to develop on a world scale. Additionally, multinational and medium-sized corporations must develop strategies for regional economic blocs called international regional strategy.

For a long time these global levels were prominent in the development of governmental foreign-policy strategies, but national economic strategies were traditionally—albeit poorly—developed without a global aspect practically until the twenty-first century. Multilateral institutions like the IMF, World Bank, and WTO have almost always missed a key aspect of strategy—the international regional level. This is largely because multilateral institutions do not have any formal mechanism for dealing with regional economic organizations and, furthermore, do not cooperate with many of them. The national level of the system of strategy can be broken down into sectorial (industrial) and regional aspects. However, a typical mistake made by national strategists is ignoring the strategies of domestic and foreign corporations operating within its borders. Ignoring this strategic aspect decreases the efficiency of both corporate and national strategies. By including the corporate aspect within an entity's national and regional strategies, and in security strategies, cooperation between corporations and national and regional governments will inevitably improve. This is absolutely necessary in order to increase the role of corporations in the resolution of major national and regional challenges. The final or initial level of the system of strategy (depending on the strategic approach) is the unit strategy, which applies to corporate subsidiaries, military units, regional and local authorities, and governmental departments (ministries, agencies, etc.).

Globalization encouraged all strategists throughout the world to develop global strategy for all multilateral institutions, national governments, security structures, and for almost all businesses—even medium-sized companies—if they are looking for opportunities and threats on the global marketplace. National governments' and internationalized companies' global strategy required multilateral levels in the strategic hierarchy. The international level did not disappear as a result of the birth of global strategy; rather, it continued to exist as an important stratum. The trend of globalization and the increasing role of international regional economic organizations made it necessary to develop an international-regional stratum within the strategic system. A company's, region's, or country's issues on a bilateral or multilateral level typically develop in this stratum, but within the framework of regional economic organizations. The national stratum was—and is—a prominent part of governmental, regional, and corporate strategy. Only the integration of businesses into the global marketplace made this level necessary even for smaller companies. National strategy must be developed in two dimensions: regional, in terms of domestic regions, and sectorial, in terms of industry and including military and security strategies. Any entity has to develop its pure internal strategy, which for businesses is a corporate strategy. Medium-sized and, obviously, larger corporations need to have a business strategy for all of their units, and that strategy should be developed under the influence of and in correspondence with the overarching corporate strategy. The described dimensions and layers can be understood as the structure of the strategy system; the ideal strategy of any strategizing object should encompass all of them.

Correlations between National Strategy and the Strategies within a Country's Internal Regions

One of the major differences between predictions, forecasts, and concepts on one side and strategies on the other is the evaluation of resources. A strategy cannot be developed without securing resources for every single priority, objective, and goal involved in its implementation. Without resources, priorities and goals are just wishes.

Often, the need to develop strategy will be triggered by an event—such as a global, national, or regional crisis, or a failure in competition for or restriction on a corporation—where resources suddenly become much more limited than they were previously. Limitations on external resources and a shortage of internal resources can drastically complicate the process of strategy implementation, and require highly gifted and hard-working, skilled strategists to develop new strategy. The formation of strategic priorities for countries, regions, military powers, and corporations during periods of shortages must be

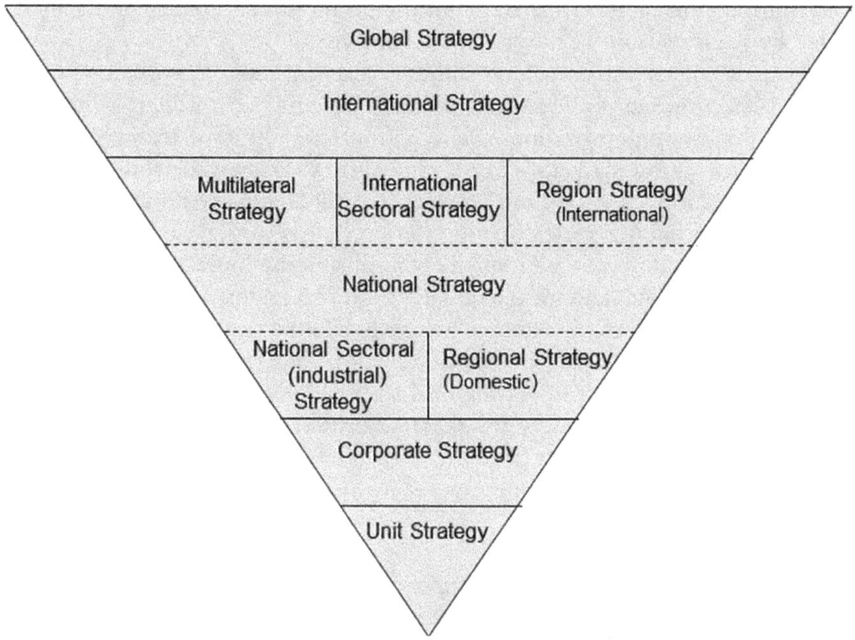

Figure 3.1 Hierarchic System of Strategy

concentrated on the highest priorities, with resources anticipatorily allocated and made available for a minimum of five to seven years. Only in the case of a successful initial strategy implementation can new resources be made available. In the initial stages of strategy implementation, strategy development creates competition for external and internal resources, and drives strategists to focus on the most limited resources and their availability. Success during these stages can create new resource opportunities.

Strategists have to carefully evaluate the trend of any forecast, and forecasts of any trend, to determine how these trends will influence the initial stage of strategy implementation. In a competitive environment, a winning strategist is the one who is knowledgeable about trends, having analyzed them and evaluated their influence on the global, regional, and sectorial scales. New technological achievements, innovations, and other notable discoveries are especially important. Since the beginning stages are a period of very limited resources, revolutionary technologies and time-sensitive maneuvers become the two major factors to successfully gain ground in a strategic competition or conflict. In this situation, an external resource analysis starts with an evaluation of strategic natural resources, raw materials, and parts that can be in short supply during a conflict. Their ecological limitations should be reevaluated as well. Moreover, an analysis of labor resources, existing production facilities, investments, and the availability of new technologies will also be needed.

An analysis of internal resources is conducted in reverse order, starting with technological, scientific, and innovative advantages that are already available to the strategized object either on a national, regional, sectorial, or corporate level. The next series of steps entails an analysis of labor resources, followed by an analysis of available raw materials and parts, and of the availability of the required capital investment, which is ideally already controlled by the leadership of the strategized object.

Both internal and external analyses indicate that the most important resources are technologies and innovations. However, all resources must go through a time-sensitive analysis. In a period of globalization, where national and regional markets are regularly integrated into the global marketplace, it is imperative to analyze the ability of the strategized object to export its goods and services, as well as import resources that will be vitally important to future operations.

All of the above rules should be implemented during the initial stages of any regional strategy development. The strategy of a country's internal region needs to be aligned with the continuing definition of the national priorities allotted to this particular region. The localization of national priorities to a specific territory not only allows for national priorities to be met, but guarantees that regional leadership will receive better funding and subsidies from the national budget for these priorities, and motivates corporations to change their strategies accordingly.

At the beginning of the strategizing process, national priorities are to be ranked in the following order:

1. Defined priorities, with secured competitive advantages, when the country has a vitally important global position, and when these priorities are brought to the attention of all national and regional leaders on its continued success.
2. National priorities, when the example country has lost its competitive advantages and needs to pay more attention to these competitive advantages, directing additional resources to them until the country returns to its previous leading position.
3. New priorities, when the country can obtain new competitive advantages, including new technological achievements, although this requires the full allocation of resources and funding.

In order to guarantee the success of these priorities, strategists must also pay attention to issues of national security and social stability after formulating national priorities according to the above order and locating them in a particular region or in available production facilities. For example, national priorities can include food and environmental security and safety, as well as sustaining and developing education, technology, and science. After national priorities are defined and the resources for them are secured, strategists can start to work on a regional strategy that develops regional-specific priorities. These priorities must also be scrutinized according to the rigid analyses outlined above. No one priority can be included in a strategic scenario if the priority does not have secure competitive advantages in the region.

During the process of defining national and regional priorities, strategists must always give special attention to current economic programs and plans that will be/may be implemented as part of previously devised strategies. When corporate planners and program managers bring on a strategist whom they formally use to create newly designed strategic scenarios, planning at the regional level can become complicated. Strategists on regional levels are immensely important, and need to be sensitive to the day-to-day needs of the regional population and the interests of the local communities.

National priorities allocated for implementation in any particular region should be superior to any regional, corporate, or sectorial priorities, including in the military sector.

When strategists and regional leadership start the process of allocating national priorities on the regional scale, they must first look for competitive advantages in a particular territory. This takes precedence over material and financial resources. Competitive advantages are required for implementing priorities (see Figure 1.3). A strategic analysis has to go through each priority from the point of view of existing competitive advantages in a given territory, region, or subregion where a strategic priority has been developed and implemented. If there are no existing competitive advantages for a particular priority, strategists must then do a thorough analysis of all new technologies, scientific achievements, patents, and required resources in that area that will impact implementing that priority.

Any competitive advantage cannot remain efficient forever. When competitors or enemies are familiar with your competitive advantages, they can respond with efficient offensives and technologies. Eventually, they will become more versed in your strategy than you are. The best example of this is Hannibal the Great's strategic use of elephants to defeat the Roman army; once the Romans became familiar with the elephant's attack formation, they adapted an offensive strategy and learned to destroy the elephants not head on, but from the sides (see Chapter 1).

If strategic advantages are not available, strategists have an alternative: to evaluate and allocate the available resources and develop a new, revolutionary solution. This solution must incorporate scientific, technological, and economic resources, and be oriented to a particular national priority. On the national level, this analysis of both national priorities and competitive advantages available in particular territories must be conducted through an interregional comparison. Strategists on the national level must decide where to allocate or reallocate national priorities based on the time and resources required for their development, implementation, and practice.

The major rule is simple: if there is no competitive advantage, and there is no efficient way to create one for a particular national priority, then this priority must either be moved to a different region or reevaluated as a priority for the strategizing period. If there is no competitive advantage, then there is no national strategic priority (see Figure 1.3).

The government of any country, be it democratic or dictatorial, faces the same issues related to different levels of prosperity and social infrastructure development among different peoples and regions under their rule. With a national budget, the government must naturally allocate some resources to regions that are lagging behind the rest of the country in basic life conditions, primarily in order to make these areas more attractive and suitable for living and working. But the first priority of any government in terms of funding should be related to national strategic priorities and to two specific territories: one where people work and one where the majority of employees live. Without this approach, national priorities would not be realized. People typically seek to work and live in reasonable proximity to each other. If an area has industry, but is unsafe for personal life, it will not succeed. The same can be true for the inverse: if an area is safe, but has no industry, it too will fail. The territories around production and living areas should therefore be prioritized for faster improvement.

However, no one country in the world—or in history—has ever had enough resources for the equal development of all territories. Resources need to be concentrated, as do national interests with corresponding competitive advantages. Some economists and other professionals have referred to this phenomenon as the pole of growth, which from a strategic position is incorrect. Here I am actually referring to poles of developed competitive advantages, which means that these competitive advantages must be supported by a corresponding level of resources; for example, it would be inefficient to use the most powerful technology available to extract scant resources. When the funding in these "poles" is sufficient, then and only then can national and regional resources be divided up between lower ranked national priorities, as well as regional, sectorial, and local priorities.

The use of allocated resources for prioritized development needs the consensus of the people through municipalities, city, and regional governments. They must understand and support the priorities presented. When a country's population is not involved in implementing these priorities, then public chaos could rule. Strategists must remember that the initial development of any strategy is the prerogative of leadership and professionals. Implementation of the strategy will be carried out by and throughout the population. Therefore, resource allocation and social infrastructure improvement can be considered part of the process to motivate the population.

Development of Strategy

Core Stages of Strategy Development

Before beginning to strategize priorities, and their division into objectives and goals, it is useful to develop benchmarks for the future. It is hard to know the end result when first developing strategy, but these realistic benchmarks must be put in place for the assumed moment of the strategic process's completion. I often provide strategists with one hint in order to set realistic benchmarks, which I already briefly mentioned in Chapter 2: They must have the foresight and mental capacity to determine the political, economic, and technological conditions, among others, that will exist in an easily visible future-constructed outcome—roughly six months ahead of time—when the strategy will have been mostly developed, and the process of implementing the new strategy in practice will have begun. Credible strategists must condition themselves to envision potential events and feel as though they live in the conditions of the future more so than in the current state of affairs. By imagining distant future conditions as a landing platform for any newly implemented strategy, strategic orientation can become more accurate and tenable.

Correlations between Forecasting, Strategizing, and Planning

It is a common misconception in the field of strategy that the processes of forecasting, strategizing, and planning are the same. Even among professional forecasters and planners, these terms are used interchangeably. This is an incorrect conflation; in fact, these three terms describe three unique activities that result in very different products.

The process of strategizing ends with a newly developed and implementable strategy. Forecasting through using predictions builds a developed prognostication. Planning is a different topic entirely: it is focused more on managerial activities by nature, resulting in a detailed and strict outline and plan. Planning shares characteristics with the power of law in some countries and regions, and is also related to a detailed corporate document. Understanding how these three processes relate to each other will give the reader a better grasp of the stages of development needed for success (see Figure 3.2).

An analysis, understanding, and recognition of the future economic and social potential of any strategized object starts with a knowledge of the general dynamic characteristics of the object that will carry it from the present to future periods anywhere from several

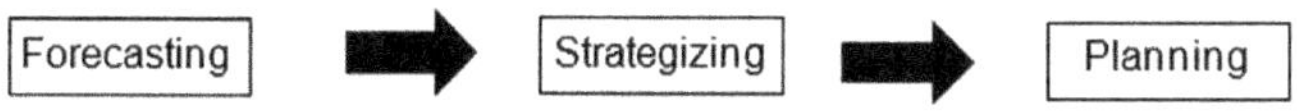

Figure 3.2 Correlation between Forecasting, Strategizing, and Planning
© Dr. Vladimir Kvint, 2014

years to several decades or even 100 years from now. This process is forecasting. The documents produced as a result—i.e., forecasts—will primarily describe the external environment, but will provide some information on the internal characteristics as well.

When strategizing, the strategist uses forecasts to help orient strategy development and implementation. When a strategy is ready for implementation, the evaluated resources and long-term time table should be given to a professional planner, who will then develop a horizon plan for the next one to five years and an operational plan that focuses on the subsequent twelve-month period, which can be even further calculated to weeks, days, and even hours.

Simply put: strategy lies between the forecast and the plan.

Scanning and Forecasting the Dynamics of External and Internal Environments

When developing a new strategy or revising an existing one, strategists should begin with an analysis of well-known and mature trends, as well as the dynamics of their influence on the entity. More importantly, strategists must be able to recognize trends that are not yet well recognized, and strategize according to their potential impact. The most innovative and successful strategies are based on analyses of emerging and still unexplored trends. It is of equal importance to understand and analyze the relationships between different trends: how they influence each other, the global community, the GMP, and any relevant industries and regions. At the corporate and sectorial levels of strategy, key trends should be used as a guiding vector for the strategy-development process. This is one of the first priorities for the statesman, military commander, executive, and professional strategist, which should be broken down into objectives and goals.

The process begins with an analysis of global trends. This is followed by an evaluation of industry specific and regional trends. Typically, corporations monitor industry or sectorial trends but ignore regional ones. Correspondingly, national strategists ignore regional strategies. This often leads to serious mistakes, as well as to competitive losses in the location of corporate facilities. Analyses of regional trends can be easily obtained from local and regional governments. Even in emerging market countries, the majority of governments develop their own socioeconomic and technological forecasts. The analyses of global, regional, and industrial trends are then used to make a global forecast specific to the strategized object, followed by regional and industrial forecasts.

The most important function of a sectorial forecast is to project the activity of major competitors, or potential enemies in military conflicts, for the next one to five years. Special attention should be given to the possibility of the appearance of newcomers from "next door" regions or countries in conflict. Strategists should also analyze possible openings for newcomers in terms of potential windows of opportunities for their own entity. The next step in a sectorial forecast is related to products and services or strategic security actions. In this part of the forecast, technological trends should be the most closely monitored. The strategist should be very familiar with the technology of the industry and be able to predict—with the help of professional scientists and engineers—the possibility of the development of substitute products and services. The appearance of such products and services is the most threatening and resource-consuming issue for an entity. Finally, an industrial forecast must include forecasts of technological issues related to suppliers. Military sectorial forecasts should predict potential conflicts.

Regional forecasts typically begin with an analysis of social and political dynamics. Strategies are a kinematical phenomenon. Scanning external and internal environments for a better and more correct understanding of the impact changes in these areas will have on the strategized object will help to accurately change the speed of development. This is not restricted to the regions or communities in which the entity operates—trends in neighboring areas should also be monitored. Regional dynamics must also be analyzed on an inter-sectorial basis. Forecasts should focus on trends that could cause major changes in the region's industries. The main priority of regional forecasts is to monitor changes in the market. New business opportunities tend to appear when other industries in the region close facilities or open new ones. When new facilities open, businesses can often acquire cheaper raw materials and parts and, in the case of bankruptcies and closings, will have more opportunities to acquire existing production facilities. Strategists also have to analyze regional industrial development in terms of potential threats. For example, a company's ability to attract and retain talented employees may be compromised when an industrial giant unexpectedly allocates production facilities in close proximity and offers higher compensation for talented professionals. Finally, the main priority of regional forecasts is to monitor changes in the market. For the majority of companies, the regional location of their production facilities is the same as the regional market for their products. Trends in values, consumer behavior, standards of living, new industrial development, etc. should always be monitored, as they can potentially shrink or expand market shares of the company.

The ultimate result of any forecast is a new entity-specific forecast that describes the most relevant global, industrial, and regional trends for current and future entity (corporate or military power) activity. For strategists working with or within the GEM, this process is especially challenging because of the rapid pace of changes relative to the developed world. Also, it is far more difficult in the GEM to obtain accurate information from the governments of many EMCs. This creates a very high level of uncertainty and makes accurate forecasts very difficult. Some emerging market and developing countries still restrict access to political, economic, and technological information, which is openly available to the public in the developed world. In some emerging market countries, and even more so in developing and underdeveloped nations, the Internet is not yet a major source of reliable day-to-day information. All of these reasons inhibit strategists' ability to discover crucial changes and trends.

A key function of the forecasting phase is scanning the external and internal environment. Unlike an analysis of the internal environment, a scan of the external environment should begin with an evaluation of natural resources and environmental limitations. This should be followed by a forecast and scan of labor resources and existing production facilities or capital, depending if the forecast is industrial or regional. The final analyzed factors of the external environment are technological and scientific achievements. During the preparation of an industry-specific forecast, the major issues include an analysis of trends in competitors' development, forecasts of potential improvements in the industry's major products and services, and finally a forecast of suppliers' potential activities. Regional forecasts primarily incorporate the targeted community's socioeconomic characteristics or the characteristics of the area in which its facilities are located. A very important element of regional forecasts is companies' production in nearby areas that belong to different industries. Often, this stage of forecasting can lead a company to new and cheap raw materials that are the waste or byproduct of companies in different industries across the region. This regional production forecast can also open potential consumer markets for the company. Finally, regional forecasts should analyze the future performance of the regional market.

Once global, industrial, and regional forecasts and/or their updates have been prepared, strategists should start to develop entity-specific forecasts. During this phase, the major focus is the assessing and/or reevaluation of the internal environment of the entity. In this process, the order in which basic economic factors are analyzed is different from that of the external scanning process. These differences in order of analysis are due to the different approaches required for strategy implementation resources. The first step is an evaluation of the entity's technological and scientific resources, how they relate to emerging technological trends, and what these trends mean for the company or for any other entity in terms of opportunities, threats, and employees' educational opportunities due to perceived new scientific and technological advancements. The next basic economic factor to be evaluated is the entity's existing infrastructure. This should also be done within the context of upcoming trends and changes that may be influential during the forecasting period. Capital, employees (i.e., labor resources), raw materials (natural resources), and parts currently used by the entity are the final basic economic factors to be evaluated. This order illustrates that the most important issues for an entity-specific forecast are technologies and innovations, which can influence all other basic economic factors of a company's internal environment. The development of the *company-specific forecast* is actually the preliminary stage of strategy formulation because forecasting (as has already been said) is not part of strategy.

Unfortunately, in practice many corporations do not complete entity-specific forecasts. Investment banking equity groups and hedge funds, however, are more strategically focused on monitoring trends and almost always prepare industry, country, and company-specific forecasts. They then develop strategies based on these forecasts, which are protected as proprietary information. Equity groups and hedge funds are like vultures that are constantly on the lookout for weak companies, in which they see great strategic potential. They buy these companies, change their management, reengineer the companies, make them successful, and sell them at a high profit. The success of hedge funds and equity groups of investment banking companies demonstrates the effectiveness of an intense and constant focus on monitoring trends and developing forecasts based on their analysis from global, industrial, national, regional, and even local perspectives. Regardless of the stage of one's strategy, the strategist must continue to monitor trends. However, following the approval of a strategy, the strategist typically narrows the focus to trends related to the approved strategy. After only a few months, the monitoring of trends widens its scope. This is especially related to technological discoveries, revolutionary political changes, new or aggravated environmental issues, and natural or technological disasters that have major technological, economic, political, environmental, and business implications.

Opportunities, Threats, Strengths, and Weaknesses (OTSW) versus SWOT

Strategic business books typically use the SWOT analysis, usually accredited to Albert Humphrey (1927–2005) of the Stanford Research Institute. SWOT is a simple abbreviation that is easy to remember: strengths, weaknesses, opportunities, and threats. However,

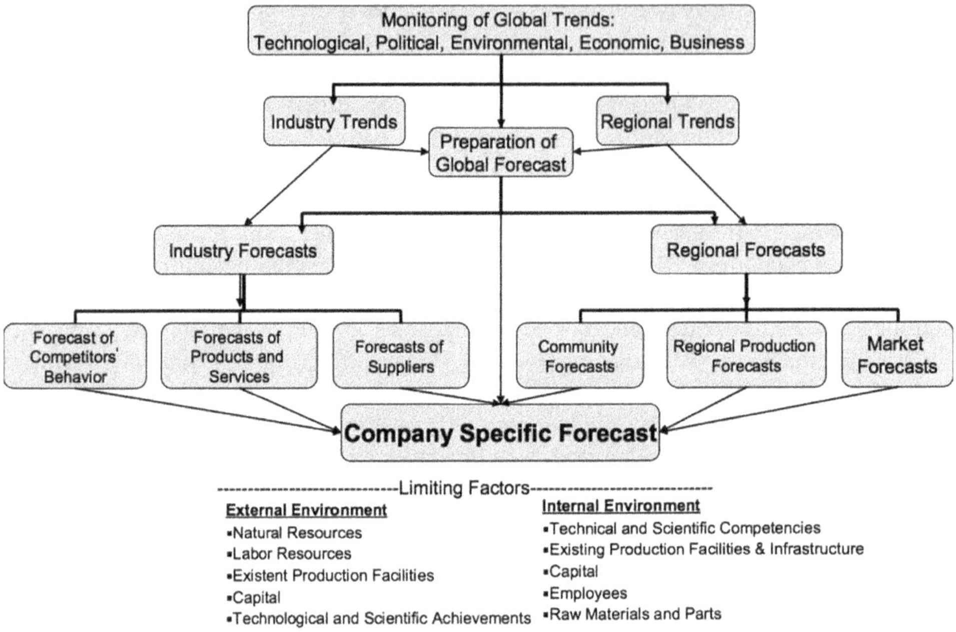

Figure 3.3 Stages of Development of Business Strategy: Scanning and Forecasting External and Internal Environments

my experience has shown me that, while this method may work on paper, it does not efficiently work in practical applications. SWOT fails because a strategist must first look for opportunities that usually exist only for a brief time. It is common knowledge that competitors quickly shut any perceived windows of opportunity. After analyzing opportunities, a strategist can then turn his attention to strengths, which can be more accurately defined as the competitive advantage of the strategized object. Only in this way is it strategically efficient to analyze threats and strategic advantages. Finally, weaknesses should be evaluated at the end of the process as they can be reinforced and made stronger. Unfortunately, OTSW is not as easy to remember as SWOT, but it is the more accurate acronym to delineate the order in which strategists need to analyze internal and external environments. (See Figure 3.3) Leaders can have incredible strategic advantages over their competition, but strength is useless without opportunity. As emphasized in a quote attributed to Napoleon, "Ability is of little account without opportunity."[3]

OTSW analysis is usually a much better method for enriching priorities and creating a strategic vision that includes breaking down these priorities into objectives, as it more efficiently allows a company, region, military, or country to be prepared for either opportunities or threats. It is especially useful for the global emerging market, where both opportunities and threats are immense. An OTSW analysis will provide time advantages for companies to recognize opportunities and identify threats, and allow them to be positioned ahead of competitors in the marketplace.

The OTSW approach can be especially useful for companies with high appetites for risk, such as a company from the developed world seeking opportunities in Iraq. While Iraq is beginning to show signs of improvement in its political stability and business climate, it is still clearly under fire, which means that it is in a state of war and armed civil unrest. Trade companies are usually better suited to operate in markets with such high levels of instability; it is less risky to buy and sell products than it is to invest. However, when a company becomes more familiar with a country, gains local experience, develops a relationship with national and local authorities, and better understands the local culture and consumer behavior, it is only logical for the company's strategist to evaluate investment opportunities. Below is an example of an OSTW analysis of Iraq.

Opportunities

- Gradual political and economic stabilization
- Possible diversification of company's export to Iraq
- Company's import development of specific Iraqi products

Threats

- Terrorism
- Regional instability
- Corruption
- Inflation
- Currency inconvertibility
- Barriers to expatriation of profits

Strengths

- Excess capacity of existing production facilities
- Surplus inventory
- New sources of inexpensive raw materials and parts

Weaknesses

- High prices due to production costs for the majority of the Iraqi population
- Deficiency of bilingual (Arabic-English) employees
- Poor knowledge of Iraqi culture, consumer behavior, and educational system

Major Stages and Documents of Strategy Formulation

MISSION STATEMENT

The mission statement is the first practical document created as a result of analyses and forecasts of the external and internal environment. The mission statement is the simplest and most straightforward way to communicate the essence of a business venture to consumers and potential partners. The mission statement must describe the *service* that the company will deliver to society. It is a brief explanation of how the entity will satisfy the values, interests, and needs of society on a global, regional, or local scale. Unlike the following stage of development—vision—the mission statement is oriented exclusively for outsiders of the entity. The mission statement should never describe how employees are compensated, what benefits shareholders or executives enjoy, or the company's profitability. The mission statement is also not a venue to express ambition or to highlight one particular product or service line within the company. The mission statement is a document that has to be prepared for the long term. Companies make substantial investments to tie the mission statement to the company brand; it is not a document that should be constantly revised to reflect new products or service lines. Skyworth, a leading consumer-electronics developer and manufacturer, is publicly held and listed on the Hong Kong Stock Exchange. In 2002, the Skyworth mission statement expressed the desire to be the No. 1 consumer-electronics company. Declarations of ambition such as this do not belong in the mission statement. Potential consumers and partners seek the leading companies of their respective industries. Declaring the desire to be a leading company tacitly concedes that one's products or services are not the best on the market and invites outsiders to question their assumption of the quality of the company's goods and services. It is especially important for companies like Skyworth, which sells expensive, high-end electronics, to present themselves properly to consumers. Skyworth revised its mission statement in 2003 as part of an improvement of its entire strategy.

In only a few sentences, the mission statement should convey the company's industry, the company's region, and the company's reason for existence, i.e., what this particular entity's value is for buyers and customers. Every successful company, even those with ordinary products or services, occupies a unique niche in the market. Companies must compete for this niche from the beginning stages of developing its entry strategy. As the great German leader and "Iron Chancellor" Otto von Bismarck once said, "All treaties between great states cease to be binding when they come in conflict with the struggle for existence."[4] It is clear from these words that the reason for existence is a vital issue and that leaders in the company will be willing to sacrifice anything for this. From this perspective, the mission statement also addresses employees, but only for one reason: to ensure their understanding of the entity's service to its country, society, and customers. The mission statement has to clearly explain the company's uniqueness—how it differs from others, and even from its subsidiaries, which may have similar functions but different locations. For example, despite the fact that the Marriott Marquis Hotel located in the theater district of Manhattan and the New York Marriott East Side are separated by roughly five blocks, they both have unique mission statements. Although the mission statement must cover a lot of information, it is important to keep it as short as possible. It should not exceed 275 words; an ideal target is roughly 150 words when modeled by best practice.

Writing a mission statement requires encapsulating into easy-to-understand language the major strategic idea. Unfortunately for many years, writing a mission statement was not many developed countries' top priority. It was almost ignored in business planning and during strategy development. In many cases, an accountant would hastily write it at the last minute after completing the 10-k report. Since the formation of the global marketplace and the subsequent groundswell of international competition, the importance of the mission statement has substantially increased; it is the first message from the entity to all outsiders.

The mission statement is often the base for an entity's slogan, logo, and other branding documents (for example, brand guidelines, pictograms, etc.) Most importantly, the drafting of the mission statement is a key stage in strategy development and a major signpost for fleshing out all subsequent steps. Although the intended audience of a mission statement is not shareholders, executives, or employees, one of its functions is to unite all of them behind the implementation of the company's responsibilities to society. Foreign companies' mission statements receive a great deal of attention in the GEM, the population of which is less familiar with international companies than that of the developed world. As a result, they have to be crafted with particular care, especially taking into account local culture, religion, and foreign-language comprehension. The majority of the GEM's population has a limited understanding of foreign languages, including English.

By the end of the twentieth century, practically all leading corporations began to invest time and resources in the formulation of mission statements. Many even hired outside consultants to rewrite or write their mission statements from scratch. As a result of this increased attention, the quality of mission statements has improved noticeably. The progression of the mission statement of Dow Jones & Company is indicative of this general trend. Prior to its recent revision, the Dow Jones mission statement stated the following:

> [P]ublish the world's most vital business and financial news and information—in any form, time or place—to create the greatest value for our customers, employees and shareholders and for the benefit of free people and free markets. Also publish high-quality community newspapers.[5]

This mission statement includes several typical mistakes. Most important, it is not directed to the proper audience, as indicated by the declaration to "create the greatest value … for employees and shareholders." The target audience of a mission statement should be outsiders, not employees and shareholders of the company. As of 2008, Dow Jones's mission statement has been revised and substantially improved: "[T]o be the world's best provider of business content and information services across all consumer and enterprise media channels."[6] This mission statement is definitely addressed to the global community, which is the appropriate audience. Nonetheless, some ambitions are often apparent. Despite the widely acknowledged importance of the mission statement, there are still some major companies that have not revised their mission statements appropriately. For example, Merrill Lynch's 2006 annual report does not even mention a mission statement.[7] This may actually be an improvement from the very poorly written mission statement in its 2001 annual report:

> Our goal is to be a leader in our chosen markets: wealth management, global markets and investment banking, and asset management. Our future is about growth—growth built on a culture of excellence. A culture that extends from how we think, to how we behave, to how we measure performance. By achieving excellence—in everything we do, every time we do it—we will deliver the full value of Merrill Lynch for our clients, shareholders and employees.[8]

First of all, it begins with an explanation of a goal, which should not be included in the mission statement; all goals should be stated in the goal-setting stage of strategy formation. As previously stated, the expression of ambition in the mission statement is never a good idea. Second, there is no mention of ethics or fair play in financial markets, both of which are of great importance. Merrill Lynch learned this the hard way from the serious legal trouble in which it found itself in 2002.[9] To be fair, this mission statement does have some positive aspects, such as its focus on the future and corporate culture. However, it does not describe how these elements are related to their customers. It also makes the mistake of speaking about shareholders and employees' interests because the mission statement is overwhelmingly addressed to customers, buyers, at any rate, to outsiders of the entity, and they could not care less about the profits of shareholders and employee compensation. They are thinking about the higher quality of goods and services at a fair price. Without a clear and correct mission statement it is always quite difficult to develop a sufficient and strong vision with all of its vital elements.

VISION: VALUES, INTERESTS, AND PRIORITIES

In the theory of strategy, vision is one of the most misunderstood elements of strategy development. Often, vision is called the philosophy of a particular strategy. As the philosopher Philo once said about Apollo, a prophet who had the capability of making predictions to assuage people so they would not be overshadowed by uncertainty:

> For Apollo is said to have been not only a physician but also an excellent prophet, by his oracular predictions announcing what was likely to conduce to the advantage of mankind, in order that no one, being overshadowed by uncertainty, going on without seeing his way before him like a blind man, might hastily fall into unexpected evils as if they were the greatest benefits; but that men having previously acquired a knowledge of the future as if it were really present, and looking at it with the eye of their mind, might guard against future evils just as they can see evils actually before them with the bodily eye, and in this way secure themselves against any irremediable disaster.[10]

In a nutshell, Philo said that a vision is a creation of a clear path through an uncertain future.

Vision is the second elemental core of strategy and the second stage of strategy development. It is incorrect to say that this is the stage where strategists find connections between values, interests, and priorities of the strategized object. From the beginning of strategic development, a strategist must always bear in mind that it is up to him or her to find and enrich the connections between these three key elements, primarily through developing and defining the strategic vision.

When developing a vision for any strategy, chaos is an ever-present component. Chaos is a major obstacle that a strategist must overcome during the development of vision and all following elements of strategy. As Nobel Laureate in Economics Douglass C. North once wrote, "[E]conomists seldom put the problem of order and disorder at the center of inquiry. Historical—and contemporary—experience suggests that they should. Establishing and maintaining social order in the context of dynamic change has been an age-old dilemma of societies and continues to be a central problem in the modern world."[11] North clearly connects strategy with order and chaos, and developing a vision through chaos will help establish order to any strategized subject.

Beyond order and chaos, vision is always about the future of strategizing systems. The strategist's required capacity when creating a vision is to build a bridge from the past to future priorities and goals. Once again, according to North: "We have not only a vision of the way an economy and society is working but a normative view of how it should be working and views about how it could be restructured to work better."[12] From a strategic point of view, "how it should" and "how it could" are already two different scenarios. "How it should" never works in strategy, since it's an ideal scenario and suggests that strategists see the future so clearly that they predicted, forecast, and strategized future scenarios as if seeing them on a computer screen. "How it could" illustrates a more realistic scenario, taking into consideration the fact that the perfect scenario in strategic practice does not exist, at least if this strategy is not about tomorrow or next week. The strategist can also

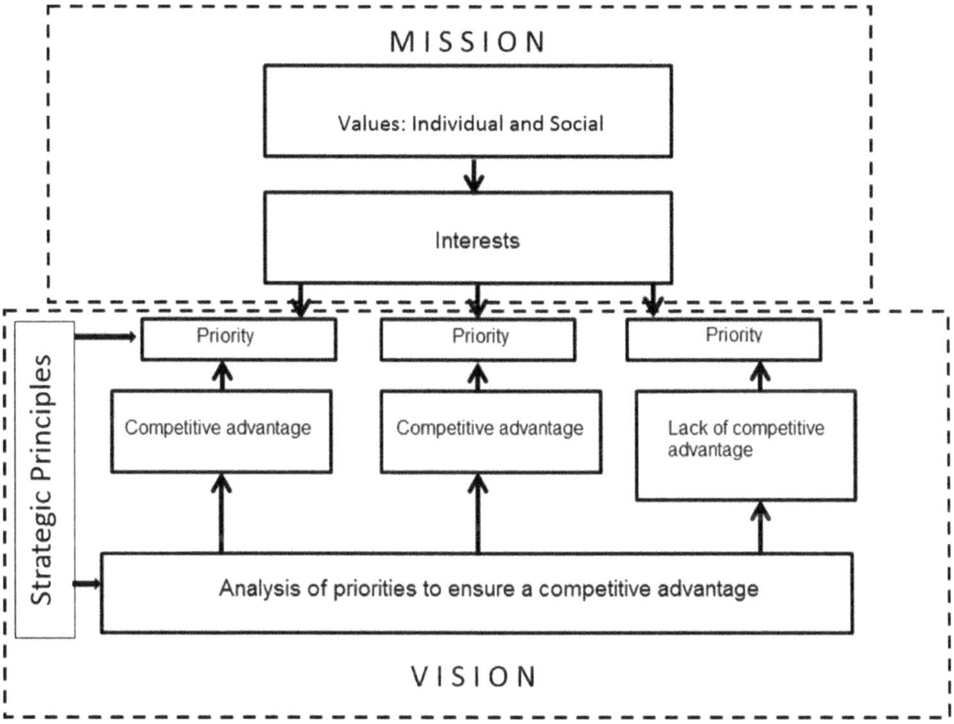

Figure 3.4 The Mission and Major Contents of the Vision
© Dr. Vladimir Kvint, 2014

create a third scenario: how it *will* work in a future high-pressure situation with limited resources due to difficulties predicting all related risks. When the strategist focuses on how a strategy works, he or she is mostly applying past experience to the future. Psychologists Keith Stanovich and Richard West divided ways of thinking into System 1 (fast and intuitive) and System 2 (slow and rational), a theory that was then adopted by Kahneman in his study on the psychology of predictions, which is obviously very useful for understanding and organizing strategic ways of thinking.[13] According to Stanovich and West, the experience of strategists and the practice of strategic expertise belong to System 1, in which thinking is fast, instinctive, and emotional. When analyzing strategic ideas, the first immediate and "quick fix" solution to a problem we are facing often comes to our mind based on our previous experience, which our intuition at the beginning quickly adopts. But this immediate solution, as Dr. Kahneman writes, can be dangerous because it can be too extreme, and too obviously a thoughtless repetition of past successful experiences. The readymade and immediate solution can be too obvious for competitors and enemies, since they can effortlessly find preventive measures to use through an asymmetric strategy for a victorious end in competition or military fight. According to Kahneman:

> Extreme predictions and a willingness to predict rare events from weak evidence are both manifestations of System 1 ... And it is natural for System 1 to generate overconfident judgments, because confidence, as we have seen, is determined by the

> coherence of the best story you can tell from the evidence at hand. Be warned: your intuitions will deliver predictions that are too extreme and you will be inclined to put far too much faith in them.[14]

Applying past experiences directly to salvage future problems is also too simplified a suggestion for solutions in future strategy. Kahneman calls it a regressive way of thinking: "Regression is also a problem for System 2. The very idea of regression to the mean is alien and difficult to communicate and comprehend … even when regression is identified … it will be given a casual interpretation that is almost always wrong."[15]

Every strategist uses intuition in addition to knowledge and calculations during all stages of strategy development and implementation. Strategists obviously cannot always ignore their intuition, even though intuitive thought can be insufficient and incorrect. Intuitive predictions are part of the psychological activities of forecasters and strategists. To understand how intuition works and how best to use it involves a very important process of maturity of mind. Perhaps with years of experience to use and analyze his or her own intuition, a strategist will gain wisdom. It is interesting how Kahneman structures different predictive judgments, some of which include intuition:

> Some predictive judgments, such as those made by engineers, rely largely on look-up tables, precise calculations, and explicit analyses of outcomes observed on similar occasions. Others involve intuition and System 1, in two main varieties. Some intuitions draw primarily on skill and expertise, acquired by repeated experience. The rapid and automatic judgments and choices of chess masters, foreground commanders, and physicians that Gary Klein has described in *Sources of Power* and elsewhere illustrate these skilled intuitions, in which a solution to the current problem comes to mind quickly because familiar cues are reorganized.[16]

Strategists use another type of intuition during the selection of priorities and goals when a lack of information often does not given them a full basis for optimal solutions. In these situations, strategists have to use modern mathematical modeling as much as possible, which, together with intuition, can help to reach the right setting of priorities and goals. During the entire process of strategy development, as well as some stages of strategy implementation and even monitoring, strategists use their imagination for understanding and describing the objectives and future results of successful strategy, and even for the description of potential dangers. This "basic resource" of strategists, as Edmund Phelps writes, "is the *imaginativeness,* or *creativity*, to conceive of things not conceived already."[17] The ability to imagine strategic results is

> another way or another goal, or if no one can imagine the chance of beneficial outcomes. Imaginativeness is fundamental to successful change, as David Hume saw in his profound work so fundamental to the modern era.[18] The innovative capacity also requires *insight*—insight into a new direction that might turn out to meet desires or needs that could not have been known beforehand. That insight is often called strategic vision—an intuition we cannot explain and a sense of whether other enterprises will be adopting the same strategy. Steve Jobs owed his huge success to his creativity and deep insights. Curiosity to explore and the courage to do something different must also be mentioned.[19]

Obviously Phelps' way of understanding strategic vision can be applied to any process of strategizing beyond business and economics. The nature of strategic vision is the same in the development of military or state strategy, or even in the strategy of one's personal life.

It is interesting to note that both Kahneman and Phelps did not dedicate their economic writing to strategy, but that their works separately provide an understanding of the processes of prediction and strategic vision that can be applied to understanding and developing a strategic mindset and even strategies themselves. According to Phelps, "creativity and vision are resources."[20] From a strategic point of view, creativity is definitely a resource and vision is a method and a vitally important stage of strategy development. Every single strategist has to have both creativity and imagination.

"How it should" leaves too much to the imagination and is too distant from reality. Knowing how a strategy will work allows the strategist to factor in every conceivable known scenario, and even a few unknown scenarios as well. It allows the strategy to become workable and stable for the long term. Regarding strategy as a philosophy assigns high importance to the term, especially in corporate strategies that will be turned into an empirical idea or even a corporate slogan. Orit Gadiesh and James Gilbert present one such example of this understanding of strategy in "Transforming Corner-Office Strategy into Frontline Action." In this essay, they describe the slogans of several multinational companies as "strategic principles" and include examples of America Online ("Consumer connectivity first—anytime, anywhere"), Dell ("Be direct"), eBay ("Focus on trading communities"), Vanguard ("Unmatchable value for the investor-owner"), and Walmart ("Low prices, everyday").[21] Not one of these slogans should be considered a strategic principle, regardless of what Gadiesh and Gilbert determine. Instead, they are derivative of a component of a strategic idea, just as a popular slogan should remain: a slogan, not a mission statement. The deep meaning of "strategic principle" doesn't exist in these pop phrases.

Strategic principles influence the rules and internal constructions vital to the creation of a strategy. Implementation of strategic principles—particularly state, military, or corporate—transfers the methods and usage of the general principle of strategy. A change of strategic principles during strategic implementation shows a complete and total misunderstanding of the very definition of strategy. You can alter the strategic priorities, objectives, goals, tasks, and resource allocation, but strategic principles must stay intact. Otherwise, the entire strategic construction will fail. Gadiesh and Gilbert incorrectly identify this concept when they state, "leaders of long-standing multinationals, like GE, crafted their strategic principles at a critical juncture: when increasing corporate complexity threatened to confuse priorities on the front line and obscure the essence that truly differentiated their strategy from that of their rivals."[22] If the authors are correct about GE losing sight of its priorities, they are mistaken, because the principles of their strategy were not correctly developed and did not reflect the priorities of the company. Napoleon once defined three basic principles for successful strategy in a letter to Marshal of France and diplomat Jacques Lauriston (1768–1828) in 1804. His rules were: "concentration of force, activity, and a firm resolve to perish gloriously." To underline their importance, he stated, "[T]hey are the three principles of the military art that have disposed luck in my favor in all operations. Death is nothing, but to live defeated is to die every day."[23] Eventually, Napoleon added a fourth principle: "[S]urprise the enemy by strategy and secrecy, by the unexpectedness and rapidity of your operations."[24] The strategic principles are not necessarily related to any particular long-term opposition, war, battle, competition, or circumstance. They should be considered general successful rules in any and all strategy.

Quite often the leaders of a country, region, corporation, or military unit will work isolated in their offices, developing strategy and priorities that are blatantly wrong for the strategized object. But because of this leader's power, all subordinate structures find themselves under pressure to fall in line and implement an inefficient or even absurd strategy. Beyond the power of the leader, there is also a lack of developed strategic priorities. The principles of strategic development were never declared or even created. All previously declared principles no longer apply to this new agenda.

Priorities are the final product of vision. Priorities are a concentration of values and interests, presented in a condensed final version. Those who are influenced by the process of strategy implementation ought to be familiar with how strategic priorities represent their interests. As Napoleon stated, "A man will fight harder for his interests than for his rights."[25] This is one of the reasons why the process of strategy development should always start with an exploration of the current values and interests held by those who will be implementing the finalized strategy. However, the only interests that should be incorporated into priorities are ones that will ensure that the strategy will be successful. The beginning of strategy implementation is nowhere near the final successful result. This is why Napoleon said, "To win confidence in advance of success, is the most difficult political accomplishment."[26] Napoleon knew very well that it takes a great deal of political maneuvering to keep a population together from the beginning of strategy implementation to the final successes.

The process begins with an elicitation of values, followed by the conversion of these values into interests, which are then divided and formulated into particular priorities. When priorities are not clearly and properly formulated in the initial stages of strategy development, then all continuation of work on the strategy will just be a waste of time. As Donald Rumsfeld said regarding this matter, "If you don't know what your top three priorities are, you don't have priorities."[27] Strategy is always more than one priority and, especially for major ideas, incorporates multiple priorities. It is important to note that strategy has to develop from priorities and not from any current problems the strategized object may currently face. Only with this approach can strategy be used as a long-term plan. Problems often have a short lifespan; priorities, however, represent the long-term vision of the strategists, as well as the deep interests and values of the corresponding population.

Without this stage of priority development, it is next to impossible to find strategic objectives. If the strategic objectives are not based on present values and interests, it is difficult to mobilize people to reach these objectives, as people—be they employees, citizens, or all of humanity—need to feel the objective is both attainable and a practical implementation of their values in order to be enthusiastic about reaching it. Values and interests are a major component of priorities. Therefore, vision predetermines the future objectives that must then be enriched by strategy.

A durable vision is a typical characteristic assigned to prophets, seers, and predictors to highlight their superhuman capacity. Why does Philo attribute his prophetic ability to Apollo? Because associating his ability with Apollo, a Greek god, designates it as supernatural. The most gifted human prophets have this ability; without it, they could not be described as prophets. If this ability is found to be fake through a false prophecy, they are called pseudo-prophets. A classic example of a pseudo-prophet is illustrated in the biblical book of Jeremiah, where the strategic leader and prophet of the same name calls into question the prophecies of Hananiah (Jeremiah 28). Jeremiah was right to declare that a liar certainly cannot be a prophet because one of his prophecies was wrong and misled the people.

Following the mission statement, the vision of the entity is the next step in strategy formulation. The vision is the philosophy of the entity. Many of the aspects that mistakenly appear in the mission statement actually belong in the vision. By including them in the vision, the mission statement is streamlined and focused only on outsiders' perceptions of the company. Typically, an entity's vision describes ideology and principles. Regarding its importance, it is best to defer to Bill Gates, one of the most successful business leaders of the twenty-first century:

> People often ask me to explain Microsoft's success. They want to know the secret of getting from a two-man, shoestring operation to a company with 17,000 employees and more than $6 billion a year in sales. Of course, there is no simple answer, and luck played a role, but I think the most important element was our *original vision* [emphasis added].[28]

In addition to the entity's philosophy, the vision should address how the leadership of the company will benefit employees and shareholders. However, it should not include quantitative estimations. These issues belong in the company's goals and tasks. An entity's vision is the best place to briefly describe its social responsibilities. Unlike in the mission statement, in which an entity's service to society is described, social responsibility should be described in the vision as a part of the philosophy, principles, and priorities of its strategy. In the vision, the priorities of a company must be clearly substantiated and explained. The principles of a company's business ethics and culture should also be part of the vision. The vision should be a concise summary of all of the above topics, and should consist of no more than 900 words. Outsiders will never read an overly lengthy vision, and outsiders are still one of its main audiences. Detailed explanations of the key aspects of the vision should be reserved for later phases of strategy development. According to Professor Willie Pietersen of Columbia Business School:

> [I]t is a common misconception that a firm can simply invent a new direction for itself in a vacuum, express it in a galvanizing vision statement, and implement it the next day. If only life were so simple … [I]t is essential to develop key insights first and *then* develop a vision statement based on those insights … A company's vision and its strategy are intertwined. A vision statement, after all, is an extension of a firm's winning proposition—an aspirational statement of where that winning proposition can take them in the future. To treat them as separate entities is a serious mistake.[29]

Pietersen's characterization of vision as an indivisible part of strategy is quite accurate. The key insights to which he refers come from scanning the external and internal environment of an entity. More than being a part of strategy, the development of a company's vision has to occur after the mission statement and prior to the formation of objectives, goals, and tasks. It functions as a bridge between the brief mission statement and the more comprehensive objectives. A company's mission statement and vision lay the philosophical foundation for a company's objectives and goals. It is a logical progression from the mission statement to the vision, and then to the objectives, goals, and tasks. A revision of any of these elements of strategy formation requires all subsequent and previous elements to be revised as well.

As the vision is a public document, it should not divulge any information that the company needs to keep secret from its competitors. A certain level of secrecy is crucial for any successful strategy. As Sun-Tzu said, "All men can see these tactics whereby I conquer, but what none can see is the strategy out of which victory is evolved."[30] Once a strategy becomes public, one must anticipate symmetric and asymmetric responses from competitors.

BREAKING DOWN PRIORITIES INTO OBJECTIVES AND GOALS

OBJECTIVES

Losing sight of one's objective is a realistic threat during the process of strategy development and implementation and is far worse than a total lack of strategy. When there is no objective, there are no results. Having no objective is an exercise of futility, which results in wasting a strategist's most limited resource—time. Strategizing around a false objective is even worse, as it leads to artificial results and a strategy completely based on fiction. A false objective leads to a dangerous strategizing system that must be completely scrapped and started again with a real objective. If a strategist completes the work of a false strategy, and even rallies others around the designed objective, he or she will lose everything.

This is a common occurrence, though not because the strategist recognizes his or her error. Objectives are usually in the distant future, and can be difficult to predict and achieve. There will be simpler benchmarks with closer deadlines, but they will not be as grandiose as an all-encompassing objective. Quite often an experienced strategist or leader of a strategized object will decide to pursue these smaller tasks instead of the objectives and goals needed for a well-developed strategy. This is a common mistake with huge strategic losses. Even in the most perilous situations, Napoleon always remained focused on his goal. He even developed strategic ideas of conceptual maneuvering around a central position. It is important to establish objectives early on and regularly align strategic work with them, regardless of the difficulties or of attractive smaller goals not originally part of the initial strategy. As expressed in a quote attributed to Napoleon, "The reason most people fail instead of succeed is they trade what they want most for what they want at the moment."[31]

The more difficult the objective, the more important the role of the leader is in reaching this objective. The leader is essential in attaining a strategic objective. If the objective and goals are easily obtainable, then it was not technically a strategic objective. Typically, a strategic objective seems to be unreachable at first glance, but is more realistic after a well-developed strategy and through inspiring leadership. In the movie *Conquest 1453,* Sultan Mehmet II (1432–1481) says, "Either I will conquer Istanbul or Istanbul will conquer me."[32] The underlying thought is true, despite the fact that Mehmet could not have said precisely this; at the time, Constantinople only had one name and it was not Istanbul. He grabbed an unreachable goal and changed history forever by ending the Byzantine Empire and starting the modern era of history. His actions marked the beginning of the Renaissance. Constantinople was such an important city that victory was his only solution. Mehmet was willing to put all of his resources on the line to obtain this objective. To him, it was larger than life. But this desire did lead to a victory, and bestowed on him the nickname "Mehmet the Conqueror" and the title "Caesar of the Roman Empire."

Objectives mark the beginning of a strategy's qualitative measurements. Building upon the mission statement and vision, the objectives present the orientation, priorities, and aim of a strategy. This phase of strategy formation must describe where the entity will be following the successful implementation of the strategy. Objectives provide the qualitative orientation for the goal-setting process. The mission statement, vision, and objectives together form the strategy's concept. The selection and enrichment of objectives and goals are usually the first stage in which strategists face criticism and arguments when presenting to executives and the board of directors, as these documents clearly present changes in the direction of the entity's strategy. The objectives within the strategy development document can vary from bullet points to several dozen pages, describing all objectives in detail. Regardless of the document's length, it should only be presented in qualitative terms. How does one define the appropriate strategic objectives and goals? More so than an analysis of resources and competitors, wisdom is the light that guides the direction to strategic objectives. Strategists will struggle to progress through the strategic development process without this very important quality.

Another problem arises when objectives are too small for the resources managed by the strategist or for the talent of the strategic leader. The leader can then find it difficult to set new objectives. This is what happened with Alexander the Great in 329 BCE at the age of 26, when he realized that he had "fully [accomplished] the great objectives which had been the aim of his ambition."[33] Alexander needed to develop new objectives, but by that time he had lost much of his objectivity:

> He lost the simplicity, the temperance, the moderation and the sense of justice which characterized his earliest years ... In a word, he was no longer the same man. The decision, the energy of character, the steady pursuit of great ends by prudence, forethought, patient effort and self-denial, all disappeared; nothing now seemed to interest him but banquets, carousal, parties of pleasure, and whole days and nights spent in dissipation and vice.[34]

These changes in personality destroyed Alexander the Great's ability to plan future objectives. It also alienated him from his officers, who did not carry on his mission. This situation illustrates the importance of objective development. During this development period, the strategist should plan to pursue more difficult objectives than the ones that originally seemed challenging and almost impossible.

GOAL SETTING

Goal setting is the first part of strategy that presents quantitative targets for production, sales, employees, etc. for strategy implementation. Building on all previous stages of strategy formation, goal setting provides a measuring stick to guide further stages of strategy development and implementation. If a strategy will require a company to downsize or expand its business, goal setting is the developmental phase in which this should be detailed. All goals are set within the context of an entity's resource limitations. The great Chinese thinker Confucius is said to have argued, "[W]hen it is obvious that the tasks cannot be reached, don't adjust the goals; adjust the action steps."[35] These words attributed to Confucius are inspiring but have little relevance in the practical world of strategy; strategists must be flexible. Natural or technogenic disasters, unexpected technological developments, changes in consumer behavior, or the appearance of a substitute product may make the initial tasks set impossible to reach or obsolete. In these cases, doing anything but reevaluating the entity's tasks is an inefficient use of resources. In extenuating circumstances, strategists may even be forced to reevaluate strategic objectives.

Once the mission statement, strategic vision, objectives, and goal setting are complete and approved, the next step in the strategic process is the selection of at least three scenarios through which the approved goals and objectives can be reached. This step also includes the development of a strategic plan. Economic-mathematical analyses are very useful for selecting these three scenarios, and for determining which will be most successful. This type of analysis is also a very effective way of determining which scenarios will not work due to limited internal or external resources. The most important limitations are those of the external environment because they are beyond the control of an entity, unlike internal resources that can be augmented if necessary. The external environment is a type of systematic risk; some experts believe that this type of risk is mostly unpredictable. Contrary to this point of view, it is actually possible to predict systematic risk, although it cannot be managed. Mathematical models can be used to forecast and provide insight into processes of the external environment that have both linear and non-linear characteristics. Conceptual and optimizational mathematical modeling should be employed to verify the feasibility of a strategic scenario, in terms of resource and time limitations. For example, imitational mathematical economic models are very good at narrowing down possible strategic scenarios. However, some experts argue that "it is more important whom one imitates rather than how."[36] These models are inevitably influenced by the quality of information provided and the biases of the strategist. The quality of the strategist and his or her strategic mindset also play a role in the interpretation of these modeling results. One data set can result in a multitude of different conclusions. In order to avoid misinterpretation, a hierarchic system of different mathematical models of sectorial and regional conditions should be used. Agent-based models are also very effective, especially for eliminating unworkable scenarios.

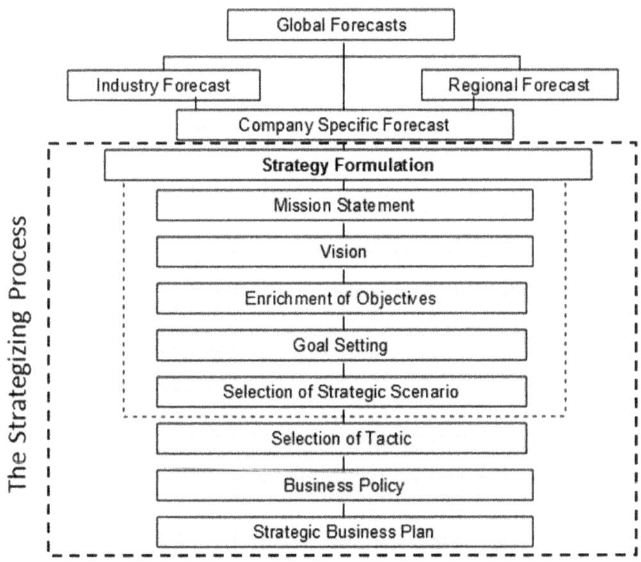

Figure 3.5 Major Stages and Resulting Documents of Strategy Formation
© Dr. Vladimir Kvint, 2008

SELECTION OF STRATEGIC SCENARIOS

The three particular strategic scenarios and plans address different levels of risk and success: low risk, moderate risk, and extreme risk, each of which provides potential returns relative to the risk level. The extreme risk scenario usually requires all resources that the entity can obtain, within reason. For each of these three scenarios the strategist develops an aggregated tactical bloc, which consists of three possible tactics. Risk isn't the only criteria for different scenarios and corresponding strategic plans. Strategic scenarios can be implemented according to different technologies, different strategic advantages, or the most major strategic criteria: time. In *Military Spending: Facts and Figures, Worldwide Implications and Future Outlook*, written with Fay Duchin (1944–), Nobel Laureate Wassily Leontief (1906–1999) categorized and analyzed a wide variety of different scenarios by the limitations of different resources. In some of his strategies for the Institute for the World Economy, which he developed at the request of the United Nations, Leontief used six different scenarios. Some of his scenarios were categorized according to the consequences on national economies of military scenarios.[37]

When presenting a strategy to clients, executives, commanders, boards of directors, etc., strategists should provide three strategic scenarios, with a total of nine possible aggregated tactics. From these options, decision-makers select a single strategic scenario and a single tactic for its implementation, which form the basis of the strategic policy. At this point all elements and subsystems of the policy are substantiated with specific details, coming together in the entity's adopted working strategic plan.

Strategic Plan

A strategic plan is very different from an operational or annual plan. There are many important factors to keep in mind when formulating the strategic plan. A strategic plan has a longer time frame, usually between five and fifteen years. The plans of any entity must incorporate financial and capital measures on both the regional and state level, especially in their budgets. Strategic planning as a part of the strategizing process starts after the strategic concept is developed. Strategic plans have to be discussed and must be the major compasses guiding annual and operational planning. They do not exist without resources and time constraints. The strategic plan must be more flexible and less detailed than annual and operational plans, allowing for adaptations to future conditions. It is this document that consolidates strategists' attention on the crucial points of strategy implementation: time, space, and the resources of basic economic factors. The strategic plan constructs an entity-specific framework under which the five basic economic factors are analyzed. This provides an analysis of the scale of raw materials and parts, workpower availability (military officers and soldiers or professionals and laborers), capital (in the form of a large-scale budget), and the capacity of production facilities necessary to meet the goals of the strategy. One of the most important elements determining a company's strategic location is the local availability of existing infrastructure, especially rail, water, and air transportation, as well as communications and high-tech infrastructure. But the key element of a strategic plan is a schedule. A workable time frame should be established for everything from the entry strategy to the exit strategy, including all basic economic factors, their allocation, and their combinations for use in the production of goods or services reaching any other goals. Strategic planning consists of a "hierarchy of endeavors … starting at the largest, the strategic plan, followed by the portfolio, the program, the project, and even the subproject."[38] Typically, in large entities—corporations,

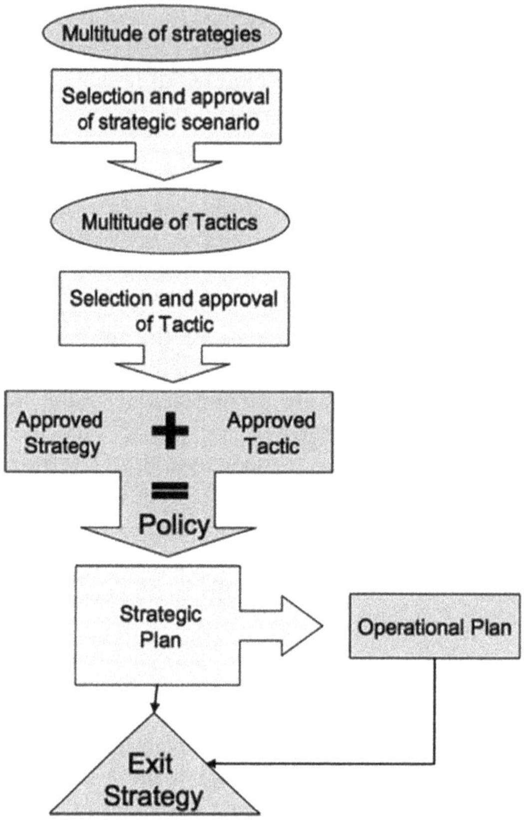

Figure 3.6 Selection of Strategic Scenario, Tactic, and Policy

armies, political parties, or governments, etc.—the strategic plan combines several projects as part of strategy development and implementation. One of the first and best examples of strategic planning was the *Program Evaluation and Review Technique* (PERT). The Virginia-based consulting company Booz Allen Hamilton Inc. created this strategic planning method for the US Navy Special Projects Office in order to plan the development and construction of the first US submarine-launched nuclear-armed ballistic missile, Polaris, in 1958. As of the twenty-first century, the PERT approach has been revitalized with modern computers and information technology. It is also important to include leadership within the strategic plan, in the form of a schedule and recommended incentives for effective implementation. The strategist must monitor the implementation of the strategic plan, as well as figure out how to avoid unanticipated obstacles as they arise and how to deal with those obstacles that are unavoidable. The practical system of all required strategic documents connected with each other (see Figure 3.5) will lead strategists from the stage of strategic forecasting to the development of a strategic plan. This is a systematic presentation of strategy. When strategists present a strategy, the following set of documents (illustrated in Figure 3.6) has to be delivered to clients (i.e., executives, board of directors, governments, etc.).

A great strategic plan and its consistent monitoring, nonetheless, can bring a strategized object to failure and doom if the initial wrong character of values, interests, and chosen priorities is totally ignored. An example of this is the well-developed four-year economic plan of Nazi Germany, under the leadership of Hermann Göring (1893–1946), which brought the nation to fiasco, not even speaking about the immoral and inhuman objectives and goals of this plan. This typically happens when dictatorial leaderships point to wrong concepts in the development of their strategic plans without consulting professionals and ignoring true societal values. The best example of this is the Juche strategy in North Korea, which has caused self-isolation from the entire world on the basis of using only internal resources. This strategy of autarchy is chosen mostly in order to ignore other nations' opinions and to concentrate all resources on producing weapons of mass destruction. Speaking about planning technology, this has been done pretty well in both historical Nazi Germany and current-day North Korea. In North Korea, a Soviet five-year planning system was used as the model, with its good and bad qualities. The good side of the Soviet five-year plan was the use of an input/output metrics system for inter-industrial inter-regional cooperation; however, the very negative and too detailed production orders, with pre-set prices, were the bad qualities that offset the positive features of the system. In conclusion, any entity's strategic plan is a strong and very powerful instrument if it is aimed to implement and practice correctly developed strategic concepts, which should be accepted by its subunits on one side and by societies through the meeting of public values on the other.

Strategy of Subordinate Units

Whether the entity is a multinational corporation with its various subsidiaries or a national government with its various ministries and committees, regional bodies, military, etc., it is important for subordinate units to develop strategies under the guidance of the main organization's strategy. Subordinate strategies can be precisely tailored to the conditions of the subordinate unit, and can focus on very specific technological and organizational trends that may be too narrow for unified corporate-level entities' strategies.

Feedback of an entity level (after analysis and integration of unit strategies) provided to subordinate units is often related exclusively to resource limitations, rather than revisions of strategic concepts. This generally results in a corporate strategy that is uncoordinated and even a contradictory summary of its various unit strategies, making it very difficult to provide leadership.

This siloed approach to strategy is actually quite prevalent among multinational corporations, military groups, and governmental bodies. However, to call such an approach a strategy is an abuse of the term; it is actually an indication of a lack of entity strategy. In order to prevent a strategy from becoming siloed, executives, commanders, and strategists should maintain an open line of communication with their subordinates, especially regarding implementation. Nonetheless, it would be naïve to assume that it is even remotely possible to avoid conflicts of interest between entity leadership and its subsidiary leadership. Conflicts typically occur over the amount of resources, the investment allocated to the unit during development, the amount of time allotted for implementation, and finally over "sales" territories, for which subunits may compete among one another. Corporate leadership often questions the unit leadership's projections of productivity and efficiency, arguing, for example, that the average of their growth rates in emerging markets are five times higher than those suggested by the unit leadership.

The unit leaders will counter that this rate of productivity is possible, but only with substantially higher levels of corporate investment. The basic conflict is over the ratio of expected production profitability and time versus investment and emerging market shares of the subsidiary. The more familiar the board of directors is with the unit leadership, the more influence they will have, making it easier for them to argue successfully for the allocation of the necessary resources for the proposed unit strategy. Annual evaluations of strategy are always aggravating times for the leadership of these two levels, especially when objectives are not being met. When the unit meets priorities and objectives, and operates efficiently, there is still conflict, though of a different nature: entity leadership wants to appropriate higher shares of the unit's profits to the mutual budget. For obvious reasons, the unit leadership will always be loath to support this. While, to a certain extent, these kinds of conflict are unavoidable, they can be substantially mitigated through coordinated development of unit and corporate strategy, which benefits both parties. Strategists have to be aware of these conflicts during the process of strategy development and especially during implementation, when the conflict usually intensifies, regardless of the level of success. From the perspective of employees, it is important to pose questions to superiors regarding the strategy of their particular unit (branch, ministry, etc.), as well as the overall strategy of the company, military organization, or government. This increases employees' knowledge of their organization and demonstrates their seriousness and ambition to superiors.

Consultant and author Clive Reading astutely described the importance of strategy for each unit of an organization:

> The old idea of strategy, as an ivory tower exercise handed down for the managers to implement, just does not work. The leadership team and the managers have to be their own strategists. The practitioners have to be planners. Therefore they need a system that they can follow, that will be comprehensive and exhaustive, yet understandable. They need a model that simplifies the situation, but does not ignore the complexities.[39]

In an attempt to diversify the company and to constantly search for more profitable activity, General Electric (GE), like other large multinational corporations, has subsidiaries in a wide range of industries. Nevertheless, among subsidiaries as diverse as GE Power Generation and the National Broadcast Corporation (NBC), there is a shared strategic business cultural understanding of success and failure. Typically, if any division of GE is not in the top two in the world in its industry, it is considered a failure. When GE Insurance Solutions did not reach these criteria, GE sold it in 2006 for $6.8 billion to Swiss Re.[40]

When some authors describe their own system of strategic thoughts, it is often the result of readdressing previous strategists' thoughts and developed ideas, and attributing works to authors who may not have originally written them. For example, in the 1966 book *The Campaigns of Napoleon*, David Chandler wrote about Napoleon's system of five principles for opening a campaign.[41] Yet these principles look to be the direct result of Chandler's systemization, not Napoleon's. We can find these ideas individually through much of Napoleon's work, but we do not know if Napoleon would have wanted to present these five principles together. While the five principles do not contradict each other, Napoleon may not have intended to group them together. Perhaps this is a type of historical editing, where we can take the ideas of great historical strategists and systematically alter them in a way they could not do themselves.

Order of Strategically Important External and Internal Factors: Influence and Analysis

When developing a new strategy or revising an existing one, strategists should begin with an analysis of existing and well-recognized trends relevant to the entity while monitoring the dynamics of their influence. More importantly, strategists have to be able to anticipate trends that are not yet recognized and plan accordingly for their influence. Strategists do not create trends—they discover existing ones. But the most innovative and successful strategies are based on analyses of undiscovered trends. It is of equal importance to understand and analyze the relationships between different trends—how they influence each other, the GMP, and any relevant industries and regions. At the corporate level of strategy, key trends should be used as a guiding vector for the strategy-development process. This is one of the first priorities for executives and strategists.

The process begins with an analysis of global trends. This is followed by an evaluation of industry and regional trends. Typically, corporations monitor industry or sectorial trends but ignore regional ones. This often leads to serious mistakes, as well as competitive losses in the location of their corporate facilities. Analyses of regional trends can be easily obtained from local and regional governments. Even in emerging market countries, the majority of governments develop their own socioeconomic and technological forecasts. The analyses of global, regional, and industrial trends are then used to make a global *forecast*, followed by regional and industrial forecasts.

The most important function of an industrial forecast is the projection of major competitors' activities for the next one to five years. Special attention should be given to the possibility of the appearance of newcomers in the sector, especially from "next door" industries. Strategists should also analyze possible openings for newcomers in terms of potential windows of opportunities for their own entity. The next step in a sectorial forecast is related to products and services. In this part of the forecast, the trends that have to be most closely monitored are technological. The strategist should be very familiar with the technology of the industry and be able to predict—with the help of professional engineers and scientists—the possibility of the development of substitute products and services. The appearance of such products and services is the most threatening and resource-consuming issue for an entity. Finally, an industrial forecast has to include forecasts of technological issues related to suppliers.

Regional forecasts typically begin with an analysis of social and political dynamics. This is not restricted to the regions and communities in which the entity operates; trends in neighboring areas should also be monitored. Regional dynamics must also be analyzed on an inter-sectorial basis. Forecasts have to focus on trends that could cause major changes in regional industries and infrastructure. New business opportunities tend to appear when other industries in the region close facilities or open new ones. Strategists also have to analyze regional industrial development in terms of potential threats. For example, a company's ability to attract and retain talented employees may be compromised when an industrial giant unexpectedly allocates production facilities in close proximity, offering higher compensation for talented professionals. Finally, the main priority of regional forecasts is to monitor changes in the market. For the majority of companies, the regional location of their production facilities is the same as the regional market for their products. Tendencies in consumer behavior, in standards of living, and new industrial development should always be monitored, as they can potentially shrink or expand market shares of the company.

The ultimate result of all this activity is a company-specific forecast that describes the most relevant global, industrial, and regional trends for current and future corporate activity. For strategists working with or within the GEM, this process is especially challenging because of the rapid pace of changes relative to the developed world. Also, it is far more difficult in the GEM to obtain accurate information from the governments of many EMCs. This creates a very high level of uncertainty and makes accurate forecasts very difficult. Some emerging markets and especially developing countries still restrict access to political, economic, and technological information, which is openly available to the public in the developed world. In many emerging market countries and even more so in developing and underdeveloped nations, the Internet is not yet a major source of reliable day-to-day information. All of these reasons inhibit strategists' ability to discover crucial changes and trends.

Unfortunately, in practice many corporations do not complete company-specific forecasts. For a strategist, resources are the most limited factor. The beginning of strategy development must make acquiring resources a top priority, and then analyzing which of these priorities have the most strategic competitive advantage and can contribute most successfully to the entire strategy. When a list of priorities is compared to a list of strategic competitive advantages, the priorities that do not contribute to the overall strategy will become evident.

Strategists always face a certain dilemma: Do they develop competitive advantages through investment in new technology? Do they develop them through an understanding of available natural resources? Or do they abolish all priorities that offer no competitive advantages and focus all resources and time on the remaining ones? There are pros and cons to each scenario.

National and long-term military strategists must work with national economists to reshuffle resources between different industries, corporations, and territories. This can lead to the creation of new companies, civilian contracts, and territories with special, prioritized functions. Foreign trade strategy should also be focused on generating resources for major strategic priorities and goals.

Financial support for developing competitive advantages is not necessarily related to additional investments and governmental spending. Often governments can use different motivation to generate funding, such as tax holidays and social infrastructure investment opportunities. However, national and regional budgets must concurrently include resources and money for emergency situations or unexpected needs. These extra funds can make all the difference between a successful and a failed strategy.

This kind of planning comes from ancient strategic agendas. Thucydides mentioned such funds in his account of the Peloponnesian War: "[Athenians] resolved to set apart a special fund ... [T]his was not to be spent, but the current expenses of the war were to be otherwise provided for."[42] This is an early example of a strategist financially preparing for unexpected situations in war, although such examples are not uncommon in ancient strategy: Sun-Tzu mentions such special funds as well. Napoleon himself rarely paid attention to economics, but appointed proven leaders in those fields to manage these situations. In his memoirs, Napoleon mentions the reign of Henry IV and credits his advisor, the Duke of Sully, with restoring France after civil war: "The organizing genius of Maximillian of Bethune, Duke of Sully, restored the finances, and agriculture, manufactures, and commerce made marvelous advances."[43] Obviously, Napoleon understood the importance of financial advisors and economic caution when leading a country.

Strategy Implementation

From the very beginning of strategy implementation, approved strategy must be bolstered by the power of law. It must be implemented and practiced without excuse, including any unforeseen expenses during initial strategy development. The only justification for additional expenses will be a final successful result. Obviously, effective strategy implementation requires flexible tactics. The best way to control and monitor priority and goal implementation of authorized formal strategy is to develop an individual program for every single goal. For the number of goals within strategic scenarios, there must be an equal number of programs to match these goals in order to implement them through regular management and monitoring. For example, a strategizing entity has 5 priorities, which are broken down into 17 goals. This means that each of 17 programs will oversee 1 goal in order to implement this strategy, including its detailed tasks and all required resources—according to a time schedule. Technological platforms and organizational mechanisms, which help to establish cooperation, compatibility of technologies, and unification of all equipment in all programs are the most important instruments in the framework of these programs. Participants at the corporate level can include technologists of different subordinate units. On the regional level, the coordinator of these programs has to work collaboratively with technologists from different companies—participants in this regional strategy who are particularly responsible and involved in the practical implementation of specified strategic goals and tasks. The technological platform used on the national, or even international, level is organized in the same way. Coordinators must help in the creation and distribution of comparable technologies from all companies from different regions in national strategy or from different companies on the scale of integrated regional unions like the European Union, Mercosur, ASEAN, etc. The technological platform is a relatively new instrument that was first widely used at the beginning of the twenty-first century. Due to the fact that it is a new concept with very limited applicable experience, it holds various meanings in different countries and international regions. For example, the concept of technological platforms in the US is mostly focused on minimizing costs and abolishing the development of any extra technologies that are already held by some platform participants. This concept of the technological platform is the closest to its intended meaning and function. Alternatively, the concept of technological platforms developed by the European Commission focuses on aiding the development of roadmaps and collaborative forms of research with all participants in a particular program. In several emerging market countries that started to use this integrated instrument by the end of the first decade of this century, technological platforms were mostly used for summits between state representatives, research organizations, and industrial companies that participated in particular national programs. As of 2003, for example, the European Union established 38 such programs, but it is difficult to evaluate how many of them were used and monitored for implementation and practice.[44] In 2010, the Russian Federation governmental commission, a semi-government body, registered 30 such technological platforms.[45] However, the problem with these platforms in emerging markets, including in Russia, is that they were established without any allocation of resources. They can thus be considered only as a declaration and forum for regular meetings between platform participants, and not a working and formal mechanism. Nonetheless, this organizational instrument of technological development can be activated and used efficiently, especially on the regional level. On the basis of technological platforms, regions can develop centers of research coordination and shared technological activities with all companies participating in the implementation of particular regional strategic goals. Technological platforms can also be useful in orientating regional educational institutions, especially those that specialize in preparing blue-collar workers for the particular needs of professionals, according to each program of regional strategy implementation. In the US, technological platforms help to decrease waste from companies belonging to program participants because the waste of one company can be used as raw materials for another participant. Companies specializing in different technological equipment can increase their sales according to the needs of customers and members of this platform. Technological platforms build ways of developing relationships between research organizations, industrial companies, educational institutions, and regional governmental bodies.

Unfortunately, even the most detailed strategy needs improvisation and flexibility during implementation. A good strategy will react to unexpected difficulties through a series of strategic landmarks and reference points, and will be capable of quickly overcoming surprises through efficient tactical decisions. Initially, it is difficult to get support for a strategy when it exists only on paper. People are generally critical of ideas that may require change. It is much more difficult to get a strategy approved than it is to gain support for it while it is being implemented and is beginning to deliver results. Some strategists overemphasize the process of implementation, often misinterpreting the strategic plan as a foundation for achieving goals. Goals are actually developed before the strategic plan, under the guidance of the mission statement and vision. The strategic plan lays out a timetable of goals for the implementation of the strategic objectives.

It is very important for strategists to understand the social dynamism and personalities of the actors who will be responsible for the strategy's application. Successful implementation of a strategy is not only determined by economic and technological factors, but by the personal influence of key decision-makers as well. The strategist should have a firm grasp of the guiding principles, underlying morality, and overall mindset that encompass the character traits of key decision-makers. When possible, it is a good idea to anticipate key decision-makers' reactions as well.

Figure 3.7 Stages of Strategy Implementation
© Dr. Vladimir Kvint, 2011

Correlation between Strategy, Tactics, and Policy

A systematic approach to strategy requires a clearly defined understanding of all of its aspects and strata. The relationship and distinction between strategy, tactic, and policy is often a stumbling point for practitioners. This is not surprising, as in economic and strategic literature it is possible to find descriptions that totally contradict one another. Quite often, policy is presented as the practical implementation of strategy. In this case, it is difficult to explain how tactics fit in, and what the difference is between tactics and policy. In some sources, especially in business literature, business policy and business strategy are treated as synonyms, with tactics presented as the practical implementation of strategy or policy. In this book, policy, strategy, and tactic are three distinct yet related aspects, layers, and stages of strategic management: once strategy is approved and becomes the orientation of an entity's practice, tactics dictate its daily, monthly, and annual implementation. Policy is the aggregate of the strategy and the tactic; or to put it another way: Strategy + Tactic = Policy.

Quantitative Limitations of Strategy

The following is an example of how conceptual modeling can be used in preliminary evaluation to analyze resource limitations. Assume that a corporation is strategizing on entering a region in an emerging market with a policy involving new technology, which will be referred to as a regional technological policy. The technological base of the policy must be very closely scrutinized, as it is a major determinant of the required resources. In this case, the regional technological policy P in k region may be implemented by means of a multitude of strategies and accordingly, a multitude of tactics. In this case:

P_k is the multitude of possible scenarios for the regional technological policy in k region;
p_k^j is j scenario of the regional technological policy in k region;
Q_k^j is the multitude of scenarios in the k region according to j regional technological policy;
q_{ik}^j is i strategy in k region according to j policy;
Z_{ik}^j is the multitude of tactics according to i strategy, j policy in k region;
z_{sik}^j is S scenario of tactics according to i strategy, j policy in k region;
$\in$ is the Greek symbol meaning "element of."

Based on these descriptions, the following hierarchy of correlation can be presented to decision-makers as a possible strategic scenario in region k of an emerging market country:

$$z_{sik}^j \in Z_{ik}^j \Leftarrow q_{ik}^j \in Q_k^j \Leftarrow p_k^j \in P_k$$

where:

k is the index of the region;
j is the index of the regional technological policy;
i is the index of the strategy of the preliminarily selected policy;
s is the index of the tactic of the preliminarily selected strategy.

Based on the above conceptual model, a system of optimizational models can be formed. The purpose of this model is to maximize the economic impact within the context of the scenario of the policy's resource limitations and the corresponding scenarios of the strategy and tactic. The model for selecting the optimal tactic is the following:

$$\sum_{s} f\left(z_{sik}^{j}\right) \times \eta_{sik}^{j} \rightarrow \max,$$

where:

$f\left(z_{sik}^{j}\right)$ is the integral economic and social effect from the implementation of the selected tactic *s*, according to *i* strategy, *j* scenario, and P policy in *k* region. The effect is oriented to the main objectives of the corporation's regional technological policy;

η_{sik}^{j} is the Boolean variable, the value of which describes choice according to tactic: 1 if *s* tactic was selected, 0 in all other cases. (The Boolean variable is named after George Boole, the great British mathematician and philosopher. It is used to hold the integer values 0 or 1, or the C++ literals true and false). [46]

In the view of interchangeability between the versions of the policy, limits are:

$$\sum_{s} \eta_{sik}^{j} = 1 \forall i, j, k$$

Besides these, there can be other limited resources:

$$\sum_{s} \partial \ell \left(z_{sik}^{j}\right) \times {}_{sik}^{j} \leq R_{\kappa}^{\ell} \forall \ell, i, j, k,$$

where:

$\partial \ell \left(z_{sik}^{j}\right)$ is the expense of resource *l* during the implementation of *s* tactic.

R_{k}^{ℓ} is the maximum expenditure of resource *l* in *k* region. "Resource" can be understood very widely—from basic economic factors to the influence of environmental, labor, and even cultural limitations.

The following model can be used to select the optimal strategy out of the three scenarios presented to the board of directors:

$$\sum_{i} U\left(q_{ik}^{j}\right) \times \gamma_{ik}^{j} \rightarrow \max,$$

where:

$U\left(q_{ik}^{j}\right)$ is the integral economic and social effect with the single intensive exploitation of *i* scenario of strategy with *j* scenario of the regional technological policy P in the *k* region;

γ_{ik}^{j} is 1 if *i* strategy was selected, 0 in all other cases;

$$\sum_{i} \gamma_{ik}^{j} = 1;$$

$$\sum_{i} h_{e}\left(q_{ik}^{j}\right) \times \gamma_{ik}^{j} \leq D_{e}.$$

After that, the selection of the optimal scenario of the company policy in the particular region can be done according to the following model:

$$\sum_j c\left(p_k^j\right) \times x_k^j \rightarrow \max,$$

where:

$c\left(p_k^j\right)$ is the integral social and economic effect from implementing j scenario, P policy, in k region;
x_k^j is 1 if j selected scenario, P policy in k region, was selected and 0 in all other cases;

$$\sum_j x_k^j = 1;$$

$$\sum_j m_e\left(p_k^j\right) \times x_k^j \leq N_e.$$

The given model shows a simplified case when there is a rigid hierarchical order in the model "company regional entry policy => strategy => tactic." In other words, one tactic, one strategy, and one entry policy scenario may be implemented simultaneously. The same tactic may also be implemented according to only one strategy, and the same strategy may be implemented according to only one scenario of the policy. In reality, more complicated cases may take place. In these situations, the given models should be modified accordingly.

However, even this simplified situation allows one to proceed to executing the concrete calculations for choosing the most profitable version of the regional entry policy. This can be done after formulating all necessary normative information, describing essential versions of the multitudes of scenarios of regional policy, strategy, and tactic, and defining the type of functions of the effect of *f, U, c*; functions of *e, h, m* resource expenditure and of *R, D, N* limits.

Any entity can use this modeling system to compare the effectiveness of a particular strategy in two regions of the same country, or between two countries with different resource limitations. For example, region k_1 may be attractive due to its inexpensive and appropriately trained labor resources, while region k_2 may have much cheaper and more widely available energy resources. In this case, the index of strategy for region k_1 will be i_1, and will be oriented towards employing inexpensive work power and increasing the production of the company based on this work power. Index i_2, for region k_2, due to its cheap energy but shortage of available labor resources, will be oriented towards the use of energy and should be based on the use of automation and robotic systems. In this case, index *f* can be the symbol for the increasing energy use per employee. This is how optimal models of a company's strategy for a particular region should be developed. Then strategists and decision-makers have to compare the entry strategies for the two different regions.

The next stage in the strategic process is the implementation phase. However, this is assuming that the entity already has an appropriate management system. If not, the development of a strategic management system is the next priority (see Chapter 4).

Qualitative Limitations of Strategy

Quantitative analysis should always be supplemented by qualitative evaluations, which are of equal importance for strategic success. The many opportunities in GEM and the GMP have brought executives and strategists of companies operating exclusively in domestic markets to a crossroad; they can allocate their resources domestically, as they have throughout the history of their company, or they can allocate resources in countries and regions of the GEM, an unfamiliar, but potentially very lucrative market. Any venture into the GEM should be made with the following issues in mind:

1. A foreign venture should improve the level of economic development in the host country, thus benefiting the local population and, in this way, meeting its values and national interests. At the very least, the priorities of the local population should not be harmed.
2. In order to ensure this, corporate leaders should be willing to seek compromises with trade unions. Trade unions' unresolved grievances can be serious obstacles to strategic success.
3. Foreign companies should ensure that the global or foreign cultural trends coexist with the local cultural values. For example, fast-food franchises should adapt their standard menu to accommodate local tastes, sanitation and health limitations, and preferences. This is in the interest of the company, the host country, and the global marketplace.
4. The entry strategy of a company into the GEM must be developed within the context of the particular EMC or its region's political dynamics and basic economic factors, including business infrastructure and level of technological development.

Another limitation that concerns many companies when investing in an emerging market country is that potential subsidiaries or branches in the GEM will be isolated from the major global business hubs, such as New York City and London. Actually, there are already several major global business hubs in the GEM, such as Moscow and St. Petersburg, Beijing and Shanghai, São Paulo, Mexico City, and Singapore. In fact, subsidiaries in these GEM hubs may be more closely connected to global business trends than subsidiaries in developed countries that have relocated to suburban campuses in order to cut costs. Advancements in telecommunications and IT have definitely reduced the importance of location. However, suburban headquarters do not benefit from the creative energy that exists in major cities, as there tends to be less social or professional interaction among executives and managers of different companies. From a different perspective, the exodus of companies from major cities does not bode well for these cities. Many of the best high-tech and financial companies have already left New York City. Even the New York Stock Exchange has considered relocating. This would have a profoundly negative impact on the creative spirit of what is considered the capital of the world.

For research companies in different scientific fields, it can be very fruitful to be within close proximity to one other and slightly removed from major urban hubs, in what are now called scientific parks. Historically, Silicon Valley could be considered the first scientific park, where many technological and later research and educational institutions were established. This happened over a matter of decades, though it was not planned. In the beginning of the 1960s, the same technological agglomeration took place outside of Boston along Route 128, which later became the catalyst for the "Massachusetts Miracle" technological-based development. One of the earliest examples of a planned "think tank town" was Akademgorodok, an academic town located 20 kilometers outside of the Siberian city of Novosibirsk. Established in 1957, the Siberian branch of the Russian Academy of Sciences is headquartered here, along with dozens of other research institutions from all spectrums of science, technology, and social studies. All institutes share facilities, including clubs, restaurants, discussion halls, etc. Scholars benefit tremendously from interdisciplinary exchanges, as they are kept up to date on cutting-edge academic thought and activity throughout the world. The Siberian branch of the Russian Academy of Sciences has been a pioneer in many research fields. For example, the leader of the Siberian economic school, Dr. Leonid Kantorovich (1912–1986), won the 1975 Nobel Prize in Economics. It is very important for strategists to have the opportunity not only to collaborate with leading scholars of their specialization through the Internet and publications, but also to interact with them face to face, as well as with researchers from other fields, and to share the spirit of innovative ideas.

In 1980, Professor Michael E. Porter of Harvard University and the head of the Institute for Strategy and Competitiveness proposed a method of evaluating strategic factors that focuses primarily on the "five competitive forces" (see Chapter 1). This is an important but incomplete evaluation of strategic factors, based mostly only on common sense. The free-market conditions of the GEM are obviously extremely competitive, as it is open to companies from any part of the GMP. A new, innovative competitor can enter an EMC and render the product for which a strategy is being developed obsolete or substantially change the bargaining power of consumers and suppliers. Porter's five competitive forces are a necessary aspect of the process of scanning the external environment,[47] but they are only part of the preliminary stages when the company is choosing the country or region to allocate its resources:

a. bargaining power of suppliers;
b. bargaining power of buyers;
c. threat of new entrants;
d. threat of substitute products;
e. existing competitors.

An analysis of these forces is also a good practice in order to set the mind of decision-makers to a strategic tune. These forces are only related in a passive way to some characteristics of competitive advantages and disadvantages and do not provide enough data and empirical evidence for an informed decision about the political, social, cultural, and financial (exchange rate, taxes, etc.) environments. Porter's five forces totally ignore the values of a population in the immediate area and of its own employees. As a result, it is difficult to select proper priorities based strictly on these five forces, but they are nonetheless very useful for an analysis to guide the decision to choose sufficient priorities. For these reasons, once a decision-maker comes to the practical development stage of strategy and its implementation, it is important to follow the processes mentioned earlier in this chapter, including, of course, quantitative evaluations of all limitations.

Strategic Economics: Time-Sensitive Resource Analysis

As mentioned earlier, the predetermined role of time in strategy development and implementation and the important role of some economic factors (first of all space) is a conceptual approach to the analysis of any strategy. The genius of Napoleon made him the first practical strategist who so directly and strongly underlined the role of time. As he stated, "Strategy is the art of making use of time and space. I am less concerned about the latter than the former. Space we can recover, lost time, never."[48] A time-sensitive analysis of any strategic decision is crucial. It has the ability to change or even prevent the continuation or implementation of particular strategic scenarios. From the point of view of quantitative time-sensitive strategic analysis, all changes will be related to the use of particular types of resources.

Changes are typically concentrated around particular benchmarks in the life of a strategy: the period of strategy development, the period of strategy implementation, the period of capital return and the return on other resources invested into the strategy, and the period of efficiency when the strategic scenario is implemented. This last period is divided into two subperiods: the life of the scenario during its development, and the life of the scenario during its practical use. To divide it even further, the practical use subperiod also includes the period of current strategic scenario exit.

A time-sensitive resource analysis is an evaluation of the correlation between increases in capital investment and reduction during the strategy-implementation phase. It is a very useful tool for strategists. This analysis is closely related to the economy of time. Despite the fact that many economists consider that first law of economics to be "the greater the demand the higher the price,"[49] in strategy, both demand and price categories can be fundamentally altered by the influence of time. For this reason the *first law of strategy is the law of economizing time.*

As mentioned in Rule 14 of strategic thinking (see Chapter 2), the ratio of time and expenses or investment is among the most important dilemmas that strategists deal with in all stages of strategy development, implementation, and monitoring in terms of the strategic investment recovery period.[50] This ratio should always be evaluated in terms of the first law of strategy/law of time.[51] The following example demonstrates the implications of the law of economizing time by evaluating the economic efficiency of accelerating the strategy-implementation period by investing more resources. State and military unit leaders, corporate executives, boards of directors, and professional strategists themselves can employ the formulas used in this evaluation for a quick and preliminary evaluation of a time versus resource investment ratio for the implementation of a strategy.

During the first stage of this evaluation, the annual economic impact (or annual economic effect) of the new strategy's application is calculated using the following formula:

$$E_{ann} = \left[\frac{Y_2 - Y_1}{Y_1} \times \Pi_1 + \frac{C_1 - C_2}{100} \times Y_2\right] - E_s C_d^i$$

where:

E_{ann} is the annual economic impact;

Y_1, Y_2 are the volumes of goods sold the year before and after the implementation of the new strategy and applied technology ($1,000);

C_1, C_2 are the investments per $1.00 of goods sold before and after the implementation of the new strategy and technology (in cents);

Π_1 is the annual profit from goods sold before the implementation of the new strategy and technology ($1,000);

E_s is the standard (.18) coefficient of a capital investment's economic effectiveness. This coefficient means that the return on investment should take no longer than five and a half years, which in general is appropriate for large-scale strategic projects. It can be changed according to the country's regulations, practices or the corporate entity's strategy.

where:

C_d^i is the cost of the new strategy's development and implementation, including innovative technology ($1,000);

$$C_{d=}^{i}C_i + C_d$$

where:

C_i is the cost of implementation and C_d is the cost of development.

In this case,

$$\Delta\Pi = \left[\left(\frac{Y_2 - Y_1}{Y_1}\right)\times \Pi_1 + \left(\frac{C_1 - C_2}{100}\right)\times Y_2\right]$$

$\Delta\Pi$ is the annual increase in profits.

The annual economic impact gives an idea of the extent of the economic effectiveness of the new strategy's development and implementation, as well as the required innovative technology, with consideration given to all costs.

The effectiveness of these costs can be defined according to the following formulas:

$$E_e = \frac{\Delta\Pi}{C_d^i} = \frac{\left[\frac{Y_2 - Y_1}{Y_1}\times \Pi_1 + \frac{C_1 - C_2}{100}\times Y_2\right]}{C_i + C_d}; E_e > E_s$$

where:

E_e is the estimated coefficient of cost (investment) effectiveness.

While cost (investment) recovery time is

$$T = \frac{C_i + C_d}{\Delta\Pi},$$

where:

T is the cost-recovery time in terms of years.

If, to reduce the cost-recovery time (T), one minimizes development and implementation costs (C_d^i) as much as possible, thereby making E_e larger than E_s, the time factor would not be accounted for. The completion time of the cost-recovery period of the new strategy and technology (T) is then postponed. The time factor is very significant in economics and strategy (in fact, this book considers time economization to be the most important law of strategy and economics), because it strongly affects the growth rate of the entity. The overall economic benefit of the new strategy implementation, which accumulates over a long period of time, is not proportionate to the benefit gained in the initial stages, starting from the beginning of the implementation process.

In this case, the problem transfers to the evaluation of the time factor with varying implementation costs. Nonetheless, in considering increasing investment to accelerate a new strategy's implementation with the aim of reaching the period of sales of goods produced based on the strategy, one should not require the condition of increasing the absolute sum of costs of this process. Instead, one should increase costs in a particular time unit of the implementation period that would intensify all operations at this stage of the development and application of strategy and the production preparation. Since increasing investments in the time unit will require an increase of total costs and, therefore, will lengthen the cost-recovery time, the challenge is to determine the optimal limits that will make increasing implementation costs economically effective. For example, Y_1 = \$3,000,000 and Y_2 = \$4,000,000 respectively. C_1, C_2 = \$0.90 and \$0.75 respectively; Π_1 = \$1,200,000. In this case, the increase in profit after the implementation of the new strategy and new technology will equal

$$\Delta\Pi = \left(\frac{Y_2 - Y_1}{Y_1}\right) \times \Pi_1 + \left(\frac{C_1 - C_2}{100}\right) \times Y_2 = \$1,000,000$$

Assume that the costs of development and implementation of the new strategy and new technology (or innovation) amount to \$900,000 and \$1,600,000; concurrently,

$$C_d^i = C_i + C_d = \$900,000 + \$1,600,000.$$

In this case, cost (investment) recovery time will equal:

$$T_1 = \frac{C_d^i}{\Delta\Pi} = \frac{\$2,500,000}{\$1,000,000(annual)} = 2.5\text{years}$$

Processes of development, implementation of strategy, and the period of investment recovery can be presented graphically, which is always useful for meetings with top executives and boards of directors, in order to increase mutual discussion and understanding (see Figure 3.8).

Where $T_1^{'}$ (time of strategy development) is two years, and $T_1^{''}$ (time of strategy implementation) is one and a half years, the total time of development, implementation, and strategic investment recovery is six years.

Assuming that the implementation costs (C_i) increase by \$400,00, this becomes:

$$C_d^{1i} = C_d + C_i^1 = \$900,000 + (\$1,600,000 + \$400,000) = \$2,900,000$$

Meanwhile, cost (investment) recovery time gets longer:

$$T_2 = \frac{C_d^{1i}}{\Delta\Pi} = 2.9\text{years}$$

This means that due to intensification of the time of the strategy implementation on the basis of increasing investment, the time of strategy implementation decreases by 0.6 years (see Figure 3.9).

However, due to increasing the time recovery period by 0.4 years in the second scenario, executives are forced to decrease the economic efficiency of the strategy. With the increased time of expense recovery, executives using this method decrease the period of strategy implementation from 1.5 years to 0.5 years. Because of this, the company starts to sell goods produced on the base of new technology and strategy 0.6 years earlier. The economic effect of this can be calculated by the following formula.

The sum of the effect from the earlier entry to the market equals:

$$E_{add} = \Delta\Pi \times \Delta T = \$1,000,000 \times 0.6 = \$600,000$$

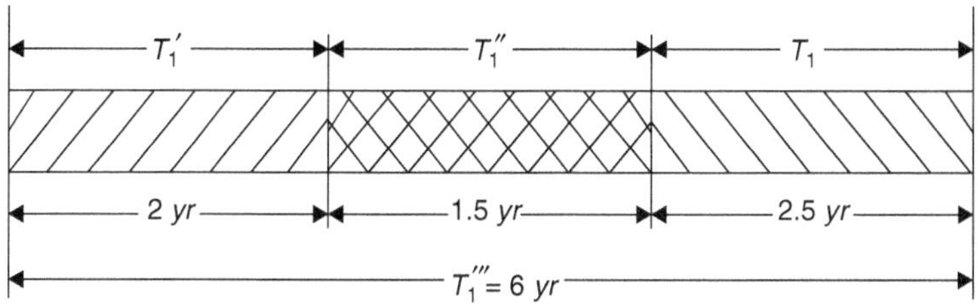

Figure 3.8 Schedule of Strategy Development, Implementation, and Strategic Investment Recovery
© Dr. Vladimir Kvint, 2008

where:

$$\Delta T = T_1''' - T_2'''.$$

Despite increasing both costs and the cost-recovery period in the second scenario, additional profits obtained by the end of the six-year period equal:

$$\Pi_2 = E_{add} - \Delta C_i = \$600{,}000 - \$400{,}000 = \$200{,}000$$

where:

$$\Delta C_i = C_i^1 - C_i.$$

In some instances it is useful to increase strategy implementation costs on the condition that there will be a decrease in the implementation time period as a result. But the total amount of this time decrease will exceed (by absolute numbers) the decrease of the cost-recovery period.

This is a simple method for strategists to show the advantages of increasing expenses during the time of entry strategy implementation, including an earlier appearance on the market, earlier occupation of the particular new market niche, and earlier sales of the goods and services produced on the basis of the new strategy and installed technology. This method of estimation is also effective for executives when presenting strategy to the board of directors (or for commanders presenting to the joint chiefs of staff).

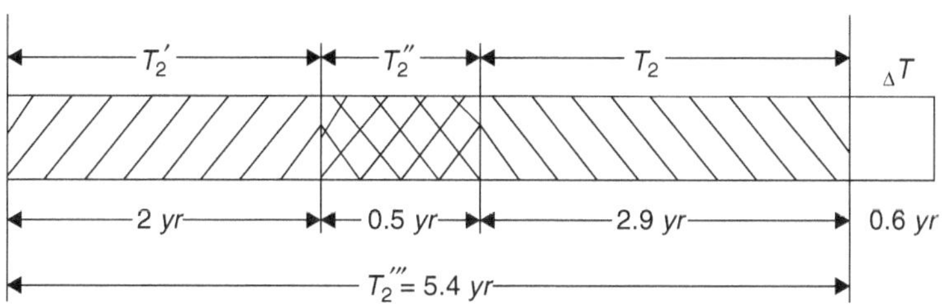

Figure 3.9 Schedule of Intensification of Strategic Investment with Accelerated Period of Strategy Implementation by 0.6 Years
© Dr. Vladimir Kvint, 2008

In addition, it is important to underline that the uncalculated effect is much larger; due to the faster period of implementation of the entry strategy, a company appears earlier on the marketplace and competitors may lose the initiative to enter the market or its new niche with the same product. As a result, the company will have a much wider market segment for its goods and services, and will have the opportunity to increase production with lower competition for some time. Reducing the application period is even more effective for EMCs. Seeing that a company has already entered the market, many competitors will not even attempt to enter this EMC. In many EMCs, competition is less intense between companies from developed countries. Consumers in these countries become familiar with the first company to enter their market with quality products (relative to local purchasing powers) and are reluctant to change their allegiance. Brand loyalty is particularly strong in the GEM; it is not uncommon for goods to be referred to by brand names rather than by proper names. For example, copy machines are generally referred to as Xeroxes in the GEM, and in many Eastern European countries in the 1980s VCRs were known as Panasonics, regardless of what company actually produced them.

Cultural and Religious Environment of Strategy

Globalization has very important cultural and religious implications that must be understood by strategists operating in the global marketplace. Its critics often argue that it is causing a global conversion of cultures that dilutes the authenticity and uniqueness of local culture. In fact, strategists have to take into consideration two paradoxical cultural dynamics: a global conversion of cultures and, at the same time, an embrace and protection of local cultural idiosyncrasies and values. A successful strategist must understand that globalization, as a trend, has very important long-term cultural and religious consequences. These consequences must be understood and used by strategists who operate on the global marketplace and its national and regional subsystems. A strictly economic approach will frequently fail if societal factors are ignored.

While English has practically been established as the standard means of communication in the GMP, there are several regional languages of great importance: Spanish in Latin America, Russian in territories of the former Soviet Union, and Arabic in the Middle East and North Africa. In addition, there are languages that represent significant markets of people dispersed throughout the world—the French market (extends to every inhabited continent), the German market (several European and African countries), the Portuguese market (Portugal, Brazil, and several African and Asian countries), the Italian market (Italy, Ethiopia, Eritrea, and Albania) and the Arabic market (the Middle East and the Arabic diaspora throughout Europe, Africa, and North America). The GMP has created a need for widespread comprehension of key foreign languages and comprehension of foreign cultures. Nevertheless, English is the language of business. As editor-in-chief of *Forbes*, Steve Forbes wrote, "English is the language of economic opportunity ... If you know English, the Information Age is your friend. If you know English, the doors of opportunity are wide open. But if you don't, you're stuck—and in danger of being left behind."[52] The same goods, services, and technologies are being used throughout the world, which is contributing to further global integration and unification and is both a factor in and a consequence of the GMP. The GMP accelerates global progress because innovation and new ideas become widely accepted and implemented. The cross-cultural exchange of ideas and technology is thus both a result and factor of the global marketplace (GMP). It creates a process of constant evolution and optimization of strategies and operations. This process is leading to the creation of a more unified, peaceful, and tolerant world. But at the same time, different political and ideological environments and varying consumer behavior throughout the GMP present a challenge to the process of global integration and strategists trying to build success in this changing environment. This requires companies to have a global strategy that takes into account differences in consumer behavior in national and regional markets.

Cultural convergence is a two-way street. The success of corporate global strategy is related to the growing influence of GEM business cultures and its convergence with the well-established business ethics and practices of companies from developed countries. A great example of this phenomenon is ArcelorMittal, the world's largest steel-producing company, owned by the British-Indian Mittal family. This family used a hybrid of Indian and British values to become one of the most successful family-owned and operated businesses in the world. Their success is reminiscent of the DuPont family in America in the nineteenth century, who merged French ethics with American business culture. Executives throughout the world, not just those from India or the GEM, should study the business culture of the Mittal family. When the Mittal family purchased Arcelor, a leading European steel company, it was one of the first examples of insourcing by an emerging market company in the developed world as a new global trend, which can be defined as "an allocation or reallocation of resources internally within the same organization, even if the allocation is in different geographic locations."[53]

Another significant cultural trend is related to the mass culture of the US as a superpower: Americanization. American behavioral norms have spread throughout the global marketplace and workplace. For example, diplomas on the walls of executives' offices in Albania or Brazil are a symbol of their interaction with partners and clients from American companies; prior to this trend, people from the GEM kept their awards and diplomas at home and did not display them in corporate offices. However, there are limits to Americanization, even on small-scale issues. In the US, it is not uncommon when buying a car to kick the tires as a kind of perfunctory test of the car's quality. This is not advisable in many EMCs, especially Ukraine, Moldova, and Georgia. When looking at a new car, if someone were to kick the tires in one of these countries, the salesman would likely (at the very least) kick that person back. The aim of this joke is just to show foreign investors that even day-to-day behavior varies substantially among cultures and can be the source of misunderstanding. As the saying goes, the devil is in the details. Professional behavior is a conglomeration of many small cultural issues to which foreigners have to be sensitive in order to develop a positive office atmosphere.

McDonald's is often portrayed as an instrument of the Americanization of foreign countries. To a certain extent, McDonald's is one vehicle through which American consumer culture has spread throughout the world, but its international success is based on its ability to cater to local tastes and preferences, often with the help of local partners. McDonald's does not enter new markets expecting to replace local cuisine with hamburgers—such a strategy would inevitably result in failure. In fact, McDonald's corporate strategists develop a variety of entry strategies in EMCs in accordance with regional, national, and local cultural and religious values. For example, in Muslim countries McDonald's provides Halal cuisine, and in Israel the menu is strictly kosher. Another important part of McDonald's global strategy is to always hire local people and to integrate local traditions and culture into its advertising. The successful application of McDonald's strategy is related to its ability to cater to local tastes and preferences. This is the model for strategists who are developing entry strategies for countries in the GEM.

The diversity of the GEM and the role of cultural traditions are much stronger and more relevant than in developed countries, which have reached a much higher level of cultural conversion.

Culture as a Strategic Risk Factor

Cultural risk, as a phenomenon, factor, and strategic category, should be the subject of joint studies among strategists, economists, and culturologists. Ignoring the influence of this phenomenon on the development and implementation of strategy could lead to decreased efficiency, as well as to complicated, negative social and economic consequences. For example, Alexander the Great understood the importance of considering the impact of cultural risk, and reflected in the following passage on the consequences of conquering regions that embodied cultural practices different from his Hellenistic homeland:

> If it were not my purpose to combine foreign things with things Greek, to traverse and civilize every continent, to search out the uttermost parts of land and sea, to push the bounds of Macedonia to the farthest Ocean, and to disseminate and shower the blessings of Greek justice and peace over every nation, I should not be content to sit quietly in the luxury of idle power, but I should emulate the frugality of Diogenes. But as things are, forgive me, Diogenes, that I imitate Heracles, and emulate Perseus, and follow in the footsteps of Dionysus, the divine author and progenitor of my family, and desire that victorious Greeks should dance again in India and revive the memory of the Bacchic revels among the savage mountain tribes beyond the Caucasus.[54]

The problem with any winning military strategy is what follows afterwards; namely, coexistence with the conquered population. Military and state leaders rarely think about how the cultures of their new territories will influence their own. The longer this relationship continues, the deeper the convergence will be between the conquered and the conquerors' values, until they create a new culture of values and traditions. Once again, as Alexander the Great stated, "Are you still to learn that the end and perfection of our victories is to avoid the vices and infirmities of those whom we subdue?"[55] Unfortunately, this quote demonstrates that Alexander only understood the effects of bringing his nation's values to others. Historically, this did not occur in his strategy, despite his claims. He was one of the most tolerant conquerors in history, almost never destroying houses of worship or other cultural necessities. All that mattered to him was the obedience of vanquished populations and their subordination to Hellenistic Greece.

In economics and business, the variety of different cultural, historical, and religious traditions pose certain challenges and even threats to international investors and companies, which can be referred to as cultural risk. This basically refers to the cultural gap between a foreign investor, merchant, or entity and the society of a potential recipient of investment or business activity. The greatest challenge comes in understanding the mentality of people with completely different cultural, religious, and historical traditions. The very different political and business cultures of EMCs compared to developed countries deeply affect people's mentalities. For example, words such as *democracy*, *elections*, *public opinion*, etc. that are universally embraced in developed countries have completely different connotations among the populations of EMCs. Many of these people have not rejected democracy outright, but associate it with the chaotic transition period after the fall of dictatorships up to and during the liberalization of command economies. Furthermore, what to strategists and executives from developed countries may seem like an oppressive dictatorship disguised by transparent democratic slogans may be a tremendously positive step forward from the brutal dictatorship that people were once forced to endure. The legacy of dictatorship deeply affects the business culture of the GEM. Many foreign managers and executives would be shocked by the lack of employee initiative in EMCs. This is a result of generations of risk-averse behavior that understandably occurred under dictatorships. In many EMC societies, there is only one correct answer—whatever the boss thinks.

The rapid pace of urbanization in the majority of EMCs deepens the cultural gap faced by foreign strategists. Large portions of urban populations are recent arrivals from provincial villages. These people experience a double culture shock: the first in experiencing the more sophisticated urban culture including museums, theaters, libraries, etc. and, second, the shock of dealing with foreigners and interacting with international culture for the first time. This is the source of a great deal of conflict between foreign executives and managers and their local blue-collar employees.

The best way for foreign companies to handle cultural risk is not to try and change the mentality of local populations. Rather, it is a gradual process that happens slowly as they interact with people from different regions. An integral part of a successful entry strategy is for foreign companies to make the effort to understand local traditions, histories, and political and business cultures. Foreign companies must be willing to change their typical practices in order to work more efficiently in and with the local society.

It is also very important that strategists of foreign companies do not misinterpret backwards political and business cultures as a reflection of a society's knowledge of high culture, such as art, literature, and film. An entry strategy for the GEM has to be developed with respect to the very deep literary and artistic traditions of such EMCs as Russia, Eastern Europe, Argentina, and India. Strategists should expect that many people with whom foreign businessmen interact will be very knowledgeable about high culture of the world. American strategists may not be familiar with the writers that Europeans (and most people of the former Soviet Union) grew up on, such as the French novelist Guy de Maupassant (1850–1893) or the German writer Erich Maria Remarque (1898–1970). It would be very difficult to find Latin American executives who are not intimately familiar with the works of the Colombian Nobel Laureate in literature Gabriel García Márquez (1927–2014) or the Brazilian author Jorge Amado (1912–2001). It would be equally difficult to find Chinese executives and strategists who do not embrace the teachings of the ancient philosopher Confucius. Any leaders unfamiliar with the Italian political philosopher and Renaissance man Niccolò Machiavelli will struggle to be successful in the Byzantine business cultures of the Balkans and the Maghreb. Foreign executives and strategists should study EMCs' high culture, especially in literature, as it can be a very effective means of bridging cultural gaps during the implementation of strategy.

There are many examples of the disastrous results of a failure to address cultural strategic risks. The Walt Disney Company theme parks were very successful in the US and even Japan, but due to an entry strategy that inadequately evaluated cultural factors, initially failed miserably in France. In 1992, Disney opened a theme park outside Paris that failed to meet projected earnings and attendance and lost a great deal of money. Disney made the mistake of assuming that the French would spend the same amount of money on entertainment, pay the same entrance fees, and enjoy the same food as

Americans and Japanese. All of these cultural assumptions were strategically wrong; Disneyland Paris became successful only after making certain adjustments, like serving alcohol, which would be inappropriate according to US cultural norms.

Cultural risk is an especially important aspect for entity-specific strategy development and implementation. This does not only apply to entities that are located in foreign countries; it can also apply to consumer culture towards particular products and services in certain industries. For example, in January 2007, when Microsoft released its newest operating system, Microsoft Vista, it was the result of several years of strategy development and implementation to combat Apple computers. They focused substantial attention on making sure that Vista would be simpler and take less time to load. Microsoft also used a tactical step: delaying the release of Vista in order to build up customer anticipation and to increase initial demand. Without evaluating the success or failure of the Vista operating system, this example is very appropriate for introducing a new product into emerging market countries, where people first need to be familiarized with the existence of the product, then need to believe that it is easy to use, and finally should anticipate the product for some time before they are able to purchase it. Cultural risk as a phenomenon, factor, and new strategic category could be fruitfully studied by strategists in cooperation with economists and scholars of culture. Ignoring cultural and religious traditions and their influence on society will inevitably lead to lower efficiency, a negative influence on economic and social consequences, and even to strategic failure.

Entry Strategy

When beginning to apply strategic theory and its practical recommendations, it is essential to follow the wisdom of geniuses and to emulate their best practices. Although few historical strategic geniuses left behind their own written thoughts, experiences, and practices (even Napoleon, who lived in the not-too-distant past of the nineteenth century), analysis of their initial actions, when they started to practically apply their long-term vision, shows that they all thought about the unexpected entrance to the fight or about the decisive move towards their enemy or competitor. An unexpected strategy is always one of the most important instruments for strategic success. If the strategist's competitors or enemies are not expecting a strategic move, then they are more likely to make a mistake in response. This though has its origins in Cao Cao (155–220), the great Chinese strategist and general of the Three Kingdoms period, who said, "While the enemy is still formulating his strategy,[56] it is easy to attack."[57] It is ideal to have an unexpected-entrance strategic scenario, as that will set the tone for the rest of the strategy implementation.

When facing an enemy who is unprepared, it is wise to remember the words of Napoleon: "Never interrupt your enemy when he is making a mistake."[58] This advice is actually more useful for tactical issues, but is applicable for entry strategy as well. Any entry strategy must be launched with the practical application of a limited number of goals and specified allocated resources.

Strategy implementation provides a framework for the entry strategy and subsequent tactical steps. Entry strategy in the GEM differs a great deal from entry strategy in developed countries. In the developed world, with minor adjustments, successful entry strategies can be effectively replicated in other foreign markets. In the GEM, if an entry strategy is not crafted to the specifics of the particular EMC, it is likely to fail. It is crucial to locate and target the demographic that will likely be most responsive to the new product. In the GEM, the majority of the population, even the middle class, may be considered poor in terms of purchasing power and economic interests by developed country standards. However, these standards are largely irrelevant in the GEM, where people's purchasing power should not be underestimated. Bottom of the pyramid strategies can be very effective in the GEM. The success of an entry strategy in an EMC is largely a result of finding the most responsive segment of society, which is likely very different from a company's experiences in developed countries.

Marketing and advertising studies are vital for the development of a successful entry strategy. It is very difficult for foreign executives, who have spent all of their life in developed countries, to understand the cultural traditions and consumer preferences of different EMCs. Initially, multinational corporations relied completely on experienced executives from developed countries to lead their ventures in the GEM. Eventually, most realized that it was extremely difficult for foreigners to understand the complex cultural and religious traditions and unfamiliar consumer behavior of EMCs. In the twenty-first century, most multinational corporations employ executives from the EMC in which they are operating, people who are already familiar with the idiosyncrasies of certain EMCs. Corporations usually train important employees from EMCs in their education facilities and headquarters. Not only does this help the corporation to better understand consumer behavior, but it also appeals to the protectionist instincts of EMCs, which are much more willing to work with native-born executives than with foreign executives. However, financial and investment departments of companies are a different story. Domestic owners prefer foreign professionals from developed countries to run these departments. The entry strategy is only as good as a company's strategic understanding of the culture, religious traditions, and consumer preferences of the EMC in which it would like to operate. The process of acquiring partners and allies in a new market is a crucial issue that should be dealt with in the entry strategy and, to some extent, is similar to getting strategic military allies. Ignorance of these issues will inevitably lead to failure.

The process of acquiring partners and allies in a new market is a crucial issue that should be dealt with in the entry strategy. Establishing these relationships can be time-consuming, but it is extremely important in the GEM. Despite the large territories and populations of many EMCs, the purchasing power is often not as large as that of many developed countries. Protectionist policies (and in some cases, lax intellectual property laws that allow domestic companies to copy international brands) have allowed some domestic companies to establish brands that are more recognized in their native countries than some of the most famous global brands. This makes the implementation of entry strategy into certain markets very difficult for foreign companies without some form of cooperation with domestic entities. When military forces are about to approach unknown territories, they often try to align with military partners or other allies familiar with the "terrain" to obtain respective military intelligence. This is also an important step for foreign companies entering unknown territories.

The delayed entry of Starbucks into the Russian market is an illustration of the difficulties of penetrating EMCs. In Russia, Starbucks has struggled to achieve the success that it has enjoyed in much of the world, primarily because of a flawed entry strategy. As a result, two domestic brands that offer consumer experiences very similar to Starbucks have already firmly established themselves as the leaders of the Russian coffee shop market. Many in the West are under the false impression that "it will take time to build a coffee-house culture in Russia similar to that now seen in the UK and US."[59] In fact, Russia has a very long tradition of coffee drinking, beginning from the Russian Renaissance in the eighteenth century, when Peter the Great brought the coffeehouse culture (in addition to other traditions) to Russia from Western Europe. This tradition was reinforced by immigration from neighboring states such as Azerbaijan, Armenia, Georgia, Uzbekistan, and other Central Asian and Baltic States, which have centuries of coffee-drinking traditions. Unlike executives and strategists from the developed world, domestic entrepreneurs were well aware of the coffee-drinking tradition in Russia, which is why a Koffee Haus and Chokoladnitza—and not a Starbucks—occupy every corner in Moscow and St. Petersburg. The Russian market is very big, and Starbucks still has an opportunity to gain access to it, but its delayed entry will make this process more difficult than it has to be. The September 2007 opening of the first Starbucks store in Russia, just north of Moscow, was a non-event. According to Adrian Blomfield, a Russian correspondent for the British newspaper *The Telegraph,* "much richer and far more brand savvy, Russians can barely muster an indifferent shrug now that another American landmark, the Starbucks coffee chain, has arrived."[60] Had Starbucks followed the examples of McDonald's in Moscow or Burger King in Warsaw, it likely would have enjoyed similar success. These two franchises employed well-crafted entry strategies for these markets and, as a result, enjoyed a great deal of success. The leadership of McDonald's was initially skeptical of the extra expenses needed to set up shop in Moscow—which was done through its Canadian branch—but quickly realized that the free public relations the company enjoyed as a result of the global media coverage of the opening more than made up for it. As of 2008, McDonald's can be found in Moscow, St. Petersburg, and even in Siberia; it is a household name across the entire GEM.

Many multinational corporations from developed countries do not have an understanding of local traditions and culture in EMCs, causing them to miss out on huge potential profits. While, to a certain extent, there is a trend of cultural convergence, whereby people of the GEM are beginning to adopt consumer behavior characteristic of parts of the developed world, nation-specific traditions will always be an important factor for entry strategies in EMCs. The most successful multinational corporations will be those that can integrate local traditions with global brands and products. Coca-Cola, for example, sells its products made famous in the United States throughout the GEM, but it also has brands targeted specifically for local populations, like Limca in India. Success in the GEM is closely related to understanding local consumption traditions, which are usually driven by cultural and religious norms.

An important part of an entry strategy is the development of a system of strategic motivation, strategic monitoring, and control. At this stage, an understanding of cultural and religious differences must be taken into consideration. A system of motivation has to be specifically adapted to local business practices. Otherwise, the motivation will be ineffective and the strategic business plan will not be properly implemented.

Quite frequently, leaders of corporations do not make a distinction between entry strategy, which should be a very detailed and precise document, and tactics. This, however, is not the case among the premier executive strategists, such as Jack Welch, who has stated: "you have to be careful in China, and you have to use certain cautions because it's going to be a tough, long way. Tactically I'm not particularly in favor of making large investments in China at present, but I'm very much in favor of taking a very determined entry strategy, being patient, and being there when the time is right."[61] From this statement it is clear that Welsh makes a firm distinction between the tactics of a currently used strategy and upcoming strategy, the entry stage of which is likely just being developed.

Tactics

Tactics are developed in order to determine how to handle the major challenges of implementation. Policy consists of a strategy and its tactics. Three tactics should be prepared: one with a minimum level of risk and lower results, one with a moderate level of risk, and one with an extreme level of risk, which is feasible but requires a large amount of resources all at once. Tactics are a detailed roadmap for strategy implementation; a document on tactics is more meticulous and focused than a document on entry strategy. In terms of scope, tactics cover all details of strategy development, implementation, formulation of strategic management systems, and the least understood aspect of a policy—the exit strategy. One of the most important tactical functions is as a guideline for chief executives' regular monitoring of the effectiveness of the strategy. Tactics are not as detailed as an operational plan. A tactical document aggregates the elements described in the operational plan. Many authors confuse tactics and strategy, mistakenly citing objectives as a separate, extrinsic part of strategy. For example, William E. Rothschild, the author of several books and articles on strategy, wrote, "What do you want to achieve or avoid? The answer to this question are objectives. How will you go about achieving your desired results? The answer to this, you can call strategy."[62] In fact, Rothschild is not actually speaking about strategy—he is speaking about tactics. More specifically, he is referring not only to tactics, but also to a strategic plan, tactical implementation, and, finally, the operational plan. Without these, objectives cannot be achieved.

Tactics play a crucial role in strategic success. As the ancient Chinese military strategist Sun-Tzu said, "Strategy without tactics is the slowest route to victory. Tactics without strategy is the noise before defeat." Sun-Tzu is absolutely correct. Strategy without tactics is almost guaranteed to fail. At the very least, its implementation will be slow and unsystematic. Tactics without strategy will most likely lead the entity that follows it to a disaster and market failure. The great statesman, strategist, and former US secretary of defense, William Cohen, expressed this point very eloquently:

> Years ago, another academic strategist, writing about marketing strategy, claimed that good tactical implementation can overcome a bad strategy. That notion is ridiculous. If the strategy is bad or wrong, the only thing good tactical implementation will do is make a bad strategy result in something worse. The bad strategy may succeed, but it would be better if it failed.[63]

For all strategists, but especially military strategists, the implementation of strategy and the development of tactic and policy are related to resource allocation. This explains one more aspect of why knowledge of the physical terrain has been a strategic issue since ancient times. Biblical leaders like Moses and Joshua, as well as the great Sun-Tzu, were all concerned with the importance of terrain and the spread and delivery of resources. Eventually, maps became vitally important from a strategic point of view, as they allowed leaders to visualize the area. Cesare Borgia, a military architect and the Duke of Valentinois, used Leonardo da Vinci's genius to produce maps of the different areas in and around Tuscany in order to "give a better overlay of the land and greater strategic position."[64] Da Vinci "created this map in conjunction with his other project of constructing a dam from the sea to Florence in order to allow a supply of water to sustain the canal during all seasons."[65] Da Vinci connected maps with Borgia's strategy and, even more importantly, included water sources, which are a vital resource for any military campaign.

A tactical document can be referred to as an implementation plan. However, in this case, implementation has a much wider meaning and includes the practical implementation of every job during development and implementation. Strategic reengineering is an important part of a tactical document. This can be understood as "a complete restructuring of technical services operations."[66] The practice of reengineering became very popular in the 1990s when several consulting companies began to specialize in it, including Andersen Consulting. Andersen Consulting later continued this service under its new name, Accenture, and helped lead many of its clients to success:

> Accenture enabled pump and valve manufacturer KSB to improve, streamline and optimize its business processes in addition to implementing SAP R/3. KSB now outperforms its peers and has outsourced its application management to Accenture as part of its drive to achieve high performance.[67]

In this particular case, reengineering is Accenture's product, but it is a tactical element for the company KSB. When the results of reengineering are successfully implemented, the entity moves on to the next stage of the tactical implementation of the strategy. According to the results of reengineering and an evaluation of the current success of the strategy implementation, the company should strategically revise its management system. The final tactical stage of strategy implementation is the monitoring and controlling of the strategy realization, which continues until the end of the current strategy. At this point, the previously developed exit strategy should begin to be implemented.

As important as tactic is, tactical success without a strategic understanding of the future is a direct route to failure. Any success that is achieved without spending time and effort to define a strategy is like treating the symptoms instead of the disease. A detailed analysis of tactic is not one of the aims of this book. However, all elements described above in regards to strategy development and implementation form a guideline for the development of tactics.

Exit Strategy

Even the most successful strategies come to a point at which changing conditions or needs necessitate the transition to a new strategy. If a strategy is failing, or the strategist can see a failure in the near future, the strategy has to be revised or stopped. Even very profitable businesses have to have an exit strategy in case they would like to sell their business or merge with others during peak profitability. Successful strategists should be prepared for this moment and employ the exit strategy, which is mostly developed during strategy implementation. Typically, an exit strategy is the most forgotten part of the strategic system. The majority of companies do not have pre-prepared exit strategies. According to a survey by Massachusetts Mutual Life Insurance Company (MassMutual), 67 percent of small businesses do not have an exit plan or a plan for exactly when and how to sell the business.[68] In some companies, executives and strategists think that they are "too good" to need an exit strategy. When they unexpectedly encounter a situation needing such a strategy, they find themselves completely unprepared. This is especially the case regarding liquidation exits, one of several methods of leaving the marketplace. This is exactly what happened in May 2002 to the largest professional auditing and consulting firm in the world (at that time), Arthur Andersen, LLP, with more than 100,000 employees and about 100,000 clients in almost 80 countries. Its leadership could not imagine that they would be forced out of business and that the US Securities and Exchange Commission would revoke their Certified Public Account license, per a court decision. The liquidation of this firm was sudden and very harmful to current and former employees, as well as for many clients. It was the absence of an exit strategy that allowed the firm's conviction in the first place, as four years later this decision was overturned by the Supreme Court.[69] By that time, out of 100,000 employees, there only remained a couple hundred. If an exit strategy had existed, Arthur Andersen would have been prepared for such a situation and could have defended itself from the initial accusations, thereby preventing the liquidation. Instead, years of litigation resulted in the destruction of the company's once highly respected name.

Another example of the tremendously negative consequences of not having an exit strategy is the experience of Metromedia Fiber Network Inc. This group was part of the "empire" of John Kluge, a great business visionary and one of the richest entrepreneurs and executives in the history of the United States. According to its business profile, "The Group has international operations in Europe and Japan. On February 8th, 2011, the Group merged with SiteSmith, Inc. On May 20th, 2012, the Group filed for reorganization under Chapter 11 of the United States Bankruptcy Code."[70] This bankruptcy happened to a company that was once very successful, only because it lacked an exit strategy from a market that was no longer lucrative. The desire to hold on to the business, no matter what, is a major barrier to the right and properly timed exit from a market. Due to the high volatility of the GEM compared with the developed world, an exit strategy must be prepared no later than the strategy implementation portion because the exit period of companies in the GEM is significantly shorter.

It is equally important to have an exit strategy for owners of small and family-run businesses, because life is a time-sensitive issue. As MassMutual states, "The idea that someday, someone else will be running your business may be a difficult one to consider,"[71] but it is an issue that must be addressed prior to the development of an exit strategy. This allows owners to transfer their business to relatives, friends, or colleagues, preventing the immediate liquidation of the entity to which they dedicated their life. As Steve Robbins said in his article "Exit Strategies for Your Business": "It's not enough to build a business worth a fortune; you have to make sure you have an exit strategy, a way to get the money back out."[72]

For partnerships, an effective exit strategy is one that prevents liquidation in order to sell some shares to outstanding employees to raise the capital necessary to prolong the firm's existence with an extended partnership. Typically, the name of the partnership will change as a result. In legal terms, the previous firm exits the market and is replaced by the new partnership. Some partners may prefer to have an exit strategy related to the full sale of their rights and shares. In these cases, it is important in the preparation of the exit strategy to have measures preventing the loss of clients and the market share. The most successful exit strategy for companies under private ownership is the preparation of an initial public offering (IPO). Other exit strategies can be related to a long-term vision to merge with certain competitors or to create a joint venture with them.

One of the main functions of the exit strategy is to deal with exit barriers, which "can be economic, strategic, or emotional factors that keep companies from leaving an industry even though they are earning a low—or possibly negative—return on their investment."[73] Among the major reasons for these barriers can be a strategic vacuum that prevented the company from developing an exit strategy prior to the emergence of major problems. These barriers include long-term contracts with buyers or suppliers, tenants, and long-term lease agreements, the termination of which can force the company to provide huge compensations to the agreement's counterparts. Strategic exit barriers can also be the result of special agreements with trade unions, the cancellation of which can bring a company immediately to court and arbitration, resulting in huge compensations for grievances. A corporation may not have enough resources to become a new entrant in nearby industries or regions, practically preventing an exit from its current area of activity. Successful corporations employ their exit strategies as a result of monitoring internal and external policy. Otherwise, the company's exit is usually caused by unexpected threats. Ideally, strategists will be prepared for any of these scenarios and can just take the exit strategy, developed far in advance and oftentimes prior to strategy implementation, from the shelf.

A successful exit strategy is no less important than an entry strategy for complete victory. Often, a successfully accomplished strategy can immediately cause new fights and struggles. This is not because the competitor or newly vanquished enemies have a heretofore unknown strategy to fight after a battle is done, but because of the fear that this victory will destroy the status quo. In order to combat this, the strategist must also calculate the consequences that come with a successfully accomplished strategy. Part of the exit strategy has to be the prevention of new competition, unrest, or conflict. After Mehmet II conquered Constantinople, leaders in Morea, located in present day southern Greece, were so worried about his next move that they began to consider their surrender without ever developing a strategy. Mehmet II won not with strategy and battle but through the emotions of the leaders who strove to preemptively appease him. In his letter to the leaders, he promised: "[O]f your possessions, and your children, and your heads, and anything of your possessions that remain to you, I will touch nothing, but I will leave you in peace so that you are better than before."[74]

Having tremendous resistance on many small fronts after a victory is a common and important issue. This resistance drains resources and times, and dilutes the power of a victory for the leader and his or her followers. It happens on battlefields and after military campaigns, but also in company takeovers, or even during the process of mergers and acquisitions. It happened with Napoleon in Russia, as well as after the initial American victories in both Iraq and Afghanistan at the beginning of the twenty-first century. Any strategic plan must have a well-developed exit strategy that must include "peaceful proposals" after the conflict. It is interesting to note that shady corporations or unprofessional military gambles or adventures never have an exit strategy and overwhelmingly finish as a failure. To a certain extent, without a successful exit strategy, the strategy cannot be totally successful. Prior to his election as president, Governor George W. Bush said regarding the conflict in Kosovo in April 1999: "Victory means exit strategy, and it's important for the president to explain to us what the exit strategy is."[75] Unfortunately, when US military forces very successfully took over Iraq, US leadership obviously did not have either a strategy to maintain success in Iraq or a strategy for exiting. Very soon after the first victorious days, this became apparent.

In some stages of corporate activity, an exit strategy is the most important part of strategy. This is especially the case when owners, shareholders, or executives decide to sell their business. The better the exit strategy, the higher the company's market price at the moment when ownership changes. In this case, the exit strategy has to present the company, like an admiral bringing a ship for a parade with a raised flag, in the best possible condition. However, even in the beginning stages of corporate activity, formulating an exit strategy is integral to the formal strategy development and the overall success of the company.

Once a formal strategy has been developed, including an entry and exit strategy, its implementation can only occur through a strategic management plan. This managerial process is an integral part of strategy formulation as a document and its design can lead to the success or failure of a well-thought-out strategic scenario and its plan.

Notes

1 Cited by Webber, E., and Feinsilber, M. (1999). *Merriam-Webster's Dictionary of Allusions*. Springfield, MA: Merriam-Webster, p. 59.
2 Burnett, F.H. (1911). *The Secret Garden*. New York: F.A. Stokes, p. 353.
3 Mieder, W., Kingsbury, S.A., and Harder, K.B. (1992). *Dictionary of American Proverbs*. New York: Oxford University Press, p. xii.
4 Cited by Seldes, G. (1996). *The Great Thoughts*. Revised edition. New York: Ballantine Books.
5 "Man on a Mission" (2005). Dow Jones mission statement. April 26. Retrieved from http://manonamission.blogspot.com/2005/04/dow-jones-dj-mission-values-statements.html
6 Dow Jones. (n.d.) "Core values." Retrieved from www.dowjones.com/TheCompany/CoreValues.htm
7 Merrill Lynch. (2006). Annual Report. Retrieved from www.ml.com/annualmeetingmaterials/2006/ar/pdfs/annual_report_2006_complete.pdf
8 Merrill Lynch. (2001). "Building a Culture of Excellence." Retrieved from www.ml.com/annualmeetingmaterials/annrep2001/ar/
9 Valdmanis, T. (2002). Mighty Merrill Lynch Bogs Down in Legal Troubles. *USA Today*. October 10. Retrieved from http://securities.stanford.edu/news-archive/2002/20021010_Settlement03_Valdmanis.htm
10 Philo. (1854). "A Treatise on Virtues and on the Office of Ambassadors. Addressed to Caius." *Works of Philo*. C.D Yonge (Trans). London: H.G. Bohn, vol. 4, p. 123.
11 North, D.C. (2010). *Understanding the Process of Economic Change*. Princeton, NJ: Princeton University Press, p. 103.
12 North, D.C. (2010). *Understanding the Process of Economic Change*. Princeton, NJ: Princeton University Press, p. 103.
13 Kahneman, D. (2013). *Thinking, Fast and Slow*. New York: Farrar, Strauss, and Giroux, p. 20.
14 Kahneman, D. (2013). *Thinking, Fast and Slow*. New York: Farrar, Strauss, and Giroux, p. 194.
15 Kahneman, D. (2013). *Thinking, Fast and Slow*. New York: Farrar, Strauss, and Giroux, pp. 194–195.
16 Kahneman, D. (2013). *Thinking, Fast and Slow*. New York: Farrar, Strauss, and Giroux, p. 184.
17 Phelps, E.S. (2013). *Mass Flourishing: How Grassroots Innovation Created Jobs, Challenge, and Change*. Princeton, NJ. Princeton University Press, p. 28.
18 The philosopher David Hume, who was also an economist, belonged to the metaphysical school of empiricism, which, as we mentioned in Chapter 1, is a root of the theory of strategy.
19 Phelps, E.S. (2013). *Mass Flourishing: How Grassroots Innovation Created Jobs, Challenge, and Change*. Princeton, NJ: Princeton University Press, p. 28.
20 Phelps, E.S. (2013). *Mass Flourishing: How Grassroots Innovation Created Jobs, Challenge, and Change*. Princeton, NJ: Princeton University Press, p. 35.
21 Gadiesh, O. and Gilbert, J.L. (2011). "Transforming Corner-Office Strategy into Frontline Action." *On Strategy*. Cambridge, MA: Harvard Business School Press, p. 199.
22 Gadiesh, O. and Gilbert, J.L. (2011). "Transforming Corner-Office Strategy into Frontline Action." *On Strategy*. Cambridge, MA: Harvard Business School Press, p. 204.
23 Napoleon. (1870). *Correspondence de Napoleon premier*. Paris: Plon, vol. X, p. 69.
24 Vacheé, C. (2007). *Napoleon at Work*, Dublin: Nonesuch Publishing, p. 17.
25 Bertaut, Jules. (1916). *Napoleon in His Own Words*. H.E. Law and C.L Rhodes (Trans.). Chicago: A.C. McClurg and Co, p. 95.
26 Bertaut, Jules. (1916). *Napoleon in His Own Words*. H.E. Law and C.L Rhodes (Trans.). Chicago: A.C. McClurg and Co, p. 95.
27 Rumsfeld, D. (2013). *Rumsfeld's Rules: Leadership Lessons in Business, Politics, War, and Life*. New York: Broadside Books.
28 Gates, B. (1995). *The Road Ahead*. New York: Viking Penguin, p. 18.

29 Pietersen, W. (2002). *Reinventing Strategy: Using Strategic Learning to Create and Sustain Breakthrough Performance.* New York: J. Wiley and Sons, p. 76.
30 Cited by Philips, T.R. (Ed.). (1985). *Roots of Strategy. The 5 Great Military Classics of All Time.* T.R Phillips (Ed.). Harrisburg, PA: Stackpole Press, p. 36.
31 This quote is attributed to Napoleon, but the veracity of that claim is in dispute.
32 Aksoy, F. (producer and director). (2012). *Conquest 1453.* Istanbul; Neoclassics Film.
33 Abbott, J. (1879). *Alexander the Great,* Kindle edition, p. 367.
34 Abbott, J. (1879). *Alexander the Great,* Kindle edition, pp. 368–369.
35 As cited in Dippel, T.H. (2012). *The Wisdom of Generations: Using the Lessons of History to Create a Values-based Future.* Brenham, TX: Texas Peacemaker Publications, p. 309.
36 Apesteguia, J., Huck, S., and Echssler, P. (2007). "Imitation—Theory and Experimental Evidence," *Journal of Economic Theory,* vol. 1, pp. 217–235.
37 Leontief, W.W. (1983). *Military Spending: Facts and Figures, Worldwide Implications and Future Outlook.* New York: Oxford University Press, p. 51.
38 Newell, M.W. (2005). *Preparing for the Project Management Professional (PMP) Certification.* New York: AMACOM/American Management Association, p. 3.
39 Reading, C. (2002). *Strategic Business Planning: A Dynamic System for Improving Performance.* London: Kogan Press, p. 366.
40 "General Electric Exits Insurance; Sells Insurance Solutions, Employers Re to Swiss Re." (2005). *Insurance Journal.* November 18.
41 Chander, D. (1966). *The Campaigns of Napoleon.* New York: the Macmillan Company, p. 162.
42 Thucydides. (2006). *The Peloponnesian War.* Book 2. XXIV. New York: Barnes & Noble Classics, p. 109.
43 Bertaut, J. (1916). *Napoleon in His Own Words.* H.E. Law and C.L Rhodes (Trans.). Chicago: A.C. McClurg and Co., pp. 243–244.
44 "Strategy for European technology platforms: ETP 2020." (2013). July 12. Brussels: European Commission. p. 272.
45 "Decision of Governmental Commission for High Technologists and Innovations of the Government of the Russian Federation." (2012.) February 21.
46 IBM. Boolean Variables. Retrieved from http://publib.boulder.ibm.com/infocenter/comphelp/v7v91/index.jsp?topic=/com.ibm.vacpp7a.doc/language/ref/clrc03boolean_variables.htm
47 Van Den Bosh, F.A.J. (1997). *Perspectives on Strategy: Contributions of Michael E. Porter.* F.A.J. Van Den Bosh, and A.P. De Man (Eds.). New York: Springer, p. 9.
48 Attributed to Napoleon Bonaparte in Bruce, R.B., Dickie, I., Khey, K., Pavkovic, M.F., and Schneid, F. C. (2008). *Fighting Techniques of the Napoleonic Age 1792–1815: Equipment, Combat Skills, and Tactic.* New York; St. Martin's Press, p. 150.
49 Haynes, W. (1953). *Cellulose, the Chemical that Grows.* Garden City, NJ: Doubleday, p. 303.
50 Here and through all following examples, the period of recovery is calculated (without discounts such as allowed expense, sales, income, etc.) in the interest of simplicity.
51 This is despite the opinion of many economists that the first law of economics is concentrated in the ratio "the greater the demand, the higher the price."
52 Forbes, S. (1999). *A New Birth of Freedom.* Washington, DC: Regnery Publishing, Inc. p. 59.
53 Schniederjans, D.G., Schniederjans, M.J., and Schniederjans, A.M. (2005). Outsourcing and Insourcing in an International Context. New York: Routledge, p. 3.
54 Plutarch. (1936). *On the Fortune of Alexander the Great.* F.C. Babbitt (Trans.). N.p.: Loeb Classical Library, p. 413. Retrieved from http://penelope.uchicago.edu/Thayer/E/Roman/Texts/Plutarch/Moralia/Fortuna_Alexandri★/1.html
55 Alexander the Great as cited in Plutarch. (2001). *Lives.* A.H. Clough (Trans.). New York; Random House, p. 172.
56 The word "strategy" here will be left to the responsibility of the translator. As I demonstrated in Chapter 1, it does not appear in any extant text before the Byzantine Emperor Maurice in the sixth and seventh centuries.
57 Cited by Sun-Tzu. (2002). *The Art of War.* J. Minford. (Trans.). New York.: Penguin Group, p. 134.
58 Napoleon Bonaparte, quoted in Charlton, J. (Ed.) (2002). *The Military Quotation Book.* New York; St. Martin's Press, p. 93.

59 Drujinina, A. (2005). "Starbucks Targets Russia after Trademark Win." *CEE-Foodindustry.com*. August 19. Retrieved from www.cee-foodindustry.com/news/ng.asp?id=62002-starbucks-russia-trademark
60 Blomfield, A. (2007). "Starbucks Opens Quietly in Moscow." *The Telegraph*. November 9. Retrieved from www.telegraph.co.uk/news/main.jhtml?xml=/news/2007/09/10/wrussia110.xml
61 Cited by Slater, R. (1998). *Jack Welch and the GE Way*. Columbus, OH: McGraw-Hill, p. 200.
62 Cited by Harvard Business School. (2010). *Thinking Strategically: Expert Solutions to Everyday Challenges*. Boston: Harvard Business Press, p. 24.
63 Cohen, W. (2004). *The Art of the Strategist: 10 Essential Principles for Leading Your Company*. New York: AMACOM, p. ix.
64 *Leonardo Da Vinci*. (2012). Series 1. N.p.: TouchInside Publishers, p. 7.
65 *Leonardo Da Vinci*. (2012). Series 1. N.p.: TouchInside Publishers, p. 7.
66 Lass, A. and Quandt, R. (Eds.) (2000). *Library Automation in Transitional Societies: Lessons from Eastern Europe*. New York: Oxford University Press, p. 431.
67 Accenture. KSB: Reengineering. Retrieved from http://www.accenture.com/Global/Services/By_Industry/Industrial_Equipment/Client_Successes/KSBReengineering.htm
68 MassMutual Financial Group. (2007). "New Report: Women Entrepreneurs Should Plan Early on How to Sell their Businesses. October 9. Retrieved from www.massmutual.com/mmfg/about/pr_2007/10_09_07.html
69 Arthur Andersen LLP v. United States. Retrieved from www.oyez.org/cases/2000-2009/2004/2004_04_368/
70 Business.com. Metromedia Fiber Network–MFNXQ-Profile. Retrieved from www.business.com/directory/telecommunications/business_solutions/metromedia_fiber_network/profile/
71 MassMutual Financial Group. (2006). "Where there's a plan, there's a continued business." Retrieved fromwww.massmutual.com/mmfg/prepare/articles/business.html
72 Robbins, S. (2005). "Exit Strategies for Your Business." *Entrepreneur.com*. June. Retrieved from www.entrepreneur.com/management/operations/article78512.html
73 Wright, P., Pringle, C.D., and Kroll, M.J. (1992). *Strategic Management: Text and Cases*. Boston: Allyn and Bacon in partnership with Ginn Press, p. 27
74 Mehmet II (1454). Contemporary Copy of the Letter of Mehmet II to the Greek Archons. December 26. ASV Documenti Turchi B.1/11. Retrieved from http://langzeitarchivierung.bib-bvb.de/wayback/20120117081752/http://angiolello.net/ARCHONS.pdf
75 Cited by Ratcliffe, R.G. (1999). "Bush Toughens His Stance on NATO Bombing." *Houston Chronicle*, Austin Bureau. April 9.

4 Strategic Management Systems

When you become a leader, success is all about growing others.[1]

Jack Welch, former chairman and CEO of General Electric (b. 1935)

From a management standpoint, it is very important to know how to unleash people's inborn creativity. My concept is that anybody has creative ability, but very few people know how to use it.[2]

Akio Morita, cofounder of the Sony Corporation (1921–1999)

Keynote Definitions

A **Strategic Management System** is a managerial process of strategy formulation, implementation, and functioning aimed at establishing or improving and enlarging the strategizing object's priorities according to its fundamental values and interests.

Concept of a Strategic Management System

One of the most important qualities for a strategist to have is a systematic strategy-oriented mindset. It is of equal importance for strategists to apply this mindset to the practice of management. However, if MBA students and even experienced executives were asked to describe a management system, or, to be more precise, to cite the major elements of a management system, the answer would likely reveal a completely unsystematic understanding of management. The knowledge gained from an MBA and years of experience as an executive cannot be fully exploited without a clearly ordered understanding of management system structure. All information relevant to the strategist's activity should be organized within the mental framework of this management system. The clear and systematic understanding of the basic elements of a management system—the managerial function of planning, control and motivation, basic organizational structures, and indicators of the efficiency of the decision-making process—are of immeasurable value to a strategist.

Developing a strategic and systematic understanding of management begins with an explanation of its two basic parts: formation and implementation. Let's say the strategy has already been developed and the entity's board has approved the allocation of resources accordingly and within the stated timetable. What is then needed to implement this strategy? The answer to this question is the first element of a management system: *leadership*. Even if the corporation is flush with cash, has a wealthy investor to finance the next step, and its board is in unanimous agreement, nothing will be accomplished without strategic leadership. Immediately following the approval of a strategy, or, ideally, during discussion of the new strategy and its priorities and tactical implementation, a leader or a small group of top executives should be selected to head the new project. What is the first step for this leader or group? Some argue that the leadership should first hire subordinate directors and managerial staff. However, this will provoke a flurry of detail-oriented questions from the human resources department: Why two executives instead of three or one? Why five managers and not seven? What is the required level of education? Why two assistants and one secretary and not one assistant and two secretaries? The leadership is not ready to deal with these minute issues. Prior to hiring people, the organizational structure must be developed and approved; at that point the process of hiring executives, managers, and staff according to this structure should begin. The next element to be developed is the formal decision-making process, i.e., the responsibilities, rights, and division of power among members of the managerial team. Once the first three elements—the organizational structure, requirements for executives, managers, and staff, and the establishment of the decision-making process—are formalized, funding should be allocated for managerial tools, managerial aids, and information systems, including office space, supplies, and, most importantly, innovative information technology. In correlation with this, requirements for information systems have to be developed as both the "raw materials" for the decision-making process and, at the same time, the only "product" of the properly functioning strategic management system.

Once all of these elements are developed, their role in the major functions of the management system should be detailed. The three most important functions of a strategic management system are strategic *planning*, *motivation*, and *control*. The way in which these major elements and functions of strategic management work together is illustrated in Figure 4.1.

Finally, prior to a strategy becoming part of an implemented policy, strategists must figure out what organizational forms (vehicles) can be used to bring the management system and the approved strategy itself into practice. This is the process by which new entities and subsidiaries are established.

Major Elements of a Strategic Management System

Strategic Leadership in Strategy Formulation, Implementation, and Education

A systematic understanding of a strategic management system begins with an explanation of its major elements, within the context of its two fundamental processes—formation and implementation. The first element of a strategic management system is *leadership*.

Leadership is a core issue during the early stages of strategy development. After all, it is up to leaders to put the development of a new strategy or the improvement of an existing one on the entity's agenda. Furthermore, without leadership a strategy cannot begin to be developed and implemented or it will not succeed due to inertia—the majority's resistance to any changes in the existing order of things. In these situations, if the leader is not strong, he or she will follow the majority and not vice versa. The importance of strong leadership is highlighted in the following expression: "I am not afraid of an army of lions led by a sheep; I am afraid of an army of sheep led by a lion." This quote is often attributed to Alexander the Great, but has also been credited to the Athenian general Chabrias (fourth century BCE) who lived just before Alexander, and even to Niccolò Machiavelli (1469–1527). Whoever coined this expression, it does reflect Alexander's mindset that the role of leaders cannot be understated in strategy development and implementation. As another strategic genius, Napoleon, said about the required character traits of a leader: "[He] must possess as much character as intellect—the base must equal the height."[3] I hope that the opinion of these two great strategists proves the point. One of the fundamental predicaments of any organization's leadership is how to balance their attention between operational, tactical, and strategic issues. When leaders ignore current events, it tends to result in declining performance and, subsequently, the loss of their leadership position. However, as previously stated, for strategists the present is already the past. For leaders, even just evaluating current and annual results can be a major obstacle to strategic issues. Leaders who lack a strategic orientation will inevitably be criticized for their shortsighted vision; they must achieve a balance between the current and future needs of a particular entity. As Brent Davies, Professor of International Leadership Development at the University of Hull, puts it, "strategic leaders are concerned with not just managing the now but setting up a framework of where the organization needs to be in the future, setting a direction for the organization. The function of strategy is to translate the moral purpose and vision into reality."[4] In the twenty-first century, the larger the organization the more it is internationalized and operates on a global scale, and the more important it is for the leadership to focus on long-term strategic issues. When a large or small entity decides to enter an emerging market country, this decision is innately strategic. It is closely tied to issues of substantially higher risk (political, economic, and business) and uncertainty than in the developed world. For many leaders, routines and assumptions acquired from operations in developed markets will be a serious impediment to success in the GEM. Even technology that operates effectively in the conditions of a developed market will often not function properly in emerging markets due to variances in the quality of raw materials, climate, and employee training regarding the maintenance of equipment and other issues.

Figure 4.1 Concept of a Strategic Management System
© Dr. Vladimir Kvint, 2008

It is not unusual during the early stages of strategy formation, even for leaders of giant multinational corporations, to simultaneously lead small strategic groups that focus on the development of strategic scenarios for the future. The required leadership qualities in small groups and large corporations are undoubtedly very different (or with deep similarities in nature, as Sun-Tzu several times underlined). The first challenge for corporate leaders is to find out how to be a global corporate head and, at the same time, a leader of a small strategic group. While within these small strategic groups some may assume that the professional strategist is the leader, in reality this is not typically the case. Usually, the leader of these groups is the deputy of one of the top corporate executives—a president, chief executive officer, or executive chairman. These deputies typically divide their time between operational and strategic issues. Even when chief strategists or the global head of strategic affairs have high-ranking positions in the corporation, like the vice-president for strategic affairs, it does not mean that reporting to the chief executive or president of the corporation is not at least a weekly routine. The chief strategist regularly reports to the leader of the corporation. Corporate leaders often make the mistake of interpreting strategic ideas from the chief strategist in the light of corporate operational preferences and problems.

Chief executives usually spend more time on operational issues and tend to be more influenced by operational officers. Additionally, in many medium-sized and especially small corporations, the chief executive and chief operating officer are the same person, and the position of chief strategist does not exist. Only leaders with a powerful strategic vision can overcome this strategic challenge; these leaders alone have the ability to bring long-term success to their entities. Quite often, the leaders who supervise the development of the entry strategy also conduct its implementation and continue their leadership role throughout the corporate operations of the implemented strategy. This results in a somewhat inefficient situation in which strategists are in charge of operations or, at the very least, of tactical activity. With mindsets oriented to long-term strategic issues, they are usually not very efficient as operational heads. This causes the entity to miss opportunities and can even result in its failure, despite the fact that it developed and implemented the proper strategy. Leaders who were closely involved with the development and implementation of the strategy tend to be attached to the current scenario to the extent that they suffer from tunnel vision, failing to see new opportunities in the marketplace and new innovations and technological advancements. In order to avoid this, an entity of any size should have two top-level officers who are both responsible for current success and for strategic issues. Once the strategy is successfully implemented, the responsibilities of these two leaders should be split, with one assuming the role of the CEO—i.e., managing the entity's activity according to current and operational tasks—and the other assuming the role of the chief strategist—i.e., initially monitoring the progress of the current strategy as well as heading the development of strategic revisions. This structure applies only to leaders of existing entities.

The primary influence on the unit or subsidiary leadership comes from the corporate or parental body leadership. A strategic leader must be truthful at all times, but especially when delivering strategic priorities, objectives, and goals to subordinates. In this instance, leaders cannot be modest because modesty for strategists and strategic leaders is a lie. In strategy, a modest approach is not a truthful approach. The truth will be found in the middle. Too far to the right and the leader will exaggerate the ability or his or her strategy. Too far to the left and it will minimize the power of corporate strategy and deflate the leader's own capability. The strategic leader must be as truthful as light. Light is not modest; neither is the sun. Strategists and strategic leaders will not die by telling the truth. For example, Alexander the Great showed his own strength and honesty in a speech to his troops during their perilous fight with the Persians:

> Our enemies are Medes and Persians, men who for centuries have lived soft and luxurious lives; we of Macedon for generations past have been trained in the hard school of danger and war. Above all, we are free men, and they are slaves. There are Greek troops, to be sure, in Persian service—but how different is their cause from ours! They will be fighting for pay—and not much of it at that; we, on the contrary, shall fight for Greece, and our hearts will be in it. As for our foreign troops—Thracians, Paeonians, Illyrians, Agrianes—they are the best and stoutest soldiers in Europe, and they will find as their opponents the slackest and softest of the tribes of Asia. And what, finally, of the two men in supreme command? You have Alexander, they—Darius![5]

Alexander was not alone in ascribing importance to honesty during strategic battles. Timur, the great Turko-Mongol conquerer and the founder of the Timurid dynasty, understood the role of honesty in forming great leaders even during his youth. When Timur was a subordinate to Tukluk Timurhan in his younger years, he conceived of three major qualities needed to be a masterful strategic leader: to be fair, to be fearless, and to be truthful. These requirements correspond with my strategic Rule 8: "A Successful Strategy Cannot Be Dishonest" (see Chapter 2). Apparently, none of these leaders were reflecting on the moral implications of leadership directly, but the seeds for it were there all along.

In addition to corporate or parental body leadership, unit leaders can also influence an entire entity or parental strategy. The theory of strategic contingencies developed by D.J. Hickson, professor of Organizational Analysis at the University of Bradford (UK), suggests that "the power of a subunit depends on three factors: (1) expertise in coping with important problems, (2) centrality of the subunit within the workflow and (3) the extent to which the subunit's expertise is unique rather than substitutable."[6] Most unit leaders tend to think of their own particular strategy as unique and non-substitutable. However, in reality, the extent to which unit strategies are valued by their parental strategy is usually related to the personal influence of the unit leader, the distinctiveness of the mission of the unit and its products, and the importance of the product for the corporation's production of "ready to go" goods and services. When the unit leader has a high level of personal influence with corporate leaders and is in charge of unique and important products, he or she is often promoted to the corporate level. Unit leadership also influences corporate leadership in cases when units and divisions have stronger leaders than those at the corporate level. This situation is often both the cause and result of siloed strategic management systems, which almost inevitably hinder the competitiveness of an entity.

Great strategic leaders can unify even the most opposed forces. Hannibal led an army against Rome that did not speak a mutual language or share a culture, and did not even have all the proper weapons or armor. It was an army made in large part of former slaves and subjects of the Romans and, as such, most of them lacked even basic military training. While crossing the Alps, Hannibal lost more than 30 percent of his army, as well as many elephants. Yet he was able to take the Gauls and Celts and unify them, defeating the Romans several times. In fact, he never lost to the Roman Republic armies while on the Apennine Peninsula.

In cases when the unit has a remote location in an emerging market country, its strategy is usually much more independent and specific. The leaders of units that achieve success in these situations have a great deal of leverage during annual corporate meetings. They tend to occupy their position for a long time, whether they like it or not. Corporate leadership usually assumes the unit's success is a result of the specific conditions of the country or region within which the unit is located and its relationship with local political and business leaders. Corporate leaders often doubt the ability of particular unit leaders to replicate their success on the corporate level. However, unit leaders in this situation are in a very strong position if the corporation decides to expand its activity in the GEM to emerging market countries with similar political and economic conditions.

There are a number of unique issues that arise in cases of strategic leadership of not-yet-existing entities. The greatest benefit of leading such entities is the ability to completely focus on strategic issues. At this point, strategic leadership and leadership are practically one and the same. As soon as the strategy is developed and the implementation process begins, operational problems tend to take the leadership's attention away from most strategic issues. There are also unique characteristics to strategic leadership in emerging market countries, depending on whether the executive is local or a foreign expatriate. While local executives try to leverage specific and unique local and regional characteristics, foreign expatriates usually try to implement strategies that have been proven efficient in developed countries. This approach is generally less effective due to substantially different conditions in the GEM. However, expatriate executives have other advantages, especially when the parent company is in a developed country. Expatriate executives tend to be much better at securing funds for the subsidiary and using reporting systems, and tend to be more adept with financial strategy. Despite the fact that domestic entrepreneurs have a better knowledge of local conditions and deeper connections, foreign executives in emerging market countries also tend to more actively address national and regional social issues, business ethics, environmental protection, and other relevant matters.

Strategic Leadership in Strategy Implementation

The first responsibility of any strategic leader during the strategy implementation phase is the development and implementation of the major elements of a management system, of which strategic leadership is an innate part. This process starts with the formation of the organizational structure, including the strategic organizational structure, according to the vision and objectives of the entity's strategy. Strategic leadership is crucial to the overall success of the strategy from the beginning of its development to the exit from the current strategic scenario. According to Mike Freedman and Benjamin Tregoe in their book, *The Art and Discipline of Strategic Leadership*, "The twenty-first century demands, as has no other, that corporate leaders create both strategic literacy and a robust process to ensure strategic constancy."[7] Leadership has to develop a collective, well-organized mindset shared by all employees involved in the processes of strategy development and implementation. According to Marius Leibold, Gilbert Probst, and Michael Gibbert, in *Strategic Management in the Knowledge Economy*:

> "Systemic thinking" is the basis of this mindset, i.e., understanding of a phenomenon within the context of a larger whole. The recent great shock to strategic management has been that systems cannot be understood by analysis. The properties of the parts are not intrinsic properties, but can be understood only within the context of the

> larger whole. Accordingly, systems thinking does not concentrate on basic building blocks, but rather on basic principles of organization—it is the whole that determines the behavior of the parts.[8]

Successful leadership in the development and implementation of this collective mindset is an important means by which modern civilization has achieved technological progression. Nevertheless, for heads of strategic departments, it is not very productive to develop strategy solely from the point of view of a unified system. Strategy as a system always contains elements of the strategic scenarios of its units, as well as substrategies developed for particular prospects and projects. For example, governments develop a national strategy for 10 to 15 years in the future, as well as substrategies on energy independence, ecological protection, and other national issues. Companies develop substrategies on certain vital issues like the supply of unique innovative materials and parts. Strategy should be understood in terms of its overall system as well as its innate elements. The success of strategic leadership is closely related to the ability to assimilate the knowledge, suggestions, and strategic proposals of leaders of units and subsystems. Many authors, such as Freedman and Tregoe, describe leadership as a synthesis of art and science:

> A crucial lesson we have learned over many years of strategy engagement is that strategic leadership requires a combination of art and discipline. By art, we mean thinking that is creative, out of the box, and blue sky. Examples include the creation of alternative strategic visions for top team assessment, new product development, the crafting of what-if scenarios, the identification of decision-making criteria, and the design of a new culture that is strategically aligned. Creativity is also required in other activities such as communicating the strategy and supporting ownership of and commitment to it ... Discipline is essential, both in the thought processes involved in strategy and in its execution. For example, it is not easy to craft and implement a plan that may include hundreds of projects and thousands of subprojects as the prerequisites to strategy implementation. Difficult too are the needs to ensure consistency of decision making throughout the organization; keep focused when so many options are available for consideration; and regularly to monitor, review, and update strategy when operational or financial imperatives are knocking at the door.[9]

If honesty and discipline are integral leadership qualities, so too is creativity. While it takes discipline to correctly implement strategy, creativity is also needed to bring governments and companies to success in an ever-changing marketplace.

Strategic Leadership and Education

Along with the other leadership qualities mentioned, successful strategic leaders also often possess higher than average education levels compared to their contemporaries. It is a well-established fact that Alexander the Great had the best teachers in the known world at that time, assigned to him by his father, Phillip of Macedonia. It was a smart strategic move on Phillip's part to attach such importance to education and seek out teachers like Aristotle for his son.

It is a common trend in history for great strategists and leaders to have a strong educational upbringing provided by their parents and mentors. Hamilcar and Hasdrubal the

Elder—Hannibal's father and uncle, respectively—both assigned several strong mentors to the young leader, including the Greek historian Sosylus (third and second Century BCE), who accompanied Hannibal on his military campaigns.

Both Julius Caesar and Napoleon received a systematic education in their youth. Napoleon had a very systematic military training and also spoke several languages. Before changing the course of human history, Vladimir Ilyich Ulyanov (1870–1924), also known as Lenin, was well educated, speaking and writing in several languages including Ancient Greek and Hebrew. Genghis Khan and Timur both obtained a high level of knowledge throughout their lives, acquiring it from their many different conquests and advisors.

Sultan Murat II (1404–1451), the father of future sultan Mehmet II, the conqueror of Constantinople and creator of the Ottoman Empire, also prioritized education for his son. Murat appointed many tutors for Mehmet, including Ilyas Efendi, a Serbian prisoner of war who later became a teacher of theology. Starting from Efendi, Mehmet

> studied foreign languages, philosophy and geography as well as Islamic, Latin and Greek history and literature, his foreign tutors supposedly including the renowned Italian humanist Cyriacus of Ancona. Cyriacus was at the Ottoman court in Edirne in the mid to late 1440s, but although he was in contact with Mehmet there is no evidence that he served as his tutor, or, as also alleged, his secretary. Mehmet was reputed to have known, apart from Turkish, some five languages, and a contemporary, Giacomo da Langusco, credits him with being fluent in Turkish, Greek and Slavic.[10]

Once Murat saw that his son was ready to lead with the help of his education, Murat abdicated the throne in order to allow Mehmet a chance to rule under his leadership. By the time Mehmet was of age to rule on his own, he already had years of experience. Scholar Julian Raby comments on Mehmet's education: "Mehmet must certainly have had an initial familiarity with Greek because he copied both the Greek and the Arabic alphabets in one of his schoolbooks, preserved in the Topkapt, but knowledge of foreign languages is a matter of degree."[11]

Not every military leader can be considered a military strategist. Many of them are heroic—like the mythical Samson, the legendary king of England, Richard I "the Lion-heart" (1157–1119), the talented commanders Leonidas I and Pompey the Great, and the great Roman Republic political and military leader Gnaeus Pompeius Magnus (106–48 BCE)—but they are not all strategists according to the required qualities of strategists or the characteristics of particular strategic decisions, which I will discuss later in this book. Personally, I find it difficult to consider the Japanese samurai Miyamoto Musashi a strategist, though most scholars do. Similarly, the Swedish King Charles XII, whose military campaigns and failures were the overwhelming result of tactical ideas without deep strategic visions and objectives, should not be considered a strategist either. But there are also several military leaders, typically viewed only as field commanders, who should be considered great strategists, no matter the subject on which they strategized. Any practitioner, field commander, or corporate leader who spends time and energy contemplating strategic terminology, ideas, and deep research is working not only with a strategic mindset, but also with a strong research capability. Practitioner-strategists, like Napoleon or Jack Welch, usually have a very strong theoretical base; they can go back to theory, stay forever in strategic practice, or return to their studies and later go back to practice. Strategy as a science is just in its initial stage of development. As a result, the great historical strategists did not have enough theoretical work to study. They were well taught, although they were not as educated in strategy as Alexander the Great, Hannibal, or Winston Churchill. Rather, these strategists were taught mathematics, philosophy, political science, history, tactical ideas, and some aspects of strategy, although not strategy as we know it today.

Although it might seem an unusual combination, some of the greatest historical strategic minds possessed the qualities of both practitioners and scholars, if not in equal proportions, like Frontinus, Jomini, Moltke, Bismarck, Emperor Maurice, and Clausewitz. It is important to note that Clausewitz was not a successful practitioner during his military leadership positions in both the Prussian and Russian armies. He never garnered top military appointments and was not considered great in his time. After Austerlitz, he was captured with dozens of other Prussian and Russian generals and held by Napoleon, who overwhelmingly won the battle with a smaller army, mostly vanquished the Russian army, and eradicated the Holy Roman Empire.

To summarize, we can conclude that **leadership is a science to be used along with artistic creativity in order to achieve the leader's vision of the future**.

Organizational Structure

The development of an organizational structure relates directly to crucial strategic issues. An inadequate organizational structure is a typical barrier against implementing an effective strategy. Organizational structures should be developed with an eye for efficiency and the delegation of some leadership functions to lower levels. This structure helps prevent the leadership from being overwhelmed, which can result in careless mistakes.

In order for a strategic scenario to be successful, strategic leaders must keep their obligations. Timur (Tamerlane) wrote about this in his *Autobiography*: "If a leader faces a big problem and sends in his subordinate to solve it, he is facing two problems. If a leader goes in by himself, it will be only one problem. A clever person always should prefer one danger to two."[12] When two competing strategic leaders come to the same conclusion that a strategic leader must lead an army or company, then the outcome will determine who is more competent in executing a strategy from beginning to end. An example of this scenario comes from Timur's own life, when, on July 28, 1402, he personally led his army to victory against the Ottoman army. His victory against this large and capable army—led by Sultan Beyazit and five of his sons—shows Timur's strong strategic capability.

The organizational structure is the blueprint for the construction and operation of the entire management system and is very different from the operational structure. The prior term is related to two different issues—the development of an organizational structure specifically for processes of strategy implementation or for the development of corporate strategy in general. The organizational structure determines the requirements for all subsequent elements of a strategic management system and the efficiency of managerial functions. An organizational structure is a form of the management system as well as one of its main functions.

Organizational structures are to be designed in such a way that they reflect the influential characteristics of the environment in which the entity operates. The organizational structure of an entity operating in an emerging market country has to take into account the higher level of uncertainty and risk found in these markets, as well as the specific local political and economic conditions, and especially the level of economic freedom.

Likewise, a country's civil and financial court of laws, corporate and financial regulations, and established reporting system must also be accounted for in an entity's organizational structure. An entity's organizational structure has to both reflect its own strategic objectives and be useful in order to build cooperation with outside authorities.

Strategists from the developed world have to be mindful of the impact of the legacy of command-economy systems on organizational structures in the GEM. Companies in EMCs lose a lot of potential foreign investment because their strategies are still influenced by the vestiges of old organizational structures. Entrepreneurial spirit and freedom in the decision-making process are rising in EMCs, but most organizational structures do not yet reflect this. One of the lingering influences of command economies is an excess of unnecessary positions in the organizational structure. The proliferation of useless appointments and positions is a significant hindrance to the decision-making process—one that's very common in Balkan countries like Romania and small Latin American countries, such as Uruguay and Paraguay, as well as in the Philippines, Egypt, and nowadays, Tunisia. It is also a function of the relatively poor compensation and meager salaries for managers and staff, which leads companies to hire more people—complicating the organizational structure—rather than intensifying the workload of a smaller group of managers. Managerial functions are often widely dispersed and the organizational structure has too many elements, which slows down the decision-making process. The governments of emerging market countries often suffer from the same poorly organized structures. It is exceedingly difficult for the myriad deputies, ministers, and even prime ministers to be effective because they do not have full authority even in the areas of their designated responsibility, as the duties of a number of other vice-presidents, deputy prime ministers, and prime ministers overlap. In 2004, Russia declared in the framework of administrative reform that they would decrease the number of deputy ministers in each federal ministry to a maximum of two people. It was implemented in practice but between 2008 and 2014 the number of deputy ministers on average in federal ministries increased up to eight to ten people. For example, at the end of 2014, the Ministry of Economic Development of the Russian Federation had on hand 12 deputy ministers, which I assume is a world record for a non-military ministry, and, in addition, 25 heads of departments and a superfluous number of subordinate structures. As a result of this pseudo-reform, the governments of 85 Russian regions were overwhelmed with requests from ministerial bureaucrats to send various reports and information to the ministry. These people "on the ground" lost most of their work time on this unnecessary paperwork, instead of solving problems and improving real economic life.

Another issue in emerging market countries is a general preference for vertical subordination instead of dual responsibility, which is a major characteristic of modern organizational structures. Under modern structures, such as matrix organizational systems, there are double and even triple reporting systems from employees to operational, functional, and project superiors. For example, a senior engineer in a workshop has to report to the head of the workshop according to the administrative line of responsibilities, to the chief technologist of the corporation regarding engineering issues, and to the head of particular projects. Employees in the strategic department also often have triple responsibilities: to the head of the strategic department, to the head of the particular branch of the company for which they are developing a strategy, and to the chief professional in their area of expertise, such as the chief technologist, chief economist, head of design, etc. The situation in the GEM is starting to improve, especially in countries like India, China, Turkey, the Czech Republic, Hungary, Estonia, and even Colombia,

Bahrain, and Tunisia. Furthermore, organizational structures in countries like Taiwan and Singapore—especially those oriented to strategic innovation—are often more efficient than the traditional organizational structures of corporations from developed countries.

There are several key concepts to the formation and role of the strategic organizational structure. According to Professor Robert Mockler of St. John's University's Graduate School of Business:

> [The] somewhat paradoxical view of organization structure—that the formal structure is and is not important—is only one of many multinational strategic management paradoxes. However, the paradox exists only if one insists on too formal a solution. When viewed from a contingency perspective, the solution to organization, as in other task areas, is that the preferred form is a basic structure (for example, a three-way matrix organization) flexible enough to be tailored to each business unit's needs ... This perspective enables developing an organization that balances situation factors: the firm's core competencies, the local country, the global scope of operations, the changing competitive market, the business processes, the people, the communications systems, and other relevant situation factors. One result of this is that organizations often change over time as situation factors change.[13]

In emerging market countries, the organizational structure traditionally plays a more important role, with less room for flexibility than in developed countries. The organizational structure is an anchor of stability. Foreign investors can use it as a basis for understanding corporations and influencing national authorities on corporate leadership. At the same time, during the transition from command economy and dictatorship to the free-market economy and democracy, the organizational structure of governments and heads of state rapidly changes due to fluctuations in the role of the state in economics and business. In general, managerial functions decrease and regulating services increase. Organizational structures have to reflect this transformation process. One would assume that privatization and the declining number of state-owned entities and businesses would lead to changes in the governmental organizational structure; however, in practice, it is quite different. Despite the decreasing number of state-owned companies and the managerial authority of the government over businesses, it does not necessarily lead to a decrease in the number of bureaucrats and state officials. In countries like Russia, Pakistan, Azerbaijan, Venezuela, Greece, and, still to some extent, Ukraine, regulatory bodies have mushroomed. They are mostly oriented to collect bribes by creating artificial barriers for companies. In some countries, this problem is so endemic that it is more accurate to describe it as a racket, rather than as mere bribe collecting.

Many strategists argue that the implementation of strategic management systems should begin with managerial functions, prior to the organizational structure. In fact, it is practically impossible to delegate administrative duties and make the management system operational before the implementation of the organizational structure. In the words of Professor John C. Camillus of the University of Pittsburgh:

> Discussing the planning and control system without considering organizational structure is inappropriate, if not impossible. Sociologists tend to view *control* and *structure* as synonymous. In a management control system, organizational structure serves as a key determinant of what is appropriate. The structure of organizations directly affects the processes and perspectives of formal strategic planning ...

> Organization structure therefore represents a set of variables or choices that top management can influence or make that are fundamentally related to the planning and control system and also clearly affect the organization's performance. In short, in order to describe top management's responsibilities, it is necessary not only to consider the design of the planning and control system but also the chosen form of organizational structure.[14]

Camillus directs our attention to the differences in processes of strategy development and strategy implementation. The development of strategic management systems should start with an analysis of strategic managerial functions because the strategic management system and the organizational structure are organized according to the effective realization of strategic managerial functions. However, the implementation of strategic management systems always starts with the establishment of the organizational structure as a form that must reflect the internal characteristics of the strategic management system.

The strategic organizational structure is not oriented to operational management. It is oriented to the formation, development, and application of strategy. A strategic organizational structure is not a closed-end system. In existing organizations, it should have connections with operational management and should function under the general executive bodies, like the president, chief executive officer, the board of directors, etc. Copying American organizational structures, most emerging market countries establish a board of trustees or directors. In emerging market countries, this model is more popular than the British one, where the organizational structure is oriented around the executive chairman, a combination of chairman of the board and chief executive officer. US-based multinational corporations have another problem: very few of them, even those heavily involved in the GEM, have positions such as the global head of EMCs. It is good to have such a position for specific coverage, better collaboration, and "best practice" exchange in this huge market. The advantages and drawbacks of these systems will be described later in the section on the decision-making process.

Executives and Their Managerial Subordinates

Once the organizational structure is developed and approved by the appropriate authorities, the leadership should begin to hire or reallocate executives, managers, and support staff. In newly formed companies, leaders of the strategy development process usually will occupy the executive positions in the new entity. In existing corporations, the leadership of parental companies or the direction at the corporate level will be responsible for the selection and appointment of new subsidiary and unit executives. It should go without saying that every single executive should be a leader by nature. While heads of departments or subsidiaries may be the subordinates of corporate executives, they still must lead their employees. Again according to Robert Mockler:

> In practice, it is often difficult to distinguish between managers and leaders. In general, managers guide staff and control an enterprise's operations … That is, they manage a new or existing enterprise within a short- to medium-range perspective. Managers also plan and guide plan implementation, and so at times must inspire and energize or lead and show the way. Managers, therefore, need some leadership skills and must perform some leadership tasks. Leaders, on the other hand, create visions and inspire (show the way), lead by example (by going before), and energize a firm and its

> people within a longer-range perspective. They also have to do some managing (guiding and controlling), when enterprise-wide crises arise[15]

In the developed world, it is typical to hire executive-search firms and consultant companies to find executives and top managers. In EMCs, this is not often the case. In some EMCs, executive search firms have not been established, or executive search companies from developed countries have not yet established branches. Since the beginning of the twenty-first century, in some cases, executive search companies have started to fill these niches. Nonetheless, it is still common practice for the search for executives to be the sole responsibility of leaders of the existing bodies and personnel departments. Unfortunately, nepotism and corruption often take place during this process. In this situation, new executives are appointed based not on their qualities, but on their relationship with the entity's leadership. Their personal loyalty to each other enables and supports corruption. After the birth of the first EMCs in the 1980s, a young new generation of executives arose. They were less influenced by the legacy of their country's history, which led to positive changes in the management of companies in the GEM. This generation of executives grew up and climbed the ranks during the time of transition from dictatorship and a command economy to democracy and a free-market economy, a time of drastic structural changes to society. As a result of this transition, the political leadership of the old regime was replaced by a new generation of leaders. But it is too naïve to say that this is an inevitable process. Still, from time to time, and from country to country, old regime cronies have appeared in executive structures in the twenty-first century. But the years of their influence are numbered. However, the situation in the business community is quite different than it was in command economies. While the business arena may change drastically, the cast of characters remains the same. It is practically impossible to replace executives and managers immediately despite the fact that their mentalities may be completely out of date. Eventually, the younger generation of lower-level executives inherits leadership positions, as they are quicker to adapt to the new business environment than the old guard. This is usually preceded by a period of reshuffling the old regime's business leadership, as executives move from company to company. This can be seen as a byproduct of inexperienced and rapidly changing ownership as businesses seek new sources of capital. In general, EMCs and firms that operate in these markets experience a shortage of qualified, experienced, and responsible domestic executives and managers. For this reason, it is practically impossible for mergers or acquisitions to prevent the loss of talented and experienced executives and managers who will be useful for the company's new strategic direction.

For decades, executives at the beginning of their careers in emerging market countries were trained professionals in the industry or field of their corporation's activity. For example, in the mining industry, practically 100 percent of the heads of companies are mining engineers; in machinery-building companies, the same is true with mechanical engineers; in restaurant franchises, culinary experts, and so on. This is not the case in the United States or Western Europe, where top executives are mostly educated in finance, law, economics, and in the business schools rather than in the company's particular field. The majority of senior executives in emerging market countries are not trained to manage people and finances or to navigate legal situations. This is inefficient on a number of levels; they are not putting their education and expertise to use and they were not trained for what they are actually doing. During the transition to free-market economies in emerging market countries, many institutions and departments of continuing and professional education, which provide current and future executives with knowledge of managerial finance, accounting, business, and civil law, etc., began to appear. Among the young generation in emerging market countries, unlike during the times of dictatorship, the most appealing academic paths are related to finance, business, and law. Engineering has become much less popular. This has also led to changes in compensation between financiers and economists on one side, and engineers and teachers on the other, who, unfortunately, lost their prestige in society, which is not good for the quality of education.

A newly hired executive's first priority is to become very familiar with the implementation of strategy that was used by the firm to locate fresh talent, which led to their being hired in the first place. The next step is to source talented deputies and other subordinates, including the heads of units and chief professionals. The appointment of a new staff is where the first conflict of interest usually occurs. Corporate and parental company leadership influences subsidiary and unit leaders in the hiring of deputies, while, at the same time, domestic leaders and executives also experience the push from local regional and even national authorities to hire their colleagues and even their cronies. Compromise during this phase will often result in the entry strategy's lower efficiency and even in the failure of the strategy implementation altogether. Once all the necessary executives are in place, the next step is to hire managerial staff, assistants and executive assistants, secretaries, and even corporate chauffeurs. Unlike in the developed world, where corporations use limousine or car services, companies in the GEM usually keep a driver on staff, due both to a lack of efficient car services and to the prestige of having a corporate chauffeur.

The system of compensation for executives and managers in emerging market countries is much less sophisticated than that of the developed world, but most importantly it is less diversified. Typically, people with the same title in different organizations have almost the same compensation. IPO processes and the development of publicly held companies in EMCs are leading to the systematization of compensation for executives and other employees. This is also leading to a paradox: strategists are much less established and strategy as a profession is much less common in the corporate world and in the governmental structures of emerging markets. This is especially true for consulting companies, which can be found in only a few EMCs. Their practice and services are still much less popular and less respected than in the developed world. Despite the fact that executives in the developed world usually have much better professional education and more extensive experience in free-market conditions, they still use consulting services far more than executives from EMCs. Corporate leaders in emerging market countries typically believe that using consulting services implies that they do not know what they are doing or how to achieve success. They have trouble believing that reputable executives and owners in the US, Great Britain, and Japan do not take a step without listening to their strategists and getting a second opinion from outside consulting firms. Even a person as highly respected as Jack Welch, the former president of General Electric, would not make a strategic decision without first checking with GE's Department of Strategic Initiative, as well as with independent consultants. When an important strategic decision fails, the board of directors and shareholders will demand to know whose idea the move was and why they did not consult with outside strategists. Executives in this situation will likely find themselves in need of a job.

There are special requirements in emerging market countries regarding administrative staff. Typically, there are two basic requirements for applicants: computer application skills and English proficiency. In particular parts of the GEM, administrative employees need more extensive foreign-language skills. In Albania, for example, due to its proximity to Italy, many companies require that their executive assistants speak Italian as well as English. In Brazil, many secretaries are required to speak Spanish, the language of most neighboring countries, in addition to English and, of course, their native tongue, Portuguese. In India, this is not a major issue since most of the country is equally comfortable with their native language as well as with English.

In the GEM, executive education and MBA programs are among the most prestigious academic paths for young students. It is impossible to find a university in an emerging market country without business, economics, and law majors. The study of law is also very popular among the younger generation. The wide presence of firms in EMCs that offer professional services, like accounting and auditing, business consulting, and legal services (mentioned in Chapter 9) is increasing the demand for people in these professions and motivating the popularity of these degrees. Traditionally, emerging market countries place a higher value on the role of higher education than in developed countries, because, historically, good education was one of the primary paths out of poverty under dictatorships.

One of the major difficulties in finding executives and managers in emerging market countries is the lower professional ethics and integrity of applicants due to the legacy of tyrants and dictatorships, as well as a lack of understanding of strategy's role and importance and its precise implementation. This lack has spurred graduates and young professionals from the developed world to build their careers in emerging market countries. This is due especially to the fact that strategic education in EMCs lags behind developed standards and practical needs in such countries. In 2007, Moscow State University, the leading educational center in Russia, established the Department of Financial Strategy in its Moscow School of Economics, the first such school in Russia as well as in any other Eastern European country; this new course of study is very popular among potential Masters students. In 2014, the framework for the Northwestern Institute of Management's Department of Territorial Strategy was established in St. Petersburg. This department is involved in teaching strategy, as well as developing regional strategists in the northwestern regions of Russia. Due to the shortage of professional strategists, a trend is already beginning to emerge for more and more graduates of American and Western European universities to look for open managerial and even executive positions in companies in EMCs, where the number of these positions is increasing ten times faster than in developed countries. The rate of growth for these positions in EMCs has been 20 to 40 percent annually during the first 12 years of the twenty-first century. Demand for professionals, especially those trained to work with or within emerging market countries, is sky-high due to the fact that there is no single university in the developed world that has management in emerging markets as a major, despite the hundreds of universities throughout the world that already have courses related to emerging market studies. Graduates who would like to be employed in a strategic department or in strategically important positions have to think about themselves from the point of view of employers and must develop an appropriate mindset. According to a publication from the Harvard Business School:

> [A] strategic mindset in HR [human resources] offers important benefits on many levels—such as greater profitability for your company, access to needed resources for your HR department, and personal advantages such as more opportunities for career advancement and lower levels of on-the-job stress.[16]

The attitude described in this quote is very helpful, not only for finding employment but also for increasing productivity and usefulness as a part of a strategic and managerial team.

Strategic Decision-Making Process

The strategic decision-making process is one of the major components of strategy and strategizing. It requires an able and focused strategic leader and capable and disciplined subordinates. The decision-making process is the pinnacle of the strategic mindset. As Napoleon once said, "Nothing is more difficult, and therefore more precious, than to be able to decide."[17] There are not many people who can take on the responsibility of decision-making, and even fewer who have the ability, capacity, and the *chutzpah* to make strategic decisions. The consequences of strategic decisions are extreme, and a strategist can stand to lose big. This is why the strategic decision-making process requires transparency for all those involved in the process, as well as communal responsibility. Otherwise, all decisions will be delegated up the hierarchy to the top leader, who will most likely be overwhelmed with small problems and unable to concentrate on strategically vital decisions.

The strategic decision-making process is the prerogative of top-level managerial bodies and executives. From the moment when decisions are made about the development of a new strategy or a new scenario of an existing strategy, top executives and boards of directors are fully responsible for the acceleration, funding, analysis, and implementation of the strategy. At the same time, both the context and timing of this decision are kept secret, unless executives decide to make the "when" and "what" of the new strategy public. These obligations are the major responsibility of the chairman of the board and the board of directors. In emerging market countries, the development of a board of directors as an institution has led to its increasing role in this process. While the monitoring, development, and implementation of strategy is the responsibility of executives, the new strategy's acceptance and evaluation is the responsibility of the board of directors, joint chiefs of staff, national and regional governments, and other collective bodies. Attention to strategic development and implementation is among the key criteria during the process of evaluating executives and hiring new ones.

There are several unique characteristics to the decision-making process in emerging market countries. First and foremost is a general lack of initiative in subordinates, especially in bringing strategic ideas and suggestions to top executives. This is the legacy of dictatorships and command economies, from which all emerging markets originate. Understandably, people living under these conditions become very risk averse, and believe that taking the initiative is an unnecessary risk. As a result, it is difficult for executives to gain an understanding of the success or failure of an existing strategy and the required needs for the development of a new or updated one because their employees are hesitant to be critical. Managers and executives are often afraid to take responsibility and be proactive. There is a proverb in many EMCs that says that initiative is punishable. As a result, even the smallest issues gradually are pushed up the chain of command—eventually forcing top executives to deal with myriad insignificant time-wasting issues. Expatriates working as top executives in companies from EMCs very often become overwhelmed with unimportant day-to-day issues. They are forced to motivate subordinates to take on responsibilities and make decisions or punish them for not doing so. This results in decision-making processes that are rigid and restrictive for employees in many cases. The lack of freedom in the decision-making process becomes a base for corruption and nepotism. Bosses will often place their cronies and close relatives below them, valuing obedience over competency. In some EMCs, such relationships dominate the decision-making process and organizational structure of companies. It is extremely difficult to reform these processes and structures. People's options are limited and they are willing to do whatever is necessary to keep their jobs, even bribing their bosses. For those from the developed world, it is hard to imagine employees going to their bosses on payday only to receive 10 percent of their compensation, but this is not unusual in some EMCs. This is one of the reasons why it is very important for pay to be deposited directly into bank accounts and not distributed in cash. A cash economy in general is a petri dish for corruption. The large number of chief executives' deputies is another lingering effect of dictatorships on the decision-making process in EMCs. The responsibility for major strategic issues is so widely dispersed that it complicates evaluating implemented strategies and makes it difficult to deliver a company-wide systematic understanding of new strategic ideas to the board of directors. As a result of many unnecessary positions, the strategic decision-making process is significantly slower than it could be. However, companies from the GEM are beginning to accept more modern organizational structures and decision-making processes, which will benefit them greatly, especially during the initial stages of strategy formation and development.

An efficient strategic decision-making process requires detailed descriptions of the strategic rights and responsibilities of top executives and boards of directors. Who is responsible for proposing strategic decisions related to the beginning of strategy development and implementation? What is the division of strategic responsibilities between the board of directors and corporate executives and their subsidiary and unit leaders? All of these issues have to be clearly explained when formalizing the decision-making process. This is also an appropriate point to formalize the basic ethics of a company. Professor Laure Paquette of Lakehead University in Ontario, Canada, presents the following rules regarding business ethics and the decision-making process:

> [1] [K]eep it simple and keep it honest … [2] When it comes to goal selection, go with the flow of events, not against it, unless you are very early in the process … If you cannot go with the flow, try to divert it or redirect to use that momentum to reach your own goals … [3] Watch the timing of your strategy … take the time to assess if a better time might not be just around the corner … [4] Watch for unintended consequences flowing from your actions … Unintended consequences have to be managed; you cannot afford to ignore them.[18]

Nevertheless, many companies do not have a formal structure for strategic decision-making processes, i.e., who initiates this process, how strategic orders go from one layer of the entity's management system to another, and who is responsible for the decision-making process on the corporate level, as well as for its coordination with local, regional, and national authorities of the country in which the strategy is developed and implemented. Subsidiaries of foreign companies in emerging market countries have even more complicated issues related to strategy development. They have to coordinate their strategic priorities and processes with parent companies abroad, as well as with the regional and national authorities of the country where their facilities are located and with their suppliers and buyers in the GEM, the developed world, and maybe in developing countries as well. These problems are innate characteristics of matrix organizational structures. Often, corporate employees in professional departments (technology, patents pending, human resources, etc.) are responsible and have to report to the head of the subsidiary in the GEM or to the respective supervisory department of the parent company in a developed country. In many cases, large multinational corporations unify professionals from different subsidiaries in several countries to create a task force while all professionals also continue to work in their offices. Cutting-edge video teleconferencing (e.g. Cisco's TelePresence) practically teleports employees from around the world to the same conference room.

In the GEM, large companies tend to operate according to the same organizational structures and decision-making processes as small companies. Regardless of the size, most companies from the GEM tend to be slow in accepting Western practices in their decision-making processes. Even in the developed world, the strategic decision-making process is not a priority for boards of directors' practice, nor is it on the daily schedule of top executives, although it should be. Business schools do not place sufficient emphasis on the value of a well-defined and formalized strategic decision-making process. These schools insufficiently focus students' attention on clearly defining and formalizing the process of strategic economic and financial decisions. As a result, during financial strategy development, financial analysts in very few entities make comparisons between future income and balances of profits of previous periods. This is why the economic efficiency of strategies that assess strategy effectiveness is often underestimated and the pressures of history, or the balances of profit, oppress strategic decision-makers.

Incorporating Global Risk Management in the Strategic Decision-Making Process

For any entity operating in the GEM, decision-making processes must be oriented to deal with higher risks, especially of the political, business, and technological varieties. For example, when governments are more involved in business activity there is a higher probability of greater political risk, which can result in breached contracts. Due to the complex history of privatization in emerging market countries, the risk of expropriation and nationalization is substantially higher than in developed countries. These issues apply not only to investment and foreign direct investment, but also to companies' trade and operational activities.

The formalization of the strategic decision-making process for companies entering emerging markets should begin prior to an evaluation of basic economic factors with an analysis of major rating—and credit agencies' evaluations of country risk, sovereign risk, national credit risk, etc. All of these issues have to be analyzed in terms of the company's objectives and goals until the point of the development of an entry strategy. It is important to keep in mind that there are noticeable differences in the analytical methods used to determine national credit risk in EMCs by different rating agencies and multilateral institutions. Disparities in their ratings cannot simply be ignored; the reasons for these discrepancies have to be identified and understood. The significance of these differences is amplified when institutional, and even public, investors use this information to make investment decisions. Publishing the results of these analyses can mislead members of the business community who are not very knowledgeable about the GEM. In addition, for professionals working with the GEM, the results of these different analyses often lead to more questions than answers. The decision-making process in corporations that work domestically, prior to entering the GEM, has to be altered. New employees who are familiar with the particular EMC have to participate in this process, as well as executives who will supervise this activity abroad and managers and professionals who most likely will work in the EMC, at least during the establishment of the subsidiary.

Risk-management analyses should always be revised to reflect shifts in local, regional, and national governance, regulations, and practice. However, the priority of risk management is to analyze technological advancements that have implications for the cost of production, possible substitute goods, etc., and then report to the board of directors. In EMCs, decisions regarding risk often lie not with the board of directors but with shareholders, who are more influential in the GEM. This can be particularly complicated when governments are substantial shareholders, which is more common in the GEM than in the developed world. Even when private minority owners do have a controlling share in such mixed state-private ownership companies, their input in strategic decisions quite often goes ignored. Foreign companies and entrepreneurs who would like to invest or cooperate with such companies have to take this issue into consideration.

The strategic decision-making process regarding business risk in EMCs is especially important for companies listed on stock exchanges in an EMC. The regulating agencies of these exchanges do not have enough control over the corporation, and, furthermore, the agencies can change the rules so frequently and in such unexpected directions that the strategic decision-making process cannot respond fast enough. This is one of the reasons why high risk and uncertainty are major factors of the strategic decision-making process for companies in not only this market, but also for those companies that are heavily involved in the market from beyond its national boundaries. Any strategic decision should factor in forecasting and strategizing the dynamics of changes to laws and under-law regulations. For this reason, it is not unusual to invite government officials or those with strong connections to authorities to participate in meetings with the board of directors. This is a key explanation as to why compensation for members of the board is usually relatively high in emerging market countries and will sometimes exceed the salaries of their primary occupations. Foreign participants in boards of directors and especially owners who do not participate in strategic decision meetings have to be aware of the high personal influence of top-level officials if they take part in strategic decisions. But their opinion is not always the best one to use as the basis of a strategic decision. Their loyalty to the corporation is always an obstacle to the close examination of company issues. However, the more shares any board member has, the greater their loyalty to the corporation will be. Because of the higher risk in the GEM, the decision-making process in emerging market countries should always take into account unexpected force majeure, which can be extraordinary situations such as unforeseen political, economic, business, technological, and environmental changes, disasters, and catastrophes. The World Bank defines force majeure as

> any event beyond the reasonable control of the Project Company, the occurrence of which could not have been reasonably foreseen, and typically includes: war, whether declared or not; revolution; riot; insurrection; strikes (except strikes by employees of (a) the Project Company, (b) the Contractor and/or its subcontractors, or (c) any other company undertaking any part of the operation and maintenance of the Project); invasion; armed conflict; hostile act of foreign enemy; act of terrorism; sabotage; radiation or chemical contamination; ionizing radiation; act of God; explosion; flood; storm; tempest; earthquake; plague or other serious epidemics; and which: (i) causes material and unavoidable physical damage or destruction to the Project or, without limitation, its toll facilities or functions; (ii) materially delays the scheduled time of completion of the Project without opportunity to otherwise repair the schedule; or (iii) materially interrupts the full and regular operation of all

or any material portion of the Project, including without limitation its toll collection facilities or functions. Notwithstanding the foregoing, the inability of the Project Company to pay money as required by the Loan or other documents, by itself, constitute a Force Majeure Event.[19]

The World Bank's definition relates to issues to which the corporation must react, although these difficulties can only be predicted with great difficulty if, indeed, at all, and to which the corporation is practically powerless to change: e.g. a coup d'état, the sinking of a shipment of important cargo, or the occurrence of technogenic or natural disasters, among the difficulties listed above. Despite the fact that many of these incidents or disasters are practically impossible to predict, the functioning of the decision-making process in force majeure situations has to be described in advance in as much detail as possible. Quite often, the strategic managerial approach to force majeure processes is detailed in the exit strategy. A strategic approach to force majeure situations has to be substantially predetermined during the process of strategizing the consequences of such situations.

Tools of Strategic Management

In addition to a shortage of strategists, well-trained executives, and capital, management systems in the GEM also experience a lack of modern information technologies and even office supplies. The ability to send pictures, graphics, maps, tables, and text instantaneously throughout the world via the Internet is a remarkable phenomenon and a helpful addition to the strategist's toolbox. These tools increase the strategist's ability to prove, demonstrate, and use the most accurate and up-to-date information during strategy implementation. The old American saying that "a picture is worth a thousand words" is correct. This causes certain behavior that would be completely unheard of in the developed world. For example, when executives in the GEM move from office to office, it is not uncommon for them to bring their chairs with them. The quality of executive offices in emerging market countries varies a great deal. Foreigners should be prepared to encounter the most opulent and technologically advanced executive offices in the world, as well as facilities that would not even qualify as offices in the developed world. The production of office furniture is an underdeveloped industry in the GEM, with a lower quality of products. In many EMCs, roughly 90 percent of office supplies are imported. Leading information technology companies are very active in emerging market countries. The most successful companies in the GEM employ the products and services of these IT companies.

Despite breakneck growth in information technology, it is hard to argue with Dr. Gary Hamel, a professor at the London Business School, who states that "management is out of date ... Like the combustion engine, it's a technology that has largely stopped evolving, and that's not good."[20] The theory of management systems and strategic management in general has not adapted to reflect technological advancements or the new challenges and opportunities in the GMP and the GEM. Nonetheless, a few companies, such as Cisco Systems, have specialized in IT for strategic management and have come up with several technological solutions that have been successfully implemented in parts of the GEM. However, many governmental and corporate executives underestimated the value of this technology and have not allocated the necessary funds to purchase these expensive but very efficient products, such as the comprehensive technology infrastructure and wireless initiatives that support the policy objectives of particular entities provided by Cisco.

Clients of Cisco include national presidents and prime ministers, heads of governmental agencies, as well as executives and board members of leading companies. Unfortunately, the majority of corporations in emerging market countries cannot afford the services of companies like Cisco or IBM. Cisco's TelePresence System,[21] for instance, is expensive but can save money and reduce the corporation's environmental impact by allowing executives to collaborate as if they were in the same conference room despite being thousands of miles apart. Entities in the GEM often lack IT systems and have to do their best with incompatible computers, outdated software, printers, scanners, and other equipment. However, the trend is clear: big and medium-sized companies in emerging markets are attempting to catch up with the technological standards of developed countries. In this market, specialized technological leasing companies have even appeared. Due to the very low competition for these services, these companies are almost always profitable.

The new generation of information technology is also increasing the capability and efficiency of twentieth-century office technologies. This is occurring now with PERT (Program Evaluation and Review Technique), which initially revolutionized the strategic planning function in the middle of the twentieth century. By the end of the twentieth century, more complex technologies appeared, like COSO (Committee of Sponsoring Organizations), which was developed in 1985. COSO is a corporate guidance system for the development of internal control systems to reduce fraudulent financial reporting and to use various financial instruments like derivatives and risk management, among other functions. Among the major sponsors of this system are the American Accounting Association, the American Institute of Certified Public Accountants, Financial Executives International, the Institute of Internal Auditors, and the Institute of Management Accountants.[22]

The Internet, to which top-level executives in the GEM barely had access at the beginning of the twenty-first century, is universally available in the offices of most companies as of 2008. Access to Internet resources is the most efficient and inexpensive source of reliable strategic information. However, the exigencies of digital cloud technologies also bring challenges to top executives, especially in EMCs, with the lack of initiative of subordinates. Some executives get as many as 400 e-mails per day, most of which they do not need. Everyone who sends these e-mails thinks that their concerns are of the utmost priority and expects an immediate response. But of course, the executives are totally overwhelmed by so much e-mail. This is a good opportunity to use motivational systems by rewarding those who make the appropriate decisions on their own and remonstrate with those who bring menial issues to the top of the chain of command. The habit of bringing every single issue to superiors is symptomatic of employees who wish to avoid sharing responsibility for minor decisions.

Subscriptions to major business publications like *Forbes*, *Businessweek*, *Fortune*, and *The Economist* have also increased tremendously in the GEM. Many of these magazines are published in the major languages of the GEM, including Mandarin, Hindi, Russian, Spanish, Arabic, and Portuguese, and even in languages of smaller nations, such as Ukrainian, Bulgarian, Czech, Hungarian, and Filipino.

Information is the raw material of the decision-making process. To be able to analyze myriad sources, types, and forms of information, strategists must employ the ninth rule of strategic thinking, "Strategists Must Be Able to Convert Future Chaos into Systems of Successful Prospects" (see Chapter 2), and systematize their approach. For example, economic information should be organized according to the order of basic economic factors, starting with natural resources and followed by labor and capital resources, infrastructure, production facilities, innovations, and technology. Indicators of basic economic factors have to be analyzed in the context of political, economic, and social systems. Management systems have to be analyzed by the order of their major elements (leadership, organizational structure, executives, decision-making process, etc.) and major functions. When systematizing various sources and types of information, it is crucial for strategists to focus on dynamics in order to discover, recognize, and describe technological, environmental, economic, and political trends. GDP growth rate is an important indicator for displaying the basic trend of economic development. This dynamic illustrates the health of the economy: GDP per head is an integrated indicator of the efficiency of a national or regional economy, and the GDP also shows its scale.

As access to strategic information increases in the GEM, so too will the efficiency of strategic management systems. This also applies to companies in the US, Western Europe, Australia, and Japan that also suffer from a lack of accurate strategic information about EMCs. It is not always easy to get access to updated and properly translated laws and under-law regulations, which, of course, can have major implications for strategy formulation and other decision-making activities. Continued advancements in information technology will greatly increase the efficiency of strategic management systems throughout the world. As Professors Robert Galliers and Dorothy Leidner from the London School of Economics and Baylor University (US), respectively, state:

> [T]he subject of strategic information management is diverse and complex. It is not simply concerned with technological issues—far from it in fact. The subject domain incorporates aspects of strategic management, globalization, the management of change and human/cultural issues which may not at first sight have been considered as being directly relevant in the world of information technology.[23]

While the Internet is improving access to information, executives from EMCs still suffer from a lack of professional strategic analyses, which hinders the efficiency of their management systems. They are often unwilling to pay for access to proprietary reports that are widely used in the developed world. Nevertheless the role of information technology departments in corporate management systems is rapidly expanding, even in the GEM. Again according to Galliers and Leidner:

> Information can now be delivered to the right people at the right time, thus enabling well-informed decisions to be made. Previously, due to the limited information-gathering capability of organizations, decision makers could seldom rely on up-to-date information but instead made important decisions based on past results and their own experience. This no longer needs to be the case. With the right technology in place to collect the necessary data automatically, up-to-date information can be accessed whenever the need arises. This is the informating quality of IT. …
>
> With the growth in the usage of IT to support information provision within organizations, the political nature of information has come into sharper focus. Gatekeepers of information are powerful people; they can decide when and if to convey vital information, and to whom. They are likely to be either highly respected, or despised for the power that they have at their fingertips.[24]

Regardless of the implications of the growing importance of IT on office politics, the impact of modern information technology usage is undeniably positive. It benefits corporations not only by improving access to information, but also by improving communication among its worldwide subsidiaries and reducing travel costs and the stresses endured by employees as a result of extensive international travel. Society benefits from this via reductions in the carbon footprint of corporations.

Major Functions of Strategic Management Systems

When establishing an entity's strategic management system, it is imperative to divide the processes of its formation from those of its operations. There are several management system functions that can be understood as stages of the decision-making processes, including planning, motivation, and control; or that can be divided among major professional areas of the management system, such as accounting, finance, and legal; or that can be divided among internal and external corporate governance, including governmental relations and supervising of subsidiaries and units. There are easily several hundred different functions that managerial bodies are supposed to fulfill. However, they are all essentially part of the three major functions, without which management systems—and especially strategic management systems—cannot be considered fully operational: strategic planning, strategic motivation, and strategic monitoring and control. If any one of these major managerial functions does not operate properly, neither will the other two; as a result, the entity as a whole will suffer.

Strategic Planning

Strategic planning is the most important function of strategic management. After strategic prediction, forecasting, and strategizing, planning may seem an afterthought. But prediction and forecasting are part of the pre-strategic stage, not the core of the strategizing process. Forecasting is a specialized profession and an instrument that is very useful during the strategizing process. Forecasts, which, as detailed in Chapter 2, are not to be confused with prophecies, can be anything from broad and general to incredibly detailed. It all depends on the field of studies, development, and use of the forecast. For financiers, 72 hours is a long-distance forecasting period. We are concerned with a different kind of forecast in this book, but it is important to note that there are normally three types of financial forecasting and planning:

- Forecasting of foreign markets' macroeconomic performance
- Forecasting exchange and inflation rates, as well as the balance of payments
- Forecasting of competitors and companies with specific shares on the market.[25]

The following prediction classifications are too practical for the narrow vision needed in finance forecasting. Forecasting for strategy is classified by a longer period of years, by political, economic, social, or technological fields, or by its level of accuracy and uses of mathematical methods and data.

A strategist must deal with predictions and forecasting before the development of a strategic mission and vision. Strategic planning as a part of the strategizing process can only start after the objectives and goals have already been determined. Through all of the processes involved in strategic development and implementation, a strategist must use the rules for strategic thinking (see Chapter 2). Rule 12 of strategic thinking is particularly relevant to this function: during strategic planning, always overestimate danger, the difficulties that arise from different circumstances, and the power of the enemy or competitor. Before every campaign, Napoleon considered all possible outcomes. He wrote:

> There is no man more pusillanimous than I when I am planning a campaign. I purposely exaggerate all the dangers and all the calamities that the circumstances make possible. I am in a thoroughly painful state of agitation. This does not keep me from looking quite serene in front of my entourage.[26]

Napoleon was not afraid. Rather, he was overestimating the capability of his enemy, predicting and almost strategizing all possible scenarios. A fully developed strategy will be ready for any of the unforeseen difficulties that will always appear during strategy implementation, especially during the tactical stages when strategy goes from a more or less abstract paper document to practical reality. Strategy must be able to sustain real-world practice and not function only in a strategist's mind.

The product of the strategic-planning process is the strategic plan as an executive document. This document reflects the utmost concentration of all elements of strategy and their implementation, presented in a timetable, and it is among the most proprietary and secretive of corporate documents. It details all current and future corporate activity of strategic importance. The strategic plan is prepared not only in terms of time but also in terms of resource allocations for specific objectives. Of equal importance to the strategic plan as a document is the process of strategic planning itself. According to Leonard Goodstein, Timothy Nolan, and William Pfeiffer, authors of several books on strategic planning:

> [T]o be successful, a strategic planning process should provide the criteria for making day-to-day organizational decisions and should provide a template against which all such decisions can be evaluated … All too often, strategic planning is seen as a top-management exercise that has little or nothing to do with the actual running of the organization.[27]

The authors of this quote correctly state that strategic planning does not deal with daily decisions; it only suggests criteria, formats, and rules for a one-year plan and operational activity. The difference between the strategic and operational plan is that the strategic plan has a quarterly or annual timetable, as opposed to the daily, weekly, and, in some cases, monthly timetable of the tactical and operational plans. The same authors of the above quote go on to describe the distinction between strategic planning and planning:

> Planning is the process of establishing objectives and choosing the most suitable means for achieving these objectives prior to taking actions … [I]n contrast, we define strategic planning as "the process by which the guiding members of an organization envision its future and develop the necessary procedures and operations to achieve that future."[28]

The strategic plan should have three major sections: strategy development, strategy implementation (including the entry strategy), and the exit strategy. This document describes only activities, events, and preliminary and final results of strategic relevance. Board members and executives have to be regularly updated or briefed with the implementation of the strategic plan. According to IBM's 2006 global CEO study, industry-leading companies ("outperformers") place almost twice as much importance upon "the business model" as companies that are less efficient and less competitive. According to this study, these "underperformers" place twice as much emphasis on operations relative to "outperformers." This example, which is based on operating margin growth over five years, is a clear illustration of the improved results entities achieve when they value strategic issues over operational ones.[29]

For entities that have a strategy department, it is their responsibility to develop and monitor the strategic plan. For these departments, strategic planning is a daily activity. In entities without such divisions, strategic planning is a discrete, or non-continuous, activity. Executives, managers, and professionals have other responsibilities and deal with strategic planning only during the processes of strategy development and implementation. On a governmental level, strategic planning often takes the form of national programs, which can be developed for specific industries and regions. However, even these programs usually are prepared without a proper and required volume of resource allocation. Governments of emerging market countries are more familiar with this concept from the planning processes and documents of command economies. However, it should come as no surprise that plans made under command economies totally lacked in strategy and were largely not even based in reality and never fully implemented, although they were not without some successes.

Strategic Motivation

Without a motivation system, it is impossible to implement any efficient strategic plan. In the words of C. Davis Fogg, an experienced executive and author:

> [A]lthough strategic planning may seem a sterile, intellectual analytical process, it's not … [T]he human element is critically important. Strategic planning requires the organization's intimate and enthusiastic involvement, often using formal and informal teams, in providing information, making decisions and successfully implementing them.[30]

It is obvious that in order for the development of a strategic plan to be efficient, motivation is required. But without motivation, the successful implementation of this plan is even problematic and close to impossible. The specifics of strategic planning largely determine the details of motivation systems. First and foremost, this system has to inspire employees involved in the processes of strategy development and implementation to orient themselves to strategic ways of thinking. In the words of the famous Japanese strategist Kenichi Ohmae:

> Strategic thinking in business must break out of the limited scope of vision that entraps deer on the highway. It must be backed by the daily use of imagination and by constant training in logical thought processes. Success must be summoned; it will not come unbidden and unplanned. Top management and its corporate planners cannot sensibly base their day-to-day work on blind optimism and apply strategic thinking only when confronted by unexpected obstacles. They must develop the habit of thinking strategically, and they must do it as a matter of course. Ideally, they should approach it with real enthusiasm as a stimulating mental exercise. To become an effective strategist requires constant practice in strategic thinking. It is a daily

> discipline, not a resource that can be left dormant in normal times and tapped at will in an emergency.[31]

Formalizing the strategic motivation system includes establishing a system of daily incentives for employees, especially those who are responsible for strategy development and implementation. The formal system is presented in a document in which all suggestions about motivation and incentives are developed and described; it includes all moral, social, and financial instruments of motivation for both individuals and groups of employees. Special recognition and awards should be granted to those who go above and beyond in creating and implementing strategic ideas.

As already discussed, a lack of initiative is one of the main challenges that motivational systems in the GEM face; this has implications for all major functions of management systems. It obviously makes it very difficult for executives to delegate operational decisions to managers. Thus, one of the main objectives of management systems in the GEM is to break the following two ironclad managerial rules that still linger from dictatorships:

1. The boss is always right.
2. In all other cases, see rule No. 1.

In an attempt to destroy this mentality and encourage an independent, initiative-taking attitude, the mayor of a city in an oil-rich province of Russia officially prohibited the use of the following phrases by any employee when meeting with superiors:

- "I don't know."
- "Why would I need that?"
- "That's impossible."
- "That would cut into my lunch break."
- "That's not my responsibility."
- "My secretary made an error."
- "I don't recall you telling me that."

This example illustrates how, in emerging market countries, a system of negative repercussions for employees must supplement the positive reinforcement of strategy. Before implementing additional motivational systems, it is always important to establish a proper system of regular compensation for employee initiative and day-to-day work. Throughout history, national leaders have always been challenged to establish such a system of payment to prevent top-level bureaucrats from corruption. For example, the famous eleventh-century governmental official and prime minister of the Seljuk Empire, Niẓām al-Mulk, wrote that each official has to be "paid a salary according to his position, so that he will have no excuse for dishonesty."[32] This is one way to decrease, if not prevent, corruption, although it does not work alone. In certain EMCs, corruption is so high that, during the last 20 years, the market was stolen all together.

In establishing motivational systems, many executives and managers overemphasize financial incentives and ignore social incentives, which can be equally powerful. It goes without saying that employees will respond to changes in their pay. However, many managers ignore the effectiveness of social incentives, like public recognition of accomplishments and mistakes, without any reason. Under dictatorships, managers and executives developed tendencies toward cautious privacy; individual employees' accomplishments were not celebrated. However, it was not unusual for mistakes to be publicly punished. In EMCs, it is not uncommon for executives of state companies with private shareholder partnerships to have former state officials on the board of directors, who still take a bureaucratic approach to the strategic decision-making process. These board members understand how to punish people but not how to positively motivate them. However, this general attitude is beginning to change; managers and executives are starting to use tools like diplomas and certificates of appreciation in order to positively motivate their employees.

A strategic motivation system consists of a set of methods, procedures, and instruments to efficiently implement strategic plans. The most difficult and important function is to motivate executives, managers, and even professionals to think strategically and to permanently develop a vision of the future. In the words of Michael McGrath, a well-known author and the CEO of Thomas Group, Inc.:

> [A]n effective core strategic vision can motivate people to work not just smarter but also harder. If the engineers have confidence that management knows where the company is going and has a good vision of the future, they will put in the extra effort to ensure that the company gets there with new products at the right time. Nothing helps motivate a product development team better than a crisp, well-thought-out strategic vision. If a development team lacks confidence in a company's vision, it is difficult to keep the members committed. The dilemma is how to communicate the core strategic vision. If a company tells everyone its strategic vision, competitors might learn about it. This points out one of the differences between core strategic vision and product strategy. The vision does not describe specific details. While it can be of some help to competitors, it is not specific competitive intelligence.[33]

This statement describes a very special kind of motivation, which occurs when strategic ideas, vision, or a strategic plan can motivate people to follow them and to be strategically creative. Motivation is not only related to financial and morale incentives; ideas can sometimes be the most powerful means of inspiration for employees to demonstrate their initiative.

Strategic Monitoring and Control: Evaluating Strategy and Strategists

Once a strategy has been developed, approved, and is beginning to be implemented, the strategist must monitor this process, noting successes and failures, and incorporate this information into the next strategic step. In order to do so, the strategist must gather feedback from the executives and managers who implement the strategy. Feedback is used to make any necessary corrections and updates to the approved strategic scenario. Just because the strategic scenario is constantly updated does not mean that the strategy and its strategic plan are constantly changing. The major elements of the strategy—its mission, vision, objectives, and goals—remain unchanged. However, some aspects of the strategic business plan can be shifted in order to make the strategy more effective and virile. During the monitoring of all stages of strategy formation and implementation, it is also important to find any mistakes and incorrect or misleading information. COSO (described above) is widely used for this purpose, especially by the Big Four auditing firms, including PricewaterhouseCoopers. The COSO system has similarities to General Electric's Six Sigma. However, while Six Sigma is related to the management quality of manufacturing, COSO primarily addresses information and reports risk management. Implementing this system during the strategic development of the management system can prevent inefficient, unethical, and misleading business operations. Quite often, operational executives and even chief risk officers do not realize that they could avoid a lot of problems in their day-to-day activity if operational risk were analyzed during the strategic development of organizational structures, the decision-making process, and information technology systems. For example, cases like the Enron Corporation implosion, which occurred due to misreporting, and the 2007–08 case of Jérôme Kerviel, a trader at the French corporate and investment banking company Société Générale, whose unmonitored activity resulted in losses of €4.9 billion, would never have occurred or would have been caught immediately if a system of monitoring and control had been designed during the stage of strategic management development. Some scholars think that it is unnecessary and even impossible to differentiate strategic planning from strategic motivation and then to differentiate both of these activities from control. The words of Dr. John C. Camillus, Professor of Strategic Management at the University of Pittsburgh, explain this point of view:

> [C]ertain kinds of planning and control activities are so intertwined that it is difficult to label them as one or the other. My approach to design sidesteps the subjective and somewhat unnecessary task of categorizing activities such as defining the organizations' mission or raison d'être as either planning or control. It is a planning activity in that it charts the future directions of the organization. It is also a control activity in that it limits the range of businesses or programs that the organization can consider.[34]

However, Camillus misses the point that, for practical strategic management, it is necessary for the efficiency of all stages of the strategizing process to divide these functions: development, application, planning, and control. Otherwise, it is impossible to structure a strategy, and the decision-making process itself, as well as to identify the responsibilities and rights among decision-makers. In political, economic, and business life, it is very difficult to find issues that are strictly divided, even by invisible borders, but strategists and executives divide them for analytical and managerial purposes. For example, it is practically unrealistic to divide political, economic, and business risk from one another, but, for purposes of allocation, evaluation, and management, the analytical division is necessary.

An important part of strategic monitoring and control is the regular evaluation of the executives and managers responsible for the strategy, as well as of the strategy itself. Ideally, appointed evaluators, or auditors, ought to have a level of separation from the strategic plan's developers. However, this is usually only possible in large organizations. As a result, in small organizations, it is even more important to understand planning, motivation, and monitoring and control as separate functions. Strategy implementation must be closely monitored in order to bring attention to any needed adjustments or revisions. Strategy assessment is one of the elements of effective control and monitoring; strategic adjustment based on the findings from the control and monitoring stage is the beginning of the improvement of strategic planning, if not the entire strategy. Information technology can be helpful in carrying out this function. According to author Michael Reed:

> Information and communication control systems are designed and implemented in such a way that total and complete transparency of organizational behavior becomes a realizable, if not realized, managerial aspiration. While poor design, system overload

> and operational breakdown are routine aspects of organizational life … the "drive to automate," underpinning managerial rationality in the domain of technological change, is well taken to the extent that it highlights the control imperatives at the ideological and political core of the latter. The managerial desire to "transmit the presence of the omniscient observer and to induce compliance without the messy conflict-prone exertions of reciprocal relations" (Zuboff 1988: 323) may be corrupted and deformed by all sorts of cognitive, political and cultural contingencies.[35]

A key aspect of monitoring and control is evaluating the individuals involved in its development and implementation. The application of a new strategy is a very risky time for an executive and board of directors—there is always the danger that the strategy could fail. In order to successfully monitor the implementation of the strategy, executives and the board of directors must have a clear understanding not only of the strategy, but also of the strategist who developed it. How intelligent, experienced, innovative, and practical is the strategist? One of the most important characteristics to look for in a strategist is integrity. There is nothing more dangerous than a strategist who promises to deliver more than what he or she has proven to be possible through intense research. Some strategists are not entirely dishonest but will give recommendations that they have not fully researched. In these cases, an executive need not see a pattern of arbitrary decisions from a strategist. If a strategist proposes even one unstudied recommendation, he or she should not be trusted with the future of the strategizing entity. Unlike executives, strategists do not have the luxury—or the grounds—to promise something that they will not necessarily be able to deliver. Leaders and executives do this in order to make themselves stand out in interviews or elections. However, such behavior is completely inappropriate for a strategist, especially since a baseless recommendation will be implemented by the hard (and wasted) work of many other people. The strategist must give practical advice that can also be applicable. While the best strategy is always just shy of perfect, perfection is what strategists must strive to achieve even if it is not fully realistic. Dedication to this approach is what makes a strategist useful.

The International Joint Venture as a Strategic Organizational Vehicle of Globalization

Finally, prior to a strategy being incorporated into an implemented policy, the strategist must figure out what organizational forms, or vehicles, can be used to bring the management system and the approved strategy itself into practice. This is the process by which new entities and subsidiaries are established.

The global marketplace created unprecedented opportunities for private and public companies to operate and cooperate globally. Foreign trade is flourishing and, since 2002, the rate of growth of foreign trade has surpassed the growth rate of gross world product (GWP). The GWP has also grown steadily over the past 15 years due to new opportunities related to the establishment of the global marketplace and increasing consumption power. Prior to the formation of the global marketplace, companies developed many different organizational and legal forms to take their products, services, and investments abroad in order to participate and compete internationally. All of these business forms, like international agreements of cooperation, trade contracts, cross-border mergers and acquisitions, and the establishment of international joint ventures, became even more efficient with the birth of the global marketplace. The liberalization of international trade,

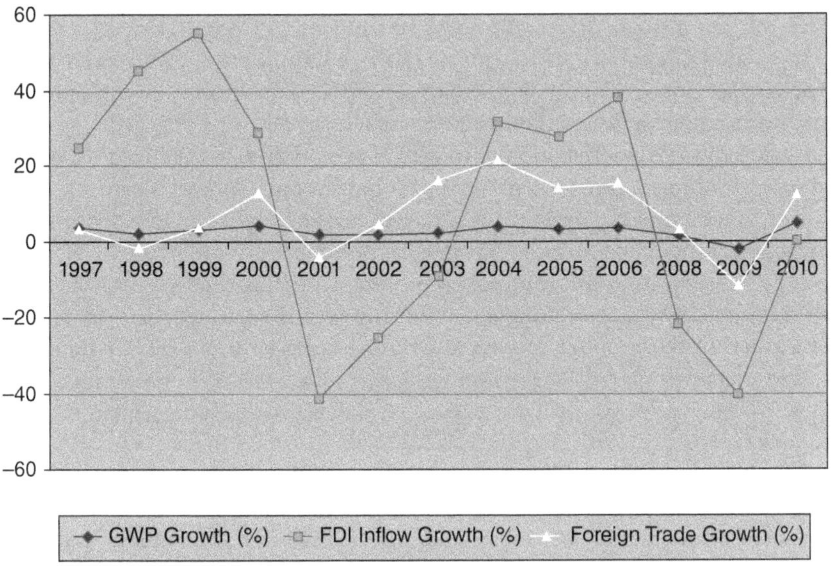

Figure 4.2 Growth Rate of FDI, GWP, and Foreign Trade

the establishment of rules by the WTO, which has already been accepted by 153 countries, the harmonization of regulations for competition and even production by major countries and regional groups like the European Union and NAFTA, as well as within regional economic organizations, has made the global workplace more productive and more predictable as a part of GMP and the global marketplace itself more open for goods and services throughout the world. All of this increased the role of cross-border transactions, trade, and investment, which developed on a faster track than the growth of domestic economies' investment and trade.

Economic Genesis of the International Joint Venture

Among the major organizational business forms of global activity, the international joint venture (IJV) was the last one to fully develop. IJVs are primarily new legal entities established by two or more parent companies from two or more countries. In most cases, one or more of the partners is from a country where the joint venture is located. It is important to underline that the establishment of a new legal entity does not result in the disappearance of the parent companies, which normally only occurs in mergers and acquisitions. In some cases, this term can refer to strategic cooperation agreements between partners from two or more countries without the establishment of a new legal entity. IJVs are particularly efficient when companies operate in political, economic, and business systems with very different characteristics from those with which one or more of the parties are familiar. They became especially relevant when dictatorships started to fail around the world and roughly 100 countries began establishing free-market economies and opening themselves to international business; this signaled the birth of the global emerging market. Companies from the developed world started to create IJVs with partners from countries that were once closed to foreigners. For example, prior to 1976 there was not a single dollar of foreign investment in China. There was no foreign investment in all 15 republics of the former Soviet Union until 1987. Even India, the most populated democracy in the world, had very strict regulations that inhibited foreign businesses from entering its market. India's reluctance was, of course, the result of its strict emulation of the Soviet economic model. Many other dictatorships throughout the world restricted foreign investment as well. In Greece, Turkey, Portugal, Paraguay, Spain, Brazil, and Argentina, foreign investment existed only on a very small scale. The transition to a free-market economy did not happen suddenly in any of these countries. Rather, most restrictions were gradually removed, a process that was slowed by many legal and economic limitations along the way. However, the greatest barriers were invisible; they existed in the mindset of people whose countries were slowly emerging from isolation and dictatorship. At the beginning of this process, the overwhelming majority of attempts by American, Western European, Japanese, and Australian investors to enter these markets failed.

Between 1988 and 1992, during the initial stages of the internationalization of what would become the GEM, only 8 out of every 100 companies from Western Europe and the United States that attempted to enter emerging markets in Eastern and Southern European countries, the former Soviet Union, Latin America, India, and China ended up being successful. It should be noted that "successful" means nothing beyond a signed international joint venture agreement. Ninety-two companies could not even accomplish this.

An analysis of the reasons for the failure of IJVs from 1988 to 1992 yielded somewhat surprising results. The most commonly cited reason was related to difficulties in finding the right partner in the foreign market. The new class of entrepreneurs in EMCs was extremely inexperienced and had no international business track record, which was further complicated by a wealth of commonly held superstitions, stereotypes, and false images regarding foreigners. They were all victims of many years of dictatorial propaganda and brainwashing. Entrepreneurs and executives from the developed world were also partially to blame for their inability to find appropriate partners. They also had no experience conducting business operations in these parts of the world and were often unable to convince local people of the benefits of signing an IJV. To make matters worse, local entrepreneurs and the general population were not totally off base with their suspicions. It was not unusual for foreigners to try to take advantage of local people and their

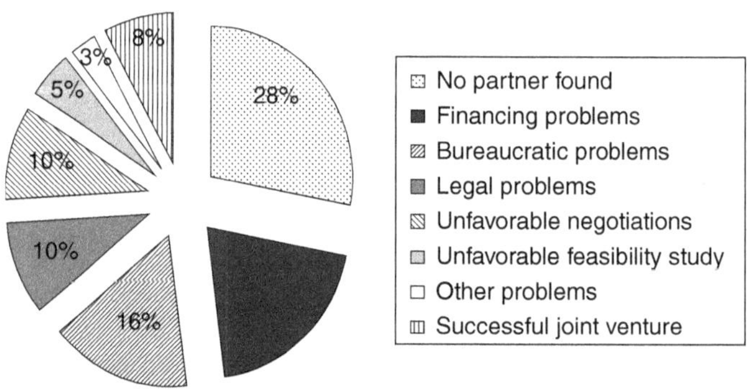

Figure 4.3 Reasons for Failure of International Joint Ventures (%), 1988–1992
© Dr. Vladimir Kvint, 2008

inexperience. As a result, an invisible wall of distrust appeared between both parties, leading to the failure of almost 30 percent of IJV agreements.

The second major reason for the widespread failure of IJVs was related to financial challenges. Financial obstacles during that time included currency inconvertibility in all emerging market countries, strict regulation of cross-border transactions and repatriation of profits, as well as the overregulation of foreign currency circulation. In the majority of EMCs, repatriation of profits in inconvertible currencies was illegal. Profits had almost no financial value to foreigners. But some entrepreneurs started to bring these inconvertible currencies abroad or to privately convert them in EMCs. Foreigners demanded the currencies of EMCs, despite their inconvertibility, because the domestic purchasing power of these currencies was stronger than that of convertible currencies. Several factors brought this about, including the fact that the official price for raw materials was usually several times lower in domestic currencies than in foreign ones. This also applied to food, fertilizer, timber, and construction materials. Some entrepreneurs recognized this situation and began collecting inconvertible currencies, which they would then exchange at a very favorable rate for themselves.

The fact that there was no operational presence of globally recognized commercial and investment banks compounded financial obstacles in the overwhelming majority of EMCs at that time. Their representative offices in these countries did not have the right to carry out any operational activity related to customer service and investment. Their purpose was only to monitor the situation and develop relationships with the rising business class and governmental authorities.

The third most commonly cited cause of failure for IJV agreements was bureaucratic barriers, which were again mostly related to the mentality, as well as the inexperience, of governmental officials and employees of regulating bodies. They were more afraid to give permission than to say no. Their inhibition to cooperate could be overcome only via bribes, which did not sit well with individuals from law-abiding countries of the developed world. This was when corruption began to flourish in EMCs.

The next most commonly cited reason for failure involved legal issues. Although many restrictions were lifted and foreign capital was allowed to operate, legal regulations in these countries were still far from being conducive to foreign business. More troublesome, in some countries, was the fact that any operations involving a foreign currency were considered illegal. Some foreigners understood how lucrative these markets could be and tried to make speculative investments in local currency, although they were inconvertible, only to find out that this was also considered illegal. This led to the widescale use of barter trade. Foreign companies would earn a profit even if they did not invest and only sold goods and services to emerging market countries without convertible currency. They reinvested these profits in local currencies into goods and commodities like oil, coal, and fertilizers, which they would then sell to companies from the developed world to finally get hard, convertible currency. Despite all of the barriers and extra effort required, companies that took the risk of providing their product for markets with inconvertible currencies made huge profits. Yet another legal issue was, and still remains today, the rapidly changing legal systems in EMCs. This is especially dangerous to foreigners because there is often a lag time between the establishment of these laws and their translation into English and other foreign languages, making it very difficult for foreigners to adhere to them.

During this period, many negotiations were ruined from the onset because each side was unfamiliar with the other's traditions and business ethics. For entrepreneurs from

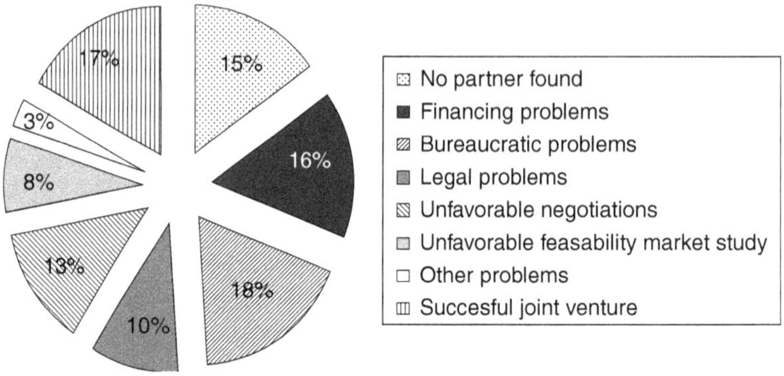

Figure 4.4 Reasons for Failure of International Joint Ventures (%), 1993
© Dr. Vladimir Kvint, 2008

many emerging market countries, especially at that time, a verbal promise meant a lot, and they did not have much respect for signed papers. American lawyers tend to want to put all details on paper. The result was awkward and embarrassing negotiations for both sides.

At that time, the results of feasibility studies were not a common cause of failure in IJV negotiations for several reasons. First of all, competition in emerging markets between companies from the developed world was very low. Second, the level of profitability was so high that as long as the company could successfully sign a joint venture agreement, it was almost a given that it would be very profitable. During that period, feasibility studies were not a significant part of IJV negotiations. It was more important to develop a trusting relationship, familiarize both parties with the respective business, and negotiate cultural differences.

By 1993, not being able to find a partner as a cause for the collapse of IJV negotiations decreased substantially from 28 percent in the previous study to 15 percent. This was the result of several factors. First, regulations in emerging market countries substantially changed, making it significantly easier for companies from the developed world to operate. In most EMCs, for example, it was no longer required to get special permission from national authorities to form an IJV, and many companies were already creating wholly owned subsidiaries or acquiring domestic companies through privatization processes. Nonetheless, if a company decided to form an IJV with a local partner(s), the procedure was the same as incorporating any other business. Partners from both sides of the negotiating table had already become more familiar with each other. In addition, currency issues became less contentious. However, the bureaucratization of EMCs continued. A certain level of anarchy in some EMCs led to an increased role for government officials, giving them more opportunities to collect bribes. Bribe-seeking bureaucrats created artificial barriers for foreigners. Despite the continued existence of these challenges, among others, after several years of internationalization in the GEM, the success rate of IJV negotiations more than doubled from 8 percent to over 16 percent.

By 1998, the reasons cited for failure began to coincide with the challenges faced during the formation of any new business entity. Of the six major causes of failure during joint venture negotiations, three were essentially taxation issues. This indicates that the focus during negotiations was not only on possible opportunities for IJVs, but also on the actual financial success of these ventures. Licensing and property law issues became

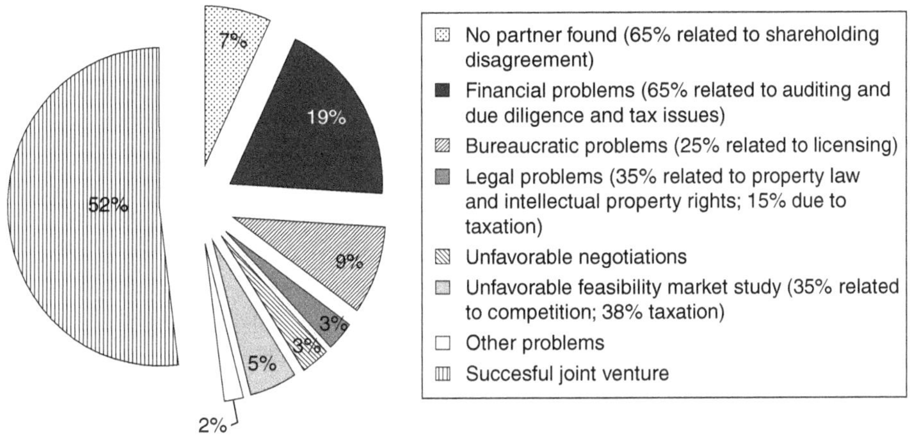

Figure 4.5 Reasons for Failure of International Joint Ventures (%), 1998
© Dr. Vladimir Kvint, 2008

a regular topic of discussion during IJV negotiations. As of 2008, in the overwhelming majority of EMCs, it is still a very difficult process to obtain ownership not only of companies and their production facilities but also of the land on which these facilities are located. In the majority of EMCs, it is more common for foreign investors to accept long-term land leases or concession agreements in place of outright land ownership. This is a serious issue during IJV negotiations that has turned off many investors, especially individuals interested in real estate. Although a more recent study has not been conducted, one could conclude, anecdotally, that by the beginning of the twenty-first century, IJVs as an organizational and legal form of global business had practically completed their maturation process.

The Letter of Intent or Memorandum of Understanding for IJV Establishment

The most important document for an international joint venture is the IJV agreement, which is usually based on the first document signed by potential partners—the letter of intent (LOI) or memorandum of understanding (MU). These non-binding documents are very important for future business relationships between partners and are used as a guideline for the IJV agreement. Although there are some exceptions, the LOI or MU is a legally unenforceable document. In most cases, the LOI or MU is the result of successful initial negotiations between potential partners. This document is used first of all to express an interest in further developing the business relationship to the level of IJV creation, and second, to agree upon an agenda for future follow-up meetings. In some cases, it will include a schedule for the introduction of all parties to each other and for the drafting of the IJV agreements. Despite the fact that these documents are non-binding, they affirm both parties' obligations to continue the development of their cooperation with each other, establishing a certain level of loyalty and trust. Signing the LOI or MU is an important step in the creation of a successful IJV.

The LOI and MU should include the official legal names and addresses of the potential partners of the IJV. The names of the partners must match the names under which they are legally registered. The companies represented by the negotiating parties must be registered before the LOI or MU is signed. These documents should also include a clear description of the potential IJV's objectives and fields of activity. Some negotiators try to keep the objectives of the company's future activity very general. There is an upside to doing this: When several general objectives are mentioned in the agreement, the company will be more flexible in later changing the direction of its business activity. On the other hand, the initial negotiations will be less focused. Nevertheless, in general, it is not a good idea to apply too many limits to potential IJV activities.

In both the LOI/MU and the IJV agreement, the role of each party must be clearly set forth—briefly in the LOI/MU and extensively in the IJV agreement. The schedule for the establishment of the IJV found in the LOI/MU does not appear in the IJV agreement. Nonetheless, the IJV agreement includes different schedules, such as an investment to registered capital ratio, the delivery of equipment, etc.

International Joint Ventures' Market Entry Strategy

IJVs became an extremely popular organizational vehicle in EMCs and a good approach for companies from the developed world to enter the GEM because they decreased uncertainty and political and economic risk for all parties. Foreign companies from the developed world gained experienced local partners who were well connected with national and local authorities. Domestic companies also provided them with existing production facilities, access to infrastructure and natural resources, and the ability to obtain licenses to access these resources. Furthermore, these domestic companies already had the appropriate personnel and could be very helpful in hiring key people to help deal with local, regional, and national authorities. Through their international foreign counterparts, on the other hand, domestic partners would get easy access to direct and indirect channels of distribution for their goods and services in the global marketplace, as well as to operational capital with lower interest rates relative to the conditions they would get from domestic commercial banks. Foreign companies also could provide them with modern information technologies and cutting-edge management systems. All of these reasons explain why IJVs have been quite successful.

For the first 20 years or so of the GEM's existence, IJVs were usually the result of the creation of new legal entities by foreign and local partners. In certain circumstances after this initial period, a new type of IJV appeared in which partners from one or more foreign countries established their own joint venture in the GEM without a local partner. This usually occurred between partners with many years of experience operating in the GEM. In this case, people who would have been partners years ago are now hired just as employees. Another new trend in IJVs is insourcing, as previously discussed, which occurs when companies and individual entrepreneurs from the GEM establish joint ventures in developed countries.

All IJVs can be divided into two major groups: equity-related and non-equity-related. Whenever a separate legal entity is established, this involves an equity-related IJV. The establishment of a long-term agreement on shared activity in emerging market countries by corporations and entrepreneurs of different national origins is a non-equity-related IJV. These can be created in order to share access to raw materials or to amicably share markets for their goods and services. The most common form of joint venture involves the creation of a new legal entity by foreign and domestic parent companies. In order to attract foreign investors, governments of EMCs developed a wide spectrum of incentives, from tax exemptions to governmental investment in infrastructure, special regimes for profit expatriation, and the import of parts and raw materials with or without lower custom duties and quotas. In order to be recognized as an IJV by a particular government, there is typically a minimum amount of foreign investment required. In some countries for a joint venture to be considered international, it must have a minimum of $100,000 of foreign direct investment (FDI). Another typical requirement is that the percentage ownership by the foreign partner cannot be less than 30. If it is less than 30, then it is treated as a domestic entity, which has its pros and cons. In many cases, an IJV forms at the end of a merger or acquisition, and never arises from a hostile takeover.

Key Factors in Considering an IJV

The first step for a foreign investor contemplating an IJV is to make a series of decisions as to the industries, countries, and particular regions in which it seeks to invest. The reasons for foreign investment have substantially changed since the initial stages of globalization. While traditional reasons, such as lower production costs and the search for new markets, still exist today, new factors have also appeared. The twenty-first century consumer demands quality products at reasonable prices. Thus, companies must produce high-quality goods at modest cost or lose their competitive advantage. This means that it is practically impossible to succeed with a GEM entry strategy of producing low-quality products while reducing production cost.

The location of an IJV within a particular EMC is a very important strategic issue. In the overwhelming majority of EMCs, territories and regions have different jurisdictions, tax regulations, and structures in terms of local and regional governmental authorities. The first priority is to learn about the existence of any territories of special jurisdiction like free-trade zones, special economic and technological zones, and domestic offshore technological parks in a potential location. In many EMCs, in order to attract foreign companies, the government and even regional authorities develop free-trade zones near seaports and around large aviation hubs. EMCs have also been eager to develop special gambling or technological zones. This trend took off in southeastern China in the 1980s in places like Shenzhen and Guangzhou. China also has other territories with special economic regulations and authorities, such as Hong Kong Special Administrative Region (SAR). One of the most well-known territories of special management and regulation outside of China is the Interoceanic Region Authority in Panama. On some occasions, when a country transitions from developing to emerging market status, the leadership of the country overestimates the opportunities for these special economic zones. For example, in the 1990s, the Republic of Georgia declared the entire country a free economic zone. Soon the government recognized that it needed taxes to finance its budget, and this regulation was officially abolished. Later, in the twenty-first century, Georgia more reasonably established a free economic zone in the Black Sea port of Poti. It is always preferable for an IJV to be located in a special economic zone.

Whether the IJV prospers depends in part on the resources available where it is located. For example, the initiator of an IJV may enter a new market with a chemical technology that consumes large amounts of water. The location of the IJV obviously must be able to provide a steady supply of suitable water, which would eliminate several potential locations. The expenses required for production in a location that suffers from water shortages would make production too difficult to render it profitable. The same holds true for an investor entering the market with an energy-intensive technology. It is crucial for investors to have detailed knowledge of the resources available in an IJV's potential location. A mistake frequently made by electro-technical companies or clothing manufacturers is to select a new market and simply assume that they can readily acquire a cheap labor force because of the low cost of living. In many EMC and developing countries, there is a shortage of skilled workers and relatively low unemployment rates. This causes the wages necessary to recruit competent workers to rise much higher than initially expected.

There are several important factors to consider when deciding on the location of an IJV, such as the development of the region (international or domestic), the presence or absence of capitalist institutions, and the availability of necessary services. The level of development of the region's capital and financial infrastructures, the host nation's trade and distribution systems, and the level of development of its telecommunications, transportation, and energy services are also key factors. For example, while China is one of the world's richest countries in labor, the low cost of this resource has often been offset by costs resulting from its poor and unreliable transportation systems, which make it difficult to obtain such resources. Because most foreign companies are located in free economic zones in coastal cities, they find it cheaper to import resources from nearby countries rather than to transport them from inland China. Another important factor is the level of development of the social infrastructure in and around the region of the potential IJV. It is important to anticipate where employees will live, eat, and find entertainment, as well as the availability of hotels, dormitories, apartment buildings, cafeterias, restaurants, movie theaters, cleaning services, among other concerns.

Management Systems of International Joint Ventures

The economic and business nature of an IJV predetermines its management system. Significant pitfalls can appear during the IJV agreement's initial negotiations and preparation. The IJV agreement, as mentioned previously, is one of the three major documents of IJV operations. The other two documents are the IJV bylaws, which are, for the most part, a reiteration of the IJV agreement except for some temporary issues related to the establishment of the company, and the IJV permission for operations from authorities of the IJV's location. The major managerial issues for IJVs are mostly related to the representation of partners on the board of directors and in its executive structure. Typically, the ratio of representation on the board of directors reflects the ratio of the IJV's initial registered capital. This does not mean that foreign partners dominate IJV boards. In most cases, foreign partners hire reputable domestic people to represent them on the board of directors. Intense discussion usually occurs about two positions: the chairman of the board of directors and the CEO. The final decision is always the result of a compromise between all parties involved. It is typical for the foreign partner to keep the chairman of the board (non-executive) position for him or herself, conceding the CEO position to the domestic partner or to his or her nominee. Some positions are relatively easy to determine. For example, it is common practice for the partner from a developed country to nominate his or her compatriots to the position of chief financial officer because EMC financiers are less familiar with international transactions and the requirements of regulating authorities in developed countries. The continuing internationalization of the GEM and its workplace will eventually lead to a situation whereby financial officers are also from EMCs.

Strategic decisions regarding the establishment of new IJVs must be consistent with the internal policy of the company considering an IJV. It is possible to use computer models to make these decisions in a process guided by experience, wisdom, and the strategist's rules mentioned in Chapter 6. Modeling allows one to choose from a variety of potential scenarios and an infinite number of possible outcomes.

An alternative to an IJV is a wholly owned venture. Sometimes wholly owned structures, rather than IJVs, are the best vehicles to facilitate a transaction. This is particularly true when those involved expect that the goals of IJV partners may diverge after a certain period or when a company seeks unadulterated control to better integrate the subsidiary into the parent company's production, sales, and marketing plans. The establishment of an investment by a new wholly owned subsidiary is often a complex and costly process, but the advantages described above may make the problems worth addressing. In the decision-making process, one must consider how difficult or easy it will be to acquire the knowledge typically supplied by IJV partners to operate alone in a foreign market.

IJV Business Negotiations as a Decision-Making Process

Executives of all entities—whether governments, small private businesses, or multinational corporations—must engage in the negotiating process at some point. But in IJVs, due to the nature of this organizational form, negotiating is almost a day-to-day activity. In the strategic management of IJVs, the negotiating process begins once the board of directors, by executive request or of its own accord, decides to develop a new strategy or revise an existing one. This process cannot begin, and a new strategic scenario cannot be implemented, without extensive discussion of this issue among all relevant parties. Due to the participation of partners from different countries, this discussion more closely resembles a negotiating process than a typical board meeting. Negotiations among IJV partners frequently unravel for several basic reasons. When two parties have equal knowledge of the market, negotiations can become overwhelmed with details, which unreasonably prolong the process. Another cause of extensive negotiation is the inability to resolve the question of how much each participant will invest. A lack of candor between partners can be a major issue as well. Too often, partners from developed countries spend a considerable amount of capital on negotiations and travel expenses only to discover that their partners have misled them or vice versa. Many companies, for instance, claim to be very profitable when they have, in fact, earned nothing. This situation is mostly a result of differences in reporting and accounting systems in EMCs and especially in developing countries. Prospective IJV partners should request documentation supporting claims of past profitability, which should be audited in accordance with internationally accepted accounting standards. Partners should agree on an auditor or a third-party fairness opinion and decide to whom, when, and how the service will be recompensed. One needs to be aware of the poor quality of a great deal of financial information in the GEM. In many cases, the accounting systems in the GEM, while improving, do not provide a realistic appraisal of products or assets. In some EMCs, concepts like current market value or liabilities barely exist. The difficulty in obtaining accurate financial data makes independent auditors all the more necessary. For this reason, parent companies' information technology and systems of collecting and analyzing data should be substantially improved and upgraded when making an IJV. In general, prospective investors who would like more information about a company from the GEM than what is included in formal reports are more likely to get accurate data from lower-level executives, such as team leaders and heads of workshops. When information is reported from lower to higher levels via several strata of the managerial hierarchy, data is intentionally or unintentionally doctored. Where possible, all data provided by the local company should be supplemented by data from national and regional authorities.

While foreigners who are victims of fraud are able to seek litigation, the amount of the settlement or judgment will probably not justify the costs and the injury to the plaintiff's reputation in the international business community. A better approach is rigorous, up-front due diligence. Foreign investors in IJVs have to try to find ways to compromise with their partners from the GEM. Even if foreigners manage to get the upper hand through the courts, depending on the EMC and the level of law and order in the country, this may not translate to a settlement in real business life. Unfortunately, in some cases, these disagreements are still resolved with bullets. The American businessman Paul Tatum, former co-owner of the Radisson Slavyanskaya Hotel in Moscow, was gunned down near the hotel in 1996, after complaining about several threats following a long series of disagreements with his local partners.[36]

The leadership's ability to understand cultural differences often determines the success or failure of an IJV. This is certainly true of IJV agreement preparation with the boards of directors of existing IJVs. Cultural differences can play a major role in the outcome of this meeting. Subject to the limitations of all generalizations, there are some basic cultural stereotypes to note. For example, Germans tend to approach the negotiation process in a thorough, systematic, but sometimes rigid manner. This results in the need for a high degree of preparation, as well as clarity and precision in communications. French and Belgian negotiators have been known to shift the course of negotiations, preferring to discuss different options of general principles before considering the specifics, which is actually a very good approach for strategic negotiations with partners from the GEM, who themselves very often fluctuate too much. The British have been known to be informal in style—flexible and open to suggestions. The danger of this approach in the GEM is that their EMC counterparts' suggestions can be too unrealistic and overly optimistic. Chinese partners may appear tediously slow to US businessmen, who may at their peril become impatient and press their partners too aggressively toward closure. Japanese negotiators often demand a close interpersonal relationship characterized by mutual trust, whereas US partners often view the development of personal relationships as needless and even harmful. It is not unheard of for partners from Korea to assent and nod their heads throughout negotiations out of politeness; in the final moment, however, they will reserve the right to say no. On entering negotiations, partners from the developed world and the GEM must be aware of the differing nuances in approaches to bargaining and should try to understand the other party's expectations.

Reliance on trust as a substitute for a formal agreement requires either strong cultural norms, under which trust is so institutionalized as to be a viable proxy for a contract, or a history of ongoing relations between the parties of the IJV. In such instances, mutual confidence compensates for a cultural environment of mistrust. Therefore, where the partner's culture is resistant to a formal contract, it may be advisable to replace the formal contract process with a negotiation and planning process.

IJV Management System Implementation: The Ignition of Strategy

The implementation of an IJV management system, as with any entity, begins with the approval of the organizational structure. Like many elements of an IJV, this structure is typically a compromise between the norms of EMCs and those of developed countries. Typically, the organizational structure of an IJV is more centralized than that of companies in developed countries; matrix systems are less common. At the beginning of its establishment and operation, an IJV typically hires many foreigners to move this project forward. In some EMCs, authorities, by both pleasant and not so pleasant means, motivate companies to hire domestic executives and managers. It is common for IJVs to employ foreigners from developed countries as executive assistants, due to their knowledge of business ethics in developed countries and their native grasp of English.

IJVs have greater flexibility in compensating employees compared with domestic companies as they can pay in the domestic currency or in foreign currencies. Most employees view such an option favorably, which makes it easier to attract more talented staff. Economic, cultural, and social differences must be considered when setting salary levels for local employees. For example, the average Russian or Ukrainian worker is often better educated than his or her US counterpart and can be an excellent employee given the proper conditions. But the average salary of a Ukrainian employee is far below that of US employees. Employers can supply amenities such as apartments, which are difficult to afford or are in short supply in many emerging market countries, to fill some of the gaps. Such amenities represent excellent ways to motivate workers and strengthen relationships between employer and employee. However, there are a number of financial obstacles that IJVs in the GEM have to deal with, such as a deficit of convertible currency, a limited number of financial institutions whose guarantees can be accepted in developed countries, and a scarcity of cash. The risk of fraud in banking transactions, which was a serious problem in the 1990s, made many European and especially American banks at the beginning of the twenty-first century substantially decrease the number of corresponding accounts in emerging market banks. In turn, this significantly complicated trade transactions between companies from the GEM and developed countries. Without corresponding accounts, even 24- to 48-hour operational loans became unavailable for companies from EMCs. Of all transactions in big international commercial banks, those related to EMCs account for 2 to 5 percent. These banks have no desire to compromise their financial reputation by having problems in corresponding relations with banks from EMCs. From this point of view, IJVs are in much better situations than the majority of domestic companies in the GEM; they can still operate with foreign counterparts, thanks to their parent companies abroad or through using their guarantee. Some of them have even had IPOs in developed countries or have been listed there via depository receipts (American-ADR or International-IDR). Few banks in the GEM accept western letters of credit because they lack working capital. Even if banks do accept letters of credit, some lend only a part of the required amount. A common practice for addressing this problem, although now decreasing in prevalence, is for foreign firms to buy raw materials from companies in the GEM and pay for them with equipment instead of cash, pursuant to a predetermined agreement. This kind of transaction is called countertrade, and is a kind of export-import operation without the direct involvement of currency.

Another form of international lending has the local manufacturer pledge a title documenting interest in a precious metal or other commodity to a bank in a third country, a practice that permits the borrower from the GEM to acquire foreign-made machinery and equipment. As the business begins to generate profit, the borrower repays the loan and, upon full payment, is returned the pledged title.

The share of initial capital investment each party contributes is important for the IJV to determine. This has very significant implications for the IJV, such as determining the division of profits. Foreign parent companies should calculate the purchasing power of currencies from emerging markets during the negotiations and recognize the value of any contributed property.

From the time of entry strategy implementation, the IJV's board of directors gathers on a regular schedule, though less often than the board of directors of domestic companies in the developed world. This is mostly due to the travel required for foreign partners. IJVs often mitigate travel costs by using IT service companies, like Cisco. There has been substantial progress in teleconferencing technologies, which has helped to reduce travel costs for IJVs. Nonetheless, in general, face-to-face board meetings take place no less than once every 45 days. A typical mistake made by foreigners from the developed world is to invite the chief executive officer to be a member of the board of directors. This obviously makes it very difficult when the board of directors has to evaluate the CEO's performance, especially since in many EMCs boards of directors have to conduct their decisions on the basis of a consensus. This is the typical situation that results in golden parachutes for fired CEOs.

During the initial stages of IJV management system implementation in the GEM, it is not unusual to have to deal with issues regarding the confidentiality of proprietary information. This is primarily related to the board of directors' decisions and materials. In some industries, foreigners have limited or no access to certain materials of strategic national importance. In other cases, governments and local authorities require that certain information be reported if it compromises the confidentiality of the board's decisions. In some EMCs, if a government creates the IJV as its partner and if the state controls more than 50 percent of shares, foreigners are not allowed to be a chairman of the board or the CEO. This has to be taken into consideration during the formation and preparation of the IJV's bylaws. Of course, the regulations cannot contradict the law of the land in which the IJV operates.

The decision-making process in IJVs is typically more efficient than that of domestic companies in the GEM. IJVs usually have much fewer managerial staff and executives compared with local companies in EMCs with similar output. Office discipline, office supplies, and information technology are almost always much higher in IJV offices. This is usually not the case in IJV offices that are the partnership solely of companies from the GEM. Nevertheless, IJVs in the GEM are still a kind of centaur—a hybrid of developed and GEM practices and traditions. Clashes related to the different cultural backgrounds of employees, their different languages, and subsequent miscommunications are a daily occurrence in IJVs. Nonetheless, this centaur is still powerful and very much alive. A key issue for IJVs is the relationship between parent companies, which are usually of different cultural backgrounds, especially during IJV strategy development and implementation. The cultural environment of the IJV's location, which may be different than that of both parent companies, often further complicates this relationship. To allow the IJV to function efficiently, it is best if the parent companies have direct control only during strategy formation and goal setting. The authority of parent companies is a very delicate issue because, legally, the IJV is an independent entity and not a subsidiary. It is especially sensitive when the parent companies do not have a shared understanding of processes of strategy formation—especially the determination of objectives and goals.

As the GEM continues to develop and mature in economic terms, a somewhat paradoxical trend is beginning to appear: EMCs are aggressively seeking foreign investment but are offering less and less special treatment to foreign companies. Companies with foreign capital are still, and will continue to be, treated somewhat differently from purely domestic companies in EMCs, be it de facto or de jure. IJVs will continue to be a very popular organizational vehicle for expanding a company's international activity, and the reasons for their failure, presented in the analysis of the 1998 IJV activities in the EMCs, will most likely not change substantially.

Notes

1 Welch, J., and Welch, S. (2007). *Winning the Answers: Confronting 74 of the Toughest Questions in Business Today*. New York: HarperCollins, p. 50.
2 Morita, A., Reingold, E.M., and Shimomura, M. (1997). *Made in Japan: Akio Morita and Sony*. New York: Penguin Group, p. 164.
3 Jung, T.H. (Ed.). (1836). *Lucien Bonaparte et ses memoires*, Paris: n.p., vol. II. p. 162.
4 Davies, B. and Davies, B.J. (2005). "Strategic Leadership." In B. Davies (Ed.), *The Essentials of School Leadership*. Thousand Oaks, CA: Paul Chapman Educational Publishing, p. 12.
5 Attributed to Alexander the Great. In Arrian. (2007). *Anabasis Alexandri*. N.p: Read How You Want Publishing, p. 7.
6 Hickson, D.J., Hinings, C.R., Lee, C.A., Schneck, R.R., and Pennings, J.M. (1971). "A Strategic Contingencies Theory of Intra-organizational Power." *Administrative Science Quarterly*, 16. pp. 216–229.
7 Freedman, M., and Tregoe, B.B. (2003). *The Art and Discipline of Strategic Leadership*. New York: McGraw-Hill, p. xv.
8 Leibold, M., Probst, G.J.B., and Gibbert, M. (2007). *Strategic Management in the Knowledge Economy: New Approaches and Business Applications*. Erlangen: Wiley-VCH, p. 136.
9 Freedman, M., and Tregoe, B.B. (2003). *The Art and Discipline of Strategic Leadership*. New York: McGraw-Hill, p. 3
10 Freely, J. (2009). *The Grand Turk: Sultan Mehmet II—Conqueror of Constantinople and Master of an Empire*. New York: Overlook Press, p. 12.
11 Raby, J. (1980). "Cyriacus of Acona and the Ottoman Sultan Mehmet II," *Journal of the Warburg and Courtauld Institutes* 43, pp. 242–246.
12 Timur. (2004). *Autobiography*. Sir H.M. Elliot (Trans.). Lahore: Sang-e-Meel Productions, vol. 1, p. 12.
13 Mockler, R.J. (2002). *Multinational Strategic Management: An Integrative Entrepreneurial Context-specific Process*. Binghampton, UK: Haworth Press, p. 230.
14 Camillus, J.C. (1998). *Strategic Planning and Management Control: Systems for Survival and Success*. Lanham, MD: Lexington Books, pp. 231–232.
15 Mockler, R.J. (2002). *Multinational Strategic Management: An Integrative Entrepreneurial Context specific Process*. Binghampton, UK: Haworth Press, p. 281.
16 *The Essentials of Strategy*. (2006). Watertown: Harvard Business School Press, p. 275.
17 Attributed to Napoleon. Cited by Sweeney, J. (1997). *Incredible Quotations: 230 Thought-Provoking Quotes with Prompts to Spark Students' Writing, Thinking, and Discussion*. New York: Scholastic Professional Books, p. 30.
18 Paquette, L. (2002). *Political Strategy and Tactics: A Practical Guide*. Hauppauge: Nova Science Publishers, Inc., p. 121.
19 World Bank. Force Majeure definition. Retrieved from http://rru.worldbank.org/Documents/Toolkits/Highways/0_outils/glossary/f.htm
20 "Kicking Ass in an Unflat World." (2007). *The Economist*. November 1. Retrieved from www.economist.com/business/displaystory.cfm?story_id=10063865
21 Cisco. Cisco TelePresence System 3200. Retrieved from www.cisco.com/en/US/products/ps9573/index.html
22 COSO. About us. Retrieved from www.coso.org/aboutus.htm
23 Galliers, R.D., and Leidner, D.E. (Eds.). (2003). *Strategic Information Management: Challenges and Strategies in Managing Information Systems*. Boston: Butterworth-Heineman, p. xi.
24 Galliers, R.D., and Leidner, D.E. (Eds.). (2003). *Strategic Information Management: Challenges and Strategies in Managing Information Systems*. Boston: Butterworth-Heineman, p. 2.

25 Hawkins, R., and Ingo, W. (1980). "Planning Multinational Operations." *Handbook of Organizational Design*. New York: Oxford University Press, pp. 253–257.
26 Attributed to Napoleon Bonaparte. Cited by Colegrove, M.B. (2005). *Distant Voices: Listening to the Leadership Lessons of the Past*. New York; iUniverse, Inc., p. 31.
27 Goodstein, L., Nolan, T., and Pfeiffer, J.W. (1992). *Applied Strategic Planning: A Comprehensive Guide*. Hoboken, NJ: Pfeiffer & Co., p. 3.
28 Goodstein, L., Nolan, T., and Pfeiffer, J.W. (1992). *Applied Strategic Planning: A Comprehensive Guide*. Hoboken, NJ: Pfeiffer & Co., p. 1.
29 "The Fading Lustre of Clusters." (2007). *The Economist*. October 11. Retrieved from www.economist.com/surveys/displaystory.cfm?story_id=9928211
30 Fogg, C.D (1994). *Team-based Strategic Planning: A Complete Guide to Structuring, Facilitating and Implementing the Process*. Boston: AMACOM, p. 3.
31 Ohmae, K. (1982). *The Mind of the Strategist: The Art of Japanese Business*. Columbus, OH: McGraw-Hill, p. 78.
32 Niẓām, M. (2002). *The Book of Government or Rules for Kings: The siyar al muluk or siyasat-nama*. Richmond, UK: Curzon Press, p. 42.
33 McGrath, M.E. (2001). *Product Strategy for High Technology Companies*. Columbus, OH: McGraw-Hill, p. 21.
34 Camillus, J.C. (1998). *Strategic Planning and Management Control: Systems for Survival and Success*. Lanham, MD: Lexington Books, p. 4.
35 Reed, M. (2002). "From the 'Cage' to the 'Gaze'? The Dynamics of Organizational Control in Late Modernity." In G. Morgan and L. Engwall (Eds.). *Regulation and Organizations: International Perspectives*. London: Taylor and Francis Group, p. 24. Referencing Zuboff, S. (1988). *In the Age of the Smart Machine: The Future of Work and Power*.
36 Kvint, V. (2005). "The Scary Business of Russia." *Forbes Magazine*. May 23. Retrieved from www.forbes.com/business/forbes/2005/0523/042.html

Part III

The Strategic Role of the Global Emerging Market in the Global Marketplace

5 A Strategic Evaluation of the Global Marketplace

A human being is part of a whole, called by us the "Universe," a part limited in time and space. He experiences himself, his thoughts and feelings, as something separated from the rest—a kind of optical delusion of his consciousness. This delusion is a kind of prison for us, restricting us to our personal desires and to affection for a few persons nearest us. Our task must be to free ourselves from this prison by widening our circles of compassion to embrace all living creatures and the whole of nature in its beauty.[1]

Albert Einstein (1879–1955)

The whole world and every human being in it is everybody's business.[2]

William Saroyan, American author and 1940 Pulitzer Prize winner (1908–1981)

Keynote Definitions

The Global Marketplace (GMP) is a strategic system of economic relationships between consumers, companies, governments, and multilateral institutions from around the world that allows real-time cooperation and competition regardless of location.

Genesis of the Global Marketplace

The formation and interaction of national economies and economies of international regions laid the foundation of the global marketplace (GMP) in the twenty-first century, a process that began more than 2,000 years ago. Through this interaction, international economic integration gradually reached a level of intensity that created a true *world economy* and the basis for the development and formation of the *global community*. Key stages of world history are typically characterized by major economic developments. In the fourth century BCE, Alexander the Great initiated economic connections between Europe, the Middle East, and Asia. Significant economic ties within and between Europe and North Africa were later created by ancient Rome. This area of the world, 2,500 years ago, known as the *ecumene*, was practically the entire known world of the Romans and Greeks. A thousand years later, by developing economic activity in Central Asia, Genghis Khan and after him Tamerlane linked the economies of Eastern and Southern Europe with those of China and the Indian subcontinent. In the fifteenth century, Christopher Columbus indelibly linked the economies of Europe and the Americas. One hundred years later, Ivan the Terrible extended economic activity to Asian Siberia, a territory larger than Europe, China, or the United States. This was one of the most important hegemonic expansions of the world economy in terms of the territory involved, second only to the discoveries of Columbus. Westernized Peter the Great, the first Emperor of Russia, established stable economic relations between Europe and Russia. Napoleon, who not only spread democracy with the sword, increased the intensity of economic integration of European nations with each other and with Russia. The Monroe Doctrine, the 1823 declaration by US President James Monroe (1758–1831), created a base for regional economic cooperation of the nations of the Americas and was later used by US President Theodore Roosevelt (1858–1919) to improve regional economic stability.[3] World War I and World War II provided the impetus for the reallocation of production facilities, and economically new territories became active and permanently involved in international business. The Bretton Woods conference in 1944 laid the foundation for the establishment of a new global order. This order rejuvenated international economic cooperation, which had been ruined by World War II and wartime economics, and caused the leading countries of the world to neglect civilian and social values, interests, and related programs. At the time, the entire world was divided into two fighting or conflicted camps; protectionism was a far less damaging issue to international economic cooperation than the impact of the war itself. The global order created at the Bretton Woods conference significantly increased and improved the world economy.

Not even the barriers to international economic activity created by the Cold War were enough to stop the boost to the world economy provided by the new global order designed at the Bretton Woods conference. In his famous Fulton Speech of 1946, Winston Churchill, the prime minister of Great Britain and Northern Ireland, referred to these barriers to international cooperation as the "Iron Curtain." This historic speech is viewed as the symbolic recognition of the Cold War, which had existed for only a few months at that time. Although the Iron Curtain did not entirely halt the birth of the global marketplace (GMP), it did significantly slow the development of international economic and business cooperation. Figure 5.2 clearly illustrates that the role of international trade in global output more than doubled after the most frigid years of the Cold War in the 1960s, allowing the GMP to become truly operational at the turn of the twenty-first century.

After World War II, the conversion of military technologies to civilian purposes brought revolutionary technological advances. This, together with relative global stability, the improvement of national economic systems in the developed world, and the

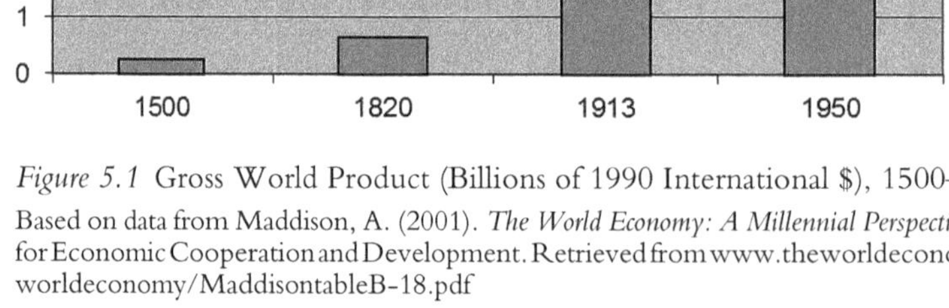

Figure 5.1 Gross World Product (Billions of 1990 International $), 1500–1950

Based on data from Maddison, A. (2001). *The World Economy: A Millennial Perspective*. Paris: Organization for Economic Cooperation and Development. Retrieved from www.theworldeconomy.org/publications/worldeconomy/MaddisontableB-18.pdf

Note: In this text GWP and global gross domestic product (GDP) are synonymous, as both indicators are a summary of the annual national GDP of all countries that annually report their GDP.

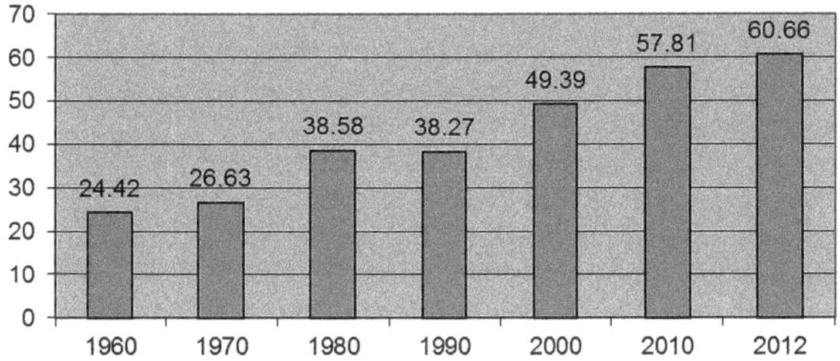

Figure 5.2 Trade as a Percentage of GWP, 1960–2012

Based on data from the World Bank World Development Indicators. Retrieved from http://data.worldbank.org/indicator/NE.EXP.GNFS.ZS

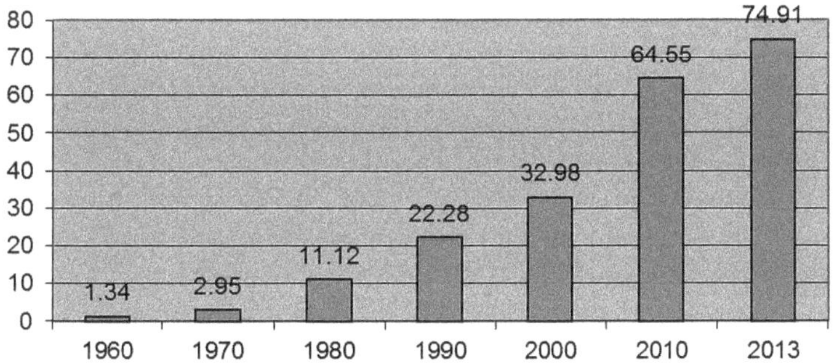

Figure 5.3 GWP (Millions of $*), 1960–2013.

Based on data from the World Bank World Development Indicators. Retrieved from http://data.worldbank.org/indicator/NY.GDP.MKTP.CD

*All figures in dollars throughout this book relate to US$ unless otherwise mentioned.

beginning of the internationalization of business, caused an immediate boost in the rate of growth of world output and greatly benefited the world economy.

During the last 20 years of the twentieth century and the first decade of the twenty-first, the global business world has gone through dramatic changes. In addition to developed and developing countries, a new economic phenomenon, emerging market countries (EMCs), has appeared and become a significant force in the world economy. This new category of countries—EMCs—is characterized by an orientation toward economic freedom and market-based economic reforms as well as by a legacy of political, social, and economic problems from their recent history as *developing countries*. In order for EMCs to reach their full economic and political maturity, these problems have to be addressed. EMCs have become partners and even competitors with developed countries. They are found in North, Central, and South America, Pacific Asia, the Indian subcontinent, Central, Eastern, and Southern Europe, in Central Eurasia in the territory of the former Soviet Union, and Northern, Central, and Southern Africa. Simultaneously, EMCs have become partners and beacons for *underdeveloped* and developing countries, which are attempting to build market-oriented economies and establish economic freedom. While they are not homogenous, EMCs share many important political, social, economic, and technological characteristics and have established significant economic ties with one another. Furthermore, the futures they seek—free-market economies and prosperity—unite them. EMCs are part of a very important new economic phenomenon—the global emerging market (GEM).

The GEM is a term that reflects a shifting economic paradigm and, to a certain extent, a new political phenomenon (see Chapter 2). The GEM has become a significant economic force as a result of the extension of the territory of global economic cooperation, i.e., the global marketplace. The formation of the GMP dramatically expanded the territory and population that participates in international economic cooperation. Opportunities found in the GEM attract entrepreneurs, business leaders, governmental officials, and even blue-collar workers to invest their money and time and in doing so bring countries of the GEM closer to the level of economic maturity of developed countries. Economic freedom in EMCs inevitably brings a new level of political freedom, according to or despite the wishes of political elites in these countries. Most EMCs are transitioning from dictatorships to free-market economies and are continuously becoming more integrated into the world economy, demonstrating a substantial level of stability, which attracts a large amount of foreign investment. EMCs organically formed the GEM, which led to the birth of a major new economic phenomenon in world economic history, the global marketplace.

The new phenomenon of the global marketplace and the involvement of EMCs in the world economy changed the pattern of global economic development. It is especially clear through the rapid expansion of the growth rate of the world economy, which began after the 1980s as a result of the failure of dictatorships, the birth of the global emerging market, and the beginning of the practical operation of the global marketplace (for a detailed analysis of this process, see Chapter 6). The average growth rate of EMCs between 1999 and 2007 was 6.5 percent. The average growth rate of developed countries was 2.75 percent during the same period.[4]

In order to understand the global marketplace, one must first understand the environment from which it arose. While it is difficult to assign the GEM an exact date of birth, it is obvious that the existence of the global marketplace (of which the GEM is a part) became possible only after the end of the Cold War, when the fall of the Berlin Wall symbolized and signaled the end of other barriers, which for many years divided national and regional businesses in the international arena and prevented them from operating on a unified territory. The collapse of the Soviet Union and other dictatorships throughout

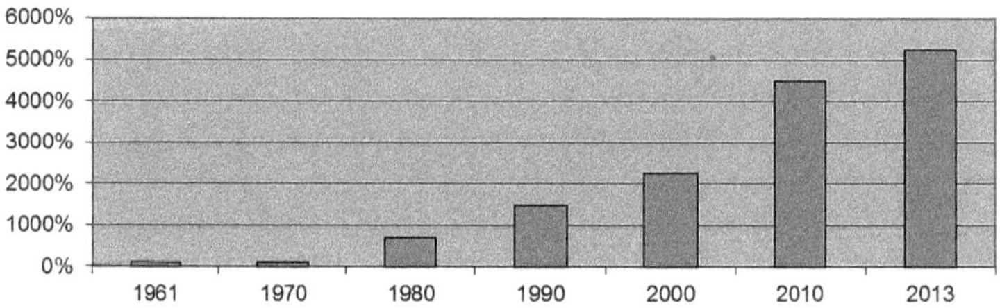

Figure 5.4 Dynamics of GWP During its Internationalization

Based on data from the World Bank World Development Indicators. Retrieved from http://data.worldbank.org/indicator/NY.GDP.MKTP.CD

Note: 1961 as 100 percent.

the world ushered in a period of unprecedented peace and prosperity, which initiated the rapid development of the unified global marketplace. While there were local and regional conflicts in many parts of the world, they were not on the global scale of the world wars or even the Cold War.

The number of people enjoying at least the basic conditions of democracy and economic freedom is unprecedented in the history of civilization, despite the remaining communist one-party system in China and Vietnam, as well as the existence of various forms of dictatorships in several other countries. Never before have individual freedoms and quality of life been valued highly by so many political and economic, national and multilateral structures. The general acceptance of democratic values, technological advancements (especially in communication), and international economic integration have created an unprecedented level of global consciousness regarding human rights, cultural and religious tolerance, environmental protection, and other "quality of life" issues. This is at once both a cause and a result of a new wave of increased political cooperation, economic integration, and the widespread dispersion of technological advancements, creating a virtuous cycle, leading to extraordinary improvements in the standard of living of most of the global population, despite the sad fact that the majority of the world's people still live in poverty. For the first time, the majority of nations share an orientation toward the achievement of prosperity for their people and global cooperation. These processes lead to the formation of not only the global marketplace but also its very important subsystem, the global workplace, in which companies cooperate in development and production of goods and services. The products of this cooperation are marketed, advertised, distributed, and sold in the global marketplace. Increasing standards of living across the globe are largely a result of these integration processes. All of this is an incredible achievement of human civilization that cannot be overemphasized. Of course, the world is far from perfect, and substantial segments of the world population do not enjoy these accomplishments. Extending prosperity to these segments is one of the most formidable challenges facing contemporary civilization; attempts to solve these challenges are leading to the creation of a new global order.

The World Economy and the Global Marketplace

Although they share some mutual characteristics, the global marketplace and the world economy are two distinct economic phenomena and terms. The world economy consists of the sum of human economic activity. Ever since humans began hunting and gathering and domesticating plants and animals, the world economy has existed. At that point in human history, of course, most of the planet's surface was uninhabited or covered in permafrost or water. Although it was clearly far from global, a primitive world economy existed. For centuries, several nations and regions demonstrated economic growth and failure in the Middle East, North Africa, the Americas, Southeast Asia, Central Eurasia and Europe. In the fourteenth century, human economic activity became increasingly sophisticated, especially in Europe under the influence of the Renaissance. However, the world economy was still not global, as European civilization was largely ignorant to the existence of American, African, Far Eastern, and Australian civilizations and vice versa. The world economy began to globalize toward the end of the eighteenth century as major geographic discoveries started influencing everyday business life. However, the world economy consisted of several distinct domestic economies that were essentially isolated from one another. The necessities that economic interests and technological advancement generated were not yet in place to integrate these economies. Political conflict and war throughout the twentieth century further hindered economic integration and the creation of a unified marketplace that included most of the world. The end of the Cold War and failures of most dictatorships throughout the world, the widespread utilization of new technological achievements in transportation and telecommunication, and the increasing liberalization of international trade and other cross-border economic relations led to continuous cooperation of almost all countries in the world economy. All of these drastic changes led to the moment when the critical mass of international economic cooperation brought the business world to a new level of tight economic integration—the global marketplace and its subsystem, the global workplace. At that moment civilization had become so unified in economic terms that some authors described the world economy as the global economy due to the fact that the world economy has many unique characteristics that, alone, any single nation does not. This is, for example, the opinion of Professor Horst Siebert, of Johns Hopkins University, who presents the world economy as a single entity under the influence of globalization, the increasing role of multilateral institutions, and regional integration. Despite these trends, he also underlines conflicts between states related to the development of the world order. The key issues that have affected the world trade system since the turn of the millennium are thus very much to the fore.[5] However, Professor Siebert's opinion actually describes some characteristics of the world economy's segmentation. The world economy still consists of national economies at extremely different levels of maturity. This point can be illustrated by a comparison of the economy of the United States to that of Afghanistan. Some countries are still economically self-isolated, as Myanmar is from Canada or any European nation. In technological terms many national economies cannot be described by characteristics of the so-called global economy. In some countries, such as Bangladesh, the majority of people have never made a telephone call. Even within individual countries, especially those with large territories and/or populations, there is a great deal of disparity in terms of economic and technological development. In India, despite sophisticated information technology in many cities, as of 2007 less than 10 percent of households in rural areas have telephone access. In Eastern Europe and the poorest areas of some of the former Soviet Republics, electricity is still not available in every village. In sub-Saharan Africa, only 8 percent of people in rural areas have access to electricity.[6] The world economy is still in the process of strengthening integration, and is not truly global. More than that, the differences in the development of national economies are still increasing, not decreasing. The process of economic development of the world economy has been

> uneven in space as well as time. The rise in life expectation and income has been most rapid in Western Europe, North America, Australasia and Japan. By 1820, this group had forged ahead to an income level twice that in the rest of the world. By 1998, this gap was 7:1. Between the United States (the present world leader) and Africa (the poorest region) the gap is now 20:1. This gap is still widening.[7]

However, in terms of the global integration of companies from different countries, the development of a world economy is a reality. Despite a lack of global economic harmonization, businesses, even from countries as self-isolated as Myanmar or Belarus, cooperate with international companies. The cooperation of individual businesses from *all* national economies initiated the creation of the global marketplace. The potential creation of the global economy is a different story. A truly global economy would require the complete economic integration of national economies, which will not happen for a long time. This is why there are two related but distinct phenomena—the world economy and the global marketplace. The GMP is part of the world economy, where businesses from around the world cooperate, compete, and merge with each other. One day this will lead to the formation of the global economy.

Defining the Global Marketplace (GMP)

Companies have conducted international activity for hundreds of years. The first economic transactions of a global scale occurred in the sixteenth century, when companies from Europe, Asia, America, and even Australia occasionally conducted intercontinental transactions. However, the global marketplace began to take form only when technological advancements in telecommunications and information technology (IT) allowed the practically instant transmission of business information, regardless of distance. This occurred when the necessity for the physical delivery of paper confirming business transactions no longer existed, and telegraph, fax, and, eventually, the Internet could immediately confirm transactions.

The first and most symbolically important instantaneous international business transaction occurred on March 30, 1867, in the intercontinental marketplace, the precursor of the global marketplace. On this date, US Secretary of State William Seward sent a cable to the president, Andrew Johnson, from St. Petersburg, Russia. The cable announced the US purchase of Alaska from Russia for $7.2 million. Immediate transfer of information was possible only because of the completion of the transatlantic telegraph cable, which occurred less than a year earlier on July 18, 1866. This established the technological conditions necessary for the formation of the intercontinental marketplace. The technological conditions necessary for the global marketplace emerged 36 years later, when in 1902 a telegraph connection was established across the Pacific Ocean. The world was unified by people's ability to send and receive practically instant information regarding any transaction to and from all major business centers of the world.

The emergence of the global marketplace can be described through an understanding of its various stages of development. Although international-trade transactions first occurred centuries before the implementation of overseas telegraph lines, it was the ability to get instant information about business transactions and to make immediate payments that provided the technological conditions necessary for the birth of the global marketplace.

The first basic conditions for global trade were established at least by 1522 when Ferdinand Magellan completed his voyage around the world. The widespread practice of international economic and business transactions between governments, businesses, and with individual customers on a regular basis, and the establishment of long-term agreements regarding these transactions, was the next stage of the GMP's development. The final stage took place when economic liberalization advanced to the point when transportation between countries and continents became part of the production process. When raw materials, energy resources, components, parts, and all other types of supplies, regardless of their place of origin, were delivered on schedule anywhere in the world to be enriched, assembled, and sold, the GMP reached its current stage of maturity. This created the global supply chain, which is an essential aspect of the GMP. Distance and time are no longer significant barriers to international supply chains, production, sales, and marketing. However, it is very important to note that there is one crucial element needed in order for the GMP to function—economic freedom. Without economic freedom, consumers and producers would be incapable of taking advantage of technological conditions. Prior to the end of the twentieth century and the collapse of most dictatorships, such was the case. Most consumers and producers were incapable of exploiting technological advances, which greatly inhibited the development of the GMP. The global marketplace is a child of technological advancement and economic freedom.

The key historical events that allowed the GMP to become operational were the internationalization of the Chinese economy (initiated by Deng Xiaoping in 1976), the fall of the Berlin Wall in 1989, and the opening of India to international business in the mid-1990s. The development of international regional economic and trade blocs at the end of the twentieth century and the establishment of the World Trade Organization in December 1994 significantly aided the formation of the GMP. The constant improvement of international communications and information technology continue to expand the GMP's reach, while the continuing development of the GMP is increasing global supply-chain efficiency and vice versa. The GMP is a venue without borders, owned by no one. It is open 24 hours a day, year round to anyone who would like to participate in international business as a producer, salesperson, or buyer and has access to the necessary technology, funds, and economic freedom. The global marketplace is the major engine of the world economy of the twenty-first century and can be defined as a strategic system of economic relationships between consumers, companies, governments, and multilateral institutions from around the world that allows real-time cooperation and competition regardless of location.

It is difficult to give an exact date of birth for the GMP. Nonetheless, its existence is indisputable. It became operational on the border of the twentieth and twenty-first centuries. Further development of the GMP will be the result of new technological achievements and the continued liberalization of national and international laws and under-law regulations. These processes will improve general standards of the quality of life by facilitating tighter business cooperation, improving the efficiency of the world economy, global business, and all participants of the GMP in general.

Economic Integration in the Global Marketplace

Local, regional, and even national markets have all been integrated within the GMP. This has created new challenges not only for national governments, multilateral institutions, and multinational corporations, but also even for small companies operating in local or regional markets. Small companies have had to drastically reassess their strategies, in terms of sources of raw materials, scale of production, price setting, marketing, advertising, etc. Even when a company operates exclusively in a local market, it must be strategically prepared for global competition. In the GMP, individual entrepreneurs, companies of all sizes, governments, and multilateral institutions cooperate and compete for the utilization of basic economic factors. Through these processes these various players must efficiently achieve the appropriate balance between global supply and demand and further global economic integration.

In addition to the above-mentioned processes, the creation of the global financial system has significantly increased the level of global integration. Financial transactions can be made from the most remote parts of the world via the Internet. Vendors can buy, sell, and deliver products to and from consumers and producers around the world, cheaper and faster than ever before. Experts from around the world, once separated by distance and national borders, can collaborate, further accelerating technological progress and innovations. Peter Mandelson, commissioner for external trade of the European Union, emphasized the significance of the process of global economic integration in his Alcuin Lecture in February 2008:

> In 1990 two in 10 people on this planet lived in societies that were significantly integrated into a global economy ... Today about nine in 10 do. That is more than three billion people and probably one billion workers entering the global economy—pretty much creating the modern global economy—in less than two decades. This is the single most important change you need to grasp to understand the modern world. We are living in the wake of an openness boom.[8]

The development of the knowledge-based economy (discussed later in this chapter) is a direct result of such collaboration and could not exist without the GMP. Distance-learning programs and virtual universities allow students in South African desserts, Siberian taiga, and the Brazilian jungles to participate in classrooms of the best universities of the world without leaving their native area. Constant cross-cultural exchange in the GMP is both a factor and product of global integration. The scale of the impact of the GMP on humanity is unprecedented. People and companies, once divided by time, space, and national borders, have deeper economic and business connections than next-door neighbors of a typical village two centuries ago.

In the few remaining dictatorships, it is almost impossible to keep entrepreneurs, companies, and economies totally isolated from the GMP. Information no longer recognizes national borders. Practically all vertical industries and regional economies collaborate under one global economic system. Under the Iranian dictatorship, for example, Iranian companies experience two types of barriers—those created by their own government and those created by international sanctions against the Iranian regime. Nonetheless, even Iranian companies conduct some international transactions. Despite the desire of the military junta of Myanmar to be self-isolated, it cannot avoid international collaboration. In order to control its population, the junta imports military equipment. By doing so it has begun to pull back its iron curtain and collaborate with the GMP, as military helicopters imported from India contain technology and components produced in six European countries.[9] The Chinese Communist Party may be able to maintain political restrictions, but unlike in Iran, Chinese companies, as well as the Chinese economy and financial system, actively participate within the GMP.

The business community of the GMP is more inclusive than ever before. It is no longer a club of the elite entrepreneurs and companies of rich nations. Companies and individuals can access the GMP regardless of their size, wealth, or country of origin. The equalizing effects of the GMP cannot be overemphasized. Prior to its existence, there was not a single billionaire outside of the developed world. In August 2007, the richest man in the world was Carlos Slim,[10] who amassed his fortune in Mexico, an EMC. Slim is a product of globalization himself, as the descendant of an émigré from Lebanon. Prior to 1987, the Soviet Union, which covered one-fifth of the Earth's surface, did not receive a single dollar of foreign investment, nor did it have a single domestic millionaire. Twenty years later, in Moscow alone there are more billionaires than in New York City. It is, however, important to point out that individual entrepreneurs and small companies do not participate in the GMP in the same way as multinational corporations. Multinational corporations have always been involved in international business, unlike individuals and small businesses, which have traditionally focused on domestic markets or even futilely attempted to isolate themselves from the GMP.

The GMP provides an arena for foreign and domestic producers of goods and services to compete for consumers' purchasing power throughout the world. Increased efficiency, lower prices, and a constant search for innovation are a direct result of global competition. This is obviously very beneficial to consumers. However, one should not make the mistake of romanticizing economic liberalization. While the GMP could not function without it, national governments still play a crucial role in the GMP. Governments, especially in EMCs, enforce law and order, the standards of cross-border trade and investment, the protection of property and intellectual rights, as well as the maintenance of crucial infrastructure. Without governmental regulation there would be complete anarchy, which would make it impossible for the GMP to function. Yet no government controls the GMP itself, and nor can any national government be forced upon it. Not even the most influential multilateral institutions, whether the World Trade Organization, the World Bank, or the IMF, have the authority or ability to manage the GMP. However, they do have the right to regulate the activity of individual companies and national governments. Global institutions are given this right by the national governments of their member countries, which in turn are authorized by their citizens and companies through the democratic process (although in some countries the process is still only semi-democratic or not democratic at all). Nonetheless, international laws allow national governments to approve or disapprove decisions of multilateral institutions if the country is a member of the institution. Voluntary cooperation and competition resulted in the GMP. Governments and regional managerial bodies initiate and provide a dialectic response to global economic liberalization. They aim to protect domestic and regional markets and producers from unfair competition and unsafe products from abroad and create easy entry conditions into foreign markers for their exports. A proper balance between government intervention and economic liberalization allows consumers around the world to enjoy a more efficient, prosperous, and safe life as a result of the GMP. However, conditions in the GMP as a whole are far from uniform—the opportunities for rich and poor countries vary substantially. The GMP is not only a network of goods and services but also, most important, a system of economic relationships between consumers, companies, and governments that produce and exchange goods, services, and knowledge through a multitude of channels.

For centuries, international business was much less valuable than domestic business. But today it is very difficult to find a business that is exclusively domestic. The GMP is far from the mere sum of global national economic activity, however. After all, the GMP exists even in neutral territories that do not belong to a country, such as international waters.

Many individuals and companies that never intended to engage in international business are active participants in the GMP. In a small corner grocery store in Manhattan there are products from an average of 40 different countries, which are sold to customers who have come to New York from around the world. Even when entrepreneurs or companies try to isolate themselves from the GMP or are ignorant of its existence, in reality, it is impossible to operate without interacting (through cooperating or competing) with players of the GMP. But most companies and individuals purposefully increased their global business because it is more efficient and profitable. The GMP provides unprecedented access to the benefits of international trade. However, with such deep cooperation, the implications of political, economic, and financial events are more widespread than at any point in human history.

It would be naïve to argue that international business and the GMP have had only a positive impact on humanity. Some of the most daunting challenges facing contemporary civilization, such as global terrorism, the global trade of illicit goods (especially drugs), illegal immigration on a global scale, large-scale ecological destruction, etc., would not exist without the GMP. The resolution of these challenges will require collaboration between private companies, governments, and multilateral institutions. The GMP is a global sea of business, where the ripple effect of both positive and negative actions and decisions reaches all shores. As a result, there is a need for new regulations for all participants.

Technological advancement, increasing economic liberalization, and cross-cultural exchange are the driving forces behind the maturation of the GMP. However, there is an important cultural aspect to the GMP. Nevertheless, the dominant forces are economic and business related.

Strategic Evaluation of the World Economy and the Global Marketplace

The formation and operation of the global marketplace gave a boost to world economic development, increasing the sustainability and rate of growth of the world economy. Figure 5.5 demonstrates the growth of gross world production (GWP) in absolute numbers in terms of the exchange rate since 1990.

Prior to the birth of the GMP, when international business activity was limited to North America, Western Europe, Japan, and Australia, comparisons of GDP provided an accurate picture of the relative strength of different national economies (see Figure 5.5). Comparing GDP per capita (GDP divided by national population) was a simple and practical way to evaluate the efficiency of different economies, their stages of development, and the standards of living of their populations relative to other countries. This indicator is still a relatively efficient means of comparing the economic power of different countries. With time, the majority of the world's largest economies will be EMCs.

Among the traditional participants of international business (developed countries), there were well-established ratios between respective currency values, interests, economic and industrial structures, consumption, and quality of life. This situation totally changed when the

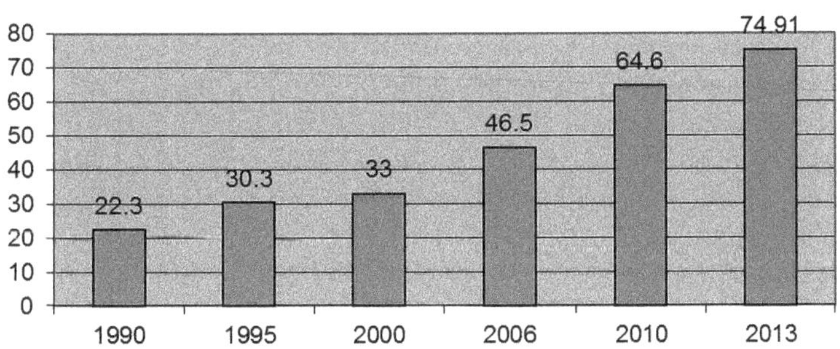

Figure 5.5 Development of GWP During the Formation of the GMP (Trillions of $)

Based on data from the World Bank World Development Indicators. Retrieved from http://data.worldbank.org/indicator/NY.GDP.MKTP.CD

Table 5.1 GDP (Exchange Rate) of the Ten Largest Economies ($), 2014

Rank	*Country*	*Gross Domestic Product (Trillions of $)*
1	United States	16.8
2	**China**	9.24
3	Japan	4.9
4	Germany	3.63
5	France	2.73
6	United Kingdom	2.52
7	**Brazil**	2.25
8	**Russian Federation**	2.1
9	Italy	2.07
10	**India**	1.87

Based on data from the World Bank World Development Indicators. Retrieved from http://econ.worldbank.org/WBSITE/EXTERNAL/EXTDEC/0,,menuPK:476823~pagePK:64165236~piPK:64165141~theSitePK:469372,00.html
Note: in all tables in this book, EMCs will appear in bold.

Table 5.2 GDP per Capita (International $), 2014

Rank	*Country*	*Gross Domestic Product per Capita (International $), 2013*
1	Luxembourg	111161.6877
2	Norway	100818.5032
3	**Qatar**	93352.02408
4	**Macao SAR, China**	91376.02254
5	Switzerland	80477.42753
6	Australia	67468.06871
7	Denmark	58893.99899
8	Sweden	58269.03005
9	**Singapore**	55182.48279
10	United States	53142.88963

Based on data from the World Bank World Development Indicators. Retrieved from http://econ.worldbank.org/WBSITE/EXTERNAL/EXTDEC/0,,menuPK:476823~pagePK:64165236~piPK:64165141~theSitePK:469372,00.html

GMP became operational. As of January 2014, the GEM accounts for 56.3 percent of the GWP in purchasing power parity (PPP). Since 2008, the GEM is continuously producing more than 50 percent of GWP in PPP. Evaluation of the same indicators, not in PPP, but in exchange rate or even calculated in current US dollars gives three substantially different answers. Table 5.3 demonstrates the role of the GEM in 2007 according to calculations by US$ in the exchange rate. Successful development of the GEM during the following five years can be significantly taken off when calculations will be done in current US$. With use of this measurement, the total GDP of the GEM as of 2013 is equal to $31,807 billion, which counts for 41.5 percent of the role of EMCs in the GWP (see Table 5.4). Nonetheless, evaluation of this indicator by any of these three measurements clearly demonstrates continuous enforcement of the role of the GEM in the world economy.

The economic and industrial structure and standards of living in emerging market countries are diverse and substantially different from those of developed countries. In the developed world, when GDP per capita increases, it means that GDP growth has

Table 5.3 The Role of the GEM and Developed Countries in the GMP (in Exchange Rate of US$), 2007

Total GDP of the GEM (Billions $)	$29,908	Total GDP of Developed Countries (Billions $)	$30,356
GEM GDP as a % of GWP	45.44%	Total GDP of Developed Countries as a % of GWP	46.02%
Developed Countries and EMCs GDP as a % of GWP	91.64%	Total GDP of Developing Countries as a % of GWP	8.44%

 Calculations based on statistics from the World Bank World Development Indicators, 2007. Retrieved from http://econ.worldbank.org/WBSITE/EXTERNAL/EXTDEC/0,,menuPK:476823~pagePK:64165236~piPK:64165141~theSitePK:469372,00.html

Table 5.4 The Role of the GEM and Developed Countries in the GMP (in Current US$), 2013

Total GDP of the GEM (Billions, Current $)	$31,807	Total GDP of Developed Countries (Billions, Current $)	$40,873
GEM GDP as a % of GWP	41.50%	Total GDP of Developed Countries as a % of GWP	53.40%
Developed Countries and EMCs GDP as a % of GWP	94.90%	Total GDP of Developing Countries as a % of GWP	5.10%

 Based on data from the World Bank (2014). GDP (current US$). Retrieved from http://data.worldbank.org/indicator/NY.GDP.MKTP.CD

outpaced population growth. This indicates an overall improvement in standards of living. However, in all EMCs the cost of living varies among regions and strata of society to the extent that national GDP per capita growth does not necessarily indicate a general improvement in average standard of living. In the GEM extreme wealth and extreme poverty occur within a single national economy. In fact, the city with the highest cost of living is not New York, Zurich, or London, but one from the GEM—Moscow. Furthermore, it is difficult to compare the economic quality of life of people in countries with limited convertible or inconvertible currencies with that of people in developed countries who have freely convertible currencies in their pockets. Such comparisons are of great importance when a company is developing its strategy to enter or expand its activity in the GMP.

As cultural, economic, business, and financial ties strengthened between the developed world and the GEM, the practical needs of strategists led to the use of more-sophisticated economic indicators, such as the purchasing power parity (PPP) methodology. Although the Swedish economist Gustav Cassel developed this concept in 1920, its application to GDP and GDP per capita[11] was widely implemented and studied as a result of the expansion of international business and the formation of the GMP. Purchasing power parities (PPPs) are currency conversion rates that both convert to a common currency and equalize the purchasing power of different currencies. In other words, they eliminate the differences in price levels between countries in the process of conversion. This makes it much easier for strategists, executives, investors, etc., to compare the economies of different countries. Table 5.5 lists the ten largest economies in the world in terms of purchasing power parity. The GDP of the GEM as a whole in terms of PPP is more than double the US GDP. It is important to note that the GEM does not include the input of developing and underdeveloped countries.

Table 5.5 GDP PPP (Billions of $), January 2014

Rank	*Economy*	*Gross Domestic Product, PPP (Billions $), 2013*
	World	99,169
	GEM	55,030
1	United States	16,768
2	**China**	16,161
3	**India**	6,776
4	Japan	4,641
5	Germany	3,585
6	**Russian Federation**	3,460
7	**Brazil**	3,012
8	France	2,500
9	United Kingdom	2,464
10	**Indonesia**	2,389

© Dr. Vladimir Kvint, 2015. Based on data from the World Bank World Development Indicators. Retrieved fromhttp://data.worldbank.org/indicator/NY.GDP.MKTP.PP.CD?order=wbapi_data_value_2013+wbapi_data_value+wbapi_data_value-last&sort=desc

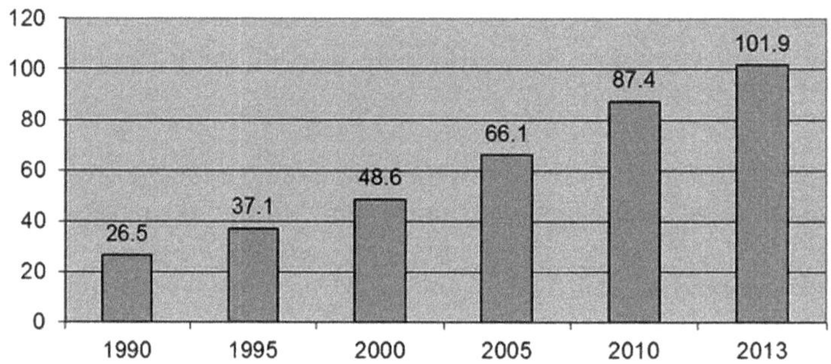

Figure 5.6 GWP PPP During the Period of the Formation of the GEM (Trillions of Current $)
Based on data from the World Bank World Development Indicators. Retrieved from www.imf.org/external/pubs/ft/weo/2014/02/weodata/weorept.aspx

Table 5.5 differs substantially from Table 5.1, which lists the top ten national GDPs in terms of exchange rate. In terms of GDP PPP, China is the second biggest economy in the world; its economy is already more than twice the size of Japan's (even before the tragic events of 2011). The same comparison in terms of exchange rate provides strategists with the same picture in different colors. China is slightly ahead of Japan, and has surpassed three European economic giants, Germany, Great Britain, and France. Because the aim of purchasing power parity is to adjust the exchange rate to equalize the price of the same products in different countries, it tremendously increases GDP figures of countries with lower-priced goods. This is why, with the increasing role of the GEM in the world economy, the GWP rate of growth will accelerate.

GDP PPP per capita is an even more integrated economic indicator. First, it provides a better understanding of the efficiency of national economies. And it is more effective to use this indicator to compare economies than an evaluation of GDP in terms of exchange rate. Different dynamics of dollar and national currency values and their

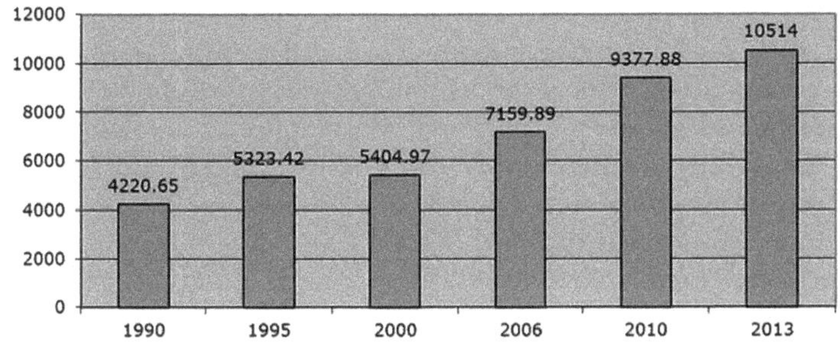

Figure 5.7 GWP per Capita (Current $).

Based on data from the World Bank World Development Indicators. Retrieved from http://data.worldbank.org/indicator/NY.GDP.MKTP.CD

differing purchasing power can distort the actual efficiency of national economies. Regardless, the GWP per capita has also risen steadily and rapidly since 1990, during the formation and operation of the GMP.

An evaluation of GDP in terms of exchange rate reflects the strengths of a particular country's currency relative to the world banking currency—the US dollar. However, it does not represent the purchasing power of currency for the general population of a given country. The exchange rate is heavily influenced by the global money market. If the currency of an economy is strong, international financial speculators will invest in this currency.

A number of factors can influence the strength of national currencies. Significant foreign-currency reserves attract international financial speculators, which changes the ratio of that country's currency to the dollar. A large foreign-trade surplus and a high volume of international trade also increase the ratio of the domestic currency to the dollar. Contrary to popular opinion, the consumer purchasing power tends to decrease as national currency strengthens. The stronger a currency, the more expensive a nation's exports become, making them less competitive internationally. This causes an increase in imports for the country with the strong currency, which results in an increase in the cost of first-necessity goods and food. The more people buy imported goods, the more they have to pay when their currency gets stronger, relative to the dollar and other foreign currencies. For regular consumers, a stronger domestic currency results in more expensive goods also because the company importing goods from abroad has to pay more for the same product. This will also factor in to the rise in consumer prices. None of these issues are accounted for when GDP is presented in terms of exchange rate.

While GDP and GDP per capita in terms of PPP are very useful indicators for academic and practical purposes, they do not take into account several factors, such as varying rates of inflation in different industries and goods, which can have a profound impact on the standard of living and business environment of an economy. When using these indicators for any purpose, it is important to consider the different industrial structures and production costs across economies. Two countries may have the same GDP per capita in terms of PPP but substantially different ratios of investment, employee compensation, or energy consumption per unit of GDP. Variations in these factors create substantially different business environments. In December 2007, the World Bank's International Comparison Program, in cooperation with the statistical office of the European Union (EU),

Eurostat, and the Organization of Economic Cooperation and Development (OECD), released a report on comparative price data. This report established a new estimation of purchasing power parities for 146 national economies based on economic data from 2005. Previous purchasing-power estimations were based on data as much as 30 years old. During this period, individual and governmental consumption have totally changed, especially in EMCs, due to improvements in standards of living and the decreasing role of governments during privatization processes. In order to reflect these changes, the new estimation surveyed prices for approximately 1,000 products and services in emerging and developing economies. The reevaluation of PPP has tremendously changed the relative size of many national economies. For some countries, such as China, this was the first collection of accurate information, since previous estimates were done during the time of totalitarian regimes or the early stages of free-market development. The survey and its updated data decreased estimations of China's GDP PPP by 40 percent and found that

> China still ranks as the world's second largest economy with around 10 percent of world production and India is the fourth largest with over 4 percent of the world total. Overall, the 2005 benchmark results show that the size of the world economy measured in PPP terms is smaller than previously estimated. The Asian and African economies (excluding high-income and oil-exporting economies) are one-third and one-fifth smaller, respectively. However, Asia still accounts for over 20 percent of the world's output. [12]

Prior to the expansion of the GMP, far fewer countries participated in international business. In order to more accurately reflect the scale of the GMP, the survey collected data and estimated the purchasing power parity of individuals and governments in 39 countries for which these estimates had never been made.[13] The International Monetary Fund also revised its estimates of global economic growth in PPP by an average of half a percentage point each year from 2002 to 2007. "In 2007, for example, the IMF's estimate of global growth was revised down to 4.7 percent from 5.2 percent in the October 2007 *World Economic Outlook*" (see Figure 5.8).[14]

Aggregate data, such as GDP or GDP per capita, can be analyzed using several methods. One approach is to analyze *the industrial structure of GDP or GWP*. The industrial structure of GWP has gone through many changes over the past 70 years. Following World War II, the leading economies of the world were still undergoing the process of industrialization. Most GDP in the majority of countries came from agriculture, followed by industry and services. A country's economy was considered very modern if more GDP came from the industrial sector than the agricultural sector. By the late 1970s and early 1980s, the world's most modern economies had entered the post-industrial stage of development, and the service sector accounted for the largest percentage of national GDP. In addition to the obvious economic importance of this achievement, there are significant social implications, as "a post-industrial society, being primarily a technical society, awards place less on the basis of inheritance or property (though these can command wealth or cultural advantage) than on education and skill."[15]

In the twenty-first century, all developed countries are post-industrial and service-based economies. For example, the historically first industrial economy in the world—Great Britain—in 2011 owed about 13 percent of GDP to light and heavy industry. Some countries have already entered a new stage—the knowledge-based

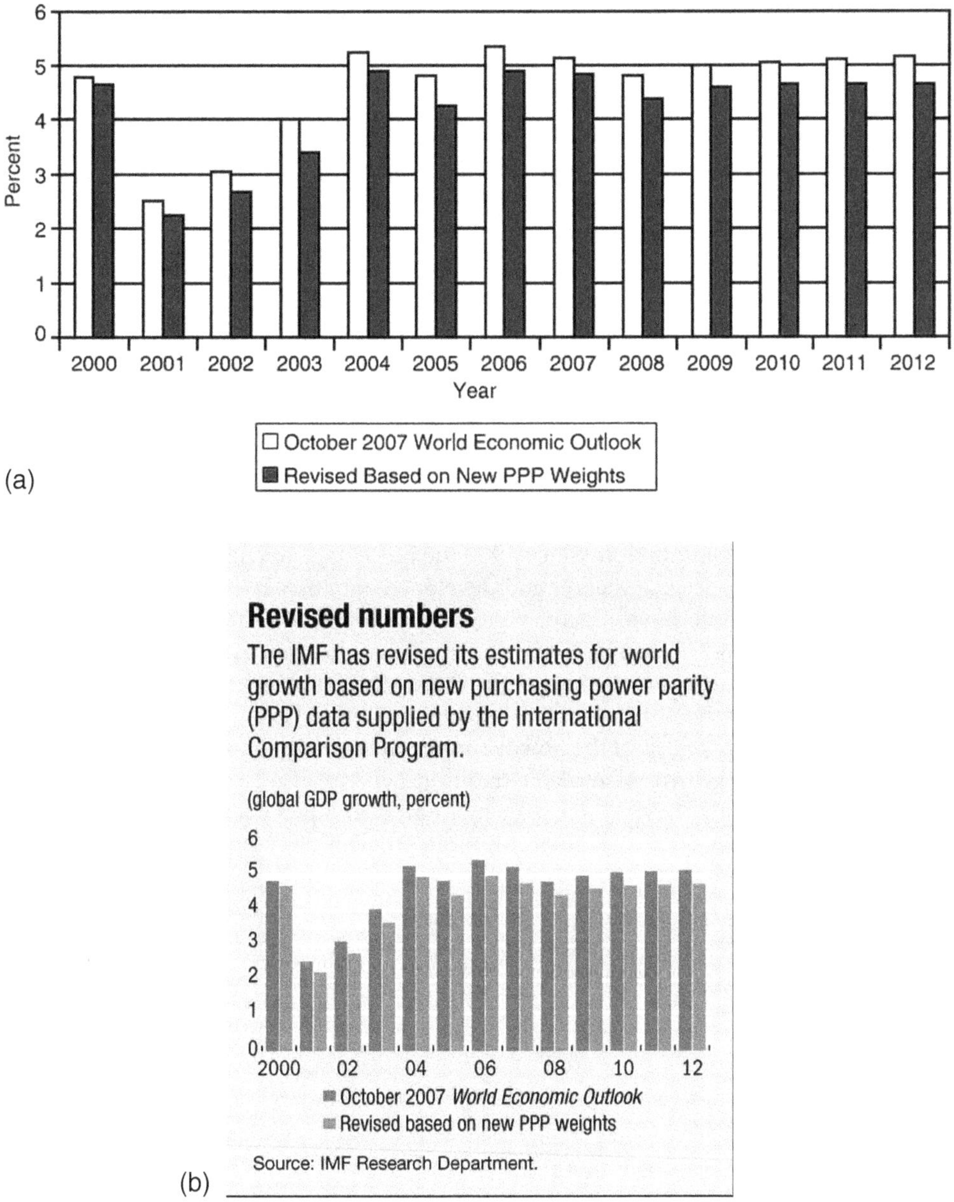

Figure 5.8a and 5.8b Revised GWP Growth by New PPP Methodology

Elekdag, S. and Lall, S. (2008,). "Global Growth Estimates Trimmed After PPP." *IMF Survey Magazine*. January 8. Retrieved from www.imf.org/external/pubs/ft/survey/so/2008/RES018A.htm

economy (or knowledge economy). This transition occurs when a substantial part of national GDP comes from the science, technology, and education sectors. A few EMCs, such as the Czech Republic, Israel, Slovenia, Taiwan, Hungary, and South Korea have also reached this stage of development and can be considered knowledge economies.[16]

As a whole EMCs are a diverse group, and most are far less advanced. Some, in fact, are still agricultural economies—Ghana, Guatemala, and India—whereby agriculture accounts for about 40, 21, and 37 percent of GDP, respectively.[17] However, many have transitioned to industrial economies (China, Brazil, and Morocco), whereby industry accounts for about 50, 32, and 30 percent of GDP, respectively. Others have progressed to the post-industrial stage of development, like Croatia, Uruguay, Ukraine, and Indonesia; the service sector accounts for about 65, 63, 49, and 48 percent of GDP, respectively, and the role of this sector is growing rapidly. This is commendable progress for newly independent and newly market-oriented countries.

Globally, the strategic role of the agricultural sector is declining. In the first decade of the twenty-first century it accounts for less than 3.5 percent of GWP. The role of industry in GWP is also declining, despite the rapid industrial development in many GEM countries. Services are definitely the only sector of the GMP besides the knowledge-based economy (which is still insignificant in terms of its percentage) whose role in GWP is increasing (see Figure 5.9). During a crisis period, these tendencies can be broken up, but only for a short time. The general dynamics of this trend—which is only important for long-term strategies—will not change.

The structure of the GWP shown above in Figure 5.9 is reflected by the changing dynamics of energy consumption. Since 1980 the percentage of energy consumed by the service sector in all emerging market and developed countries has steadily increased. In developed countries, the service sector's energy consumption is already greater than that of the industrial sector. In many EMCs, this is still not the case. For example, in Russia in 2012, the industrial sector accounted for more than 50 percent of total final energy consumption, while the service sector, including transportation, consumed less than 40 percent. For the strategists of the global business community, it is important to understand that the rate of growth of available traditional energy resources from 2000 to 2006 will not increase during the next ten years by more than 2 percent annually. This means that energy strategies will have to focus on more efficient consumption.

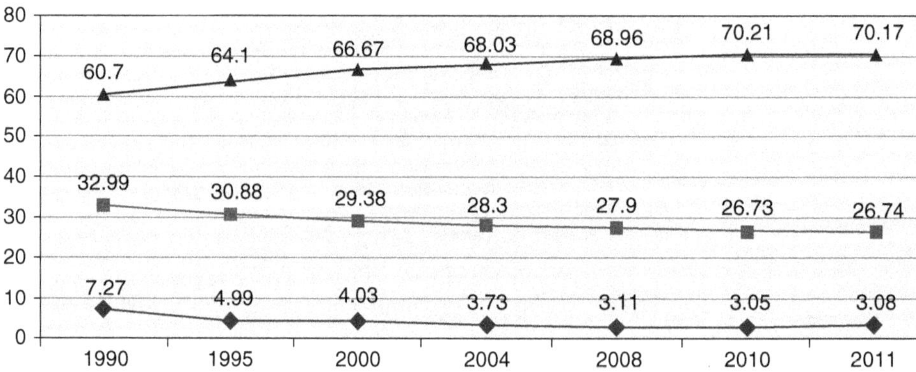

Figure 5.9 Industrial Structure of GWP

 Based on data from the World Bank World Development Indicators (up to year 2011, inclusive). Retrieved from http://data.worldbank.org/indicator/NV.IND.TOTL.ZS/countries

Note: The bottom line illustrates the role of the agricultural sector in the gross world product (GWP); the middle line illustrates the role of industry in the GWP; and the top line illustrates the role of the service industry in the GWP.

Another strategically important method of evaluating an economy's efficiency is an analysis of energy consumption per unit of GDP. This can also be used to strategize the standards of living and quality of life for people in different economies (further discussed later in this chapter). An evaluation of income by industry yields a totally different perspective on GDP or GWP. However, during strategizing processes it is important to note that variations in cost of products and production will have a substantial impact on the strategic recommendations. A widely accepted way of evaluating GDP is to analyze public and private consumption. GDP is the sum of consumption, investment (business expenditures on capital), and net foreign trade (if the balance of foreign trade is positive, then GDP will increase by the net excess of exports over imports). Different ratios of these aspects of GDP have important strategic implications for a national economy.

For strategists, GDP is not the only indicator of the total production of an economy; gross national product (GNP) can also be a useful indicator. GNP summarizes the economic activity of a country's citizens regardless of whether they work abroad or domestically. It helps strategists correctly represent public values in strategic vision and priorities. GDP accounts only for economic activity within national orders. Gross national income (GNI) is yet another indicator, but as they are relatively similar, it is not necessary to analyze both GNP and GNI.

Unfortunately, no matter how thoroughly strategists and economists analyze GDP/GNP figures, the numbers never completely illustrate the economic and business environment of an EMC. This is because the informal sector accounts for as much as 25 to 50 percent of GDP in some EMCs.[18] Such economic activity is obviously not included in official statistics. In order to get an accurate understanding of an economy's size and efficiency, it is crucial to acknowledge the significance of unreported economic activity. In every single country, substantial parts of the economy, such as all black-market operations, as well as gray-market operations (legal but unregistered activity, i.e., companies that seek to avoid taxes), are left out of official statistics. During the initial transition from dictatorships and command economies to free-market-oriented economies, private business matured at a faster pace than the improvement of a legal system. A free-market economy emerged ahead of an appropriate legal structure, and many companies that would be perfectly legitimate in developed countries were considered illegal in EMCs because of lingering regulations and restrictions from dictatorships and command economies. The legal system eventually evolves the appropriate structure for a free-market economy, but because many of these companies do not report their activity for several years, their leaders worry that if they do start reporting, they will face prosecution for past infractions. As a result, the economic activity of these companies is obviously not included in official statistics. Governments of EMCs should conduct economic and financial amnesty, with the goal of legitimizing these businesses and their payrolls. Bringing these companies and employees into the mainstream economy is more important than the additional tax revenue that an amnesty program will eventually generate. Of course, the informal economy is also significant in developed countries. For example, according to the US Department of Health and Human Services, the estimated retail value of the annual marijuana crop in the US is $36 billion.[19]

The following issues are typical causes of miscalculations and misinterpretations of economic data and should be taken into consideration during a strategic analysis:

- In order to avoid and minimize taxes, companies often sell their products substantially below market value to subsidiaries that are officially registered in offshore zones with lower or non-existent tax rates.

- There are several intermediaries that would buy the product as cheaply as possible, and after several iterations, the government loses track of companies' real output. The solution is simply to register intermediaries or implement a regulation to decrease them. This problem also occurs with delivery systems, as they are a separate line of GDP and are usually underreported by statistics. Here, the solution is to register all players in the delivery system.
- In order to avoid and minimize taxes, entrepreneurs create large conglomerates from several formerly independent companies and report only the final product, not including all of the products that were used during the production process. For example, a mining conglomerate could consist of one company that extracts the raw materials, another that enriches these raw materials, a metallurgical company that produces the final metal product, and one that delivers the end product.

An analysis of GDP and GWP can also be done through the use of the achievements of Russian-born and -educated American economist Wassily Leontief. Dr. Leontief developed the matrix input-output economic analysis, which breaks down an economy by region and industry. Typically, this method can be used to understand the connections and relationships between different industries in the world, national, or regional economy and illustrate what part of the product of one industry is consumed as a raw material or component by another industry. For this work, Leontief received the Nobel Prize in Economics in 1973. His method can be used by strategists and economists for an interregional-interindustrial analysis. Dr. Leontief used this approach when he worked for the United Nations in the 1970s and for the development of his global forecast for the year 2000.

> "The United Nations had been pressing for an international development strategy for the 1970s ... In particular, the organization wished this strategy to aim at reducing the disparities between rich and poor countries and to take account of the new consciousness of the limited capacity of the earth. The interesting progress of modeling these relevant topics moved the United Nations to launch a study dealing with environmental issues raised by world development and looking for "possible alternative policies to promote development while at the same time preserving and improving the environment"[19a] ... To embark on such a study, the United Nations required a solid methodological basis. Wassily Leontief, who had already analyzed the relations between the economy and the environment ... was, therefore, the United Nations' first choice ... The model was built around a hypothetical case of two regions (developed and less developed countries), three commodities (the product of the extraction industry, other production, and pollution abatement), two components of final demand (domestic and trade), and two components of value added (labor and capital returns). Its theoretical formulation included both a quantity model and a dual price model, relying on the basic input-output relations."[19b]

Strategic Evaluations of the Basic Economic Factors of the World Economy

After an analysis of the most integrated and aggregated economic indicators such as GWP, GDP, GDP PPP, GNP, and their per capita equivalents, the next step is a strategic analysis of the basic economic factors. The underlying economic factors of a country or the GMP play an extremely important role in the decision-making process of a company considering expansion of its international business activity.

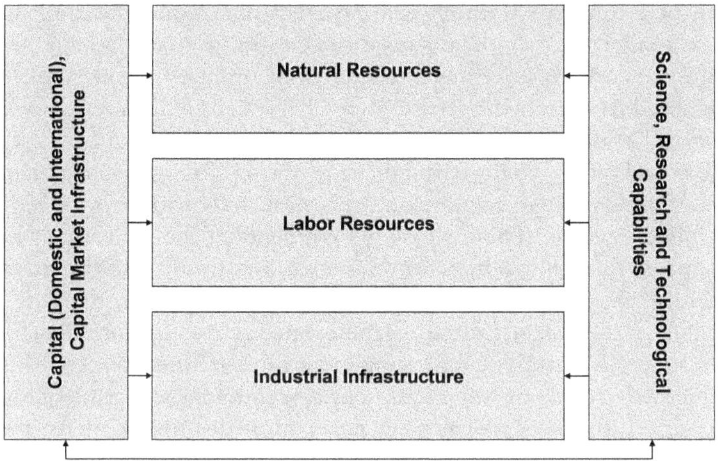

Figure 5.10 System of Basic Economic Factors for Strategic Evaluation

The economic and technological development of the world economy and the formation of the GMP have even changed the structure of basic economic factors. In addition to the traditional basic economic factors such as natural resources, labor, and capital, opportunities created by the GMP and modern technological innovations make it necessary to analyze other factors, such as existing production facilities, industrial infrastructure, and science and technology. The following five modern basic economic factors are key stages of a strategic analysis (see Figure 5.10).

An analysis of these factors should be conducted on global, national, and regional levels, as well as for vertical industries and even individual companies. When this analysis is focused on the company level, the basic economic factors take a different form, but their economic nature does not change. For example, the natural resources for a company can take the form of raw materials, parts, or even assembled components (such as an engine for a car or plane). Industrial infrastructure on a company level can be understood as corporate hardware, software, network technology, etc.

The following section presents the global allocation of the basic economic factors and their distribution in the processes of production and consumption in the GMP. Two important points should be conveyed. First, the formation of the GMP makes resources from around the world available to any country or company; and second, the role of the GEM is steadily increasing in terms of production and use of the basic economic factors.

Natural Resources (Including Land) of the Global Marketplace

THE STRATEGIC FACTOR OF TERRITORY IN THE GMP

Territory is the most important natural resource. The role of this factor, and its scale and location, is heavily influenced by different dynamics of labor resources and capital and is constantly changing due to technological innovation. Nonetheless, there is no more strategically important factor than territory, especially in terms of national pride and economic interests! For business concerns, the scale of territory is less important, though the size or location of a country's territory is always part of national tradition, which strategists often mistakenly ignore. In the twenty-first century, an overwhelming majority of countries are not looking to extend territories by military means; still, some countries have attempted to appropriate territories solely for economic interests without extending their national borders. The Arctic zone and in the future Antarctica are possible regions of the world where countries might seek out possible national extensions. Needless to say, all of these changes can be done only peacefully and with the required approvals of the United Nations. The national governments of the majority of EMCs are looking to encourage foreign investors for their territories to increase export capacity and thereby increase the standards of living of the population. With this aim some states are developing special strategies using several economic and organizational vehicles to achieve their strategic objectives: for example, they declare these territories as free economic zones, free trade zones, or zones with special technological regimes. Governments are using a variety of motivational mechanisms in order to encourage foreign investors; among these stimuli include tax-free holidays for as long as up to ten years, custom- and duty-free charges on equipment, raw materials, and parts that are required to establish efficient productions in these territories. The same economic motivations can be applied to foreign capital or land ownership. When the interests of the national economy need to develop particular territory as fast as possible—and make these territories attractive for domestic and foreign investors—governments can declare these zones as areas of accelerated economic development. These areas typically have newly established special administrations for the coordination and protection of upcoming investments.

The most important incentives to draw entrepreneurs and their corporate interests to these territories include: governmental investments in preparation of industrial, transportational, communicational, and social infrastructures of these territories that substantially decrease expenses for upcoming investors, special regulations for land and property ownership, and the most liberal code of tax for these areas. Quite often these territories are located near national borders or on the coast of major rivers, seas, and oceans in the framework of national boundaries. These areas can play a role as bridges between national economies and the global marketplace. I can see a lot of potential for these areas of accelerated development on the coastal regions of Brazil, China, Russia, South Korea, and some other countries, but with one required pre-condition: they need to develop special strategies for these economically accelerated areas. The regional allocation of resources and businesses, the allocation of construction sites of a new development of a company, and the geopolitical location of a country of current or potential business activity are always crucial elements of a strategic analysis. The scale of a nation's territory is almost always correlated to the potential agricultural capacity of the country. From this perspective, the percentage of arable land is a major characteristic of territory. For centuries the quality of soil predetermined the prosperity of a nation. However, the Green Revolution, which occurred during the twentieth century, reduced the importance of soil quality. But there are new factors. By the year 2050, the global population will double, and territories with high-quality soil will decrease by 60 percent, forcing strategists to reevaluate the role of soil as a natural resource. According to a study by Professor Bo R. Döös, chairman of Global Environmental Management, by 2030 "the loss of cropland is likely to be between 30 and 60 million hectares; the reserve land utilized will be about 100–200 million hectares; and the reserve land still in use by that

Table 5.6 Largest National Territories

Rank	*Country*	*Square Kilometers*
1	**Russia**	17,098,242
2	Canada	9,984,670
3	United States	9,826,675
4	**China**	9,596,960
5	**Brazil**	8,514,877
6	Australia	7,741,220
7	**India**	3,287,263
8	**Argentina**	2,780,400
9	**Kazakhstan**	2,724,900
10	**Algeria**	2,381,741

CIA. (n.d.). "World Factbook". Retrieved from https://www.cia.gov/library/publications/the-world-factbook/rankorder/2147rank.html

time will be about 50–100 million hectares."[20] Out of the ten largest countries in the world in terms of territory, seven are from the GEM. This is one of many indications of its strategic importance (see Table 5.4).

The formation of the GMP has had very important strategic implications regarding the allocation of natural resources. Prior to the GMP's existence, the location of global natural resources was understood as a summary of natural resources that belonged to particular nations. In the GMP, the location of most natural resources is much less significant. They are no longer understood solely as resources available to a certain country, but as resources available for any company in the world. And access to them is much less determined by national identity. The only restrictions are legal regulations, environmental requirements, and the cost of production and transportation. National governments controlling territories with these resources are always checking out how foreign investments or investments with foreign participation will influence and meet national interests. This is important to keep in mind when analyzing the global distribution of natural resources.

THE STRATEGIC FACTOR OF FRESHWATER IN THE GMP

Access to freshwater resources has always been a major issue for particular regions and countries. However, strategists should realize that in the twenty-first century humanity will experience a serious shortage of freshwater on a global scale. This is unprecedented in the history of modern civilization. Rapid population growth and improvements in standards of living in emerging market, developing, and underdeveloped countries will result in a surge in demand for freshwater resources in absolute and per capita terms, especially in China, India, countries of the Maghreb, and the majority of African states, among others. It is possible that technological innovations will satisfy this growing demand via more efficient distribution systems and desalination techniques. This problem is not limited to emerging and developing countries. The majority of developed countries will have to deal with freshwater-supply issues for much of the twenty-first century, with the possible exceptions of Australia, Canada, and a few European nations like Norway, Switzerland, and Austria. In 2008, in response to several years of drought conditions, two of the largest desalination plants in Europe were installed, with the capacity to produce between 200,000 and 240,000 cubic meters of water a day.[21] Despite increasing numbers of water-desalination projects throughout the world, barring significant technological progress, freshwater shortages will continue on a regional level and eventually on a global one. Unfortunately, control of and access to freshwater resources may be the cause of intense local and regional wars in the near future. As Plate 5.1 indicates, freshwater resources are distributed very unequally throughout the world. The availability of freshwater resources will have important implications for the intensity and location of business activity in the GMP of the twenty-first century.

As indicated by comparison with Table 5.7, most of the countries with the largest freshwater resources are EMCs (8 of the top 15). The US and Canada are the only two developed countries among the world leaders in terms of freshwater resources. A nation's freshwater resources should also be understood in terms of exploitability. A country's exploitable water resources are determined by

> the economic and environmental feasibility of storing floodwater behind dams or extracting groundwater, the physical possibility of catching water which naturally flows out to the sea, the minimum flow requirements for navigation, environmental services, aquatic life, etc. Methods to assess exploitable water resources vary from country to country depending on the country's situation.[22]

This indicator has very important implications for a country's economic development. For example, while China has recently been one of the fastest-growing economies and is currently considered (in terms of PPP) the second largest economy in the world, it is ranked 88th in the world in terms of exploitable water resources. This will be a major hindrance to China's continued development. Furthermore, the uneven territorial distribution of China's freshwater resources will limit the development of certain regions. This will be an issue for the Northwest Territories. There is already a scarcity of freshwater in this region (usually less than 1,000 cubic meters of water per

Table 5.7 Countries with Largest Total Renewable Water Resources, 2014 (10^9 m^3/yr)

Rank	*Country*	*Total Renewable Water Resources*
1	**Brazil**	8,647
2	**Russian Federation**	4,508
3	United States	3,069
4	Canada	2,902
5	**China**	2,840
6	**Colombia**	2,360
7	**India**	2,081
8	**Indonesia**	2,019
9	**Peru**	1,894
10	Venezuela	1,325
11	Democratic Republic of the Congo	1,283
12	Bangladesh	1,227
13	Myanmar	1,168
14	**Chile**	923
15	**Vietnam**	884

Based on data from the Aquastat database of the Food and Agriculture Organization of the United Nations. Retrieved from www.fao.org/nr/water/aquastat/dbase/index.stm

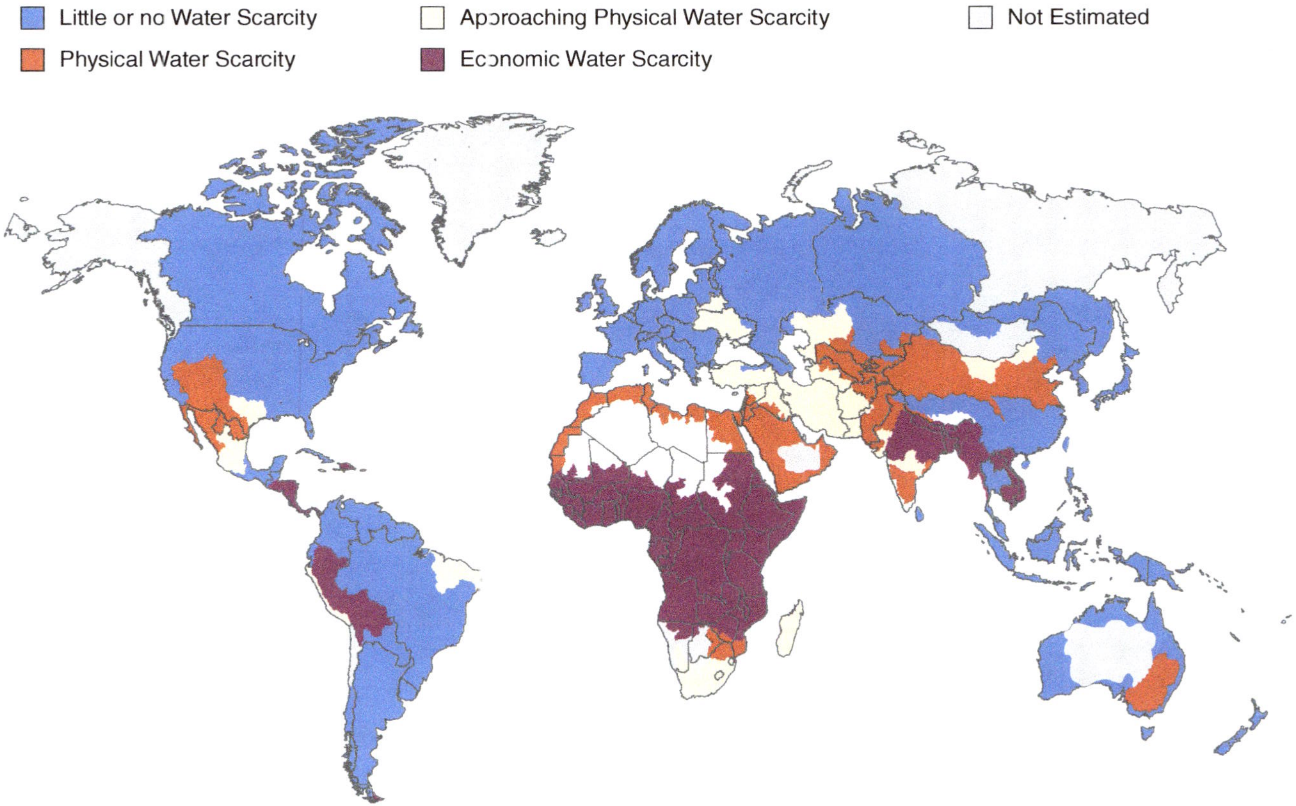

Plate 5.1 Global Distribution of Freshwater Resources

 From Molden, D., Frenken, K., Barker, R., de Fraiture, C., Mati, B., Svendsen, M., Sadoff, C., and Finlayson, C. M. (2007). "Trends in Water and Agricultural Development." In D. Molden (Ed.), *Water for Food, Water for Life: The Comprehensive Assessment of Water Management in Agriculture*. London: Earthscan and the International Water Management Institute, p. 63. Retrieved from www.iwmi.cgiar.org/assessment/Water%20for%20Food%20Water%20for%20Life/Chapters/Chapter%202%20Trends.pdf

Notes: See p.269 for detailed notes

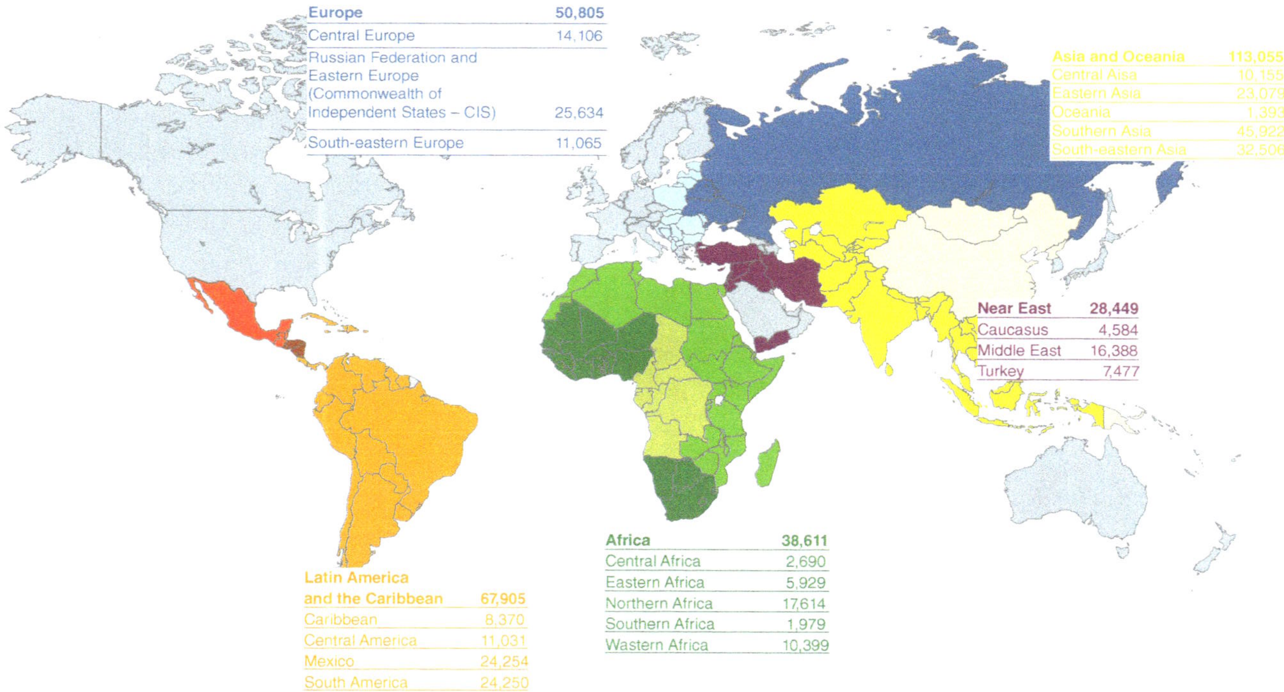

Plate 5.2 Worldwide Distribution of Remittances, Continents, Regions, and Country ($), 2006

*International Fund for Agricultural Development. (2007). "Sending Money Home: Worldwide Remittance Flows to Developing Countries." Retrieved November 19, 2007, from http://ifad.org/events/remittances/maps/index.htm

capita is considered to be a scarcity of freshwater resources. Such situations exist mostly in sub-Saharan Africa and in some areas of the Middle East). By 2030, China will have roughly 1.76 cubic meters of water per capita. Although this is not technically considered a scarcity of freshwater resources, it will substantially hinder both economic growth and social cohesion.

Scarcity of freshwater resources will lead strategists to develop a new economic practice: the mass cross-border trade of freshwater resources on a global scale. Exporting freshwater resources will be a very profitable undertaking for countries with excess resources, such as those listed in Table 5.7. However, in addition to analyzing freshwater resources per capita, it is very important to strategize freshwater resources in terms of domestic regional economic strategies and the industrial structure of a national economy. The consumption of freshwater resources by industrial and agricultural sectors is usually strategically more significant than freshwater consumption by individuals.

The countries from Table 5.8 will likely receive exports of freshwater from countries with surpluses of this resource. The oil-rich countries listed in Table 5.9, such as Kuwait, United Arab Emirates, Qatar, Saudi Arabia, Libya, and Bahrain, as well as the relatively rich countries like Singapore and Israel, will be able to import large volumes of freshwater. However, some countries, such as the Maldives, Yemen, Burundi, Cape

Table 5.8 Countries with the Largest Total Renewable Water Resources per Capita (m^3/inhab/yr), 2014

Rank	*Country*	*Total Renewable Water Resources per Capita*
1	Iceland	515,152
2	**Guyana**	338,750
3	Congo	187,050
4	Suriname	183,673
5	Papua New Guinea	109,411
6	Bhutan	103,448
7	**Gabon**	99,282
8	Canada	82,485
9	Solomon Islands	79,679
10	Norway	77,930
11	New Zealand	72,570
12	**Belize**	65,452
13	**Peru**	62,352
14	Paraguay	57,013
15	Liberia	54,029
16	**Bolivia**	53,791
17	**Chile**	52,389
18	**Uruguay**	50,543
19	Laos	49,261
20	**Colombia**	48,840
21	Venezuela	43,578
22	**Brazil**	43,157
23	**Panama**	36,051
24	Equatorial Guinea	34,346
25	Fiji	32,406

Based on data from the Aquastat database of the Food and Agriculture Organization of the United Nations. Retrieved from www.fao.org/nr/water/aquastat/dbase/index.stm

Table 5.9 Countries with the Lowest Total Renewable Water Resources per Capita (m^3/inhab/yr), 2014

Rank	*Country*	*Total Renewable Water Resources per Capita*
1	Kuwait	5.936
2	**United Arab Emirates**	16.05
3	**Qatar**	26.74
4	**The Bahamas**	53.05
5	**Saudi Arabia**	83.25
6	Yemen	86.04
7	Maldives	86.96
8	**Bahrain**	87.09
9	**Singapore**	110.9
10	Libya	112.9
11	**Malta**	117.7
12	**Jordan**	128.8
13	Occupied Palestinian Territory	193.5
14	**Israel**	230.2
15	**Barbados**	280.7
16	**Algeria**	297.6
17	Djibouti	343.6
18	Oman	385.5
19	Tunisia	419.7
20	**Saint Kitts and Nevis**	444.4
21	Antigua and Barbuda	577.8
22	Cape Verde	601.2
23	**Cyprus**	683.6
24	Kenya	692.2
25	**Egypt**	710.5

Based on data from the Aquastat database of the Food and Agriculture Organization of the United Nations. Retrieved from www.fao.org/nr/water/aquastat/dbase/index.stm

Verde, and Rwanda, will likely be in desperate need of international aid in order to provide an adequate supply of freshwater to meet the minimum health needs of their citizens. Meeting the demand of industry for freshwater in these countries will be extremely difficult.

An analysis of the freshwater dependency ratio of a country also has important strategic implications for future economic development and even political independence. This indicator reflects the amount of freshwater resources that originate from abroad. This is not an indication of the amount of imported freshwater, but rather a result of the geographical location of the source of a country's rivers. A high freshwater dependency ratio complicates bilateral relations with neighboring countries that control the source of another country's freshwater resources. There have been multiple times in history when the acquisition of new territory via military force damaged the victor's economy due to the fact that the new territory required more freshwater resources than could be delivered. In this scenario, military success was short-lived and a strategic failure. In another strategic issue, the country that controls the source of a neighbor's freshwater can seriously threaten that neighbor's welfare by diverting freshwater for its own non-vital industrial purposes or by creating an artificial reservoir.

In order to avoid conflicts over this issue, some countries that share freshwater resources have already signed bilateral and multilateral agreements. The Nile Basin Initiative is one of the best examples of such an agreement. While the Nile is traditionally associated with Egypt, its waters pass through the territories of Uganda, Sudan, the Democratic Republic of Congo, Ethiopia, Eritrea, Zaire, Kenya, Tanzanian, Rwanda, and Burundi. The White Nile, which originates from Lake Victoria (shared by Tanzania, Uganda, and Kenya) and the Blue Nile, which originates from Lake Tana in Ethiopia, converge to form *the* Nile. However, the ultimate source of the Nile is the Ruvyironza River in Burundi. In order to avoid potential conflicts and to assure the steady supply of freshwater to the 300 million people who depend on the Nile, all of the above-mentioned countries (with the exception of Eritrea) signed the Nile Basin Initiative in 1999. The vision of this initiative is "to achieve sustainable socioeconomic development through the equitable utilization of, and benefit from, the common Nile Basin water resources."[23] Later, in June 2001, the International Consortium for Cooperation on the Nile was established to improve economic development and fight poverty in this area, in cooperation with other multilateral organizations. The ability of these countries to come to a consensus regarding the use of the Nile as a source of freshwater is heartening. Nevertheless, it is also an illustration of the complexities of managing internationally shared water resources.

Table 5.10 Countries with the Highest Total Renewable Water Dependency Ratio, 2014

Rank	*Country*	*Dependency ratio (%)*
1	Kuwait	100
2	**Turkmenistan**	97
3	**Egypt**	96.91
4	**Bahrain**	96.55
5	Mauritania	96.49
6	Sudan	96.13
7	**Hungary**	94.23
8	Bangladesh	91.44
9	**Republic of Moldova**	91.42
10	Niger	89.72
11	Netherlands	87.91
12	Namibia	84.79
13	**Botswana**	80.39
14	Uzbekistan	80.07
15	**Romania**	80.04
16	**Pakistan**	77.71
17	**Azerbaijan**	76.60
18	**Slovakia**	74.85
19	Cambodia	74..67
20	Congo	73.32
21	Syrian Arab Republic	72.36
22	Luxembourg	71.43
23	Paraguay	69.83
24	Chad	67.18
25	**Argentina**	66.67

Based on data from the Aquastat database of the Food and Agriculture Organization of the United Nations. Retrieved from www.fao.org/nr/water/aquastat/dbase/index.stm

Table 5.11 Countries with a Total Renewable Water Dependency Ratio of Less than 1 Percent, 2014

Rank	*Country*
1	**China**
2	Lebanon
3	**Estonia**
4	Angola
5	**Spain**
6	Cape Verde
7	Central African Republic
8	Comoros
9	Djibouti
10	Equatorial Guinea
11	Ethiopia
12	Guinea
13	Lesotho
14	Libya
15	**Madagascar**
16	**Mauritius**
17	**Morocco**
18	Sao Tome and Principe
19	Seychelles
20	Sierra Leone
21	Antigua and Barbuda
22	**The Bahamas**
23	**Barbados**
24	**Costa Rica**
25	Cuba
26	Dominica
27	Dominican Republic
28	Grenada
29	**Jamaica**
30	Puerto Rico

Based on data from the Aquastat database of the Food and Agriculture Organization of the United Nations. Retrieved from www.fao.org/nr/water/aquastat/dbase/index.stm

It is also important to realize that a low dependency ratio does not mean that a country has an adequate supply of freshwater. It only signifies that all freshwater resources, be they extremely limited or vast, originate within national borders. Nations such as Cape Verde and Singapore have low dependency ratios as well as low freshwater resources. Table 5.11 consists mostly of small island nations, which for obvious reasons do not have rivers that originate in foreign countries. It is important for strategists to consider several indicators regarding freshwater to get a complete and accurate understanding of the situation.

THE STRATEGIC FACTOR OF ENERGY IN THE GMP

The rate of development of any civilization is determined and at the same time can be characterized by its production and use of energy. The majority of technological achievements are incorporated into energy production, delivery, distribution, and consumption. Intensive use of energy per unit of production or per capita of an economy is usually a good indicator of its maturity. Energy intensity accumulates in any economic and industrial product, and even in the intellectual results of a society's development. The energy intensity of an economy can be strategically evaluated via energy consumption per capita or per unit of GDP.

In developed countries, energy consumption per unit of GDP is decreasing, although it refers only to oil consumption. Developed countries have begun to implement energy-saving technologies, causing the overall downward trend in energy intensity. For future reference, primary energy consumption is typically evaluated in British thermal units (BTU).

Despite substantial improvements in energy efficiency in the developed world, global energy consumption increased by 33.2 percent from 347.424 quadrillion BTU in 1990, to 462.798 quadrillion BTU in 2005.[24] Strategically, this is a result of the rapid development of the GEM economies. Unlike in the developed world, energy consumption as a percentage of GDP is increasing in much of the GEM, as a result of the use of oil, gas, and coal and their price dynamics.

The energy intensity of a national economy and the global distribution of production facilities are strategically determined by the allocation of major natural energy resources like coal, oil, natural gas, and geothermal energy. Despite the fact that the GMP makes energy resources more widely transportable and available than ever before, national policies and legal systems can prevent foreign or even domestic companies from exploring and/or extracting natural resources. For example, the United States has not developed its largest oil and coal reserves due to (rightly or wrongly) evaluated environmental consequences and the strategy of energy preservation for the future. The national strategy of a country may not allow companies, especially foreign ones, to directly utilize natural resources or invest in certain related projects.

For strategic evaluation, it is important to note that when a company sells raw materials or semi-products, its national government gets much less from foreign trade revenue than it would have from the sale of final products abroad. This was the cause of the negative foreign trade balance in the United States, until 1888.[25] Many EMCs have found themselves in similar situations in the late twentieth and early twenty-first centuries.

Figure 5.11 demonstrates the overwhelming role of Middle Eastern oil reserves. As a result, Middle Eastern countries often try to use oil not only as a source of economic strength but also as a bargaining chip in political negotiations. At the same time, it is important to realize that actual oil reserves may be distributed differently than indicated

Table 5.12 Proven Energy Reserves by Region as a Percentage of World Total, 2013

Region	*Oil (as a % of World Total)*	*Natural Gas (as a % of World Total)*	*Recoverable Coal (as a % of World Total)*
North America	13.00%	5.75%	27.29%
Central and South America	19.80%	3.93%	1.65%
Europe	0.73%	2.13%	9.26%
Eurasia	7.22%	31.81%	25.65%
Middle East	48.73%	41.24%	0.13%
Africa	7.76%	7.52%	3.58%
Asia and Oceania	2.76%	7.62%	32.44%

Compiled from several sources by the Energy Information Administration. Retrieved from www.eia.gov/cfapps/ipdbproject/IEDIndex3.cfm?tid=5&pid=57&aid=6html; www.eia.gov/cfapps/ipdbproject/IEDIndex3.cfm?tid=3&pid=3&aid=6; www.eia.gov/cfapps/ipdbproject/IEDIndex3.cfm?tid=1&pid=7&aid=6

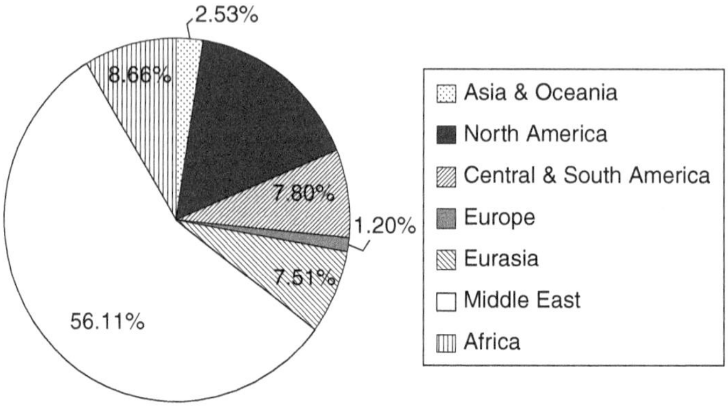

Figure 5.11 Estimates of Proven Oil Reserves by World Region as a Percentage of World Total

PennWell Corporation. (2006). *Oil & Gas Journal*. December 18 (except for the United States). Oil includes crude oil and condensate. Data for the United States are from the Energy Information Administration, US Crude Oil, Natural Gas, and Natural Gas Liquids Reserves, *2005 Annual Report*, DOE/EIA-0216 (2005) (November 2006). *Oil & Gas Journal*'s oil reserve estimate for Canada includes 5.2 billion barrels of conventional crude oil and condensate reserves and 174.0 billion barrels of oil sands reserves.

by Figure 5.11. There is some foundation for the estimation that the overwhelming majority of oil fields are still undiscovered. Some have been discovered but are still not measured by certain geological categories and are not proven; proven reserves "are estimated quantities that analysis of geologic and engineering data demonstrates with reasonable certainty are recoverable under existing economic and operating conditions."[26] This is the case in Russia, for example, whose role is underestimated in Figure 5.11, due to a lack of investment in geological studies over the past 20 years. The existence of oil reserves is not enough to draw a conclusion about the ability of a country to exploit these resources. Oil fields may be located in economically undeveloped regions that require large investments in industrial and social infrastructure in order to exploit these fields. In some cases, the required investment makes exploitation of an oil field economically inefficient. At the beginning of the twenty-first century, unexplored oil fields typically lie in very remote or geographically isolated (by desert, permafrost, etc.) areas. For this reason, it is possible to predict that oil reserves in the Arctic zone of Russia (which accounts for more than 45 percent of Russian territory) are larger than those in Central and South America. Due to this fact, Russian oil reserves are likely much larger than currently estimated. New technologies and innovations invented and implemented by the end of the twentieth century have made economically efficient several shale, oil, and gas reserves which prior to the development of new technologies were not economically efficient for their development. From the beginning of the twenty-first century, the United States, and then Canada, started to develop these shale reserves. Between only two years, 2006 and 2008, estimated natural gas reserves in the US increased by 35 percent,[27] which I assume is an unprecedented rate of growth. This made the US by the year 2012 the world's largest producer of oil and gas and created immense potential for the export of these resources to Europe and other world regions. In 2014, this new development tremendously increased and changed competition and decreased prices on the oil and gas

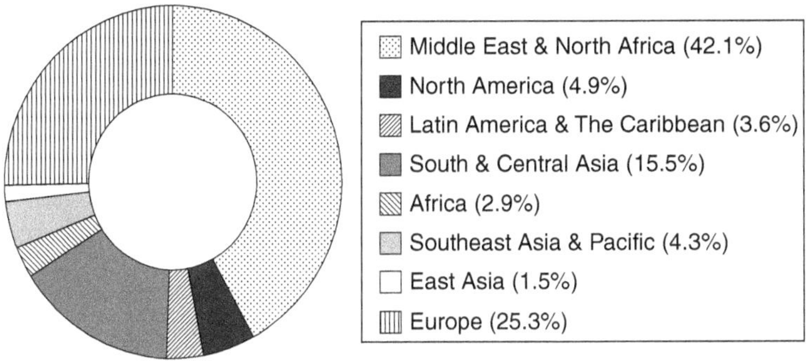

Figure 5.12 Gas Recoverable Reserves by Region as a Percentage of World Total, 2014
Based on data from the World Energy Council. (2014). Retrieved from www.worldenergy.org/data/resources/resource/coal/

global markets. In other technological developments that made economically efficient deep shelf oil and gas reserves, increased national interests of countries with Arctic coasts like Greenland (in care of Denmark), Norway, Canada, Russia, and the United States have tried to extend their national territories in the Arctic. All of these countries are preparing special researches and feasibility studies to demonstrate that these territories, according to their geographical nature and historical evidence, should belong to their sovereignty. These states are sending "bullet-proof" petitions with these requests for approval by the United Nations. These countries' interest in territories with Arctic coasts has increased also due to dramatic climate changes in the Arctic region, which has made economic development of these territories efficient and easier. These new developments will change the ratio of potential oil, gas, and other productions capacities of this world region.

As indicated in Figure 5.12, the largest share of proven reserves of natural gas belongs to Russia—the most significant part of the "Europe" category. Despite huge domestic consumption of this resource, Russia is a major supplier to the EU and other European states. Like the countries of the Middle East, Russia attempts to exploit its natural gas in bilateral and multilateral political relationships. For different countries, Russia establishes and changes prices per cubic meter of natural gas. The more or less similar practice is used by natural gas–rich Turkmenistan and Azerbaijan. The world's leading producer of natural gas is the Russian state-controlled monopoly Gazprom. Without clearly developed strategy this company allowed drastic decrease of its market value by the end of December 2014. This happened despite Gazprom's leaders' declared but not strategy-based ambitions to increase the corporate market value up to one trillion dollars. As of 2014, Russia is still the leading producer of natural gas in the GEM. The high profitability of this company encouraged more than $100 billion of FDI to Russia between 1993 and 2008. During 2007, Gazprom began to buy gas-distributing companies abroad in order to control the entire technological process, from gas extraction to its distribution in Europe. This attempt motivates the Europe Union to diversify its supplier of natural gas and to develop its own strategy of energy independence and security.

At the end of the twentieth century, under the influence of stricter ecological requirements, the role of coal as a source of energy was declining. However, new

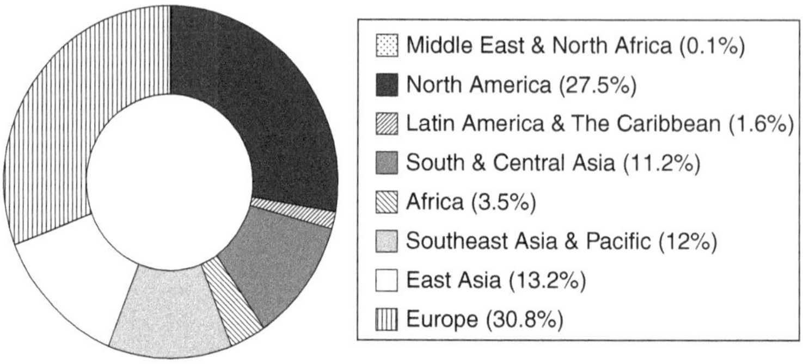

Figure 5.13 Estimated Recoverable Coal Reserves by World Region as a Percentage of World Total, 2014

World Energy Council. (2014). Retrieved from www.worldenergy.org/data/resources/resource/coal/

technological achievements renewed coal as an important source of energy. Because of modern twenty-first technology, there is a new trend: small coal fields and those with a low quantity of coal in ore are considered economically exploitable. The US, as a major consumer of mineral energy resources, has the largest recoverable coal reserves in the world, a major source of their energy security.

Developing an understanding of the geopolitical allocation of traditional energy resources in the GMP is only the first step in a strategic analysis of the availability of energy resources for a particular company. It is also important to analyze the allocation of alternative energy resources like biological, wind, tidal, etc.

ENERGY PRODUCTION IN THE GMP

A strategic analysis of the allocation of energy resources is quite different from an analysis of energy production. Despite political and legal barriers, it is not uncommon for primary energy resources to be exported to different countries and continents for further enrichment and final production. Iran is the perfect example of this scenario. Despite the fact that this country is the No. 4 producer in the world of crude oil (5.5 percent of total world production as of 2007) and the No. 3 exporter of it, Iran produced less than 50 percent of its domestic consumption of gasoline. As a result, Iran "imported over 192,000 bbl/d of gasoline … costing $5 billion."[28] Countries with large primary energy resources are typically not the biggest producers of final energy products and are almost never the biggest consumers of energy (see Map 5.1).

Figure 5.14 shows the major sources of fuel in the world economy from 1973 to 2013. Since 1973 there have been no major changes in the relative production of different sources of fuel. Oil is still the leading fuel produced, though its role has declined by 11 percent. The other major change occurred in nuclear fuel. Its share increased from less than 1 percent to 6.3 percent. The tremendous rise in the production of natural gas in Russia, Turkmenistan, and Iran is the cause of the 4.7 percent increase in the role of natural gas in the fuel energy balance. Clearly, there have been no revolutionary changes during this period. However, a focus on alternative sources of fuel, especially ethanol and biodiesel in countries like Brazil, the US, Germany, China, and India, will likely

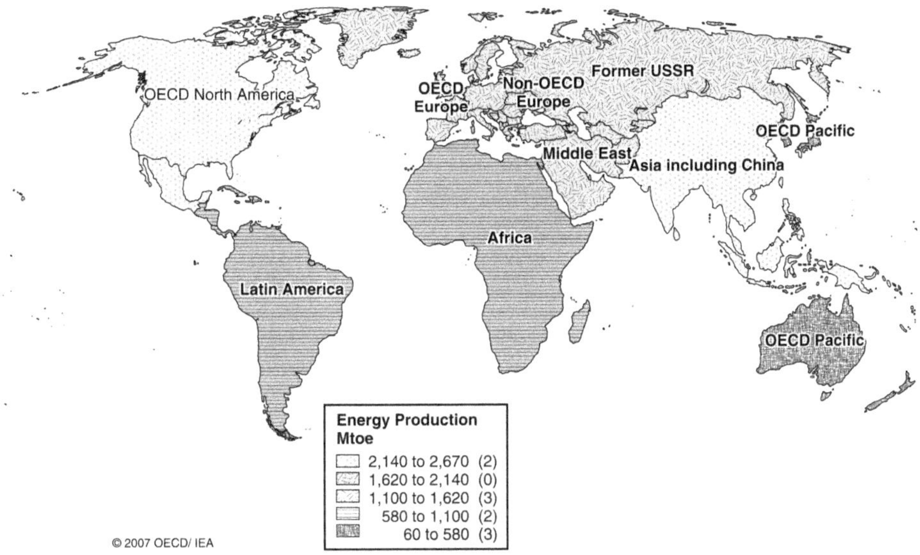

Map 5.1 Energy Production in the GMP, 2005

IEA Statistics © OECD/IEA; www.iea.org/textbase/stats/index.asp. International Energy Agency. Map of World Energy Production. Retrieved from www.iea.org/Textbase/country/maps/world/prod.htm

Note: Energy production = Total production of primary energy, i.e., hard coal, lignite, peat, crude oil, natural gas liquids, natural gas, combustible renewables and waste, nuclear hydro, geothermal, solar, and the heat from heat pumps, that is extracted from the ambient environment. Production is calculated after removal of impurities.

substantially change the global balance of fuel production and use by 2020. For example, in 2007 President Bush announced the "Twenty in Ten" initiative. This initiative aims to reduce US gasoline usage by 20 percent from 2007 to 2017 by dramatically increasing the domestic production of ethanol and other renewable fuels, as well as increasing automobile fuel efficiency standards.[29]

ELECTRICITY GENERATION IN THE GMP

The production of electricity is one of the most energy-intensive industries of the GMP. It consumes almost all hydropower generation and more than two-thirds of world coal production. According to projections from the International Energy Outlook from the Energy Information Administration of the US government, "Coal and natural gas remain the most important fuels for electricity generation throughout the projection period, together accounting for 80 percent of the total increment in world electric power generation from 2004 to 2030."[30] It is important to realize that the role of certain energy resources in electricity generation differs from their role in energy production.

Although hydropower accounts for only 16 percent of world electricity generation, it is a very significant source of electricity. Hydropower plants reduce the use of other sources of electricity during peak times. In the morning and during working hours, hydropower plants increase the stability of energy systems and play a very important role in energy balance and consumption in different regions connected by electrical networks.

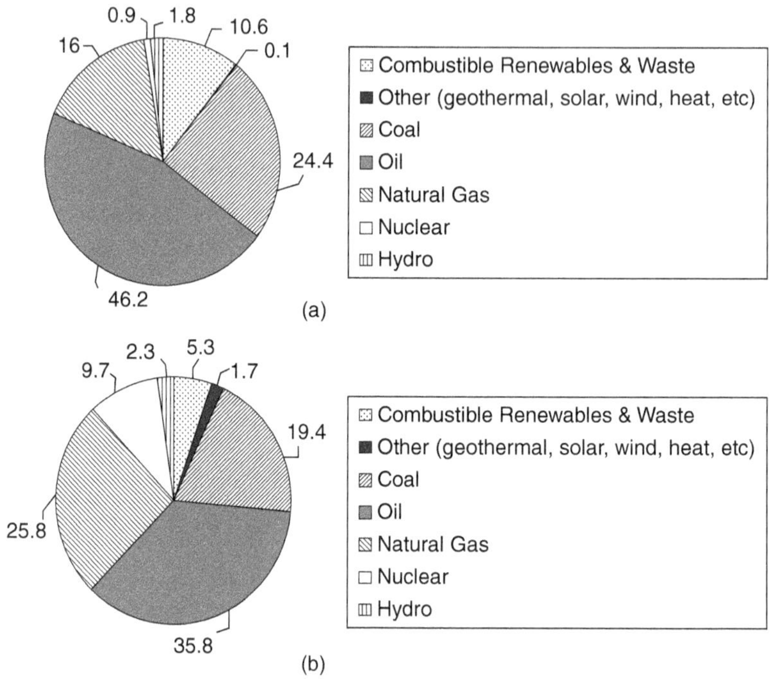

Figure 5.14a and 5.14b Changes in Fuel Shares of Total Primary Energy Supply (TPES), 1973–2013

International Energy Agency. (2014). *Key World Energy Statistics 2014*. Retrieved from www.iea.org/publications/freepublications/publication/KeyWorld2014.pdf

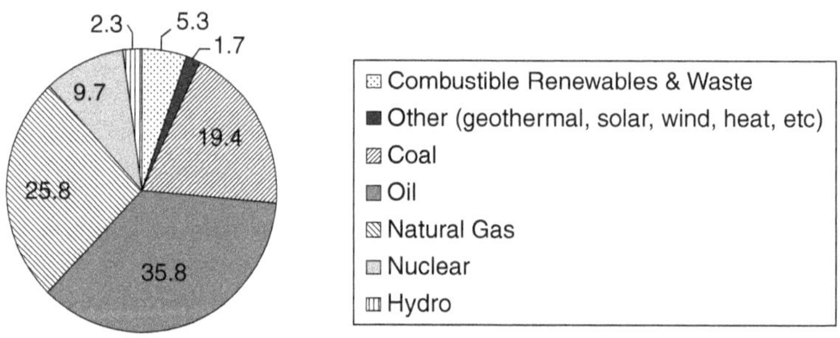

Figure 5.15 Sources of World Electricity Generation, 2013

International Energy Agency. (2014). *Key World Energy Statistics 2014*. Retrieved from www.iea.org/publications/freepublications/publication/KeyWorld2014.pdf

Typically, among regions that share an electrical grid, during periods of reduced energy consumption (daily, weekly, etc.), electricity from a hydropower plant can be diverted to another region that experiences a peak in power consumption during this period.

EMCs are among the world leaders in terms of hydropower resources and production. China is the largest producer of hydropower electricity, accounting for

13.3 percent of the world total. As part of a national initiative, China will triple the capacity of its hydropower stations to 300 gigawatts by 2020.[31] That will be six times the hydropower capacity of Russia, which accounts for 9 percent of global hydropower resources, as of January 2008. Brazil is the leading producer of hydropower electricity in Latin America, accounting for 11.3 percent of the world total. Despite the fact that EMCs are the leading producers of hydropower, in terms of utilization of total capacity, they lag behind developed countries. For example, in Japan, 99 percent of hydropower resources are utilized; in the US, 82 percent; in Canada, 65 percent; and in Eastern Europe, 60 percent. By comparison, Russia utilizes only 20 percent. But in Siberia and the Russian Far East, where the major hydropower resources are located, only 4 percent of resources are utilized. Nevertheless, hydro energy accounts for 50 percent of Siberian energy consumption. Since 2003 India has implemented a national program to utilize hydropower energy and aims to build 50 gigawatts of hydropower stations by 2012 (which is also more than the total capacity of all hydropower stations in Russia as of January 2008).

The hydro energy sector is typically owned or regulated by governments, even in developed countries. In the twenty-first century, most of these stations will be privatized, and national governments will act only as regulators. Developments in the hydropower industry are of great economic importance, and strategists should understand hydropower plants as centers of regional economic development. According to the author's estimate, hydropower stations are typically constructed with the capacity to accommodate a 50 to 200 percent increase in economic activity in the surrounding area.

PRODUCTION OF NUCLEAR ELECTRICITY IN THE GMP

In terms of energy production, the most dynamic changes in the last 30 years of the twentieth century took place in nuclear energy. Over 32 years, the role of this high-tech sector in electricity generation increased by 1,363.5 percent. No other source of electricity increased by an amount even close to this figure. During this period, the role of EMCs in nuclear electricity generation has more than doubled. As of 2005, the GEM accounts for 15 percent of this industry. This trend will likely increase due to ambitious nuclear energy programs in several EMCs, including Armenia, Brazil, Bulgaria, Chile, China, the

Table 5.13 Production of Hydro Electricity, as a Percentage of World Total, 2012

Country	*Percentage of World Total, 2011*
China	20.2
Brazil	12.4
Canada	10.8
United States	9.3
Russian Federation	7.8
India	3.8
Norway	3.5
Venezuela	2.4
Japan	2.4
Sweden	1.9
Rest of the World	28.6

Based on data from International Energy Agency. (2014). *Key World Energy Statistics 2014*. Retrieved from www.iea.org/publications/freepublications/publication/KeyWorld2014.pdf

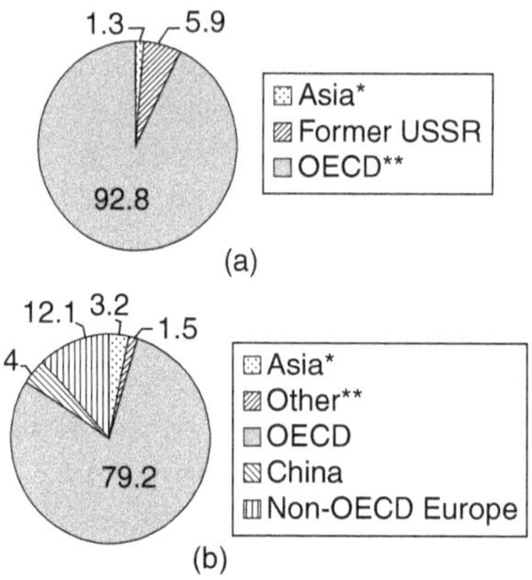

Figures 5.16a and 5.16b Changes in Regional Shares of Nuclear Production, 1973–2012

International Energy Agency. (2014). *Key World Energy Statistics 2014*. Retrieved from www.iea.org/publications/freepublications/publication/KeyWorld2014.pdf

* Asia excludes China

** Others includes Africa, Latin America, and China

Czech Republic, Egypt, India, Israel, Jordan, Kazakhstan, Lithuania, Pakistan, South Africa, and Turkey, among others. China will achieve a "fivefold increase in nuclear capacity to 40 GWe [Gigawatts electrical] by 2020."[32] For China the nuclear industry is especially important because the country's current registered coal resources will last only until roughly the year 2100. Replacing coal as a source of electricity is a major goal of the Chinese government.

By 2005, of the ten leading producers of nuclear electricity, three were EMCs. By 2020 more than half of all nuclear energy will be produced by EMCs. Any strategic analysis of the allocation of energy-consuming industries and production facilities should take into account these countries and the growth of their nuclear programs. Typically, when the location of energy-intensive projects is under consideration, an analysis of the current balance of energy in the potential location has to be supplemented by an analysis of the energy balance of that region over the next three to five years. By the time the proposed project will be implemented in practice, the energy balance may substantially change. It is also important to consider the impact of the diversification of the primary energy resources, a key trend of the twenty-first century.

ENERGY CONSUMPTION IN THE GMP

A high production and consumption of energy is obviously not an indication of a highly efficient economy. While EMCs are among the world leaders in terms of energy resources and production, they trail developed countries by a great distance when it comes to energy consumption. However, the steady economic development of EMCs is increasing their role in global energy consumption. According to the *Economist*, "The oil price has risen mainly because of strong demand in emerging economies, which have accounted for as much as four-fifths of the total increase in oil consumption in the past five years."[33]

Table 5.14 Production of Electricity from Nuclear Energy, 2012

Country Producer	*Percentage of World Total, 2011*
United States	31.8
France	17.1
Russian Federation	6.7
South Korea	6.0
Germany	4.2
Japan	4.0
Canada	3.6
Ukraine	3.5
China	3.3
United Kingdom	2.7
Sweden	2.3
Rest of the World	14.8

International Energy Agency. (2007). *Key World Energy Statistics 2007*. p. 19. Retrieved from www.iea.org/stats/index.asp

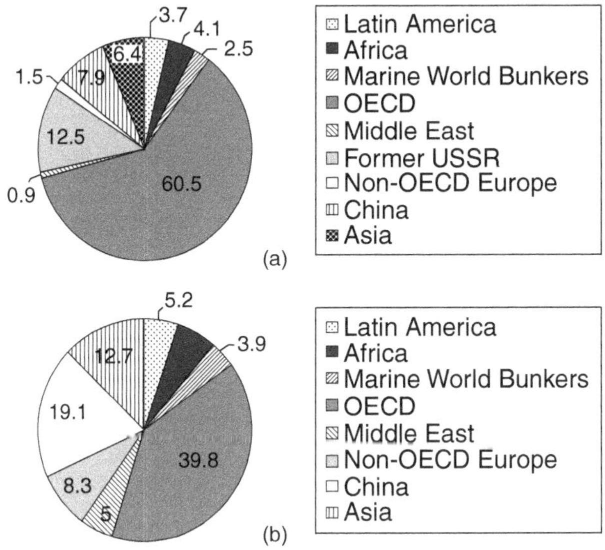

Figures 5.17a and 5.17b Changes in Regional Shares of Total Final Energy Consumption, 1973–2012

International Energy Agency. (2014). *Key World Energy Statistics 2014*. Retrieved from www.iea.org/publications/freepublications/publication/KeyWorld2014.pdf

Figures 5.17a and 5.17b demonstrates the tremendous extent to which energy consumption has increased in Latin America and Asia (especially China). Obviously, this does not indicate any increase in efficiency. Nonetheless, the increasing energy consumption in EMCs does reflect their growing clout and importance in the GMP. The category "former USSR" does not contain the same countries in 2005 as it did in 1973, because for political reasons the three Baltic states are no longer considered part of the "former USSR."

ENERGY INTENSITY IN THE GMP

Energy intensity describes total primary energy consumption per unit of GDP. An analysis of national energy intensities yields somewhat unexpected results. Of the 30 countries with the lowest use of energy per unit of GDP, there is not a single developed country and only three EMCs (Burkina Faso, Sri Lanka, and Saint Kitts and Nevis). These three countries barely meet the requirements of an EMC and are actually considered developing countries by some estimates. This illustrates the limited ability of energy intensity as an indicator of the actual energy efficiency of an economy. In the case of the countries listed in Table 5.15, a lower level of consumption of energy per unit of GDP is not the result of a national policy of energy efficiency, but of a tremendous lack of energy, underdeveloped industrial sectors, and widespread poverty.

However, as indicated by Table 5.16, high national energy intensity is not correlated with a high level of economic development. However, half of the countries on this table

Table 5.15 Thirty Countries with the Lowest National Energy Intensity (Use of Energy per One Unit of GDP), 2012

Country	*Energy Intensity (BTU per 2000 US $), 2011*
Chad	195
Mali	515
Rwanda	597
Guinea	697
Macau, China	766
Burundi	914
Ethiopia	934
Burma (Myanmar)	985
Niger	994
Central Africa Republic	1,004
Uganda	1,047
Burkina Faso	1,089
Haiti	1,125
Sierra Leone	1400
Cape Verde	1424
Kiribati	1429
Eritrea	1433
Cambodia	1496
Sri Lanka	1501
Comoros	1554
Malawi	1655
The Gambia	1841
Swaziland	1876
Cameroon	1897
Timor-L'Este (East Timor)	1910
Solomon Islands	1913
Madagascar	1916
Vanuatu	1927
Bangladesh	2164
Equatorial Guinea	2204

Energy Information Administration. International Total Primary Energy Consumption and Energy Intensity. Retrieved from www.eia.gov/cfapps/ipdbproject/iedindex3.cfm?tid=92&pid=47&aid=2&cid=regions&syid=2007&eyid=2011&unit=BTUPUSDM

Table 5.16 Energy Intensity (Use of Energy per One Unit of GDP) of Major Economies of the GMP, 2005

Rank	*Country*	*Energy Intensity (BTU per 2005 US $)*
1	**Russia**	**14,501**
2	**China**	**10,252**
3	United States	7,328
4	**Indonesia**	**6,380**
5	**Brazil**	**6,048**
6	**India**	**5,829**
7	France	5,412
8	Japan	5,378
9	Germany	4,983
10	United Kingdom	3,912

Based on data from Energy Information Administration. International Total Primary Energy Consumption and Energy Intensity. Retrieved from www.eia.gov/cfapps/ipdbproject/IEDIndex3.cfm

are from the GEM. Out of these 15 EMCs, only 2 do not produce enough oil for their domestic consumption. This indicates that the overwhelming majority of EMCs have high energy intensity as a result of inefficient use of primary energy rather than a lack of energy, which is the case in the developing and underdeveloped countries listed in Table 5.15. Typically, developing and underdeveloped countries have outdated and inefficient technologies and as a result use much more energy than necessary per unit of production, despite a shortage of energy resources.

The economies that actually use energy most efficiently are not found on the top or bottom 30 in terms of energy intensity. Tables 5.15 and 5.16 both include countries that lack a national energy strategy. Many of them totally lack energy resources and/or modern machinery, technology, etc. All of them have standards of living far below the level of developed countries, with the exception of Kuwait and Qatar, which have high levels of energy consumption due to abundant oil reserves, and the Virgin Islands and the Netherlands Antilles, which have extremely expensive energy due to transportation costs. Both of these tables illustrate why strategists should not rely too heavily on a single indicator when assessing a country's economic maturity and business climate.

Among the largest economies in the world, Russia has the highest energy intensity. This is caused by inefficient and outdated technologies and machinery, a lack of energy strategy, and the increasing energy transportation costs in Russia's vast territory.

Since 1990, several important trends have affected global energy intensity. The most important development during this period was the formation of the GMP and the GEM. This is reflected in the decreasing energy intensity in the former Soviet Union, where the majority of countries are EMCs, transitioning from industrial to service-based economies. However, in Central and South America, where the overwhelming majority of countries are also EMCs, energy intensity has remained relatively stable. This is a result of the somewhat slower process of technological development, which itself results from a shortage of investment in science, technology, and education in this part of the world. Energy intensity increased during this period in the Middle East, where the majority of countries were in the process of industrializing their economies. North America experienced a substantial decrease in energy intensity, as did the GMP as a whole. In both cases, this is a direct result of the utilization of modern technologies and machinery, a trend that will likely continue in the foreseeable future.

Table 5.17 Energy Intensity (Use of Energy per One Unit of GDP) by Region (BTU per $2,000)

Region	*1990*	*1995*	*2000*	*2005*	*2011*
North America	10,362	9,980	8,771	7,990	7,384
Central & South America	6248.23	6,249	6,596	6,421	5,876
Europe	6979	6,815	6,230	5,908	5,271
Territory of the Former USSR	22214	26,059	22,228	17,540	14,586
Middle East	9,917	10,361	10,100	10,992	11,204
Africa	6,409	6,755	6,355	5,998	5,269
Asia & Oceania	8,751	8,629	8,100	8,186	7,749
Global Marketplace	9503	9,005	8,202	7,860	7,317

Based on data from Energy Information Administration. International Total Primary Energy Consumption and Energy Intensity. Retrieved from www.eia.gov/cfapps/ipdbproject/IEDIndex3.cfm

ENERGY CONSUMPTION PER CAPITA

It is important to analyze energy consumption on a per capita basis, in addition to per unit of GDP. The difference in consumption per capita of the least-energy-consuming countries and the most-energy-consuming countries varies by a factor of roughly 1,000. The average of the ten countries with the lowest energy consumption per capita is only 1.032 BTU. Not surprisingly, all of these countries are underdeveloped and developing, with the exception of Burkina Faso, which is among the poorest of all EMCs.

Table 5.19, which lists the countries that consume the most energy per capita, consists entirely of developed and emerging market countries, with the exception of Brunei and Nauru (indicators from these two countries are always distorted by extreme wealth imbalances and tiny populations). The highest per capita consumers of energy are mostly countries rich in primary energy resources, such as Qatar, Kuwait, Norway, and Canada; countries with very high standards of living, such as Iceland, Luxembourg, and the United States; or countries with poor energy-consumption practices, due to outdated machinery and technology, such as Trinidad and Tobago. The average energy consumption per capita of the top ten countries is 856.9 BTU. In general, energy consumption per capita is directly correlated with standard of living.

From 1990 to 2005, on a regional basis, there have been some important trends in energy consumption per capita. In North America and the former Soviet Union, there is no discernable pattern. However, in Central and South America, energy consumption per capita has increased steadily, due to the industrial development of EMCs of this region, which is occurring without modern energy-saving technologies as well as slowing of demographic trends. A similar dynamic occurred in Europe, the Middle East, Africa, and Asia. As a result, the efficiency of energy use is declining, while at the same time energy consumption is increasing. At the beginning of the twenty-first century, some countries have started to develop national energy-saving programs, but as of 2008, they have not yielded any tangible results.

After the initial stages of capitalization in EMCs and the completion of the initial processes of industrialization in underdeveloped and developing countries, energy consumption per capita tends to stabilize and eventually decrease, due to the use of energy-saving modern technologies and structural changes in the economies of these countries.

However, the interconnected use of technologies of varying levels of efficiency in processes of production, delivery, distribution, and consumption makes it very difficult to improve the energy efficiency of a national economy as whole. It is very difficult

Table 5.18 Thirty Countries with the Lowest Energy Consumption per Capita, 2014.

Rank	*Country*	*Consumption per Capita (Million BTU)*
1	Chad	0.3
2	Burundi	0.5
3	Eritrea	1.0
4	Rwanda	1.1
5	Mali	1.1
6	Niger	1.2
7	Somalia	1.2
8	Central African Republic	1.2
9	**Madagascar**	**1.5**
10	Congo (Kinshasa)	1.5
11	**Burkina Faso**	**1.6**
12	Ethiopia	1.8
13	Uganda	1.9
14	Sierra Leone	1.9
15	Malawi	2.0
16	Liberia	2.2
17	Guinea	2.2
18	Timor-Leste (East Timor)	2.4
19	Tanzania	2.7
20	Comoros	2.9
21	Nepal	3.0
22	Haiti	3.1
23	Gambia, The	3.4
24	Guinea-Bissau	3.5
25	Togo	3.6
26	Afghanistan	4.1
27	Burma (Myanmar)	5.0
28	Nigeria	5.0
29	Cambodia	5.1
30	Solomon Islands	5.3

Based on data from Energy Information Administration. International Energy Statistics. Retrieved from www.eia.gov/cfapps/ipdbproject/IEDIndex3.cfm

to optimize the efficiency of installed and currently used technologies. While each individual phase of these processes can be optimized based on linear programming, the optimization of such complex interconnected processes (which consist of many different industries, companies, and projects based on a variety of technologies and sources of energy) can be done only with non-linear modeling. For this reason, the participation of professionals and economists with high-level mathematical skills is needed to craft a strategy for multihierarchical scenarios.

Transportation (and even the transportation of energy itself) is one of the most energy-consuming industries in the GMP. However, significant progress has been made since the beginning of the twenty-first century, especially toward the development of more-efficient vehicles. The governments of developed countries like the United States, the European Union and its member-states, as well as those of emerging market countries like Brazil, China, and India, are developing national initiatives to motivate companies to develop energy-efficient technologies and machinery. The largest engine, airplane, locomotive, and automobile manufacturers are responding to these initiatives

Table 5.19 Thirty Countries with the Highest Energy Consumption per Capita, 2014

Rank	*Country*	*Consumption per Capita (BTU)*
1	**Qatar**	**790.3**
2	**Trinidad and Tobago**	**757.5**
3	**United Arab Emirates**	**728.4**
4	Iceland	688.3
5	**Singapore**	**578.6**
6	Kuwait	577.3
7	**Bahrain**	**451.2**
8	Canada	393.7
9	Norway	386.8
10	Luxembourg	385.8
11	Brunei	378.4
12	**Saudi Arabia**	**339.0**
13	**United States**	**313.0**
14	Oman	291.9
15	Australia	282.6
16	Belgium	257.5
17	Netherlands	244.8
18	Sweden	235.8
19	Finland	233.8
20	**Korea, South**	**232.0**
21	Malta	226.0
22	**Nauru**	**220.0**
23	**Russian Federation**	**213.4**
24	**Taiwan**	**210.0**
25	New Zealand	202.4
26	**Turkmenistan**	**187.1**
27	**Hong Kong**	**180.7**
28	Austria	179.1
29	France	165.9
30	Germany	165.4

Based on data from Energy Information Administration. International Energy Statistics. Retrieved from www.eia.gov/cfapps/ipdbproject/IEDIndex3.cfm

Table 5.20 Energy Consumption per Capita (Millions of BTU) by Region, 1990–2011

Region	*1990*	*1995*	*2000*	*2005*	*2011*
North America	276.3	279.0	286.1	278.2	258.2
Central & South America	40.7	45.3	49.7	52.3	58.5
Europe	136.8	134.5	139.8	143.6	134.4
Former Soviet Union Countries	210.7	144.6	134.7	148.8	154.9
Middle East	82.1	89.4	100.2	121.4	142.2
Africa	15.2	15.0	15.0	15.9	15.9
Asia & Oceania	25.2	29.7	32.1	40.2	51.9
Global Marketplace	65.7	63.9	65.4	70.3	74.9

Based on data from Energy Information Administration. International Energy Statistics. Retrieved from www.eia.gov/cfapps/ipdbproject/IEDIndex3.cfm

with more-efficient products. Even small companies have begun to play an important role in the development of key energy-saving technologies. According to the *Venture Capital Journal*, between 2006 and 2007 roughly $220 million was invested in small companies that are developing electric cars.[34] Small countries are also developing their own strategies to use renewable and environmentally friendly technologies. Iceland is one of the best examples. In 1998 this country announced an initiative to become the first hydrogen society, and by 2007 local buses were running on hydrogen fuel cells, as were many private cars. Iceland's scientists are among the leading experts in this field.

ENERGY-RELATED ENVIRONMENTAL POLLUTION IN THE WORLD

Many countries are following Iceland's lead, and the global community is becoming more focused on protecting the environment by implementing alternative energy strategies. The most ecologically and socially responsible countries have already begun to implement technology and other measures to decrease the negative influence of their energy consumption on the environment. In most emerging market and developing countries, these concerns have not yet resulted in high-priority national clean-energy and efficiency programs. As a result, the GEM has become responsible for a growing share of global pollution. As indicated by Figure 5.18, Asia's (and especially China's) share of global CO_2 emissions has more than tripled. Emissions of CO_2 have also increased in the EMCs of Latin America and Africa. The largest increase occurred in the Middle East, where CO_2 emissions have quadrupled since 1973.

The unique issues of economic development and environmental protection experienced by EMCs require coordinated cooperation to overcome similar challenges of their

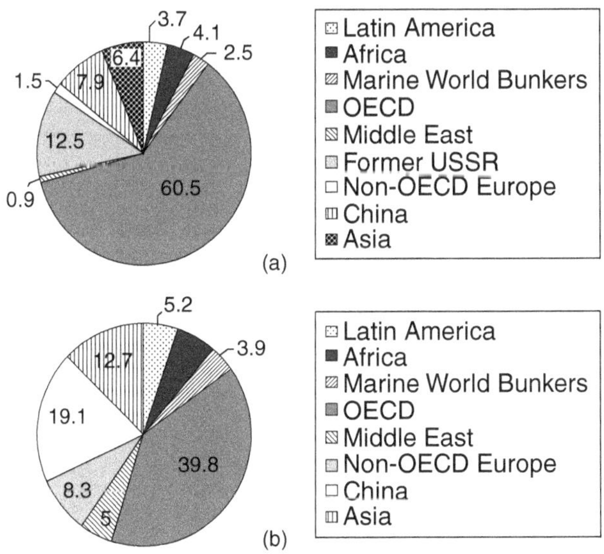

Figures 5.18a and 5.18b Change in World Energy-Related Carbon Dioxide Emissions by World Region and Country, 1973–2012

International Energy Agency. (2014). *Key World Energy Statistics 2014*. Retrieved from www.iea.org/publications/freepublications/publication/KeyWorld2014.pdf

development. It would be very beneficial to EMCs to establish a multilateral institution, which would monitor, coordinate, and provide recommendations for all countries of the GEM. This organization could be known as the Global Emerging Market Monitoring and Coordinating Agency (GEMMCA).

THE FACTOR OF NON-FERROUS METALS IN THE GMP

A comprehensive presentation of metal resources of the GMP is an immense task, and not the goal of this section. There are a number of encyclopedic source books and websites that can provide the appropriate information. This section focuses on the most economically important metals for major industries of the GMP. As a result of the formation of the GEM, competition for these metals, their reserves, and their production facilities is extremely high. In coming decades, competition for these resources will only intensify, as demand for their final products will continue to increase in the GEM and the developing world. Prices for metal-based products will undoubtedly rise, and available reserves will eventually decline. This is why it is very important to strategically evaluate the scale of current production and consumption of these metals and their allocation in the GMP. The analysis of these metals is based primarily on data from the United States Geological Survey of the US Department of the Interior. The tables are only slightly modified to highlight the role of EMCs for the reader's convenience.

ALUMINIUM

Typically, major aluminium production facilities are not located in the countries with large amounts of the mineral resource for aluminium (bauxite). The process of aluminium production is extremely energy intensive. As a result, bauxite is usually delivered to countries with powerful hydroelectric plants. One of the most significant changes in the aluminium industry is the emergence of China as the leading producer of this metal,

Table 5.21 World Aluminium Production (Thousands of Metric Tons), 2013

Rank	*Country*	*Production**
1	**China**	**21,500**
2	**Russia**	**3,950**
3	Canada	2,900
4	United States	1,950
5	**United Arab Emirates, Dubai**	**1,800**
6	Australia	1,750
7	**India**	**1,700**
8	**Brazil**	**1,330**
9	Norway	1,200
10	**Bahrain**	**900**
11	Iceland	825
12	**South Africa**	**820**
13	**Qatar**	600
14	Mozambique	560
	World Total	47,300

United States Geological Survey. "Aluminium." Retrieved from http://minerals.usgs.gov/minerals/pubs/commodity/aluminium/alumimcs07.pdf
*Estimated.

recently surpassing Russia. Its high established capacity and very low production costs practically ensure China's continued dominance of this industry, despite its very limited bauxite resources (only 3 percent of global bauxite reserves are located in China). This emerging Asian giant already consumes 14.3 percent of world aluminium, second only to the US. Interestingly, China produces enough aluminium for its domestic needs but still imports it from any available sources to store as reserves. This is one of many examples of China's sophisticated long-term strategy.

COPPER

The overwhelming majority of reserves and production of copper come from EMCs, with Chile as the unchallenged leader. At the beginning of this century, a geological evaluation of global copper reserves using more sophisticated technology resulted in a doubling of estimated reserves. Nevertheless, because of the continuing industrialization of many developing and emerging market countries, the demand for copper will continue to surpass the supply. Among the leading consumers of this heavy non-ferrous metal are China, followed by the European Union, the United States, Japan, South Korea, and Taiwan. Russia and Kazakhstan are not only among the leading producers but also among the leading consumers.

NICKEL

Two of the most potentially dangerous metal shortages for the European and US economies are deficits of nickel and cobalt. Neither the US nor the EU has substantial natural reserves or production facilities of nickel, which has been in high demand for many years

Table 5.22 World Copper Mine Production and Reserves (Ordered by Production) (Thousands of Metric Tons), 2014.

Rank	*Country*	*Production**	*Reserves***
1	**Chile**	5,434	190,000
2	**China**	1,642	30,000
3	**Peru**	1,299	70,000
4	United States	1,170	39,000
5	Australia	914	87,000
6	**Russia**	720	30,000
7	Zambia	629	20,000
8	Congo	608	20,000
9	Canada	579	10,000
10	**Mexico**	500	38,000
11	**Poland**	427	26,000
12	**Kazakhstan**	424	7,000
13	**Indonesia**	398	28,000
	World Total	16,800	690,000

United States Geological Survey. "Copper." Retrieved from http://minerals.usgs.gov/minerals/pubs/commodity/copper/coppemcs07.pdf

*Estimated.

**The part of the reserve base that could be economically extracted or produced at the time of determination. The term "reserves" need not signify that extraction facilities are in place and operative. Reserves include only recoverable materials.

Table 5.23 World Nickel Mine Production and Reserves (Ordered by Production) (Metric Tons), 2014

Rank	*Country*	*Production**	*Reserves***
1	United States	–	7,100
2	**Philippines**	330,000	1,100,000
3	**Indonesia**	320,000	3,900,000
4	**Russia**	270,000	6,100,000
5	Australia	230,000	20,000,000
6	Canada	220,000	3,300,000
7	New Caledonia	140,000	12,000,000
8	Other countries	120,000	4,600,000
9	**Colombia**	80,000	1,100,000
10	**China**	79,000	3,000,000
11	**Brazil**	74,200	7,500,000
12	Cuba	72,000	5,500,000
13	**South Africa**	42,000	3,700,000
14	Dominican Republic	24,000	970,000
15	**Madagascar**	22,000	1,600,000
	World Total	2,100,000	75,000,000

United States Geological Survey. "Nickel." Retrieved from http://minerals.usgs.gov/minerals/pubs/commodity/nickel/nickemcs07.pdf

*Estimated.

**The part of the reserve base that could be economically extracted or produced at the time of determination. The term "reserves" need not signify that extraction facilities are in place and operative. Reserves include only recoverable materials.

due to its use for the production of stainless steel. The importance of nickel increased substantially when major car manufacturers began production of nickel-metal hydride batteries for gasoline-electric hybrid cars at the beginning of this century. The only two countries that have actually implemented an aggressive long-term strategy in the nickel industry are Russia and China.

China's demand for nickel has grown substantially in recent years. As of 2005, it accounts for 17 percent of global primary nickel consumption.[35] China is seeking and signing long-term contracts in order to guarantee a sufficient supply for the needs of its economy and to increase its share in the global consumption of nickel. Russia has a different strategy. Already one of the largest producers of nickel, Russia acquired nickel-production facilities in Canada, another leading producer. This will have important strategic implications for the United States. By 2007 Russia already accounted for 17 percent of US imports of nickel. As a result, all imports from Canada (which account for 41 percent of total US imports of nickel) are also under the control and ownership of the Russian nickel-cobalt-platinum giant, Norilsk Nickel.

COBALT

The lack of domestic production of cobalt from primary raw materials will also have significant implications for the US and the EU. The United States consumes more than 350 million tons of this heavy metal annually, mostly for engine and machinery building and aircraft production. Most imports to the US and the EU are from developing and emerging market countries. The world leader by far is the Democratic Republic of Congo (Kinshasa). However, due to strategic agreements made by the Chinese government with the Congo, a substantial amount of cobalt ore goes directly to refineries in China. In 2005, China became the world's largest producer of refined cobalt. Ninety percent of cobalt ore used to produce final products in China comes from the Congo. Only one-quarter of raw materials (including scrap) for refined cobalt production comes from domestic Chinese sources.

Among developed countries, only the United States and Australia have substantial natural cobalt reserves. However, due to a lower amount of cobalt per unit of raw, extraction is much more expensive and requires very sophisticated technologies. Furthermore, there are much stricter environmental regulations in these countries, further increasing extraction costs. It appears that the US government does not have a strategy to motivate the development of cobalt production. For example, in 2006, a plant in North Carolina that produced extra-fine cobalt powder relocated to Belgium, Canada, and China.[36] Even from this decision, the role of imports from China is again increasing for the US economy.

PLATINUM GROUP METALS

A global shortage of platinum group metals will have serious strategic implications for several major industries of the GMP. Platinum group metals include platinum, palladium, rhodium, ruthenium, iridium, and osmium. Despite the fact that the majority of readers may have never heard of some of these metals, demand for them has risen markedly, due to increasing production of catalytic converters for environmentally friendly technologies and engines. These metals will also be used heavily for the removal of organic vapors, odors, and carbon monoxide. Unlike other non-ferrous metals, which were mentioned above, the production of platinum group metals is estimated not in millions of tons, or even tons, but in kilograms. Only five countries are major producers of these metals. Among developed countries, only the US has reserves and production facilities of platinum and palladium. But even the US imports more than 70 percent of its palladium. Thirty-seven percent of these imports come from Russia.

In a few countries, platinum is a popular jewelry metal. Japan and China are by far the leading consumers of platinum for the jewelry industry. Until 2001 Japan accounted for 25 percent of global sales of platinum jewelry. However, as the standard of living in China

Table 5.24 World Cobalt Production and Reserves (Ordered by Production) (Metric Tons), 2012

Rank	*Country*	*Production*	*Reserves*
1	Congo (Kinshasa)	52,000	3,400,000
2	Zambia	5,700	270,000
3	Australia	4,000	1,400,000
4	Canada	7,200	130,000
5	**Russia**	5,100	250,000
6	Cuba	4,000	1,000,000
7	**Morocco**	1,500	20,000
8	**China**	6,500	80,000
9	New Caledonia	2,000	370,000
10	**Brazil**	1,700	87,000
	World Total	98,000	7,500,000

United States Geological Survey. "Cobalt." Retrieved from http://minerals.usgs.gov/minerals/pubs/commodity/cobalt/cobalmcs07.pdf

improved, its consumption of platinum jewelry surpassed Japan's. It is important to underline that being one of the largest consumers of platinum, China has only 0.3 percent of global platinum reserves. For industrial purposes, the US, Germany, Japan, South Korea, China, Italy, France, Brazil, Sweden, India, Iran, and the Czech Republic, among others, will compete intensely for platinum, and especially palladium. According to the US Geological Survey,

> An increase in diesel car sales in Europe can be expected to cause a strong increase in use of platinum ... The tightening of emissions regulations in China, Europe, Japan and other parts of the world is also expected to lead to higher average platinum loadings on catalysts, especially on light-duty diesel vehicles, as particulate matter emissions become more closely controlled.[37]

In the first quarter of the twenty-first century, the world will continue to face an increasing shortage of palladium because this precious metal will play a crucial role in the upcoming mass production of hydrogen fuel cells and converters. All major scientific advances have already been completed for this technology. Scientists and engineers are working on the development of commercially viable products. In this context, the acquisition of Stillwater Mining Company from Columbus, Montana, by Norilsk Nickel (the largest producer of palladium in the world) is an example of Russia's aggressive cross-border economic strategy.

Norilsk Nickel (Norilsk Mining-Metallurgical Concern), even during the time of the Soviet command economy, was and still is the largest producer of palladium and nickel, and one of the largest of cobalt, platinum, osmium, and gold in the world. It is one of Russia's most efficient companies and one of the most profitable in the world. Prior to the disintegration of the Soviet Union, this company, with 125,000 employees, had an annual profit of about \$1.5 billion, and an annual total value of production of non-ferrous and precious metals of about \$3.2 billion. The privatization of the Norilsk Concern is an example of mismanagement and possibly corruption by the Russian government. In 1996 it sold for only \$170 million, and it is not even clear if this money was ever actually delivered. These numbers would be comical if it weren't so tragic for the national budget of Russia and the standard of living of its people. At that time, any company in the world, at least from this industry, would be happy to buy 10 percent of this company for \$1 billion. In order to increase production of nickel, copper, platinum, or any other metals produced by Norilsk, any company would have to invest in geological explorations, the development of the mines, construction of enrichment and metallurgical plants, and development of an infrastructure (transportation, telecommunication, and housing, etc. for employees—the location of ore and raw material are far from existing housing areas). These investments require billions of dollars and substantial time. Any company would not hesitate to seize the opportunity to buy Norilsk Nickel, with its huge proven and registered reserves, established production facilities, and developed infrastructure.

GOLD

The primary value of gold in the GMP is its use as a banking metal. With the extension of capital markets to the GEM and other areas of the global marketplace, it is important to consider the limited production of gold. As more EMCs attempt to make their national currencies stable and convertible, the importance of gold as a banking metal is increasing.

Table 5.25 World Platinum Group Metals Production and Reserves (Ordered by Reserves) (Kilograms*)

		Mine Production				
		Platinum		*Palladium*		*Platinum Group Metals*
Rank	*Country*	*2012*	*2013***	*2012*	*2013***	*Reserves****
1	**South Africa**	**133,000**	**140,000**	**74,000**	**82,000**	**63,000,000**
2	**Russia**	**24,600**	**25,000**	**82,000**	**82,000**	**1,100,000**
3	United States	3,670	3,700	12,300	12,500	900,000
4	Canada	7,000	7,000	12,200	13,000	310,000
5	Zimbabwe	11,000	12,000	9,000	9,000	NA****
	Other countries	3,480	4,000	11,500	12,000	800,000
	World Total (rounded)	183,000	192,000	201,000	211,000	66,000,000

United States Geological Survey. "Platinum Group Metals." Retrieved from http://minerals.usgs.gov/minerals/pubs/commodity/platinum/platimcs07.pdf

* Table organized by reserves.
** Estimated.
*** The part of the reserve base that could be economically extracted or produced at the time of determination. The term "reserves" does not signify that extraction facilities are in place and operative. Reserves include only recoverable materials.
**** Included with "World Total."

Gold reserves, together with foreign currency reserves, act as a backup of any currency. It is different for the United States because the US dollar is the leading banking currency, and practically all countries try to accumulate it in their reserves. As a result, despite strong competition from the euro, the US dollar is still an equivalent of gold in several economic functions. Thus the US Department of Treasury has only about $47 billion worth of foreign currency reserves, which, for example, is 22.5 times less than Chinese reserves and 8.2 times less than Russian reserves. Both of these countries keep 40 to 45 percent of their foreign currency reserves in US dollars. This is why the United States, the emitter country of dollars, does not need huge foreign currency reserves. Instead it has the largest gold stocks in the world: 261.50 millions of fine troy ounces stored in Fort Knox and other vaults around the country.[38] However, I question the official numbers of national gold reserves of several countries, but first and foremost China. I estimate that China has two or three times more gold than it officially states. A quarter century ago, in the Soviet Union, on several occasions I was witness to similarly exaggerated statements about gold reserves. I have since begun to question if the United States still has the biggest gold reserves, due to the huge quantity of undeclared gold in China. Even though the gold standard was abolished in 1971, gold reserves still play a very important role in the global banking system, especially for currencies that are not freely convertible. Out of the eight major gold-producing countries, five are EMCs, accounting for about three-quarters of world gold production. The biggest individual gold mine, the Muruntau, is in Uzbekistan, which by many indicators can still be considered a developing country. Regardless, the GMP will not experience a shortage of gold for industrial purposes, but in terms of its role as a banking metal, gold can at least be partially replaced by platinum group metals if it is required by the global monetary system.

Gold production is a very sensitive and often secretive issue. I have basis for doubting the real value of gold production in several countries of the GEM and in some

Table 5.26 World Gold Production and Reserves (Metric Tons), 2013*

Rank	*Country*	*Production***	*Reserves****
1	**China**	**420**	**1,900**
2	Australia	255	9,900
3	United States	227	3,000
4	**Russia**	**220**	**5,000**
5	**Peru**	**150**	**3,500**
6	**South Africa**	**145**	**6,000**
7	Canada	120	920
8	**Mexico**	**100**	**1,400**
9	Uzbekistan	93	1,700
10	**Ghana**	**85**	**2,000**
11	**Brazil**	**75**	**2,400**
12	Papua New Guinea	62	1,200
13	**Indonesia**	**60**	**3,000**
14	**Chili**	**55**	**3,900**
	Other countries	700	10,000
	World total (rounded)	2,770	54,000

United States Geological Survey. "Gold." Retrieved January 13, 2015 from http://minerals.usgs.gov/minerals/pubs/commodity/gold/mcs-2014-gold.pdf

*Table organized by production.

**Estimated.

***The part of the reserve base that could be economically extracted or produced at the time of determination. The term "reserves" need not signify that extraction facilities are in place and operative. Reserves include only recoverable materials.

developing states. It is important to verify statistics by multiple sources. With increasing demand for gold from EMCs (who are most interested in holding gold as a back-up for their national currencies) some EMCs have reported very rapid increases in production, despite the fact that total world production is not increasing. According to some sources, China increased its production by 12 percent in 2007, becoming the leading producer of gold in the world.[39] However, this information needs further verification.

There are other important metals, such as titanium and molybdenum, and some minerals, such as metallic uranium, which there may be shortages of in the future. In general the GMP will be able to find substitutes or make alloys that can replace minerals and metals in extreme shortage. In addition to being aware of the location of reserves and existing production facilities for key metals and minerals, it is also important to analyze their capacities and percentage of use. Of course, technological advancements will likely make many existing production facilities obsolete. It is also important to realize that not all reserves are economically feasible to extract. The reserves could be located in areas with a lack of transportation infrastructure, which is the case for at least 35 percent of Russian mineral resources, which are located in permafrost above the Arctic Circle. The world has tremendous reserves of minerals on and under the ocean floor, but there are no existing technologies to efficiently exploit them. The production of metal as well as of all other natural resources as an essential economic factor is very heavily influenced by two other economic factors: technological development and available capital.

When evaluating natural reserves, it is important for strategists to consult several sources. Corporate reports on reserves, for instance, are not always accurate.

In order to avoid taxes, companies in EMCs sometimes underreport the scale of their reserves. On the other hand, reserves may be over-reported in the interest of attracting investors. It is a good idea to consult independent organizations that specialize in the particular mineral or natural resource. For example, the Society of Petroleum Engineers, a professional association of energy, is a good resource when evaluating oil reserves. Evaluations based solely on company reports should always be reevaluated based on actual geological studies when possible, in order to avoid potentially serious strategic blunders.

THE FACTOR OF FORESTRY

Forestry is among the most important natural resources for any country and its inhabitants. Since the beginning of the industrial revolution in the eighteenth century, forestry has been considered only as a source of industrial production. However, by the end of the twentieth century, as concern for the impact of humankind on the environment increased, forestry has become a major factor in environmental quality and health standards. With time and technological development, the ecological value of forestry will overwhelm its value as a source of timber and pulp production. For example, forestry reserves can be artificially augmented in order to prevent environmental threats like desertification, which is a danger in roughly 32 percent of the world's territory. This could substantially improve standards of living, as population growth in areas of desertification is growing faster than the world average. Among the countries with the largest reserves of forestry, there are only a few developed countries (Canada, the US, Australia, and, much further behind, ranked 22nd in the world, Sweden).

Table 5.27 lists countries with the largest forest areas. This data should also be interpreted on a per capita basis. For example, while China has the fifth most abundant forest areas in the world, this country is six times below the world average on a per capita basis. As when analyzing the allocation of all natural resources, it is important to evaluate forestry resources in terms of their location relative to existing production facilities, infrastructure, etc.

Having the largest reserves of forestry does not guarantee that a country will be a major producer of wood-based final goods. Japan, which is the 23rd country in terms of forestry, is the third-largest producer of paper and paperboard. Japan gets much more revenue from these final products than countries with larger forestry reserves that export more timber or logs (i.e., raw material). Japan exports only high-value-added final products, not raw materials. Not surprisingly, China is at the forefront of national strategies in the forestry industry as well. This is clearly illustrated by the fact that China has a quarter of the forestry resources of Russia (the world's leading country), but Russia produces only 13 percent as much paper and paperboard products as China. Russia totally lacks a strategy in this industry, as it primarily exports logs (without any value added) and timber, rather than more sophisticated final products. This trend is increasing, as more logs are imported to China from Russia. The percentage of total Chinese log imports from Russia increased in two years, from 43.6 percent in 2000 to 60.7 percent in 2002. It is important to note that 93 percent of these imports are of pine and larch, the highest-quality wood.[40] The strategic success of China is even more clearly demonstrated by the fact that the combined production of paper and paperboard of the two world-leading countries by forestry (Russia and Brazil) is only 28.7 percent of China's production. China has also made strategic investments in the timber industry of many countries of South America,

Table 5.27 Top 25 Countries in Terms of Forest Area (Square Kilometers)

Rank	*Country*	*Forest Area (Sq. Km)*
1	**Russia**	8,087,900
2	**Brazil**	4,776,980
3	Canada	3,101,340
4	United States	3,030,890
5	**China**	1,972,900
6	Australia	1,636,780
7	Congo, Dem. Rep.	1,336,100
8	**Indonesia**	884,950
9	**Peru**	687,420
10	**India**	677,010
11	Sudan	675,460
12	**Mexico**	642,380
13	**Colombia**	607,280
14	Angola	591,040
15	**Bolivia**	587,400
16	Venezuela, RB	477,130
17	Zambia	424,520
18	Tanzania	352,570
19	**Argentina**	330,210
20	Myanmar	322,220
21	Papua New Guinea	294,370
22	Sweden	275,280
23	Japan	248,680
24	Central African Republic	227,550
25	Finland	225,000

Based on data from the World Bank World Development Indicators. Retrieved from http://econ.worldbank.org/WBSITE/EXTERNAL/EXTDEC/0,,menuPK:476823~pagePK:64165236~piPK:64165141~theSitePK:469372,00.html

Africa as well as Russia. China has established more than 30 companies related to forestry and timber in these areas. Forty percent of timber consumption in China is imported. At the same time, China is developing a strategy to spare its own natural forestry from industrial purposes, and instead is developing artificial forestry farms, which account for 26 percent of the world total, covering 160 million hectares.[41]

The exploitation of natural resources without a proper strategy can do more harm than good to a national economy. Countries like Brazil, Indonesia, Romania, and Russia still do not have correctly developed national strategies for the use of natural resources. Some of these countries have developed documents called strategies, but they have not allocated to them the required investments and technologies, making them just empty declarations. When a country sells raw materials or semi-products instead of final goods, the country loses a significant amount of potential revenue. Out of the 25 leading countries in terms of forestry, 19 are emerging market, developing, or even underdeveloped. In terms of production of much more profitable goods, such as paper and paperboard, out of the top 25 countries, less than half (11) belong to the GEM, and none are developing or underdeveloped. Countries that lack strategic vision sell raw materials. Sophisticated countries sell final products. A key element of successful strategy in the GMP is the use of technology, which allows the export of more sophisticated and expensive final products.

Table 5.28 Paper and Paperboard Production (Tons), 2012

Rank	*Country*	*Millions of Tons of Production*
1	United States of America	75.90
2	**China**	92.60
3	Japan	27.30
4	Germany	23.10
5	Canada	12.80
6	Finland	11.80
7	Sweden	11.40
8	**Korea, Republic of**	11.10
9	France	8.80
10	Italy	9.10
11	**Brazil**	9.80
12	**Indonesia**	10.00
13	**Russian Federation**	7.60
14	United Kingdom	4.30
15	**Spain**	6.20
16	Austria	5.00
17	**Mexico**	4.80
18	**India**	9.20
21	**Thailand**	4.70

Based on data from the FAOSTAT database of the Food and Agriculture Organization of the United Nations. Retrieved from http://faostat.fao.org/site/381/default.aspx

LABOR RESOURCES OF THE GLOBAL MARKETPLACE

Labor is a key basic economic factor and the most important in terms of a country's future prosperity. For strategists and executives, dynamics and qualitative indicators of this factor, such as population growth or decline, literacy level, level of higher educational attainment, dynamics and development of the middle class, and the level of social unity and tolerance in society are more important than quantitative indicators. Labor resources are not only a key basic economic factor, but they are also a bridge between economic analysis and broader evaluations of a country. Strategists often make the mistake of looking at a country, region, or corporation only through the prism of economic indicators. It is important not to underestimate, or fail to estimate at all, the role of social, cultural, and religious issues in a society. All of these concerns are key to understanding the current and future labor market, required compensation, and the quality of potential employees. These factors also have crucial implications for the development of a country. Low-cost, quality labor resources attract foreign investment. China is an obvious example. The overwhelming majority of foreign investment in China is not there because of the country's natural resources or its existing production facilities. China's main lure is its inexpensive and practically unlimited number of hardworking employees. Despite the fact that China's consumer market is rapidly growing and already large, it is not a major draw for foreign investors; 80 percent of goods produced in China are export oriented.

The role of labor resources of developed countries in the global labor market is diminishing due to fast-growing populations in emerging, developing, and underdeveloped countries. Out of the ten countries with the highest populations, only two are developed—the United States and Japan. Within a matter of five years, Japan's population will likely be surpassed by Mexico's.

Table 5.29 Ten Largest Countries in Terms of Population, 2015

Rank	*Country*	*2014 Population*
1	**China**	1,355,692,576
2	**India**	1,236,344,631
3	United States	318,892,103
4	**Indonesia**	253,609,643
5	**Brazil**	202,656,788
6	**Pakistan**	196,174,380
7	Nigeria	177,155,754
8	Bangladesh	166,820,712
9	**Russian Federation**	142,470,272
10	Japan	127,103,388
	Other Countries	3,005,478,372

Compiled from Internet World Stats. Retrieved from www.internetworldstats.com

Table 5.30 Fastest-Growing National Populations, 2014

Rank	*Country*	*Population Growth Rate (%)*
1	Oman	9.17
2	**Qatar**	**5.60**
3	South Sudan	4.14
4	Niger	3.85
5	Kuwait	3.57
6	Uganda	3.34
7	Eritrea	3.25
8	Zambia	3.24
9	Gambia, The	3.19
10	Burundi	3.13
11	Angola	3.08
12	Zimbabwe	3.05
13	Tanzania	3.03
14	Chad	2.98
15	West Bank and Gaza	2.98

Based on data from the World Bank World Development Indicators. Retrieved from http://data.worldbank.org/indicator/SP.POP.GROW/countries?order=wbapi_data_value_2013+wbapi_data_value+wbapi_data_value-last&sort=desc

Among the 15 fastest growing national populations there is not a single developed country, and only 1 country that barely qualifies as an EMC. The fastest growing nations require a great deal of international support in terms of health and education, as well as the creation of conditions conducive to business activity.

Contrary to popular opinion, among the top ten countries with the most rapidly declining populations there is also not a single developed country. The high standard of living and low birth rates (below the 2.15 per woman replacement rate) usually associated with developed countries are not necessarily causes of a rapidly declining population. Also contrary to popular opinion, there is only one sub-Saharan nation, Swaziland, among the most rapidly declining national populations. Even the extreme hunger, mass disease, and low standards of living that plague much of sub-Saharan Africa do not necessarily cause rapid decline in national populations. Out of the ten fastest-declining

Table 5.31 Most Rapidly Declining National Population, 2014

Rank	*Country*	*Population Growth Rate (%)*
1	**Lithuania**	**-1.07**
2	**Latvia**	**-1.03**
3	**Albania**	**-1.01**
4	**Romania**	**-0.57**
5	**Bulgaria**	**-0.56**
6	**Greece**	**-0.55**
7	**Portugal**	**-0.52**
8	**Serbia**	**-0.49**
9	**Croatia**	**-0.35**
10	**Georgia**	**-0.31**
11	**Spain**	**-0.24**
12	**Hungary**	**-0.23**
13	**Ukraine**	**-0.23**
14	Japan	-0.17
15	**Bosnia and Herzegovina**	**-0.12**

Based on data from the World Bank World Development Indicators. Retrieved from http://data.worldbank.org/indicator/SP.POP.GROW/countries?order=wbapi_data_value_2013+wbapi_data_value+wbapi_data_value-last&sort=desc

national populations, eight are countries of the former Soviet Union. They are all from Eastern Europe, with moderate standards of living, decent health care systems, a high level of education and literacy, and a developing middle class. This regional phenomenon should be further examined from a strategic economic point of view.

Another counterintuitive trend regarding population dynamics is the rapid growth in populations in areas near deserts. The productivity of this population as a labor resource is strongly tied to the issue of freshwater resources, especially for water-consuming processes like agriculture and chemical industries. Typically, desert areas also suffer from a shortage of energy resources, which is an issue for the labor productivity and cost of this growing segment of the world's population.

Of course there are a number of factors beyond the size of a national population that determine its productivity as a labor resource. For strategists it is important to calculate the percentage of people of working age (between age 16 and 65). Typically in countries with high standards of living there is a high percentage of elderly people (65 and older), who are generally not considered a productive part of the labor force. However, there is an emerging trend of continued employment for people of retirement age due to health improvements of the population of this age. Among the ten oldest national populations, there are four European EMCs—Greece, Croatia, Portugal, and Latvia. Among the top 20, half are EMCs. This is also a reflection of improvements in health care and standards of living and longer life expectancies in the GEM.

An extremely young national population also has important strategic implications for business and government. Practically all national populations with a high percentage of people age 15 or younger are very poor, with low standards of living and low life expectancies. These countries require special attention from the global community to support the establishment of health care and education systems. These countries also require specially designed microfinance systems to help develop domestic companies. Some of these countries are already attracting foreign investment—Burkina Faso and the

Table 5.32 Countries with Largest Percentage of National Population Age 65 and Above, 2014

Rank	*Country*	*National Population 65 and Above (%)*
1	Japan	25.08
2	Germany	21.14
3	Italy	21.13
4	**Greece**	**19.67**
5	Sweden	19.33
6	**Bulgaria**	**19.31**
7	Finland	19.04
8	**Portugal**	**18.77**
9	**Latvia**	**18.57**
10	Austria	18.36
11	**Croatia**	**18.29**
12	**Estonia**	**18.04**
13	Belgium	17.98
14	Denmark	17.90
15	France	17.86
16	**Spain**	**17.76**
17	Switzerland	17.71
18	United Kingdom	17.49
19	**Slovenia**	**17.24**
20	**Hungary**	**17.22**

Based on data from the World Bank World Development Indicators. Retrieved from http://data.worldbank.org/indicator/SP.POP.65UP.TO.ZS

Democratic Republic of Congo, for example—but this investment is neither sustainable nor big enough to be a significant factor of economic development. Nonetheless, strategists have already found a way to address these countries as a market. This approach is known as the bottom of pyramid (BOP). People in these countries have the same essential needs as anyone else—basic consumer and durable goods, education for themselves and their children, etc. A strategy crafted for this particular business environment can yield substantial profit for companies in certain industries. In doing so, companies from the GMP participate in the improvement of the standards of living of these countries. The poorest countries' most desperate need is more permanent jobs with innovational background.

Life expectancy is another issue worth exploring by strategists in order to properly evaluate the labor resources of a country. Among the ten countries with the lowest life expectancy, only 1 belongs to the GEM: South Africa. The other countries listed in Table 5.34 are underdeveloped and developing. Beyond the implications of this indicator for the labor resources of these countries, it is a further illustration of the unique needs of developing and underdeveloped countries. Many multilateral and research institutions falsely group all non-developed countries into the category of developing countries. This is extremely counterproductive, as the needs of developing and underdeveloped countries are totally different from those of emerging market countries. Each of these categories has substantially different business, social, and political environments. If EMCs mostly seek cooperation from and even fair competition with the developed world, the developing and especially underdeveloped countries seek foreign aid more than anything else. An entry strategy for companies going to underdeveloped and developing countries is also unique. Companies investing in these groups of countries have to make

Table 5.33 Countries with Largest Percentage of National Population Age 15 and Below, 2014

Rank	*Country*	*National Population Age 15 and Below (%)*
1	Niger	50.1
2	Chad	48.4
3	Uganda	48.4
4	Angola	47.5
5	Mali	47.4
6	Somalia	47.2
7	Afghanistan	46.6
8	Zambia	46.6
9	Gambia, The	45.9
10	Timor-Leste	45.8

Based on data from the World Bank World Development Indicators. Retrieved from http://data.worldbank.org/indicator/SP.POP.0014.TO.ZS

Table 5.34 Countries with the Lowest Life Expectancies, 2014

Rank	*Country*	*Life Expectancy at Birth*
1	Sierra Leone	45.3
2	Botswana	47.0
3	Lesotho	48.8
4	Swaziland	48.9
5	Central African Republic	49.5
6	Congo, Dem. Rep.	49.6
7	Mozambique	49.8
8	Cote d'Ivoire	50.4
9	Chad	50.7
10	Angola	51.5

Based on data from the World Bank World Development Indicators. Retrieved from http://data.worldbank.org/indicator/SP.DYN.LE00.IN

investments in the social infrastructure in addition to their main industrial investment. Social investment and the creation of new jobs are not only extremely beneficial to the people of these countries, but also to the companies themselves. They establish a positive relationship with the local population and improve the lives of the company's employees, who would otherwise struggle to afford housing, health care, transportation, and education.

Literacy

The well-educated populations of many EMCs are the basis for the nations' innovative potential and a major lure for foreign investment. Among the ten most literate populations, there are two EMCs: Latvia and Estonia. Among the countries with the most illiterate populations, there is not a single EMC.

Contrary to popular opinion, developed countries do not dominate the list of countries with the highest percentage of the national population with university-level educations. Half of the top ten countries in this category are EMCs. Four of them have a higher percentage of people with university degrees than that of the US and Japan. Out of the

Table 5.35 Countries with the Highest Literacy Rates, 2014

Rank	*Country*	*Literacy Rate (%)*
1	Andorra	100.0
2	Finland	100.0
3	Korea, North	100.0
4	Liechtenstein	100.0
5	Luxembourg	100.0
6	Norway	100.0
7	**Azerbaijan**	**99.8**
8	Cuba	99.8
9	**Estonia**	**99.8**
10	**Latvia**	**99.8**
11	**Barbados**	**99.7**
12	**Georgia**	**99.7**

CIA. (n.d.). "World Factbook." "Literacy Rates." Retrieved from www.cia.gov/library/publications/the-world-factbook/fields/2103.html

Table 5.36 Countries with the Lowest Literacy Rates, 2014

Rank	*Country*	*Literacy Rate (%)*
1	South Sudan	27.0
2	Mali	27.7
3	Afghanistan	28.1
4	**Burkina Faso**	28.7
5	Niger	28.7
6	Sierra Leone	35.1
7	Chad	35.4
8	Ethiopia	39.0
9	Senegal	39.3
10	Guinea	41.0
11	Benin	42.4
12	The Gambia	50.0
13	Wallis and Futuna	50.0
14	Bhutan	52.8
15	Haiti	52.9

CIA. (n.d.). "World Factbook." "Literacy Rates." Retrieved from www.cia.gov/library/publications/the-world-factbook/fields/2103.html

top 20 countries with the most educated population, more than half (11) are from the GEM. The highest level of kinematical effect in education as far as I can see is demonstrated in South Korea, India, Hong Kong, and China as a whole. Education leadership of the US most related to higher education, but with less and less widening gap in comparison with the nations mentioned above.

Distribution of Wealth

The formation of the GMP, about 50 percent of which consists of the GEM (in terms of GDP PPP), has made it more difficult for strategists to understand traditional statistical data. In EMCs, average and median statistics give a less accurate portrayal of economic and social conditions for the majority of the population than equivalent data of developed countries. The numbers are distorted due to the very unequal distributions of

Table 5.37 Countries with Highest Level of Educational Attainment (Ordered by Graduates as a Percentage of Population), 2012

Rank	*Country*	*Total University (Tertiary) Graduates for Year 2012*	*Total Year 2012 Graduates as a Percentage of Population*
1	Australia	386,625	1.68
2	**Poland**	**638,957**	**1.67**
3	New Zealand	71,931	1.61
4	**Ukraine**	**642,387**	**1.41**
5	**Lithuania**	**42,379**	**1.40**
6	**Russian Federation**	**1,970,883**	**1.38**
7	**Belarus**	**126,028**	**1.34**
8	Slovakia	72,374	1.33
9	Ireland	60,022	1.31
10	Cuba	145,275	1.29
11	**Mongolia**	**35,847**	**1.28**
12	**Armenia**	**37,815**	**1.27**
13	**Republic of Korea**	**618,281**	**1.26**
14	United Kingdom of Great Britain and Northern Ireland	754,310	1.20
15	**Romania**	**259,634**	**1.19**
16	France	697,193	1.09
17	Denmark	58,667	1.05
18	**Latvia**	**21,472**	**1.04**
19	United States of America	3,308,494	1.04
20	**Czech Republic**	**107,773**	**1.01**

Based on data from UNESCO Education Statistics. Retrieved from http://data.uis.unesco.org

wealth, corruption, and the diminished role of the middle class (relative to developed countries). In EMCs, standards of living of the top 10 percent and bottom 10 percent vary by a factor of at least 15 in most cases. Any indicator related to the average quality of life in an EMC (life expectancy, for example) is distorted by the substantial gap between the rich and the poor and is not indicative of the conditions experienced by most people. Unlike in underdeveloped countries, where the dynamic is different, in EMCs increasing social polarization typically leads to decreased birth rates, shrinking populations, and decreasing life expectancy.

The correlations between all of these factors were the focus of many studies of states and groups, such as the Luxembourg Income Study. This project examined more than 30 countries, including 14 EMCs from Europe, Asia, and Latin America. Studies like this, analyzing a limited number of countries from all areas of the GMP, are useful to help strategists evaluate the role of a particular country or group of countries in the GMP relative to others. The general conclusions from the Luxembourg Income Study are that the poorer the country, the wider the gap between the rich and poor, the more social tension and the worse conditions are for international business.

Among the top ten countries with the highest polarization of wealth distribution, the first four are underdeveloped, and only four are EMCs. None of them are from Europe or North America, where the standards of living are higher than those of Latin America and Africa. One of the most efficient methods of evaluating income inequality is the Gini index, developed by Italian statistician Corrado Gini in 1912. This index became especially popular at the end of the 1980s, as EMCs became more important in the international business community. The growing role of the GEM created a demand to evaluate variations in income equality. The Gini index is essentially a coefficient of income concentration; the Gini coefficient can also be used to compare different regions within a country. The Gini method is a simple means of providing a *static* picture of income distribution. However, Dr. Simon Kuznets, the Nobel Laureate in Economics (1971), developed a hypothesis that deals with the *dynamic* of income distribution. The Gini coefficient is an extremely useful method to understand income inequality. Many economists have attempted to develop an economic law that determines the distribution of income; the most successful of them are Nobel Laureates Maurice Allias (awarded in 1988) and Amartya Sen (awarded in 1998). These attempts substantially built upon the Gini coefficient.

Employment

One of the most important indicators of a labor market is the level of national unemployment. This indicator provides an evaluation of stability, political and economic risk of investment, and has important implications for human resource policy, potential level of

Table 5.38 Countries with the Most Unequal Distribution of Wealth—Gini Index, 2014

Rank	*Country*	*Gini Index*
1	Lesotho	63.2
2	**South Africa**	**63.1**
3	**Botswana**	**63**
4	Sierra Leone	62.9
5	Central African Republic	61.3
6	Namibia	59.7
7	Haiti	59.2
8	Honduras	57.7
9	Zambia	57.5
10	**Colombia**	**55.9**

CIA. (n.d.). "World Factbook." "Country Comparison. Distribution of Family Income—Gini Index." Retrieved from www.cia.gov/library/publications/the-world-factbook/rankorder/2172rank.html

Table 5.39 Countries with the Most Equitable Distribution of Wealth—Gini Index, 2014

Rank	*Country*	*Gini Index*
1	Sweden	23
2	**Slovenia**	**23.7**
3	**Montenegro**	**24.3**
4	**Hungary**	**24.7**
5	Denmark	24.8
6	**Czech Republic**	**24.9**
7	Norway	25
8	Luxembourg	26
9	**Slovakia**	**26**
10	Austria	26.3

CIA. (n.d.) "World Factbook." "Country Comparison. Distribution of Family Income—Gini Index." Retrieved from www.cia.gov/library/publications/the-world-factbook/rankorder/2172rank.html

compensation, etc. The unemployment rate in the world economy has been steadily declining since 1997. However, the terrorist attacks on September 11, 2001, had a very negative impact on this indicator. It took another three years for the world economy to recover its positive dynamic. In terms of regions of the GMP, the highest unemployment can be found in the EU, which is higher than the average in the world, and even higher than in the GEM. According to the author's evaluation, as of January 1, 2008, average unemployment in the GEM is 7.4 percent, which is higher than the rate in the US, but lower than that of Europe.

The general dynamics from the graph and diagram in Figures 5.19 and 5.20 indicate a decreasing level of unemployment in the world and in all major categories of countries of the GMP from 2004 to 2008. After the global financial crisis of 2008, the US and GEM recovered much more quickly than both the European Union and the world average overall. As of 2015, unemployment in the GEM and the United States continues to decline, while the role of the GEM in world unemployment is increasing. Emerging market countries which engage in international trade with the US see a faster decline in unemployment than those who trade with the European Union, such as the countries of Southern and Central Europe, several of which are members of the EU. The above figures also demonstrate the increasing influence of international trade and cross-border FDI on both employment and unemployment. Increased economic cooperation between the EU and US on one side and the GEM on the other has led to a faster decrease in unemployment for the former. This cooperation takes a substantial portion of foreign investment from the GEM and moves it primarily to the US and to a much lesser extent the EU. As a result, there is an increase in developed market workplaces.

Another very important indicator for an evaluation of employment is the productivity of labor. However, this indicator can be difficult to interpret. For example, the United States has a higher productivity of labor than Germany. But this indicator does not factor in the working hours of employees in these countries, which has important implications

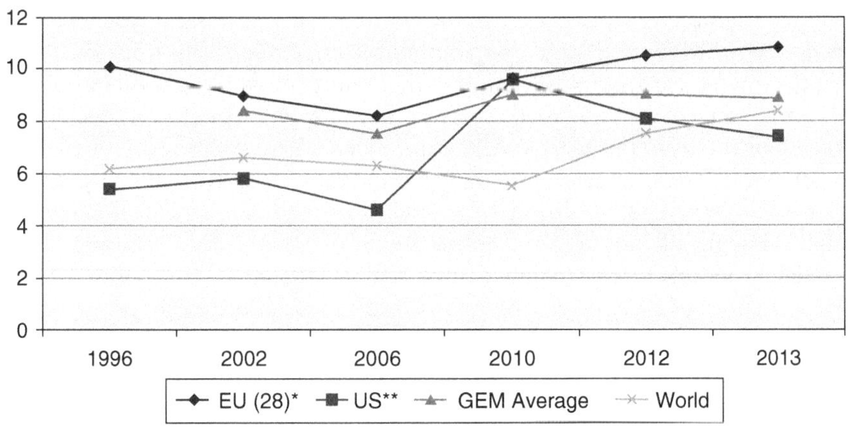

Figure 5.19 World, GEM, United States and EU Unemployment Rates, 2013

 Based on statistics from the CIA. (n.d.). "World Factbook." "Unemployment rate." Retrieved from www.cia.gov/library/publications/the-world-factbook/rankorder/2129rank.html/

*Eurostat

**US Bureau of Labor Statistics

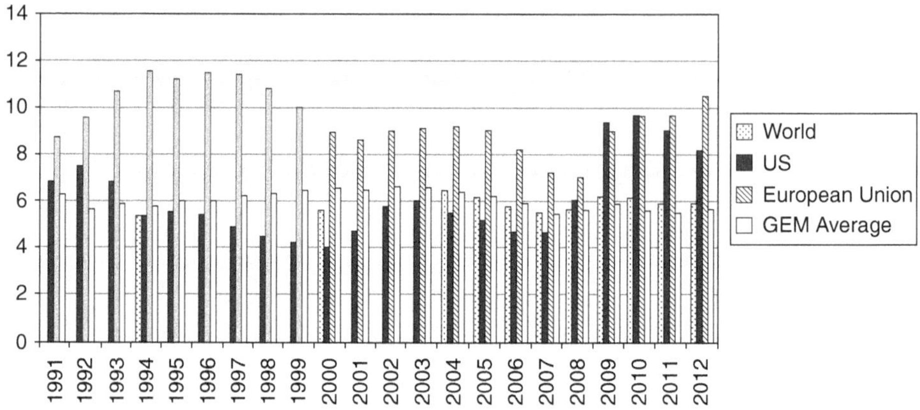

Figure 5.20 World, GEM, United States and EU Unemployment Rates, 2012

Based on statistics from the International Labour Organization. (2007). *Key Indicators of the Labour Market*. September. Retrieved from www.ilo.org/public/english/employment/strat/kilm/

for the efficiency of a labor force. In the United States the average annual hours worked per employee is about 1,708. In Germany it is about 1,433, about 19 percent lower. These numbers demonstrate both the strong work ethic of American employees and the efficiency of German employees. Employees in EMCs actually have long working days. The top six countries by this indicator are EMCs from Asia, Europe, and Latin America. The integration of EMCs in the global marketplace and the unification of the global and regional labor markets increased the influence of the GEM on labor productivity of developed countries. There is a direct correlation between the number of immigrants in a developed country and the number of hours worked annually. This correlation is the cause of Italy's surpassing Japan on the list below (see Table 5.40), as it received an influx of workers from EMCs of Eastern and Southern Europe, especially from Balkan countries. All the top ten hard-working countries by number of working hours are EMCs. In general, during the last 20 years working hours have had the tendency to decline, with a few exceptions found in the United Kingdom, Sweden, Austria, and Mexico.

In an attempt to create a method to objectively compare standards of living in different countries, in 1990 the United Nations began publishing the Human Development Index. This highly integrated indicator incorporates statistics that reflect economic strength, inflation, life expectancy, access to freshwater, health care, literacy, education, electricity, as well as a number of other quality of life indicators. This index provides strategists with a great deal of information and can be very useful when analyzing the labor resources of an economy. As of 2006, there are six EMCs in the top 25 countries on the Human Development Index (see Table 5.41). At the bottom of the list are only developing and underdeveloped countries, with the exception of Burkina Faso, which barely qualifies as an EMC. Eight years later, EMCs are showing some progress, with Singapore among the top ten HDI countries. In the top 25 there are still six EMCs, but there are changes. Greece and Spain fell down in the rankings, replaced by Israel and Slovenia. On the bottom of the list there is still only one EMC, Burkina Faso, which most likely represents the lack of progress in this category. In general, the HDI is very useful for strategists

Table 5.40 Working Hours by Country (Average Annual Hours Worked per Employee), 1995, 2006, and 2013

Rank	*Country*	*1995*	*2006*	*2013*
1	**Mexico**	1857	1883	2237
2	**Greece**	2658	2357	2037
3	**Chile**	2154	2052	2015
4	**Russian Federation**	2039	1989	1980
5	**Poland**	1875	1640	1918
6	**Hungary**	1733	1708	1883
7	**Estonia**	2064	1997	1868
8	**Israel**	1879	1758	1867
9	**Turkey**	1842	1787	1832
10	**Ireland**	1859	1800	1815
11	United States	1884	1784	1788
12	**Czech Republic**	1897	1985	1772
13	**Slovak Republic**	1775	1736	1770
14	New Zealand	1832	1794	1760
15	Italy	1793	1728	1752
16	Japan	1743	1669	1735
17	**Portugal**	1776	1716	1712
18	Canada	1733	1656	1706
19	Iceland	1719	1604	1704
20	Australia	1647	1659	1676
21	United Kingdom	1656	1601	1669
22	Finland	1702	1651	1666
23	**Spain**	1580	1571	1665
24	Luxembourg	1651	1555	1643
25	Austria	1499	1584	1623
26	Sweden	1534	1433	1607

OECD iLibrary. "Average annual hours actually worked per worker." Retrieved from http://stats.oecd.org/index.aspx?DataSetCode=ANHRS

analyzing the values of people and societies prior to formulated national and regional interests, which in turn influence strategic priorities.

An analysis of indicators, less integrated than the HDI, illustrates that in some social categories the standards of living of EMCs are not far behind those of developed countries. The clearest example of this may be life expectancy. Among the top 20 countries by this indicator, 6 belong to the GEM—Singapore, Hong Kong, Spain, Israel, Greece, and Malta. This also can be related to access to freshwater resources, or free or affordable higher education and health care. This means that any integrated indicator always has to be supplemented by an analysis of more specific economic and business indicators and characteristics. The HDI, for example, has flaws, as it does not illustrate the access that people of varying income levels have to an assortment of services or specific energy-consumption patterns of different groups of people. However, there are limitations to the use of statistics to compare quality of life. As previously discussed, any average or median statistic of a given country (especially EMCs) does not take into account disparities between the rich and the poor. Socioeconomic indicators are most effective when they are analyzed from several angles and used in conjunction with extensive market research and expert consultation.

Table 5.41 HDI Ranking, 2006

Highest 25 Scores		*Lowest 25 Scores*	
Rank	*Country*	*Rank*	*Country*
1	Iceland	1	Burundi
2	Norway	2	Congo (Democratic Republic of)
3	Australia	3	Ethiopia
4	Canada	4	Chad
5	**Ireland**	5	Central African Republic
6	Sweden	6	Mozambique
7	Switzerland	7	Mali
8	Japan	8	Niger
9	Netherlands	9	Guinea-Bissau
10	France	10	**Burkina Faso**
11	Finland	11	Sierra Leone
12	United States		
13	**Spain**		
14	Denmark		
15	Austria		
16	United Kingdom		
17	Belgium		
18	Luxembourg		
19	New Zealand		
20	Italy		
21	**Hong Kong**		
22	Germany		
23	**Israel**		
24	**Greece**		
25	**Singapore**		

United Nations Development Programme. (2007). "Human Development Index Rankings." November. Retrieved from http://hdr.undp.org/hdr2006/statistics/

Capital as a Basic Economic Factor of the Global Marketplace

A NEW PARADIGM FOR GLOBAL FINANCIAL STRATEGISTS

The creation and development of the GMP tremendously increased the access of financial strategists and executives to capital from around the world. Prior to the integration of local markets into regional and national markets, a company's access to capital was mostly determined by the quality and scale of the local capital market; companies operated on a local market, using local capital in the domestic currency. This was the paradigm prior to the birth of the GMP and the formation of the global financial system. As a result of the internationalization of financial markets and their eventual globalization, new opportunities appeared for corporate leadership and even for national economies. These processes tremendously changed requirements for financial strategies. In the nineteenth century and most of the twentieth, financial strategists and executives considered foreign financial markets only in terms of uncertainty, risk, and extra costs. Debt and profit in foreign currency was always associated with extra expenses and was not desirable. Expatriation of profits made in foreign countries required expenses related to currency exchange and the difficulties in forecasting fluctuations in exchange rates and price transfers. Variations in financial regulations of different countries and even regions

Table 5.42 HDI Ranking, 2014

Rank	*Top 25 countries with the highest HDI*	*Rank*	*Top 25 countries with the lowest HDI*
1	Norway	1	Niger
2	Australia	2	Congo (Democratic Republic of the)
3	Switzerland	3	Central African Republic
4	Netherlands	4	Chad
5	United States	5	Sierra Leone
6	Germany	6	Eritrea
7	New Zealand	7	Burkina Faso
8	Canada	8	Burundi
9	**Singapore**	9	Guinea
10	Denmark	10	Mozambique
11	**Ireland**	11	Guinea-Bissau
12	Sweden	12	Mali
13	Iceland	13	Liberia
14	United Kingdom	14	Malawi
15	**Hong Kong, China (SAR)**	15	Ethiopia
16	**Korea (Republic of)**	16	Gambia
17	Japan	17	Côte d'Ivoire
18	Liechtenstein	18	Djibouti
19	**Israel**	19	Afghanistan
20	France	20	Haiti
21	Austria	21	Sudan
22	Belgium	22	Togo
23	Luxembourg	23	Benin
24	Finland	24	Uganda
25	**Slovenia**	25	Senegal

United Nations Development Programme (2014). *Human Development Reports*. "Human Development Index." Retrieved from http://hdr.undp.org/en/content/table-1-human-development-index-and-its-components

compounded the level of risk and uncertainty. While there is still a certain amount of disharmony among national fiscal and monetary systems, prior to the birth of the GMP these systems were very disparate.

During the initial stages of international economic integration, multinational corporations were the main force driving local and national financial markets beyond domestic boundaries. With the birth of the GMP, practically every company is tied, to some extent, to the global financial market. This has created new professional requirements for financial and money managers and greatly complicated financial strategy and its development. By the late 1990s, the existence of the integrated global financial market was not fully acknowledged and understood. This made it nearly impossible to stop the global spread of what is often referred to as the Asian financial crisis. This crisis of currencies and stock markets began in 1997 in Thailand, Malaysia, the Philippines, Indonesia, and other Asian economies. It was not a national or regional crisis however: it was global. Due to a poor understanding of the global financial system and a lack of appropriate strategy, it was not recognized as such, and its contagion spread. This crisis marched from Asia through the vast territory of Russia, ruining its national currency in August 1998 (the so-called "ruble default"), through European financial markets, finally making its way to Latin America in December 2001 with the Argentinean peso crisis. This crisis led to the recognition of the integration of the global financial system and a reevaluation of the rejuvenating role of government and central banks in this sphere. It clearly demonstrated the necessity of cooperation between national financial institutions and private business, national governments and central banks with global multilateral institutions, in order to properly manage the global financial system. This cooperation can help to prevent future crises.

THE GLOBAL FINANCIAL MARKET

The global financial market requires a new dialectical attitude from executives, economists, strategists, and political leaders. This new approach requires an understanding of the appropriate balance between a high level of economic freedom and strict enforcement of widely accepted regulations, i.e., tighter monitoring, clearer international rules, global harmonization of national rules, and defined functions and responsibilities of multilateral institutions. The global financial and monetary systems are not well defined and are the most informal of all international economic regimes. They are mostly based on established practice and national laws and under-law regulations, which do not coincide with one another. Essentially, "the money and banking system of the world—usually called the international monetary system—is not a coherent, nor even well-organized system. There are no convenient sets of laws or regulations."[42] The international monetary system is not well organized despite the existence of the International Monetary Fund, which is supposed to establish clear international financial regulations. Even international financial institutions themselves do not a have well-defined role, function, or even a universally accepted legal base for cooperation with national financial systems and private companies. One of the best examples of this is the Basel Committee, which was created by the central banks of ten Western European countries and the United States in 1974. The committee aims to encourage "convergence towards common approaches and common standards without attempting detailed harmonization of member countries' supervisory techniques."[43] The committee has gone through several stages of development in order to promote appropriate global supervisory standards. The limited number of countries memberes undermines the committee's goal to be a global "standard-setting body on all aspects of banking supervision."[44] Nonetheless, the Basel Committee can be very useful for banking supervisory bodies from EMCs; the secretariat of the committee and its many subcommittees are open to giving advice to representatives of any country.

Globalization actually changed traditional practices of transferring prices, currency exchanges, stock market regulations, etc. Companies began to address their strategies toward the global financial market in order to increase production, profit, and market values. Strategists began to find solutions to local financial and business problems in the GMP, beyond not only local but even national borders. The combination of modern technologies and a new level of informatization in financial systems, multiplied by slightly more transparent regulations of global financial transactions, worked to increase the speed and frequency of these transactions. As a result, at the beginning of the twenty-first century, remarkable opportunities for companies in all corners of the GMP appeared.

The integration of emerging market countries (with limitedly convertible or totally inconvertible currencies) to the GMP and their cooperation with developed countries (with convertible currencies) further multiplied the complexity of the global monetary system. The global financial system is complicated by a very narrow spectrum of financial instruments in national capital markets of EMCs, restrictions on foreign capital, and a lack of protection of minority shareholders. However, this system has created new strategic opportunities to use capital as a basic factor of economic development. Integration of companies and national economies to the global monetary system increases the necessity of international exchanges between different currencies, and complicates the dynamics of national currencies in comparison with each other. National emitters (like central banks), national supervisory securities and exchange bodies started to face new challenges in banking, stock market, and currency regulation and practice. The integration of financial systems of EMCs into the GMP expedited the rate of growth of capitalization of their national economies. It also increased financial stability and eventually decreased the number of inconvertible and limitedly convertible currencies. In order to make currencies freely convertible, financial systems more stable, and to prevent a lack of liquidity, countries began to amass foreign currency and gold reserves (see Figure 5.21). The largest currency reserves are held by countries that would eventually like to render convertible their limitedly or inconvertible currency—China, Japan, South Korea, Russia, and Taiwan. By the beginning of the twenty-first century, a few EMCs already have convertible currencies: the Czech koruna, the Hong Kong dollar, among others.

After 2007, China's declared foreign currency and gold reserves practically quadrupled (see Figure 5.21 and Figure 5.22). As of January 2014, seven of the top ten country-holders of convertible currency and gold reserves are EMCs. The fastest growing holders of any country besides China are Saudi Arabia, Switzerland, and the US.

To make the strategists' understanding about the division of gold reserves on the global marketplace more robust, it is important to note that many countries keep their gold reserves in the United States for security reasons. The same can be said for multinational corporations and even medium-sized companies operating in EMCs. This means that the physical distribution of gold reserves does not reflect ownership, an arrangement that has both positive and negative implications for EMCs. For instance, if a country demonstrates continued regression in human rights, or is increasingly hostile towards other

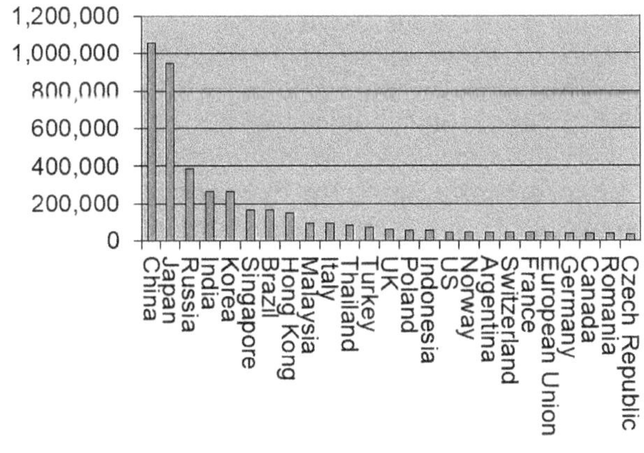

Figure 5.21 Foreign Currency Reserves in Convertible Currencies* (Millions of US$), January 2008

Based on data from the World Bank (2014). Data Template on International Reserves and Foreign Currency Liquidity. Retrieved from http://data.worldbank.org/indicator/FI.RES.TOTL.CD/countries

*Convertible currencies are defined as currencies that are freely bought and sold globally and are usable for settlements of international transactions.

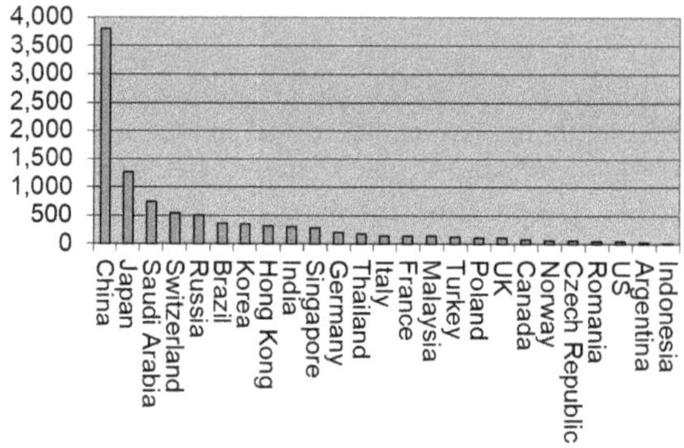

Figure 5.22 Total Reserves (Includes Gold and Convertible Foreign Currencies, Billions of US$), 2014

Based on data from the World Bank. Total Reserves. Retrieved from http://data.worldbank.org/indicator/FI.RES.TOTL.CD

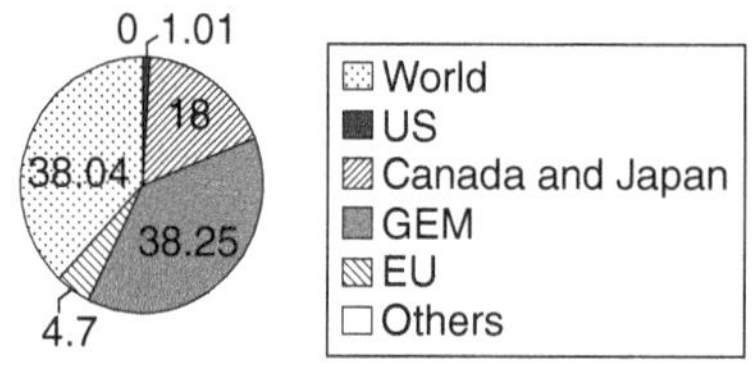

Figure 5.23 Foreign Currency Reserves as a Share of Global Total, 2007

Based on data from the International Monetary Fund. (2007). "Global Financial Stability Report: Financial Market Turbulence: Causes, Consequences and Policies." October. Statistical Appendix, p. 139. Retrieved from www.imf.org/external/pubs/ft/gfsr/2007/02/pdf/statappx.pdf

countries, it may find itself under US and international sanctions via the United Nations, and their reserves held as part of negotiations and punishment.

As indicated in Figures 5.23 and 5.24, the GEM is the main holder of foreign currency reserves (without gold); it has surpassed Canada, the EU, Japan, and the US *combined*. Based on this information from 2007, the continuous changes in these indicators during the next six years led to an increased domination of the GEM as a holder of foreign currency reserves to an unprecedented level. The GEM increased its leadership by more than 50 percent, and as of 2014 holds 65.9 percent of all global foreign currency reserves. I conjecture that this does not include all of China, due to suspected underreporting of their total assets, which are in all likelihood closer to $4 trillion! No one country in the world has *ever* had such a large amount of foreign reserves. Of course, the United States doesn't need vast amounts of foreign reserves as it is a country that engages in dollar emission. In 2014–2015, Russian foreign currency reserves—as well as their gold reserves—have drastically declined due to substantial spending to increase the value of the Russian national currency (ruble), the need for additional investment in crucial industries like the military, and for continued social support for the poorest sections of the population.

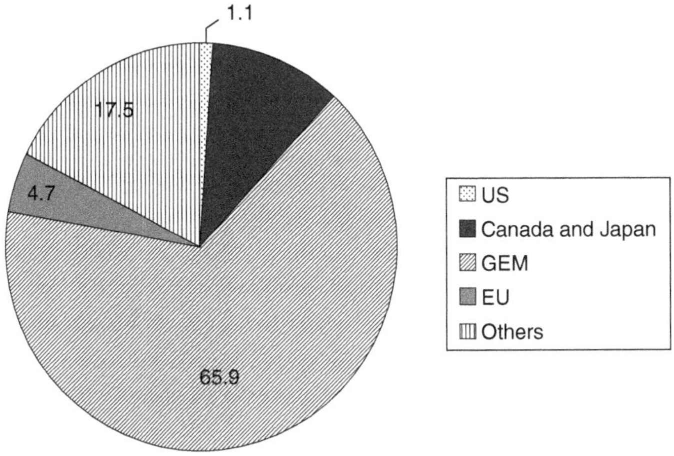

Figure 5.24 Foreign Currency Reserves (Without Gold) as a Share of Global Total, 2013

Based on data from the International Monetary Fund. (2014). "Global Stability Report." Retrieved January 17, 2015 www.imf.org/external/pubs/ft/gfsr/2014/02/pdf/text.pdf

Large accumulations of foreign currency and gold increase the value of gold stocks worldwide. Even the International Monetary Fund has increased its gold assets, one of the largest stores in the world: as of October 2007, the IMF holds 103.4 million ounces of gold.[45] With the increasing instability of the global marketplace in 2007, countries began to increase their banking stocks of other precious metals, such as platinum and palladium. Table 5.43 demonstrates global gold reserves, special drawing right (SDR), where the leading countries are of the GEM, as well as the United States, and, recently, Switzerland.

An understanding of the global financial market and its trends is a major requirement for strategists, especially those who would like to use globally available capital as the dominant factor of economic success in the GMP. Prior to the birth of the GEM and the integration of this market to the GMP, developed countries with excess capital competed intensely for the most interesting and lucrative investment projects. Of course, their options were restricted to the relatively small international marketplace of the 1980s that consisted of 17 developed countries. After the formation of the GMP and the GEM, a new trend became evident—the increasing shortage of capital. Strategists stopped considering foreign currencies as an unnecessary risk and began evaluating their supplies and demands. The role of local financial markets and their authorities started to decrease as they became integrated with the global financial system. This process increased the speed of international transactions and developed a global network of foreign currency exchanges. It even created new functions for the oldest international financial institution, the Bank for International Settlements (BIS), which was established in 1930.

According to the Bank for International Settlements,

> BIS financial services are provided out of two linked trading rooms: one at its Basel head office and one at its office in Hong Kong SAR.[45a]

The Bank continually adapts its product range in order to respond more effectively to the evolving needs of central banks. Besides standard services such as sight/notice

Table 5.43 Global Gold Reserves Special Drawing Right (SDR)*

Year	1998	2001	2005	2008	2010	2011	2012	2013	March 2014
Global Gold Reserves (SDR)	1,446,450	1,915,340	3,285,100	4,836,000	8,080,000	8,952,000	9,875,000	7,224,000	7,711,000

Based on data from the International Monetary Fund. International Reserves. Retrieved from www.imf.org/external/pubs/ft/ar/2014/eng/pdf/a1.pdf

*The SDR is an international reserve asset, created by the IMF in 1969 to supplement the existing official reserves of member countries. The value of the SDR will continue to be based on a weighted average of the values of a basket including the US dollar, euro, Japanese yen, and pound sterling, evaluated on a daily basis. See http://www.imf.org/external/np/exr/facts/sdr.htm.

accounts and fixed-term deposits, the Bank has developed a range of more sophisticated financial products which central banks can actively trade with the BIS to increase the return on their foreign assets. The Bank also transacts foreign exchange and gold on behalf of its customers.

In addition, the BIS offers a range of asset-management services in sovereign securities or high-grade assets. These may be either a specific portfolio mandate negotiated between the BIS and a central bank or an open-end fund structure—the BIS Investment Pool (BISIP)—allowing customers to invest in a common pool of assets. The two Asian Bond Funds (ABF1 and ABF2) are administered by the BIS under the BISIP umbrella: ABF1 is managed by the BIS and ABF2 by a group of external fund managers.

The BIS extends short-term credits to central banks, usually on a collateralised basis. From time to time, the BIS also coordinates emergency short-term lending to countries in financial crisis. In these circumstances, the BIS advances funds on behalf of, and with the backing and guarantee of, a group of supporting central banks. The Bank's Statutes do not allow the Bank to open current accounts in the name of, or make advances to, governments.[46]

Unfortunately for private companies, "the BIS does not accept deposits from, or generally provide financial services to, private individuals or corporate entities."[47] The globalization of the monetary system also increased the fluctuations of exchange rates and value of different currencies. One of the major roles of financial strategists in the global environment became financial risk management. Each strategy in the GMP requires a hedging strategy as an important sub-element. Even traditional instruments against currency fluctuations, such as forward markets, money market systems, and restructuring systems, have changed. Global operations of companies have complicated traditional evaluations of labor productivity, cost production, quality of goods, and the efficiency of technology. It happened because of the necessity to evaluate all of these strategic issues within the scale of the GMP, rather than in isolated local, regional, or national markets. Debt restructuring of companies has to be analyzed by the different countries and even continents where this company and its subsidiaries operate or from which its goods and services are supplied and sold.

The increasing role, stability, and maturity of the GEM accelerated the development of banking systems in EMCs. At the initial stages of democratization and market-oriented reforms in these countries, the banking sectors were limited to state-owned banks with a few insignificant private exceptions. Economic development, processes of privatization, and increasing numbers of entrepreneurs drastically raised the need for commercial and investment-banking services. Like mushrooms after rain, many private banks emerged with small amounts of assets and capital. Typically, it takes several years, or even a couple of decades of development, for the processes of concentration and the regulation of the banking sector to see even a few sophisticated private banks established in EMCs. At the end of the twentieth century, the initial stage of development of the banking sector was completed in EMCs. National banking systems developed according to the requirements of international regulations and the needs of domestic entrepreneurs and companies. At the beginning of the twenty-first century, banking assets in EMCs are substantially greater than those of the United States—the dominant banking power of the world (see Figure 5.25). After 2006, these dynamics proved that the leading international banks from developed countries were moving more and more of their assets to friendly EMCs. As a result, the role of the GEM increased from 21.7 to 30.6 percent over the next seven years, decreasing the gap between the banking assets of the GEM and the European Union (see Figure 5.26).

The role of the US, Australia, and other developed countries' banking assets began to decline, with notable exceptions seen in Japan and Canada. This is due to vastly improved banking conditions in emerging market countries, many of which have dedicated

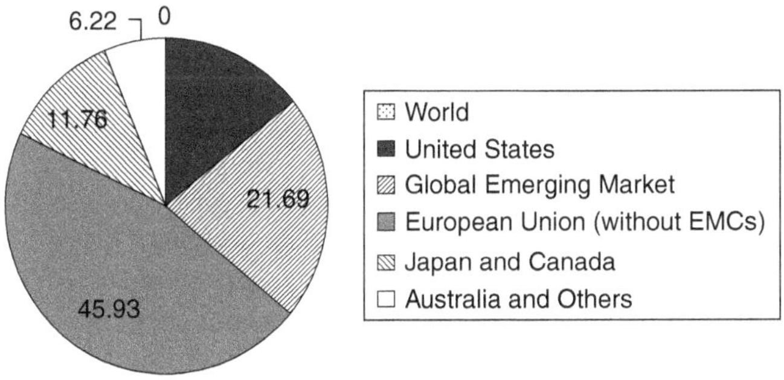

Figure 5.25 Bank Assets as a Share of the Global Total, 2006

© Dr. Vladimir Kvint, 2008. Based on data from the International Monetary Fund. (2007). "Global Financial Stability Report: Financial Market Turbulence: Causes, Consequences and Policies." Statistical Appendix. Retrieved from www.imf.org/external/pubs/ft/gfsr/2007/02/pdf/statappx.pdf

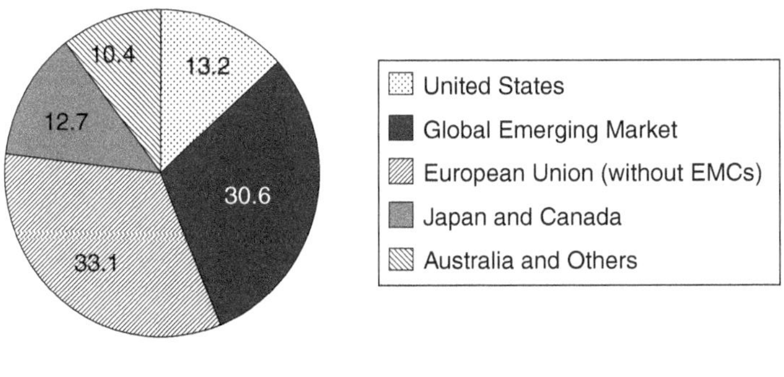

Figure 5.26 Bank Assets as a Share of the Global Total, 2013

© Dr. Vladimir Kvint, 2014. Based on data from the International Monetary Fund. (2014). "Global Stability Report" Retrieved from www.imf.org/external/pubs/ft/gfsr/2014/02/pdf/text.pdf

national strategists who are focused on improving conditions for international bank operations and the safety of its assets. This strategy to develop national financial centers that can rival international financial hubs has been successful in several EMCs, like Singapore, Hong Kong (China), Argentina, and South Korea. The Russian government has repeatedly expressed interest in creating more hospitable market conditions for foreign investment, but has yet to improve conditions for international banking operations or increase the ratings of their banks to match the high international levels of stability, reliability, and safety. Their intent to convert Moscow into a global financial hub is still only on paper.

What is especially important for private businesses in EMCs is the fact that the growth in capitalization and assets of the banking sector is increasing the role and capacity of private financial institutions in short-term lending. However, in the bond market, private banks are still far behind state and governmental institutions. Despite the increasing maturity of the banking sector in the GEM, and the continuing growth of capitalization in these countries, the scale of domestic capital is still relatively low, and far behind the similar role of domestic capital in developed countries. This explains why the factor of foreign investors in bond markets in EMCs as of 2008 is still increasing. In some EMCs—United Arab Emirates, Uruguay, Hungary, and Poland—foreign investment accounts form more than a quarter of the total domestic bond market.

THE GLOBAL CAPITAL MARKET

Financial assets of companies have become more international and in some cases global. But the liabilities of a company have been even more heavily influenced by globalization. The manner in which financial strategists evaluate the costs of preparation and development of new production facilities and the production process itself relative to income and profitability has changed dramatically. All of this is leading to constant changes in the theory of capitalization and its national and international practice. Capitalization is essentially the conversion of potential income into capital. However, this simple concept has been greatly complicated by the dialectical relationship between the dynamics of the global capital market and regional and national capital trends. Different patterns of global capitalization are determining factors of national and regional dynamics of capitalization. For example, financial decline or crisis in one part of the GMP tremendously influences tendencies and even the scale of capitalization in distant national and local markets. Figure 5.27 shows the stock market capitalization of the GMP in 2006. The GEM

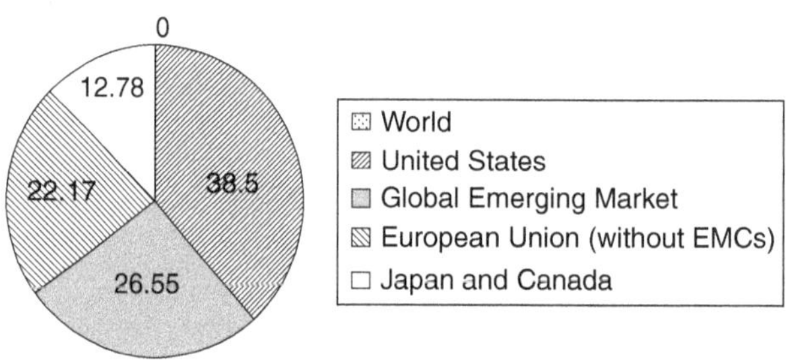

Figure 5.27 Stock Market Capitalization of the Global Marketplace Regional Shares, 2006

© Dr. Vladimir Kvint, 2007. Based on data from the International Monetary Fund. (2007). "Global Financial Stability Report: Financial Market Turbulence: Causes, Consequences and Policies." Statistical Appendix. Retrieved from www.imf.org/external/pubs/ft/gfsr/2007/02/pdf/statappx.pdf

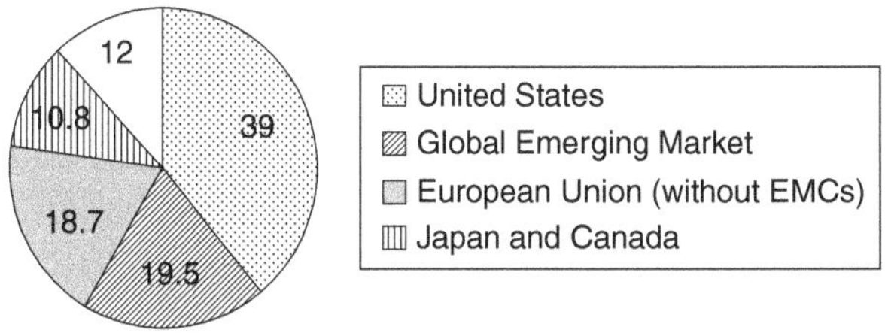

Figure 5.28 Stock Market Capitalization of the Global Marketplace Regional Shares, 2013

© Dr. Vladimir Kvint, 2014. Based on data from the International Monetary Fund. (2014). "Global Stability Report" Retrieved from www.imf.org/external/pubs/ft/gfsr/2014/02/pdf/text.pdf

occupied the second leading position after the US as the global leader of stock markets, easily surpassing the European Union without their EMC members.

During the next seven years, stock markets in the GEM increased in absolute numbers, but shares in the various stock markets didn't increase, due to the powerful sway held by the NYSE, NASDAQ, and the regional exchanges in different US cities like Chicago, Philadelphia, etc. (see Figure 5.28). Stock exchanges in other countries—like the EU, Japan, and Canada—gradually declined in this seven-year period. Stock exchanges of European and Latin America EMCs (with the exception of Buenos Aires) have not produced a well-developed strategy to improve their positions in the global competition between major stock exchanges. Hong Kong is one of the few that has demonstrated a well-designed attempt to rival the stock exchanges of developed countries that are found in the Asia-Pacific region.

Rapid capitalization in the GEM positively influences global capitalization. During the last decade of the twentieth century, companies from EMCs began to be listed on major international stock exchanges in developed countries, directly or indirectly. Due to the uncertainty of domestic markets in EMCs and a lack of knowledge in developed countries about brands and even names of companies from EMCs, some were able to be listed on major stock exchanges through international depository receipts (IDR). If a company would like to be listed, for example, on the New York Stock Exchange, this company has to give a US financial institution its stock in trust and create and issue American depositary receipts (ADR) in the United States. These receipts offer potential holders the same rights as regular shareholders have, including the right to vote. Only this kind of ADR, usually called a sponsored ADR, can be listed on the New York Stock Exchange. But unsponsored ADRs issued by any US financial institution, without official relationships with the foreign company, can also be traded in the US, but only over the counter, like on the NASDAQ. The use of these instruments, among others, has expedited processes of global capitalization. Figure 5.29 illustrates the fact that the dynamics of global capitalization would be at least five times slower without the input of BRIC (Brazil, Russia, India, and China)—the leading countries of the GEM. The rate of growth of capitalization in developed countries is far below the world average.

In developed countries, net savings as a percentage of GDP is roughly negative 1.25; in EMCs, it is 4.5 percent.[48] This ratio actually represents the current account balances of these categories of countries. As a result, domestic spending in the GEM is closely tied to GDP, which is why budget deficits are decreasing in these countries.

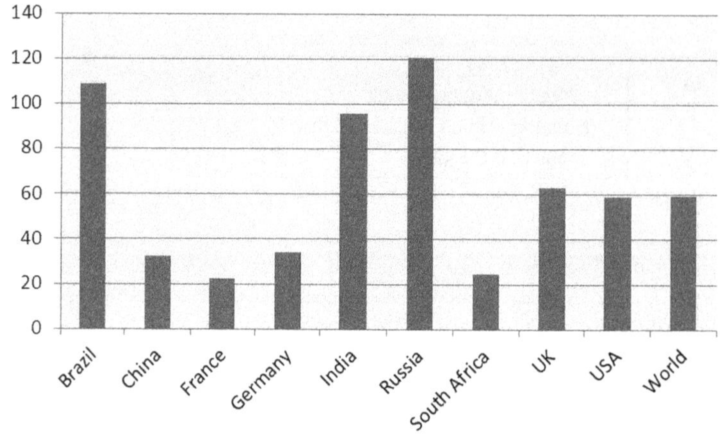

Figure 5.29 Capitalization Growth Rates of Major Economies, 2012*

Based on data from the International Monetary Fund. (2014). "Global Financial Stability Report: Financial Market Turbulence: Causes, Consequences and Policies." Statistical Appendix. Retrieved from www.quandl.com/c/economics/stock-market-capitalization-by-country

*100 percent is level of indicators of 2007.

Table 5.44 US and GEM Capital Inflows (Billions of US$), 1996–2006

United States	*2000*	*2001*	*2002*	*2003*	*2004*	*2005*	*2006*	*2007*	*2008*	*2009*
Direct Investment	321.3	167	84.4	63.8	146	112.6	243.2	271.2	134.7	328.3
Portfolio Investment	436.6	428.3	427.6	550.2	867.3	832	1126.7	1156.6	366.7	520.1
Other Investment	280.4	187.5	283.2	244.4	519.9	302.7	695.3	679.8	–195.7	–393.7
Total capital flows	1038.2	782.9	795.2	858.3	1533.2	1,247.3	2065.2	2107.7	305.6	454.7
Emerging Market and Developed Countries	*2000*	*2001*	*2002*	*2003*	*2004*	*2005*	*2006*	*2007*	*2008*	*2009*
Direct Investment	169.9	182.6	173	174.5	251.5	337.5	420.8	615.9	410.7	695.4
Portfolio Investment	30.5	2	–5,4	57.1	109.5	179.9	297.7	421.1	196.7	12.7(?)
Other Investment	28.3	1.7	8.7	75.1	105	121.7	189.9	693.7	63.3	148
Total capital flows	228.7	186.2	176.3	306.8	466	639	908.4	1730.6	670.6	856.2

Based on data from the International Monetary Fund (2010). "Global Financial Stability Report." Retrieved from http://www.imf.org/external/pubs/ft/gfsr/2010/02/pdf/statappx.pdf

Table 5.44 provides an understanding of the scale, structure, and dynamics of global movements of capital during a GEM's maturity, including portfolio and direct investment, and capital in national reserves. International investors still view the GEM as an area suited for direct investment. Since 2001, the GEM countries have steadily overtaken the United States as the highest recipients of FDI inflow. This is a result of a much faster rate of return on the FDI invested in EMCs. In the Asian EMCs, for instance, the speed of return is two times faster than it is in either the EU or the US. Rising capitalization of companies and listings in stock exchanges of the GEM is increasing portfolio investments, but at a pace about three times slower than in the United States. As of 2008, the dynamic of capitalization and the inflow of portfolio investment in the GEM do not coincide. Access of public companies from the GEM to international stock exchanges will change this ratio during the second decade of the twenty-first century. Outflow of capital from the GEM to other regions of the GMP will always occur, but with increasing number of stock exchanges in the GEM and the names of major international companies appearing on these stock exchanges, the outflow in portfolio investment will decrease.

In Figure 5.29—where the data of 2007 is marked as 100 percent on the x-axis—several trends can be seen. Brazil and Russia are seen as the leaders of capitalization in their markets. This is despite the fact that the Russian market is still incredibly shallow, unlike the Brazilian public capital market. The rate of growth in the Russian market declined rapidly after 2013 due to political tensions with western countries, Japan, and Australia, as well as due to the lack of domestic and technological strategies. Only in 2014 did the net outflow of capital from Russia increase by 2.5 times to the level of $151.5 billion, according to the Central Bank of Russia.[49] India demonstrates positive dynamics and has a capitalization rate of growth in its market that is four times that of China, and two times the world average. However, in absolute numbers, China is still very much ahead of India. Positive economic dynamics in the US helped to increase the capitalization rate of growth in its market. The average European indicators of capitalization rate of growth include the leading European economy—Germany—yet are still behind the world average. The only European exception is the United Kingdom. Unfortunately, the last eight years do not clearly demonstrate the leading growth positions of the GEM in comparison to the rate of growth of capitalization developed countries already had in place during the end of the twentieth century and first five years of the twenty-first.

During the twenty-first century major developed countries (as well as the EMCs China, Singapore, and South Korea) started to heavily invest in stable and efficiently developed emerging market countries. These EMCs had either proven natural resources and/or well-developed technological and knowledge-based economic sectors. Germany became a leading exporter of capital, with a substantial portion going to China, Turkey, Russia, and Eastern European countries. China in turn invested in capital-hungry nations, such as Russia, Kazakhstan, Brazil, Mongolia, and other EMCs that proved to have strategic interest to China.

There are a wide range of motivations behind these capital investment projects. Turkey encouraged inflow of capital through the drastic improvement of higher education, creating nearly 100 new universities and visibly improving infrastructure. Turkey also increased its capital import by boosting its tourism industry, providing vastly improved resorts and attractions. Brazil is another country attracting billions in foreign investment, primarily through the sports industry on the international level and the related hospitality infrastructure. These investments have increased tremendously with both the World Cup in 2014 and the upcoming summer Olympic Games in 2016.

EMCs are not the only countries to benefit from an inflow of capital. The United States has returned to its position as the global leader of importing capital by improving its economic climate, growing its economic indicators, fostering a community of low corruption, and providing protection of foreign investments. The United Kingdom has implemented a strategy to encourage foreign investment in science, technology, education, and the sports industry. Canada is also a good harbor for the inflow of direct foreign investment, due to a combination of the positive factors found in both the US and UK.

China, Russia, Ukraine, and Egypt have failed to draw the attention of foreign investment to their respective countries for a variety of different economic and political reasons. China has seen a lack of interest due to the slowdown of its economy, and Russia and the Ukraine have serious political drawbacks. Egypt, despite apparent stabilization, still does not provide any protection of foreign investments. This same situation can also be found in Hungary.

In addition to the integration of regional and national financial systems, unique regional cultural and religious traditions have also been integrated within the global capital market. This has created new challenges for executives and managers from the developed world who are unaccustomed to the idiosyncrasies of certain traditional capital-market practices. The most obvious example is the Islamic prohibition of generating profit from interest. In order to avoid violating this principle, Islamic financiers developed interest-free financial instruments known as *sukuk*. Sukuk returns are tied directly to purchased or constructed assets, such as equity in an existing company. The largest sukuk market is in Malaysia; it accounts for two-thirds of outstanding global Islamic bonds with an estimated value of $47 billion.[50] Islamic finance is one of many challenges that capital market executives in EMCs face.

PRODUCTION FACILITIES OF THE GLOBAL MARKETPLACE

AUTOMOBILE PRODUCTION FACILITIES

Production facilities and infrastructure are important basic economic factors. For this reason, companies are rarely created in uninhabited islands, deserts, or frozen wastelands. Companies generally need existing transportation or telecommunication infrastructure, nearby human settlements, and existing production facilities. However, with modern technology, even uninhabited islands can access telecommunications infrastructure via satellites. The aim of this section is to underline internationalization and globalization of production facilities. In the GMP, it is nearly impossible to find in the twenty-first century totally domestic production facilities, technologies without any foreign influence or elements from abroad, and infrastructure not internationally connected. Out of the 14 major production facilities of light vehicles in North America, 11 originate in Europe or Asia. Even the automobiles assembled in domestically owned production facilities contain at least 30 percent of parts and components of foreign origin.[51] Western European automobile production is just as globalized as that of North America. Out of the 15 major automobile production facilities in Western Europe, eight are of direct foreign origin. Just as in North America, domestically owned facilities contain a significant number of foreign parts and components.[52]

Automobile production in emerging market countries has experienced the same trends as in North America and Western Europe. In EMCs, high-quality and high-tech production are almost always a result of international collaboration. Out of the 16 major automobile-production facilities in the emerging markets of Eastern Europe, Russia, Turkey, and Central Asia, 13 are of direct foreign origin, from the US, Western Europe, and Asia. The automobile industry is only one of many that have been substantially globalized. Production facilities of heavy, light, and agricultural industries, low- and high-tech products, services, and industries are the result of international cooperation and globalization. International cooperation is one of the most important factors in the creation of modern production facilities. Globalization made these facilities available to companies and consumers from all corners of the GMP.[53]

Production facilities of the GMP are experiencing the influence of many political, economic, and global trends. With the increasing role of infrastructure, the role of

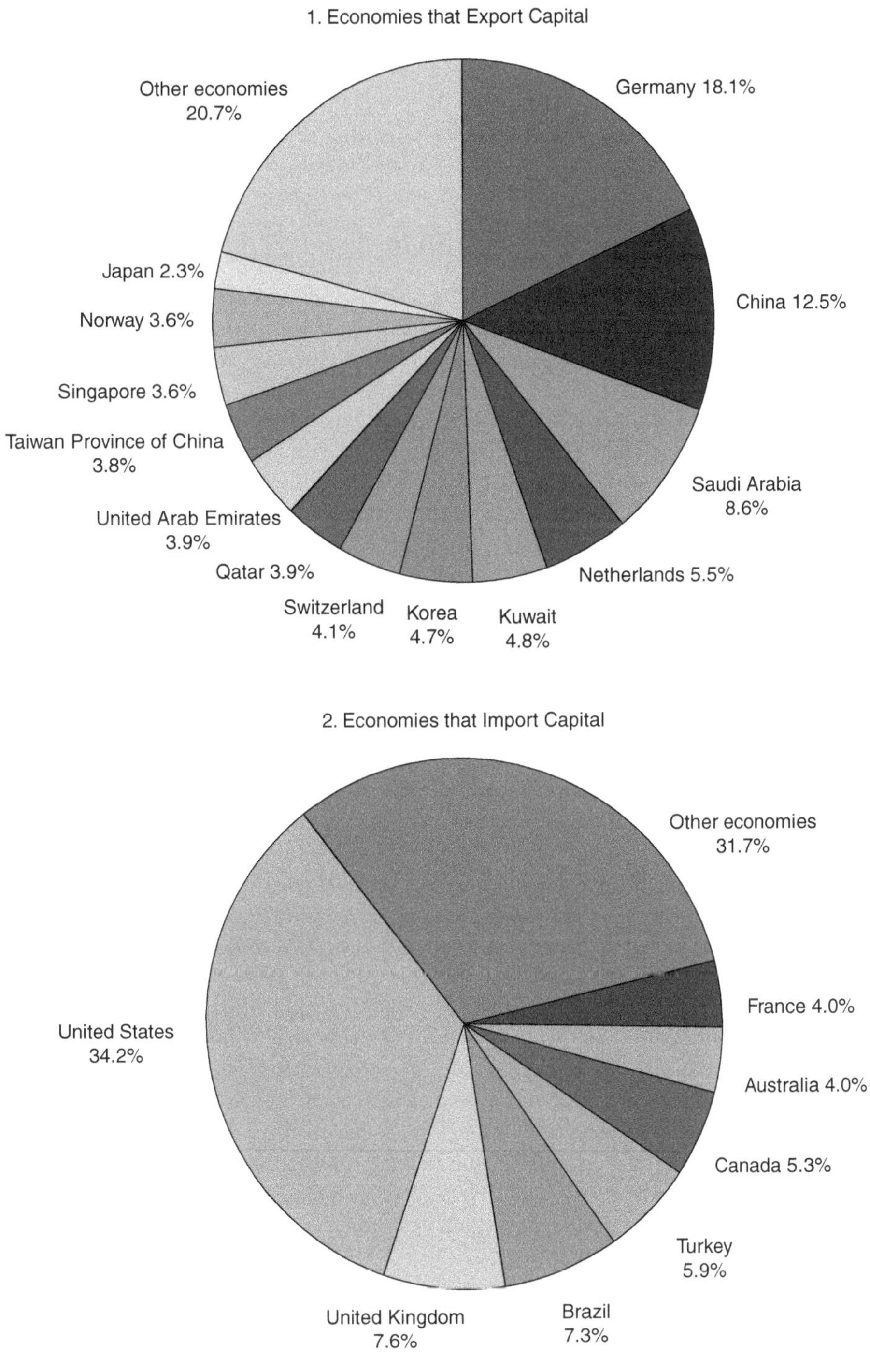

Figure 5.30 Major Net Exporters and Importers of Capital, 2013

Based on data from the International Monetary Fund (2014). "Global Financial Stability Report: Moving from Liquidity to Growth Driven Markets." April, p. 145. Retrieved from www.imf.org/External/Pubs/FT/GFSR/2014/01/pdf/text.pdf

production facilities as an economic factor is increasing. But it always has to be analyzed together with the most modern basic economic factor—research and technology.

Science, Research and Technology Strategic Capabilities of the Global Marketplace

Knowledge-Based Economy

The industrial structure of global production will change radically in the twenty-first century. Science and technology will no longer function only as instruments for other industries; they will become major industries themselves. Over the past 50 years, the world has transitioned from an agriculturally based economy to an industrialized one, and then to a service-based economy. In the twenty-first century, the service-based economy has already started to be replaced by the knowledge-based economy. This will create new opportunities, higher standards of living, and the expansion of economic activity beyond planet Earth through dual and nano-technologies. Of course, the technology of the knowledge-based economy will also present tremendous threats to civilization as it can be used for war and destruction. The economy of war and the military-industrial complex will unfortunately continue to be an indivisible part of the GMP. Newly empowered countries from the GEM will direct a substantial amount of investment toward this effort.

There are many interesting patterns to note. All of the Nordic states, including Sweden, Finland, Denmark, as well as the Netherlands and Switzerland, are considered knowledge-based economies or knowledge economies. In the top ten knowledge economies, according to the World Bank's Knowledge Economy Index of 2012 (see Table 5.45), all are developed nations. During the past 15 years, Sweden has oriented their national economy towards the sciences and knowledge-based industries. Finland, Germany, and the Netherlands have made similar strategically based changes. Among EMCs, the countries that devote the highest percentage of their national economy to the knowledge economy are Ireland, Taiwan, Hong Kong, and Estonia. Surprisingly, the level devoted to the knowledge economy has declined in the technological-leading EMCs of Israel and South Korea. For me, it is especially strange to see this negative dynamic indicator in South Korea, due to the fact that South Korea once had a strategy devoted to the development of the knowledge-based economy, and even a special Ministry of Knowledge Economy. Hungary has demonstrated very little progress in support of the knowledge economy over the past years. After a decline in their own knowledge economies in the 1990s, Romania and Bulgaria experienced a substantial increase during the twenty-first century. Unfortunately, since 2007 the Russian Federation—which used to be a technological leader in the former Soviet Bloc—has fallen from position 47 to 55, due to the total lack of scientific strategy and decline in related investments. Ukraine lost 5 positions since 2007, and is now at 66. Yet Belarus has seen a slight increase in the role of the knowledge economy in their own national economy, moving from 61 in 2007 to 59 in 2012. This is important to note because before 2007 they had been consistently declining. Among the top 25 countries, according to this index, 8 are from the GEM, Ireland having the highest rank, followed by Taiwan, Hong Kong, and Estonia. In these countries, high-tech industry, science, and education generate a substantial segment of the GDP.

The position of Israel and Canada would be much higher in this ranking if they were not evaluated so high in another ranking: Israel and Canada are the top countries in terms of the ratio of their scientists who work abroad. The primary recipient of these scientists is the United States. According to Professor Dan Ben-David of Tel Aviv University, "the number of Israeli academics in U.S. universities has already reached 25 percent of the scholars still remaining in Israel."[54] The example of Israel and Canada shows how the science- and knowledge-based industries are already an integrated sector of the global marketplace. In some of the EMCs in Table 5.45, knowledge-based technologies have already penetrated society to the point that they can be considered knowledge-based societies, such as Estonia, Hungary,[55] and Taiwan. In February 2007 the European Federation of National Academies of Humanities discussed the role of research in knowledge-based societies, arguing that it should be the "basis for strategies; the instruments—mobility, infrastructure, cooperation—should be tuned in harmony with fundamental objectives."[56] At the bottom of the Knowledge Economy Index, among the 25 countries there is only one—Burkina Faso—which this book considers to be an EMC. All others are developing (Bangladesh, Nepal, and Ethiopia) and underdeveloped countries (Guinea and Sierra Leone). In the KEI of 2007, Singapore came in at position 138, which was highly questionable. I issued several requests to ensure that this position was correct. Now, eight years later, Singapore occupies a more realistic position towards the top of the table. This success also can be addressed to the technological strategy that the country has persistently implemented and practiced.

Table 5.45 The Knowledge Economy Index (KEI), 2012

Country/ Economy	*2012 Rank*	*KEI 2012*	*2000 Rank*	*Change from 2000*	*Country/ Economy*	*2012 Rank*	*KEI 2012*	*2000 Rank*	*Change from 2000*
Sweden	1	9.43	1	0	Slovenia	28	8.01	28	0
Finland	2	9.33	8	6	Korea, Rep.	29	7.97	24	−5
Denmark	3	9.16	3	0	Italy	30	7.89	27	−3
Netherlands	4	9.11	2	−2	Malta	31	7.88	39	8
Norway	5	9.11	7	2	Lithuania	32	7.8	34	2
New Zealand	6	8.97	9	3	Slovak Republic	33	7.64	40	7
Canada	7	8.92	10	3	Portugal	34	7.61	30	−4
Germany	8	8.9	15	7	Cyprus	35	7.56	32	−3
Australia	9	8.88	6	−3	Greece	36	7.51	31	−5
Switzerland	10	8.87	5	−5	Latvia	37	7.41	37	0
Ireland	11	8.86	11	0	Poland	38	7.41	35	−3
United States	12	8.77	4	−8	Croatia	39	7.29	43	4
Taiwan, China	13	8.77	16	3	Chile	40	7.21	38	−2
United Kingdom	14	8.76	12	−2	Barbados	41	7.18	36	−5
Belgium	15	8.71	14	−1	United Arab Emirates	42	6.94	48	6
Iceland	16	8.62	19	3	Bahrain	43	6.9	41	−2
Austria	17	8.61	13	−4	Romania	44	6.82	53	9
Hong Kong, China	18	8.52	25	7	Bulgaria	45	6.8	51	6
Estonia	19	8.4	26	7	Uruguay	46	6.39	42	−4
Luxembourg	20	8.37	22	2	Oman	47	6.14	65	18
Spain	21	8.35	23	2	Malaysia	48	6.1	45	−3
Japan	22	8.28	17	−5	Serbia	49	6.02	144	95
Singapore	23	8.26	20	−3	Saudi Arabia	50	5.96	76	26
France	24	8.21	21	−3	Costa Rica	51	5.93	47	−4
Israel	25	8.14	18	−7	Trinidad and Tobago	52	5.91	56	4
Czech Republic	26	8.14	33	7	Aruba	53	5.89	145	n/a
Hungary	27	8.02	29	2	Qatar	54	5.84	49	−5

(Continued)

Table 5.45 The Knowledge Economy Index (KEI), 2012 (Continued)

Country/ Economy	*2012 Rank*	*KEI 2012*	*2000 Rank*	*Change from 2000*	*Country/ Economy*	*2012 Rank*	*KEI 2012*	*2000 Rank*	*Change from 2000*
Russian Federation	55	5.78	64	9	Sri Lanka	101	3.63	87	−14
Ukraine	56	5.73	54	−2	Morocco	102	3.61	92	−10
Macedonia, FYR	57	5.65	73	16	Cape Verde	103	3.59	98	n/a
Jamaica	58	5.65	55	−3	Vietnam	104	3.4	113	9
Belarus	59	5.59	70	11	Uzbekistan	105	3.14	101	−4
Brazil	60	5.58	59	−1	Tajikistan	106	3.13	102	−4
Dominica	61	5.56	146	n/a	Swaziland	107	3.13	97	−10
Mauritius	62	5.52	63	1	Indonesia	108	3.11	105	−3
Argentina	63	5.43	44	−19	Honduras	109	3.08	99	−10
Kuwait	64	5.33	46	−18	India	110	3.06	104	−6
Panama	65	5.3	50	−15	Kenya	111	2.88	108	−3
Thailand	66	5.21	60	−6	Syrian Arab Republic	112	2.77	111	−1
South Africa	67	5.21	52	−15	Ghana	113	2.72	106	−7
Georgia	68	5.19	75	7	Senegal	114	2.7	103	−11
Turkey	69	5.16	62	−7	Nicaragua	115	2.61	107	−8
Bosnia and Herzegovina	70	5.12	143	73	Zambia	116	2.56	112	−4
Armenia	71	5.08	58	−13	Pakistan	117	2.45	122	5
Mexico	72	5.07	61	−11	Uganda	118	2.37	120	2
Kazakhstan	73	5.04	78	5	Nigeria	119	2.2	124	5
Peru	74	5.01	66	−8	Zimbabwe	120	2.17	114	−6
Jordan	75	4.95	57	−18	Lesotho	121	1.95	109	−12
Colombia	76	4.94	79	3	Yemen, Rep.	122	1.92	128	6
Moldova	77	4.92	69	−8	Malawi	123	1.92	117	−6
Guyana	78	4.67	81	3	Burkina Faso	124	1.91	133	9
Azerbaijan	79	4.56	94	15	Benin	125	1.88	115	−10
Tunisia	80	4.56	89	9	Mali	126	1.86	119	−7
Lebanon	81	4.56	68	−13	Rwanda	127	1.83	141	14
Albania	82	4.53	96	14	Tanzania	128	1.79	126	−2
Mongolia	83	4.42	86	3	Madagascar	129	1.77	127	−2
China	84	4.37	91	7	Mozambique	130	1.76	135	5
Botswana	85	4.31	67	−18	Lao PDR	131	1.75	129	−2
Venezuela, RB	86	4.2	72	−14	Cambodia	132	1.71	116	−16
Cuba	87	4.19	83	−4	Cameroon	133	1.69	118	−15
El Salvador	88	4.17	84	−4	Mauritania	134	1.65	123	−11
Namibia	89	4.1	80	−9	Nepal	135	1.58	125	−10
Dominican Republic	96	4.05	85	−5	Cote d'Ivoire	136	1.54	121	−15
Paraguay	91	3.95	93	2	Bangladesh	137	1.49	134	−3
Philippines	92	3.94	77	−15	Sudan	138	1.48	139	1
Fiji	93	3.94	74	−19	Djibouti	139	1.34	136	−3
Iran, Islamic Rep.	94	3.91	95	1	Ethiopia	140	1.27	138	−2
Kyrgyz Rep.	95	3.82	82	−13	Guinea	141	1.22	132	−9
Algeria	96	3.79	110	14	Eritrea	142	1.14	131	n/a
Egypt, Arab Rep.	97	3.78	88	−9	Angola	143	1.08	142	−1
Ecuador	98	3.72	90	−8	Sierra Leone	144	0.97	140	−4
Guatemala	99	3.7	100	1	Myanmar	145	0.90	137	−8
Bolivia	100	3.68	71	−29	Haiti	n/a	n/a	130	n/a

World Bank. (2014). "Knowledge Assessment Methodology." Retrieved from http://siteresources.worldbank.org/INTUNIKAM/Resources/2012.pdf/

Technological processes of production are not the only systems that are being changed by the knowledge economy. Technology will soon integrate the human mind in a global network of knowledge. The development of the Internet is the first step in this process. Before the end of the twenty-first century, everyone will be constantly integrated as users and contributors within this network. Unprecedented availability of individual knowledge and experience will create incredible opportunities and serious challenges for human civilization in the GMP.

Global Industry of Research and Development

Research and development are a central part of any strategy that seeks future prosperity for a country. The results of investments in this field are usually not immediately tangible and are very difficult to measure. There is still not an adequate measurement system to estimate the long-term impact of fundamental science, which produces theoretical results of long-term economic consequences. It takes time to implement the discoveries of groundbreaking and revolutionary studies for the betterment of society. However, every generation is profoundly indebted to past scholars and governmental and business leaders who invested in the future by conducting and financing scientific research. When the British scientist Michael Faraday discovered electromagnetic induction in 1845, everyone (including himself) thought its only practical application was in circus performances. Of course, only a few decades later, thanks to the genius of Thomas Edison, Faraday's discoveries brought light and heat to homes and offices, laying the foundation for the modern economy. Due to the strong influence of scientific achievements on global economic dynamics, the World Bank developed

> a **summary index of technology** that includes a much wider range of indicators than included in other technology indexes. This index is derived from three sub-indexes that measure four dimensions of technological achievement:

- The extent of scientific invention and innovation.
- The diffusion of older technologies.
- The diffusion of newer technologies.
- The intensity with which foreign technologies are employed in domestic production.[57]

One of the leading countries in the world in terms of R&D spending as a percentage of GDP is Germany. At the beginning of the new millennium, Germany's prime minister, Angela Merkel, gave special attention to science policy and prepared an editorial about German priorities in scientific strategy. In this editorial she claimed, "By 2010, we aim to increase spending on R&D to 3 percent of gross domestic product. Science and research will be one of the priorities of Germany's European Union (EU) presidency."[58] But by far, the leading region in the world in terms of budgetary expenses on R&D as a percentage of GDP is the EMC—Israel, followed by the Scandinavian countries, Japan with several other EMCs close behind, like South Korea, Taiwan, and Singapore.[59] In terms of total expenses on science, research, and development, in 2007 China surpassed Japan and Germany and is second only to the US. Among the top 15 countries in terms of gross domestic expenditure on R&D are also India, South Korea, Taiwan, Russia, and Spain.[60] It has to be clear that the difference in expenses on science between China and the other EMCs is so large that they are barely comparable. For example, Russia spends almost 15 times less than China, with declining dynamics as Russia is steadily decreasing its budget investment in R&D, and Russian corporations do not spend any amount of money for R&D whatsoever. Russian and Ukrainian companies mostly consume results of outdated Soviet research. In 2013, without any objective reasoning, Russian leadership took control of all major research institutions, which previously had been under the control of the leading Russian research think tank, the Russian Academy of Science. I have no doubt that this decision will one day be overturned. It has to be; otherwise Russian sciences will continue to decline. In the twentieth century Russia was a leader in the exact sciences. As of 2015, the country has only one Nobel Laureate in physics, and none in the other scientific fields.

Regarding other EMCs, I must point out that Thailand, Taiwan, Singapore, and South Korea have seen a markedly increased investment in science. Over the last ten years, South Korea has increased investment in R&D eightfold; Thailand by six times, and Taiwan by five. These countries are on the way to being leaders in the future technological age, not only in their competitive region, but in the global arena. These strategic investments have attracted scientists and scholars from all over the world. I have visited hi-tech companies in South Korea, Taiwan, and Turkey, and have met scholars from Russia, Ukraine, Hungary, Israel, and Bulgaria who have found a supportive environment for their work and life. Countries who refuse to create efficient and productive conditions to best utilize and nourish their scholars' talents will not have a place in the future. Globalization increases international cooperation in this leading economic sector. Developed countries, from this perspective, play an imperative role in the global distribution of scientific achievements. One of the major vehicles of this process is the multinational

Table 5.46 Research & Development Performed Abroad by Majority Owned Foreign Affiliates of US Multilateral Corporations, (Millions of US$) 2010

Economy	*1994*	*1995*	*1996*	*1997*	*1998*	*1999*	*2000*	*2001*	*2002*	*2007*	*2010*
All Countries	11877	12582	14039	14593	14664	18144	20457	19702	21151	28484	39470
Asia	1538	1569	1651	1482	1298	2923	3587	3908	3552	5575	8313
China	**58**	**68**	**63**	**117**	**118**	**553**	*	*	*	**909**	**1452**
Mainland	**7**	**13**	**25**	**35**	**52**	**319**	**506**	*	**646**	**804**	**1299**
Hong Kong	**51**	**55**	**38**	**82**	**66**	**214**	*	**289**	*	**105**	**153**
India	**5**	**5**	**9**	**22**	**23**	**20**	*	**26**	**80**	**310**	**1644**
Indonesia	**5**	**9**	**6**	**5**	**4**	**1**	**2**	**3**	**3**	*	**28**
Japan	1130	1286	1333	1089	962	1523	1630	1507	1433	1739	1855
Malaysia	**27**	**21**	**23**	**32**	**30**	**161**	**218**	*	*	**249**	**376**
Philippines	**14**	**23**	**14**	**12**	**10**	**31**	**40**	**48**	**50**	*	**55**
Singapore	**167**	**63**	**88**	**73**	**62**	**426**	**551**	**755**	**589**	**850**	**753**
South Korea	**17**	**29**	**34**	**41**	**29**	**101**	**143**	**157**	**167**	**729**	**835**
Taiwan	**110**	**61**	**75**	**84**	**55**	**122**	**143**	**139**	**70**	*	**235**
Thailand	**3**	**5**	**5**	**5**	**4**	**7**	**13**	**18**	**22**	*	**106**
EU	8271	8852	9386	9691	10058	11900	12472	11253	12142	12142	24406
Other	2068	2161	3002	3420	3308	3321	4398	4541	5457	4281	6751

National Science Foundation, Division of Science Resources Statistics. (2007). *Asia's Rising Science and Technology Strength: Comparative Indicators for Asia, the European Union, and the United States*. NSF 07–319. Arlington, VA. Retrieved from www.nsf.gov/statistics/nsf07319/content.cfm?pub_id=1874&id=4/

*Suppressed to avoid disclosure of confidential information.

Note: Data is for non-bank overseas majority-owned affiliates of non-bank US parent companies. Majority-owned affiliates are those in which combined ownership of all US parents is more than 50 percent. Data includes research and development (R&D) performed by affiliates, whether for themselves or others, and excludes R&D expenditures made by others for affiliates. European Union includes 12 countries for 1994 and 15 countries thereafter. Data for 2002 is estimated.

corporation, the overwhelming majority of which originated from developed countries like the US and EU countries.

According to calculations of the World Bank, "technological progress in developing countries between the 1990s and 2000s has been very strong."[61] It is important to underline that in the category of developing countries, in this statistic the leading role is carried out by EMCs, as they are categorized in this book. In EMCs from very different regions of the GEM, such as "Chile, Hungary, and Poland, the overall level of technological achievement increased by more than 125 percent during the 1990s."[62] However, a regional analysis of technological and innovative development in the GEM shows that in the majority of Asian and Eastern European countries, technological progress is moving much faster than in Latin America, Africa, and the Middle East. In terms of know-how, the GEM is still behind developed countries. In terms of the global know-how market, the United States accounts for 35 percent; Japan, 30; Germany, 16; and Russia, only 0.3 percent.[63]

An interesting tendency should be underlined: the most modern technologies and innovations spread through countries of the GEM at a much faster pace than traditional technologies. For example, Internet bandwidth more than doubled between 1999 and 2004 in middle- and lower-income countries.[64] But, the more and more expensive access is, the slower its dispersion through society.

Innovation—especially technological innovation—is based on the most cutting-edge scientific achievements. One of the major indicators of a nation's potential success, and an important strategic competitive advantage for nations and corporations alike, is the accumulation of granted patents. These represent innovative thinking and collaboration between the government and its citizens. The United States leads the world in granted patents by a staggering amount, with 5.5 million patents received from 1963 to the end of 2013. Japan comes in a distant second with fewer than one million patents in the same amount of time, and the innovative Germany comes in third with less than 400,000

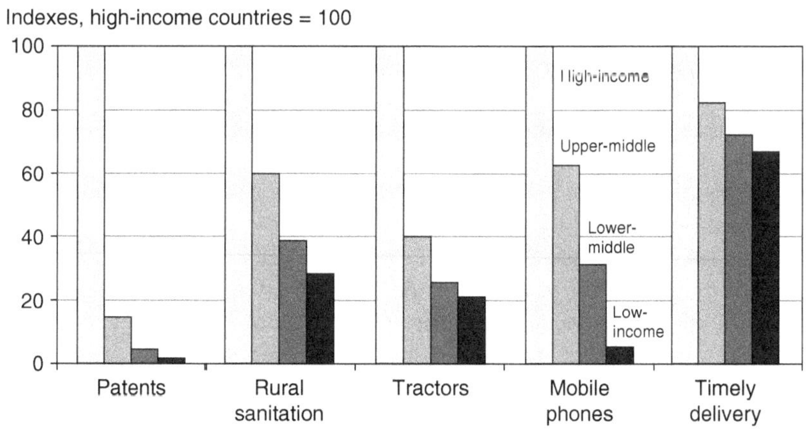

Figure 5.31 Disparities in Use of Patents and Various Technologies, 2008

World Bank. (2008). *Global Economic Prospects 2008: Technology Diffusion in the Developing World*. Retrieved from http://econ.worldbank.org/WBSITE/EXTERNAL/EXTDEC/EXTDECPROSPECTS/GEPEXT/EXTGEP2008/0,,contentMDK:21602245~isCURL:Y~noSURL:Y~pagePK:64167689~piPK:64167673~theSitePK:4503324,00.html/

patents. In 2013 alone, this gap increased: the US was granted 277,835 new patents, and Japan received 51,919.

From 2000 to 2008, EMCs demonstrated substantial, steady progress in technological innovations, and as such were granted many more patents than in the twentieth century. Two EMCs—South Korea and Taiwan—are now among the top 10 leading countries in patent granting. In the top 20 globally leading countries, we see Israel, followed by China and India. In terms of patents granted per capita, the world leader is Israel. Since 2008, China overcame Israel in terms of absolute numbers of granted patents and is now a distant third behind South Korea and Taiwan in patent-receiving EMCs, even if related Hong Kong statistics are added to the statistics of mainland China. Government support of the sciences and technology in Singapore and Ireland helped bump up their standing worldwide to surpass Russia in terms of this indicator. Among BRICS countries, Russia is in third place, and still has more than twice the amount of patents of South Africa. During the first part of the twenty-first century Malaysia, Czech Republic, Poland, Turkey, Portugal, and Egypt increased the most number of patents among GEM states, while Syria, Uzbekistan, and Venezuela by this indicator are in decline, with Venezuela receiving twice as few patents in 2014 than in 2002. Finally, some EMCs have remained steadily low and have not demonstrated progress in patent registering: Bolivia, Kazakhstan, Armenia, Morocco, and Zimbabwe.[65]

An entry strategy and strategy development in general of different areas and industries of the GMP is not necessarily used in the same order of basic economic factors as presented in this book. For example, an analysis of high-tech industries has to begin with the last (and most modern) basic economic factors: science, research, technologies and innovations that predetermine the dynamism of the strategizing entity. Regions and countries rich with natural resources and industries related to these resources must be analyzed from the starting point of their territory and natural resources. However, any strategic analysis related to bringing businesses (or increased military presence) to a new country or region, or to increase one's presence and investments, should include a discussion of all basic economic factors, followed by an analysis of the main elements of strategic management systems in these regions, countries, and industries. These basic economic factors play an important role not only in purely economic analysis but in strategic analysis as well. Any priorities of a social nature and improvements in the standards of living of the population can be based only on the achievements in facing economic and technological priorities of strategy. These priorities are a source for the salvation of social issues and improvements in the standards of living for people, and not vice versa. Otherwise, all dreams about enriched quality of life will be just wishful thinking.

It is understandable that basic economic factors are major components of any economic, social, or military strategy. There is one marked difference: in strategy, time is a principle factor, unlike in economics. Innovation and technological achievements on the basis of new patents create new opportunities for tremendous improvement of the quality of life for the global community, but the lack of well-developed strategy and the strategic weakness of leadership found in major multilateral institutions and NGOs will often stand in the way of progress. For example, the millennium summit in 2000 correctly predicted a huge increase of wealth in the new century, but incorrectly surmised that this would lead to an eradication of poverty, mass disease, and improvement of the quality of life for the poorest 1.5 billion people in the world. This did not happen by 2015—the horizon for which millennium goals were set. Powerful, instrumental strategy is still underestimated and underused by global leadership. Lack of well-developed strategy is slowing the development of the GMP and the improvement of the global community.

Notes

1 Rucker, R. (1977). *Geometry, Relativity and the Fourth Dimension.* Mineola, NY: Dover Publications, p. 118.
2 Saroyan, W. (1968). *I Used to Believe I Had Forever, Now I'm Not So Sure.* Spokane, WA: Cowles, p. 166.
3 Theodore Roosevelt was the first American and first US president awarded the Nobel Peace Prize in 1906.
4 Kalter, E. (2008). "Local Capital Markets: Emerging Market Investment Opportunities. Executive Summary." Medford, MA: Center for Emerging Market Enterprises.
5 Siebert, H. (2002). The World Economy. 2nd edition. London: Routledge, p. i.
6 The World Bank. (2008). Global Economic Prospects 2008: Technology Diffusion in the Developing World. Retrieved from http://siteresource.worldbank.org/INTGEP2008/Resources/complete-repost.pdf
7 Maddison, A. (2001). The World Economy: A Millennial Perspective. Paris: Organization for Economic Cooperation and Development. p. 19.
8 Mandelson, P. (2008) Alcuin Lecture. Retrieved February 19, 2008 from http://ec.europa.eu/commission_barroso/mandelson/
9 EU NGOs. (2007). "Indian Helicopters for Myanmar." July. Amnesty International UK and Saferworld. Retrieved from www.saferworld.org.uk/publications.php/270/indian_helicopters_for_myanmar
10 Mehta, S.N. (2007). "Carlos Slim, the Richest Man in the World. Fortune. August 20. Retrieved from http://money.cnn.com/2007/08/03/news/international/carlosslim.fortune/index.htm
11 The GDP indicator was developed by Nobel Laureate in Economics Simon Kuznets for the US Congress in 1934. The GDP together with the PPP are good indicators of the national product of any country. However, the impending domination of the knowledge economy requires these integrated indicators to be updated.
12 The International Comparison Program. (2005). International Comparison Program preliminary results. Retrieved from http://siteresources.worldbank.org/ICPINT/Resources/backgrounder FAQ.pdf
13 The International Comparison Program. (2005). International Comparison Program preliminary results. Retrieved from http://siteresources.worldbank.org/ICPINT/Resources/backgrounderFAQ.pdf
14 Elekdag, S. and Lall, S. (2008,). "Global Growth Estimates Trimmed After PPP." IMF Survey Magazine. January 8. Retrieved from www.imf.org/external/pubs/ft/survey/so/2008/RES018A.htm
15 Bell, D. (1999). *The Coming of the Post-Industrial Society.* New York: Basic Books, p. xcvi.
16 In 2009 I met with the Minister of Knowledge Economy (MKE) in South Korea. By that time the Ministry of Economy had been abolished and replaced with this new government department. It indicates that South Korea is already dedicated to a knowledge-based economy.
17 Based on data from the World Bank World Development Indicators. Retrieved from http://databank.worldbank.org/data/reports.aspx?source=world-development-indicators
18 Vaknin, S. (2000). "The Blessings of the Informal Economy." Central Europe Review. January 17. Retrieved from www.ce-review.org/00/40/vaknin40.html
19 Gettman, J.B. of the US Department of Health and Human Services, quoted in M. Burke. (2007). "Inside Dope," Forbes, March 26, p. 81.
19a Leontief, W. (1984). *Input-output Economics.* Oxford: Oxford University Press. p. 322.
19b Fontela, E. (2004). "Leontief and the Future of the World Economy." In *Wassily Leontief and Input-Output Econimics.* Dietzenbacher, Erik and Lahr, Michael (eds). Cambridge: Cambridge University Press. p. 3.
20 Döös, B.R. (2002). "Population Growth and Loss of Arable Land." Global Environmental Change, volume 12, issue 4. pp. 303–311.
21 Bold, A. (2007). "440,000 m/day—SWRO Desalination Plants in Spain Saving Energy with PX Technology." Retrieved from www.energyrecovery.com/news/documents/440K_Spainaward%20PR_FINAL101107.pdf

22 Food and Agriculture Organization of the United Nations. (n.d.). "Aquastat." Retrieved from www.fao.org/nr/water/aquastat/dbase/index.stm
23 Nile Basin Initiative. (n.d.).Retrieved from www.nilebasin.org/
24 Energy Information Administration. (n.d.). "International Total Primary Energy Consumption and Energy Intensity." Retrieved from www.eia.doe.gov/emeu/international/energyconsumption.html
25 Sampson, R.J. and Calmus, T.W. (1974). *Economics: Concepts, Applications, Analysis.* Boston: Houghton Mifflin Company. p. 384.
26 Energy Information Administration. (2007). "World Proved Reserves of Oil and Natural Gas, Most Recent Estimates." January 9. Retrieved from www.eia.doe.gov/emeu/international/Notes%20for%20Most%20Recent%20Estimates%20of%20Proved%20Oil%20and%20Natural%20Gas%20Reserves.html
27 US Energy Information Adminstration. (n.d.). "Top 100 Oil and Gas Fields." Retrieved from www.eia.gov/pub/oil_gas/natural_gas/data_publications/crude_oil_natural_gas_reserves/current/pdf/top100fields.pdf/
28 Energy Information Administration. (n.d.). "Country Analysis Briefs: Iran." Retrieved from www.eia.doe.gov/emeu/cabs/Iran/Oil.html
29 The White House. (2007). "State of the Union: Twenty in Ten: Strengthening America's Energy Security." Retrieved from www.whitehouse.gov/stateoftheunion/2007/initiatives/energy.html
30 Energy Information Administration. (2007). International Energy Outlook 2007. Retrieved from www.eia.doe.gov/oiaf/ieo/highlights.html
31 Yardley, J. (2007). "China Banks on Hydropower to Cut Emissions, but at Huge Human Cost." The International Herald Tribune- Asia Pacific. November 18.
32 World Nuclear Association. (2008). "Nuclear Power in China." February. Retrieved from www.world-nuclear.org/info/inf63.html
33 "America's Vulnerable Economy." (2007). The Economist. November 15. Retrieved from www.economist.com/opinion/displaystory.cfm?story_id=10134118
34 "Wingless Migration." (2007). The Economist. November 1. Retrieved from www.economist.com/science/displaystory.cfm?story_id=10062451
35 Hunt, G. and B.H.P. Bilton. (2007). "Growth Through Optionality." June 6. Retrieved from www.bhpbilliton.com/bbContentRepository/070531GhUbs2007ConfLondon.pdf
36 United States Geological Survey. (n.d.). "Cobalt." Retrieved from http://minerals.usgs.gov/minerals/pubs/commodity/cobalt/cobalmcs07.pdf
37 United States Geological Survey. (n.d.). "Platinum Group Metals." Retrieved from http://minerals.usgs.gov/minerals/pubs/commodity/platinum/platimcs07.pdf
38 United States Geological Survey. (n.d.). "Gold." Retrieved January 13, 2015 from http://minerals.usgs.gov/minerals/pubs/commodity/gold/mcs-2014-gold.pdf
39 "Gold." (2008). The Economist. January 26, p. 94, based on data from GFMS, a precious metals consultancy.
40 Shaparev, N. (2007). "Natural Resources of China." Herald of the Russian Academy of Sciences, vol. 77, no. 10. p. 928.
41 Jingrong, Li. (2003). "China's Artificial Forest Area Ranks First in the World." China through a Lens. October 28. Retrieved from http://japanese.china.org.cn/english/2003/Oct/78535.htm
42 August, R. (1993). *International Business Law: Text, Cases and Readings.* Upper Saddle River, NJ: Prentice Hall, p. 369.
43 Bank for International Settlements. (n.d.). "History of the Basel Committee and Its Membership." Retrieved from www.bis.org/bcbs/history.htm
44 Bank for International Settlements. (n.d.). "Fact Sheet Basel Committee on Banking Supervision." Retrieved from www.bis.org/about/factbcbs.htm
45 International Monetary Fund. (2008). "Gold in the IMF." Retrieved from www.imf.org/external/np/exr/facts/gold.htm
45a Bank for International Settlements. (n.d.). Banking Services for Central Banks. Retrieved from www.bis.org/banking/index.html
46 Bank for International Settlements. (n.d.). Banking Services for Central Banks. Retrieved from www.bis.org/banking/index.htm
47 Bank for International Settlements. (n.d.). Banking Services for Central Banks. Retrieved from www.bis.org/banking/index.htm

48 Kalter, E. (2008). "Local Capital Markets: Emerging Market Investment Opportunities Executive Summary." Bretton Woods Committee Meeting.

49 Gazeta, R. (2015). "Central Bank of Russia Declaration." January 16. Retrieved from www.gazeta.ru/news

50 Sy, A. (2007). "Malaysia: An Islamic Capital Market Hub." Islamic Finance. September 18. Retrieved from www.imf.org/external/pubs/ft/survey/so/2007/CAR0919A.htm

51 J.D. Power Automotive. (2008). "North American Light Vehicle Production Update." January Retrieved from http://128.121.187.28/publicData/prodEstimate_northamerica.htm

52 J.D. Power Automotive. (2008). "Estimated Pan-European Passenger Car Assembly by Model." January. Retrieved from http://128.121.187.28/publicData/prodEstimate_europe.htm

53 J.D. Power Automotive. (2008). "Estimated Pan-European Passenger Car Assembly by Model." January. Retrieved from http://128.121.187.28/publicData/prodEstimate_europe.htm

54 Ben-David, D. (2008). "Brain Drained: A Tale of Two Countries." VOX . Retrieved from www.voxeu.org/index.php?q=node/984

55 World Science Forum. (2003). "Knowledge and Society." Budapest. November 8–10. Summaries: Knowledge-Based Society.

56 European Federation of National Academies of Sciences and Humanities. (n.d.). "News." Retrieved from www.allea.org/cfdata/output/news_archive.cfm/

57 World Bank. (2008). Global Economic Prospects 2008: Technology Diffusion in the Developing World. Retrieved from http://siteresource.worldbank.org/INTGEP2008/Resources/complete-repost.pdf

58 Merkel, A. (2006). "German Science Policy 2006." Science AAAS. July 14, p. 147.

59 Duga, J. and Study, T. (2008). "Globalization Distributes More of the R&D Wealth." Global R&D Report 2008. Retrieved from www.rdmag.com/pdf/RD79GlobalReport.pdf

60 Duga, J. and Study, T. (2008). "Globalization Distributes More of the R&D Wealth." Global R&D Report 2008. Retrieved from www.rdmag.com/pdf/RD79GlobalReport.pdf

61 World Bank. (2008). Global Economic Prospects 2008: Technology Diffusion in the Developing World. Retrieved from http://siteresource.worldbank.org/INTGEP2008/Resources/complete-repost.pdf

62 World Bank. (2008). Global Economic Prospects 2008: Technology Diffusion in the Developing World. Retrieved from http://siteresource.worldbank.org/INTGEP2008/Resources/complete-repost.pdf

63 Speech of First Deputy Prime Minister S. Ivanov at the Ministry of Education and Science of the Russian Federation. February 19, 2008. From the Russian Information Agency Novosti.

64 World Bank. (2008). Global Economic Prospects 2008: Technology Diffusion in the Developing World. Retrieved from http://siteresource.worldbank.org/INTGEP2008/Resources/complete-repost.pdf

65 Based on data from the United States Patent and Trademark Office. Patents by Country, State, and Year—Utility Patents (January 1, 1963–December 31, 2013). Retrieved from www.uspto.gov/web/offices/ac/ido/oeip/taf/cst_utl.htm/

Notes on Plate 5.1

Little or No Water Scarcity: Abundant water resources relative to use, with less than 25 percent of water from rivers withdrawn for human purposes.

Physical Water Scarcity (water resources development is approaching or has exceeded sustainable limits): More than 75 percent of river flows are withdrawn for agriculture, industry, and domestic purposes (accounting for recycling of return flows). This definition—relating water availability to water demand—implies that dry areas are not necessarily water scarce.

Approaching Physical Water Scarcity: More than 60 percent of river flows are withdrawn. These basins will experience physical water scarcity in the near future.

Economic Water Scarcity (human, institutional, and financial capital limit access to water even though water in nature is available locally to meet human demands): Water resources are abundant relative to water use, with less than 25 percent of water from rivers withdrawn for human purposes, but malnutrition exists.

6 The Global Emerging Market

Definition, Characteristics, and Dynamics

> If we began with certainties, we shall end in doubts, but if we begin with doubts, and are patient in them, we shall end in certainties.[1]
>
> Francis Bacon, English philosopher and lord high chancellor of Great Britain (1561–1626)

> All the like us are We,
> And everyone else is They.
> And They live over the sea,
> While We live over the way.
> But—would you believe it?—
> They look upon We
> As only a sort of They.[2]
>
> Rudyard Kipling, English author and 1907 Nobel Prize winner in Literature (1865–1936)

Keynote Definitions

An **Emerging Market Country (EMC)** is a society transitioning from a dictatorship to a free market–oriented economy, with increasing economic freedom, gradual integration within the GMP and with other members of the global emerging market, an expanding middle class, improving standards of living, social stability, and tolerance, as well as an increase in cooperation with multilateral institutions.

The **Global Emerging Market (GEM)** is a new economic, strategic, and political phenomenon of the world economy and the global marketplace, encompassing emerging market countries and their regional blocs, which, despite varying geopolitical characteristics, are united by comparable levels of risk and developing free-market infrastructure. These factors of the GEM unify vectors of development of emerging market countries toward economic freedom and global integration, attracting international economic and business cooperation and competition.

Preconditions for the Birth of the Global Emerging Market

Despite the fact that the global emerging market has existed for about 30 years, the first definition of GEM and emerging market countries was published only in 2009 for the first time in my previous book on this subject.[3] It is what economists and strategists are supposed to do: to discover new or unrecognized trends, economic and strategic phenomena, opportunities and threats, and to explain correlations between them, describe their characteristics, and use them to increase the efficiency of companies and regional economies, and the prosperity of nations.

Historical Precedents of the Creation of Emerging Economies

Human civilization has gone through several turning points in history. These crucial milestones were almost always marked by the expansion of the frontiers of major civilizations into unknown or barely known countries and uninhabited territories, from the time of Alexander the Great and his "expeditions" deep into Asia, to the borders of Punjab; to the extension of the Roman Empire to Africa and Britain; the creation of the empires of Genghis Khan and Tamerlane (who unified Central Asia for the first time); and to the opening for Europeans of the "New World" by Columbus, among other great geographical explorations. These expeditions throughout Eurasia and the Americas spurred the emergence of new economies and subsequent opportunities and challenges.

Leaders tend to think that the borders and new frontiers of their empires will last forever. Alexander, for example, assumed that the "fusion" of his people's culture with that of conquered nations would maintain the borders of his empire. The Spanish and Portuguese royalty assumed that the economic resources and markets of the Americas would always be under the control of their protectionist duopoly. Of course, global orders never last forever. In just the twentieth century, for example, the global order went through three drastic changes: the global order prior to World War I, between the two world wars, and the aftermath of World War II. The second decade of the twenty-first century has been a period of formation of a new global order and the materialization of new challenges, causing some regional superpowers to question the existence of one polar world.

In December 1975, the US, Canada, and the countries of Western Europe met with the Soviet Union at the Conference on Security and Co-operation in Europe. From this conference, the Helsinki Accords, signed by 35 countries, officially recognized the territorial integrity and sovereignty of all European states, acknowledging and seemingly condoning the expansion of the Soviet Union into Eastern Europe following World War II. Of course, within less than two decades, the Berlin Wall fell, and the Soviet empire disintegrated into 15 independent states (all of which have since become members of the United Nations), again radically altering the global order. During the same general period, dictatorships throughout the world, including those in Greece (1973), Spain (1975), Turkey (1982), Argentina (1982), and Brazil (1985), and the personal dictatorships of Ferdinand Marcos in the Philippines (1986) and of Alfredo Stroessner in Paraguay (1989) failed. People and political and business leaders who assumed that past global orders would become the permanent status quo ignored a basic strategic principle and one of the rules of strategic thinking: nothing lasts forever. Strategists always have to try to discover and evaluate new trends with the potential to change the political, economic, and business order and redesign their strategies according to upcoming opportunities and thunderstorms.

The Strategic, Economic, and Philosophical Inevitability of the Failure of Dictatorships and Command Economies

The overwhelming majority of people living under dictatorships of the twentieth century were isolated from the world beyond their national borders. Travel and most forms of communication (mail, radio, television, etc.) were severely restricted. Only high-level government officials and their relatives and cronies were able to see firsthand the lifestyles and standard of living enjoyed by people in free societies. In return for this privilege, as well as access to consumer and luxury goods from capitalist countries, and in order to maintain their own power, these bureaucrats endorsed the official propaganda about their "imperialist enemies."

But why was access to foreign-made goods such a coveted privilege of the top-level bureaucrats and decision-makers of dictatorships (this was correctly referred to as the "nomenclature" in countries of the Soviet bloc—a term that can be used for any dictatorship)? Why did people living under dictatorships prefer used foreign cars to new domestic ones? Indeed, why did most dictatorships not even attempt to produce cars or other sophisticated consumer goods?

As previously discussed in this book, command-economy dictatorships were incapable of producing these high-quality and technologically advanced goods because of the direct relationship between motivation and the availability of goods and services on one side of the equation, and freedom and variations in the quality of goods and services on the other. These relationships are the source of the fundamental distinction between command-economy dictatorships and free-market economies. Quality of life (and standards of living) is determined by the availability of quality goods and services appropriate to varying individual preferences and needs. The production of high-quality goods and services requires a high quality of labor. High-quality labor is the result of effective motivation throughout the process of production. Effective motivation, in turn, helps ensure attentive, thorough, and professional workers. A fundamental ideal of communism and a staple of all command economies is the equality of wages, salaries, and other forms of compensation regardless of a worker's level of output. This practice removes effective incentives for worker efficiency, innovation, or leadership, and often even integrity. When motivation is removed from the process of production, the result is low-quality labor, goods, and services and, subsequently, a much lower quality of life. Furthermore, there is also a constant deficit of the various goods and services required by different individuals, which negatively affects quality of life. Consumers totally lack options. This absence of consumer choice allows goods and services to be produced and consumed, regardless of their quality. The inevitable poverty and low quality of life of command economies and dictatorships are tangible results of the suppression of motivation. Most important, beyond the political repression characteristic of dictatorships, the results of a lack of motivation repress the freedom of individuals to make choices that determine the quality of their lives. This is the structural weakness of command economies and dictatorships as well as the fundamental distinction between them and the liberty of free markets.

If a dictatorship were to introduce motivation to the production processes via differentiated compensation that reflects productive input, the ensuing variation in product quality and standards of living, as well as consumer's freedom of choice, would seriously contradict the ideology and relevance of the dictatorship. This introduction inevitably leads to the destruction of the dictatorship or at the very least a major revision of its ideology, such as the Chinese Communist Party's embrace of free-market principles.

Why do dictatorships always repress free thinkers? The answer to this question was given by the great philosopher Jean-Paul Sartre. In the following quote from *Les Mouches* (*The Flies*), King Aegistheus describes how destructive freedom can be to dictatorships: "A man who is free is like a mangy sheep in a herd. He will contaminate my entire kingdom and ruin my work."[4] Individual freedom of choice is the defining quality of a free society; any ruling structure that represses this freedom sows the seeds of its own destruction. The blunt names of the stores in the Siberian city of Krasnoyarsk illustrate the lack of freedom of choice and constant deficit of goods in dictatorships: "Meat" or "Fish"; "Shoes," "Dress," "Furniture," etc. One particular store, when it first opened in the 1960s, was called "Meat-Fish." When the shortage of meat became severe, the name changed to "Fish-Chicken." When there was a shortage of fish, the store was renamed "Chicken-Eggs," then both words disappeared for the same reason and the name was changed to "Vegetable-Fruits." Finally, it was called only "Vegetables." A more accurate name would have been "Potato-Cabbage."

In addition to ensuring an impoverished and miserable material existence for the majority of the populace, the anemic economic performance of command economies makes it increasingly difficult for the self-appointed leadership to maintain power. Poverty combined with a lack of freedom, repression of minorities, government-sponsored nationalism and intolerance, and economic as well as political self-isolation create conditions that cannot be endured for very long, and that almost inevitably lead to democratic change. The form of these changes varies from country to country. However, in general, democratic changes began to occur during the same period, due to the influence of one of the most powerful global trends—democratization. The convergence of this trend with globalization and revolutions in global information technology made it practically impossible for the overwhelming majority of dictatorships to resist democratic pressures. It is important, however, to point out that there are exceptions to this scenario. Dictatorships in unusually wealthy countries, typically with smaller populations, can maintain control for longer periods, primarily due to income derived from the sale of natural resources. Dictatorships and repressive regimes financed by petrodollars are an obvious present-day example. But the recent example of Iraq shows that even oil-rich dictatorships cannot last forever. Nevertheless, in most command-economy dictatorships, it becomes practically impossible to generate the revenue necessary to dominate, appease, and/or placate the public. But it was the dramatic improvement in information technologies, an external factor almost completely beyond the control of any government, that has made it exceedingly difficult for dictatorships to exist and will likely be the proverbial nail in the coffin. Dictatorships' ability to control information has been seriously compromised. Global communication systems made it exceedingly difficult for dictators to keep their populations isolated from and ignorant of the superior standard of living that exists in free-market democracies. This was the beginning of the end for the majority of dictatorships throughout the world. Two obvious exceptions to this trend are China and Vietnam. The communist parties of these two countries introduced economic freedom and motivation to the productive process and allowed foreign investment. Subsequently, the quality of goods and services and standard of living has improved steadily in these two countries. However, in most dictatorships political unrest led to the eventual replacement of dictatorial regimes with elected leaders, democratic governments, and economic freedom. The newly elected leaders looked abroad for proven methods to create economic growth and improve the standard of living. This led to a wave of market-oriented economic reforms, the appearance of the first modern emerging market countries (EMCs), and eventually to a new economic and political phenomenon, the global emerging market (GEM). In any emerging market democracy, in order for a political regime to be sustainable, its major strategic concept should include preferences which reflect the basic needs and choices of the public. In the words of Dr. Alexander Nekipelov, "The problem of public preferences, influence upon the strategy of economic development of a country is a permanent one."[5]

The Global Emerging Market

Initial Understanding of the Global Emerging Market as a New Economic, Strategic, and Political Phenomenon

The creation of the global emerging market cannot be given a precise date of birth. The terms "emerging stock markets" and "emerging markets" first appeared in financial literature at the end of the 1980s to describe stock, equity, debt, and security markets outside of developed countries.[6] At that time there were already 43 countries outside of the developed world with stock exchanges, and the term "emerging stock markets" referred mostly to markets of shares in these countries. However, there were no defined terms used to describe the maturity of national economies until the 1990s. This initial terminology demonstrated a vague understanding of the development of emerging market countries, but not of the GEM, and lacked a real theoretical framework. For example, the International Finance Corporation (IFC) considers all countries with a gross national income (GNI) per capita below the World Bank's minimum requirement for high-income countries to be emerging markets (see current classifications below).[7] (For a more detailed analysis of classification systems of major multilateral institutions, see Chapter 4). The current classification of the World Bank by GNI per capita is as follows:

World Bank classification of countries according to 2006 and 2013 GNI per capita.

2006[8]	2013[9]
Low Income: < $905	< $1,035 or less
Lower Middle Income: $905 > $3,595	$1,036 > $4,085
Upper Middle Income: $3,595 > $11,115	$4,086 > $12,615
High Income: > $11,115	$12,616

As the above data demonstrates, during the last seven years the world economy led to tremendous progress in the quality of life and standards of living according to one of the most integrated indicators, GNI per capita. What used to be income for the lower middle class has become income for people in the low income bracket. What used to be high income in 2006 became in 2013 just upper middle-class income, and the high income class increased annually by $1,500. This progress would be impossible without a new level of integration of economic cooperation on the global marketplace. It is also demonstrates a continuing decreasing of the gap between the incomes of people in developed and emerging market countries. Strategists have to evaluate and extend these dynamics for the strategizing horizon by inserting required coefficients. It will definitely help them secure a better vision for the strategizing object in the distant future.

When the IFC, by the initiative of Antoine van Agtmael, renamed the Third World Database the Emerging Market Database[10] (which would later appear as two indices: the S&P/IFC Investable Emerging Markets Index covering 22 markets, and the S&P/IFC Global Index, which covers 33 markets[11]), it incorrectly equated these two terms. Nonetheless, it was a step in the right direction toward recognizing the birth of a new economic phenomenon, which was later described as the global emerging market.[12]

Any attempt to classify a national economy purely by the above-mentioned limited financial approach does not explain the distinctions between different categories of non-developed countries. There are fundamental differences between those countries that have become an important part of the global marketplace (all categories of emerging market countries—economies in bloom, emerging market democracies, oligarchic emerging markets, emerging market dictatorships, and, to a limited extent, pre-emerging markets) and those that still are not a comfortable option for foreign and even domestic businesses (developing and underdeveloped countries). Developing countries are in the early stages of opening up for international business, while underdeveloped countries typically have economic and business agendas that are not conducive to any international business activity whatsoever. Even at the beginning of the twenty-first century, the unique needs and characteristics of EMCs and both developing and underdeveloped countries are ignored by most country classification. Ignoring these distinctions distorts the conclusions and results of studies of the global marketplace. For example, a 2006 special report on EMCs in *The Economist*[13] arbitrarily blurs the lines between emerging market, developing, and underdeveloped countries into one category, rendering all of the survey's statistics inaccurate. Due to a lack of understanding of the distinctions between EMCs and developing countries, the real emerging market economies appeared to be less efficient than they were in reality, as the population and economies of developing and underdeveloped countries falsely augmented the population of the GEM. This also falsely reduced the productivity of labor and GDP per capita of EMCs (see Chapter 4 for a detailed analysis of current country classification systems and their flaws).

Unlike emerging market countries, developing and underdeveloped countries still need special attention from multilateral institutions and aid associations to prevent starvation, mass diseases, and political instability, which can easily create conditions for the temporary return of some softer form of dictatorship. Developing countries need special attention from the international community to improve their education systems, because the quality of this system has very important implications for the future of these countries—as well as the pace of economic and political reform. They need assistance in the formation of their national economic strategies, with the goal of transitioning into the GEM. This is also an important mission of companies from developed and emerging market countries. Companies from EMCs can be especially helpful to those in developing countries, as they have a great deal of experience operating in conditions of non-developed markets. For example, China is playing an instrumental role in strategy development in Nigeria, as is Taiwan in Swaziland.

Ratings and Evaluations of the Maturity of Emerging Market Countries

A single indicator, even one as integrated as GNI or GDP per capita, cannot adequately categorize an EMC. It is very important to consider the vector of change of GNI per capita. Obviously, the pace and direction of a statistic such as GNI per capita has significant implications for a country's economic maturation. There are examples of countries that were once categorized as EMCs that have reverted to the developing and/or underdeveloped category. Take Zimbabwe, Uzbekistan, and Venezuela, where the government changed the political and economic course and attitude toward international cooperation. However, even describing a country solely in terms of the vector of GNI per capita will not give an adequate basis to analyze economic maturity or a sufficient basis upon which to determine the correct categorization of development. A much more comprehensive analysis is required, such as the Strategic Comprehensive Country Classification System proposed, laid a foundation for, and described in my previous book.[14]

The first periodicals dedicated specifically to the study of EMCs were introduced at the World Economic Development Congress and the Joint Annual Meeting of the World Bank and IMF in October 1994 in Madrid. The international community specifically focused its attention on EMCs in October 1995 at the World Economic Development Forum and the Joint Annual Meeting of the World Bank and IMF in Washington, DC. Also in 1995, the US Department of Commerce and the International Trade Administration demonstrated an understanding of the new role of EMCs and organized a seminar called "Beyond Borders: Big Emerging Markets." The seminar listed Argentina, Brazil, China, Hong Kong, Mexico, Poland, Turkey, South Korea, South Africa, and Taiwan. Initially, experts debated over what exactly qualified as an EMC. Furthermore, the fact that EMCs were part of a global phenomenon—the GEM—was scarcely understood at all. Unique historical legacies make the countries of the GEM a diverse bunch, and the level of economic and political freedom and standards of living vary a great deal among them. Nevertheless, EMCs can be grouped together because of a present orientation and a long-term trend toward economic freedom and integration with the GMP. While some EMCs may temporarily veer off course (such as Venezuela, Bolivia, Zimbabwe, Belarus, and, until 2007, Turkmenistan), and the pace of progress varies, all paths in the GEM eventually lead to economic and political freedom and improved standards of living.

In order to determine the level of a country's economic maturity, its level of integration into the GMP, and whether or not it can be categorized as an EMC, strategists should consult several sources. There are a multitude of sources for data, including multilateral institutions, rating agencies, and various research organizations; the key to successfully understanding EMCs, the global emerging market, and the global marketplace is the ability to critically analyze and compare data, evaluations, and opinions from multiple sources. It is also important to understand the rationale behind the differences in ratings and opinions from various agencies regarding the same country, industry, or company. In the end strategists must draw their own conclusions regarding the status of a national economy. There are a number of organizations and agencies that regularly publish ratings and/or data that can be strategically analyzed to decide the maturity of a country. Among them are the World Bank Group, Moody's, Standard and Poor's (S&P), Fitch, Dun and Bradstreet, the Heritage Foundation, the *Wall Street Journal*, the Economist Intelligence Unit, the Morgan Stanley Capital International Barra (MSCI Barra), and others.

The World Bank Group and IMF regularly update the World Development Indicators and the World Economic Outlook Database, International Financial Statistics, and Direction of Trade Statistics, among others. The World Economic Forum, an annual meeting of political and economic leaders and experts from a number of fields, annually publishes its *Global Competitiveness Report*, which measures "the set of institutions, policies, and factors that set the sustainable current and medium-term levels of economic prosperity"[15] of national economies. The International Institute for Management Development (IMD), a Swiss business school, publishes a similar annual report, *The World Competitiveness Yearbook,* which ranks national economies based on how they create and sustain the competitiveness of enterprises. There are also a number of organizations that publish rankings of economic freedom annually. The Hong Kong Center for Economic Research's annual report on the *Economic Freedom of the World* and the *Index of Economic Freedom*, published annually by the *Wall Street Journal* and the *Heritage Foundation*, are two of the most widely respected. Each year Transparency International publishes the *Global Corruption Report*, which is a reliable indicator of the openness of an economy and demonstrates its level of economic and political freedom. Major rating agencies are an excellent source of data that can be used to determine the degree to which a country is developing. Standard & Poor's offers independent national credit ratings, international indices, and risk evaluation, in addition to other extensive research. When it comes to sovereign credit risk, S&P's opinion is especially useful. This rating is so widely respected that it influences corporate credit ratings in the country where the sovereign credit risk evaluation occurs. S&P basically issues an opinion regarding possible future scenarios in a country or of a company that it's evaluating. Fitch provides a number of ratings, such as the Country Ceiling Ratings, which indicate transfer and convertibility risk. The International Credit Ratings reflect a government's ability to meet foreign or local currency commitments. Moody's has offices throughout the world in developed countries as well as in EMCs, such as Hong Kong and Singapore. One index with particularly important implications for EMCs is Moody's National Scale Ratings, which assigns an evaluation to "certain countries in which investors have found the global rating scale provides inadequate differentiation among credits or is inconsistent with a rating scale already in common use in the country."[16] Dun & Bradstreet is one of the best sources for information on particular companies that work with or within the GEM. The United States Trade Representative publishes the annual *National Trade Estimate Report on Foreign Trade Barriers*, which is a very good indicator of a country's openness to international business activity and to its overall economic maturity. Similar agencies from other countries can also provide useful information on EMCs. The *globalEDGE*,[17] a website of the International Business Center of Michigan University, is also a useful source. Since 2002, it has published an index and rankings that evaluate countries considered to be emerging markets by *The Economist*. Of course, all of these ratings have to be reevaluated with one's own critical analysis and compared with those of other agencies. For example, in the *globalEDGE* rating, China correctly shifted from the fifth-ranked EMC in 2002 into the No. 1 position in 2007. But the market potential indicator does not reflect the progress that India and Brazil have made; both fell in the rankings, as did South Korea, one of the most efficient EMCs in economic terms. It is also very hard to believe that Brazil is ranked below Pakistan, Saudi Arabia, and Russia, and that Russia has a lower rating for economic freedom than Venezuela followed by the recipes for economic disaster of Hugo Chavez. The fact that Taiwan was not rated until 2005 (it was ranked fourth) brings into question the accuracy of all previous rankings. Nevertheless, the index incorporates the opinion of several professional publications and should not be ignored.

Strategists must compare the rankings of different agencies, find discrepancies, and understand the reasons behind them. In order to do so, one must have a great deal of theoretical and practical knowledge. It is absolutely crucial to underline the fact that all of the agencies and organizations mentioned above lack clearly defined country-classification systems upon which to base their ratings, forecasts, evaluations, etc. As a result, strategists must be very careful when these organizations and agencies describe groups of countries, like emerging markets, developing, or developed countries. These categories are almost never well-defined and/or based on a comprehensive methodology, which distorts the results and conclusions of these organizations and agencies regarding specific country groups. The Strategic Comprehensive Country Classification System mentioned above should be used to help organize and strategically analyze data received from the above-mentioned agencies, organizations, and institutions.

It is important to analyze not only absolute ranks of countries but also the relative rank of a country compared with others. Strategists should compare the opinions of domestic and foreign experts and analyze any discrepancies. Due to the fact that EMCs benefit from being ranked by major rating agencies—it attracts investment—many governments respond to the requirements of the major agencies. This is a direct and positive impact of rating agencies on the economic and financial situation of a country and the world. Investors can benefit from this by developing a strategy oriented to entering a country that it expects to be ranked by a major rating agency. Once the country appears on this list, its assets will immediately increase in market value.

Major Characteristics of an Emerging Market Country

What are the major requirements and characteristics that a country must have or achieve in order to be qualified as a part of the GEM? First of all, it is important to note that the process of acquiring the necessary characteristics is non-linear. As an economy develops into an EMC and continues to mature, some characteristics are gained, others are lost. From the beginning of the practical use of the term "emerging markets" by financiers, economists, and business executives (even before the creation of the term *emerging market country*), there has always been a need to understand the general characteristics of this economic phenomenon. It was especially necessary because initially, when the term was not clearly defined, "emerging stock market" and "emerging market" were used interchangeably. A typical example can be found in Margaret M. Price's *Emerging Stock Markets: A Complete Investment Guide to New Markets around the World.* In the section "Characteristics of Emerging Markets," the author states that emerging markets "include countries experiencing or having the potential for high economic growth but facing substantial political, economic and/or market-specific risks."[18] The author's characteristics are clearly not specific enough to differentiate emerging markets from other categories of national economies. It is also important to remember that none of the key characteristics remains static in a growing national economy. Below is a list of major characteristics that all EMCs have, had, or will have at some stage during their process of economic maturation and development. All of these characteristics (indicators of maturity) are enriched from empirical and comparative analysis with characteristics of developed and developing countries. While it is not necessary for all of the following characteristics to be present for a national economy to be considered an EMC, all EMCs experience the following characteristics and processes at some point in their development:

Forty-Five Major Strategic, Economic, and Political Characteristics of an EMC

1. A difficult search for the path to democracy from dictatorship.
2. A rapid transition from a command economy to a free-market economy.
3. An expeditiously increasing level of economic freedom.
4. Often, but not always, an increasing level of political freedom.
5. A brief anarchic period during the initial transition from a dictatorship to a free-market economy, which quickly ends as law and order is better enforced.
6. The replacement of a one-party system with a multiparty system (unless there were multiple parties under the dictatorship).
7. The emergence of a more transparent society.
8. An initial increase in corruption but a decrease in nepotism, and an eventual reduction of both as transparency increases.
9. The replacement of the legal framework of the dictatorship with a free market–oriented legal system that protects private property and interests.
10. Poor protection of intellectual property rights.

11. A reduction in the differences of legal treatment of foreign and domestic businesses.
12. An initial rise in crime followed by a gradual improvement of law and order as the government gains strength.
13. A rapidly changing legal, business, and economic environment that makes investment risky, even when these changes have a positive vector.
14. A transition from a society in which rulers are above the law to a government that is accountable to the law and society.
15. A search for spiritual tolerance and unification of different political and ethnic groups based on a rising interest in historical roots and national memories.
16. Decentralization of many economic functions from the national government to regional and local authorities.
17. Large-scale privatization.
18. Increasing productivity of labor.
19. Increasing economic growth, usually at a faster rate that the average of the global marketplace.
20. Deregulation of the creation and operation of businesses and other legal entities.
21. Establishment of free-market institutions such as commercial and investment banks; insurance companies; auditing, accounting, and legal-services firms, etc.
22. Creation and development of capital-market institutions (stock, currency and commodity exchanges, trust and custodian organizations, security and exchange oversight bodies, etc.)
23. Increasing convertibility of national currency.
24. Gradual economic integration with other members of the GEM and the GMP.
25. Manifestations of the global trend of regionalization via increasing economic cooperation in regional blocs, and on a multilateral and bilateral basis.
26. Integration of domestic regional economies within the national economy, but at a slower rate than the integration of the national economy with foreign economies, especially of developed countries.
27. Removal of the majority of remaining command economy restrictions on foreign investment.
28. An influx of foreign direct investment that gradually replaces foreign aid.
29. An outflow of domestic and, periodically, foreign capital.
30. Diversification from an economy predominantly oriented to natural resources and raw materials to more sophisticated and high-tech industries and services.
31. Decreasing role of the production of raw materials in GDP and exports.
32. An increasing national and personal emphasis on ecology and green technologies.
33. A general move toward a more efficient, consumer-based economic structure.
34. An expansion of the tourism and hospitality industries.
35. Increasing number and role of small and medium-size companies.
36. The existence of a positive trade balance, initially a result of inability to afford imports. As the economy matures, there is a growing need for more sophisticated goods and services that cannot be produced domestically. In general, the poorer the EMC, the more positive the trade balance.
37. Development and expansion of the middle class.
38. A proportion of roughly 15 to 20 percent of the population lives below the poverty line.
39. An increase in income disparities and inequality during the initial development of a market economy.

40. An increase in emigration of blue-collar workers as well as scholars and scientists (the brain drain) when national borders are first opened. Many return later, when the economy and level of freedom improve.
41. Improvements in the industrial infrastructure, telecommunications, transportation, and energy-distribution networks with significant governmental investment.
42. An exponential increase in the development of the telecom and IT industries as the demand for access to information increases dramatically.
43. A higher level of general education than in developing and underdeveloped countries and a lower level of illiteracy.
44. A major deficit of financial professionals, but a tremendous increase in the interest of students in economic and financial studies, as well as a dramatic improvement in these areas of education.
45. An increase in the acceptance of English as the language of business in parallel with local languages.

These 45 major characteristics of an EMC can be used as a checklist to evaluate if a particular country belongs to the GEM or not. However, as previously stated, a country does not need to exhibit all of these characteristics at a given time to be considered an EMC.

A critical mass of these major characteristics creates a comfortable and often attractive environment for global business, foreign investment, and international trade. Based on this understanding, it is possible to define two business, economic, and political phenomena: an *emerging market country* and the *global emerging market.*

Classification of Emerging Market Countries

It is important to understand that there are 83 different emerging market countries in the world economy. However, there is only one global emerging market, which is a subset of the global marketplace. The GEM is in constant cooperation with other subsets of the global marketplace, i.e., developed, developing, and underdeveloped countries. In the majority of cases, EMCs differ greatly from one another in terms of their maturity, economic and industrial structure, and the development of a middle-class and democratic institutions, etc. They can be classified by several different methods. The following classification categorizes EMCs based on their level of maturity during the transition from developing to developed countries. It does not mean that every EMC has to go through these stages of transition. Each EMC has its own "starting point." The starting point of a country considered an oligarchic emerging market may have been an emerging market dictatorship, while another country may have started as a developing country—the category prior to the first stage of the emerging market group of countries. In the end all EMCs are headed toward the same goal: becoming a developed country.

The GEM consists of a variety countries, some of which never before existed in history as independent states (Kazakhstan, Kosovo, etc.) or briefly existed for a very short period (Ukraine), as well as countries that have had statehood for thousands of years, such as China, Egypt, India, and Russia. Regardless of the various histories of these EMCs, all of them have only recently developed conditions conducive to international business activity, and thus have only recently become part of the GEM.

A typical mistake is to combine the terms "EMC" and "GEM" to create the pseudo-term "global emerging markets." An example of this pseudo-term can be found in the name of companies like *Global Emerging Markets* and in academic databases like the *Global*

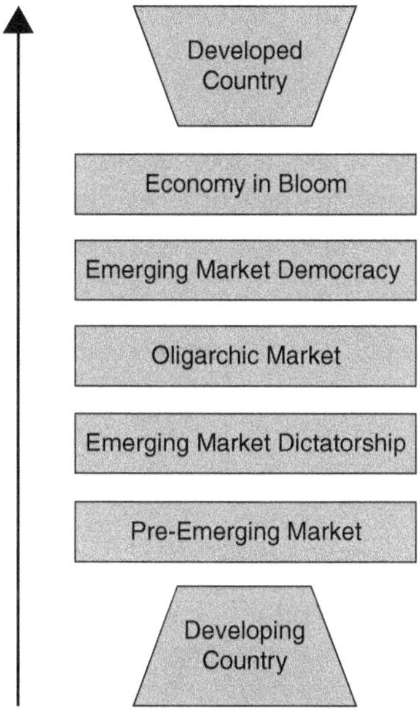

Figure 6.1 EMC Classification by Economic and Social Maturity
© Dr.Vladimir Kvint, 2008

Emerging Market Database, which on its homepage uses the correct term, "GEM," and the wrong term, "GEMs," interchangeably. It is very important for future analysis to understand that there is only one GEM. It is global and cannot be plural.

With the increasing economic and political power of EMCs and their regional blocs and improving levels of political stability and democracy, the role of the GEM is growing in the global marketplace. While in a given EMC, democracy may not be growing, it definitely is in the GEM in general. The overwhelming majority of EMCs are democratizing and liberalizing their societies. Most EMCs are also diversifying their national economies, although this trend is occurring at a slower pace. While not every EMC is undergoing this process, the majority of EMCs are transitioning from mono-industry economies dominated by a single industry or from an inefficient industrial structure to a more efficient, diversified economy. This process requires tremendous investment and political will. Some EMCs, such as Argentina, Brazil, the Philippines, and Egypt, had a few major free-market institutions—commercial and investment banks and accounting and law firms—even prior to the internationalization of their economies. However, in general, EMCs are in the early stages of creating these institutions. Not all EMCs are constantly experiencing a high speed of economic development, but the GEM as a whole is. EMCs can have very different GDP per capita and, as a result, very different standards of living. In some cases the standard of living of an EMC may be closer to standards of developed countries, while in other cases the standard of living may be comparable to that of a developing country. However, the GEM average GDP per head and standard of living are unique to the GEM, i.e., below those of developed countries and above those of developing countries. It is important to realize that the GEM as a whole has specific characteristics that may differ from individual EMC members of the GEM.

The GEM, as previously stated, is a new phenomenon. Professionals, experts, and even special publications dedicated to this subject often have conflicting opinions as to which countries qualify as part of the GEM. Table 6.1 shows the opinion of major periodicals dedicated to EMCs. (The opinion of *The Economist* appears in this table because until January 2007 it dedicated its last page to emerging market indicators). Out of 45 countries listed in Table 6.1, only 17 countries received the consensus opinion of all 5 periodicals regarding their status as an EMC. This is why an analyst, strategist, or executive should study the opinion of all available rating agencies, professionals, and leading publications and draw their own conclusion regarding a country's level of maturity. Although a country may have all the characteristics of an emerging market, it does not mean that this market has actually "emerged" for all foreign companies. Not all companies are prepared to work in the conditions of a particular EMC.

The Genesis of the Global Emerging Market

Growing Input of the Global Emerging Market in the World Economy

The GEM is developing at a much faster rate than the world economy as a whole and faster than developed countries. More than that, the slowest developing EMCs of Eastern Europe and the former Soviet Union are on average still growing at a faster rate than the world economy, as indicated by Table 6.2. Since 2003 the output of emerging economies "has grown by 35 percent; the developed world's by only 10 percent. More than ever before, emerging economies are being relied upon to help lift the world economy."[19] Actually, for most of economic history, emerging economies have developed at a faster pace than developed economies. The explanation for this is simple: growing from a very low level of development is much easier than growing from a higher level of economic development. Each percentage point during the initial stages of development consists of much less economic input and output. But, of course, economic crises and downturns happen more frequently in non-developed economies than in developed economies. In 2007, "for the fourth year running, all of the 32 emerging economies tracked by

Table 6.1 EMC Classifications According to Professional Publications

Europe	*The Emerging Markets Monitor*		*JP Morgan Emerging Markets Economic Outlook*	*Standard & Poor's Emerging Markets*	*Emerging Markets Investor*		*The Economist*		*Total*
Date	*Oct-94*	*Oct-01*	*Oct-94*	*Oct-94*	*Oct-94*	*Oct-01*	*Oct-94*	*Oct-01*	
Bulgaria	x	x	x						3
Czech Republic	x	x	x	x	x	x	x	x	8
Greece			x	x	x	x	x		5
Hungary	x	x	x	x	x	x	x	x	8
Poland	x	x	x		x	x	x	x	7
Portugal	x	x	x	x			x		5
Russia	x	x	x		x	x	x	x	7
Turkey	x	x	x	x	x	x	x	x	8
Romania	x	x				x			3
Slovakia	x	x		x					3

(Continued)

Table 6.1 EMC Classifications According to Professional Publications (Continued)

Latin America	*The Emerging Markets Monitor*		*JP Morgan Emerging Markets Economic Outlook*		*Standard & Poor's Emerging Markets*		*Emerging Markets Investor*		*The Economist*		*Changes*
	Oct-94	*Sep-06*	*Oct-94*	*Sep-06*	*Oct-94*	*Sep-06*	*Oct-94*	*Sep-06*	*Oct-94*	*Sep-06*	
Argentina	x	x	x	x	x	x	x	x	x	x	0
Brazil	x	x	x	x			x	x	x	x	0
Cuba								x			1
Chile	x	x	x	x	x	x	x	x	x	x	0
Colombia	x	x	x	x	x	x	x	x		x	1
Ecuador			x	x			x	x			0
Mexico	x	x	x	x	x	x	x	x	x	x	0
Peru	x	x	x	x			x	x		x	1
Panama					x	x					0
Uruguay				x	x	x					0
Venezuela	x	x	x	x	x	x	x	x	x	x	0

Asia/Pacific	*The Emerging Markets Monitor*		*JP Morgan Emerging Markets Economic Outlook*	*Standard & Poor's Emerging Markets*	*Emerging Markets Investor*		*The Economist*		*Total*
	Oct-94	*Oct-01*	*Oct-94*	*Oct-94*	*Oct-94*	*Oct-01*	*Oct-94*	*Oct-01*	
Bangladesh					x	x			2
China	x	x	x	x	x	x	x	x	8
Hong Kong	x	x	x		x	x	x	x	7
India	x	x	x	x	x	x	x	x	8
Indonesia	x	x	x	x	x	x	x	x	8
South Korea	x	x	x	x	x	x	x	x	8
Malaysia	x	x	x	x	x	x	x	x	8
Mongolia						x			1
Pakistan		x			x	x			3
Philippines	x	x	x	x	x	x	x	x	8
Singapore	x	x	x		x	x	x	x	7
Taiwan (R.O.C.)	x	x	x	x	x	x	x	x	8
Thailand	x	x	x	x	x	x	x	x	8
Vietnam	x	x							2

© Dr. Vladimir Kvint, 2008

The Economist show[ed] positive growth. This is a remarkable turnabout: in every previous year since the 1970s at least one suffered a recession, if not a severe financial crisis."[20] As is evident from Table 6.1, *The Economist* evaluates 29 EMCs on a regular basis and not 32, as in the above quote, at least prior to 2007. The *globalEDGE* of Michigan University's International Business Center stated that the focus of its study is to rank "the market potential of twenty-seven countries identified as an 'Emerging Market' by The Economist."[21] Clearly, even rating agencies do not have consistent positions regarding which countries qualify as emerging markets, which is important to take into consideration.

Table 6.2 Global and Central and Eastern Europe (CEE)/Commonwealth of Independent States (CIS) Growth Outlook, 2005–2012

	2005	*2006*	*2007f*	*2008f*	*2009*	*2010*	*2011*	*2012*
World	3.4	3.96	3.2	3.4	-0.7	5.1	4.0	4.0
Euro Area	1.5	2.76	2.3	2.2	-4.3	1.8	1.6	1.1
Emerging Europe	5.9	6.6	5.7	5.4	2.8	7.3	6.4	6.1
CEE5	**4.2**	**5.6**	**4.9**	**4.5**	**-3.6**	**4.5**	**4.3**	**2.7**
CIS6	6.5	7.3	6.8	6.2	-6.4	4.6	4.6	4.4

Adapted from data from the World Bank. Retrieved from http://data.worldbank.org/indicator/NY.GDP.MKTP.KD.ZG

Note: Emerging Europe: CEE5, 3 Baltic states (Estonia, Latvia, Lithuania), CIS6, Turkey
CEE5: Czech Republic, Hungary, Poland, Slovakia, Slovenia
CIS6: Armenia, Azerbaijan, Kazakhstan, Moldova, Russia, Ukraine

This observation is correct, not only for the faster growing economies of Southeast Asia and Russia, but also for emerging Europe—old economies, which are reemerging after communist dictatorships. This is one more indication that despite different geographical locations, all EMCs share many similar characteristics and development dynamics.

But even in terms of GDP value, the global emerging market has already reached, and will soon overcome, the cumulative GDP of developed countries. According to *The Economist*, "The best hope that global growth can stay strong lies … with emerging economies … [In 2007] … they will contribute half of the globe's GDP growth, measured at market exchange rates, over three times as much as America."[22]

As of May 2014, the input of the 83 countries of the GEM in the world economy is approaching 56.3 percent of total global output, and it will soon overcome the total GDP of developed countries. However, estimates of this figure vary substantially, due to the lack of a universally recognized structure of categorization of national economies.

According to *The Economist*:

> Emerging economies account for 30 percent of world GDP at market exchange rates (and over half using purchasing-power parity to take account of price differences). At market exchange rates they already account for half of global GDP growth. And by a wide range of measures, their weight is looming larger. Their exports are 45 percent of the world total; they consume over half of the world's energy and have accounted for four-fifths of the growth in oil demand in the past five years (explaining why oil prices are so high); and they are sitting on 75 percent of global foreign-exchange reserves.[23]

To break down the source of EMCs' 56.3 percent role in the world economy, Table 6.3 offers a list of countries that are considered by the author to be EMCs and their cumulative GDP as a percentage of global GDP in purchasing power parity (PPP).

The Strategic Business Perspective

Strategically, the leadership of EMCs should strive to develop conditions that create opportunities for their citizens to improve their quality of life on the basis of economic success. This is usually achieved by promoting freedom and market-oriented reforms,

Table 6.3 EMCs by GDP in PPP (Billions of $), 2013

Rank	*Country and Rank by GDP PPP*	*GDP PPP (Billions $), 2013*
1	China	16,158
2	India	6,774
3	Russian Federation	3,461
4	Brazil	3,012
5	Indonesia	2,388
6	Mexico	2,014
7	Korea, Rep.	1,664
8	Saudi Arabia	1,550
9	Spain	1,498
10	Turkey	1,422
11	Taiwan	971
12	Thailand	964
13	Argentina	928
14	Egypt, Arab Rep.	910
15	Poland	897
16	Pakistan	856
17	Malaysia	692
18	South Africa	662
19	Philippines	643
20	Colombia	598
21	United Arab Emirates	534
22	Algeria	522
23	Iraq	508
24	Vietnam	475
25	Singapore	425
26	Ukraine	400
27	Kazakhstan	395
28	Chile	386
29	Hong Kong SAR, China	382
30	Romania	372
31	Peru	358
32	Czech Republic	288
33	Qatar	286
34	Greece	283
35	Portugal	271
36	Israel	264
37	Morocco	242
38	Hungary	226
39	Sri Lanka	199
40	Ireland	199
41	Ecuador	165
42	Azerbaijan	161
43	Slovak Republic	141
44	Tunisia	121
45	Bulgaria	116
46	Guatemala	113
47	Ghana	103
48	Croatia	89
49	Serbia	89
50	Jordan	76
51	Lithuania	75
52	Panama	75
53	Turkmenistan	73
54	Costa Rica	68
55	Uruguay	67

(Continued)

Table 6.3 EMCs by GDP in PPP (Billions of $), 2013 (Continued)

Rank	*Country and Rank by GDP PPP*	*GDP PPP (Billions $), 2013*
56	Bolivia	65
57	Bahrain	58
58	Slovenia	58
59	El Salvador	49
60	Latvia	46
61	Trinidad and Tobago	41
62	Estonia	33
63	Gabon	32
64	Georgia	32
65	Madagascar	32
66	Botswana	32
67	Albania	29
68	Burkina Faso	28
69	Mongolia	27
70	Cyprus	26
71	Macedonia, FYR	25
72	Jamaica	24
73	Armenia	23
74	Mauritius	22
75	Moldova	17
76	Malta	13
77	Montenegro	9
78	Bahamas, The	9
79	Guyana	5
80	Belize	3
81	St. Lucia	2
82	St. Kitts and Nevis	1
83	Barbados	0
	Total	57,350
	% of World	56.3

Adapted from data from the World Bank. Retrieved from http://data.worldbank.org/indicator/NY.GDP.MKTP.PP.CD

which eventually leads to a true freedom of choice for individuals and companies. This is the source of a high standard of living. In existential terms, the production of a variety of quality of goods and services of any company is determined by the freedom of choice of individual consumers and their preferences. But, on the other hand, freedom of choice cannot exist without the production of a variety of different quality of goods and services, in order for consumers to actually have choices. Different standards of living and/or different preferences of consumers of the same purchasing power group generate differences in demands. As Kenneth Arrow (1921–), the 1972 Nobel Laureate in Economics, stated in his famous book, *Social Choice, and Individual Values*, "The relation of 'known preference or indifference' is clearly transitive, but it is not connected since, for example, it does not tell us how the individual compares two social alternatives, one of which yields him more of one commodity than the second, while the second yields him more of a second commodity than the first."[24]

This assumption of Arrow, which may be difficult to comprehend at first, works only when an individual or company has the opportunity to make choices. Under command economies, choices are very limited—if they exist at all—because of shortages of goods and services, especially higher quality ones. Freedom of choice is created in EMCs by the development of a free-market economy, which responds to individual consumer demands and interests. Of course, the goal of companies entering the GEM is to generate profits. But in doing so, a wider variety of goods and services is produced, which benefits society by increasing freedom of choice for individuals. Companies seek profit by responding to the constantly differentiating demands of consumers in a free market. When a strategist positions a company in the market, an evaluation should be made of all current and potential competitors, in order to identify consumer demands that are not totally, if at all, addressed. By addressing consumer demands that current producers are not satisfying, companies increase freedom of choice, and a wider variety of goods and services is produced. This is how free-market economies address private and public interests. But first and foremost in the GEM, strategy should define and publicly announce, via a mission statement and the non-proprietary part of the vision, a company's social orientation, part of its priorities (that of social concern) and responsibilities to society and to regional and local communities, and the services that the company will provide. It will help the entity to be strategically more efficient and experience support of the population.

Environmental Protection in Entry Strategy to the Global Emerging Market

When companies from developed countries made their first ventures in the GEM, they were barely cognizant of the potential opportunities that lay ahead. Initially, companies expanded into the GEM in search of competitive advantages that would make them more successful in their domestic or traditional markets of operations. When they unexpectedly found huge markets of consumers and producers, new, inexpensive production facilities, and access to a practically unlimited supply of cheap labor, the development and role of the GEM in the GMP grew exponentially. However, in some cases, a lack of strategic vision and especially principles of strategy can turn short-term profits into long-term liabilities. Some companies took advantage of inexperienced and ineffective governments and local executives in the GEM to maximize short-term profits. In many cases, this resulted in the loss of access to markets, resources, production facilities, etc., once governments matured and the general population had a better understanding of the situation. Many companies entered EMCs when they were actually pre-emerging markets, still under some form of dictatorship. At this time democracy was little more than a pipe dream for the people of these countries. In these conditions a handshake from the dictator was practically all that was required for foreign companies to operate. The social and ecological impact of a foreign company was totally ignored. When these dictatorships collapsed and democracy began to emerge, companies accustomed to dealing with the dictatorship made the mistake of ignoring the birth of a new social force: public opinion. In many cases freedom of speech and assembly seriously hindered the operations of a foreign company of which local populations did not approve, whether formally or informally. Ignoring the social and ecological impact of a company's activities is a reflection of a lack of strategic vision with its principles and priorities.

The experience of Tengizchevroil (TCO) in Kazakhstan is a clear example of the dangers of ignoring ecological issues. Tengizchevroil, a joint venture of Chevron, ExxonMobile, Lukarco, and KazMunayGas, produces oil from one of the world's biggest oil fields, the Tengiz in western Kazakhstan. For several years TCO spent only about one cent per metric ton of oil produced in Kazakhstan to address ecological issues, such as the disposal of sulfur byproducts from crude-oil production. TCO maintained that these byproducts were harmless.[25] Such a shortsighted approach eventually cost them a great deal. When the national government began to focus on the environment, TCO was forced to pay much more than they would have if they had addressed the sulfur-byproduct issue from the beginning of their venture. In February 2007 the minister of ecology of the Republic of Kazakhstan threatened to suspend the operational license of the joint venture. TCO subsequently agreed to pay $300 million a year to the national government for environmental protection.[26]

Even more serious charges were brought against Shell Petroleum Development Corp. (SPDC), a joint venture of Royal Dutch Shell in Nigeria, by the national government. SPDC was forced to "pay $1.5bn (£830m) compensation to communities affected by oil pollution in the country ... SPDC was to compensate the Ijaw tribe in the southern Bayelsa state. SPDC has long been accused by activists of not cleaning up oil spills and complicity in human rights abuses."[27]

Increasing competition among EMCs and developing countries to produce and export more energy resources has led many of them to implement less restrictive environmental policies which attract foreign direct investment (FDI) from major international energy-producing companies. These shifts of FDI suddenly decrease or increase the role of a particular EMC in the global energy balance. For example, the Gulf of Mexico has been experiencing a shortage of offshore drilling equipment (jack-up and deep-water rigs) as a result of multinational corporations relocating their equipment in search of more profitable projects in areas with less restrictive environmental regulations. The richest and most accessible reserves of the Gulf of Mexico have already been drilled. Many foreign companies do not want to bother with the more expensive remaining deep-water and ultra-deep-water reserves, especially because of the relatively higher environmental standards. This further increases the expenses and prices to lease oil rigs. It will be more difficult for the Gulf region, which produces one quarter of US oil, to curtail its annual decline in output.[28]

In order to decrease energy shortages, many countries of the EU have enacted very restrictive domestic energy policies and aggressive foreign energy policies in order to gain access to more energy resources. One of the very few exceptions to this rule is Bulgaria, which has the most liberal energy policy in the EU, and one that is less environmentally restrictive. It exports some electrical energy to Turkey, among other countries, while also acting as a hub in the North Balkan region. Several pipelines already connect Bulgaria (and more are planned) with the countries of the Black, Caspian, and Adriatic Seas via its Black Sea coast with an attempt to encourage Russia.

The experience of Global Fishing, a producer of seafood products headquartered in the US that operates in the GEM, offers an example from a different industry. Global Fishing was accused of illegally poaching. According to one report, "The small leg size of some Russian product sold in the United States indicated that young, undersize crab have sometimes been part of the haul."[29] One former Alaskan crabber added, "If we had landed crab like that in Dutch Harbor [Alaska], we would have ended up in jail."[30] Any company that ignores ecological regulations takes the systematic risk of putting short-term profits (which are generally affiliated with unacceptable levels of systematic risk) over long-term strategy. This has very serious implications. It is strategically unwise for companies from developed countries operating in the GEM to take advantage of the lower standards and regulations or a lack of their enforcement. From a long-term strategic vision, it is not worth it. The same recommendations can be addressed to EMCs who ignore potential ecologically related expenses, domestically and abroad.

Emerging Market Countries' Regional Integration into the Global Marketplace

International business activity is the locomotive that drives the development of the GEM, integrating the economies of EMCs with those of developed countries at an incredible pace. But among EMCs themselves within the GEM, there is not yet a great deal of political and economic integration. Even the most advanced regions within individual EMCs often have more economic ties with developed countries than with nearby domestic regions. This is because developed countries are the main source of investment, modern managerial skills, and technologies, and, in some cases, even funding for operational activity, for companies in EMCs. This is a very important dynamic both within the GEM and between it and developed countries.

In general, the larger the territory of an EMC, the wider the gaps in economic development among its domestic regions. This is the case in Brazil, Russia, China, Argentina, South Africa, and Ukraine. In these large EMCs, the location and deficit of the five basic economic factors is the main cause of the disproportionate regional economic development (see Chapter 3). Natural resources, labor, and production facilities are often concentrated in certain regions, separated from one another by great distances and usually a lack of infrastructure. A domestic deficit of the two remaining basic economic factors, technology and capital, further isolates regions from one another.

By the author's estimation, 65 percent of the basic economic factors of Russia, China, and Brazil are concentrated in particular regions, isolated from each other by the previously mentioned factors. In China the natural resources are concentrated in the northwest, the production facilities in the southeast, and the cheap labor resources in the central region. More than 25 percent of China's forestry is located in the northeast, while most industrial facilities are roughly 2,000 miles south, or in Inner Mongolia. In Russia about 40 percent of all natural resources are located above the Arctic Circle, where only about 5 percent of the population resides. Most production facilities in Brazil are located in the southern part of the country, with a few exceptions on the Atlantic coast, while all natural resources, including those of the rainforests, are in central Brazil, thus separated from these facilities by thousands of kilometers. Furthermore, in all of these countries, the local population in natural resource–rich regions, in many cases, is unprepared culturally and professionally to utilize the industrial resources needed to exploit natural resources. Most productive facilities in these big EMCs are separated from natural resources by roughly 2000 to 3000 kilometers of uninhabited territory and a lack of transportational communications.

As a result of the location of substantially accessible resources within EMCs, companies from developed economies focus their investment and activity in certain regions of a particular EMC. Not surprisingly, regions with abundant natural resources tend to experience the fastest industrial growth and increasing level of quality of life. These regions often develop almost independently from other parts of the country, due to the lack of domestic capital and modern technology needed to integrate the productive forces of different domestic regions with the rest of the country. As a result, foreign economic interests have weakened inter-regional domestic economic connections in large EMCs.

A lack of domestic-regional integration is also evident in EMCs with smaller territories, such as those of Eastern and Southern Europe. Since 2004, 13 Eastern, Central, and South European EMCs have joined the EU. These countries are being integrated with the developed Western European member-states of the European Union (EU) at a much faster rate than between each other. Even Ukraine, which is not a member of the EU,

Table 6.4 EMCs by Size of Territory

Rank	*Country*	*Area (Sq. Km)*
1	Russia	17,075,200
2	China	9,596,960
3	Brazil	8,511,965
4	India	3,287,590
5	Argentina	2,766,890
6	Kazakhstan	2,717,300
7	Algeria	2,381,740
8	Saudi Arabia	2,149,690
9	Mexico	1,972,550
10	Indonesia	1,919,440
11	Mongolia	1,565,000
12	Peru	1,285,220
13	South Africa	1,219,912
14	Colombia	1,138,910
15	Bolivia	1,098,580
16	Egypt	1,001,450
17	Pakistan	803,940
18	Turkey	780,580
19	Chile	756,950
20	Ukraine	603,700
21	Botswana	600,370
22	Madagascar	587,040
23	Thailand	514,000
24	Spain	504,782
25	Turkmenistan	488,100
26	Morocco	446,550
27	Iraq	437,072
28	Malaysia	329,750
29	Vietnam	329,560
30	Poland	312,685
31	Philippines	300,000
32	Ecuador	283,560
33	Burkina Faso	274,200
34	Gabon	267,667
35	Ghana	239,460
36	Romania	237,500
37	Guyana	214,970
38	Uruguay	176,220
39	Tunisia	163,610
40	Greece	131,940
41	Bulgaria	110,910
42	Guatemala	108,890
43	Korea, South	98,480
44	Hungary	93,030
45	Portugal	92,391
46	Jordan	92,300
47	Serbia	88,361
48	Azerbaijan	86,600
49	United Arab Emirates	82,000
50	Czech Republic	78,866
51	Panama	78,200
52	Ireland	70,280
53	Georgia	69,700
54	Sri Lanka	65,610
55	Lithuania	65,200

(Continued)

Table 6.4 EMCs by Size of Territory (Continued)

Rank	*Country*	*Area (Sq. Km)*
56	Latvia	64,589
57	Croatia	56,542
58	Costa Rica	51,100
59	Slovak Republic	48,845
60	Estonia	45,226
61	Taiwan	35,980
62	Moldova	33,843
63	Armenia	29,800
64	Albania	28,748
65	Macedonia	25,333
66	Belize	22,966
67	El Salvador	21,040
68	Israel	20,770
69	Slovenia	20,273
70	Montenegro	14,026
71	Bahamas, The	13,940
72	Qatar	11,437
73	Jamaica	10,991
74	Cyprus	9,250
75	Trinidad and Tobago	5,128
76	Mauritius	2,030
77	China, Hong Kong SAR	1,092
78	Singapore	693
79	Bahrain	665
80	Saint Lucia	616
81	Barbados	431
82	Malta	316
83	Saint Kitts and Nevis	261
	Totals	71,329,352
	% of World	47.89

CIA. (n.d.). "World Factbook". Retrieved from www.cia.gov/library/publications/the-world-factbook/

exports more to the EU than to Russia. Russia is only the seventh biggest investor in Ukraine, far behind Germany, Cyprus, Austria, Great Britain, the Netherlands, and the United States.[31] The cumulative investment of Russia in Ukraine is only 4.6 percent of all cumulative foreign investment in Ukraine. The role of Ukrainian exports to Russia has decreased from 43 percent in 1995 to 22.5 percent of total exports in 2007.[32] The EU accounts for one-third[33] of Ukrainian external trade.[34] During May and June of 2014, as a result of the Russian-Ukrainian conflict, Ukrainian exports to the EU grew over 25 percent,[35] but exports to Russia fell over 50 percent, with a continued decline in dynamics after this period. In my opinion, it is premature to draw any serious strategic conclusions about the consequences of the conflict on Ukrainian exports until at least 2017, when serious directional changes will take place.

According to *The Economist,* "rich economies' trade with developing countries is growing twice as fast as their trade with one another."[36] This acceleration is occurring because the removal of barriers and tariffs between different (and even neighboring) EMCs happens at a much slower pace than the removal of barriers and tariffs between EMCs and developed countries. EMCs are competing with each other for foreign direct investment from developed countries and for cooperation with them. There is a much stronger incentive to liberalize economic relations with the developed world than with other less-developed competitors, i.e., EMCs. Lower inter-industrial connections among

EMCs are one of the key factors that decrease domestic inter-regional integration and increase international integration of emerging market countries' regions with developed nations and within the global marketplace.

In order to optimize economic development, EMCs must achieve a balance between foreign-led growth and growth initiated by internal factors. The most prosperous EMCs, such as Ireland, the Czech Republic, South Korea, and Argentina have achieved this balance. But as of 2015, many EMCs still export more raw materials than processed products. Producers of raw materials in EMCs tend to be more tightly integrated with processing companies in developed countries than they are with domestic processing companies. This prevents companies from EMCs and the EMC itself from receiving higher profits, as the profits from sales of final products are always higher than those from raw materials. This dynamic is an obstacle for more balanced economic development and faster economic and social improvements in EMCs.

Integration of the Labor Resources of the GEM into the Global Marketplace

Labor resources of EMCs have several similar characteristics such as long working hours, higher unemployment, much lower wages, and faster growing productivity of labor relative to developed countries. On the other hand, each EMC has many unique characteristics regarding its labor resources, rooted in its distinctive economic history. For example, levels of education vary substantially, with a high level of professional and general education in Central and Eastern Europe and Russia, compared to the Indian subcontinent and Latin America. The productivity of labor resources and the levels of unemployment and wages are also quite different among some EMCs due to variations in their economic maturity. The earlier a country begins the transition from a totalitarian regime and command economy, the closer its productivity of labor, education, and wages will be to developed countries and to economies in bloom.

During the initial stages of transition to the free market, the rate of growth of productivity of labor is not as high as one would assume. Low levels of education and technological development slow the growth rate productivity. For example, during the 1980s and 1990s, the growth rate of labor productivity in China was only about 4.5 percent. India suffered from a slow growth rate of labor productivity during the initial stages of its relatively late transition from a command economy to a free market economy. Despite the fact that it had been the largest democracy in the world for several decades, it only began to embrace the free market at the end of the twentieth century. After the initial transition period EMCs generally surge in labor productivity growth. In the first decade of the twenty-first century, the average growth rate of productivity of labor in the GEM has been roughly four times faster than that of the developed world. During this period, labor productivity has increased at an average annual rate of 8 percent in Central and Eastern Europe, China, and Russia. This is mostly a result of increasing access to modern technology and equipment, growing familiarity with free market conditions, and improvements in motivation systems. During the same period, most developed countries experienced a slowdown in the growth of labor productivity to less than 2 percent. Some EMCs, despite their early entrance to the GEM, have not experienced rapid growth in productivity of labor. For example, Mexico has been very slow to adopt modern technologies and improve general educational levels. The growth rate of its productivity of labor has been about 1 percent, which is almost two times lower than that of the US, though still higher than that of Western Europe.

The rapid growth in labor productivity of the GEM is actually one of the causes of its higher unemployment relative to the developed world. From another strategic perspective, high unemployment is a cause of the rapid growth rate of labor productivity in the GEM. This can be seen in the more rapid pay increase in EMCs than in the developed world. According to the Mercer Global Compensation Planning Report, prepared by Mercer LLC, India, Vietnam, Bulgaria, Turkey, China, South Korea, Romania, and Ireland will have a higher rate of growth of compensation than the US and other developed countries.[37] The fast growth of labor productivity in EMCs can also be explained due to the hiring of top-level high-quality executives from developed countries, as well as keeping their own best domestically grown CEOs and compensating them with a much higher difference in remuneration compared to professionals in EMCs. This wide difference in compensation does not exist in developed countries. At a first glance, it may seem like unfair compensation, but this wide disparity in many cases pays off through the rapidly increasing productivity of labor. Without this attractive pay scale, many executives from developed countries who choose to work in the GEM would not take on this risky endeavor. According to Mercer's 2014 Compensation Planning Report, "Eastern European countries such as Russia show a clear differentiation in salary increases between low and top performers. Further differentiations include vertical differences in the annual base salary, meaning that a CEO in Poland is paid 22 times more than a professional, compared with Germany, where the ratio is 1-to-6."[38]

A negative side effect of the increasing freedom that inevitably comes as countries embrace democracy and the free market is the widespread emigration of its citizens, who seek more stable economic conditions. As EMCs stabilize and economic conditions improve, émigrés usually return. In cases of the most successful economic reforms, in addition to the return of émigrés, migrants from other EMC also come, looking for stability and prosperity. Such was the case of Ireland, the so-called Celtic Tiger, which experienced a wave of émigrés returning to their homeland as well as of migrants from Eastern Europe at the beginning of the twenty-first century.

The liberalization of the global labor market is characterized by a similarly outward-oriented phenomenon. A tighter relationship and more open cooperation with developed

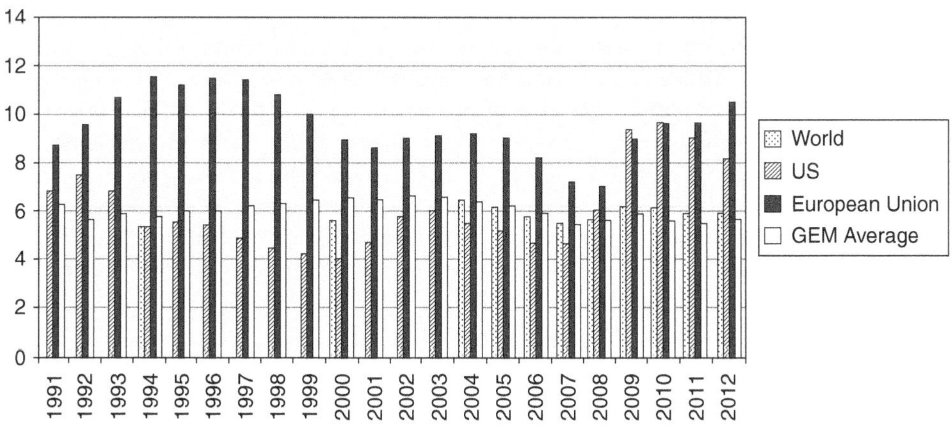

Figure 6.2 Unemployment in the US, EU, GEM, and the GMP

© Dr. Vladimir Kvint, 2014. Adapted from data from the Eurostat Database. Retrieved from http://ec.europa.eu/eurostat/tgm/table.do?tab=table&init=1&language=en&pcode=tsdec450&plugin=1

countries motivates and gives more opportunities for unemployed or underemployed people in EMCs to permanently or temporarily emigrate to developed countries in search of employment. Due to their intensive and extensive work ethic, they are often willing to do any work, even if they are overqualified for the job. They compete successfully with local work power in the countries to which they emigrate. Aging work forces in developed countries also make it difficult for domestic workers to compete with younger émigrés from the GEM. When and if these émigrés find employment, a significant portion of their wages is sent back to their relatives in their country of origin, a practice called *remittances*. According to the International Fund for Agricultural Development, remittances which were sent by 150 million migrants back to their domestic emerging market and developing countries usually were done through small shipments of $100 to $300, which can be cumulatively estimated as of 2006 as $300 billion.[39]

> Remittances by international migrants from developing countries are on course for strong growth this year, while at the same time forced migration due to violence and conflict has reached unprecedented levels, says the World Bank's latest issue of Migration and Development Brief, released today.
>
> Officially recorded remittances to developing countries are expected to reach $435 billion this year, an increase of 5 percent over 2013. The growth rate this year is substantially faster than the 3.4 percent growth recorded in 2013, driven largely by remittances to Asia and Latin America.
>
> Remittances to developing countries will continue climbing in the medium term, reaching an estimated $454 billion in 2015.[40]

Many émigrés from the GEM in developed countries realize themselves not only as employees but also as entrepreneurs. With easier access to financial resources via commercial and investment banks in developed countries, they are able to implement their business ideas, know-how, and even patents. A lack of capital, overpowering bureaucracy, and corruption make such achievements practically impossible in their native countries. Remittances sent home by these émigrés have a very positive impact on the standard of living of the poorest and most vulnerable segments of society in the GEM. In addition, they increase the consumption power of EMCs and the role of consumption in the GDP of emerging market countries. In some countries the role of remittances is comparable to the GDP itself. In Moldova, remittances account for one-third of the GDP. Since 2007, Moldova has kept record high indicators of the role of remittances in the national economy among all EMCs. However, in developing countries the share of remittances of GDP can be even higher. In Guinea-Bissau remittances account for 48.7 percent of GDP. However, remittances also have a negative impact. They can contribute to inequality of income distribution, which is discussed further in the following section. Plate 5.2 and Figures 6.3, 6.4, and 6.5 present the geographical distribution of remittances and their role in the economies of different EMCs.

According to a special report from *The Economist*,

> Tim Jones of Innovaro, a European innovation consultancy, points out that Africa is about to take the lead in using mobile phones for payments and remittances, thanks to the introduction of schemes like the M-PESA money-transfer service introduced by Vodafone and Citigroup in Kenya. These allow people to send money using text messages.[41]

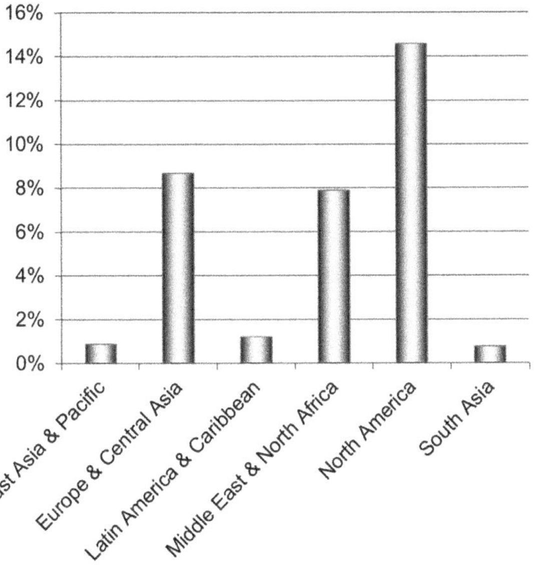

Figure 6.3 Size of Diaspora as a Percentage of Origin Country Population

© Dr. Vladimir Kvint, 2014. The World Bank (2010–2014). International Migrant Stock, Total. Retrieved from http://data.worldbank.org/indicator/SM.POP.TOTL/

Income Inequality, Uncertainty, and Risk

The outflow of labor resources from the GEM to developed countries can accelerate income inequality in EMCs. The more citizens of a particular EMC emigrate to work in developed countries, the more remittances are sent to their country of origin. Their compensation or profit in developed countries is substantially higher than in their native countries—up to ten times more than the average compensation. This is one factor that can contribute to increases of income-distribution inequality in EMCs.

One of the strongest factors causing increasing income-distribution inequality in EMCs is corruption and nepotism. Corruption and income inequality are directly related.

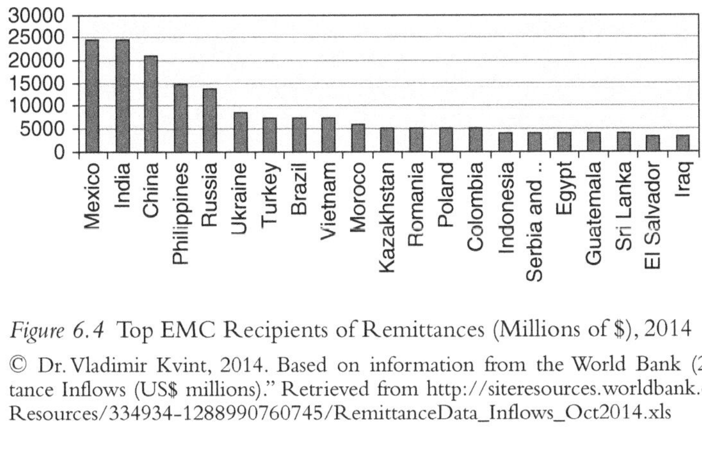

Figure 6.4 Top EMC Recipients of Remittances (Millions of $), 2014

© Dr. Vladimir Kvint, 2014. Based on information from the World Bank (2014). "Migrant Remittance Inflows (US$ millions)." Retrieved from http://siteresources.worldbank.org/INTPROSPECTS/Resources/334934-1288990760745/RemittanceData_Inflows_Oct2014.xls

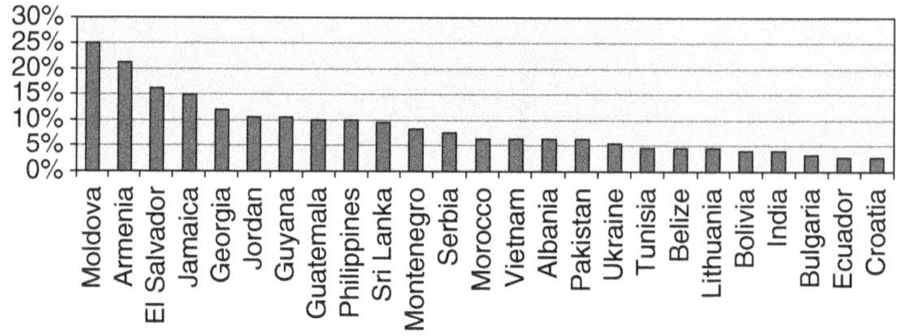

Figure 6.5 Top EMC Recipients of Remittances (Percentage of GDP), 2013

© Dr. Vladimir Kvint, 2014. Based on information from the World Bank (2014). "Migrant Remittance Inflows (US$ millions)." Retrieved from http://siteresources.worldbank.org/INTPROSPECTS/Resources/334934-1288990760745/RemittanceData_Inflows_Oct2014.xls

As corruption increases so does income inequality, to a certain point. While there are many detailed studies of income inequality,[42] it is very difficult to apply them to EMCs because of the strong negative influence of informal and unreported underground economies.[43] These statistics are obviously not reflected in official statistics. However, ultimately, as economic freedom increases, so does average income per capita, but not equally. Nonetheless, this gradually leads to a more equitable distribution of income. This process progresses at a substantially slower pace in EMCs than in developed countries (discussed further below).

The need for FDI from developed countries is helping to reduce corruption and, as a result, income inequality. Investors from developed countries seek stability and predictability in potential recipients of investment, even more so than democracy. Widespread corruption is a significant deterrent to FDI. As corruption is reduced by national governments seeking FDI, so is income inequality.

Nevertheless, the high level of corruption and unreported economic activity not reflected in official financial statistics and balance sheets of companies in the GEM causes a great deal of uncertainty and limited and/or inaccurate information for investors, companies, and entrepreneurs. Not having an accurate understanding of existing companies and the business environment or information about economic and financial processes and legal entities has a very negative impact on the initial risk of investment and operational risk in a country. This is especially the case for companies that are not officially registered. They do not pay taxes or insurance, and they put their employees and customers at an unmeasured risk. These unregistered companies greatly complicate the business environment for investors. If uncertainty is related to a lack of understanding and limited information of the economic and business reality, risk is related to lost or negative results of economic and business activity in conditions of uncertainty. In *Risk, Uncertainty, and Profit*, Frank Knight wrote, "If we are to understand the workings of the economic system we must examine the meaning and significance of uncertainty; and to this end some inquiry into the nature and function of knowledge itself is necessary."[44] Economic statistics, business reporting, and auditing and due diligence systems in EMCs are far behind those of developed countries. This is one of the identifying characteristics of countries that are not yet developed. An analysis of official governmental and business statistics from EMCs should never be made without understanding how the data was gathered. Typically, business and economic statistics in the GEM diverge from reality from the very beginning—from workshops, through the processes of feasibility studies, architectural design, and construction activity, to the headquarters of the biggest multinational corporations. Incorrect or manipulated information almost always hides corruption, bribery, kickbacks, and the non-reported gray or black sectors of the economy. This is one of the major causes of inefficiency for companies operating in the GEM. All of the above conditions in the GEM create not only the economic strategic phenomenon as a whole but *economies of uncertainty* as well. Strategic studies related to this economic reality formed entirely new and very important research directions. Any strategist, executive, or investor operating in or with the GEM should be familiar with Dr. Harry Markowitz's studies on the economics of uncertainty, for which he received the Nobel Prize in Economics in 1990. Uncertainty is a main focus of strategy. Without uncertainty, the future would be clear to everyone, and there would scarcely be a need for strategy and strategists. But because uncertainty is so prevalent in business, economics, and politics, it is vitally important (and extremely difficult) to forecast and predict the future. As President Franklin Delano Roosevelt said, "The only limit to our realization of tomorrow will be our doubts of today."[45]

The Strategic Role of the Global Emerging Market in the World

The relatively different economic, political, and geographic conditions of EMCs have important implications for the processes of strategizing their development and the speed and progress of reaching their objectives. However, what allows all EMCs to be understood as a part of the GEM is the uniform direction of their progress toward economic freedom, global integration, and, in the best cases, democracy. As EMCs develop, they are beginning to become more and more integrated with one another. The global trend of regionalization, which leads to the creation of regional blocs and economic unions, furthers this process (this trend is discussed in detail in Chapter 8). As of 2015, emerging market countries are found in North, Central, and South America; Pacific and Central Asia; the Indian subcontinent; Central, Eastern, and Southern Europe; the territory of the former Soviet Union; and Northern, Central, and Southern Africa. It is impossible to overestimate the scale of the global emerging market. As of May 2014, the GEM consists of 83 countries, which account for nearly 67.92 percent of the global population, and about 47.89 percent of the Earth's land surface. The input of the global emerging market in the world's output is 56.3 percent, and about 40 percent of foreign direct investment goes to EMCs. The GEM capitalization has more than tripled since 1995, growing from less than $2 trillion to more than $5 trillion in 2006—12 percent of GMP capitalization,[46] up from 3 percent in 1981 and 5 percent in 1990.[47] In 2008, in terms of market capitalization, among the top three largest companies in the world were the Russian natural gas semi-state monopoly OAO Gazprom, which surpassed another company from the GEM, China Mobile Ltd, as well as a non-GEM company, General Electric.[48] Revolutionary innovations drastically changed the members who have reached this pinnacle by 2015. High-tech firms such as Apple are the global corporate leaders by market capitalization, followed by Exxon Mobile Corp., Microsoft, and Google. Even General Electric fell to ninth place, while China Mobile Ltd. went down to eleventh place. This has happened for several reasons, not only due to the technological achievements mentioned above, but also because of a total lack of coherent strategy on the part of Gazprom. This Russian industrial giant underestimated the role of shale oil and shale gas due to new, efficient technologies of their exploration and enrichment. Gazprom also underestimated economics and the capacity of alternative sources of energy and the organizational efficiency of the use of energy in European countries and the United States. Put under pressure by these strategic mistakes, Gazprom not only lost its position among the top global companies by market cap, but also this corporate indicator decreased in absolute numbers.

Countries of the GEM are a beacon for the remaining underdeveloped (Sudan, Democratic Republic of Congo, and, at some moment in time, North Korea, etc.) and developing countries (Afghanistan, Somalia, etc.) that strive, or one day will strive, to build market-oriented economies.

The GEM contains all the major characteristics of individual EMCs. However, collectively, there is a synergy among EMCs that creates an environment more conducive to global business. Different resources and factors attract developed countries and encourage their companies to develop aggressive strategies with the aim to cooperate with and within emerging markets. The integration of EMCs into a unified GEM creates a distinct, cumulative, joined power of all EMCs that draws companies to the GEM. The integration of EMCs within the GEM is an example of the conversion of a critical mass of quantity to a new, higher quality.

The development of the GEM decreased the importance of American, European, and Japanese businesses and the economic triangle that dominated the second half of the twentieth century. In terms of economic power and foreign trade, the dominant forces of the GMP in the twenty-first century are the US, the EU, and the GEM. In several categories of the production of goods and services, the GEM as a whole and even some individual EMCs have surpassed the US, individual EU member-states, and Japan. The increasing importance of the GEM can also be seen in Table 6.5, which shows the largest countries in the world economy by GDP; out of the top ten countries in terms of GDP in purchasing power parity (PPP), five are emerging market countries. Out of the top 20 countries of the GMP, 10 are emerging market countries. Finally, out of the top 30 countries in terms of GDP in PPP, 18 are emerging market countries.

From the strategic perspective of companies of the developed world, the GEM represents new markets with substantial purchasing power and new sources of labor and natural resources that can be harnessed to achieve high returns on investment. From the strategic perspective of countries of the GEM, companies from the developed world represent sources of new investment and operational capital, managerial skills, technology, and new jobs that can lead to further economic and social development and, subsequently, more tax revenue. This revenue provides the funding for the construction of new nurseries, kindergartens, schools, retirement communities, hospitals, theaters, athletic complexes, and other entertainment facilities, which results in an increase in the local quality of life. This vector of strategic development leads to further integration of emerging market countries into the GEM and of the GEM into the GMP. This in turn improves the global optimum (see Chapter 5) of the world economy by decreasing poverty, mass disease, and migration, and improving the standard of living of all individuals through increases of global output, and international economic cooperation via the utilization of new technological advancements. This is how the standard of living of Earth's 6.5 billion people will eventually improve.

Despite the substantial risks offered by the global emerging market, no company in the global marketplace can ignore the strategic opportunities. There are an endless number of examples of companies that went out of business after a lack of strategy saw them fail to compete with rivals who took advantage of opportunities offered by the global emerging market. The risks and opportunities offered by the GEM have also led to the rise in importance of risk management systems in order to understand, evaluate, measure, and adjust in order to manage risk.

Table 6.5 Largest Countries in Terms of GDP PPP (Billions of $), 2013

Rank	*Country*	*GDP PPP, 2013 (Billions $)*
1	United States	$16,800
2	**China**	**$16,158**
3	**India**	**$6,774**
4	Japan	$4,624
5	Germany	$3,493
6	**Russian Federation**	**$3,461**
7	**Brazil**	**$3,012**
8	France	$2,437
9	**Indonesia**	**$2,388**
10	United Kingdom	$2,320
11	Italy	$2,052
12	**Mexico**	**$2,014**
13	**Korea, Rep.**	**$1,664**
14	**Saudi Arabia**	**$1,550**
15	Canada	$1,520
16	**Spain**	**$1,498**
17	**Turkey**	**$1,422**
18	Iran, Islamic Rep.	$1,207
19	Australia	$1,007
20	Nigeria	$972
21	**Thailand**	**$964**
22	**Egypt, Arab Rep.**	**$910**
23	**Poland**	**$897**
24	**Pakistan**	**$856**
25	Netherlands	$729
26	**Malaysia**	**$692**
27	**South Africa**	**$662**
28	**Philippines**	**$643**
29	**Colombia**	**$598**
30	Venezuela, RB	$553

Adapted from data from the World Bank, with my own updates. Retrieved from http://data.worldbank.org/indicator/NY.GDP.MKTP.PP.CD

Global business risk management is one of the major functions of strategic and tactical business practices. In the past, risk was something to avoid. But the GEM has resulted in a fundamental change in how international business strategy considers risk. While the opportunities are incredible in the GEM, risk is to some degree inherent in EMCs. Instead of avoiding risk altogether, in cases of investment strategy, strategists aim to utilize risk-management systems and convert new opportunities into profit and success, despite threats (see Chapter 9).

The geopolitical location of some EMCs essentially ensures them a key and lucrative strategic role as a bridge between developed countries and the GEM as a whole. Bulgaria, Turkey, Ukraine, and Spain are important crossroads between the developed countries of Europe and EMCs of Southern and Eastern Europe, the Middle East, Russia, and Africa. Mexico is an important intermediary between developed North America and the emerging markets of Latin America. Kazakhstan is a key entrance to Central Asia and China, as is China to Southeast Asia. Azerbaijan occupies a very strategic location, the role of which will only increase when Iran's dictatorship eventually collapses or drastically changes its course of action. As stability increases in Iraq, so will its strategic value—the country will play an integral role in the twenty-first-century GMP; and the role of Turkey will only increase as a strategic crossroad with markedly improved education and quality of life. Of course, strategic geopolitical locations are not always taken advantage of. Portugal has failed to exploit its cultural ties to the world's substantial Portuguese-speaking market and especially Brazil. It did not follow the lead of its neighbor Spain, which realized the potential of South America and was one of the first developed countries to establish a relationship with the newly formed economic union of the southern cone of South America—Mercosur (Mercosul). Due to extremely tense bilateral and multilateral relations with its neighbors, Israel has mostly not been able to leverage its strategic location. Despite these difficulties, Israel is improving its economic relations with some Muslim countries, such as Jordan, Egypt, Azerbaijan, Turkmenistan, Kazakhstan, and (predominately Muslim) Albania.

The integration of the GEM into the global marketplace has multiple effects on both developed and emerging market countries. Both categories, through their cooperation, investment, and increasing international trade due to liberalized economic conditions and deregulation, have most of the time experienced acceleration in their rate of growth. This resulted in an overall acceleration of world economic development, which the world has experienced since the operational existence of the GEM in the middle of the 1980s. The fact that the world economy has more than quadrupled in terms of GDP since 1980 is due directly to the growth of the GEM (see Figure 6.6).

Figure 6.7 shows the differences in the vector of economic development of emerging market and developed countries. Over the past 20 years, the rate of growth of the GEM has always outpaced that of the world economy and (with the exception of one year) of the US. At the same time, the dynamics of individual GEM members can fluctuate substantially. Figure 6.7 shows the example of Russia, which for seven of eight years beginning in the 1990s, during the transition from communism to a free-market economy, experienced economic recession and a serious downsizing of the national economy, which will have taken place in 2014 to 2016. Nonetheless, the GEM continued to grow at a faster pace than the world economy, despite Russia's slowing economy that will continue to have an influence on general trends in the GEM. Developed countries no longer dominate global production in absolute numbers and in rate of growth.[49]

Integration of the GEM into the global marketplace and increasing industrial and economic development in EMCs due to new business opportunities, foreign investment, and trade have all had a tremendous influence on the societies of EMCs, their values, and their strategic interests. These changes initiate strategically important shifts in the allocation of different basic economic factors. One of the most significant changes is the reallocation of

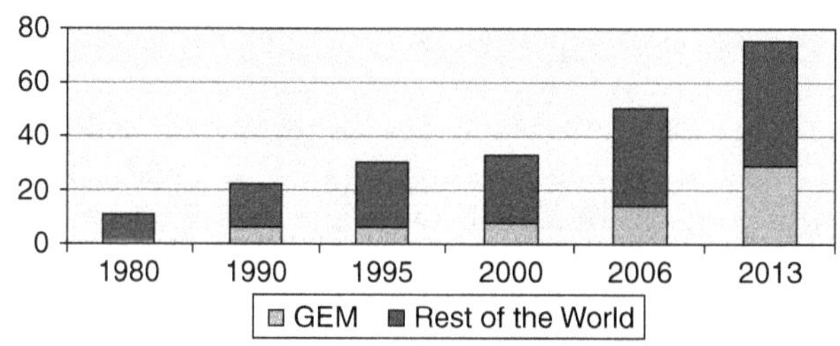

Figure 6.6 Input of GEM in Global GDP (Exchange Rate, Trillions of $)

© Dr. Vladimir Kvint, 2014. Adapted from data from the World Bank. Retrieved from http://data.worldbank.org/indicator/NY.GDP.MKTP.CD

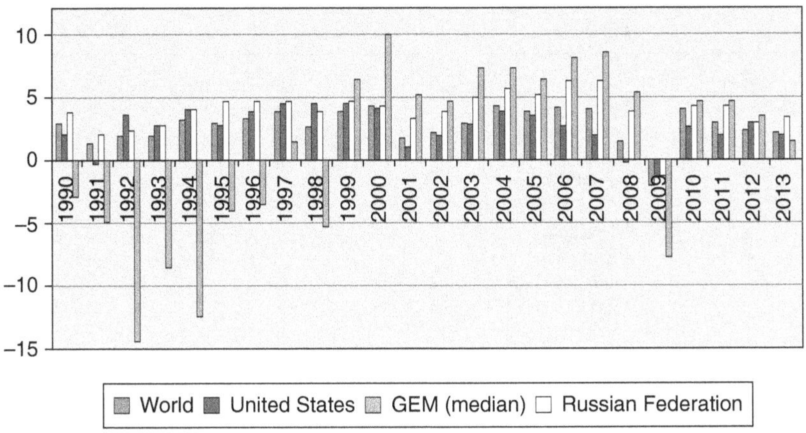

Figure 6.7 Comparison of the Rate of Growth of the World Economy with the Dynamics of Economic Development of the GEM, US, and Russia, 2013

© Dr. Vladimir Kvint, 2013. Based on data from the World Bank World Development Indicators, and the International Monetary Fund. (2013). Retrieved from http://data.worldbank.org/indicator/NY.GDP.MKTP.KD.ZG

production facilities, which in turn alters the scale and patterns of domestic migration. It is very important for strategic investors in the GEM to consider the fact that urban populations are increasing at least three times faster than in rural areas. This trend is changing strategies of companies seeking consumer markets of scale in the GEM. Because of the population growth in the GEM and increasing migration of people from villages to urban areas, the number of cities with 5 million people increased from 41 to 59 between 2000 and 2015.[50] During the same period the number of cities of more than 10 million has increased from 19 to 23.[51] This will have a powerful impact on the world economy because the population of the GEM accounts for 67.92 percent of the global population. As a result, domestic and social dynamics in EMCs are changing the process of world social development.

In the early 1980s, prior to the birth of the GEM, 70 percent of capital invested in developing countries (many of which have since become EMCs) came from developed countries as governmental aid. Due to tremendous improvements in the business environment of the GEM and increasing political stability, the private economic interests of developed countries in EMCs has skyrocketed. As a result, in 2007, 83 percent of capital invested in the GEM came from private companies.

Technological Achievements and Innovations in the GEM

Every year since 2007, the GEM has surpassed all individual developed countries, including the US, in terms of patents pending. Within the GEM, China has surpassed Russia as the leading source of new patents. In January 2008, in terms of patents pending, China ranked third for the first time, behind the US and Japan. Scientific and technological progress, as well as huge investments in research and development in the GEM, is changing the strategic objectives and goals of investors. Strategic investors used to think of the GEM as a source of natural resources, cheap labor, and consumer markets. With increasing frequency, strategists from developed countries orient investors in the GEM to utilize

Table 6.6 EMCs by Population, 2014

Rank	*Country*	*2013 Population*
1	China	1,357,380,000
2	India	1,252,139,596
3	Indonesia	249,865,631
4	Brazil	200,361,925
5	Pakistan	182,142,594
6	Russian Federation	143,499,861
7	Mexico	122,332,399
8	Philippines	98,393,574
9	Vietnam	89,708,900
10	Egypt, Arab Rep.	82,056,378
11	Turkey	74,932,641
12	Thailand	67,010,502
13	South Africa	52,981,991
14	Korea, Rep.	50,219,669
15	Colombia	48,321,405
16	Spain	46,647,421
17	Ukraine	45,489,600
18	Argentina	41,446,246
19	Algeria	39,208,194
20	Poland	38,530,725
21	Iraq	33,417,476
22	Morocco	33,008,150
23	Peru	30,375,603
24	Malaysia	29,716,965
25	Saudi Arabia	28,828,870
26	Ghana	25,904,598
27	Taiwan	23,424,615
28	Madagascar	22,924,851
29	Sri Lanka	20,483,000
30	Romania	19,963,581
31	Chile	17,619,708
32	Kazakhstan	17,037,508
33	Burkina Faso	16,934,839
34	Ecuador	15,737,878
35	Guatemala	15,468,203
36	Greece	11,032,328
37	Tunisia	10,886,500
38	Bolivia	10,671,200
39	Czech Republic	10,521,468
40	Portugal	10,459,806
41	Hungary	9,897,247
42	Azerbaijan	9,416,598
43	United Arab Emirates	9,346,129
44	Israel	8,059,400
45	Bulgaria	7,265,115
46	Hong Kong SAR, China	7,187,500
47	Serbia	7,163,976
48	Jordan	6,459,000
49	El Salvador	6,340,454
50	Slovak Republic	5,414,095
51	Singapore	5,399,200
52	Turkmenistan	5,240,072
53	Costa Rica	4,872,166
54	Ireland	4,595,281
55	Georgia	4,476,900

(Continued)

Table 6.6 EMCs by Population, 2014 (Continued)

Rank	*Country*	*2013 Population*
56	Croatia	4,252,700
57	Panama	3,864,170
58	Moldova	3,559,000
59	Uruguay	3,407,062
60	Armenia	2,976,566
61	Lithuania	2,956,121
62	Mongolia	2,839,073
63	Albania	2,773,620
64	Jamaica	2,715,000
65	Qatar	2,168,673
66	Macedonia, FYR	2,107,158
67	Slovenia	2,060,484
68	Botswana	2,021,144
69	Latvia	2,013,385
70	Gabon	1,671,711
71	Trinidad and Tobago	1,341,151
72	Bahrain	1,332,171
73	Estonia	1,324,612
74	Mauritius	1,296,303
75	Cyprus	1,141,166
76	Guyana	799,613
77	Montenegro	621,383
78	Malta	423,282
79	Bahamas, The	377,374
80	Belize	331,900
81	Barbados	284,644
82	St. Lucia	182,273
83	St. Kitts and Nevis	54,191
	Total	4,839,115,462
	% of World	67.92

Adapted from data from the World Bank. Retrieved from http://data.worldbank.org/indicator/SP.POP.TOTL

their highly developed scientific and technological resources, which due to lack of strategies in most EMCs are underutilized. Leaders of EMCs can continue this dynamic by generating revenue from foreign exploitation of domestic resources (natural and labor) to be invested in science, technology, education, and health care. Some EMCs, such as Azerbaijan, Kazakhstan, and Russia, have created strategic accounts for revenue from natural resources (mostly oil and gas) to be invested in the non-oil economy, but due to lack of strategy and governmental consistence, EMCs often do not follow this. The vulnerability of EMCs to unforeseen shocks is greatly reduced by economic diversification based on the implementation of scientific advancements and cutting-edge technologies. The level of economic diversification of an EMC is a good indicator of its level of overall development. Strategists quite often make recommendations to national governments, and corporate executives from EMCs have started to motivate their foreign partners to use their investment for new technologies and modern management systems.

National Agendas and Benefits to Society of Emerging Market Countries

Increasing cooperation with developed countries and the inflow of investment from developed states to the GEM has substantially changed public values and opinion, and

Table 6.7 FDI Inflows to EMCs, 2014

Rank	*Emerging Market Country*	*2013 FDI Inflow (Millions $)*
1	China	123,911
2	Russian Federation	79,262
3	Hong Kong SAR, China	76,633
4	Brazil	64,045
5	Singapore	63,772
6	Spain	39,167
7	Mexico	38,286
8	Ireland	35,520
9	India	28,199
10	Chile	20,258
11	Indonesia	18,444
12	Colombia	16,772
13	Thailand	12,946
14	Turkey	12,866
15	Malaysia	12,306
16	Korea, Rep.	12,221
17	Israel	11,804
18	United Arab Emirates	10,488
19	Peru	10,172
20	Kazakhstan	9,739
21	Saudi Arabia	9,298
22	Argentina	9,082
23	Vietnam	8,900
24	South Africa	8,188
25	Egypt, Arab Rep.	5,553
26	Czech Republic	4,990
27	Panama	4,651
28	Philippines	3,860
29	Ukraine	3,771
30	Taiwan	3,688
31	Romania	3,617
32	Morocco	3,358
33	Ghana	3,226
34	Portugal	3,114
35	Hungary	3,091
36	Turkmenistan	3,061
37	Iraq	2,852
38	Uruguay	2,796
39	Costa Rica	2,652
40	Azerbaijan	2,632
41	Greece	2,567
42	Mongolia	2,047
43	Jordan	1,798
44	Bolivia	1,750
45	Trinidad and Tobago	1,713
46	Algeria	1,691
47	Bulgaria	1,450
48	Serbia	1,377
49	Guatemala	1,309
50	Pakistan	1,307
51	Albania	1,225
52	Bahamas, The	1,111
53	Tunisia	1,096
54	Georgia	1,010
55	Bahrain	989

(Continued)

Table 6.7 FDI Inflows to EMCs, 2014 (Continued)

Rank	*Emerging Market Country*	*2013 FDI Inflow (Millions $)*
56	Estonia	950
57	Sri Lanka	916
58	Gabon	856
59	Madagascar	838
60	Latvia	808
61	Ecuador	703
62	Slovak Republic	591
63	Croatia	580
64	Jamaica	567
65	Cyprus	533
66	Lithuania	531
67	Montenegro	447
68	Barbados	376
69	Burkina Faso	374
70	Armenia	370
71	Macedonia, FYR	334
72	Mauritius	259
73	Guyana	240
74	Moldova	231
75	Botswana	188
76	El Salvador	140
77	St. Kitts and Nevis	112
78	Belize	89
79	St. Lucia	88
80	Slovenia	-679
81	Qatar	-840
82	Malta	-2,100
83	Poland	-6,038
	GEM Total as a Percentage of World Total (Approximately)	56

Adapted from data from the UNCTAD statistics database. Retrieved from http://unctadstat.unctad.org/wds/TableViewer/tableView.aspx?ReportId=88/

the attitude of governments of EMCs, toward foreign trade, companies, and investments. The agenda of the national government, which is a reflection of its vision, is a very good indicator of the maturity of a country. The new outlook of most EMC governments toward collaboration within the GMP is the first indicator to foreigners that they can start to strategize explorations and analysis of business opportunities in these countries. Mature EMCs develop strategies of integration within the GMP as a means to resolve domestic challenges, while less mature countries or those with specific political agendas look for internal solutions to domestic challenges and still embrace some forms of isolationism. The latter view is usually a transparent attempt to either recentralize power, such as in Putin's Russia and Morales's Bolivia, or to revert to totalitarianism, such as Mugabe's Zimbabwe and what used to be Chavez's Venezuela. When the national agenda does not mirror the population's values and/or its verified strategic interests, it can lead countries on the fast track to crisis and subsequently to strategic and economic maneuvers that generate different, and usually opposite, agendas.

Strategic Role of the Middle Class in Economic Maturation of EMCs

The creation and development of a middle class is crucial for stabilizing economic and political conditions in EMCs. The middle class plays an important role in attracting international business activity and investment. Unfortunately, in many GEMs, the rich segment of the population often allocates their money and assets abroad (both legally and illegally). This capital is not used for domestic economic activity, such as job creation, which would further expand the middle class, but would not attract foreign investors, and not improve the overall stability and quality of life of the country's population. At the beginning of the twenty-first century, the per capita income in the 20 richest countries is 37 times higher than the average per capita income in the 20 poorest countries.[52] One of the causes of this situation is an underdeveloped financial sector of national economies of the GEM and the general population's subsequent lack of trust of these institutions. This situation is mirrored in the Global Financial Centres Index.[53] Out of the top ten global financial centers, only two are from the GEM (Hong Kong and Singapore). However, of all 46 ranked financial centers, there are already 16 in EMCs; and the financial centers ranked from thirty-ninth to forty-sixth are all from EMCs.[54] Dublin stands out as a financial center that is oriented toward its customers' quality of life. More than any other EMC financial center, Dublin gives a great deal of attention to individual customers, not just corporate clients. Practical observations make it possible to conclude that the banking system is adequate to the needs of the general population once there are roughly 10 banks and their offices per 100,000 people. This ratio can be increased to 75 banks per 100,000 people in countries with much larger territories than average, like Russia, China, Brazil, India, Argentina, Kazakhstan, and South Africa.

Another factor that encourages people to move their personal and corporate financial assets abroad is high taxes. Mumbai registered the highest worldwide corporate tax with a rate of 81 percent.[55] This has created an incentive for capital to be moved abroad, which has negative implications for the development of the middle class. For EMCs, a rising and strong middle class is a key strategic factor of stability, which eventually attracts more investment and also discourages domestic companies from sending their assets abroad. For this reason strategists have to recommend strategies to the government to develop programs to motivate the expansion of the middle class. If the correct strategies are implemented, eventually the market itself will create the conditions necessary for the sustainable expansion of the middle class.

The development of the middle class also has positive implications for gender inequality. According to the director of one of Cisco Systems' Networking Academies (part of a global education initiative of CISCO), 30 percent of students and 20 percent of teachers of information technology (IT) in CISCO Academies are women. While many assume that women do not play a significant role in the GEM, this is not at all the case in many EMCs. In some EMCs, especially those of Eastern Europe, women often occupy important leadership positions in government, as well as in hospitals, academic institutions, and light and food industry companies. Among medical doctors, teachers, and engineers, the percentage of women in some EMCs is equal to that of men.

It is also important to note that the middle class of EMCs may be very different from that of developed countries in terms of quality of life, purchasing power, etc. The effects of the middle class on politics and national agendas in EMCs can be different than in developed countries. In developed countries, the middle class is the most politically active. In EMCs, the middle class often prefers the stability of the status quo, instead of the continuation of rapid political reforms. For this reason, in EMCs without a long tradition of democracy, once a certain level of political freedom is attained, the pace of democratic reform dissipates. This can be seen in China, Russia, India, Argentina, Turkey, Jordan, Singapore, and Uruguay, and with some explainable exceptions in Kazakhstan and Colombia.

The Strategic Vision of the Future of the Global Emerging Market

Strategic analysis proves that the role of the GEM in the GMP will continue to expand, at least until the end of the twenty-first century. After this period, the majority of the most mature EMCs will achieve a level of prosperity on par with median developed countries and will no longer be part of the GEM. This will obviously have a huge impact on the GMP.

By the year 2025, a few EMCs will transition into the highest category of a country's development in the GEM—economies in bloom, and even to the category of the developed country. In Europe, the Czech Republic, Greece, Portugal, Slovenia, and Slovakia will follow the lead of Spain (which is already an economy in bloom despite the crises of 2010 to 2015) and Ireland, which by that time will have completed the transition to the category of developed country. In Asia, Singapore, South Korea, UAE, Bahrain, and possibly Taiwan will also be categorized as economies in bloom. Costa Rica will be the only EMC outside of Europe and Asia to become an economy in bloom during this period. Israel, with its well-established democracy, high levels of economic freedom, and superb technological and innovative advancement, has the potential to make this transition as well. However, a very high level of political risk, as a result of extremely tense bilateral relations with its neighbors, inhibits the development of multilateral and regional agreements and may prevent Israel from completing the transition to the economy in bloom during this period.

Developing countries that have lower quality of life than those in the GEM and that lack economic and political freedom will eventually (within ten years) initiate political and economic reforms and become part of the GEM. Mostly positive processes toward democracy started in countries of the Maghreb and the Arabian Gulf, only proving strategic analysis made five years before these events.[56] This even includes economies that are "repressed" according to the *Wall Street Journal* and Heritage Fund Index of Economic Freedom, such as Libya, Myanmar, Venezuela, and Iran—nothing lasts forever. Of course, it would be equally foolish to assume that all EMCs constantly progress forward. The examples of Zimbabwe, Venezuela, and Bolivia clearly indicate how progress can be stalled and even reversed. But in all likelihood, these governments will eventually realize that there is no alternative to economic freedom and integration with the GMP.

The continuation of the spread of democracy and economic freedom will lead the most successful EMCs to become developed economies. Countries which, at the end of the first decade of the twenty-first century, are considered pre-emerging market, developing, and even underdeveloped will become part of the GEM. It is important to note, however, that the GEM is not a temporary entity composed of countries in transitional phases of their development. There will almost always be differences in the political, economic, and technological characteristics of development of countries in the GMP, and the GEM will be made up of the relatively less developed countries in terms of their political, economic, and social maturity. In the next 100 years, these countries will provide opportunities and challenges for entry strategies of companies from developed countries. What is indisputable is that all major problems of humankind, such as poverty, hunger, unemployment, mass diseases, ecological devastation, terrorism, and migration, can be solved only though a strategic partnership between national governments of different categories of countries, together with private companies and multilateral institutions. These types of global issues need to be simplified and solved on the basis of required global strategies.

Under the influence of the GEM, humanity's problems will be both aggravated and mollified, and the global order will constantly adjust in response.

Forecast of the top 20 EMCs (by attractiveness of FDI), until 2025:

1. China
2. India
3. Brazil
4. Mexico
5. South Korea
6. Russia
7. Poland
8. Vietnam
9. Israel
10. Kazakhstan
11. Egypt
12. Turkey
13. Czech Republic
14. South Africa
15. Ukraine
16. The Philippines
17. Argentina
18. Portugal
19. Romania
20. Hungary

Notes

1 Bacon, F. (2004). *Novum Organum: True Directions Concerning the Interpretation of Nature.* Whitefish, MT: Kessinger Publishing.

2 Kipling, R. (1927). *We and They. Rudyard Kipling's Verse.* Garden City, NY: Doubleday, Page & Company, p. 820.

3 Kvint, V. L. (2009). *The Global Emerging Market: Strategic Management and Economics.* New York and London: Routledge, p. 75.

4 Sartre, J.-P. (1963). *Les Mouches. Drame en trois actes.* Act 2. King Aegistheus.

5 Nekipelov, A. (2004). "Public Preferences and Their Role in Shaping Russian Economic Development." *Distinguished Lecture Series, No. 14.* October 15. Warsaw: Academy of Entrepreneurship and Management. p. 3.

6 Park, K.K.H. and Van Agtmael, A.W. (Eds.). (1993). *The World's Emerging Stock Market: Structure, Developments, Regulations and Opportunities.* Chicago and Cambridge: Probus Publishing Company.

7 International Finance Corporation Press Release (1994). November 11. Retrieved from www.ifc.org/ifcext/pressroom/ifcpressroom.nsf/PressRelease?openform&625C5388C0DB59B92852569680057A8D1

8 World Bank. (n.d.). "Country Classification." Retrieved from http://siteresources.worldbank.org/DATASTATISTICS/Resources/OGHIST.xls

9 World Bank (2013). "New Country Classifications." July 2. Retrieved from www.data.worldbank.org

10 Van Agtmael, A. (2007). *The Emerging Market Century: How a New Breed of World-Class Companies Is Overtaking the World.* New York: Free Press, p. 5.

11 Russell Investments. S&P/IFC Emerging Market Indexes. Retrieved November 2, 2007 from www.russell.com/us/glossary/indexes/s&p_ifc_emerging_markets_indexes.htm

12 Kvint, V. (1995). "A Different Perspective on Emerging Markets". *The Fourth Annual World Economic Development Congress, Addendum: A Special Summit Briefing of Some of the Speakers' Addresses*, pp. 50–54.
13 "Survey of the World Economy." (2006). *The Economist*. September 16, p. 6.
14 Kvint, V.L. (2009). *The Global Emerging Market: Strategic Management and Economics*. New York and London: Routledge, p. 75.
15 World Economic Forum. (n.d.). "Global Competitiveness Network." Retrieved from www.weforum.org/en/initiatives/gcp/FAQs/index.htm#network1
16 Moodys. (n.d.). "National Scale Ratings." Retrieved from www.moodys.com/cust/content/loadcontent.aspx?source=staticcontent/free%20pages/nsr/nsr.htm
17 globalEDGE. (n.d.). "Market Potential Index." Retrieved from http://globaledge.msu.edu/resourceDesk/mpi.asp#MarketPotential
18 Price, M. (1994). *Emerging Stock Markets: A Complete Investment Guide to New Markets around the World*. Highstown, NJ: McGraw Hill, Inc. p. 11.
19 "Dizzy in Boomtown." (2007). *The Economist*. November 15. Retrieved from www.economist.com/opinion/displaystory.cfm?story_id=10136509
20 "Dizzy in Boomtown." (2007). *The Economist*. November 15. Retrieved from www.economist.com/opinion/displaystory.cfm?story_id=10136509
21 globalEDGE. (n.d.). "Market Potential Index." Retrieved from http://globaledge.msu.edu/resourceDesk/mpi.asp#MarketPotential
22 "America's Vulnerable Economy." (2007). *The Economist*. November 15. Retrieved from www.economist.com/opinion/displaystory.cfm?story_id=10134118
23 "Dizzy in Boomtown." (2007). *The Economist*. November 15. Retrieved from www.economist.com/opinion/displaystory.cfm?story_id=10136509
24 Arrow, K.J. (1963). *Social Choice and Individual Values*. New Haven, CT and London: Yale University Press, p. 61.
25 "Kazakh Ecology Ministry Drops Chevron Tengiz Probe." (2007). Reuters. April 4. Retrieved from www.reuters.com/article/companyNewsAndPR/idUSL0433100620070404
26 "Kazakh Ecology Ministry Drops Chevron Tengiz Probe." (2007). Reuters. April 4. Retrieved from www.reuters.com/article/companyNewsAndPR/idUSL0433100620070404
27 Shah, S. (2004). "Shell Hit by $1.5bn Oil Pollution Claim from Nigerian Senate." *Energy Bulletin*. August 5. Retrieved from http://energybulletin.net/1739.html
28 Krauss, C. (2006). "Major U.S. Oil Discovery in Gulf of Mexico." *The International Herald Tribune*. September 6. Retrieved from www.iht.com/articles/2006/09/06/business/oil.php
29 Brenton, H. (2007). "Russians Arrest Crab Mogul." *The Seattle Times*. November 13. Retrieved from www.seattletimes.com/seattle-news/russians-arrest-crab-mogul/
30 Brenton, H. (2007). "Russians Arrest Crab Mogul." *The Seattle Times*. November 13. Retrieved from www.seattletimes.com/seattle-news/russians-arrest-crab-mogul/
31 Sidenko, V. (2007). "Structural Shifts in Economic Relations of Ukraine and the Russian Federation." *World Changes*, no. 3, pp. 66–67.
32 Sidenko, V. (2007). "Structural Shifts in Economic Relations of Ukraine and the Russian Federation." *World Changes*, no. 3., p. 64.
33 "EU Extends Trade Preferences for Ukraine until End of 2015." (2014) Retrieved from www.english.news.cn/
34 European Commission. (n.d.). "Bilateral Trade Relations." Retrieved from http://ec.europa.eu/trade/issues/bilateral/countries/ukraine/index_en.htm/
35 "European Union Delegation to Ukraine: Trade and Economic Section" (2014). *Ukraine—Impact on ATM Restrictions from Russia on Exports*. September 25. Retrieved from http://eeas.europa.eu/delegations/ukraine/documents/eu_ua/impact_atm_en.pdf/
36 "Survey of the World Economy." (2006). *The Economist*. September 16, pp. 2–3.
37 Mercer LLC. (2008). *2008 Global Compensation Planning Report*. Retrieved July 16, 2008 from www.imercer.com/default.aspx?page=surveydetail&surveyid=2851&menuld=344&newRegionId=3/
38 Mercer LLC. (2014). *Compensation and Planning: EMEA Forecasts and Trends*, p. 5. Retrieved from www.mercer.com/content/dam/mercer/attachments/global/Talent/human-capital-agenda/Anthology%202013/2014-compensation-planning-emea-forecasts-and-trends-europe-2013-mercer.pdf/

39 International Fund for Agricultural Development. (2007). "Sending Money Home: Worldwide Remittance Flows to Developing Countries." Retrieved from www.ifad.org/events/remittances/maps/
40 The World Bank. (2014). "Remittances to Developing Countries to Grow by 5 Percent this Year, while Conflict-related Forced Migration Is at All-time High, Says WB Report." Retrieved from www.worldbank.org/en/news/press-release/2014/10/06/remittances-developing-countries-five-percent-conflict-related-migration-all-time-high-wb-report/
41 "Special Report: Innovation." (2007). *The Economist*. October 11. Retrieved from www.economist.com/specialreports/displayStory.cfm?story_id=9928154
42 Abed, G.T. and Gupta, S. (Eds.). (2002). *Governance, Corruption and Economic Performance*. Washington, DC: IMF.
43 Treisman, D. (2000). "The Causes of Corruption: A Cross-National Study." *Journal of Public Economics*, vol. 76, no. 3. pp. 399–457.
44 Knight, F.H. (1921). *Risk, Uncertainty, and Profit*. Boston and New York: The Riverside Press.
45 Franklin D. Roosevelt, from a prepared speech for Jefferson Day on April 13, 1945. Retrieved from www.presidency.ucsb.edu/ws/?pid=16602
46 Based on data from Standard & Poor's. (2005) *Global Stock Markets Factbook*.
47 Park, K.K.H and Van Agtmael, A.W. (Eds.). (1993). *The World's Emerging Stock Market: Structure, Developments, Regulations and Opportunities*. Chicago and Cambridge: Probus Publishing Company, p. 9.
48 Walters, G. and Mauldin, W. (2008). "Gazprom Passes GE, China Mobile, Becomes World No. 3." *Bloomberg*. May 8 Retrieved from www.bloomberg.com/apps/news?pid=20601095&sid=aZomK8T5CtUs&refer=east_europe
49 "Survey of the World Economy." (2006). *The Economist*. September 16, p. 4
50 The United Nations Department of Economic and Social Affairs Population Division. (1999). *World Urbanization Report: 1999 Revision Key Findings*. Retrieved from http://157.150.195.10/esa/population/pubsarchive/urbanization/urbanization.pdf
51 The United Nations Department of Economic and Social Affairs Population Division. (1999). *World Urbanization Report: 1999 Revision Key Findings*. Retrieved from http://157.150.195.10/esa/population/pubsarchive/urbanization/urbanization.pdf
52 The World Bank. (2001). *World Development Report 2000/2001*. New York: Oxford University Press, p. 51.
53 Initiated by the city of London, and managed by Z/Yen. Retrieved from www.zyen.com/Activities/On-line%20surveys/GFCI.htm/
54 The Global Financial Centres Index of the City of London. (2007). Retrieved from http://213.86.34.248/NR/rdonlyres/0C0332C0-4CE5-4012-9AF7-2CF98A32E618/0/BC_RS_GFCI07_FR.pdf/
55 The Global Financial Centres Index of the City of London. (2007). Retrieved from http://213.86.34.248/NR/rdonlyres/0C0332C0-4CE5-4012-9AF7-2CF98A32E618/0/BC_RS_GFCI07_FR.pdf
56 Kvint, V.L. (2009). *The Global Emerging Market: Strategic Management and Economics*. New York and London: Routledge, p. 109.

7 Ten Global Trends

Political, Economic, and Technological Impacts on Strategies for Emerging Markets

Democracy is the worst form of government, except for all those other forms that have been tried from time to time.[1]

Sir Winston Leonard Spencer Churchill, the first lord of the treasury and prime minister of the United Kingdom, 1953 Nobel Prize winner in Literature (1874–1965)

Democracy means simply the bludgeoning of the people by the people for the people.[2]

Oscar Wilde, Irish author (1854–1900)

System of the Ten Global Trends

For strategists, any correctly verified objective trend is an Ariadne's thread that can help to solve many strategic problems and dilemmas through the analysis of connected and even chaotic events that form future patterns. Strategists use proven trends and tendencies to recognize conditions involving the strategizing object in the distant future.

The 10 selected key global trends of varying strength and maturity presented in this chapter influence the political, social, economic, and technological development of modern civilization. The interaction of these trends and their strategic influence on one another can be understood as a hierarchical system. At the top of this hierarchy are the super trends: *globalization* and *democratization*. These two global trends, enforced by advancements in information technology, have destroyed empires, dictatorships, and command economies, and have also given smaller and less powerful nations the strategic opportunity to achieve their own statehood and to cooperate in the global marketplace. In fact, the formation of the GMP itself is a direct result of these trends. The collapse of dictatorships on a global scale led to the emergence of the global trend of *political disintegration*. Political disintegration indelibly changed the political map of the world. Since the 1980s, new independent countries have appeared almost annually, usually with smaller and smaller populations. In an attempt to improve the quality of life among their citizens, the governments of these new nation-states looked for strategic solutions beyond their borders, causing a surge in international economic cooperation. It is quite common for leaders of newly emerging states to order strategy development that focuses on active regional cooperation.

Arising from this surge of political disintegration, this initial attempt at internationalization developed mostly between neighboring countries on a bilateral and multilateral basis. The liberalization of international economic relations, under the influence of the trends of globalization, democratization, and internationalization, initiated tighter political and economic cooperation between countries with relatively similar cultural, religious, political, and economic characteristics.

From this process another global trend was reinforced: regionalization, which is discussed later in this chapter in more detail. Regionalization is not the opposite of globalization, but rather an effect of it, and occurs when strategic economic and political connections form in the framework of regional zones. The formation of regional economic unions, free-trade areas, and special economic and technological zones for faster development was accelerated by the global trend of regional economic integration, born during iterations of regionalization. The objective need to increase the efficiency of national economies strengthened politically independent countries' regional economic integration. Regional integration develops specific characteristics when countries that were once part of a bigger state begin to reintegrate economically, while maintaining their recently gained political independence. This occurred in Europe and is ongoing among countries of the former Soviet Union, as well as in Asia, which used to be unified and were then politically divided, but continue and even improve and deepen their economic cooperation; for example, Singapore and Malaysia, Indonesia and East Timor, or Russia and Kazakhstan, Belarus, Armenia, and Kyrgyzstan. They are developing and experiencing regional economic cooperation under the umbrella of such regional unions as the Association of Southeast Asian Nations (ASEAN) or the Eurasian Economic Union (EEU), which was operationally established recently in January 2014. After several iterations, the trend of regional integration and regionalization motivated the integration of regional economic blocs, unions, and zones within the GMP.

The widespread failure of dictatorships and command economies, which resulted from globalization and democratization, catalyzed the global trend of privatization, a massive tsunami of ownership transformation from state to mostly private hands. The burgeoning number of privately held enterprises in national economies that were once overwhelmingly dominated by the state triggered a new wave of internationalization. This trend, the father of globalization, was rejuvenated in new, objective conditions. The dialectic connection between internationalization and globalization is obvious; at different stages of economic development, one of them plays the leading role. In order to increase the efficiency and profitability of their companies, private entrepreneurs and professional strategists developing and encouraging conditions and entry strategies for capital from abroad, mergers and acquisitions spread like wildfire throughout the world economy. The influence of all of these trends eventually resulted in the formation of the GMP at the edge of the third millennium.

The GMP created tremendous strategic opportunities for international investors, immediately leading to a shortage of capital in international, national, and regional markets. While the implications of this trend are not positive, neither is it the worst global trend. A deficit of capital is only a minor obstacle in the path of globalization. The most dangerous global trend, which became evident in the less restrictive international arena of the GMP, is the rebirth of terrorism and extremism. Revolutions in science and technology (especially information technologies) not only expedited the creation of the GMP and provided new instruments for international business, but also gave weapons of new and very dangerous capacities to terrorists. The combination of the last two trends tremendously increased political risk in the newly formed GMP.

As previously mentioned, the influence and maturity of these ten trends vary. Some, like democratization and political disintegration, have been influential for a long time. Their effect on society has likely already peaked. As time goes by, the influence of these two global trends is diminishing, mostly due to their successful implementation. Other trends, like economic reintegration and global terrorism and extremism, are only approaching the pinnacle of their influence. Strategists must always be aware that the global impact and existence of some trends may not yet be detectable. However, the above-mentioned 10 global trends have directed the recent dynamics of the world economy and the eventual formation of the GMP. Strategists should expect these trends to continue to influence the progress of humankind over the first quarter of the twenty-first century. Their impact on implementing strategies will continue even beyond this distant horizon to about 2035. Knowledge of powerful trends (and not necessarily global trends) helps strategists not only to develop particular entities' strategies but also to predict competitors' and enemies' secretive strategic moves on any strategizing strata.

Global trends can also be just sectorial. These sectorial specific trends can influence the future development of particular industries or even subindustries. As an example, let's take a deeper look at both the fishing industry and some of the subindustries like marine aquaculture, hydrobionics, and the caged fish-farming subindustry. The Food and Agriculture Organization of the UN (FAO) marked that climate changes and carbon emissions influence international fishing trade and fishery products.[3] Substantial climate warming has decreased negative temperatures in the Arctic zone and drastically altered the fishing industry. Fish products have occupied an important part of the world trade of livestock (see Figure 7.1). Two sectorial trends in the fishing industry are good examples. The first is a change in transportation routes that are moving further north. These northern routes have especially opened potential use of the Arctic seaway along the coasts of Norway and Russia, and have substantially decreased traditional transportation expenses for this industry. These tendencies, as of 2015, are on the strategic agenda of all major fishing companies and related governmental bodies. This trend has given new advantages and opportunities for fishing subindustries, especially within America and Russia, among other nations.

The second sectorial specific trend is related to changes in areas of fishing that have implications for the distant future. Companies from countries with Arctic coastlines are already competing with each other and even using the political leverage of national leaders to obtain broader fishing rights in Arctic waters. For example, it will be much easier

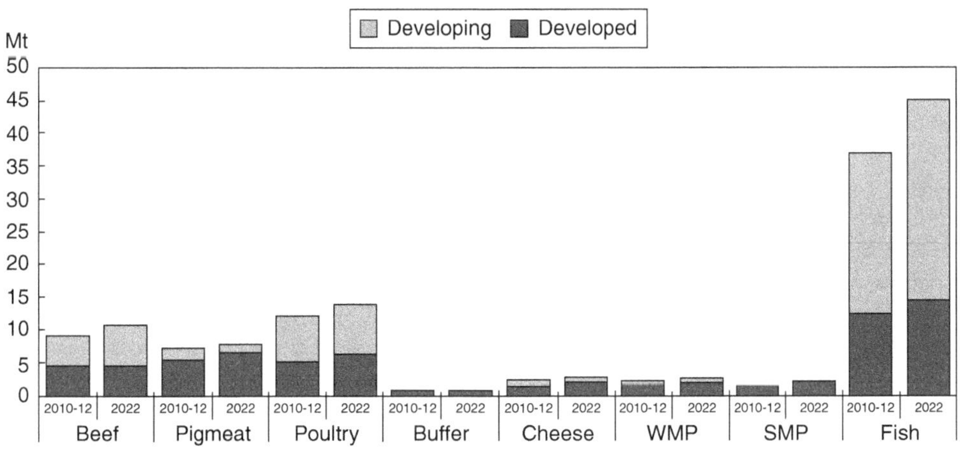

Figure 7.1 Increasing Exports of Livestock and Fish Products (in Million Tons, 2010–12 and 2022)
© Dr. Vladimir Kvint, 2014. OECD and FAO Secretariats. (2013). *OECD-FAO Agricultural Outlook 2013–2022: Highlights, OECD/FAO*, pp. 42–116. Retrieved from http://www.oecd.org/berlin/OECD-FAO%20Highlights_FINAL_with_Covers%20%283%29.pdf

for American companies to deliver frozen fish fillets to Pacific Asia, and in particular to Japan, South Korea, Singapore, and China, using the Arctic seaway, which is either in Russian waters or in a maritime economic zone.

Shorter-term trends, which I call tendencies, in the fishing industry will be related to changing prices for fishing and aquaculture products. Aquaculture, which already demonstrates much faster acceleration of its production than other fishing subindustries, is a good illustration of one of these tendencies. Of course, any of these trends and tendencies that are specifically particular to the fishing industry can be further detailed, which can substantially help strategize processes for this industry. The trajectory will intensively continue in three directions in the aquatics industry. First, the annual growth rate in the aquaculture industry will expand and vary across the different international regions, with a large bias towards Asian countries. Already we see an average annual growth rate exceeding 6 percent in the last decade, as aquaculture expansion continues to outpace that of the other food-producing industries.[4] The second subtendency will be related to innovations in hydrobionics, which will continue to help farmers raise seaweed, scallops, mussels, sea urchins, etc. Finally, farmed fish production will become a major industry within inland aquaculture. Without a doubt, the leaders in the marine aquaculture subindustry are the producers of Atlantic salmon nursed in caged salmon farms, which guarantee, as of 2015, at least 10 years of leadership to Norway and Chile (see Table 7.1). Sustainable development of marine aquaculture in the world is constrained mostly by the lack of an adequate strategy in the majority of countries with an oceanic coastline and by conflicts related to the development of recreation territories in areas useful for the fishing industry. At the same time, strategists can see a sustainable rate of growth of demand both in developed countries and in the most developed EMCs—economies in bloom—for seafood products, especially of wild origin, due to the lack of supply on the global fishing market. One fishery product that could satisfy this demand is the Pacific salmon. The Pacific salmon is an anadromous fish that is born in fresh water, spends most of its life in the open sea, and migrates back to fresh water to spawn. Using hatcheries, the maturation process is very promising for this fish. During the first decade of the twenty-first century, a summary of hatchery releases of Pacific salmon stabilized to about 5 million salmon per year.[5] Japan and Alaska are world leaders in the volume of production and the number of hatcheries that specialize in this lucrative industry. In the near future, most probably, a new trend will develop related to the growth of Pacific salmon fishing hatcheries at the same time as caged salmon farms in Norway and Chile will gradually decline.[6]

These examples illustrate to strategists that they must explore all potential trends related to the strategizing object: regional trends, country-specific trends, and even those influencing only particular economic factors. Trends and tendencies, which can at first glance look like common-sense thinking, are in fact the result of long-term statistical analysis using mathematical models. At any rate, the analysis of sectorial specific trends and tendencies can be used for any particular industry. This is the work strategists do daily to create workable and efficient strategy. Uncovering all of these trends and tendencies, and their correlations, will help to develop more sustainable strategy.

How do global trends influence multiple levels of strategies, and how are they reflected in strategies of different levels and scales? Why is it so important to study trends? Because every developed strategy is about the future, and the future is behind a curtain stronger than iron. With strategy, the future is known and unknown, predictable and unpredictable, and contains systematic and unsystematic characteristics. When we strategize, we are attempting to connect the present with the future. However, what we are actually doing

Table 7.1 Farmed Fish Production by Top 15 Producers and Main Groups of Farmed Species in 2012

Producer	*Finfish*		*Crustaceans*	*Molluscs*	*Other species*	*National total*	*Share in world total*
	Inland aquaculture	*Mariculture*					
	(Tonnes)			*(Tonnes)*			*(Percentage)*
China	23,341,134	1,028,399	3,592,588	12,343,169	803,016	41,108,306	61.7
India	3,812,420	84,164	299,926	12,905	...	4,209,415	6.3
Vietnam	2,091,200	51,000	513,100	400,000	30,200	3,085,500	4.6
Indonesia	2,097,407	582,077	387,698	...	477	3,067,660	4.6
Bangladesh	1,525,672	63,220	137,174	...	...	1,726,066	2.6
Norway	85	1,319,033	...	2,001	...	1,321,119	2.0
Thailand	380,986	19,994	623,660	205,192	4,045	1,233,877	1.9
Chile	59,527	758,587	...	253,307	...	1,071,421	1.6
Egypt	1,016,629	...	1,109	...	...	1,017,738	1.5
Myanmar	822,589	1,868	58,981	...	1,731	885,169	1.3
Philippines	310,042	361,722	72,822	46,308	...	790,894	1.2
Brazil	611,343	...	74,415	20,699	1,005	707,461	1.1
Japan	33,957	250,472	1,596	345,914	1,108	633,047	1.0
Republic of Korea	14,099	76,307	2,838	373,488	17,672	484,404	0.7
United States of America	185,598	21,169	44,928	168,329	...	420,024	0.6
Top 15 subtotal	**36,302,688**	**4,618,012**	**5,810,835**	**14,171,312**	**859,254**	**61,762,101**	**92.7**
Rest of world	2,296,562	933,893	635,983	999,426	5,288	4,871,152	7.3
World	**38,599,250**	**5,551,905**	**6,446,818**	**15,170,738**	**864,542**	**66,633,253**	**100**

FAO. (2014). *The State of World Fisheries and Aquaculture 2014. Opportunities and Challenges.* Rome, pp. 22–223.

is connecting the *past* with the future, because the present always becomes the past with strategy. Unlike the past, which can be proven through different studies, the future is always a prediction, and much more subjective than the past. The past is objective, or more or less objective, due to different interpretations under the influence of political leaders who often misinterpret the past for the benefit of their policies and wrong decisions. Even well-known facts in history books are often rewritten by rulers, scholars, or just by public opinion. Nonetheless, for strategists facts from the past can be taken into consideration during the verification of future dynamics because facts can be used as a beacon to understand the future. This beacon gives light in order to see how the past can help to predict the future. Most of the beacon's projections can be seen in possible trends if you correctly understand how different trends can influence the future of a strategized object; only then will it become easy to find a way from the known to the unknown, from the visible past to a mostly invisible future. Global trends influence the global order and strategies and, because of this, it is impossible to underestimate the importance of their analysis.

Globalization and Democratization as Objective Trends

All strategizing entities, be they macro (global, regional, etc.) or micro (corporate, workshops, army or army units, etc.), experience the following basic stages: formation, maturation, and eventual dissolution or drastic changes, which substantially alter the strategizing system. These processes are mostly predetermined by objective factors. When those factors have long-term implications, they help to define the vector of strategizing systems' dynamics. Objective factors influence any entity regardless of the wishes or efforts of politicians or executives, which can be understood as subjective factors. Objective factors, in the majority of cases, are overwhelmingly beyond the control of human beings. As a simple example, regardless of how hard one tries (a subjective factor), the laws of thermodynamics, gravity, or the absence of rich natural resources (objective factors) will never be overcome.

A strategic economic analysis must begin with a study of basic economic factors and objective global, regional, and industrial trends because these are objective influences of the global marketplace (GMP). Despite the subjective wishes of political leaders and executives, the quantity of oil, gold, and other mineral deposits cannot be increased; this is an objective factor. Because natural resources are limited and humankind continues to utilize them, the amount of available resources in the Earth is decreasing. This is not only a factor but also an objective trend. Though labor resources may change over time, at a given point of strategy development, literacy rates, life expectancies, and national demographics are what they are. However, subjective factors do influence strategizing systems to a certain extent. According to the scholar Bob Jessop, "Economic globalization is a contradictory phenomenon that necessarily produces, as its support, a space of flows and, as its nemesis, the importance of place, a source of objective and subjective resistance."[7] The quality of management systems determines the efficiency of the understanding and the use of objective factors. For example, the amount of oil in a particular field cannot be increased, but the innovative manner and technology by which it is extracted, enriched, and distributed significantly influences the actual output of the company exploiting the field.

In order to develop and implement an efficient strategy, any entity's executives, commanders, or leaders of national governments must recognize and understand the most powerful objective trends—global, sectorial, and regional—and their hierarchical breakdown. A successful strategy will work according to these trends, not against them. Strategists must figure out how to minimize the negative impact of trends or, if possible, to harness them toward the fulfillment of strategic objectives. Like the best captains, strategists must be able to use headwinds to propel ships to their destination.

The end of the twentieth century and the beginning decades of the third millennium witnessed drastic changes in modern civilization. Major dictatorships disappeared, the poverty rate has slowed down, and the birth of the Internet and mobile systems, along with the tsunami of gadgets and other technological achievements and innovations, radically changed people's daily lives. All of this development is the result of the influence of global trends. This includes scientific breakthroughs such as the unmanned Rosetta spacecraft Philae that soft-landed on a comet in November 2014 and the preparation for a manned mission to Mars.

Global trends are objective processes that predetermine the dynamics of any economic system. The hierarchy of global trends changed during the last quarter of the twentieth century, as *globalization* and *democratization* became the two most important and influential trends. Globalization emerged from the maturation of the previously dominant trend, internationalization. Globalization "involves two main features: increasing interdependency and increasing integration. Trade is most closely associated with interdependency while capital flows and investment are most closely associated with integration."[8] The strength of the trend of globalization was multiplied by cutting-edge information technologies, which eventually led to the formation of the global marketplace at the end of the twentieth century (this is discussed in detail in Chapter 5). Globalization as a trend can be understood as a process of involvement among all countries from all continents under one global order, and the GMP functions under the influence of this order. It may be impossible, in fact, to identify a single country of the world as totally separate from the GMP. Nonetheless, some professional firms and experts disagree. For example, in 2006, Morgan Stanley Capital International considered countries of Sub-Saharan Africa and Western Asia to have missed the globalization process. It is true that they are late to catch the train of globalization, but they obviously did not miss it altogether. The positive impact of globalization is obvious, but as with any new phenomenon to which people are not yet accustomed globalization also has effects that can be seen as negative, such as environmental problems, terrorism, cultural clashes, erosion of traditions, and even an influence on people's ethnicity. Nonetheless, the positive impact is unparalleled. Globalization connects all individuals, bringing billions of people the truth about freedom. The growing capabilities of globalization based on information technologies have brought the reality about democratic countries to every corner of the world. No dictatorial regime, whether personal, military, or communist, could stop the spread of information at its national borders. This was the inspiration of democratic rebellions against dictatorships throughout the world, which acted as the tipping point in the collapse of the overwhelming majority of inefficient command economies. Around this time another global trend was peaking in influence—democratization, which of course experiences tremendous resistance and has a variety of paths to realization in different countries. According to a report by the National Intelligence Council of the US:

> By 2015, key countries will have made some headway in building sturdier and more capable democratic institutions. Democratic institutions in Mexico, Argentina, Chile, and Brazil appear poised for continued incremental consolidation. In other countries, crime, public corruption, the spread of poverty, and the failure of governments to redress worsening income inequality will provide fertile ground for populist and authoritarian politicians. Soaring crime rates will contribute to vigilantism and extrajudicial killings by the police. Burgeoning criminal activity—including money laundering, alien smuggling, and narcotics trafficking—could overwhelm some Caribbean countries. Democratization in Cuba will depend upon how and when Fidel Castro passes from the scene.[9]

The confluence of globalization and democratization changed the landscape of the political and economic structures of the world. The subsequent new political and economic reality triggered the birth of several other global trends, which will be discussed in this chapter. At the end of the twentieth century, these trends changed the global order itself. According to the National Intelligence Council:

> All states will confront popular demands for greater participation in politics and attention to civil rights—pressures that will encourage greater democratization and transparency. Twenty-five years ago, less than a third of states were defined as democracies by Freedom House; today more than half of states are considered democracies, albeit with varying combinations of electoral and civil or political rights. The majority of states are likely to remain democracies in some sense over the next 15 years, but the number of new democracies that are likely to develop is uncertain.[10]

The Roots of the Global Trend of Political Disintegration

During the second half of the twentieth century, the influence and momentum of globalization and democratization steadily increased, like a snowball rolling down a hill. Democratization first emerged as a global trend in the eighteenth and nineteenth centuries due to the success of democratic principles in the United States and the democratic ideas and Civil Code of Napoleon, which he and his armies spread across Europe on the tip of their bayonets.[11] These two historical phenomena established examples for democratically oriented political leaders around the world. Democratization was an especially important trend following World War II. Its influence was greatest in Western Europe, Australia, New Zealand, and Japan; the success of these democracies demonstrated to the world the strong correlation between democracy and economic strength, efficiency, and prosperity.

In early 1992, after the failure of the Soviet Union, 15 politically independent countries appeared overnight. All of these countries became members of the United Nations (UN), and all of them eventually joined major economic multilateral institutions. The disintegration of the Soviet Union is the most profound manifestation of the global trend of political disintegration. However, the initial results of this trend were subtler; the Soviet Union's disintegration started to influence the world in an almost invisible way, when dictatorships became weaker under the influence of objective and subjective factors. In 1990, the Socialist Federal Republic of Yugoslavia disintegrated into five countries: the Federal Republic of Yugoslavia; Bosnia and Herzegovina; Macedonia (though its neighbor, Greece, refused to recognize this name); Slovenia; and Croatia. This part of the Balkans was still experiencing the influence of political disintegration when Montenegro left the State Union of Serbia and Montenegro (the successors of the Federal Republic of Yugoslavia) in 2006 and became an independent state. On February 17, 2008, Serbia, under the influence of the same trend, experienced the painful independence of the previously autonomous Serbian province of Kosovo. There are 2.2 million Kosovars, 92 percent of whom are ethnically Albanian. Kosovars have a real opportunity to improve their standard of living and to integrate economically with the global marketplace, and the people of Serbia also benefit. Cooperation in the Western Balkans is reaching a new level: after many years of ethnic and political conflict and uncertainty, a much friendlier relationship between Kosovo and Serbia will prevail. Serbian minorities in Kosovo can play a very important role as a bridge between these two independent states.

In January 1993, another example of the influence of the global trend of political integration took place when Czechoslovakia split through the "Velvet Divorce" into the Czech and Slovak republics. The reach of political disintegration is not limited only to the Soviet Union, Eastern Europe, and the Balkan states, however; it is a trend that directs political and economic processes around the world. Also in 1993, the State of Eritrea declared its independence from Ethiopia after many years of military conflict. In May 2002, after a 27-year-long fight for its independence, the Democratic Republic of Timor-Leste, which had been occupied by Indonesian armed forces, finally became the first new independent country of the new millennium. The global trend of political disintegration has to be understood as a process, not simply the declaration of independence of any new state, which results from the influence of this trend. This trend influences many countries that are still unified and may continue to be unified forever, but they also may not. Strategists cannot ignore the possibility of any new state's appearance or the rebirth of old ones as independent countries, substantially changing the strategic landscape which has to be predicted and strategized.

One of the best examples of this trend as a process is the democratic vote for independence in Quebec. The people of Quebec have already expressed their opinion on the issue of sovereignty through two transparent referendums, which took place in 1980 and 1995. During the first referendum, 40.44 percent of the population voted in favor of pursuing independence from Canada, while 59.56 voted to keep Quebec as a province of Canada. Fifteen years later, by a margin of only 1 percent, supporters of sovereignty lost (49.42 percent) to those who voted to keep Quebec as a province of Canada (50.58 percent). Quebec is still part of Canada, and it may always be. But no one knows what the next referendum will show, if it even takes place. It's certain that Canada, like many other countries, is under the strong influence of the global trend of political disintegration.

The Kingdom of Belgium is still a unified country, but at the beginning of the twenty-first century, the gap between the provinces of Wallonia and Flanders is widening, not narrowing. When on June 17, 2008, the new Benelux treaty was signed with Luxembourg and the Netherlands, on behalf of Belgium, it was signed also by ministers-president of Flanders, the Walloon region, the German-speaking community in Belgium, and the Brussels Capital Region. This clearly indicates that even in the international arena, Belgium does not present a singular unified voice.[12] This kingdom may continue its existence as a federation, but maybe not. Strategists cannot ignore this. It may come as a surprise to many, but the same situation exists in 18 other regions within European states. For example, in September 2014, an important referendum occurred in Scotland; those who voted for Scotland's independence from the United Kingdom comprised "only" 44.7 percent, unlike those who won with 55.3 percent and voted for Scotland to remain part of the United Kingdom. Strategists have to evaluate future outcomes on the same issues. Some separatist leaders of the rich northern region of Italy would like independence from the less economically developed south of the country. Leaders of this movement even established a name for the northern part of Italy: the "Republic of Padania."[13] Strategists should not totally ignore this; nor should they ignore the separatist movements in the Basque Country and in Catalonia, two of the most industrialized regions of Spain. Another European country, the United Kingdom of Denmark, is experiencing similar difficulties with Greenland, an autonomous country within the kingdom that is many times bigger than the mainland, as well as the largest island in the world. Since 1979, Greenland has sought more self-ruling authority in an amicable process, and, since 2003, the Danish-Greenlandic Commission has supervised it. This commission has recommended increasing the foreign-policy rights of Greenland, which already has its own national symbols. As a result of a referendum on Greenland's autonomy, which took place in November 2008 and in which 75.54 percent voted "yes," the Greenlandic government started to control police forces, the coast guard, judicial systems, and part of shares of all major national resources of this giant island. Again, strategists always have to monitor the potentials of these processes and remain neutral.

Similar tendencies are under way in several other European countries such as Georgia, Ukraine, and Moldova, among others, as well as in some Asian countries. The majority of these movements in Europe unfold through peaceful and democratic means. However, in Russia and Asia, these processes often occur outside of voting booths. This was the case in Chechnya, where separatists in the 1990s practically declared war on Russia and especially on neighboring provinces like Dagestan. Violence is a major means employed by similar separatist movements, such as that of the Tigers of Tamil, who seek the creation of their own country—Tamil Eelam—on the island of Sri Lanka. Two provinces within the country of Georgia, Abkhazia and South Ossetia, as well as the Transnistrian Moldovan

Republic, have for years operated as independent states and seek official international recognition. For these three regions, the recognition of Kosovo is a very promising example. All of these processes and military conflicts can be seen not only as separatist movements but also as processes under the influence of the global trend of political disintegration. This approach is more accurate for strategists, who are not taking part in any of these conflicts and must evaluate both scenarios: all of these provinces can be part of unified countries or will become independent states. This is not the approach for politicians, but it is the appropriate mindset for strategists.

The result of this trend's influence can be seen in the increasing number of countries around the world. The League of Nations, which was established by the Treaty of Versailles between 1919 and 1920, had 42 charter countries. The United Nations had 51 founding member-states that established this organization in 1945. Ten years later, the UN already had 76 member states. In 1965, there were 117 members. In 1990, 159 countries were members of the UN; in 2000 the figure was 189, and as of January 1, 2008, the UN has 193 member states.[14] Due to this dynamic, strategists always have to analyze the continuation of this global trend's influence, despite what political leaders may wish.

The transition from dictatorship or command economies to democracy is not necessarily a smooth process; a totalitarian system is never instantly swapped for democracy and a free-market economy. The process ebbs and flows, and can even reverse itself, but the one constant is usually increasing economic freedom. The former Soviet Republic of Turkmenistan offers an interesting example. Following the disintegration of the Soviet Union, all 15 former Soviet republics took their own path away from the Soviet system. The Baltic States, Estonia, Latvia, and Lithuania, which were part of the Soviet Union for only about 50 years, immediately embraced democracy and economic freedom with much success. Other countries, such as Kazakhstan, Moldova, Russia, and Ukraine, immediately began developing foundations for democracy and economic freedom, but with great difficulty. These newly independent countries straddled the line between anarchy and oligarchic capitalism, where the rule of law is often subjugated to the personal interests of a superrich minority. Countries such as Belarus, Azerbaijan, Uzbekistan, and Turkmenistan replaced the communist party's dictatorship with personal dictatorships. In Turkmenistan, the leader of the communist party, Saparmurat Atayevich Niyazov, was "elected" president by people who never experienced anything even resembling democracy, in a country that had never experienced independence. Turkmenistan's economy, with some of the richest natural gas and oil reserves in the world, was converted into Niyazov's personal empire. He changed his name to Turkmenbashi, which means "father of the Turkmens," ordered stamps from the US with his portrait on them, put his profile on currency and coins, replaced monuments to Lenin in every poor village with monuments of himself, renamed the major seaport after himself from Krasnovodsk to Turkmenbashi, made the birthday of his mother a national holiday, and made a book of his poetry required reading for all students. In 1995, "Turkmenbashi" declared Turkmenistan's neutrality, maintaining an equal distance from his neighbors Russia, China, and Iran as well as the US, and preventing economic activity with all of them. He firmly held on to power until December 2006, when he unexpectedly died of cardiac arrest. After a brief struggle for power, a medical doctor and minister of health under Turkmenbashi, 49-year-old Gurbanguly Berdymukhammedov, was elected president. Cautiously, he started to lead the country out of the ruins of Turkmenbashi's personal dictatorship and somewhat closer into the democratic world. This process is extremely complicated, and every move made by the new president sends multiple messages to allies and enemies both foreign and domestic. The many business leaders who are interested in Turkmenistan (and countries in relatively similar situations, such as Azerbaijan, Venezuela, Saudi Arabia, and China) must be able to sift through the multifaceted and subtle messages from President Berdymukhammedov. One of his first moves was to open Internet cafes with free, unlimited access to the web. He reestablished the Academy of Sciences of Turkmenistan, which Turkmenbashi had abolished, and lengthened the required years of schooling from nine to ten. However, the mass media remains in the hands of the state, but the president also appointed a third-year university student to be editor-in-chief of a major youth newspaper. The president gave the order to purchase 19,000 computers for schools and universities and has already given all universities access to the Internet. All of this took place within the first six months of his presidency. But when asked by the president of Columbia University in September 2007 if he planned on dissolving the legacy of Turkmenbashi, he replied ambiguously: "Turkmenbashi is our history." At this pace, it looks like the legacy of Turkmenbashi will be similar to that of Mao in contemporary China, whose portraits and books are prevalent in mainland China.

The transition to democracy varies by country, but is never easy and straightforward; some temporary back steps can always occur. That is why the political risk of investment is so much higher in EMCs than in countries with long democratic traditions. While it may be surprising to some, 65 percent of people in the world actually live in partially free or totally free societies. The majority of people not living in at least partially free societies are in Africa and the Middle East, where huge democratic changes and secularism have also been under way since December 2010, especially in Tunisia, Egypt, and Libya and practically every country in this international region.

Regionalization as a Global Trend

Cardinal innovations, as well as scientific and technological revolutions, during the second half of the twentieth century have led to strategic structural shifts in the world economy. This first initiated the industrialization of the world economy and, later, the development of the post-industrial, service-based economy. At the beginning of the twenty-first century, the world economy has begun a transition to a knowledge-based economy with the strategic aim to increase economic growth in developed countries; their international regional economic blocs required stable and innovative sources of raw materials and energy resources, including those from abroad, since the majority of these countries could not sustain their growth by domestic natural resources. Eventually, this situation also became relevant to EMCs that achieved a relatively high level of economic maturity and began to experience a shortage of energy and raw materials. Increasing inequality in economic development between different regions of the world economy led to a new international division of labor. Growth in developed and emerging market countries could not be sustained without the expansion of key industries related to the exploration, extraction, and enrichment of raw materials in developing and underdeveloped countries. This led to a huge strategic investment in economically underdeveloped territories, which were never before part of the world economy and were very often uninhabited, lacking basic infrastructure and modern production facilities. The allocation of investment and the development of assets in these areas began a large-scale transfer of raw materials to these newly industrializing regions. This large-scale economic shift could not and still cannot be efficient without a new regionalized form of interaction between science, technology, innovations, businesses, governments, and society within the legal framework of environmental protection, which became part of the core societal values and predetermined factors of strategic interests.

The extraction of hydrocarbon raw materials in the deserts of the Arabian Peninsula and Central Asia, in the permafrost of northern Siberia, and on the shelf of the World Ocean, as well as the development of deposits of nonferrous metals, diamonds, and coal above the Arctic Circle, forests in the tropical zone and the Arctic taiga, and fallow and virgin lands in experimental agriculture zones, all required regionalized equipment and technologies. This technological specialization according to regional conditions is a simple way of understanding the global trend of technological regionalization. In addition to the natural difficulties of exploiting resources in these environments, the fact that they are primarily located in developing and emerging market countries with insufficient infrastructures, poorly studied geological features, low population density, and shortages of skilled labor created requirements for special strategies of economic acceleration with specific economic solutions and regionally suitable environmental and social programs.

Machinery and technology that is extremely efficient in one particular region may be barely functional in another. For example, innovative technologies and equipment have been implemented in the eastern part of Russia in the brown coal deposits of the Kansko-Achinskiy and Ekibastuz (located in northeastern Kazakhstan) basins. This technology has achieved labor productivity 20 to 25 times higher than the national industry averages of these countries. However, if these technologies were implemented in any mine in Europe, Ukraine, or almost any other world region, they would not operate at their full capacity; they would be inefficient, and strategists should be aware of this. Geological conditions in a particular region—the reserves of natural resources like minerals, timber, and energy—largely determine technological development. This phenomenon is a result of the influence of regionalization, the global trend that dates from the second half of the twentieth century, but that is still very powerful today. It is important to underline that regionalization is definitely not restricted to technology and innovations used in processes of production, engineering, construction mechanics, etc. Science itself has also been influenced by this global trend, leading to the development of new theoretical disciplines like regional geology and regional geomorphology, regional sociology, regional economics, and later popular regional strategy, among other fields of study. Regionalization also has very important implications for environmental protection and revitalization.

Economic development in the Arctic zones of Scandinavia, Russia, Canada, and Alaska was particularly influenced by the trend of regionalization. These territories required specialized technology, such as frost-resistant concrete for the construction of roads, dams, and hydroelectric facilities, among many other innovations.

Region-specific strategies to economic and technological development tremendously influenced social studies and social development in areas of new economic activities, as well as the regional integration of these territories following the establishment of regional governments, unions, etc. New technologies in aircraft construction, such as a new engine that allowed direct flights between geographically remote regions, became the basis for new extra-regional economic cooperation, which substantially improved the efficiency of the GMP. Companies began to gear their products toward regional cultures, climates, and economic and business conditions and opportunities. Strategies focused on the regionalization of products increased company market share and the efficiency of regional economies. According to Professor Lin Sien Chia of the Institute of Asia-Pacific Studies:

> The addition of more powerful engines to Boeing 747-200 series in the 1990s meant that non-stop operations were possible between Southeast Asian points and Europe ... Additional non-stop options were feasible following the introduction of the Boeing 747-400 series (for example, between Bangkok and Singapore and Europe overflying the Persian Gulf). These technological developments provided scope for the region's carriers to pursue expansionist strategies and broaden their connections both within the region and with Northeast Asia. The increased regional feeder links gave airlines the potential to use key airports as hubs to mitigate weaknesses in Southeast Asia's route network.[15]

This global trend, which extended international business to new economic territories, was a topic of great interest among global leaders, strategists, and scholars, who often referred to it as regionalism. According to Shaun Breslin, Richard Higgot, and Ben Rosamund, scholars who have written extensively on regionalism:

> Early discussions about regionalism emerged from three primary sources. The first was a political-normative question about the sustainability of the nation-state as a vehicle for effective and peaceful human governance. The second was the growth and gradual formalization of the social sciences, particularly in the United States. The third, of course, was the appearance of regional integration schemes.[16]

Some mistakenly interpret the trend of regionalization as the opposite of globalization. It is not. Regionalization is one of several processes *resulting from* globalization. Regional blocs, regional economic unions, and free-trade zones and areas of accelerated strategic development play a very important role in the improvement of the GMP.

The influence of regionalization and strategies oriented on this trend has changed social and economic processes, especially in developed and emerging market countries, and has motivated innovations in governance and management systems. Akio Morita, the founder and former president of Sony, the first global Japanese company, coined the term *glocalization* to explain the relationship between regional management and governance in the global marketplace.[17] Corporate leaders operate and strategize on both levels simultaneously. The continuous improvement of strategic management systems and governmental practice in collaboration with other processes under the influence of globalization and democratization eventually led to an offspring of the modern global trend—regional decentralization. This trend is related to the decentralization of managerial functions of national governments to regional and local authorities. Dictatorships always concentrate and centralize most power in the hands of one ruler or authoritarian body. When dictatorships fail, new democratically elected leaders focus on strategic national issues, mostly preoccupied with the democratization of society, and begin to delegate many managerial functions, beginning with operational ones and then regional and then local authorities.

Like privatization, while the global trend of regional decentralization has been vital in the GEM, it was used much earlier in the developed world. This particular trend originated in France. Despite the socialist nature of the party of François Mitterrand, who won the French presidential election in 1981, his strategy to improve the efficiency of public administration and the national economy took place through the transfer of many national functions to provincial authorities. In order to do so, he formed the Ministry of the Interior and Decentralization. Mitterrand's decentralization strategy was based on his belief in the need "to develop regional economic development strategies, based upon a regionalized economic plan."[18] According to Professor Michael Keating:

> The French governmental system comprises a mixture of central and local power. The Socialist Government came to power pledged to decentralization. This is being achieved through a series of laws. Yet separating central and local affairs has raised major problems. There are contradictions within the Socialists' ideology with regard to decentralization and the implementation of the programme has been slowed down.[19]

Outside of the developed world, especially in those countries under authoritarian rulers and command economies, all governing and managerial functions are the responsibility of the national government, which is located in the country's capital city. After the fall of the dictator and/or liberalization of the economy and establishment of initial free-market conditions, these functions are then transferred to regional, local, and even municipal authorities. It is important that leaders and strategists of foreign companies that were active in the country during the dictatorship are aware of this trend. Those who ignore the implications of this trend and work exclusively with national or federal governments will suffer as a result. Increasing economic freedom does not necessarily weaken national and federal governments but it definitely improves and empowers local communities and entrepreneurs, as well as regional and local authorities. Strategists of foreign companies should pay special attention to the values and interests of local communities in which they do business. Offering assistance on local social issues can be a relatively inexpensive way to create an environment friendly to foreign businesses and to avoid potential conflicts. The Nobel Laureate in Economics Joseph Stiglitz argued that local communities were the "fourth pillar" of successful development strategies, in addition to markets, government, and individuals.[20] One successful example of this is the practice of Eli Lilly, a leading pharmaceutical company that always has offices in the capital city of the countries in which it bases its activities, as well as in the particular region in which Eli Lilly invests, especially in EMCs. The office in the capital city is responsible for the company's national strategy, while the regional office implements regional applications of this strategy through sales and the development of relationships with regional and municipal communities and authorities. It is vital for certain industries, like pharmaceuticals, to have a good relationship with local and regional authorities and communities, as the quality of health care is usually a crucial community issue and can vary a great deal regionally and even locally.

For strategists and economists, the evaluation and measurement of the practical realization of the influence of global trends is always a subject of opportunities and necessity. Regional decentralization does not have a widely accepted index to measure its impact as a global trend, although scholars have made several attempts to quantify it. In 1999 Professor Christine Kearney created the Decentralization Index, which measures "the assignment of fiscal, political, and administrative responsibilities to lower levels of government."[21] The index is based on the following nine dimensions: government structure, selection of regional executive, selection of local executive, override authority, revenue-raising authority, revenue sharing, authority for education, authority for infrastructure, and authority for policing.[22]

Regional decentralization has occurred in practically all EMCs. According to the UN Development Program, there are three challenges that arise in processes of regional decentralization:

> First, most countries are implementing reforms on an ad hoc basis, and the legal framework for decentralization is incomplete or inconsistent. Second, fiscal decentralization remains very much a work in progress. Fiscal decentralization reform is characterized by the following: one-off or piecemeal approach; lack of logical sequencing; unclear assignment of expenditure responsibilities between the different tiers of the government; ineffective local tax management; inadequate fiscal-equalization mechanisms; and inadequate regulation of local borrowing. Third, attracting and retaining professional and qualified employees in local governments continues to be a challenge. Local governments are expected to carry out decentralization, taking on new responsibilities and providing quality services. However, personnel management and employment conditions at the subnational levels have long been neglected.[23]

Indonesia's decentralization strategy introduced in 2001 is the best example after France's decentralization strategy. According to Kazuhisa Matsui, a senior research fellow from the Institute of Developing Economies of the Japan External Organization:

> Decentralization [in Indonesia] has transferred not only administrative authority but also many new vested interests from the center to regions. Local governments have become more extensive economic actors in regional economies. Regional economic actors now compete actively for such vested interests and have missed the opportunity to create market-friendly regional economies.[24]

Analysis of the consequences of this decentralization, including the example of Indonesia, leads to the clear conclusion that a properly done decentralization of power, which used to concentrate unnecessary functions in the hands of central authority, always produces an increase in democracy, economic freedom, and efficiency of national economy, and ends in the improvement of quality of life.

The Regional Economic Integration Trend in the Strategizing Process

Globalization and liberalization of international economic relations created a new environment for politically independent countries. Orientation on economic isolation and autarchy lead some nations to economic failure and declining standards of living. Countries that recently obtained their independence often attempt self-isolation—and suffer the inevitably negative consequences. In the euphoria of their fresh independence, political leaders often make the mistake of cutting not only political but even economic ties with their former dominant or sister countries. However, I hope political leaders will learn from experience and past examples, and the naïve concepts of autarchy and self-isolation will be quickly replaced by international economic cooperation.

Transnational economic cooperation and cross-border trade, which have increased on a *global* scale since the beginning of the 1980s, later, during the early 1990s, developed rapidly on a *regional* scale. The beacon for all countries that sought to improve regional cooperation was the European Communities, established in 1967 by the merger of the European Steel and Coal Community, the European Atomic Energy Community, and the European Economic Community. In fact, modern European economic integration began much earlier, when in 1958 Belgium, Luxembourg, and the Netherlands formed the Benelux Economic Union, which would be the prototype for future European integration. Benelux was formed in 1958 on the basis of the Benelux Customs Union, which had been operational since 1948. In the twenty-first century, Benelux is still very much alive. In June 2008, the leaders of these three countries signed a new Benelux treaty. This agreement is no longer restricted to issues of economic cooperation. It also focuses on the harmonization of policies on justice and law enforcement. The success of European strategy toward integration and its increasing number of member-states inspired other countries to achieve a new level of economic efficiency through regional economic integration or reintegration with neighboring countries.

Regional economic integration is most successful when it includes countries of different levels of economic development and other basic economic factors such as labor and natural resources (and especially energy). Asymmetry in strategy of regional economic cooperation creates the incentives for tighter economic and business connections. The example of North American economic cooperation is a clear illustration of this point. The high unemployment in Mexico (relative to the United States and Canada) of people with a strong work ethic was one of the reasons for the national leaders of North America to develop intracontinental economic cooperation. Another motivating strategic factor was the different allocation of natural resources and the asymmetric consumption of these resources among these three countries. For example, oil resources and oil consumption are distributed disproportionately in North America. It may come as a surprise to many that the largest and second-largest exporters of oil to the US are Canada and Mexico, respectively. The technological advancement of the United States was the basis for the beginning of the economic strategy of industrial cross-border cooperation with Mexico in 1965, when the US started to build production facilities in Mexican territory, using a duty-free regime for the delivery of equipment and raw materials and employing Mexicans. This cross-border regional cooperation was called the Border Industrialization Program, or the *Maquiladoras* Program. The success of this program provided support for President Bill Clinton, when, in 1993, he brought it through Congress and signed the North American Free Trade Agreement (NAFTA). This trilateral treaty between the United States, Canada, and Mexico was developed during the time of his predecessor, President George H.W. Bush.

After the two strategically successful precedents of NAFTA and the EU, countries from other parts of the world followed suit. The level of intensity of economic ties in different regional economic agreements varies, but the strategic concept is always the same. In 1991, formal multilateral regional economic cooperation began between the countries of the south cone of South America—Argentina, Brazil, Paraguay, and Uruguay. Later, other South American countries joined this regional economic and trade agreement, known as Mercosur (or Mercosul in Brazil), with varying statuses of membership, including Venezuela (a full member as of 2012), Bolivia, Chile, Colombia, Ecuador, and Peru (associate members) and two state observers (New Zealand and Mexico). In Asia, the Association of Southeast Asian Nations (ASEAN), which was established in 1967, began to intensify the economic component of its cooperation only in the 1990s. Its members include Brunei Darussalam, Cambodia, Indonesia, Laos, Malaysia, Philippines, Singapore, Thailand, Vietnam, and the mostly isolated country of Myanmar, which started some economic reform in 2014 and recently in 2015 declared its intent to open its first stock market. An interesting development is that ASEAN has begun to sign and participate in bilateral economic agreements between ASEAN as a whole and other non-member-countries.

Several African regional economic unions have intensified ties between member-countries, such as the Common Market for Eastern and Southern Africa (COMESA), which was established in 1994 and in 2015 has 19 member states. Another African economic bloc, the Economic Community of West African States (ECOWAS), was established much earlier in 1975 with its own parliament, the Assembly of People of the Community. It was rejuvenated, and its 15 member-countries began to expand their mutual trade and economic ties. The same dynamic occurred in the Caribbean Community (CARICOM), which was formed in 1973 (originally as the Caribbean Community and Common Market). As of 2015, CARICOM has 15 full members, 15 associate members and 7 observers, which all unified due to mutual objectives related to economic efficiency and improving standards of living.

It is interesting that republics of the former Soviet Union that were so eager to secede from the Soviet empire later in the 1990s established several regional economic organizations, like the Commonwealth of Independent States (CIS), which is based on a relatively loose agreement, and the GUAM Group, which includes Georgia, Ukraine, Azerbaijan, and Moldova and two state observers, Latvia and Turkey. These member-states signed an economic cooperation treaty in 1996. Interestingly, the member-countries of GUAM are also members of CIS, together with six other countries,[25] but the activity of GUAM (if any) is mostly unknown. In December 2014, the GUAM group switched its working language from Russian to English.

The influence of globalization has increased the geographic scale of regional economic cooperation and trade. Reflecting this trend, the Asia-Pacific Economic Cooperation (APEC) became "the premier forum for facilitating economic growth, cooperation, trade and investment in the Asia-Pacific region."[26] In 1995, during a meeting in Osaka, Japan, APEC adopted the framework for the intensification of ties in the biggest economic region in the world, "the Osaka Action Agenda (OAA), which provides a framework for ... trade and investment liberalization, business facilitation and sectoral activities, underpinned by policy dialogues, economic and technical cooperation."[27] As of 2015, APEC has 21 member-economies including Russia, the US, Japan, China (as well as Hong Kong), among others. No one regional bloc can compete with APEC, not only in the number of countries but also in terms of the economic power of its member-states, which account for 41 percent of the world's population, 56 percent of GWP, and about 49 percent of global trade.[28]

APEC is only one example of the expansion of regional economic integration in the global marketplace. Regional trade blocs throughout the world are beginning to evolve into huge regional trade and economic areas. An obvious example is the proposed Free Trade Area of the Americas, which would extend NAFTA and Mercosur, usurping the smaller regional blocs, like the Central American Free Trade Agreement (CAFTA), as well as bilateral and multilateral agreements among blocs and between blocs and individual countries (like the Dominican Republic-CAFTA free-trade agreement). In Asia, several regional blocs and individual countries have begun to formulate development strategy for the South Asia Free Trade Agreement (SAFTA). This agreement provides the legal framework for another mega-zone, which includes about 1.5 billion people. A similar trend is occurring in Africa, where the previously mentioned African trade blocs and economic agreements are in the early stages of converging into a continental free-trade area of Africa. This enlargement of the territorial and economic scale of economic integration is primarily the result of globalization, democratization, and regionalization. Countries involved in large-scale regional cooperation tear down economic barriers for each other and eliminate most custom duties, tariffs, and quotas, allowing the free movement of all basic economic factors such as raw materials, manpower, and capital as well as goods and services. Businesses in these zones and areas also benefit from the harmonization of domestic legal frameworks, unified standards, and technological requirements. At the same time, companies that originate in these mega-areas receive preferential treatment (de facto and de jure), which leads to unequal conditions for companies from other parts of the world. This is a major concern for the World Trade Organization. The strategic solution to this issue is already in regular use—intercontinental agreements, such as the signing of the framework agreement between Mercosur and the European Union and their member-countries. "Regionalization for countries and for firms is characterized by preferential trading arrangements among countries and a regional network approach to resources, markets, and organization for firms." [29]

Regional economic integration and reintegration is a major trend of increasing efficiency of the global marketplace if decisions about regional organizations' creation and development are economic and social by nature and not mostly political. Otherwise, member-countries will get mostly problems, and unions and economic blocs established without clear, mutual economic efficiency will not have a long future. The dialectic connections between global and regional integration will be on national and multinational strategic agendas throughout the twenty-first century. (Particular regional economic blocs and areas and their strategic economic and business conditions will be discussed in detail later in the book.)

The Trend of Privatization

One basic characteristic of a dictatorship is absolute and complete domination by the ruling body or individual dictator over the politics, culture, and economics of a society, which will distort its moral values. Economic domination is generally what leads directly to the collapse of dictatorships and command economies (a detailed analysis of this process can be found in Chapter 6). Absence of effective strategy and poor management of nationalized state-owned companies and the complete controlling centralization of an economy do not generate in the long run the revenue necessary to control, placate, or appease the population. When the dictatorship falls, the nascent democratic government faces a dilemma. In general, the leadership lacks the necessary experience and knowledge to efficiently run large national companies and is incapable of doing so while also focusing on the creation of democratic institutions. The leaders of these countries find themselves obliged to control the majority of a country's enterprises, most of which are on the edge of bankruptcy or barely profitable. The budgets of these countries are very limited, making it difficult for democratically elected leaders to fulfill their pledges to improve the standard of living of their citizens. The transfer of ownership of state-controlled companies to private hands—privatization—is the only option to increase national economic efficiency, and market capitalization, and improve the fiscal situation of the national government and the quality of life of its citizens. In the early 1990s, most foreign direct investment in EMCs was drawn by opportunities generated from the privatization of state-owned companies. According to Professor Bruce Wallin of Northeastern University:

> [T]he goal of privatization as contracting out is usually reduced cost, and often greater flexibility. The argument usually suggests:
>
> - government bureaucracy is inefficient and is not driven by the threat of competition, thus raising cost and lowering performance, reducing efficiency;

- civil service and public employee union contracts limit flexibility and ability to reward performance, and to punish those who don't perform, or reassign personnel;
- privatization eliminates corruption;

Critics of privatization posit:

- government workers have expertise;
- government exists to promote goals beyond low cost;
- the need to lower bids may lead to reduced service;
- government loses direct control, becoming dependent on private providers;
- "legal corruption," in the form of campaign contributions, occurs.[30]

Privatization is not a process that is restricted to the emerging and developing business and economic world. In fact, the above points were used to argue for the privatization of public services in the state of Massachusetts. Some of these arguments require further explanation. For example, it is mentioned that privatization eliminates corruption. This can be understood in the following way: when companies transfer to private hands, corruption inside companies (between executives and employees) is decreased, compared with the level of corruption while a company is state owned. However, it is important to realize that during the process of privatization itself, corruption typically skyrockets.

Unfortunately, in reality, the process of privatization is structurally very vulnerable to corruption. Typically, the bureaucrats in charge of the privatization receive modest salaries that are disproportionate to the market value of the government assets that they are bringing to the market through auction or privatization tenders. Some entrepreneurs are more than willing to offer bribes worth more than most bureaucrats have been paid for their entire career of public service in order to purchase government assets at a reduced price. This is why a substantial part of state-owned assets transfer into the hands of private entrepreneurs for a fraction of the company's market value, while the bureaucrats in charge of the privatization retire early with an unusually healthy bank account. In many cases governments actually receive only a small part of the already discounted price from the private buyer. And governments rarely enforce the agreements made with private buyers. There are some instances in which ownership of state assets was transferred to private entrepreneurs without any payment ever being delivered.

Privatization as a global trend became most powerful and practically useful, mostly during the time of the initial maturity of EMCs. As a major economic phenomenon and powerful instrument for improving the efficiency of national economies, privatization began in 1979 when Margaret Thatcher (1925–2013) became the first female prime minister in the history of Great Britain. Her main strategic objective was to improve the country's dismal economic situation and to increase employment. Privatization was central to Thatcher's strategy; she chose her close associate David Young, who later obtained a cabinet position, to oversee the process. Under his guidance, almost all companies of huge industries were successfully privatized, including coal, iron, steel, gas, electricity and water supply, real estate, trucking, railways, airlines, and telecommunications. Young did an outstanding job, and on average, privatized companies decreased cost production by 30 to 33 percent. Shipyards were able to accomplish the same jobs in the same time, but with 10 percent fewer cost expenses.[31] In 1993, speaking with Lord David Young, I asked what could be the major characteristic of privatization and his answer was very straightforward: "economic intensification and corruption."

Lack of strategy, poorly managed privatization, extreme corruption and the outright theft of government assets often provoke future governments to renationalize private but formerly state-owned assets. Although the impulse is understandable, it harms the economy. It results in low investment ratings of the country from all major international rating agencies, which leads to a great reduction of foreign investment and business activity with a following decrease of employment and efficiency. Privatization also has to be understood as an initial stage of the capitalization of EMC. The increasing capitalization is one of the major and most important results of privatization, together with the development of private and public ownership of companies that were once state owned. In general, by the mid-1990s, about 75 percent of state-owned companies in the GEM were privatized. As a result three-quarters of the GDP of the GEM was from the input of private companies. The conversion of state-owned companies to private ownership in EMCs has made the transition from state domination to economic freedom almost irreversible in the GEM. Even attempts to increase the role of the state through the creation of private-state partnerships cannot be seen as a direct analogy of state ownership during dictatorial regimes. The economic nature of private-state corporations is much different. They work for profit, and tax revenue from these profits goes toward increasing citizens' standard of living, not just military expenditures. These processes of course could not be successful without strong public oversight (like public accounting bodies, and increasing the legislative branch's role in financial issues) and transparency. This decreases corruption or any impulse by government officials to "privatize" revenue of these corporations. The last point is important to clarify. Due to the issue of corruption, a lot of governmentally connected people with deep pockets try during privatization to privatize not a company as a whole, but particularly its profits. This means that potential buyers try to get a company below the market price—even those that were profitable before privatization. This is exactly what happened, for example, with the privatization of Norilsk Nickel, a company with more than $1 billion of annual profit prior to privatization (see Chapter 5). Another example occurred during 2002, when relatives of Bulgarian officials attempted to underpay for the privatization of Bulgartabac Holding AD, a state-owned manufacturer of cigarettes and tobacco, which covers 85 percent of the Bulgarian market.[32] This holding consisted of 22 companies, which employed about 300,000 people, mostly Turkish minorities, in a country with a population of less than 8 million.[33]

The initial stages of privatization in EMCs typically proceed in very difficult conditions. On the one hand, state-owned companies have to be privatized, but on the other hand, the overwhelming majority of people cannot buy even a medium-sized company, thus beginning a tsunami of corruption. It is not hard to imagine how absurd it sounds to offer to the general population, who for generations could barely afford enough food and clothing to subsist, the opportunity to purchase multimillion-dollar enterprises. In EMCs, unlike in developed countries, privatization generally goes through the following stages:

1. Employees and the general population receive some of the shares of state-owned companies for free, according to their experience, input, and years working for the company. Another version is that every citizen receives a certificate (voucher) for a certain portion of national wealth, without any distinction between people who spent their entire life working for the country, or a child who was born a day before the declaration of privatization. Both ways have their pluses and minuses. This stage can be called *mass privatization*. Typically, foreigners are not allowed to be part of this stage. However, they can participate on the secondary market by buying shares of companies or vouchers from citizens who get them for free from the state.

2. The second stage is usually conducted a few years later, when the country has gone through the initial stages of development of market-oriented reforms and the middle class. It typically begins once some domestic entrepreneurs have enough initial capital to buy properties, and/or are capable of getting credit and loans from banks. This stage is usually called cash privatization. In this period of privatization, foreign investors actually get access to the primary market of company's shares.

Privatization is a complex and very important process for countries progressing from a command economy to a free market society. While it is vital to transfer state-owned assets to the private sector in order to prevent regression to a dictatorship, this is not the main objective of privatization and it is not always a successful strategy to stop some ambitious official with this kind of attempt. Strategically, privatization should result in intensification of the national economy on the basis of a net creation of jobs, the establishment of a new middle class of business owners and entrepreneurs, the creation of a competitive atmosphere between private and state-owned businesses, and a prevention of the appearance of a large wealth gap. The strategic transition from a state-controlled economy to a private economy in EMCs (whereby more than 50 percent of GDP is produced by private or mostly private companies) takes three to seven years. A successful privatization will go a long way toward solidifying social and economic progress. The extent to which an EMC has privatized its economy is one of several indicators of its maturity and the quality of the strategizing process.

Mass Privatization

In EMCs, during the initial stages of market-oriented reforms and capitalization, due to the general population's lack of purchasing power, governments cannot simply auction off state assets. Instead, what the government owns (anywhere from 10 to 100 percent) can be distributed among employees of state-owned companies based on the tenure and position of each employee. Often, executives of the company get an additional 10 to 15 percent of ownership, contingent on the development and implementation of a program to increase the productivity and efficiency of the company once it is privatized during a one- or two-year period. This has generally been strategically wrong and an ineffective means of motivation, as executives usually leave the company or sell their shares shortly after privatization. Of course, the government tries to limit special executive shares by time and other constraints to buy or sell shares, but with the mass scale of this privatization, and the strong atmosphere of corruption, it is difficult to control, monitor, and especially to enforce regulations in practice.

An alternative first stage of privatization in EMCs is to distribute a part of state-owned property equally among all citizens, regardless of age, position, or even employment status. This was the method used by the Russian Federation. On September 1, 1992, every living citizen received a voucher with a face value of 10,000 rubles. Unfortunately, due to the lack of strategy and following high inflation and poor management of the privatization process, within a couple of months people had no faith in the vouchers, and many threw them away or exchanged them for bottles of vodka that were worth roughly 100 rubles at the time. Most Russians were extremely pessimistic about the future. Although the vouchers represented a means to future ownership of state assets, most people were more concerned with their immediate well-being and survival. Also, people tried to sell vouchers through any means available because they were valid for only one year. In reality the expiration date was prolonged for a few months, but this did not change the situation and was one more proof of the absence of strategy. Some entrepreneurs (many of questionable backgrounds) wisely, either honestly or on the basis of initially stolen money, collected hundreds or even thousands of these vouchers, which most people thought were worthless. This class of nouveau riche was later always ready to oppose any further reforms and even to support the permanent implementation of an oligarchic system.

During the next stage of mass privatization (the "voucher tenders"), first priority was given to voucher holders to purchase the assets of state-owned companies. In some countries, the vouchers applied to specific companies, while in others they applied to all regional or national state assets. This gave entrepreneurs who had collected thousands of vouchers the ability to amass huge portfolios of state assets from voucher tenders. It is also the origin of the unprecedented disparities between the rich and poor in many EMCs. The final stage of the process of mass privatization is known as the open tenders and biddings. Typically, citizens who already held state vouchers, shares of the company, or were employees of the privatizing company participate in these tenders. Outsiders and foreigners are not allowed to participate in the initial stages of tenders and biddings, but they can buy companies or shares of privatized companies from owners who obtained their ownership at these tenders. This basic structure of mass privatization took place during the first half of the 1990s in Czechoslovakia, Bulgaria, Romania, and some other emerging markets of Europe, in the so-called transitional economies.[34] Table 7.2 shows the mass privatization programs in Central and Eastern Europe and the CIS in greater detail.

Cash Privatization

Mass privatization, above and beyond all objectives mentioned earlier, was a simple and practical way for many countries to build initial capital markets. However, according to

Table 7.2 Mass Privatization Programs in Central and Eastern Europe and the CIS

Country	*Shares in Waves or Continuous Issue*	*Vouchers Bearer, Tradable, or Non-tradable*	*Investment in PIFs Allowed, Encouraged, or Compulsory*	*Independent Fund Managers or Self-managed Funds*
Albania (1995)	C	B	E	I
Armenia (1994)	C	B	A	I
Belarus (1995)	C	B	E	S
Bulgaria (1995)	W	N	E	S
Czech Rep. (1992)	W	N	E	I
Estonia (1993)	C	T	A	I
Georgia (1995)	C	N/A	A	
Kazakstan (1994)	W	N	C	I
Kyrgyzstan (1994)	C	B	A	I
Larvia (1994)	C	T	A	
Lithuania (1993)	C	N	A	I
Moldova (1994)	W	N	E	I
Poland (1995)	W	T	C	I
Romania (1992)	C	B	C	I
Romania (1995)	W	N	A	Tbd
Russia (1992)	C	B	E	S
Slovak Republic (1992)	W	N	E	S
Slovenia (1994)	C	N	A	I
Ukraine (1995)	C	N	A	S

Estrin, S. and Stone, R. "A Taxonomy of Mass Privatization." *Transition*, vol 7, nos. 11–12.

Zuzana Fungacova of the Center for Economic Research and Graduate Education–Economics Institute, "the functioning of capital markets in mass-privatization countries would seem to lag the development of other transition economies, which we consider to be the price for establishing capital markets only as a kind of 'by-product' of mass privatization."[35] The thousands of new owners who appeared after mass privatization became a new class of investors and developers after a few years. They were eager to pay for companies and production facilities during the next stage of privatization—cash privatization. In many cases the new private owners are restricted from raising prices of goods or services that are used by domestic consumers or producers. This was the case in the 1998 privatization of Telebras, the state-owned telephone system of Brazil, and of Israeli state-owned gas companies in 2006.

The transition from centralized economies dominated by state-owned monopolies to the free market is obviously not immediate. This period is often characterized by a decline in production as state control wanes but enterprises are not yet privatized, and it offers huge investment opportunities for entrepreneurs and companies from developed countries. Many domestic companies are so strapped for cash that they do not even have enough operational capital to maintain production and pay their employees. Foreign investors can offer relatively small loans to domestic companies so that they may continue to function. This often provides foreign companies the opportunity of eventually assuming ownership of local companies that are in desperate need of operational and investment capital, companies that struggle to repay loans. This was the strategy of many multi-millionaires and tycoons from developed countries, who today can be found on the *Forbes* list of the richest people in the world, when they made their initial fortune in the GEM.

While many EMCs have legal restrictions on foreign ownership, these limits usually apply only to certain regions or strategically or militarily important industries. There are also cases in which national governments seek to protect the livelihood of people whose income is dependent on recently privatized companies, preventing new owners from drastic restructuring and downsizing. Governments of EMCs usually put together an annual privatization plan (usually without any strategy), which lists the companies that are ready to be privatized. This can be a valuable tool for strategists who are deciding between countries for a potential direct investment. Governments typically provide very detailed information on companies included in this list. However, this information should not always be taken at face value. It is not unusual for governments to include companies that are not ready to be privatized, in order to artificially balance the national budget by falsely augmenting incoming privatization revenue.

The participation of foreign investors in cash privatization tenders and bidding often leads to the following strategically unsustainable situation: 49 percent of a company's shares are available for purchase, while the other 51 percent was distributed during mass privatization among employees and executives of the company. Typically, in this situation the foreign owner promises employees to invest in further restructuring and modernization of the company only if the employees sell the remaining shares or a controlling stake to the owner. This is usually easier in companies that are not operational at the moment of privatization due to a lack of capital or broken equipment that the company cannot afford to repair. One often-used transitional method consists of a combination of ownership by foreign investors and employees. An analogy of this kind of ownership can be found even in the United States, in Avis Car Rental Company, which in 1987 became employee-owned. In EMCs, this is usually a transitional stage of ownership, eventually leading to a shareholding company with very few owners.

A high concentration of capital and ownership are two other characteristics that usually occur with processes of privatization. When new investors concentrate ownership in their hands, they have the economic interest to improve the company's efficiency, to buy new equipment (a lack of which had previously limited production), and to promote and develop marketing abroad, especially in their country of origin. These new rich business owners, whether foreign or domestic, often become company executives, try to get exclusive rights and licenses from regional or central governments, and their businesses become de facto monopolies again. A typical tactic is to promote their cronies in governmental structures and occasionally to be governmental officials themselves. They practically become oligarchs. This is the beginning of oligarchic capitalism in several EMCs, such as Russia (a global leader by the group of nouveau riche which control up to 35 percent of the nation's wealth), Indonesia, Ukraine, Mexico, Kazakhstan, and to some extent in China, at least until 2013, etc. In recent history, this was the situation in South Korea and Argentina, but this is no longer the case. Oligarchy was the usual practice in ancient Greece in the fourth century BCE. For all intents and purposes, it exists in some developed countries, such as Japan, where huge industrial conglomerates have a strong influence on political processes. In the initial stages of an EMCs development, when democracy has not firmly taken root, oligarchs are able to concentrate a considerable amount of power in their hands. The description of this process can be supplemented by the astute comments of Professors Bruce Kogut (INSEAD, France) and Andrew Spicer (University of California, Riverside). They argue that a successful privatization program depends on the development of impersonal capital markets; however,

> [M]ass privatization created the contradictory conditions of generating millions of poorly informed shareholders, with no efficient markets for the sale of the shares. The absence of financial markets created systematic pressures to move assets by illegal or non-transparent means to users who value them more. Privatization created the incentives to destroy the financial markets critical to its success … the functional necessity for these markets does not engender their own creation. In the absence of institutional mechanisms of state regulation and trust, markets become arenas for political contests and economic manipulation. The irony of these policies is that a principal lesson has been that market reforms cannot create viable markets, only institutional formation can.[36]

As democratic institutions mature in EMCs, the role of public opinion increases, and people become more acquainted with their political rights (especially during elections), the power and influence of oligarchs tends to diminish.

The Role of Initial Public Offerings (IPO) in Privatization

Following the completion of major privatization processes, new owners often still lack the necessary capital to modernize or even to make the company efficiently operational. As a result, these owners develop strategies to submit their companies to the public market. To reach this objective, the typical strategic method is to make new issues by offering securities for sale in the primary market. This is called an initial public offering (IPO). Largely as a result of the influence of the global trend of privatization, IPOs in the GEM dramatically increased in the beginning of the twenty-first century. According to a study by Ernst & Young on global IPO activity, "the so-called BRIC countries together—Brazil, Russia,

India and China—have raised $106.5 billion in 382 deals so far in 2007 [as of December 17]. More than half of those were flotations of Chinese companies, however."[37] The global value of IPOs for 2007 as of December 17 was $255 billion, and the global number was 1739.[38] The Ernst & Young report goes on to say that "seven out of the top ten IPOs and 14 out of the top 20 IPOs by capital raised were from emerging markets. Two out of the top ten IPOs were from Brazil, and three of the top 20 IPOs by capital raised were from Brazil. Two out of the top 10 IPOs were from China, and six out of the top 20 IPOs by capital raised were from China."[39] Table 7.3 clearly demonstrates the steadily increasing role percentage-wise of the GEM IPOs in this global indicator. Raising capital for IPOs in BRICS has declined by more than 50 percent during the second decade of the twenty-first century for two major reasons: first, increased shortage of capital in the global market, and second, increased time of return of investing capital in IPOs in EMCs. They are no longer attractive for venture capitalists as they were in the early 2000s. Long-term players, who usually represent the largest multinational corporations in the world, continue to engage with IPOs on the GEM and invest in the technological updates of its entities.

The number of IPOs in BRICS EMCs will continue to decrease due to the increasing political risk involved in investing, a lack of attractive IPO entities on the major exchanges of the world financial capitals, and the downgrading of sovereign and corporate ratings by major global rating agencies like Standard & Poor's, Moody's, and Fitch. This is especially true in Russia, whose sovereign bonds and corporate chairs have consistently received poor ratings. In January 2015, the Central Bank of Russia made the move to no longer use the credit ratings from the above agencies, which is an undoubtedly poor idea and a far step back from the financial progress Russia achieved prior to the spring of 2014.[40]

The concentration of this capital is in big IPOs in EMCs. The average size of IPOs in BRIC countries is almost twice the average size of those in developed countries (this ratio is made with the assumption that there are no IPOs in developing and underdeveloped countries). According to Maria Boutchkova of Concordia University and William Megginson of the University of Oklahoma:

> Privatizations have significantly improved stock market liquidity during the last ten years [from 1990 to 2000]. On average, each additional privatization deal is associated with a 2.3 percent increase over the first year and a 1.7 percent increase over the second year of the turnover ratio of the respective stock market.[41]

In general, EMCs with a strategic orientation on the increasing numbers of publicly held companies strengthen the influence of shareholders and societal values over pure business interests. They also improve the transparency of business transactions and eventually decrease corruption.

In geographic terms, due mostly to their much deeper developed strategy, companies in Europe and Asia occupy the leading positions by capital raised from IPOs.[42] The role of IPOs in raising capital in Central and South America has never exceeded 5 percent in the first decade of the twenty-first century in terms of total capital raised from IPOs worldwide. It is possible to conclude that capital raised by IPOs is directly correlated to the existence of mature and deep regional capital markets and the quality of related corporate strategies.

When IPOs of different companies proceed simultaneously in several markets, a usual occurrence in the GEM, other domestic and foreign investors have the opportunity to make money through strategic arbitrage. In this context arbitrage is the simultaneous

Table 7.3 The Role of BRIC IPOs in the GMP

	2005	*2006*	*2007*	*2012*
Number of IPOs worldwide	1537	1729	1739	837
Number of BRIC IPOs	142	302	382	246
BRIC IPOs as a Percentage of World IPOs	**9.24**	**17.47**	**21.97**	29.39068
Total Value of IPOs worldwide ($bil)	167	246	255	129
Total Value of BRIC IPOs ($bil)	29	89.6	106.5	33
Value of BRIC IPOs as a Percentage of World Total	**17.37**	**36.42**	**41.76**	25.5814

Compiled from Ernst and Young: Q1'13 Global IPO update, April 2, 2013. Retrieved from www.ey.com.br/

trade of securities in different markets with the purpose of profiting from short-term price disparities. The prevalence of this practice in the EMCs is a clear illustration of the extent to which the GEM is integrated within the GMP.

It is not unusual for oligarchs to offer portions of their privately held companies to be publicly listed on stock exchanges in order to create an air of greater legitimacy. However, they often buy back their shares from the market in the future. This is typically done through a tender offer, which involves a limited window in which the company can buy its own shares, usually at a premium to their current market value.

Oligarchs, or any investor with lots of cash, can also be influential in the IPOs of companies in which they do not yet hold shares. They typically do so by a process called averaging down, whereby a potential investor with lots of cash lowers the average share price through various tactics in order to buy more of them once the price has been sufficiently reduced. Oligarchs usually try to keep most shares under their control. Often, they will put about 30 percent of their shares on the stock market, both to raise capital and to improve their image. An example of this is the strategy of Skyworth, the biggest exporter of consumer electronics in China, and the third largest producer of these goods. The company is listed on the Hong Kong stock exchange, but its facilities are in mainland China, in the Shenzhen Special Economic Zone of the Guangdong province.

The Trend of Internationalization

Internationalization is one of the oldest global trends of modern time; it preceded and influenced globalization. Internationalization has already passed the peak of its influence but remains a very relevant global trend. Under the influence of internationalization as a *trend*, internationalization as a strategic *method* and as a strategic *form* of increasing the efficiency of national economies and corporations was developed and is now widely in use.

Strategic Reasons to Do Business Internationally

What are the major strategic reasons for companies to internationalize? This analysis can first be done in terms of the strategic factor of time and basic economic factors. Companies can internationalize in order to gain access to richer and cheaper natural resources, raw materials, or parts, and to decrease cost production by the use of cheaper, better educated, and/or specialized labor resources or just for faster occupation of a market's niche. With the development of the global capital market, companies often use strategies of internationalization in order to access venture capital and investment from abroad due to a domestic deficit of capital, which emerged as a result of the globalization of international markets (discussed later in this chapter). The failure of dictatorships and the birth of the GEM became a new triggering strategic event for companies to strategize their internationalization in order to access existing and inexpensive production facilities and infrastructure. This time-sensitive strategy allows them to avoid the cost of constructing these facilities domestically, which would require a much larger investment. For companies that are struggling in their domestic market, one of the fastest ways to improve their competitiveness is to use existing foreign facilities and infrastructure to increase production and achieve economies of scale with less costly products. With the growing importance of the knowledge economy, companies seek access to foreign scientific resources and researchers. The opposite asymmetric strategic scenario also works; a company can make its scientific research and educational facilities available to foreign companies or individuals. This strategy of internationalization was used in the UK to increase the economic efficiency and stability of its universities and colleges. At the beginning of the 1960s, there were about 28,000 foreign students in Great Britain. At that time relatively new universities developed a strategy to internationalize their operations by attracting foreign students and developing branches and subsidiaries abroad. As a result, by 2002 the number of foreign students in the UK reached 225,000.[43] Through the export of education, Great Britain received £28 billion in 2003–04, which was more than it received from financial service exports.[44] Also, the prestige of British universities, which was declining toward the end of the twentieth century, has improved markedly. In 2011–12, this number went up to 311,800, but a lack of updates to curriculum and improvement to university infrastructures in the UK and new international educational environments and improvement of higher schools in Australia, Singapore, South Korea, Hong Kong, Turkey, Poland, and some other EMCs increased competition; this caused the numbers of international students in the UK in 2012–13 to fall to 307,205.[45] In the US, by comparison, improvements in universities resulted in the increase in the number of international students to almost 900,000 in the 2013–14 academic year. This number is a record high. Behind these numbers is an obviously well-developed strategy because the number of foreign students in the US has permanently increased since 2000 and has already grown by 72 percent.[46] The majority of these students came from China (an increase of 17 percent in one year); followed by students from Kuwait, Brazil, and Saudi Arabia. Even the number of students studying in the US from Iran and Venezuela, countries that have not always been on friendly terms with the United States, have grown annually by double digits. I am positive that this educational market will grow through online teaching and strategies related to these new educational technological trends are under development.

Quite often, companies strategize internationally not for inexpensive but for unique natural resources, production facilities, skilled workers, or even for rare final products. After the US invasion of Iraq in 2003, some brave entrepreneurs traveled there to obtain traditional goods that are not produced anywhere else, such as rugs and art, to sell in American and European markets.

However, it is important to realize that there are dangers associated with this strategy of internationalization. Companies take major political and economic risks when they create subsidiaries in unknown or unfamiliar emerging markets (discussed in detail in Chapter 9). Nonetheless, less competitive environments and less costly production have the potential to generate very high profits, which can then be repatriated and used to increase production or reduce prices in a company's traditional domestic market. In many cases companies that were not willing to take the risks associated with the internationalization of their strategies struggle to compete in their domestic market with those companies that strategized its internationalization. Practically, internationalization is one of the most efficient strategic approaches to increase the volume of production by decreasing cost and price, which finally increases profit and market shares of the company in its domestic market.

It is difficult to conclude by traditional means whether internationalization is a proactive or reactive strategy. In the case of companies that go abroad due to a loss of competitiveness in domestic markets, it is predominantly a reactive strategy. But when these same companies repatriated and reinvested their profit from abroad in their domestic market, the strategy is converted and is considered proactive. The internationalization of some companies was proactive from the very beginning. Executives with great vision and fortitude saw the potential in emerging markets very early or at least saw the successful internationalization of other companies in other industries. These executives invested in the GEM, not to save their companies, but to build markets abroad and eventually increase their domestic market share. Trade companies can go abroad just to increase sales, without investments in overseas production facilities.

Companies use different organizational forms, or "vehicles," to strategize their internationalization. Options include strategic alliance with a foreign company; a cross-border merger; or, to save time (but definitely not money), acquisition, whereby a company buys an existing business or facility abroad. If the acquisition is not amicable, it is referred to as a hostile takeover. In order to decrease investment abroad while still having a strong partner overseas, one of the most popular and efficient vehicles for going abroad is the creation of an international joint venture with foreign partner(s). The following examples illustrate the possible strategic vehicles to take a company international while taking into consideration its strengths and weaknesses.

Company A, a Canadian firm, has international aspirations but lacks the experience and know-how to expand beyond its local market. The company can use the following four options:

Option 1: Strategic alliance

Company A could make a *strategic alliance* with Company B, which operates in a market of interest (Mexico, for example) and has a strategic interest in expanding its operations into Canada. A strategic alliance is an agreement between two companies not to compete against each other, for example for raw materials or market share, and to provide access to each other's facilities. Company B, from Mexico, would gain access to Company A's facilities and infrastructure in Canada, and vice versa. Both Company A and Company B would theoretically gain a strategic competitive advantage over their traditional competitors. A strategic alliance is one of the most inexpensive ways to take a company international.

An example of a strategic alliance agreement took place on February 5, 2008, when the British retailer Sports Direct announced a strategic alliance with ITAT Group. Sports Direct "operated out of 465 stores, of which 408 are located domestically, 30 in Belgium, 12 in Ireland, 11 in Slovenia and four in the Netherlands."[47] ITAT Group is a Hong Kong apparel retailer that operates in mainland China. Prior to this strategic alliance, ITAT Group had several strategic alliances with other companies, including China Resources Vanguard, Ren Ren Le, Trust Mart, Hualien, Better Life, BLC, Bailian, Walmart, Carrefour, and Chongqing New Century. Sports Direct is investing about £20 million to fit out ITAT stores in China.[48] ITAT's 700 stores in 275 Chinese cities made it an ideal ally for Sports Direct's expansion into the Chinese market.[49]

Option 2: Merger

Company A could merge with Company B, which is already international. Company B will provide the know-how, experience, and infrastructure to internationalize Company A. However, this could result in the disappearance of one of the company's brands as the more internationalized company grows dominant. An example of this is the strategic merger between the Union Bank of Switzerland and the American investment banking company PaineWebber Group, Inc., which took place in 2000. Initially, the new company was called UBS PaineWebber, Inc. But in 2003, the name of the less internationalized PaineWebber disappeared: the company's name was once again UBS, the brand of a single integrated firm.[50]

Company A could merge with a company of relatively equal size and recognition that already has a foothold in the particular market of interest. For example, Company A could orient themselves strategically toward a Mexican company with local experience, connections, and sales infrastructure that may be interested in merging with Company A in order to obtain access to its intellectual property, know-how, financial capacity, production facilities, etc. An example of a merger occurred in February 2008, when Thomson Corp's £7.9 billion bid for Reuters gained approval from US, Canadian, and European regulators. The goal of this merger was to create a more competitive rival for Bloomberg L.P., a leading provider of financial information.

Option 3: Friendly acquisition and hostile takeover

A strategic partnership or international joint venture may provide Company A with the financial capacity and desire to acquire control over Company B's business. If Company B accepts the offer, this acquisition will be friendly. It is also possible for Company A to acquire control of Company B without its approval, via a hostile takeover. Company A can secretly acquire a controlling interest (ownership of more than 50 percent of voting shares) of Company B on the stock market and gain the ability to hire and fire executives and make strategic decisions. In big business, a hostile takeover strategy can often be successful by obtaining a sufficient amount of voting shares that allow an investor to impede the operations of a company (much less than 50 percent). This aggressive strategy would allow Company A to bring the business of Company B to a halt. The amount of shares necessary for a company to have a blocking stake depends on the overall distribution of shares among owners and is typically between 10 and 25 percent. For example, in February 2008, China's state-owned aluminum producer Chinalco partnered with Alcoa, an American aluminum group, to acquire a 12 percent blocking stake in Rio Tinto, a UK-listed mining powerhouse.[51] A hostile takeover is the most expensive way to take a company international. According to an article from the *Financial Times,* since 2007, there has been a rise in hostile takeovers, largely as a result of two factors:

> The first is cyclical. Many commentators fear that the latest dealmaking cycle that began in October 2003 … is nearing an end—particularly since private equity groups have pulled in their horns because of the credit squeeze, and chief executives of corporate buyers are concerned about an economic slowdown … The second driving force has been the proliferation of hedge funds and activist investment firms.[52]

It is not difficult to find studies and textbooks describing the strategic advantages of international acquisition. However, it is not as easy to find information on the disadvantages of international acquisitions, though they are substantial. Being aware of these disadvantages is extremely helpful in avoiding pitfalls during and especially after the acquisition process. In *The Handbook of International Mergers & Acquisitions*, Professor David J. BenDaniel, together with the experienced executive Professor Arthur H. Rosenbloom, lists some of the most important drawbacks, including cultural shock, management distance, people problems, lack of local business knowledge, and poor knowledge of industry and geography.[53]

Option 4: International joint venture

Company A (from Canada) and Company B (from Mexico) could create an international joint venture (IJV) forming a new legal entity, separate from both companies. By creating and supplying the initial charter capital for a separate legal entity, Company A and Company B can benefit from each other's strategic competitive advantages, infrastructure, and unrestricted access to markets, etc., while limiting their respective liabilities. Parent companies are not held responsible for obligations made by an international joint venture. From an economic strategy perspective, an IJV is essentially the same concept as a strategic partnership or alliance. However, from a business and legal perspective, they are significantly different because pure strategic alliances do not require the creation of a new legal entity and substantial investment. IJVs are a very efficient legal form for companies going abroad to a country in which they do not have prior experience or local relationships. Well-established local partners can create substantial advantages for an IJV. An experienced and well-connected partner can make the IJV victorious over other companies with foreign capital (subsidiaries of foreign firms or other IJVs) that have already entered the market. For this strategic reason, some foreign companies seek partnerships with state-owned companies or companies with strong ties to the current government. There are advantages and disadvantages to this strategic scenario. When the IJV is very profitable, the government may force the foreign partner to sell all its shares to the local partner. One of the best examples of this is what happened in 1999 with Metromedia International Group, Inc. in China, when they received a letter from "China Unicom stating that a department of the Chinese government had requested termination of one of its four joint telecommunications projects."[54] (Details of international joint ventures as a business and legal form are analyzed in Chapter 4).

As a result of the influence of the internationalization trend, business has expanded beyond national borders to the point that a company's single "international" department can no longer manage the export of products and the import of raw materials and parts to and from all parts of the world. Well ahead of the curve, in 1990, Jack Welch, the famous CEO of General Electric (GE), shut down General Electric International, the division of GE responsible for international activity. Welch realized that the quantitative increase of GE's international business would make it impossible for one division to handle cross-border transactions for the other eleven GE divisions that existed at that time. Welch realized that in order to be globally competitive, all divisions of GE had to be international. A similar situation happened to the investment-banking company PaineWebber, which was once the fifth-largest United States securities firm.[55] It followed GE's lead and closed its subsidiary PaineWebber International. In the mid-1990s, Andersen Worldwide, the largest auditing and consulting professional firm in the world at the time, opened Arthur Andersen International (AAI). Andersen Worldwide, with more than 100,000 employees and 100,000 clients in 78 different countries, could not work through AAI, one small internationally oriented subsidiary. When I worked in the 1990s at Andersen Worldwide, it was already clear that Arthur Andersen International was insignificant and incapable of handling Andersen Worldwide's international activity, and this department closed shortly after it was opened. In the twenty-first century, the majority of multinational corporations do not have international departments. Most businesses and subsidiaries handle their own cross-border activity in the GMP. At the beginning of the internationalization of markets, new business dimensions that had been closed for decades to foreign business entities were opened. The number of creating corporations in developing countries by its dynamics overcame the number of international firms in the traditional developed world. When the most lucrative and potentially profitable efforts in countries which became emerging markets at the beginning of the 1990s were taken by western or Asian companies from the developed world, the number of internationalized firms in developed countries again overcame its initial leap of international business in EMCs (see Figure 7.2).

In terms of globally operated companies' foreign assets, businesses from the GEM do not play a major role until 2005. At that time, the company from the GEM with the most foreign assets was Spain's Repsol YPF SA, ranked only 46th on the UN list of the world's top 100 non-financial multinational corporations. The first non-European company, Petronas–Petroliam Nasional Bhd from Malaysia, was ranked 55th. Nonetheless, out of the top 100 non-financial multinational corporations, ten were from the GEM. However, it is important to understand that while almost all of these companies have a presence in the GEM, only ten of them registered their headquarters in EMCs. This situation came to a head during the next ten years. As depicted in Table 7.4, 4 of the world's top 15

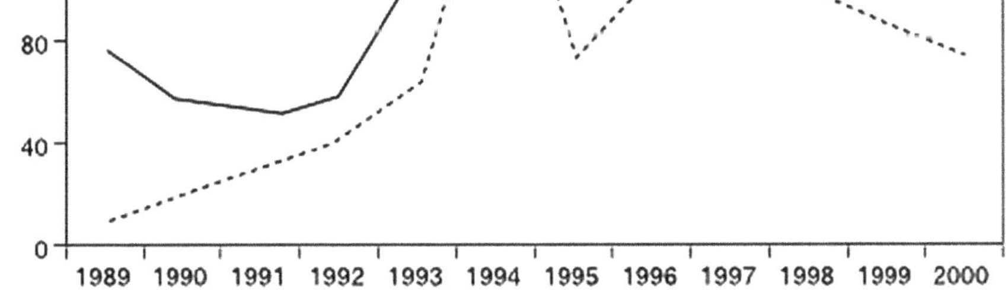

Figure 7.2 Number of New International Firms in the Global Marketplace

Claessens, S. and Schmukler, S. L. (2007). "International Financial Integration through Equity Markets: Which Firms from Which Countries Go Global?" *International Monetary Fund Working Paper WP/01/138*, p. 24. Retrieved from www.imf.org/external/pubs/ft/wp/2007/wp07138.pdf

"The United States and the United Kingdom are not included in the sample due to the classification of these countries as international financial centers. International firms are those identified as having at least one active depository receipt program, having raised equity capital in international markets, or being listed on the London Stock Exchange, NASDAQ, or NYSE. Countries are divided by income level following the classification of the World Development Indicators, World Bank at the beginning of the sample period (1989)."

Table 7.4 GEM MNC from the List of the World's Top 15 Non-Financial Transnational Corporations Ranked by Foreign Assets (Billions of US$), 2012

SO-TNCs	*Home country*	*Industry*	*State share*	*Assets*		*Sales*		*Employment*		*Transnationality Index*
				Foreign	*Total*	*Foreign*	*Total*	*Foreign*	*Total*	
GDF Suez	France	Utilities	36	175	272	79	125	110,308	219,330	0.59
Volkswagen Group	Germany	Motor vehicles	20	158	409	199	248	296,000	533,469	0.58
Eni SpA	Italy	Oil and gas	26	133	185	86	164	51,034	77,838	0.63
Enel SpA	Italy	Utilities	31	132	227	66	108	37,588	73,702	0.57
EDF SA	France	Utilities	84	103	331	39	93	30,412	154,730	0.31
Deutsche Telekom AG	Germany	Telecommunications	32	96	143	42	75	113,502	232,342	0.58
CITIC Group	China	Diversified	100	72	515	10	52	30,806	140,028	0.18
Statoil ASA	Norway	Oil and gas	67	71	141	28	121	2,842	23,028	0.29
General Motors Co	United States	Motor vehicles	16	70	149	65	152	108,000	213,000	0.47
Vattenfall AB	Sweden	Utilities	100	54	81	19	25	23,864	32,794	0.72
Orange S.A.	France	Telecommunications	27	54	119	24	56	65,492	170,531	0.42
Airbus Group	France	Aircraft	12	46	122	67	73	88,258	140,405	0.64
Vale SA	Brazil	Metal mining	3[c]	46	131	38	48	15,680	85,305	0.45
COSCO	China	Transport and storage	100	40	52	19	30	7,355	130,000	0.50
Petronas	Malaysia	Oil and gas	100	39	150	43	73	8,653	43,266	0.35

Selected from United Nations Conference on Trade and Development. (2014). *The World Investment Report: Investing in the SDGs: An Action Plan*, p. 21. Retrieved from http://unctad.org/en/publicationslibrary/wir2014_en.pdf/

Note: The Transnationality Index is calculated as the average of the following three ratios: foreign to total assets, foreign to total sale, and foreign to total employment. Foreign assets data is calculated by applying the share of foreign assets in total assets of the previous year to total assets.

non-financial TNCs are from the GEM, including 2 Chinese companies, 1 Brazilian, and Pretonas from Malaysia. State-owned does not mean 100 percent ownership; it means that at least 10 percent of the company belongs to the state or public entities, and these entities play a role as the largest shareholder in the TNCs. Strategists can then conclude that many developed countries have companies that prefer to invest where the controlling stake belongs to the government or semi-governmental corporations to decrease the risk of cross-border investment.

However, this conclusion is not always correct. Quite often, governments try to take control of foreign shares if the state-owned or partially state-owned company is highly profitable, by legal or even not-so-legal means. I remember this was the case with the US-based MetroMedia in the late twentieth century. A similar attempt was also made on behalf of the governments in Kazakhstan, Venezuela, and Bulgaria, among others. Foreign corporations are attracted to buy shares of partially state-owned entities from EMCs because of the presumption that eventually the government will put their share on the market to achieve liquidity. Then, foreign partners from developed countries will get first refusal rights for purchasing those newly extended shares. This means that corporate strategists must carefully evaluate the history of the strategic-political risk with particular EMCs, analyzing the political balance of power found in the country they are interested in investing in, and how this balance will be sustainable over the next ten years, when they can see a return on their invested capital.

For territorial analysis of the allocation of multinational corporations, the Geographical Spread Index is very interesting for strategists as a technical indicator of the globalization of multinational corporations. It is calculated as the square root of the Internationalization Index (the number of foreign affiliates divided by the number of all affiliates) multiplied by the number of countries in which a company operates. According to this calculation, only three of the most globalized multinationals originate in the GEM (two companies from Spain and one from China) as of 2005. But this 6 percent presence is only the beginning of the increasing role of multinationals from the GEM in the GMP. With rapid capitalization (see Chapter 5), there is a strong basis to expect an exponential increase of GEM multinationals on this kind of spread. Figure 7.3 is related to this indicator and shows the dynamic, which already has become visible.

A company's participation in the GMP does not necessarily mean that a company is international. The overwhelming majority of territories in developed countries and the EMC are already part of the GMP. But many companies operate locally, without even knowing that they are part of the GMP. When a company purposefully looks for international cooperation, receives foreign direct investment, or exports its goods and imports raw materials and parts from abroad, this is an example of the influence of the trend of internationalization.

The internationalization of science and technological development is proceeding even faster than the internationalization of business and investment. As described in Chapter 5 and later in this chapter, the GMP in the first half of the twenty-first century is transitioning from a service-based economy to a knowledge economy. The new role of science in this transition practically represents the approaching second scientific-technological revolution. Recognition of this has made countries pursue inflows of foreign high-tech companies and scholars, which eventually leads to the increasing role of the scientific sector in the national economies of these countries. Prosperity in these countries is highly correlated with scientific-technological progress. The influence of internationalization in these processes is represented in Figure 7.4. This figure demonstrates the increasingly

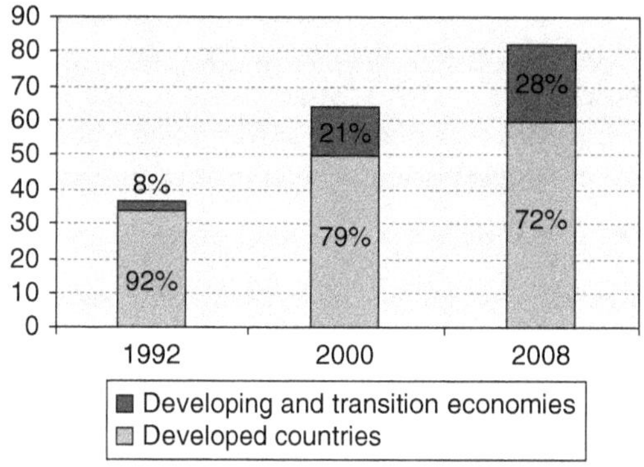

Figure 7.3 Number of MNCs from Developed, Developing, and Emerging Market Countries (Thousands), 1992–2008

© Dr. Vladimir Kvint, 2008. The United Nations Conference on Trade and Development. (2010). *The World Investment Report: Investing in a Low-Carbon Economy*, p. 17. Retrieved from http://unctad.org/en/Docs/wir2010_en.pdf

innovative role of residents and non-residents from EMCs. Among the top ten countries in this figure, four are from EMCs. It is also important to note that all member-countries of BRIC are represented.

There are many other noticeable trends. The most surprising development during the last ten years is that in terms of patents pending, China now leads the world, overcoming the global technological leader the United States by more than 100,000 patents. This demonstrates an absence of a US technological strategy, because even a poorly conceived and implemented strategy would still keep the US at the top of this figure. South Korea is not surprisingly on this list, as for the past ten years South Korea has occupied the top spot of number of patents pending per $1 billion of a country's GDP. The lack of European technological strategy is also noticeable on this chart, as the relatively small South Korea surpasses Germany (the European technological leader) and the rest of the EU combined. In terms of patents pending, the position of Russia is far better on the global scale of EMCs than its position related to registered patents. Here, Russia is above India and far ahead of Brazil.

If you include the EPO (European Patent Office, which represents not only developed European countries some EMCs as well), there are nine countries found in the GEM on this figure, which is a great success for these countries' technological strategies. If there is an absence of strategy—as in Russia—this high position is a result of talented individuals involved in technological development. The presence of North Korea can easily be explained by two concurrent reasons: first, this brutal, mostly self-isolated regime tries to remove all foreign distractions and influence, which leads to the need for the most up-to-date weapons, including WMDs. Second, in order to achieve these weapons, North Korea must ironically rely on foreign education, sending students to study abroad and learn about the cutting-edge technology available, in order to bring it back and expand upon it in isolation. I have met a few of these students while teaching in Europe, and noted that they strive to avoid any personal interaction, political discussion, or even independent thought. They remind me of the technological robotic systems often described in dystopian futures.

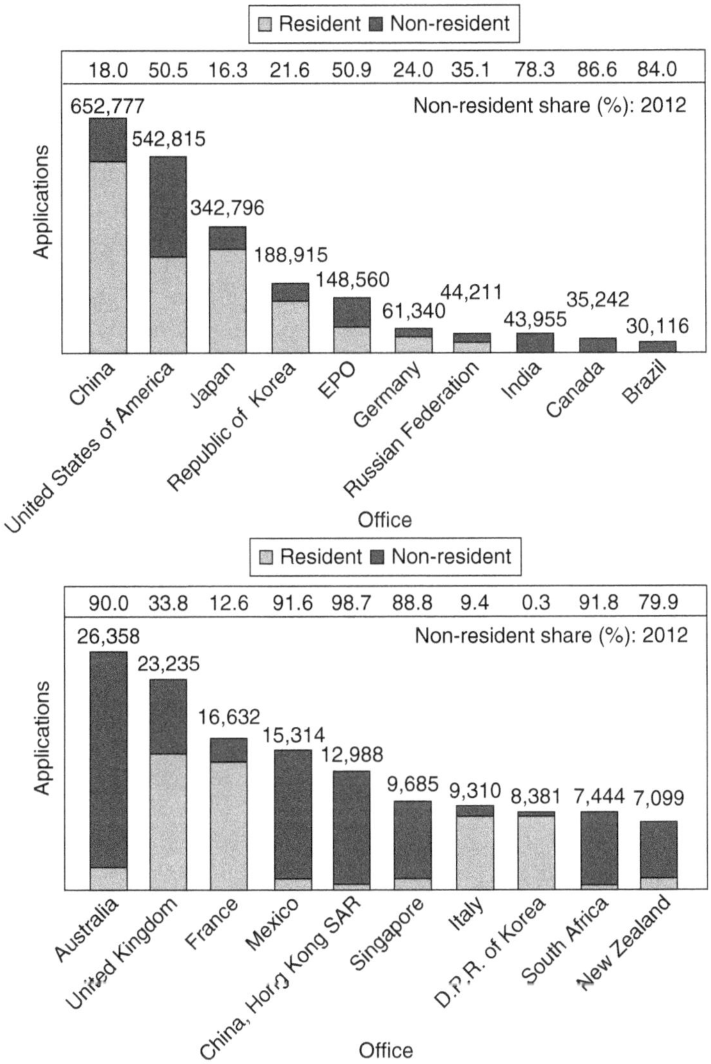

Figure 7.4 Patent Applications for the Top 20 Countries by Residents, 2012

World Intellectual Property Organization (WIPO). (2013). World Intellectual Property Indicators, p. 53. Retrieved from www.wipo.int/edocs/pubdocs/en/intproperty/941/wipo_pub_941_2013.pdf

The presence of some countries on this list is due to the creative activity of non-residents. Countries like Hong Kong, Australia, and Canada work hard to provide a scholarly environment that attracts non-residents (both individual and corporate) and allows them to contribute to the achievements of their host countries. This flow of scholars has changed direction over the past ten years, as outstanding scientists, scholars, and high-tech professionals are leaving Europe for the ideal working conditions fostered by these countries, corporations, and universities. Worldwide, an average 38 percent of all patents pending come from non-residents. That in itself reflects the high level of internationalization of science and technology. Out of 28 countries with the highest level of internationalization in this sector, 15 are EMCs—more than half. Fifteen countries have a higher level of internationalization in scientific studies than the world average. Two-thirds of these countries are EMCs. A high internationalization of science and technology is a further illustration of the new emerging stage of development in the global marketplace—the knowledge-based economy.

Deficit of Investment as a Consequence of Internationalization

Prior to the birth of the GEM at the end of the 1970s, the developed world had a surplus of cash for investment. Companies and entrepreneurs had to compete for investment projects. The birth of EMCs and formation of the GEM turned this relationship upside down, creating tremendous strategic opportunities and an unprecedented inflow of FDI, achieving a record high in 2000. Companies from the GEM sought FDI and partnership from and with companies from well-developed countries. For the majority of companies in the GEM, at the initial stage of economic liberalization, the strategy of finding a foreign partner or potential owner was like a panacea from bankruptcy or dissolution. Local executives reported to their employees about successful or failed hunts for foreign investors, partners, and even owners. Equipment was stagnant, and raw materials and parts did not arrive due to the shortage of operation cash. This forced executives and domestic companies to totally or partially sell their assets and shares to foreign owners, often for practically nothing. It is one of the major characteristics of the initial stage of integration of companies from the GEM to the GMP—and the birth of the GMP itself. For two years, the terrorist attacks of September 11, 2001 changed the situation for the worse. Investors started to take this capital back to their country of origin, or to a few tax-haven countries like Luxembourg or Panama. This was the first major impact of international terrorism on the GMP, and it took five years for the FDI to rebound after the tragic events of 9/11. In 2006, for the first time, FDI inflows surpassed the previous record set in 2000. In Chapter 9, foreign direct investment as a global trend and practice will be analyzed in detail.

The Strategic and Economic Impact of the Global Trend of Terrorism and Extremism

The Roots of Terrorism and Extremism

Globalization brought the influence of modern western culture and values to parts of the world with very different cultural and religious traditions. In some of these countries and regions, extremists exploit the western presence and influence for political purposes, creating a hostile environment for foreign business and even its products. Western values and law often contradict ingrained attitudes toward women's rights and the law of the dominant religion of the land. A new wave of terrorism and extremism emerged from this clash. Conflicts of this nature are most prevalent in regions where religion has never been separated from the state. This is why such conflicts basically do not exist, or at least are less intense, in Turkey, where in 1924 the great leader Kemal Atatürk (1881–1938) strategically made Turkey a secular state, which as of the twenty-first century still exists as strategized by Atatürk despite some counterattempts contrary to his strategic vision. The implementation of secularism on a practical level meant the closing of Islamic courts and the Islamic educational system, and the adoption of the Swiss Civil Code. But western values are not the only source of disapproval of foreign activities in regions with non-western cultural traditions (see Chapter 1). In some countries any foreign business or cultural presence is often met with animosity by small but fierce groups and movements. This is why there is a basis for saying that conflicts are inflamed by extremists and exploited by terrorists, who in any country do not represent the general sentiment of the population.

There are several other roots of terrorism, the most serious of which are poverty and illegal immigration. It is a well-known fact that the majority of the terrorists who committed the attacks of September 11, 2001, came from Saudi Arabia and Yemen. This lends credence to well-known Saudi journalist Abid Khazindar's argument that "without development, it will be impossible to attack the root causes of terrorism; they spring from poverty [and] unemployment which in turn are produced by the absence of sufficient places in our universities for our young people."[56] Poverty is definitely correlated to levels of education, but it is not true that poverty inevitably leads to terrorism. In Saudi Arabia, for example, the illiteracy rate is 21 percent and enrollment in primary schools is only 59 percent,[57] which will increase the amount of illiterate adults. As long as education is not valued, the low literacy rate will not improve. It is sad and difficult to believe that a country as rich in natural resources as Saudi Arabia can have such a poor education system. There are so many terrorist attacks on civilians in Iraq also because the illiteracy rate in this country is 26 percent.[58]

At the same time, the roots of terrorism can be found among the wealthy and well educated. According to Professor Alan B. Krueger of Princeton University:

> [C]ontrary to popular stereotype … uneducated, impoverished masses are particularly *unlikely* to participate in political processes, through either legitimate or illegitimate means … Instead of being drawn from the ranks of the poor, numerous academic and government studies find that terrorists tend to be drawn from well-educated, middle-class or high-income families.[59]

This does not contradict the previously stated link between poverty and terrorism. In fact, terrorists or those sympathetic to terrorist causes from middle-class or wealthy backgrounds use the poor by offering money to participate in terrorist attacks. State sponsors of terrorism use the same tactic. For example, Saddam Hussein offered an honorarium to the surviving poverty-stricken families of recruited terrorists. According to the report of the National Commission on Terrorist Attacks upon the United States, "Terrorism is not caused by poverty."[60] There is no doubt that this is an accurate statement, but by the same token poverty creates a vulnerable environment for the poison of terrorist money and ideology.

Illegal immigration is another root of terrorism, which is directly related to poverty. Only those who are forced by extreme poverty are willing to leave their homes to become illegal aliens in another country. According to a report from an independent research organization, the Center for Immigration Studies, "strict enforcement of immigration law—at American consulates overseas, at ports of entry, and within the United States—must be an integral part of our efforts to prevent future attacks on U.S. soil."[61] Nonetheless, even legal immigrants can come to America with non-peaceful goals.[62]

Defining Terrorism

While the existence of terrorism and extremism as a global trend is obvious to even the most casual observers of international affairs, it is a particularly challenging phenomenon to analyze. Despite a practically global consensus rejecting terrorism as a deplorable and inhuman act, terrorism is actually a very controversial issue. The US Department of Defense defines terrorism as "the unlawful use of—or threatened use of—force, or violence against individuals or property to coerce or intimidate governments or societies, often to achieve political, religious or ideological objectives."[63] Even a definition as clear-cut as this is not necessarily accepted by every international and multilateral organization and national government. As of February 2015, no one has been able to come up with a globally accepted definition of terrorism. In 2010, "the EU issued its first-ever internal security strategy, which highlights terrorism as a key threat facing the EU and aims to develop a coherent and comprehensive EU strategy to tackle terrorism as well as organized crime, cybercrime, money laundering, and natural and man-made disasters."[64] Nonetheless, even this international regional bloc did not come up with a mutually accepted definition by 29 member-countries, which substantially undermined this strategic effort.

The League of Nations was the first international institution to attempt to create a globally approved definition in the Convention for the Prevention and Punishment of Terrorism in 1937. Since then the United Nations has been unable to achieve a consensus on this term, although it has issued many conventions, some of which are relevant to international business, like the Convention for the Suppression of Financing of Terrorism (1999) and the Protocol for Suppression of Unlawful Acts against the Safety of Fixed Platforms Located on the Continental Shelf (1988), among others. The lack of a definition is a major obstacle for universally accepted countermeasures against terrorism. In 1999, two years prior to the tragic attacks of September 11, 2001, the UN made a resolution strongly condemning the practice of terrorism as criminal and unjustifiable. On September 28, 2001, the United Nations Security Council adopted Resolution 1373, which not only condemned the attacks of September 11 but also created the Counter Terrorism Committee, which monitors the implementation of the resolution and is made up of all 15 members of the Security Council. The UN's inability to come to a consensus on the definition of terrorism did not shield the organization from the impact of this global trend. In August 2003, a truck bomb exploded in the UN Headquarters in Iraq, killing 17 people and injuring 100. From a business perspective, terrorism can be understood as an unprovoked and intentional attack on unarmed civilians or non-military targets. This approach innately covers businesspeople and business and economic entities.

Strategic Responses to Terrorism and Extremism

Due to the lack of a clear definition of terrorism in conjunction with several other important issues, the legal systems of the overwhelming majority of countries could not effectively prosecute and use force against terrorist organizations. The attacks of September 11, 2001, were a monumental point in the theory, legal regulation, and practice of fighting terrorism, the catalyst for international businesses, governments, and multilateral institutions to develop antiterrorism strategies.

One of the first and most important almost strategic responses to the global trend of terrorism was the so-called USA Patriot Act (the abbreviation stands for "Uniting and Strengthening America by Providing Appropriate Tools Required to Intercept and Obstruct Terrorism"), which was signed by President Bush on October 26, 2001. In order to protect global supply chains from concealing and smuggling terrorist weapons, the US government also implemented the Customs-Trade Partnership against Terrorism (C-TPAT). Import-export companies that participate in this program can expedite the clearance process for their goods through customs and receive less intensive inspections.[65] The US Department of State also undertook special measures. In order to monitor terrorism worldwide, the secretary of state transmitted the following:

> [T]o the Speaker of the House of Representatives and the Committee on Foreign Relations of the Senate, by April 30 of each year, a full and complete report providing …
>
> (A) detailed assessments with respect to each foreign country—
> (i) in which acts of international terrorism occurred which were, in the opinion of the Secretary, of major significance;
> (ii) about which the Congress was notified during the preceding five years …
> (iii) which the Secretary determines should be the subject of such report; and
>
> (B) detailed assessments with respect to each foreign country whose territory is being used as a sanctuary for terrorists or terrorist organizations.[66]

It should be noted that, within the context of this report, the term *terrorism* is defined as "premeditated, politically motivated violence perpetrated against non-combatant targets by subnational groups or clandestine agents."[67]

Of course, any national security measures or private security activities of businesses can be seen from two points of view. In one sense they decrease international cooperation and increase business costs, but on the other hand they give people grounds for believing that they are better protected. An example of this is the Patriot Act, which focuses substantially on the prevention of and reporting systems for suspicious financial transactions that can be related to money laundering. The Patriot Act required the implementation of preventive monitoring systems. This requirement immediately increased the role of due diligence and improved the quality of the preparation of professionals for this service. Several US government agencies specialize in the prevention of money-laundering activities. Among them are the Bureau of Alcohol Tobacco and Firearms (ATF), the United States Secret Service (USSS), the Internal Revenue Service (IRS), the Immigration and Customs Enforcement agency (ICE), and the Customs and Border Protection agency (CBP). As a result of their activities, a substantial amount of money, which would have financed terrorism, landed in US government coffers. Based on the experience of the US government, in 2007 the Department of the Treasury, the Department of Justice, and the Department of Homeland Security developed the National Money Laundering Strategy.[68]

The more that governments and the private sector cooperate, the more a country will be able to minimize the economic damage of terrorism. According to Peter Jennings, a director from the Australian Strategic Policy Institute, "the best way to defeat terrorism will involve government and business borrowing some of each other's styles of operating: Governments must learn to be more open and flexible, while business must develop greater skills in strategic analysis and war gaming."[69]

The Strategic Negative Influence of Terrorism on the Global Marketplace

The terrorist attacks of 9/11 were much more than an assault on the United States; they were an attack on the GMP. This was the first real indication of the scale of the terrorist impact on the GMP. However, for the GMP, as well as for civilization in general, it is important to realize that local and regional insurgent groups are just as dangerous as global terrorist networks. In fact, local insurgents pose a particular challenge to businesses, despite the fact that their impact may be less widely felt. This is because it is harder to monitor local terrorists and thus more difficult to prevent their attacks.

The major economic impact of terrorism on the GMP is extremely wide-ranging, with strategic consequences. The disruption of financial and currency markets, of global transportation systems and infrastructure, and the distortion of global prices for key commodities are only the beginning. The burden of unprecedented expenses for security and protection drives some companies to bankruptcy. The cost of maintaining commercial and corporate transportation facilities, airplanes, and ports skyrockets as a result of terrorist activity due to increased security costs. Of course, terrorism is not only a threat to physical assets. Crucial elements of the GMP, such as the Internet and telecommunications infrastructures, are very vulnerable to attack. Terrorists can use any one of the thousands of different viruses, not to mention other cyber attacks, to harm the Internet and personal computers. Internet viruses are especially dangerous for identity fraud: in 2005 there were about 60 cases per 100,000 people. This ratio shows the vulnerability of the Internet to terrorism.

Terrorism has become one of the most important determinants and indicators of the strategic political risk of investment. Even the threat of terrorism prevented many potential international transactions that would have benefited the GMP. In the US alone, the direct economic impact of 9/11 was $75 billion, or a 0.75 percent reduction of the 2002 GDP.[70] It took seven years for the total amount of foreign direct investment (FDI) flows to surpass the pre-9/11 record and for the United States to become the leading recipient and source of FDI; this occurred in 2007, when global FDI outflows reached a record high of $1.82 trillion.[71] The tourism, transportation (especially the airlines), and insurance industries felt the brunt of 9/11. Unemployment had the largest rise during 1 month in 21 years, and 415,000 jobs were cut as a direct result of 9/11. In the hotel industry, 46,000 jobs were eliminated, and in the trade industry 81,000 jobs were cut. The surge in unemployment and declines in the above-mentioned industries were the result of cautious consumer spending and a failure in investor confidence. Nationwide consumer spending in the US fell by 6 percent and by 11 percent in New York City during the following year. Domestic spending fell by 9 percent, and international spending by 13 percent.[72] Immediately after the attacks of September 11, US airspace was closed for two days, which resulted in a daily loss of $330 million. For the following week, by different evaluations, the loss was between $1 billion and $2 billion. Following the terrorist attacks, travel to New York City dropped by 15 percent in volume compared with the previous year (a 10 percent drop in leisure travel and a 29 percent drop in business travel). International arrivals to New York City declined by 54 percent. According to the US coordinator for counterterrorism, Ambassador Francis Taylor, New York City's estimated losses in sales were $1.7 billion and in rent, $1.75 billion, following September 11, 2001, until the end of 2003.[73] Compared with September 2000, passenger miles were down by 32 percent for domestic flights and by 29 percent for international flights. Because of this, in October 2001, airlines reduced their flights by 18 percent (compared with October 2000), leading to 140,000 layoffs. New York and New Jersey Seaports were closed for two days. Freight decreased by 9 percent, and US borders with Canada and Mexico were almost shut down, which had a wide impact on the economies of both countries. For example, "the Ford Motor Company was not a direct target on September 11, but it lost US $30 million through supply chain disruptions when the US-Canada border was shut after the attack."[74] To demonstrate the scale of the negative economic impact of the closure of the US-Canada border, it is important to underline that 500,000 vehicles cross this border every day.

As a result of 9/11, the world's insurance industry parted with about $50 billion and this led to obvious strategic consequences.[75] The US government, through the Terrorist Risk Insurance Act of 2002, made the following limitations: insurers have to pay the first $5 million of losses in full; if they are between $5 million and $100 billion, the insurer pays the deductible. From the remaining losses, the insurer pays 10 percent and the US government pays 90 percent. The World Trade Center in New York alone

> holds the "worst loss ever" title for numerous individual coverages, such as Workers Compensation for which the loss has been valued at $3.5 billion. Aviation loss valued at $4 billion, and a combined property and business income interruption loss valued at $18.5 billion and life insurance payments at a cost of $2.7 billion.[76]

It is interesting from a strategic business perspective to underline that reinsurance companies consider terrorism as an uninsurable risk. This can be explained by the difficulties of rating terrorism and determining the credible profitable/possible maximum losses. Reinsurers usually support their position by the fact that terrorist attacks are unpredictable and can be too large in destruction. But strategists always have to be able to deal with and predict the unpredictable (further discussed later in this book). One of the leading experts in this area, Kenneth Hoggins, vice president of William Gallagher Associates' Property and Casualty Group, provides interesting suggestions to minimize a company's exposure to risks of terrorism, such as "increasing use of videoconferencing instead of travel, limiting the number of staff members on any single flight, and conducting more vigorous background checks on contractors and employees".[77] But one of the most important strategic objectives of global business in the struggle against terrorism is to help "to cut off money flows to terrorists."[78] Most of the money that goes to terrorist organizations goes under the cover of legal transactions. According to the United States General Accounting Office, oil smuggling and illegal surcharges between 25 and 50 cents per barrel of legal oil revenues provided funds that bolstered Saddam Hussein's regime.[79]

As of 2015, the latest evaluation of strategic economic consequences caused by the September 11, 2001, terrorist attacks is $55 billion, related to loss of life and destruction of infrastructure only in New York City. Increased expenses related to security and decline of some economic activities is estimated at $3.3 trillion by the Global Terrorism Index of the Institute for Economics and Peace.[80] For strategists, some extra time is required to evaluate the economic consequences of large-scale catastrophic events. This is why 13 years after the tragedy of September 2001, more complete damage, both indirect and direct, was measured.

The economic impact on Spain after the Madrid train bombing on March 11, 2004, on the UK after the London terrorist attack on July 7, 2005, and on France after the terrorist attacks in Paris in 2015 damaged not only these countries but also all of Europe and the world economy for a long time. Even a country as far from the US as Norway experienced damage from the September 2001 attacks. The Norwegian capital market had cumulative average losses of approximately 25 percent in the 11 days after the attack. It took 107 days for the Norwegian stock market to recover, which is the second longest recovery period among stock exchanges worldwide, behind the Johannesburg Securities Exchange, which took 162 days to recover.[81] In Mumbai, India, terrorists attacked the public transportation system twice. The July 11 attack in 2006 killed 174 people and injured 464.[82]

Despite all of the economic damage and direct business losses, the most negative impact of terrorism is psychological: the creation in the mindsets of many of barriers against globalization, liberalization, and open national borders. The mentioned decrease in tourism, and especially international tourism, is a direct result of the psychological impact of terrorism and must always be evaluated by strategists. When reported terrorist attacks occur in one part of the world, thousands of people from another part of the world will not even consider traveling to places as attractive as Madrid, London, and Paris, at least for a certain period after terrorist attacks. The World Travel and Tourism Council's Crisis Committee met in London shortly after the attacks and estimated that out of the 31 million people who visit the United Kingdom each year, a drop of about 588,000 was expected—a decline of 1.9 percent from the original 2005 forecast.[83] British carriers alone lost about $475 million due to the fact that 2,500 flights, scheduled to leave only the three major airports of London, were cancelled during the week following the attack.[84] London airports had to deal with all of these losses in addition to their 26 percent loss in passengers in 2001 after the 9/11 attacks, which had implications for Great Britain as well as the entire GMP. However, in 2005 the British government reacted quickly and allocated £4 million to the London Tourism Action Group for a marketing campaign to decrease the negative strategic influence of acts of terror. This money was spent on theatrical performances, athletic events, discount packages, etc., in order to attract tourists and the revenue they generate.

Psychological barriers caused by terrorism became real business barriers for companies from the GEM when they tried to invest in assets of high national security in developed countries. In 2006, Dubai Ports World (DP World), owned by the Dubai government, bought the British company Peninsular & Oriental Steam Navigation. For years this London-based company was a major operator of many ports in the US. When DP World became the owner of this British company, the US Congress grew anxious.[85] In order to solve the problem, DP World wisely decided to hand over control of US port operations to an American company. These fears happened despite the fact that Dubai is one of the most liberal Islamic states in the Middle East and a major trading hub of the world.

It is important to underline that there is not only Islamic terrorism in the world. There are many other streams of terrorism that negatively influence the GMP. When terrorists, motivated purely by domestic issues, attacked an oil tanker in Nigeria, the eighth largest petroleum producer in the world, oil exports were immediately reduced by 20 percent.[86] Because of this attack, Shell Oil Company removed 330 employees that were operating in Nigeria, resulting in a decline of 226,000 barrels of daily oil production.[87]

Strategic Repercussions of Terrorism in the Global Emerging Market

Terrorists usually seek to strike in developed countries, but in fact it is their activity in poor and emerging market countries that allows them to be successful. This is where they find their foot soldiers, spread their propaganda, and have the best chances of getting governmental support (national, regional, or at least local). EMCs are usually the primary location for fundraising and weapons manufacturing. In most cases, EMC governments are secular, and terrorists use this as propaganda to incite extremism with the attempt to make religious law the law of the state. Terrorist organizations usually have two artificially separated wings—one engaged in political battle against the government, and another engaged in military insurgency against the government. Hezbollah in Lebanon is an obvious example of this. Businesses are prime targets for terrorists in their attempts to create civil unrest and anti-western sentiment, and to weaken secular governments. The closer a government of an EMC moves toward democracy and western values, the more aggressive and active terrorists become. Such is the case in Lebanon, Pakistan, Bangladesh, Indonesia, and Libya, where terrorists are making last-ditch efforts to prevent the spread of prosperity and democracy. For terrorists, extremists, and for primitive anti-westerners, the presence of foreign companies, especially those from developed countries, always symbolizes the "infidels" and/or "non-patriots" of their domestic governments, which allow the foreign presence. Under fear of other terrorist attacks, during 2001–2002, net private capital inflows to EMCs decreased by 36.5 percent, from $167 billion to $106 billion. Certain industries are more attractive targets for terrorists, especially tourism, the world's largest industry in terms of input to GWP, which is approximately 11 percent. This industry employs 207 million people worldwide, 8.2 percent of employment in the GMP.[88] In the GEM, the role of tourism is even more important. In small EMCs like Morocco, Lebanon, Croatia, Albania, and small island nations, tourism is the main industry. The regional budgets of many cities in EMCs, like St. Petersburg in Russia or Dubrovnik in Croatia, among others, substantially depend on tourism. Terrorist attacks, or just the threat of terrorist attacks, negatively impact tourism by reducing the number of tourist arrivals and forcing the hospitality industry, including tourist companies, to invest heavily in protection, decreasing profits and required foreign investment. Turkey receives 1.8 percent of worldwide tourist arrivals and is ranked 20th by the World Tourism Organization by this indicator.[89] In the spring of 2006, because of terrorist attacks and threats, Turkey lost between $4 billion and $5 billion, and tourist arrivals decreased by 20 percent.[90] According to a study by the Australian Strategic Policy Institute, "in Indonesia, a 2.2 percent fall in tourist arrivals in 2002—in part reflecting the Bali bombings—led financial market analysts to predict a 1 percent reduction in national gross domestic product."[91]

Leaders of EMCs understand the danger of terrorism. Counterterrorism was once on the agenda of only a few developed countries. In the twenty-first century, the leaders of EMCs such as Algeria, Pakistan, Saudi Arabia, Russia, and China; of pre-emerging market countries like Bangladesh and Kosovo, and even of developing countries like Afghanistan and Uzbekistan devote substantial resources to fighting terrorism. Laws against terrorism appear throughout the GEM, as do laws preventing money laundering and the funding of terrorist activities. For example, the Commonwealth of Independent States (CIS), an organization of 12 of the 15 former Soviet republics, have a formal agreement on financial crimes inspired by the Office of Foreign Assets Control of the US Department of Treasury, which enforces economic and trade sanctions according to US foreign policy and implements regulations against terrorist activities and the trafficking of narcotics.

Modern technology and increasing economic integration has made it possible for domestic extremists and terrorists to operate in foreign countries and to develop networks on a global scale. Terrorism has become a major factor of political risk of investment. Consequently, the development of the future global order has and will be greatly influenced by this. Terrorism will continue to be a very important and money-consuming threat for business in the twenty-first century. But increasing economic integration can be considered one of the strategies used by businesses against terrorism. The development of private domestic businesses in Arab nations and the integration of these businesses in the GMP undoubtedly play an important role in the fight against terrorism. This strategy benefits not only the business community but also society within these countries in general.

Terrorism is a social manifestation of evil and requires complete eradication. Terrorists interpret kindness as weakness—such methodologies will not solve their malevolence. Compromising with terrorists only prolongs their ability to wage war against humanity and creates an ocean of grief and extended poverty. The existence of the plague of terrorism and extremism diverts badly needed resources from the fight against hunger and mass disease. Just as barbarians destroyed ancient Rome and plunged humankind into darkness, terrorists with modern weapons can bring a global catastrophe. But the GMP has demonstrated strength to withhold the wave of terrorism. The fast reaction of the global community, anti-terrorists, and national and international strategies helped to develop more strict regulations and to implement preventive measures and new technologies in practically every industry and region of the GMP. Despite the high cost of all these measures, during the first decade of the twenty-first century, the GMP has demonstrated steady growth and an improvement of the standards of living of the global population. What humankind needs is the development of a detailed global strategy, including: first, strategies to prevent terrorism; second, strategies of fighting and prosecuting terrorism and extremism; and third, economic and social-recovery strategies after terrorist attacks, which unfortunately will occur for the foreseeable future.

Technological Trends in Strategic Development

As a result of the scientific-technological revolution of the twentieth century, evaluation of recent and future political, social, and economic trends cannot be accurately completed without strategic factoring of the repercussions of technological trends. The most influential scientific and technological development in the twenty-first century is the transformation of the world economy from the once predominant service sector to that of knowledge-based industries. This emerging transformation is a result of the approaching second scientific-technological revolution, which will determine all aspects of social, economic, and even political development. This revolution will so profoundly change science and technology that its influence can be compared only to the scientific-technological revolution of the twentieth century. The GMP will be dominated by this revolution at least until 2050 and possibly until the twenty-second century. The development of the knowledge economy and trends in research and development are discussed in more detail in Chapter 5, and are touched upon throughout this book.

This section provides a brief analysis of the most important trends in scientific research and technological development and their impact on humankind in the twenty-first century. The technological trend with the most wide-reaching impact on the GMP is the increasing penetration of radical telecommunication capabilities and cutting-edge information technologies, which is creating an unprecedented level of interconnectivity throughout the entire GMP. The capabilities of these technologies do not even compare to those of the twentieth century. By the end of this century, practically everyone will have access to telecommunications and information technologies of fundamentally new qualities. However, at the beginning of the twenty-first century, despite very rapid growth in penetration rates, there are still substantial portions of the global population without access to basic information technologies. In Figure 7.5 both the International Telecommunication Union (ITU) World Telecommunication and the United Nations Conference on Trade and Development (UNCTAD), which adapts this information into Figure 7.5, use outdated classification terms and categories for emerging market countries, dividing them into two different groups: "Developing Economies" and "Economies in Transition."[92] These terms undermine the role EMCs play in the GMP. Combining these descriptions into the category "emerging market countries"—as we have done throughout this book—demonstrates the unquestionable leadership of GEM countries over developed nations when it comes to dynamic cell phone penetration during the first

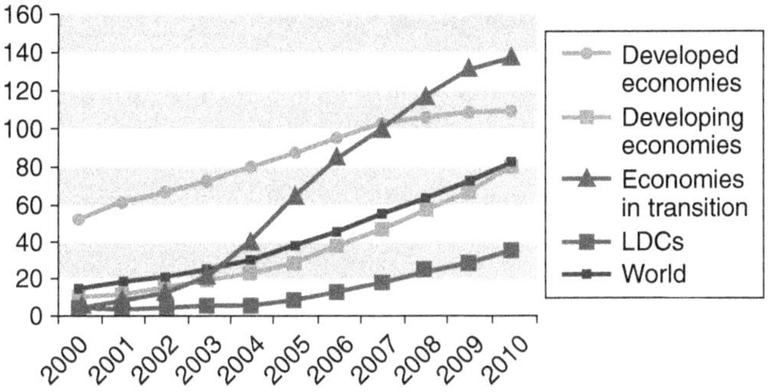

Figure 7.5 Mobile Phone Penetration by Country Categorization, 2002–2010

Adapted from United Nations Conference on Trade and Development (UNCTAD). (2011). *Information Economy Report 2011: ICTs as an Enabler for Private Sector Development.* London and Geneva: United Nations Publication, p. 19. Retrieved from http://unctad.org/en/Docs/ier2011_en.pdf

decade of the twenty-first century. This tendency will continue until at least the year 2025. Telecom strategists can and should rely on this dynamic.

The three indicators in Figure 7.6a and Figure 7.6b also demonstrate the very positive dynamics of mobile telephone penetration in EMCs compared to developed states.

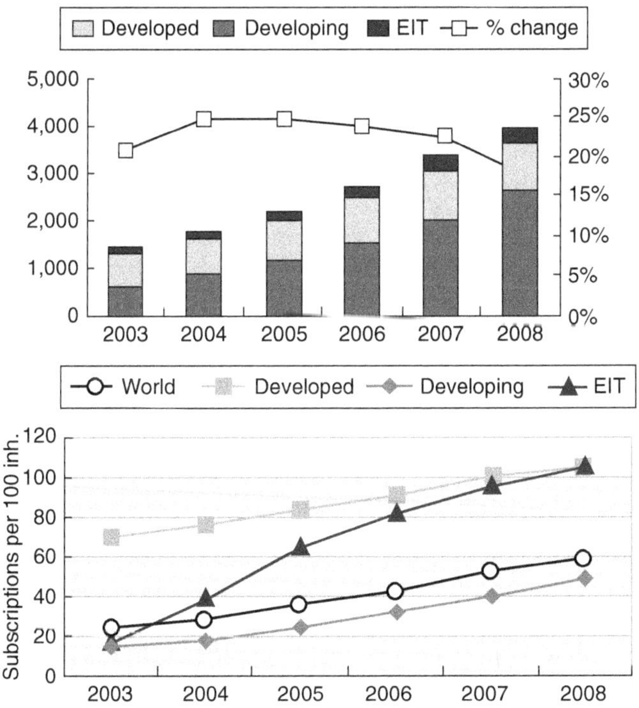

Figure 7.6a Mobile Subscribers by Country Categorization, 2002–2009[93]

UNCTAD.(2009). *Information Economy Report 2009: Trends and Outlook in Turbulent Times.* London and Geneva: United Nations Publication, p. 4. Retrieved from http://unctad.org/en/Docs/ier2009_en.pdf. Based on ITU and National Data.

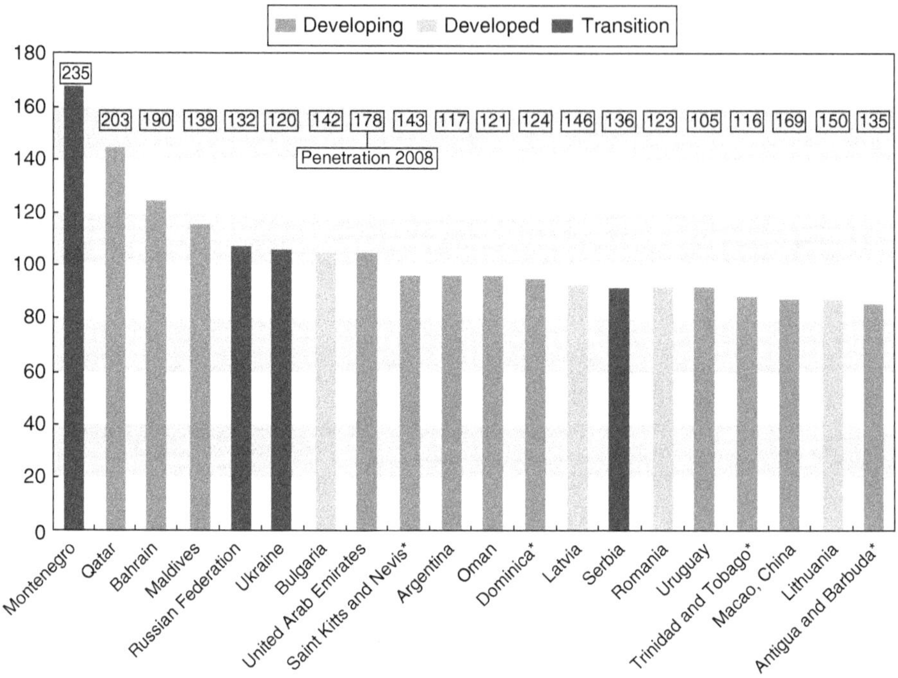

Figure 7.6b Twenty Most Dynamic Economies in Terms of Increased Mobile Penetration, 2003–2008
UNCTAD. (2009). *Information Economy Report 2009: Trends and Outlook in Turbulent Times*. London and Geneva: United Nations Publication, p .7. Retrieved from http://unctad.org/en/Docs/ier2009_en.pdf. Based on ITU and National Data.

Again as a reminder, both ITU and UNCTAD are using outdated classification terms and categories in these tables. It is easier and more conducive to research these three indicators by grouping together developing countries (because in reality only three countries out of this list still belong to the developing country category) with Eastern European States in Transition to Market Economy (or EIT) to better understand the GEM dynamics.

The statistics of all countries mentioned in the above three indicators belong to EMCs except for the following three states, which did not change their statistics substantially: Dominica, the Maldives, and Antigua and Barbuda, which still belong to developing countries according to our book's classification (which has already been discussed previously). Mobile telephone penetration in society is a very important strategic factor for several compelling reasons. First of all, it increases the quality of life of residents of these countries and their safety; and second, it lays a foundation for easy development of diversified services for people, corporations, and governmental structures on central, regional, and municipal levels. Third, mobile penetration is a very attractive factor for any foreign entrepreneur or corporate entity who may be considering cross-border investments or trade in these countries. Some other strategic reasons can be added to this line of important development drawn from these figures.

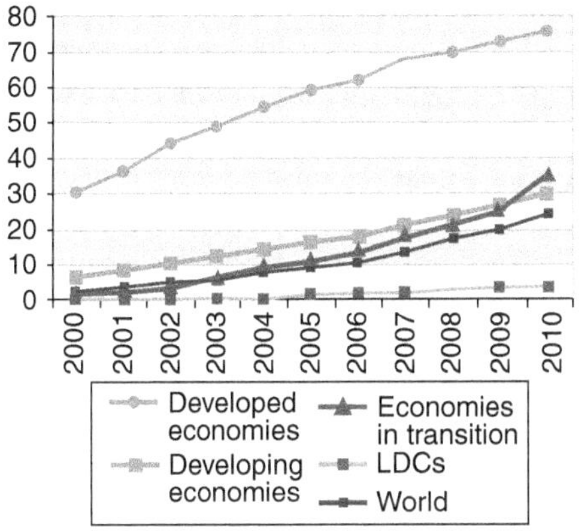

Figure 7.7a Internet Penetration by Country Categorization, 2002–2010

UNCTAD. (2011). *Information Economy Report 2011: ICTs as an Enabler for Private Sector Development*. London and Geneva: United Nations Publication, p. 26. Retrieved from http://unctad.org/en/Docs/ier2011_en.pdf

Technological trends as an accumulation of innovations are responses to the economic, social, and security needs of society. Most research and development is being used to discover technological solutions to meet the public values and practical demands of companies and entrepreneurs. This is the first major avenue of scientific achievement in the GMP and the main prospect for upcoming strategies. The second major avenue is through the national budgets of countries. Typically, research and technology sponsored

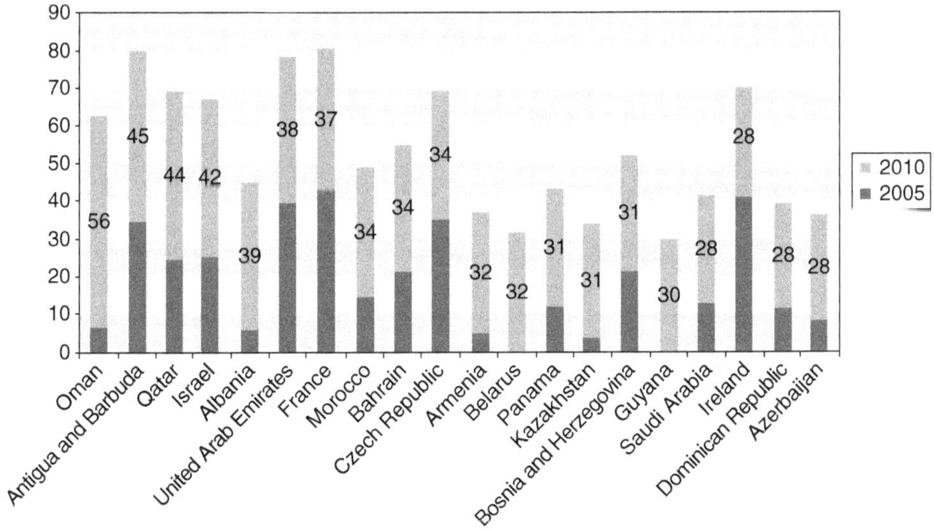

Figure 7.7b Top 20 Economies by Largest Increase in Internet Users per 100 Inhabitants, 2005–2010

UNCTAD. (2011). *Information Economy Report 2011: ICTs as an Enabler for Private Sector Development*. London and Geneva: United Nations Publication, p. 27. Retrieved from http://unctad.org/en/Docs/ier2011_en.pdf. Adapted from ITU World Telecommunication/ICT Indicators Database.

by national governments address problems shared by contemporary civilization, such as poverty, mass disease, migration, unemployment, terrorism, national security, and environmental protection. Even new technological achievements from the private sector reach their final utilization via the needs and values of the general population. More than that, military-oriented technological achievements, almost always with a certain time lag, are used in the civilian sector of the economy and finally by individual consumers. The development of scientific-technological solutions to the most challenging problems facing humankind is already underway, not only via information technology but through advancements in transportation, geological studies, civil engineering and construction, biology and genetics, and, subsequently, food production and health care. Some directions in scientific research, like nanomembrane and space technologies, are penetrating all industries as well as the social and private lives of individuals.

A 2006 RAND Corporation study sponsored by the National Intelligence Council of the United States evaluated the implementation feasibility of the following 16 most promising technological applications by the year 2020:[94]

1. *Cheap solar energy*[95]
2. *Rural wireless communications*
3. *Communication devices for ubiquitous information access anywhere, anytime*
4. Genetically modified crops
5. *Rapid bioassays*
6. *Filters and catalysts for water purification and decontamination*
7. *Targeted drug delivery*
8. Cheap autonomous housing
9. *Green manufacturing*
10. *Ubiquitous radio-frequency identification (RFID) tagging of commercial products and individuals*
11. *Hybrid vehicles*
12. Pervasive sensors
13. *Tissue engineering*
14. *Improved diagnostic and surgical methods*
15. Wearable computers
16. *Quantum cryptography*

Based on evaluations of scientists from the Massachusetts Institute of Technology, *MIT Technology Review* offers another expert opinion on the most important emerging technologies at the beginning of the twenty-first century. This publication's annual selection (since 2001) of ten revolutionary technologies is a very useful tool for strategists. Below I present two examples of selected technologies by the *MIT Technology Review* in 2008 and 2012. This is an annual selection of the following ten technologies,[96] all of which represent modern technological trends with key strategic implications. Despite the technological achievements that appeared during this five-year period—communication technologies, biological technologies, and modernization of different traditional technologies on a new innovative base—they are mostly concentrated around foreseeing the future, which is very important for strategists. Strategists always have to pay attention to the most revolutionary innovations, which are not necessarily scientific or technological. These innovations can be organizational and emerge as a result of humanity's intellectual activity to promote the increase of economic efficiency and the quality of life:

2008[97]

1. Forecasting Modeling of Unexpected Events
2. Probabilistic Chips
3. NanoRadio
4. Wireless Power
5. Atomic Magnetometers
6. Offline Web Applications
7. Graphene Transistors
8. Connectomics
9. Reality Mining
10. Cellulolytic Enzymes

2012[98]

1. Egg Stem Cells
2. A Faster Fourier Transform
3. Ultra-Efficient Solar
4. Nanopore Sequencing
5. Light-Field Photography
6. Crowdfunding
7. Solar Microgrids
8. High-Speed Materials Discovery
9. 3-D Transistors
10. Facebook's Timeline

When assessing and strategizing global technological trends, it is very important for strategists to keep in mind that the technological development of the GMP, and especially of the GEM, is an uneven process. These disparities have roots in the educational gap, age of production facilities, and level of strategy developments between different countries and even domestic regions. It can be understood through an analysis of economic history and the subsequent societal attitudes toward education. Variations of this have very important implications for economic and technological strategic development. The quality of education and the influence of technological trends are always preconditions for economic and social progress, especially in emerging market, developing, and underdeveloped countries. Some EMCs from Asia, Africa, and Latin America suffer from educational levels below the world average. However, in other EMCs, such as Ireland, the Czech and Slovak republics, Hungary, Russia, Ukraine, Poland, South Korea, and Hong Kong, the educational levels are well above that average. In countries with large territories and populations, like China, Russia, India, and Brazil, the quality of education differs profoundly by region and even ethnic group. For example, in the Chinese northwest, the quality of education is far behind that of southeastern regions of China. In Brazil a significant portion of the indigenous population in the central regions does not even speak Portuguese, the national language. Obviously, the educational levels in this region are far below the national average. Due to many years of oppression from the horribly shameful system of apartheid, the black population of South Africa has lower levels of education than the white population, in general. In many of the rural villages in Russia, children do not receive more than an elementary school education, while at the same time some of the most respected scientists and scholars of the world are Russian. In countries that are small in terms of territory, like Bahrain, UAE, or Qatar, the widest educational gap is mostly between local nationals and service expatriates, mostly from Eastern and Central Asian countries.

Surprisingly, in many EMCs, an advanced level of some technologies is a legacy of the dictatorial system, which strategically devoted most of its resources to military power in order to protect itself from internal and external threats (the greatest of which was democracy, which is vulnerable itself!). A strong military requires a sophisticated level of science and technology. Highly educated specialists were a necessity, especially in the fields of mathematics, physics, chemistry, and engineering. This is why countries from the former Soviet bloc and later China and Cuba have achieved relative success in education and in a few scientific fields. It is important to underline the fact that investments in education by dictatorships were done to protect the regime, not to benefit the people. The fall of dictatorships throughout the world has allowed a reorientation away from mostly military use of technology toward civilian and consumer use (with relapses in a few former regimes, the most dictatorial). Not surprisingly, foreign investors have become very keen to develop high-tech industries in countries from the GEM with well-educated and relatively cheap engineers and scientists. This is actually increasing the gap between the educational and technological "haves" and "have nots." Countries with rich traditions in science and education like Russia, Poland, and Hungary receive some foreign investment in this field, while technologically less-developed countries do not.

All of these disparities in education are on the one hand a major obstacle to the global strategy of modern technological implementation. On the other hand, modern technological trends are so powerful that they will eventually increase the standards of living in every single region and country of the GMP, which in turn creates a virtuous cycle of gradual and constant educational and technological advancement. This correlation always has to be taken into consideration by strategists. Figure 7.8 indicates that disparities in education lead to substantial differences in scientific and technological achievements. The top 30 countries in terms of patents filed by resident per unit of GDP does not only include developed countries.[99] Half of the countries on this list are from the GEM. Twelve of the fifteen EMCs are former command economies, which illustrates the link mentioned above between some dictatorships and investments in science and technology. As of the

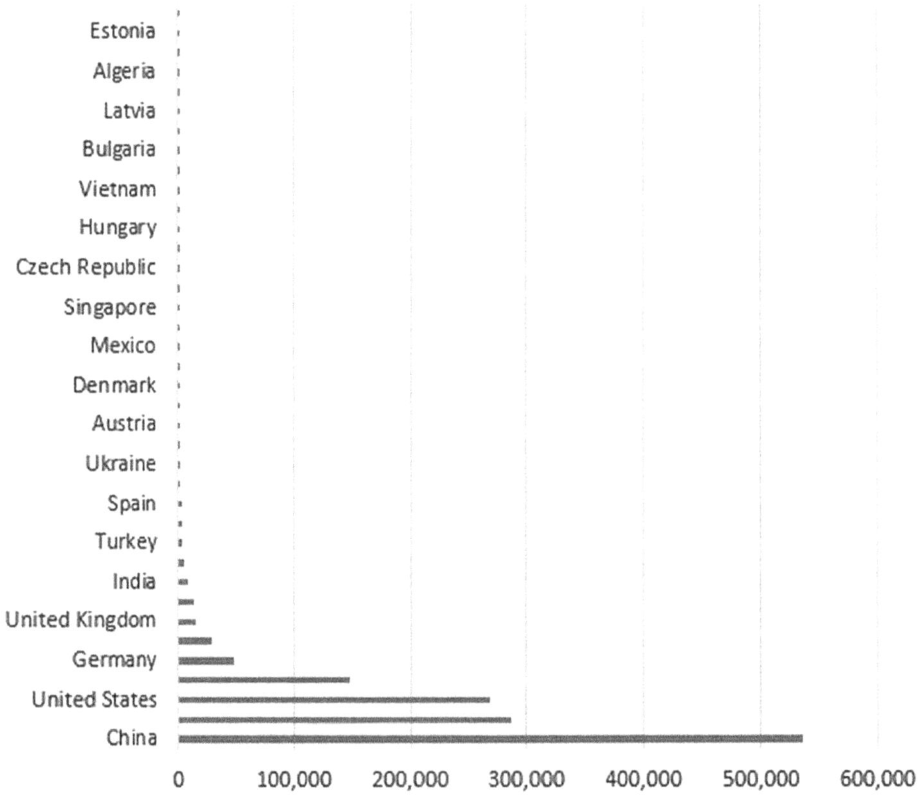

Figure 7.8 Resident Patent Filings per $1 Billion of Gross Domestic Product (PPP)

World Intellectual Property Organization (WIPO). (2009). *World Intellectual Property Indicators (2009)*, p.18. Retrieved from www.wipo.int/edocs/pubdocs/en/intproperty/941/wipo_pub_941.pdf

twenty-first century, the fastest-growing input to patent-related scientific achievements relative to GDP is in China—a country still controlled by the communist party.

> "According to a study from the RAND corporation, the twenty-first century will be revolutionized by "the growing effect of multidisciplinary technology across all dimensions of life; social, economic, political, and personal. Biotechnology will enable us to identify, understand, manipulate, improve, and control living organisms (including ourselves). The revolution of information availability and utility will continue to profoundly affect the world in all these dimensions. Smart materials, agile manufacturing, and nanotechnology will change the way we produce devices while expanding their capabilities. These technologies may also be joined by 'wild cards' ... if barriers to their development are resolved over time. The results could be astonishing. Effects may include significant improvements in human quality of life and life span, high rates of industrial turnover, lifetime worker training, continued globalization, reshuffling of wealth, cultural amalgamation or invasion with potential for increased tension and conflict, shifts in power from nation state to non-governmental organizations and individuals, mixed environmental effects, improvements in quality of life with accompanying prosperity and reduced tension, and the possibility of human eugenics and cloning".[100]

When developing a strategy for a particular entity, whether a corporation, government, or multilateral institution, it is absolutely crucial to analyze the impact of dynamic key innovations and technological trends. Political and economic goals can be achieved faster and more efficiently if the right technological means are selected. Microsoft's decades of success based on Bill Gates' ability in the 1970s to foresee technological trends in personal computers,[101] the "information superhighway," is an obvious illustration of this. As a result of Gates' strategic vision and recognition of these key trends, Microsoft had huge strategic advantages over its competitors in the development of personal computers and Internet technologies. The strategic selection of the right trends and development of a scientific-technological strategy for its research and implementation can bring great personal and commercial success—and almost always a positive social impact. A sophisticated scientific-technological strategy significantly accelerates the fulfillment of its objectives and goals. Corporate innovative scientific-technological strategy, which is part of general corporate strategy, should be developed with a focus on basic economic factors of production, as well as on the social and environmental impact of the company's activity.

Accurate selection of the most dominant technological trends influencing the strategizing object allows strategists to prepare strategic experiments, such as an analysis of a trend's influence on branches or subsidiaries. And not immediately for a five- or ten-year horizon strategy for the entire entity, but for a much shorter period of three years in one of its country's corporate facility locations. Strategic experiments help with selection of the most efficient decisions and also to eliminate from future use any unproductive or counterproductive ideas, technologies, methods, and regulations. If strategic experiments demonstrate positive results, then strategists can extend investment of this technology throughout all corporate facilities around the world (quite often with some specific adjustments). Strategic experimentation is the most underdeveloped instrument and method of evaluation of strategizing an entity's strengths and weaknesses and the evaluation of strategy potentials for full entity involvement. The same experimental approach can be used by strategists for the development of national and regional strategies.

Technological trends, discussed above in collaboration with other global, regional, and sectorial ones, are very important for strategists to survey and understand, and are leading to an increasingly interconnected world, where everyone on Earth will be online by 2020 in what is called the new digital age.[102] Due in part to these technological advancements, the global order has emerged, whereby countries, regional blocs, and corporations can engage in a system of cooperation in order to tackle global issues. This emerging global order, discussed in the next chapter, would not have been possible without the trend of technological advancements that strategists must continue to foresee, analyze, and strategize.

Notes

1 Churchill, W. (1947). Speech at the House of Commons. November 11. From *Winston S. Churchill: His Complete Speeches, 1897–1963,* in R.R. James (Ed.), vol. 7 (1974), p. 7566.
2 Wilde, O. (1915). "The Soul of Man under Socialism." Google eBook. Literary Collector Press, p. 45.
3 The Food and Agriculture Organization of the United Nations (FAO). (2014). *The State of World Fisheries and Aquaculture 2014. Opportunities and Challenges*. Rome, p. 53.
4 The Food and Agriculture Organization of the United Nations (2014). *The State of World Fisheries and Aquaculture 2014. Opportunities and Challenges*. Rome, pp. 88.
5 Irvine, J.R., Tompkins, A., Saito, T., Seong, K.B., Kim, J.K., Klovach, N., Bartlett, H., and Volk, E. (2012). "Pacific Salmon Status and Abundance Trends—2012 Update." *NPAFC,* doc. 1422. Retrieved from www.npafc.org/new/publications/Documents/PDF%202012/1422 (Canada).pdf
6 "NPAFC Hatchery Release Data." (2014). Retrieved from www.dfo-mpo.gc.ca/international/dip-NPAFC-eng.htm
7 Jessop, B. (1999). "Reflections on Globalisation and Its (il)logic(s)." In Olds, K. Dicken, P., Kelly, P.F., Kong, L. and Wai-chung Yeung, H. (Eds.), *Globalisation and the Asia Pacific: Contested Territories* (p. 37). London: Routledge.
8 Thompson, G. (2000). "The Nature and Limits of Economic Globalization." In D. Held (Ed.), *A Globalizing World? Culture, Economics, Politics* (p. 94). London: Routledge.
9 National Intelligence Council. (2000). *Global Trends 2015: A Dialogue about the Future with Nongovernment Experts*, Washington, DC. Retrieved from www.dni.gov/nic/NIC_globaltrend2015.html
10 National Intelligence Council. (2000). *Global Trends 2015: A Dialogue about the Future with Nongovernment Experts*, Washington, DC. Retrieved from www.dni.gov/nic/NIC_globaltrend2015.html
11 In fact, Napoleon's influence is not only in Europe. The Napoleonic Code has influenced the judicial system of the US state of Louisiana.
12 Ministry of General Affairs of the Netherlands. (2008). "Countries Sign New Benelux Treaty." June 9. Retrieved from http://www.minaz.nl/english/News/Press_releases_and_news_items/2008/Juni/Countries_sign_new_Benelux_Treaty
13 Tagliabue, J. (1996). "North Italy's Separatist Leader Says He Is Willing to Negotiate." *New York Times*. September 25. Retrieved from www.nytimes.com/1996/09/25/world/north-italy-s-separatist-leader-says-he-is-willing-to-negotiate.html
14 United Nations. (n.d.). "Growth in United Nations Membership 1945–present." Retrieved from www.un.org/en/members/growth.shtml
15 Chia, L.S. (2003). *Southeast Asia Transformed: A Geography of Change*. Singapore: Institute of Southeast Asian Studies, p. 303.
16 Breslin, S., Higgot, R. and Rosamond, B. (2002). "Regions in Comparative Perspective." In Breslin, S., Hughes, C.W., Phillips, N. and Rosamond, B. (Eds.), *New Regionalisms in the Global Political Economy*. London: Routledge, p. 2.

17 Manning, T. (2008). "Emerging Markets Everywhere—The Strategist's Dream Come True." *BA UpFront*. Retrieved from www.tonymanning.com/asp/downloads/articles/Tony%20Manning%20-%20Emerging%20markets%20everywhere%20-%20Sept%202005.pdf
18 Loughlin, J. and Mazey, S. (Eds.). (1995) *The End of the French Unitary State? Ten Years of Regionalization in France (1982–1992)*. London: Routledge, p. 2.
19 Keating, M. (1983). "Decentralization in Mitterrand's France." *Public Administration: An International Quarterly*, vol. 61, no. 3, pp. 237–252.
20 Stiglitz, J. (2007). *Making Globalization Work*. New York, London: W.W. Norton and Company, p. 52.
21 Litvack, J., Ahmad, J. and Bird, R. (1998). *Rethinking Decentralization in Developing Countries*. Washington, DC: The World Bank, p. 4.
22 Index compiled by Professor Christine Kearney of Saint Anselm College. December 30, 1999. Retrieved from www.econ.brown.edu/faculty/henderson/decentralization.pdf
23 United Nations Development Program. "Local Governance and Decentralization in Europe and the CIS." Retrieved from http://europeandcis.undp.org/governance/lgdc/show/F8B06B55-F203-1EE9-B73274DA527AD025
24 Matsui, K. (2005). "Post-Decentralization Regional Economies and Actors: Putting the Capacity of Local Governments to the Test." *The Developing Economies*, vol. 43, no. 1, p. 171.
25 As of 2015, Ukraine is about to retract its membership from CIS.
26 Asia-Pacific Economic Cooperation. "About APEC." Retrieved from www.apec.org/content/apec/about_apec.html
27 Asia-Pacific Economic Cooperation. "About APEC." Retrieved from www.apec.org/content/apec/about_apec.html
28 Asia-Pacific Economic Cooperation. "About APEC." Retrieved from www.apec.org/content/apec/about_apec.html
29 Mucchielli, J.-L., Buckley, P.J., Cordell, V.V. (Eds.). (1996). *Globalization and Regionalization: Strategies, Policies and Economic Environments*. New York: International Business Press, p. xi.
30 Wallin, B. (n.d.). "Privatization of State Services in Massachusetts: Politics, Policy and an Experiment that Wasn't." Prepared for the Economic Policy Institute, pp. 3–4. Retrieved from http://archive.epinet.org/real_media/010111/materials/wallin.pdf
31 See Pirie, M. (1985). *Privatization in Theory and Practice*. London: The Adam Smith Institute.
32 Bulgartabac Holding AD. Homepage. Retrieved from www.bulgartabac.bg/?&LanguageCode=en
33 Vatahov, I. (2005). "Another Bulgartabac Privatisation Attempt." *Sofia Echo*. February 18. Retrieved from www.sofiaecho.com/article/another-bulgartabac-privatisation-attempt/id_10793/catid_23
34 "Transitional economy" is a theoretically unreasonable determination for several Eastern and Southern European countries in the GEM.
35 Fungacova, Z. (2005). "Building a Castle on Sand: Effects of Mass Privatizatoin on Capital Market Creation in Transition Economies." Working Paper Series, Center for Economic Research and Graduate Education Academy of Sciences of the Czech Republic Economics Institute. Retrieved February 9, 2008 from www.cerge-ei.cz/pdf/wp/Wp256.pdf
36 Kogut, B. and Spicer, A. (2002). "Capital Market Development and Mass Privatization Are Logical Contradictions: Lessons from Russia and the Czech Republic." *Industrial and Corporate Change*, vol. 11, no. 1, abstract.
37 Lesova, P. (2007). "Emerging Markets Drive Record IPO Activity: Ernst & Young Study Documents China's 2007 Dominance." MarketWatch from DowJones. December 17. Retrieved from www.marketwatch.com/news/story/emerging-markets-drive-global-ipo/story.aspx?guid=%7B3D345195-EBA1-4A70-B837-AC31D8D14A64%7D
38 "Ernst & Young Press Release" (2007). December 17. Retrieved from www.ey.com/global/Content.nsf/International/Media_-_Press_Release_-Year_End_IPO_Activity
39 "Ernst & Young Press Release" (2007). December 17. Retrieved from www.ey.com/global/Content.nsf/International/Media_-_Press_Release_-Year_End_IPO_Activity
40 "Russia Central Bank Voids Standard & Poor's, Moody's, Fitch Ratings." (2015). *Russia Today* (RT). January 19. From www.rt.com/business/224067-russia-central-bank-rating-agencies
41 Boutchkova, M.K. and Megginson, W.L. (2000). "Privatization and the Rise of Global Capital Markets." *Financial Management*, vol. 29, no. 4. Retrieved February 19, 2008 from http://ideas.repec.org/a/fma/fmanag/maria00.html

42 Ernst & Young. (2006). "Accelerating Growth Global IPO Trends 2006," p. 2. Retrieved July 16, 2008 from www.altassets.com/pdfs/eyGlobal_IPO_Survey2006.pdf
43 Reed, S. (2003). "School Daze at British Universities." *Businessweek*. November 10. Retrieved from www.businessweek.com/magazine/content/03_45/b3857109_mz054.htm
44 MacLeod, D. (2007). "Education Worth More to British Exports than Banking." *The Guardian*. September 18. Retrieved from http://education.guardian.co.uk/students/internationalstudents/story/0,,2171234,00.html
45 Sellgren, K. (2014). "Decline of Overseas Students at England's Universities." BBC News Education Report. April 1. Retrieved from www.bbc.com/news/education-26836962
46 Paulson, A. (2014,). "Record 900,000 International Students in the US: The Top Countries They Hail From." *The Christian Science Monitor*. November 17. Retrieved from www.csmonitor.com/USA/Education/2014/1117/Record-900-000-international-students-in-US-the-top-countries-they-hail-from
47 Sports Direct International. "Overview." Retrieved from www.sports-direct-international.com/main.asp?pid=3
48 Braithwaite, T. (2008). "Sports Direct in China Alliance." *Financial Times*. February 5. Retrieved from www.ft.com/cms/s/0/a610697e-d413-11dc-a8c6-0000779fd2ac.html
49 Braithwaite, T. (2008). "Sports Direct in China Alliance." *Financial Times*. February 5. Retrieved from www.ft.com/cms/s/0/a610697e-d413-11dc-a8c6-0000779fd2ac.html
50 UBS. "History of UBS." Retrieved from www.ubs.com/1/e/about/history/2001_2006/2003.html
51 Bream, R., Burgess, K. and Saigol, L. (2008). "Dawn Raid for Rio Tinto Stuns BHP." *Financial Times*. February 1. Retrieved from www.ft.com/cms/s/0/a51f903e-d09f-11dc-953a-0000779fd2ac.html.
52 Politi, J. (2007). "Hostile Takeovers Make a Comeback." *Financial Times*. November 28. Retrieved from www.ft.com/cms/s/0/a51f903e-d09f-11dc-953a-0000779fd2ac.html?nclick_check=1
53 BenDaniel, D.J. and Rosenbloom, A.H. (1999). *The Handbook of International Mergers & Acquisitions*. Upper Saddle River, NJ: Prentice-Hall, Inc., pp. 12–13.
54 "Metromedia International Group's Ningbo Ya Mei Joint Venture Receives Notice of Project Status." (1999). Business Wire. August 4. Retrieved from http://findarticles.com/p/articles/mi_m0EIN/is_1999_August_4/ai_55341682
55 "Paine Webber's New Role." (1999). *New York Times*. June 4. Retrieved from www.nytimes.com/1999/06/04/business/paine-webber-s-new-role.html
56 Khazindar, A. (2003). "The Roots of Terrorism." *Arab News*. October 19. Retrieved February 21, 2008 from www.arabnews.com/?page=13&section=0&article=33849&d=19&m=10&y=2003
57 UNICEF. (n.d.). "At a Glance: Saudi Arabia." Retrieved February 15, 2008 from www.unicef.org/infobycountry/saudiarabia_statistics.html
58 UNICEF. (n.d.). "At a Glance: Saudi Arabia." Retrieved February 15, 2008 from www.unicef.org/infobycountry/saudiarabia_statistics.html
59 Krueger, A.B. (2007). *What Makes a Terrorist: Economics and the Roots of Terrorism*. Princeton, NJ: Princeton University Press, p. 3.
60 *The 9/11 Commission Report: Final Report of the National Commission on Terrorist Attacks Upon the United States*. (2004). New York: Norton & Company, p. 378.
61 Kephart, J.L. (2005). "Immigration and Terrorism: Moving Beyond the 9/11 Staff Report on Terrorist Travel. Executive Summary." Center for Immigration Studies. Retrieved March 1, 2008 from www.cis.org/articles/2005/kephart.html
62 Federation for American Immigration Reform. (n.d.). "Immigration and National Security." Retrieved from www.fairus.org/site/PageServer?pagename=iic_immigrationissuecentersb1c7
63 US Code of Federal Regulations 28 C.F.R. Section 0.85.
64 Archick, K. (2014). "US-EU Cooperation against Terrorism—Analysis." *The Eurasia Review*. December 19. Retrieved from www.eurasiareview.com/19122014-us-eu-cooperation-terrorism-analysis/
65 US Customs and Border Protection. (2004). "Securing the Global Supply Chain: Customs Trade Partnership against Terrorism Security Plan." Retrieved February 21, 2008 from www.cbp.gov/linkhandler/cgov/import/commercial_enforcement/ctpat/what_ctpat/ctpat_strategicplan.ctt/ctpat_strategicplan.pdf
66 Section 2656f(a) of Title 22 of the United States Code.
67 Section 2656f(d) of Title 22 of the United States Code.

68 US Department of Treasury (2007). *National Money Laundering Strategy*, p. 105. Retrieved February 14, 2008 from www.treas.gov/press/releases/docs/nmls.pdf
69 Jennings, P. (2004). *Terrorism and Australian Business*. Barton: Australian Strategic Policy Institute, p. 1.
70 Citation of the IMF in Jennings, P. (2004). *Terrorism and Australian Business*. Barton: Australian Strategic Policy Institute, p. 3.
71 "Foreign Direct Investment." (2008). *The Economist*. July 3. Retrieved July 15, 2008 from www.economist.com/markets/indicators/displaystory.cfm?story_id=11670637
72 NYC Visit.com. (n.d.). "NYC Statistics." Retrieved February 29, 2008 from www.nycvisit.com/content/index.cfm?pagePkey=57
73 Taylor, F. (2002). "The Impact of Global Terrorism. Remarks to Executives Club of Chicago Leadership Symposium." March 14. Retrieved March 14, 2002 from www.state.gov/s/ct/rls/rm/8839.htm
74 Jennings, P. (2004). *Terrorism and Australian Business*. Barton: Australian Strategic Policy Institute, p. 3.
75 Taylor, F. (2002). "The Impact of Global Terrorism. Remarks to Executives Club of Chicago Leadership Symposium." March 14. Retrieved March 14, 2002 from www.state.gov/s/ct/rls/rm/8839.htm
76 Hoggins, K. (n.d.). "A Look at Terrorism and Its Effect on the Insurance Industry." William Gallagher Associates. Retrieved February 24, 2008 from www.wgains.com/Assets/WhitePapers/Terror702.PDF
77 Hoggins, K. (n.d.). "A Look at Terrorism and Its Effect on the Insurance Industry." William Gallagher Associates. Retrieved February 24, 2008 from www.wgains.com/Assets/WhitePapers/Terror702.PDF
78 Weidenbaum, M. (2002). "Government, Business, and the Response to Terrorism." *USA Today Magazine*, vol. 130, no. 2684, p. 26.
79 Cohen, A. and O'Driscoll, G.P., Jr. (2003). "Privatization and the Oil Industry: A Strategy for Postwar Iraqi Reconstruction." In *The National Interest*. January 22. Retrieved February 26, 2008 from www.inthenationalinterest.com/Articles/Vol2Issue3/Vol2Issue3CohenDriscoll.html
80 Caulderwood, K. (2015). *The International Business Times*. January 9.
81 Chen, A.H. and Siems, T.F. (2004). "The Effects of Terrorism on Global Capital Markets." *European Journal of Political Economy*, vol. 20, no. 2, pp. 349–366.
82 CNN. (2006). "At Least 174 Killed in Indian Train Blasts." July 11. Retrieved February 12, 2008 from www.cnn.com/2006/WORLD/asiapcf/07/11/mumbai.blasts/
83 Ruggles-Brise, O. (2005). "World Travel & Tourism Council Crisis Committee Issues Estimate of London Bombing Impact." Hotel Online. July 8. Retrieved from www.hotel-online.com/News/PR2005_3rd/July05_LondonImpact.html
84 "Business Counts Cost of Terrorism." (2006). *Taipei Times*. August 17, p. 10. Retrieved from www.taipeitimes.com/News/worldbiz/archives/2006/08/17/2003323578
85 CNN. (2006). "Bush, Congress Clash over Ports Sale." February 22. Retrieved from www.cnn.com/2006/POLITICS/02/21/port.security/
86 "Nigeria Militants Fight Military." (2006). *BBC News*. March 9. Retrieved from http://news.bbc.co.uk/2/hi/africa/4789274.stm
87 "Shell's Nigeria Output Cut by 20%." (2006). *BBC News*. January 13 Retrieved from http://news.bbc.co.uk/2/hi/africa/4789274.stm
88 World Travel and Tourism Council. Home. Retrieved February 15, 2008 from www.wttc.travel/index.php?LANG=eng
89 Based on statistics from the World Tourism Organization. "International Tourist Arrivals by Country of Destination." Retrieved February 29, 2008 from www.photius.com/rankings/tourism_2001.pdf
90 Drakos, K., and Kutan, A. (2003). "Regional Effects of Terrorism on Tourism in Three Mediterranean Countries." *Journal of Conflict Resolution*, vol. 47, no. 5.
91 Jennings, P. (2004). *Terrorism and Australian Business*. Barton: Australian Strategic Policy Institute, p. 3.
92 The country categorization in this report is not according to the categorization used in this book. Because of this, in the section on developing and emerging market countries, countries from both groups are mixed together. CAGR stands for Compounded Annual Growth Rate. Under the category of transition economies in this chart are two countries, according to the categorization of this book, that are still developing—Uzbekistan and Tajikistan. The remaining countries are emerging markets of Eastern Europe, the former Soviet Union, and Central Asia.

93 As above, the country categorization in this report is not according to the categorization used in this book.

94 Silberglitt, R.S., Anton, P.S., Howell, D., Wong, A., Gassman, N., Jackson, B.A., Landree, E., Pfleeger, S.L., Newton, E.M. and Wu, F. (2006). *The Global Technology Revolution 2020, In-depth Analysis: Bio/Nano/Materials/Information Trends, Drivers, Barriers and Social Implications.* Santa Monica, CA: RAND National Security Research Division, p. xviii.

95 Those technological applications that are italicized are considered to be highly feasible or feasible by 2020 and to satisfy a strong need for a medium-size or large market without raising significant public-policy issues.

96 "The 10 Emerging Technologies of 2008." (2008). *Technology Review.* March/April. Retrieved March 29, 2008 from www.technologyreview.com/Infotech/20249/

97 "The 10 Emerging Technologies of 2008." (2008). *Technology Review.* March/April. Detailed descriptions of these emerging technologies can be found at www.technologyreview.com/Infotech/20249/

98 "The 10 Emerging Technologies of 2012." (2012). *Technology Review.* Retrieved from www2.technologyreview.com/tr10/?year=2012

99 This information is not necessarily fully presented in Figure 7.8.

100 Anton, P.S., Silberglitt, R. and Schneider, J. (2001). *The Global Technology Revolution: Bio/Nano/Materials Trends and Their Synergies with Information Technology by 2015.* Santa Monica, CA: RAND National Defense Research Institute, p. xi. Available online at www.rand.org/pubs/monograph_reports/MR1307/

101 Gates, B. (1996). *The Road Ahead.* New York: Penguin Books.

102 Gross, D. (2013). "Google Boss: Entire World Will Be Online by 2020." CNN. April 15. Retrieved from www.cnn.com/2013/04/15/tech/web/eric-schmidt-internet/

8 The Strategic Influence of the Emerging Global Economic and Business Orders

[G]overnment is not the solution to our problem; government is the problem. From time to time we've been tempted to believe that society has become too complex to be managed by self-rule, that government by an elite group is superior to government for, by, and of the people. Well, if no one among us is capable of governing himself, then who among us has the capacity to govern someone else?[1]

Ronald Reagan, US president (1911–2004)

The idea of the Reagan era that "government is the problem" just isn't going to get us anywhere. In such a complicated society as we have, you have got to have some kind of responsible, representative national authority to define priorities and allocate resources. That we can "get government off our backs" and privatize everything is at best an illusion, at worst an invitation to rapacity by selfish private interests.[2]

J. William Fulbright, US senator (1905–1995)

Keynote Definitions

The **Global Order** is a political and economic system of cooperation that emerges organically or as a result of the strategic influence of multilateral institutions, superpowers, and other nations, though not necessarily by cooperative means. The global order provides customary procedures, allowing the avoidance or mitigation of conflict while promoting stability and sustainable development by offering countries, regional blocs, and corporations a means to negotiate disputes among themselves and to develop mutually beneficial solutions to global challenges.

The **Global Business Order** is a subsystem of the global order that provides a relatively stable framework for cooperation between businesses with global, regional, and national institutions, allowing the predominantly evolutionary development of the global marketplace. It is a set of customs by which corporations compete and cooperate with other businesses in the global marketplace, exploiting opportunities offered by it without violating human rights, national interests, or regional and global standards and agreements.

Genesis of the Global Order

The terms *international order, world order, global order*, and all their variations (such as *new world order*) have been on the agenda of thinkers, scholars, and political leaders throughout modern history. According to Professor Lynn Miller of Temple University, this issue has existed for several centuries:

> [T]he game of international politics is played in the normative framework, which provides the parameters within which international actors compete for power and influence. That framework is not an accident of nature but a human invention, created to rationalize and order the relevant social and technological capabilities of increasingly sovereign actors some 350 years ago and consciously enlarged and adapted to respond to changes in those capabilities ever since. It therefore should be regarded not merely as a footnote or an afterthought in the analysis of international politics but as the ordering, ideal structure that both shapes international behavior and makes its evaluation possible.[3]

The global order is, in fact, much more than a framework for "the game of international politics." After the millions of deaths suffered during two world wars, and the extreme tension of the Cold War and its recurrences, national leaders, strategists, and scholars have come to understand the global order differently. It is not only a framework for international politics but also for strategic, peaceful economic, technological, and business cooperation and collaboration toward the resolution of major challenges that face civilization—hunger, mass disease, poverty, and international terrorism, among others.

The practice of the global order became a necessity well before any theoretical basis for it had been developed. Of course, during the seventeenth century, the aftermath of the Thirty Years' War, with the Treaty of Westphalia, offered a new, and maybe the first formal, regionally specific order of the *ecumene*. During that time, it was essentially a declaration of the world order with a series of peace treaties and a legal framework of mutual coexistence and collaboration of many European states and principalities. It should be noted that this book is published in the bicentennial year of another document that shaped the beginning of the global and regional order—the Concert of Europe, signed in 1815. This treaty substantially predetermined the current European order and planted seeds for the global order and definitely became the first canvas of the European economic order.

Two hundred years later, under the conditions of the twenty-first century, politicians are far from the only participants in the global order as it used to be. The corporate world also plays a crucial role in this process. Due to the unifying impact of the global marketplace, corporations have reached the stage of development in which their leaders and strategists understand the importance of collaboration with national governments and multilateral institutions to expand global prosperity for the sake of humankind, as well as for their own strategic business interests. In general, corporations are intrinsically selfish, as their primary function is to make a profit. The situation in 2015, however, in which only 2.5 out of the world's 7.5 billion people are part of corporations' market of buyers and clients, is not sustainable. With the increasing productivity of labor derived from cutting-edge technologies and innovations, corporate overproduction is a realistic possibility. This could cause global, national, and regional recessions, not to mention economic crises that would make the Great Depression of the 1930s look mild. In order to prevent this kind of economic disaster, it is very important for business leaders and strategists to rethink their role in the improvement of the standard of living of billions of people, with the ultimate goal of making them capable of becoming active participants in the global marketplace. Corporate executives and strategists are awakening to the link between the satisfaction of people's values and improvements in their quality of life, and potential growth in their markets and, eventually, their profits. This selfish mindset will actually be the most productive way for business leaders to understand their social responsibility as a function of business success, strategically thinking. In the global marketplace, social responsibility and business success go together. The corporate world's strategic understanding of global responsibility arose over centuries of painful experiences for all those involved—corporations, governments, multilateral institutions, and individuals.

Already at the end of the eighteenth century, financiers discussed the concept of an international order because they needed international cooperation with creditors and lenders from other countries. This concept was also interesting to financiers because of the importance of stability for international financial transactions. Unlike politicians, who may have been able to exploit instability and uncertainty and gain for themselves and even for their nations, financiers rely mostly on stability to function efficiently. However, they can also profit from instability if proper strategic approaches are used.

The false and unproductive idea of a small group of elites running the world has fascinated conspiracy "theorists" for centuries. Beginning with legends about the origins of the Masonic movement several centuries ago, the creation of international clubs and the membership of national leaders in private international organizations have always been the object of suspicion. Even in the twenty-first century, a period of unprecedented enlightenment and information-technology revolution, some still believe in the existence of secret organizations that run the world. Many point to international institutions and think tanks like the Bretton Woods Committee or the Council on Foreign Relations. In actuality, these organizations are open for public view. Their members are prominent scholars, economists, former politicians (as well as those still in office), and business leaders who use these organizations to discuss and advocate solutions to global challenges.

A common source of fascination and speculation of conspiracy "theorists" are the words and symbols found on the US one-dollar bill and Great Seal. Dan Brown's bestseller *The Da Vinci Code*, which speculated a great deal about the meaning of the dollar bill's design and that of the Seal, briefly brought this issue to the forefront of pop culture. Strategists should always ignore such "pop" explanations. A direct clarification is provided by the United States Department of Treasury:

> [T]he eye and the pyramid shown on the reverse side of the one-dollar bill are in the Great Seal of the United States ... The Department of State is the official keeper of the Seal. They believe that the most accurate explanation of a pyramid on the Great Seal is that it symbolizes strength and durability. The unfinished pyramid means that the United States will always grow, improve and build. In addition, the "All-Seeing Eye" located above the pyramid suggests the importance of divine guidance in favor of the American cause. The inscription ANNUIT COEPTIS translates as "He (God) has favored our undertakings," and refers to the many instances of Divine Providence during our Government's formation. In addition, the inscription NOVUS ORDO SECLORUM translates as "A new order of the ages," and signifies a new American era.[4]

Although these symbols have existed for more than 230 years (the US government officially adopted the Great Seal in 1782), the idea of a "new order" has never ceased to fascinate conspiracy "theorists" and the general public. In fact, it became especially interesting as the twentieth century ended. The reason for this is obvious, as at that time the world was entering a period of unprecedented change, with increasing levels of internationalization and interconnection. The number of countries had grown, and global challenges had been complicated, requiring an updated world order. The global order with which humankind entered the twenty-first century has its roots in the order developed at the end of World War II, in 1944. Four years later, when the Cold War began, the post–World War II order changed and became less efficient for humankind, which was divided into three camps—the capitalist, communist, and nonaligned countries. At one point this was the new world order, but newer political and economic developments, as well as global challenges, have brought national and corporate leaders, heads of multilateral institutions, and strategists to seek a newer and more efficient global order. This order must correctly reflect the current and future levels of development and improvement of humankind as well as its upcoming challenges—global and regional, as well as bilateral and multilateral disputes, which no entity can abolish. Strategists, of course, cannot afford to make the mistake of believing in the existence of a nefarious, all-powerful secret global body. This would completely undermine the role of strategists and executives, and it would imply that they are mere figureheads for these secret organizations, making them ineffectual and insignificant. In reality, strategists work in and collaborate with many important leaders, international organizations, think tanks, and corporations. While corporate and governmental strategies are, in general, tightly guarded after development, the "copyright" of strategic activity almost always becomes public knowledge. Corporations attempt to keep their strategies, or at least some parts of them, unknown to the public and, of course, to their competitors until a certain point. If corporate strategy becomes publicly known prior to its full implementation, competitors will inevitably find ways and means, especially asymmetric ones, to make it obsolete. Multilateral institutions also keep certain aspects of their strategies out of the public eye. This usually relates only to issues concerning the fight against terrorism, narcotic and human trafficking, national secrets of member countries, etc. However, because of the nature of these institutions, most aspects of their strategies are available to the public.

Contrary to what conspiracy "theorists" might imagine, global orders are generally the result of humanitarian visions of leaders and strategists to establish a mechanism to prevent international conflicts, promote stability, and address the major challenges facing humankind that cannot be solved or handled by national governments alone. There are certain challenges that national governments are innately unequipped to handle due to conflicts between national interests and global or regional needs. As a result of increasing shortages of various natural resources, such conflicts will be a major challenge for the global order in the twenty-first century. The freshwater resources of some countries, for instance, originate primarily from foreign sources. In such cases the ability to satisfy people's most basic need depends on the beneficence of foreign governments, which at any moment could divert freshwater flows for their own industrial purposes. This issue was discussed in greater detail in Chapter 7, but is mentioned in this chapter as an obvious illustration of the strategic need for international and interregional cooperation.

It is very important to underscore the fact that international cooperation should consist of a collaborative strategy-based relationship among multilateral institutions, national governments, and the private sector. A supernational world government is not a productive or sustainable idea. Any form of an executive supernational government has deep roots in the ideas of dialectical liberalism and neo-Marxism, "which aims merely to harmonize rather than to eliminate differences in the pursuit of equality."[5] This approach is significantly softer than Karl Marx's, but it's no more practical. For the emerging global order of the twenty-first century to be sustainable, national governments must play a dominant role. Multilateral institutions should focus on the coordination of national governments and the private sector on the basis and in the framework of different problem-oriented global strategies that work towards the resolution of global issues. However, multilateral institutions need to be able to make executive decisions, primarily on the basis of consensus, as it is imperative that national authority not be undermined. There are some cases in which decision-making by overwhelming majority is required. Protection of national sovereignty comes at a cost, as international bodies that require a consensus can be very inefficient; the United Nations General Assembly is an obvious example of this fact. Due to numerous conflicts of strategic interest among its 193 member-states, the decisions of this body act only as recommendations. In order to skirt this managerial challenge, in situations of great importance, executive decisions can be based on a supermajority (also known as a qualified majority), which requires two-thirds of all votes. Supermajorities will play a key role in the emerging global order in issues related to security and the survival of civilization.

New global orders often appear or are reorganized from previous orders after wars, multilateral sharp conflicts, or major discoveries (the geographical discoveries of the fifteenth century, for example). The development of a new global order is almost always challenged by politicization and conflicts of national interests and values. In attempting to solve these conflicts, be they political, humanitarian rights, or economic in nature, there is often a tendency to advocate for the creation of a global executive government. As previously discussed, this is completely undesirable. However, the firm intention to resolve these challenges, in addition to the influence of objective and subjective factors, is the basis upon which global orders are formed.

Ideally, the global order should be oriented toward the achievement of the global optimum, which can be understood as the equilibrium balance of the values, interests, and priorities of all participants under the global order, including national governments and international regional bodies, multilateral institutions, corporations, as well as individuals. Obviously, the global optimum is an ideal that is extremely difficult—if not impossible—to achieve. Nevertheless, the closer mankind comes to it, the more efficient, prosperous, and equitable civilization will be. The global optimum is a serious theoretical issue with very important practical implications. It provides a strategic path that the development of the global order should follow. The search for this path and the triggering events of the new global order, its design, and functions have their own kinetics and dynamics. Predicting and strategizing the global order requires analysis and understanding of the influence of objective global and regional trends determining changes of this order (see Chapter 7). According to Dr. Henry Kissinger, "Since the Renaissance the West has been deeply committed to the notion that the real world is external to the observer, that knowledge consists of recording and classifying data—the more accurately the better—and that foreign policy success depends on assessing existing realities and trends."[6] He also speaks about the necessity of "unifying principles—in which resides a cardinal distinction between Western and non-Western approaches to order." Regarding the role of principles in the global order's design and development, I totally agree with Kissinger because the western tradition of democracy stems from the time of the Magna Carta (which as of 2015 celebrates its 800-year anniversary) with its principles, individual freedoms, and protection of property. Leadership of countries that are still in Europe, geographically, but do not fully yet belong to western civilization often put principles on the side when they see immediate, but short-term gains. Because of that, this gain tends to be a pyrrhic victory. Often, politicians who make these decisions, with short-term gains, are seeing only an obvious reason for their attempt, but do not see, and ignore, deep and often tragic (due to their power) economic and moral consequences. Nonetheless, strategists obviously have to take into consideration these differences in values and principles, which will exist for quite a while between western and non-western values and mentalities. Of course, the development of regional and global communities and international economic integration in the framework of the global marketplace due to modern technological communications decreases the gap in values between people of East and West. It is where the social optimism of the global community can continue to flourish.

In the twenty-first century, civilization faces unprecedented challenges and problems that cannot be solved or even mitigated without coordination under a new, more efficient global order. The cataclysmic capabilities of humankind, as a result of the spread of nuclear technologies and other weapons of mass destruction, or total cyberattacks, as well as the increasing danger of technogenic disasters, require a global order for the survival of humankind and the prevention of the annihilation of civilization. In a time when 5 of the 6.5 billion people of the world live in relative or total poverty, global coordination is needed in order to fight poverty, for humanitarian as well as practical purposes. The increasing liberalization of international relations in a world in which the gap between wealthy and underdeveloped nations is growing exponentially requires global coordination to monitor and regulate international migration. The surge in international and global cross-border movement of people and labor raises the strategic risk of pandemic outbreaks of disease, the prevention and management of which can be done only through global coordination. The liberalization of international financial and economic relations and the global integration of both require a global order to help harmonize national regulations according to worldwide standards. Global coordination is absolutely necessary to counter new threats, such as international terrorism and the growing influence of religious extremism. The protection of the environment and the management or prevention of both global and regional natural disasters all require global strategy to harmonize international efforts. The global order should be understood as a means of improving the efficiency of civilization as a whole—it is not merely an economic or financial issue. National policies should be coordinated to promote world peace, social cohesion, prosperity, and the widespread penetration of the most important and useful technologies and knowledge. None of these issues can be addressed without a global order appropriate to the conditions of the twenty-first century. Without properly crafted strategic functions of current and upcoming new multilateral institutions and some self-restrained obligations upon national governments to coordinate their efforts with these institutions, the global order will not be able to achieve any of the aforementioned objectives. However, global and national leadership should try to reach these exceedingly difficult objectives; even attempts to do so will have a positive impact on humankind's future. Quite often, the process of reaching a worthwhile objective is no less important than its actual fulfillment.

Strategic Role of Bretton Woods Institutions in the Global Order

In the twenty-first century, strategists, as well as global and national political and business leaders, tend to be very critical of the existing global order, which is a derivative of the recommendations of the Bretton Woods Conference. This book is no exception. However, despite this well-founded criticism, it is important to acknowledge and respect the visionaries from around the world who met in 1944 in the small town of Bretton Woods, New Hampshire. Officially called the United Nations Monetary and Financial Conference, but almost universally known as the Bretton Woods Conference, the meeting engineered the strategic pattern of the global political and economic order to be implemented immediately after the end of the war. Although the Allied forces would fight the fascists from Germany, Italy, and Japan for more than a year after, the participants of the conference already considered these enemy states as future business partners and even political allies. The post-war global order would likely have been different if Joseph Stalin, the leader of the Soviet Union at the time, decided to send his representative to Bretton Woods. As a powerful member of the Allies, the Soviet Union was asked to participate and Stalin initially accepted the invitation, but however he later changed his mind. This conference gave birth to the International Monetary Fund (IMF), the International Bank for Reconstruction and Development (the major institution of the World Bank Group), and the United Nations (all known as the Bretton Woods institutions). The conference also designed the International Trade Organization, whose charter was completed in 1948, but the United States Congress never ratified the creation of this organization, due to the reluctance of Congress to give a foreign organization the ability to affect US foreign trade policy. Nonetheless, this organization was established 50 years later, in 1994, and became operational in January 1995 as the World Trade Organization (WTO). The post–World War II international gold standard system was also introduced at Bretton Woods. The conference participants' strategic vision is quite impressive. Although they were probably not looking much more than 10 or 20 years into the future, the majority of the global order strategic principles that they created functioned for about 70 years.

The broad strokes of the global political order under which humankind lived until the first decade of the twenty-first century were designed in February 1945, in the vacation palace of the Russian imperial family in the Black Sea coastal town of Yalta on the Crimean Peninsula (which in 2014 became even more widely known because of Russia taking back this territory from Ukraine). The three leaders of the anti-Nazi coalition, US President Roosevelt, UK Prime Minister Churchill, and the Soviet dictator Stalin, marked their spheres of influence in post-war Europe, the Pacific Rim, and even in continental Asia, in countries such as Mongolia and China. The Yalta Conference reinforced the recommendations of Bretton Woods and made a date for the inaugural meeting of the UN, in San Francisco, later in the year: April 25. "The Yalta Declaration contains a number of ambiguous formulas that served to bridge the gap between the positions of the U.S., Britain, and the Soviet Union vis-à-vis the post–World War II global order."[7] The Potsdam Conference of July 1945 should also be mentioned, but the focus of this conference was mostly on the post-war development of divided Germany. This meeting already demonstrated the serious disagreement between the UK and the US on one side, and the Soviet Union on the other. Potsdam was the first indicator that, after the war, the world was headed toward a bipolar global order. Nonetheless, neither the Yalta nor Potsdam Conference had as significant an influence on the global economic order as did the Bretton Woods Conference.

Several alterations with long-term strategic consequences of the Bretton Woods global economic order were made: first, at the beginning of the Cold War, in 1948; second, in 1971, when the gold-dollar standard system failed and was abolished. It failed because dollar reserves outside of the United States substantially surpassed the value of US gold reserves. The most substantial changes to the global order occurred at the end of the Cold War, with the failure of communism.

By the end of the 1980s and the beginning of the 1990s, the world had undergone drastic changes. The colonial system was destroyed, along with apartheid in South Africa. Most of the dictatorships throughout the world collapsed. The Soviet Union, the world's last empire, disintegrated into 15 independent states (and this trend is not over, as shown when Abkhazia left Georgia, for example). The Cold War was over, the Warsaw Pact no longer existed, and by 1997 three former Soviet Republics—the Baltic states—had already joined NATO, along with most of the former Soviet bloc countries. During this period the number of independent countries tripled. UN membership expanded from 1945's 44 charter members to 193 members as of 2015. The world has clearly gone through profound changes since the Bretton Woods Conference. Without these changes, a third world war likely would have taken place at some point. However, the global order and its regulating bodies, established in 1944, are no longer suited to the economic, business, and political reality of the twenty-first century. Furthermore, information technology of the twenty-first century has multiplied the capacity of global institutions to coordinate the efforts of countries, regional bodies, and corporations, and the order needs to be strategically reorganized appropriately.

According to the agreements between their member countries, a board of governors manages the activity of each Bretton Woods institution. For example, in section two of the Articles of Agreement of the IMF, it states,

> [A]ll powers under this Agreement not conferred directly on the Board of Governors, the Executive Board, or the Managing Director shall be vested in the Board of Governors. The Board of Governors shall consist of one Governor and one Alternate appointed by each member in such manner as it may determine.[8]

For the management of operational activity, these organizations have executive boards. According to section 10 of the IMF's bylaws,

> [T]he Executive Board shall have prepared for presentation to the Board of Governors an annual report in which shall be discussed the policies and activities of the Fund and which shall make recommendations to the Board of Governors on the problems confronting the Fund. The Executive Board shall review, as part of the annual report, the functioning of the international monetary system, including the adequacy of global reserves, the conduct of the business of the General Department and of the Special Drawing Rights Department, as well as the performance of financial services by the Fund, including the administration of resources contributed by members.[9]

For many years this was a moderately successful structure. However, as of the beginning of the twenty-first century, shares of different countries in the voting of these multilateral institutions are outdated and do not represent the reality of the twenty-first century; the functions of these institutions have not been appropriately updated despite several efforts in 2000–2013; and there is not enough coordination among multilateral institutions, in addition to other factors. Every year from the last week of September to the first week of October, the Joint Annual Meeting of the World Bank and IMF is conducted. At the meeting, the results of the previous year are accepted and the plan for the upcoming year is approved.

The key architect of the Bretton Woods system was the great British economist John Maynard Keynes (1883–1946), arguably one of economics' most important figures. In his speech on July 22, 1944, at the conclusion of the Bretton Woods Conference, he declared,

> [F]inally, we have perhaps accomplished here in Bretton Woods something more significant than what is embodied in this Final Act. We have shown that a concourse of forty-four nations is actually able to work together at a constructive task in amity

> and unbroken concord. Few believed it possible. If we can continue in a larger task as we have begun in this limited task, there is hope for the world.[10]

The annual meeting of the Bretton Woods Committee is basically the successor to the original Bretton Woods Conference.

The current system of multilateral intuitions is clearly not a world government. The decisions of the UN General Assembly, for example, are merely recommendations and can be (and often are) ignored even by member-countries. It is heard but not listened to. Furthermore, the General Assembly focuses primarily on international governmental relationships, and much less on strategic economic, financial, or business issues, and mostly avoids discussions on global strategies, which are predominantly absent from its agenda. The UN Security Council is a much more powerful body, but as the name suggests, it also does not directly focus on economic, financial, or business issues. Some topics with which it deals, such as terrorism and extreme nationalism, certainly affect business and economics. Because these integrated strategic factors of political risk affect not only businesses but also the United Nations itself, a relatively unified global front has been formed to counter these threats. Regardless, it is very difficult for the Security Council to reach consensus, and that is without having to listen to the voices of most countries of the world. The power of the UN General Assembly and Security Council is clearly limited. Even so, they both still play a significant role in the current global order and will continue to do so in the new, emerging global order.

The new dynamics and qualities of the influence of objective and subjective factors have rendered traditional multilateral institutions and their strategies and operational activity inefficient under twenty-first-century conditions. For this reason, leaders of the member-countries of these institutions seek new functions and structures of multilateral institutions, coordination among them, and strategic cooperation with national governments and corporate leadership.

Empirical Dynamics of the Global Order

The birth and maturation of the emerging global order of the twenty-first century is the result of the collaboration of two processes with very different dynamic characteristics—evolution and revolution. In the twenty-first century, the world economy has been almost totally empirically reorganized and integrated into the global marketplace, which is an entity of great complexity and dynamism. It consists of global, regional, national, and local elements, as well as industrial and corporate structures. The relative weight of and relationships among these elements constantly changes over time. Some countries that for many years were relatively insignificant players are beginning to assume major roles in the emerging global order, while the importance of some traditional powers is declining. The appearance of countries that did not previously exist (like Kazakhstan or South Sudan) and their rise to regional and global importance, due to various factors like unique and rich natural or technological resources, has led to further complications. New and rising powers are increasingly challenging the strategic dominance of global and regional players. Shifts in the importance of specific industries, multinational corporations, and multilateral institutions also increase complexity. All of this requires a new global order that reflects these strategically important changes and their dynamics. The dynamics of the global marketplace leave the global order in constant disequilibrium. While there may be a status quo, it is only temporary.

The global order reflects the dynamism of the global marketplace and the global workplace but at the same time influences them. At the end of the first decade of the twenty-first century there is only one superpower—the United States (based on the achievement of many, but not all, requirements in a category that is itself questionable due to its exclusivity). It is still the most influential country of the global order. However, the example of the Soviet Union illustrates that the dominance of a superpower can be fleeting when it experiences drastic declines in its efficiency, the relevance of its ideology, and then inevitably its power in the global arena and demonstrates a lack of strategy to solve these problems and tendencies. Although the global order of the first decade of the twenty-first century has been essentially a unipolar, hegemonic system, the United States is not immune to the possibility of losing its status as the global superpower, especially in a world as complex and dynamic as that of the twenty-first century. Rising regional superpowers, which can be thought of as centers of high efficiency and strong military power, with ideologies and strategic visions of different qualities of the global order which differ from that of the global superpower, are already challenging the dominance of the US in certain regions but mostly not yet on a global level. Processes of regionalization have led to a situation in which regional superpowers are not restricted to individual countries. The European Union can be considered a regional superpower, although it is very different from all others. It is based not on strategic national interests, but on the regional western values and interests of almost 30 nations. This is a radically new phenomenon of the emerging global order. Although the European Union is not a sovereign body, it has institutions that unify member countries to the extent that together they constitute a European government with loose functions and power. To a certain extent, this government is developing and implementing a European business order on the so-far short-term strategies and through under-law regulations and regulatory practices, like common bankruptcy (described in many documents, such as the Lisbon Strategy for growth and jobs) and anti-trust rules (described in the treaty establishing the European community). From this point of view, the European Union is very different from the United Nations, which does not have such integrated power and sovereignty over its member-countries. As the economic clout of regional superpowers like China, India, or Brazil grows, they are demanding with increasing assertiveness that the United States reduce its influence in different regions and structures. Neighboring countries of regional superpowers find themselves in tenuous situations because of the interplay between the global power of the US and the refusal of regional powers to delegate authority. The vacillating allegiance of neighboring countries between these competing powers increases the complexity, dynamism, and imbalance of the global order. After September 11, 2001, the leadership of the United States developed its own conceptual response to the challenge of rising regional superpowers. Stefan Halper, a senior fellow at the Centre of International Studies at Cambridge University, and Jonathan Clarke, a foreign-affairs scholar at the CATO Institute, described the following principles that they believe were developed by the neoconservative administration of George W. Bush:

1. Analyze international issues in black-and-white, absolute moral categories. They [the Bush administration] are fortified by a conviction that they alone hold the moral high ground and argue that disagreement is tantamount to defeatism.
2. Focus on the "unipolar" power of the United States, seeing the use of military force as the first, not the last option of foreign policy. They repudiate the "lessons ofVietnam," which they interpret as undermining American will toward the use

of force, and embrace the "lessons of Munich," interpreted as establishing the virtues of preemptive military action.

3. Disdain conventional diplomatic agencies such as the State Department and conventional country-specific, realist, and pragmatic analysis. They are hostile towards nonmilitary, multilateral institutions and instinctively antagonistic toward international treaties and agreements. "Global unilateralism" is their watchword. They are fortified by international criticism, believing that it confirms American virtue.
4. Look to the Reagan administration as the exemplar of all these virtues and seek to establish their version of Reagan's legacy as the Republican and national orthodoxy.[11]

The widely held critical attitude of these authors toward former President George W. Bush's administration aside, the political and economic conditions and the global order within which this administration worked made it difficult for alternative strategies to be effective, especially given the tremendous influence of the new threat of global terrorism and religious extremism. Nonetheless, this strategy can be considered an extension of the Washington Consensus, as they do not contradict one another, unlike the so-called Beijing Consensus, both of which are described in detail later in this chapter.

The Global Economic and Business Orders in the Dynamics of the Global Order

Strategists should be aware that during the last three-quarters of the twenty-first century challenges to superpowers especially from regional superpowers like Russia and China are very likely to emerge. This will undoubtedly destabilize the global order. Given this dynamic, the unipolar global order that emerged after the Cold War will most likely remain intact until approximately 2025 to 2030. At this point, one or even several regional superpowers may challenge and share the role of the United States as global superpowers, and a bipolar or, most likely, a multipolar global order and its subsystem, the global business order, will emerge. The development of the global marketplace and the birth of the global workplace—as a production platform of industrial cooperation—in conditions of a multipolar world will require a global business order, the global strategy and the rules and means of which will be incompatible with the current structure of the global marketplace. The global business order is a new phenomenon. As of 2015, in economic and business literature, this phenomenon remains undefined, although the term has appeared on a few occasions, without an explanation of its role and significance. The following quote is an example: "Since 1947 successive GATT rounds lowered macroeconomic trade barriers throughout the world, facilitating the integration of domestic economies into a global business order based on internationally deregulated capital markets, which nonetheless remained rooted in the multinational corporation's host state."[12] Some authors refer to the international economic order, but their explanations of this term as it relates to the global order show that they are actually speaking about the global business order:

> [A] new international economic order has in fact emerged. However, it was not produced by the political will of government but by the needs and perceptions of the marketplace. If I were to pick three groups of actors who have contributed more to the emergence of the new Global Order than any other, it would be central bankers, financial regulators, and credit agencies. They have already laid the foundation of

> a new financial architecture and will continue to build upon it, brick by brick, to meet market demands. If governments want to act, they should prompt and facilitate the work of these agents of change … The only practical way to deal with the profound changes taking place in the structure of the global economy is not to impose on it a new architecture. Instead, what is required is to balance the profound changes that have already occurred in the global economic and financial system with an equally profound restructuring of domestic economies.[13]

In referring to a new paradigm, Dr. Michael Gavin, author of the above quote, is also rejecting the need for structural changes in the managerial and coordinating bodies of the global marketplace which will implement this paradigm in practice. The global business order requires the activity of new institutions, which will be primarily oriented toward the coordination of private businesses with one another and with governments and government-oriented Bretton Woods multilateral institutions. The collaboration of these institutions with private business is particularly necessary in the sphere of finance.

The impact of the GEM on the global financial system has been very significant with the growing role of derivative instruments, pension and mutual funds, and currency markets throughout the GMP. The use of these instruments in the GEM requires regulation by national governments as well as multilateral institutions. Another sphere of coordination and unification is standardization and compatible technological requirements. Currently operational worldwide institutions like the International Organization for Standardization (ISO) is capable of improving its ability to the level of the global workplace.

The global business order and its structures have to be geared for cooperation between companies and traditional agencies from the business world with multilateral institutions and governments. They also have to face the threats, both ongoing and yet to emerge, that will influence the global order of the twenty-first century. In addition to the threat of terrorism and extremism, the emerging global business order has to be oriented to face another, more organized, though less threatening challenge—the formation of international cartels that intend to control strategic natural resources. This challenge first emerged in 1960, upon the creation of the most powerful international intergovernmental cartel, the Organization of the Petroleum Exporting Countries (OPEC), which accounts for about 45 percent of worldwide crude oil production and additionally for 20 percent of natural gas production.[14] Its member-countries, including oil-exporting states from the Middle East, Africa, and even Southeast Asia and Latin America, have on their territories about 81 percent of proven global oil reserves, with absolute leadership ofVenezuela and Saudi Arabia.[15] By controlling the production of one of the most crucial natural resources, OPEC is tremendously influential in the global business order as well as in the global order. The interests of this cartel are totally selfish, and they completely contradict the promotion of global prosperity and the global optimum. OPEC's stated mission is to coordinate

> oil production policies in order to help stabilise the oil market and to help oil producers achieve a reasonable rate of return on their investments. This policy is also designed to ensure that oil consumers continue to receive stable supplies of oil.[16]

From this mission statement, it is clear that OPEC's first priority is the return on investment of its member-countries. Stabilizing the oil supply of the world is an afterthought, generally ignored during world energy crises. During such times, in order to increase prices, OPEC member-countries often try to decrease production and exports or do not use existing capabilities in order to reduce oil supplies and raise prices, but the domination of OPEC was finally challenged in the second decade of the twenty-first century by shale and shelf oil production of the US, Norway, and some other states, almost newcomers to this industry like Poland.

There is a danger that other strategic natural resources will be cartelized in the twenty-first century. Several major producers of natural gas, such as Iran and Russia, are attempting to develop an OPEC-like natural gas cartel. An informal group known as the Gas Exporting Countries Forum (GECF) has already formed to discuss this issue. Among GECF member-countries are Algeria, Bolivia, Egypt, Equatorial Guinea, Iran, Libya, Nigeria, Qatar, Russia, Trinidad and Tobago, the United Arab Emirates, Venezuela, and Iraq. Kazakhstan, the Netherlands, Norway, Oman, and Peru are observer members.[17] Iran and Russia, the two leading natural gas producers, play a crucial role in the development of this group and in the appointment of the secretary general of the GECF. The formation of such a cartel is not extremely positive for the global business order because it would place 40 percent of gas production and 75 percent of reserves under the governmental control of 12 countries as of 2015.[18] If such an organization is actually created, the emergence of cartels controlling other important natural resources, like freshwater reserves, basic food commodities, or precious metals like palladium (more important for technological and hydrogen energy production than jewelry), is quite possible. One of the most dangerous precedents was the 2008 proposal of "Thailand, the world's biggest rice exporter … to form an OPEC-style cartel with Laos, Myanmar, Cambodia, and Vietnam to give them more control over international rice prices."[19] The governments of several countries interpreted this proposal as a serious threat. In order to prevent the formation of a rice cartel, the government of Japan sent thousands of tons of rice to countries like the Philippines as aid and released rice from its national stocks into the regional and global market.[20] The cartelization of the global marketplace would be, it seems to me, a very negative development for the efficiency of the global business order. The function of these organizations is hostile to global prosperity. The global order has to be oriented toward the use of all possible political and economic mechanisms to prevent the creation of new cartels and limit the influence of existing ones. The new architecture of multilateral institutions of the twenty-first century will reflect many global challenges—the threat of terrorism and the cartelization of the global marketplace, among others.

Due to these challenges, the role of national governments in the global business order will increase compared to its decline during the romantic liberalism of the last quarter of the twentieth century. The wave of economic liberalization that swept across the world following the end of the "old" Cold War began to recede after the "Asian" crisis of 1997 (contrary to common belief, this was the first global one). Proponents of romantic liberalism, like Voltaire's character Candide and several other more contemporary "experts," undermined the role of national governments to the extent that despite having the ability to prevent contagion, governments were hesitant to intervene in financial markets. As a result, the crises crossed national borders and even oceans. Only after this experience did governmental and financial leaders, scholars, and strategists start to reevaluate the role of government in a globalized world. Romantic liberalism is beginning to give way to a strategically new dynamic of global economic affairs, with a growing role for national interests and national governments structured to reflect these interests. Although it may not yet be evident by the first decade of the twenty-first century, the end of the period of romantic liberalism has already begun. Rising regional superpowers will decrease the unipolar dominance of the United States and increase the role of protectionism around multiple regional poles that are appearing.

Regional unions and blocs are already forming around these new regional poles. "Regular" members of regional blocs are constantly reevaluating the balance between their relationships with global and regional superpowers and reshuffling their allegiances accordingly. Central European countries, such as the Czech and Slovak republics and Poland, have to find a balance between the US and Germany—the regional superpower of Europe. The European Union itself is a new pole in the global order. Latin American countries balance the weight of US influence with that of their growing regional superpower, Brazil. The situation in Asia is even more complex: countries have to deal with the influence of four regional superpowers—China, India, Russia, and Japan—as well as that of the United States. Pakistan's increasing position as one of the first Muslim nations with nuclear power will make the regional equilibrium even more difficult to sustain in the environment of the increasing role of Islam. The strategy of liberalization of international relations and especially of international trade has made it possible for *regional economic organizations* (REOs) to expand at an unprecedented pace, and there are more than 100 REOs in the GMP, with varying levels of integration. The addition of new member-countries affects the politics, economics, and business of all parties involved, and the dynamics of expansion of REOs have important implications for the global order. The strength and influence and strategies of regional organizations like the EU, NAFTA, Mercosur, ASEAN, etc. vary substantially and are reflected in their respective roles in the GMP. However, the relative dynamics of these organizations change as membership expands to include neighboring countries and agreements are signed with economies of no geographic proximity. NAFTA, for example, has free-trade agreements with Jordan, Chile, Colombia, Israel, Morocco, Oman, Singapore, and several other countries (mostly of the western hemisphere). The dynamic and uneven development of regional blocs and unions complicates the GMP, the GEM, the relationships among countries of different categories, and the global order.

Regional blocs and unions are usually self-strategized, and their development is a function of their own continued survival and improvement. A lack of balance and harmony in economic and technological development within regional blocs leads to their disintegration unless the economic, social, business, and technological situation is improved and becomes sustainable in the relatively less-developed member-countries in order to maintain a balance. Development tends to be uneven within REOs, causing further disruption and disequilibrium. As this process continues, it increases the integration of member countries of regional blocs in the global marketplace. A key factor determining the extent to which a regional economic organization is integrated within the GMP is its relationship with neighboring countries. The more politically, economically similar neighboring countries are to those of the regional economic organization, the more their strategies are compatible, the more likely the organization is to have liberalized economic and financial relationships with its neighbors and eventually to add them as full member-countries. The larger a regional economic organization, and the more liberalized its relations are, the more integrated it is within the GMP. During periods of global economic liberalism, the practical significance of rapidly expanding regional blocs comes into question. In general, the more open the GMP and global workplace, the looser are REOs. One of the best examples of this is the July 2008 formation of the

Union for the Mediterranean (UfM). It was established by European commission and 43 countries, with very different agendas, including Muslim and Christian nations as well as Israel. It is great that the leaders of these diverse nations are meeting and working together, but their ability to come to a consensus regarding the most important issues is dubious. Nonetheless during five years of operation the UfM demonstrated sustainable progress and some successful examples of cooperation in several fields like alternative energy, water and environmental protection, education, and in some other areas. On the other hand, during times of reduced global economic integration, regional organizations are tighter, stronger, and more relevant. The more regional economic organizations are integrated with the GMP the less complicated is the global order, making it less region specific and more oriented toward global issues. This is the strategy behind the Transatlantic Trade and Investment Partnership (TTIP). This agreement between the US and the EU will increase satisfaction of customers in both counterparts and lead to the creation of 13 million new jobs.

The size of a regional bloc is usually proportional to the size of its member-countries but is limited by geographical and political conditions and by few but the most important strategic contradictions. The more similar the political system of a country and the closer it is geographically to the REO, the more likely that country is to join. Regional blocs are experiencing two very different and somewhat mutually opposite dynamics—internal integration between current country members (and their businesses) and external integration. The economic necessity of external business integration makes regional blocs intensify cooperation with countries that do not have mutual borders with the bloc and are even on different continents. Such integration between regional blocs as a whole and with other individual countries complicates the global order and the missions of its institutions. The demolition of economic barriers within REOs has linear characteristics and is typically proportional to the square of the territory of the REO and its country members. In terms of the GDP of its country members, this proportion is cubic. Bigger economies integrate at a slower pace within regional blocs, as they tend to already be more integrated with the GMP. At a certain level, these two different dynamics lead to the complete integration of some regional blocs within the GMP and the global workplace. The business cooperation and at a certain level integration of individual corporations to regional blocs and to the GMP occurs at a much faster pace than that of national economies. The varying rates of development of individual countries as well as of different regional blocs can be seen as a threat to the current global order, but also as a process that makes the current order sustainable. For example, the global order reflects the strong influence of the US as a reigning superpower. But it is also influenced by the rising power of China and other regional powers like Brazil, India, Russia and Germany. By 2025 the role of South Africa and Egypt as regional superpowers will also be significant. Democratic reform in Iran would likely allow it to become a regional superpower as well. At the beginning of the twenty-first century, Iran, like North Korea, represents a regional as well as a global threat, but it does not have any of the economic and social characteristics of a superpower. BRICS—Brazil, Russia, India, China, and South Africa—is a group of countries that many see as a bloc and even as a regional organization; however neither of these terms actually apply and no formal organization actually exists. The first time the leaders of these countries (at that time without the leader of South Africa) gathered in a formal setting was during the 2008 G8 summit in Japan. The BRICS cannot be considered a regional organization, as these countries are spread among four continents. Nevertheless, they share similar characteristics, and their role in the world should not be underestimated. The collective output of these countries is about $16 trillion, which is about the output of the US. The BRIC accounts for about 20 percent of GWP and 38 percent of the global population. In an attempt to be ahead of the curve, S&P established the BRIC 40 Index, providing "exposure to 40 leading companies" mostly in these four countries "through liquid stocks trading on developed market exchanges."[21] "The China portion of the index is made up of offshore stocks, H-shares and U.S.-listed ADRs/ADSes"[22] (American Depository Receipt/Shares, discussed in Chapter 9). From a strategic point of view, these countries cannot create a workable bloc, even though they declared to form The New Development Bank with $50 billion of initial capital,[23] and they should be analyzed and strategized as a part of the GEM. Regardless, all of the developments described above will allow BRICS countries to influence the global order and change its configuration, but they will not threaten its existence as a mostly unipolar world until about 2030. The hegemony and the major global multilateral institutions will deal more with strategic balancing regional superpowers between one another, especially due to the fact that the majority of these countries do not have their own well-designed (if any) national strategies.

The Evolution of the Global Order

In the unipolar global order of the first decade of the twenty-first century, a temporary balance has been achieved through the formation and development of regional blocs, usually built around regional superpowers. There are also some regional blocs, such as the ten-member Association of Southeast Asian Nations (ASEAN), that do not have a regional superpower among their member countries. ASEAN was formed largely to counter the influence of Asian regional superpowers and, as of 2015, with the aim to establish an ASEAN Economic Community (AEC) with a single market.[24] Liberalization and the fall of barriers to globalization increase entropy, which can be understood as a process of increasing disorder initially, followed by the disappearance of some elements of the status quo that are never recovered. One manifestation of this is the disintegration of countries into smaller economies, during the chaotic process of the disappearance of imperial or dictatorial systems, and their integration into the global marketplace and into the global community. The influence of this trend is waning but still significant (see Chapter 7). The self-organization around regional poles can be understood as part of the process of achieving a temporary balance in the unipolar global order. Regional self-organization has led to the creation of new organizational forms in the global marketplace—different types of regional economic organizations and communities. Regionalization, primarily under the influence of the similarly named global trend, is leading to a reorganization of the GMP and global civic institutions of the global community, which can be understood as one of the major characteristics of its *evolution*. Strategic conclusions can be drawn from the application of the morphological principle of evolution to the organizational structure of the emerging global business order. Usually, new organizational bodies appear organically, in an unsystematic process. Not surprisingly, during the initial development of any new economic, business, or societal organizational structures, more governance structures appear than are necessary for the functioning of an efficient system. Later, as a formal system begins to emerge, redundancies decrease through a process that can be understood as *oligomerization*—a process of simplification by the reduction of a structure's units and subunits. The result of this strategically ruled process is a much more efficient and sustainable system with fewer executive bodies.

This is the process that is under way at the beginning of the twenty-first century, during the formation of the new global order and the emerging of the global community and the global business order. Regionalization and political disintegration have been occurring for decades. Barring any ecological or technogenic catastrophes, both forces will continue to influence the GMP, the global community, and the current global order for some time.

The basic regional structure of the global order will continue to exist until the middle of the century, but it seems to me it will become increasingly unstable, especially from 2025 to 2050, when the formation of several global industrial-sectorial markets will collide with regional blocs in the framework of the GMP. This will happen as a result of the substantial changes in the traditional economic structure and south-north and east-west trade routes and axes. Due to the fact that alternative energy technologies and new methods of enrichment of traditional carbon energy resources started to slowly meet practical needs, in the first quarter of the twenty-first century, Russia has continued to be one of the major sources of oil and gas for Europe, but not the dominant one any more. Pipelines will continue to operate from east to west. They will also run east of Russia to China, North and South Korea, and even Japan. Pipelines are also already under development from Kazakhstan to China, and from Turkmenistan and Azerbaijan toward Europe, as alternatives to Russian oil and gas. Vertical connections will also continue, as oil will flow from the Middle East and Africa to Europe, northwest to the US, and northeast to China. In this process, the transit role of Turkey will increase. Outsourcing and offshoring are developing along similar north-south connections, from the Indian subcontinent in the south to the US and Europe in the north. Knowledge-based technologies and intellectual property will head in the opposite direction, from the high-tech industries of the US and Europe to less-developed countries of Asia and Africa. In the second quarter of the twenty-first century, these traditional axes will change and knowledge-based technologies will be more or less equally heading to old Western European nations from South Korea, Taiwan, and Singapore and slightly later from Thailand and Indonesia. Transportation in the energy sector of hydrocarbon resources from Russia, Nigeria, and even from some Middle Eastern countries (though not Saudi Arabia and Iraq) will dwindle, and new geological discoveries will not occur at the same rapid pace of the previous century. The efficiency of alternative energy technologies like bioethanol, butanol, and nuclear power production will increase, and they will eventually replace hydrocarbon resources as the primary fuel. Any strategic diversification of sources of hydrocarbon from different countries or its partial substitution by alternative sources of energy leads to a decreasing dominance in the energy sector of oil- and natural gas–rich countries, bringing more balance and stability to the global marketplace and more sustainable prosperity to the global community. Eventually, this will lead countries to leave cartels like OPEC and possibly initiate the creation of new ones. Bioenergy is not only a more environmentally friendly source of energy than oil and gas, but it will also lead to a modernization of global political and economic relations. The increasing role of unification of technological standards and requirements, and the enforcement of environmental regulations as well, will increase costs of production, especially in India and China. This process will also be enforced by the need to increase the quality of life of people in these countries in order to prevent high political instability and will eventually make the outsourcing patterns of the early twenty-first century less economical. The global orientation of international business and economic connections will be much more diversified; as a result, the traditional north-south and east-west patterns and corridors will be less visible in the global marketplace.

Nonetheless, they will still be of strategic significance. For corporate leaders and strategists, it makes sense to develop strategic international relations along these corridors to exploit the already well-developed infrastructure and agglomeration effect, which occurs when multiple companies of different industries complement each other in a particular territory or region, reducing the expenses of all parties involved in the project or regional development.

Due to global trends, almost the entire world economy has been integrated within the global marketplace, which will improve and make more evident the existence of the global community. By a similar process the GEM is expanding, as more countries embrace principles of free-market economics and become emerging markets. This is occurring at a faster pace than the most advanced EMCs (economies in bloom) transition into the developed world. More developing (and even some underdeveloped) countries are becoming emerging markets because it requires fewer resources and less time to transition from the status of developing to emerging than it does from emerging to developed. This accelerating dynamic is also causing imbalance in the world economy. However, processes are only one perspective from which to analyze and strategize the impact of the GEM on the global order. It should also be strategized in terms of the static structure of the GEM, which is a stabilizing force in the GMP. Because the GEM is classified between rich developed countries and poor developing countries, it acts as a buffer between these two categories and reduces tension. Without the GEM, inequality in the GMP and especially inside of the global community would be so overwhelming that it would lead to revolutionary changes that could destroy or substantially undermine the global order. The maturation of the GEM will provide another basis for the continuation of the major characteristics of the current global order until the middle of the twenty-first century. At the same time, the GEM's rapid expansion decreases the stability of the world economy. For the short term, the GEM reduces tension in the GMP and increases stability of the global community, but in the long term it increases instability. The global order has to reflect this dichotomy. The continued enlargement of the GEM coupled with the appearance of new countries and the subsequent expansion of the GMP and its sectorial markets further complicates the global order. However, the appearance of new countries under the influence of the trend of political disintegration has already slowed. The wave of transitions of developing countries to the GEM should also slow in the second quarter of the twenty-first century. As a result of these two dynamics, the evolutionary widening of the GMP will also slow down. However, acceleration of the global community improvement will continue with some periodic bilateral and multilateral tensions.

The Revolution of the Global Order

During the Cold War, the world was relatively balanced. There were two superpowers and the global order was organized around the tension between them. This gave the false impression that the global order would last forever, because of the danger and damage (nuclear war) that many assumed would inevitably occur in order for one side to overcome the other. How did this global order, based on the balance of two competing nuclear powers, change? Despite the consensus among experts that the loss of the bipolar balance between the United States and the Soviet Union would have devastating consequences, the end of the Cold War came about in a mostly peaceful, but *revolutionary* reorganization of the global order. This leads to the paradoxical conclusion that *balance in the global order inhibits revolutionary development and subsequent progress.* An asymmetrical global order emerged in place of the symmetrical order of the Cold War and the opinion of the majority again happened to be wrong (see Chapter 2 on rules of strategic thinking). Common sense usually argues that imbalance is dangerous, but it was the main path to progress. While it is counterintuitive, an asymmetric global order is actually more efficient. However, without the revolutionary changes, i.e., the failure of the overwhelming majority of national communist systems, including the Soviet Union, this new global order would not exist. The disappearance of the Soviet Union was the entropy of the Cold War global order. Without this, the global order would not have changed.

The emergence of the new global order allowed the global marketplace and the global community to form and mature. The failure of the old global order led to the fall of the majority of national economic barriers. The fall of the Berlin Wall is the most striking symbol of the collapse of many political and economic barriers during this period of radical change at the end of the 1980s and beginning of the 1990s. These changes were triggering events toward strategies of tighter international economic integration; they resulted in the eventual formation and maturation of the global marketplace. Starting in the last quarter of the twentieth century and the first decade of the twenty-first, the failure and disintegration of the Soviet Union was actually not the beginning of the failure of the global order set by the Bretton Woods Conference. It began much earlier when, under the influence of global trends, dictatorships disappeared throughout much of the world and international economic integration began to increase. The disappearance of the Soviet Union was the culmination of these colossal processes.

At the end of the twentieth century, only formal changes were made, without any strategic basis, to the global order, and international economic integration reached the level of the formation of the global marketplace and the global community. However, the nature of the relationships in the world economy did not change prior to the twenty-first century. At this point, there had not been enough time for political and corporate leaders, and especially for bureaucrats of multilateral institutions, to grow into their new roles and proposed strategy, which for this obvious reason was never presented. The new strategic opportunities and challenges became clear to strategists and to political, economic, and business leaders only during the first decade of the twenty-first century. According to Steven Bernstein:

> The immediate post–cold war period marked an interregnum: a brief honeymoon of optimism for a renewed multilateralism and new global bargains among old foes as well as rich and poor. International economic institutions gained in authority, a host of global issues largely buried beneath cold war priorities began to receive a serious political hearing, and a new engagement with civil society in global affairs promised to extend the reach and legitimacy of institutions of global and regional governance ... But a *global* world where transactions, ideas, and even human beings cannot easily be blocked at borders' edges, requires a reconstitution of multilateralism, at a minimum, and perhaps even a shift to a new paradigm of governance altogether.[25]

Global multilateral institutions were initiated by the Bretton Woods Conference to establish, promote, and sustain a post-war global order. For 40 years this order remained relatively intact. But as a result of the tremendous changes that occurred at the end of the 1980s and 1990s, such as the destruction of the bipolar global balance, these institutions could no longer operate efficiently enough without and systematically develop strategy with the following altering of their functions. During the first 14 years of the process of reform, after the Millennium Summit of 2000, which had established with the horizon of 2015 8 goals and 18 targets, practically none of these objectives were fully reached. It happened mostly due to the fact that there were no rules of strategy development used during the formulation of these goals and targets, and no strategy and strategic management systems were developed for their implementation and practice. All of these goals were very useful and noble:

1. Eradicate extreme poverty and hunger.
2. Achieve universal primary education.
3. Promote gender equality and empower women.
4. Reduce child mortality.
5. Improve maternal health.
6. Combat HIV/AIDS, malaria, and other diseases.
7. Ensure environmental sustainability.
8. Develop a global partnership for development.[26]

The strategic evaluation of how these goals were achievable during just 15 years is one issue; another issue is the lack of a strategic management system for their implementation. Unfortunately, professional strategists were not involved in both of these procedures. The absence of strategic professionalism is a typical barrier against channeling political will into practice. Due to the problems mentioned above with these goals and targets, inequality in the distribution of wealth by the objective year of 2016 is only increasing. As of 2016, 1 percent of the richest people in the world will exceed half the wealth of the remaining 99 percent.[27] And goal number 1, to "eradicate extreme hunger and poverty," was not reached despite the fact that during this period global wealth doubled to $263 billion. At the same time, progress on the way to the eradication of poverty is substantial because the global population that lived in poverty at the end of the twentieth century has decreased twice (by 2015). I would not use the word "only," but in the world today 16 percent of the global population still lives below the poverty line. On the one hand it is a great success that the number is no longer 30 or 40 million (as it was in the last quarter of the twentieth century), but on the other hand, due to the Millennium Summit's wrong strategizing process of its goals, preparation, and implementation, a woeful number of the world's population is still poverty stricken. Besides the fact that none of these eight goals and related targets were reached, it was the aim of the summit to reflect new developments, such as the existence of the global marketplace and the new role of emerging market countries that were non-existent at the time of the Bretton Woods Conference. Nonetheless, don't take me wrong, I am still absolutely positive that the GMP and the global community in general need multilateral institutions like the United Nations, the World Bank, and the World Trade Organization, but the existence of the International Monetary Fund as an institution separate from the World Bank is questionable for me. For the special needs of the global business community, more diverse multilateral institutions are needed. The number of multilateral institutions will grow to reflect the increasing level of economic and business integration in the GMP, as changes in any part of the world influence the overwhelming majority of other regions and industries. Another important organizational form is the international and global non-governmental organization (NGO). According to Professors David Held, Anthony McGrew, and David Goldblatt:

> Although governments and states remain, of course, powerful actors, they now share the global arena with an array of other agencies and organizations. The state is confronted by an enormous number of intergovernmental organizations (IGOs), international agencies and regimes which operate across different spatial reaches, and by quasi-supranational institutions, like the European Union. Non-state actors or transnational bodies, such as multinational corporations, transnational pressure groups, professional associations, social movements etc., also participate intensively in global politics. So too do many subnational actors and national pressure groups, whose activities often spill over into the international arena. Thus, the global arena can be conceived of as a polyarchic "mixed actor system" in which political authority and sources of political action are widely diffused ... This conception alone challenges the conventional Westphalian, state-based or realist characterization of the global political order.[28]

NGOs play an increasingly important role in the emerging global order. These organizations are funded by voluntary donations of private parties that support their humanitarian missions and orientation for the resolution of the most challenging problems of humankind. The following list offers a quick glance at examples of the different types of NGOs and their missions:

- Established in 1984, **International Medical Corps** "is a global, humanitarian, nonprofit organization dedicated to saving lives and relieving suffering through health care training and relief and development programs."[29]
- Founded in 1961, the **Academy for Educational Development** "is a nonprofit organization working globally to improve education, health, civil society and economic development—the foundation of thriving societies." It has more than 250 programs serving people in more than 150 countries.[30]
- Founded in 1971, **Doctors Without Borders/Médecins sans frontières** "is an independent international medical humanitarian organization that delivers emergency aid to people affected by armed conflict, epidemics, natural or man-made disasters, or exclusion from health care in nearly 60 countries."[31]
- Formed in 1995, **Oxfam International** "is a confederation of 13 organizations working together with over 3,000 partners in more than 100 countries to find lasting solutions to poverty and injustice."[32]
- The **NGO Committee on Migration** is an organization with the goal "to encourage the promotion and protection of migrants and their human rights, in accordance with the United Nations Charter."[33]
- It is also important to mention the function of the **International Olympic Committee** in the global community due to the role of athletics in humankind's development.

Technology is an increasingly important instrument in the formation of the global order and its subsequent influence on world affairs. Consider, for example, the power of Google, which accounts for nearly 66.4 percent of all Internet searches and therefore information flows.[34] In the relationship between corporations and global institutions, dialectics are very evident; the GMP influences these organizations and companies and vice versa. This is also true regarding the relationship of the GMP with the global community and all multilateral institutions and NGOs, the majority of which represent the global business community as well, which are all part of the global business order. Revolutionary changes in the global business community at the end of the twentieth century became the objective conditions for the birth of the global business order. According to Indu B. Singh, an author of several books on technological trends:

> The global business community is beset by incessant change. In general, the change in global business is largely the consequence of significant economic and technological revolutions of the post-industrial society. The cumulative result of these revolutions is leading the way to: (a) a new world economic order, (b) creation of the global economy and market, (c) heightened importance of electronic business communications, and (d) the blurring of industry boundaries and competitors. Two important economic and technical changes made during the 1990s will further revolutionize the business community. They are: (a) the growth of transnational corporations and (b) the integral use of global networks to meet the revolutionary needs of transnational corporations. These changes will redefine the global business order and the nature of global business communications ... Underlying the growth in the transnational corporation, global economy and markets will be the increased requirement for moving information around the world. In today's global business environment, the global networks and the value-added services they provide are critical to successful business strategies. Whatever the business, corporations in the future will run that business on the network.[35]

When the global order loses the support of the global and regional superpowers, its influence and sustainability immediately decrease, as do the institutions that represent and implement the order. This inevitably leads to the decline and disintegration of the global order, triggering the eventual revolutionary development of a new order. Quite often in human history going through revolutions of military conflicts and war, as Count Helmuth von Moltke wrote, "eternal peace is a dream, and not even a pleasant one. War is a part of God's world order ... adversity and misery are merely unavoidable elements in the world's order."[36] War is a typical instrument, but not necessarily a strategic one of revolutionary change of the global or regional order. Global order will always include war or at least conflicts. Who is in charge of the global order and prevention of bloody military conflicts? When the representatives of 44 nations met in Bretton Woods, they did not concoct a secret, self-serving organization. The delegates of this meeting were scholars, visionaries, and governmental officials. The meeting was open to all Allied member-countries. The Bretton Woods Committee, which some conspiracy "theorists" cite as a secretive body, is actually a very open organization. Detailed information and data about all major multilateral institutions and international think tanks are available via the Internet. Conflicts, disasters, etc. throughout the GMP and in the world make the absence of a global, all-powerful institution obvious and instead indicate the existence (barely) of poorly coordinated monitoring authorities of global processes. Multilateral institutions of the global order are unable to prevent global, regional, and industrial conflicts and crises and are actually quite dysfunctional. The global order needs strategies for the global community and improved coordination among its established institutions, as well as new, more effective ones. Human technological achievements have created a basis for such a global order. The harmonization of national laws, bylaws, standards, and constitutions of REOs and other regional bodies would enable the development of a global order with specific political and economic priorities as well as the innovations, technological advancements, and legal capabilities to implement them. As of 2015, the global order is an informal public, political, social, and economic phenomenon with a shortage of strategies and efficient institutions, challenging its sustainability. Nonetheless, it is not an institutional phenomenon and is more objective than subjective, due to the fact that it is the reflection of mostly objective global, regional, and other trends, basic economic factors and realities of a social, religious, and cultural nature. There is no single multilateral institution, including the United Nations, that has the definitive "global order" document, to implement in practice, and the preparation of such an order is not on the agenda of any multilateral institution. Furthermore, all multilateral institutions should develop documents with an orientation for their member-countries that establishes strategic principles, priorities, and objectives of the global order. A compendium of these documents would be a basis for a universally accepted doctrine of the global order. Is it good for humankind that strategists and leaders have not developed a doctrine of the global order's principles and priorities? It would be better for the global community if there were an annual study of the global order, which could provide an orientation for multilateral institutions, governments, and corporate and NGO leadership. Multilateral institutions, of course, can present several different observations reflecting the status quo, and even make forecasts and propose strategies of global problems. One of the first such forecasts was the global forecast for the year 2000, developed in the 1970s under the auspices of the United Nations with the leadership of the Nobel Laureate in Economics Wassily Leontief. The destiny of this document is not unusual—not a single international leader even considered employing it for practical needs. The global community as a new phenomenon is in need and forced to deal with many challenges with limited resources. Humankind needs to develop a coordinated and globally accepted order in which to use these resources for grounded priorities and objectives for the resolution of major challenges and global problems. In this way, the global order as a doctrine is definitely needed. This doctrine should not be understood as a directive but as an orientation. It should be used to organize the activity of multilateral institutions and national governments behind consensus or majority-backed strategic priorities, objectives, and goals. If the global order can emerge organically through international structures and national governments, the doctrine should be a document that lays out strategies to solve global problems with strategic principles that are endorsed by a qualified majority of multilateral institutions, national governments, and regional blocs. This document would also be very useful for corporate strategists, especially during the development of the corporate strategic vision.

Objective and Subjective Strategic Factors Influencing the Global Economic and Business Orders

The flickering global order of the first quarter of the twenty-first century has, despite its vulnerability, predetermined the infant global business order until 2025 to 2030. Prior to this period, local and regional conflicts, the appearance of new countries on the political map of the world, the maturation of the global workplace and the global marketplace, and the appearance of new technologies will most likely require the global business order to be revised and improved accordingly; the priorities of the strategic doctrine of the global order, which will most likely exist by this point despite all contemporary and potential conflicts, will also need to be changed. Insofar as the strategic interests of international businesses are concerned, the global order of the first 15 years of the twenty-first century was one of the best and most prosperous in history. The widespread liberalization of the GMP that occurred after the Cold War will continue, albeit at a slower pace due to shifts on the global political arena. The subjective role of national governments as regulators is an increasing factor, but for an overwhelming majority of states it will not reach the point where national governments negatively intervene in private businesses on a large scale. Some relapses will definitely take place, and are already taking place, but one key improvement in the global order will be the emergence of a global component in corporate strategies oriented to the resolution of the major challenges facing civilization. This will lead to the development of another influential factor in the global order: a trilateral relationship between global institutions, national governments, and corporations. This trilateral, albeit difficult, relationship will be the result of the influence of objective and subjective factors that shape the global order and its subsystems. For example, the limits and eventual depletion of certain elements of basic economic resources, such as hydrocarbon reserves, freshwater, and even territory, will have a major impact on the global order, as well as its subsystem—the global business order. Resource shortages have the potential to entirely reconfigure the global order. If leading oil- and gas-producing countries were to suddenly run out of these resources or face unexpected newcomers to this industry, their role in the GMP would change, and the global order would readjust with duress, but accordingly. Despite short-term signals in the GMP regarding the influence of oil-rich countries from the Middle East and other regions, their role and influence is actually quite limited and in some cases insignificant. Examples of other objective factors that will have a strong influence on the emerging global order are the capacity of the environment to withstand the negative impact of industry, natural and technogenic disasters, or the outbreak and pandemic spread of infectious disease.

Subjective factors also shape the global order. The impact of these factors can be both positive and negative. Examples of negative subjective factors are global terrorism, religious extremism, intolerance, territorial claims, and harsh disputes—all of which can lead to armed conflicts and even wars. An important positive subjective factor is the increasing cooperation among national governments and multilateral institutions, especially concerning environmental protection, hunger, and poverty. A few examples of this include the establishment of consensuses, such as the UN Millennium Project, the Doha Development Agenda, and the Kyoto Protocol. Although none of these multilateral agreements was universally accepted and/or enforced, they nonetheless had a significant positive impact on the global strategic agenda, which is itself a subjective factor of the global order. During the first quarter of the twenty-first century, it is likely that the Kyoto Protocol (a legally binding document unifying nations' approaches to international emissions trading and a clean development mechanism) and the Doha Agenda (a mandate on negotiations and implementation in the agriculture and service industries of developing and emerging market countries) will be updated, overwhelmingly accepted, and used as a monitoring guideline for the development and reorganization of the global order's institutions—multilateral global, regional, and national organizations, and corporate ruling structures, which themselves, to some extent, are all parts of the global order and have significant subjective factors that influence it.

Another concept, which is undoubtedly related to an understanding of the needs of the global order, especially at the time of the maturation of the global community, is the noosphere, hypothesized by the great thinker, geologist, and geochemist Vladimir Vernadsky (1863–1945). The noosphere describes when human consciousness and cognition, and societal activity in general, fundamentally change the Earth's biological environment. The influence of human cognition on the noosphere is comparable to the influence of geological processes on it because of the enormous influence of humankind on nature. At the same time, without a particularly detailed knowledge of the deep consequences of its effect on nature, the global community is confident that it has improved nature, when, in fact, it has not. Humanity takes everything from nature without "asking" its permission and, furthermore, without a clear knowledge of the consequences. The global community's ecological consciousness, unfortunately, is still evolving slowly and without the development of strategic priorities helpful to improve "cooperation" between society and nature. Without this cooperation, it will be impossible for quite some time to reach and sustain a high quality of life for individuals within the framework of the global community. This understanding of the birth and maturation of the global community is already a fundamental study, but it is also a public and vital necessity. The global community should take into consideration the concept of the noosphere as an immanent part of its required development, in order to understand the mutual influence between nature and society. In fact, this increasing and improving understanding will encourage societal hope, prevent many potential crises on the global and regional levels, and will stop processes that contribute to the demoralization of society, which, unfortunately, has already taken place. This particular issue requires the development and implementation of a focused global strategy.

The Strategic Factor of Global Trends

Ten key modern global trends and their influence were analyzed in detail in Chapter 7. The aim of this section is to underline their role as objective strategic factors affecting the emerging global order. The majority of these trends have a positive influence on the GMP. Even trends that create challenges, such as the increasing shortages of natural resources, actually create positive incentives. Such shortages force the business world to allocate resources toward the development of alternative or non-traditional sources of energy, substitutes for raw materials, and other environmentally friendly technologies. The knowledge-based economy has started to play a crucial role in developing these technologies, making it possible for even small countries to be among the leaders in these fields. The best example of this is Iceland, the first country to widely develop and sustain a hydrogen-based national economy. The knowledge economy—a term that was created by Austrian-American scholar Fritz Machlup and implemented throughout modern economic theories and practices—is analyzed throughout this book, but in this section it is important to understand its implications for the emerging global order. As the great visionary Peter Drucker said, the world needs "to develop an economic theory appropriate to a world economy in which knowledge has become the key economic resource and the dominant, if not the only, source of comparative advantage."[37] A "world/global community" realistically needs not only an economic theory oriented towards knowledge-based economies, but an updated global strategy that incorporates an analysis of state-of-the-art technology as well. On the national level, as a knowledge-based economy becomes a major driving force in the national product and wealth, it must be included in the national strategy, so that any changes to the national GDP in global output and international trade can be absorbed easily and efficiently.

The best example of this national knowledge-based economy strategy is South Korea. The orientation for building a knowledge-based economy has changed nearly all major individual and social values, as well as economic indicators, and has made creativity one of the most important components of the national spirit. During the country's transitional period, the level of illiteracy in South Korea decreased 2.5 times. Expenses for research and development (R&D) as a percentage of the GDP increased 14 times, with the amount of people involved in the R&D field growing from 2,000 people in 1962 to almost 400,000 in 2010. The role of the private sector in the national GDP increased 3.5 times, and the role of the Korean GDP in the world economy went from nearly 0 to 1.9 percent in 2014, going from well below the world average to 2.5 times greater than that same number. This is astounding for a country with a population of about 50 million.

These numbers are not accidental or lucky. During this time, South Korea had a national strategy focused on creating and developing a knowledge-based economy. This overall strategy was driven by separate but coordinating industrial strategies, trade strategies, and energy strategies.[38] This national strategy was and still is concentrated on 17 different engines of economic growth, all aggregated into 3 divisions: green technology, high-tech industries, and science-oriented services. South Korea was the first nation to establish governmental departments specifically focused on these fields—first the Ministry of Knowledge Economy and then the Ministry of Strategy and Finance, which were mainstays through two different leaders. In September 2013, the new president, Guen Hye Park, the first female South Korean president, established a new government structure that concentrated this later ministry on four strategic priorities:

1. Large corporate investment projects
2. Tourism infrastructure
3. Innovative technology
4. Venture investment and technology finances.[39]

Very few countries in the world can take as much pride as South Korea can in their development and implementation of a national strategy. Only Singapore, Taiwan, Finland, Sweden, Brazil under the leadership of Fernando Henrique Cardoso (and not after), and China since the great strategist Deng Xiaoping come to mind. Israel is a special case, where individuals and small-business strategic initiatives compensate for the lack of a national technology-based strategy. Monetary proof of the success of a knowledge-based economic strategy is a simple fact. Almost 26 percent of Korean exports are high-tech based. Korea's R&D expenses total about 4 percent of their entire national GDP.

Knowledge-based innovations and technologies are the major answer to environmental challenges. Humankind will not reduce production. In fact, as the population grows, the production of necessary foodstuffs, goods, and services will continue to increase. The best strategic option is to change the technological basis of production to improve efficiency and reduce its impact on the environment. This is the only rational method of strategy for protecting the environment without compromising world needs. Eventually, as a result of the penetration of knowledge-based innovations and technologies, the emerging global order will restrict the use of non-environmentally friendly technologies. Knowledge-based technologies are the foundation for resolving other global challenges, such as pandemics and poverty. All of these issues appeared on the global agenda at the end of the twentieth century. The collapse of most dictatorships allowed the establishment of a global consensus on the importance of human rights and human values, the only perspective from which global challenges should be strategically understood if they are to be eventually overcome. While some may argue that a global consensus on human rights does not yet exist, it must at least be conceded that the mindsets of many leaders are moving in the direction of accepting this as the highest strategic priority.

Strategically Aiming for the Global Optimum

As early as the 1970s, the idea of a global optimum was discussed among scholars and world leaders, including representatives of dictatorial regimes. Unfortunately, the mindsets of many economists and strategists regarding the global optimum were backward. Their strategic priorities were the resolution of major international challenges, such as nuclear proliferation, the establishment of agreed-upon national borders, international trade and tariffs, and the strengthening of national economies in the competitive environment of the bipolar world. While these are clearly important strategic objectives, the most important issue of all—the quality of life of individuals—was ignored. Dictatorial concepts of the global optimum were heavily influenced by a general disdain for human rights and the tension of the Cold War. The protection of human rights, routinely violated by repressive regimes, was a subject of political debate and was nowhere near a globally accepted value.

The failure of the bipolar global order provided the opportunity to establish a nearly global consensus on human rights, placing the quality of individuals' lives as the top priority on the pyramid of the global optimum (see Figure 8.1). For the most part, the emerging global order is already centered on the concept of the global optimum. The highest strategic priorities of the global agenda are essentially based on the need to improve the quality of life of every individual on the planet. The focus has shifted to issues such as the prevention of epidemics of infectious diseases, the discovery of solutions to poverty and famine, universal access to freshwater and basic education, as well as the resolution of other challenges that threaten human dignity, like issues of migration and

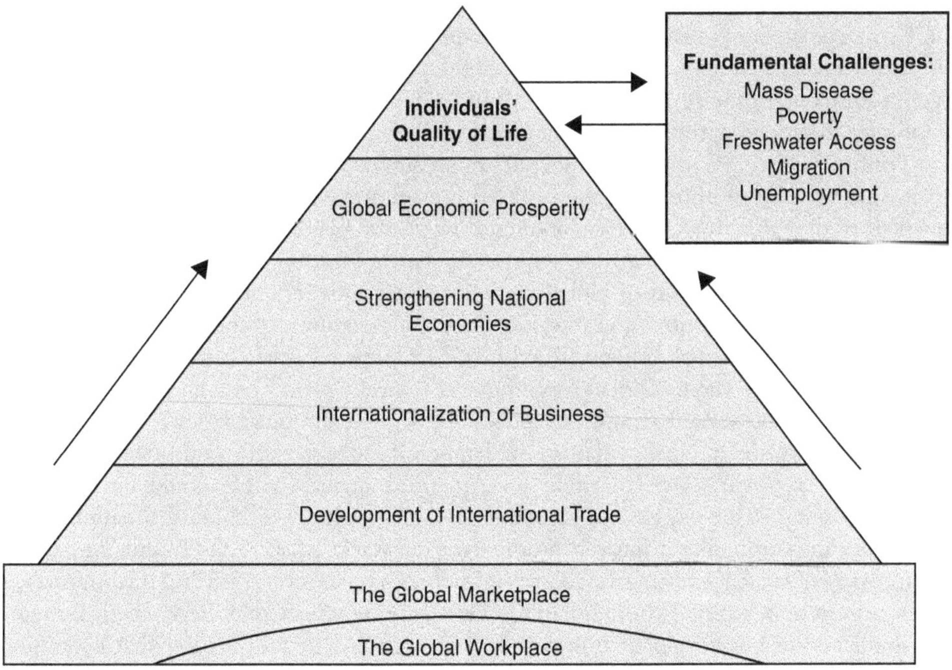

Figure 8.1 The Global Optimum in the Global Business Order

unemployment. The strengthening of national economies and their regional and global integration leads to the continued improvement of international trade and business cooperation, subsequently bringing humankind closer to the global optimum. However, these positive strategic developments are only a basis upon which the standard of living of every human being will eventually be improved: this is a pyramid that stands on its base. The concept of the global optimum asserts that global progress cannot be made if it comes at the expense of individual citizens. The continued improvement of the standard of living for people in developed countries, as well as of those in emerging markets, cannot come at the expense of individuals in developing and underdeveloped nations. This is the basic strategic vision of the great Italian-Swiss economist Vilfredo Pareto (1848–1923). He developed the "Pareto Optimum," which is based on *ophelimity*, a term invented by Pareto that can be understood as "economic gratification." In Pareto's words:

> We will say that the members of a collectivity enjoy *maximum ophelimity* in a certain position when it is impossible to find a way of moving from that position very slightly in such a manner that the ophelimity enjoyed by each of the individuals of that collectivity increases or decreases. That is to say, any small displacement in departing from that position necessarily has the effect of increasing the ophelimity which certain individuals enjoy, and decreasing that which others enjoy, of being agreeable to some, and disagreeable to others.[40]

In accordance with Pareto's ideas, the global order must be organized so that economic development occurs without negatively affecting any individuals. Although this idea was developed roughly a century ago, the critical mass of political, economic, and technological achievements have only recently emerged to enable it to become a fundamental and practical concept of the global order. Pareto's understanding of maximum ophelimity is the most efficient and equitable understanding of the global optimum, although some scholars, such as his contemporary Johan Gustav Knut Wicksell (1851–1926), criticized Pareto for confusing the social optimum with competitive equilibrium.[41] This could be understood as a confusion during Pareto and Wicksell's time, but in the twenty-first century, with the increasing priority of improving the well-being of individuals and the devastating consequences of the violation of national interests, the Pareto principle is more applicable than ever. New technologies, information systems, the harmonization of statistical and reporting systems, and the experience of global institutions have made it more possible than ever before to strategically control and monitor the implementation of the Pareto optimum by the appropriate number of dimensions of the GMP. However, various scholars have shown "that the size of the Pareto Global Optimum set typically grows with an increasing number of constraints, variables, and objectives for a general multiobjective optimization problem."[42] If this is the case, what would happen if Pareto's maximum ophelimity were achieved on a global scale—meaning that no one's quality of life could be improved without coming at the expense of someone else's? In such a hypothetical situation, technological innovation, like improved productivity of arable land, advancements in genetic engineering of food, technological solutions to draughts, etc., could expand the boundaries of maximum ophelimity. Although Pareto's ideas are theoretical, they have practical strategic implications. Future global orders must be organized in such a way that economic development occurs without creating tension and social conflict.

Economists and sociologists have developed several guidelines by which to achieve new levels of global prosperity and bring civilization closer to the global optimum.

The Washington Consensus, a term as widely known as it is criticized, is an example of such a path to future prosperity. John Williamson, an economist from the Peterson Institute of International Economics in Washington, DC, proposed this term in 1989 as a summary of the development theories advocated by Washington-based multilateral institutions. Although it originally referred to Latin America, it eventually became associated with the general development policies of Bretton Woods institutions for non-developed countries. According to a 2002 speech by Dr. Williamson, the Washington Consensus consisted of the following ten points:

1. Fiscal Discipline. This was in the context of a region where almost all the countries had run large deficits that led to balance of payments crises and high inflation that hit mainly the poor because the rich could park their money abroad.
2. Reordering Public Expenditure Priorities. This suggested switching expenditure in a pro-poor way, from things like indiscriminate subsidies to basic health and education.
3. Tax reform. Constructing a tax system that would combine a broad tax base with moderate marginal tax rates.
4. Liberalizing Interest Rates. In retrospect I wish I had formulated this in a broader way as financial liberalization, and stressed that views differed on how fast it should be achieved.
5. A Competitive Exchange Rate. I fear I indulged in wishful thinking in asserting that there was a consensus in favor of ensuring that the exchange rate would be competitive, which implies an intermediate regime; in fact Washington was already beginning to subscribe to the two-corner doctrine.
6. Trade Liberalization. I stated that there was a difference of view about how fast trade should be liberalized.
7. Liberalization of Inward Foreign Direct Investment. I specifically did not include comprehensive capital account liberalization, because that did not command a consensus in Washington.
8. Privatization. This was the one area in which what originated as a neoliberal idea had won broad acceptance. We have since been made very conscious that it matters a lot how privatization is done: it can be a highly corrupt process that transfers assets to a privileged elite for a fraction of their true value, but the evidence is that it brings benefits when done properly.
9. Deregulation. This focused specifically on easing barriers to entry and exit, not on abolishing regulations designed for safety or environmental reasons.
10. Property Rights. This was primarily about providing the informal sector with the ability to gain property rights at acceptable cost.[43]

The Washington Consensus came under attack by anti-globalization protestors and several prominent scholars, including Joseph Stiglitz, the 2001 Nobel Laureate in Economics. In response to such criticism, Dr. Willamson argued:

> [S]ome of the most vociferous of today's critics of what they call the Washington Consensus, most prominently Joe Stiglitz … do not object so much to the agenda laid out above as to the neoliberalism that they interpret the term as implying. I of course never intended my term to imply policies like capital account liberalization … monetarism, supply-side economics, or a minimal state (getting the state out of welfare provision and income redistribution), which I think of as the quintessentially neoliberal ideas.[44]

The neoliberalism to which Dr. Williamson refers can be understood as the process of liberalization of the world economy, which took place during the last quarter of the twentieth century. The negative result of this was the subversion of the role of national governments, which is especially dangerous in times of global crises. The roots of these ideas can be traced to Milton Friedman, a Nobel Laureate in Economics, though in practice his ideas were often vulgarized.

In 2004, Joshua Cooper Ramo, a member of the Council of Foreign Relations, described an emerging alternative to the Washington Consensus, which he called the "Beijing Consensus." He underlined the economic success of China and the importance of its progress, not only for China itself but also for other states that would like to model their development on China's rapid economic growth. He discusses the possibility of the replacement of the Washington Consensus by the Beijing Consensus. In his words:

> To the degree China's development is changing China it is important; but what is far more important is that China's new ideas are having a gigantic effect outside of China. China is marking a path for other nations around the world who are trying to figure out not simply how to develop their countries, but also how to fit into the international order in a way that allows them to be truly independent, to protect their way of life and political choices in a world with a single massively powerful centre of gravity. I call this new physics of power and development the Beijing Consensus. It replaces the widely-discredited Washington Consensus, an economic theory made famous in the 1990s for its prescriptive, Washington-knows-best approach to telling other nations how to run themselves.[45]

He goes on to describe the "continuing U.S. failure" to expedite "a shift from power politics to moral politics."[46] This statement really calls into question the legitimacy of Cooper Ramo's entire argument. Even the harshest critics of the United States are not so naïve as to expect the communist dictatorship of China to have a foreign policy based more on "moral politics" than that of the US. In fact, the strategy of China's communist dictatorship seems to be based solely on "power politics," with a total absence of any observable morality, at least until Xi Jinping emerged at the top of China's pyramid of power and unified for the first time in a couple of decades all the major leading positions of this giant country: the general secretary of the Communist Party of China, the president of the People's Republic of China, and the chairman of the Central Military Commission. This concentration of power has given Jinping the role of chief strategist to move China forward at a progressive pace, contingent upon whether he has a strong strategic vision.

Mr. Cooper Ramo is very critical of the Washington Consensus, but he never gives a concrete outline of the policies in the Beijing Consensus. China's strategy has definitely resulted in a substantial increase in economic development and improvement in the standard of living of the Chinese people. And it is quite possible that Chinese economic output will equal and even surpass that of the United States. However, there is no indication that the standard of living in China will even approach that of the US. Furthermore, although the Chinese communist party has implemented basic economic freedom, political freedom is obviously non-existent in China. Using the Chinese example as a development model for emerging market, developing, and underdeveloped countries would represent a major shift in priorities away from valuing individual lives to valuing economic statistics. The Beijing Consensus is heavily influenced by economic determinism, which is, as previously discussed, an inappropriate perspective by which to strategically understand the world. Economic determinism played a substantial role in the outgoing global order of Bretton Woods, but the new order has to place human rights, tolerance, and the individual's quality of life at the top of its agenda; economic prosperity is only a means to this end. This is especially important as the emerging global order is and will be experiencing the strong influence of several negative subjective factors and trends. The subjective factor that represents the greatest threat to the global order is the impact of global terrorism and extremism. According to professor Francis Fukuyama of Johns Hopkins University:

> In the international system, stateness has been under attack and eroded de facto for a variety of reasons. States throughout the less-developed world are weak, and the end of the Cold War led to the emergence of a band of failed and troubled states from Europe to South Asia. These weak states have posed threats to international order because they are the source of conflict and grave abuses of human rights and because they have become potential breeding grounds for a new kind of terrorism that can reach into the developed world. Strengthening these states has become vital to international security but is one that few developed countries have mastered.[47]

Unfortunately, for most of the twenty-first century, this global challenge will not be resolved. The terrorist attacks of September 11, 2001, accelerated the decline of romantic ideas regarding the complete liberalization of international economic and trade relations, which began during the Asian crisis of 1997. This was the moment when humankind began to understand that the plague of terrorism and extremism could not be stopped by mere words and remonstrations. The good will of humankind has to be reoriented to fight back against individuals, institutions, and national governments that even slightly support terrorism and extremism. It further underlines the fact that the value of human life has to be the top strategic priority for the emerging global order. The negative economic impact of terrorism is analyzed in Chapter 7; the focus of this section is to remind leaders and strategists that this factor always remains a crucial consideration during the development and implementation of strategy in any country or region. It is especially important for businesses or investments related to, or allocated in, countries with state-supported or state-sponsored terrorism and their neighboring countries. Unfortunately, even countries halfway across the globe are vulnerable to the destructive impact of state-sponsored terrorism and extremism, or even state-sponsored aggression. Dr. Matthew Rendall, in his article, "Defensive Realism and the Concert of Europe," raises the question, "Why do great powers expand?"[48] As an answer to this question, he quotes Professor John Mearsheimer, "There are no status quo powers in the international system … save for the occasional hegemon that wants to maintain its dominating position over potential rivals." Using Mearsheimer's reflection, Rendall concludes that, "Many realists expect bids for hegemony to backfire by provoking balancing coalitions." This is why the concepts of the balance of power and the equilibrium of the global optimum are always provocative for some of those who question the fairness of the status quo. This is a major threat for the existing global order, which can lead to, or hinder, its changes. And for the same reason, the analysis of terrorism and extremism is always an important issue for strategists.

An evaluation of new strategic objective and subjective factors of the global order that appeared at the end of the twentieth century, as well as a reevaluation of traditional factors of the global order that aim toward the global optimum, illustrate the changing balance of power between countries and international regional organizations in the global marketplace and have led to the emergence of the global business order. This also indicates the changing balance between the global order and the global business order, in which the role of politics is less central but still important. The formation and functioning of the global marketplace has created the need for a new global order and a new global business order, particularly tailored to both the twenty-first-century global marketplace and the global community.

Strategic Triggering Events Due to the Formation of the Emerging Global Economic and Business Orders

Several triggering events of a strategic nature demonstrated that the global order envisioned at Bretton Woods required more than cosmetic changes. The first major strategy-changing signal of the eroding relevance of Bretton Woods institutions was the failure of the gold-dollar standard system in 1971, when the US declined the request of France and other European nations to fulfill its obligation to unlimitedly convert dollars into gold at a fixed rate. While "the last vestiges of gold were not purged from the system until after the gold window was shut for official international transactions in 1971, the U.S. gold stock had little (if any) effective influence on the behavior of money supply after World War II."[49] However, due to the role of the United States in the world economy and of the dollar as the dominant reserve and banking currency, this first Bretton Woods crisis was solved, at least for the following 40 years. Only the birth of the euro and the growing regional role of the currencies of several emerging regional superpowers—the Japanese yen, the Chinese yuan, the Russian ruble, and the new Brazilian real (introduced in 1994)—reinforced the currency shortcomings of the Bretton Woods global order. Some regional currencies that appeared can actually strengthen the role of the dollar. For example, were the member-countries of the Cooperation Council for the Arab States of the Gulf (CCSAG or GCC)—Bahrain, Kuwait, Qatar, Oman, Saudi Arabia, and the United Arab Emirates— to establish a regional single currency, for its political and economic unity, which is a realistic possibility, it would undoubtedly be related to the dollar, though not pegged. This is because all of the economies of these countries rely on exports of crude oil, which is globally traded in US dollars. In 2014, Bahrain, Kuwait, Qatar, and Saudi Arabia started the practical implementation of Monetary Council with its own central bank. GCC members are already using a basket of its national currencies as a nominal medium of exchange, but any changes in the dollar would inevitably influence this future regional currency. In general, the unification of currencies on a regional basis, which could happen in Latin America, Africa (Afro currency), and among the countries of Oceania, could lead to a reform in the global business order, as shared currencies are always the result of strategic regional integration and the influence of the long-term continuation of this process. However, none of them would pose a challenge to the dollar's role as the ultimate banking currency at least until 2050.

The failure of most dictatorships and the subsequent demolition of many, but far from all, barriers to internationalization increased the interdependence of national economies and led to one of the most active periods of reshuffling of all national and international strategies. This period was one of the most important strategy triggering events for the development of a strategic framework to guide the continuing internationalization of business, culminating in its eventual globalization. The increasing intergovernmental economic relations among newly free-market-oriented countries and with governments and businesses of the developed world created, in the majority of bilateral and multilateral relations, a virtuous cycle of increasing momentum. Emerging market countries were in desperate need of investment, governmental aid, and a new level of cooperation with multilateral institutions. This process would not have taken place had the developed world not aggressively sought the best strategic investment opportunities in newly emerging markets. The increasing internationalization of business led to the emergence of globalized corporations, i.e., companies with more foreign than domestic affiliates. The most globalized of these operate in more than half of the countries of the world.

This phenomenon has not been restricted to the developed world. Several corporations from EMCs, some of which operate also in more than 50 countries, have become globalized. Statistics for the internationalization of global businesses require analysis with more sophisticated indicators, and while improvements are still at the initial stages of development, some progress is evident. The UN *World Investment Report* (UNCTAD) of 2007 was based on a different index than was used for the calculations for Table 8.1. The Transnationality Index (TNI) is a newer arithmetical calculation based on the evaluation of foreign assets of corporations, shares of sales abroad, and the percentage of employees of foreign branches in the total number of corporate employment, unlike the previously applied Geographical Spread Index (GSI), which was a square root of the Internalization Index multiplied by the number of host companies. GSI, as of 2015, is only now used to rank financial corporations. Of the top ten most internationalized global multinational industrial corporations, two are from emerging market countries. While both of them are registered in the United Kingdom, their operational headquarters are in South Africa (SABMiller plc) and in Ireland (WPP plc). In terms of the industrial structure of leading companies, during the last eight years, it is possible to register substantial transformation from predominately delivery and energy corporations (Deutsch Poste AG, Royal Dutch/Shell Group)—or some that disappeared from the top ten most internationalized companies, like Total, together with IBM and Phillips Electronics. The food and beverage industry company (Nestlé SA) is the only company from 2007's list that is still in the top ten of 2014, and actually is now the number one internationalized company in the world. Other top companies from this list also mostly represent the food, beverage, and brewing industry. Top mining (Anglo American plc) and gold-producing companies (Barrick Gold Corporation), the world's largest industrial gases company (Linde AG), and only one

Table 8.1 Top Ten Non-Financial Multinational Corporations Ranked by Transnationality Index, January 2015

Rank	*Corporation*	*Home Economy*	*TNI*
1	Nestlé SA	Switzerland	97.1
2	Anglo American plc	United Kingdom	95.9
3	Anheuser-Busch InBev NV	Belgium	93.3
4	British American Tobacco plc	United Kingdom	91.0
5	Linde AG	Germany	91.0
6	Barrick Gold Corporation	Canada	89.2
7	**SABMiller plc**	United Kingdom	89.1
8	ArcelorMittal	Luxembourg	89.0
9	Vodafone Group plc	United Kingdom	88.9
10	**WPP plc**	United Kingdom	87.8

Based on data from the *UNCTAD World Investment Report* (2014). Annex. Table 28. Retrieved from www.unctad.org/Sections/dite_dir/docs/WIR2014/WIR14_tab28.xls

Note: TNI, the Transnationality Index, is calculated as the average of the following three ratios: foreign assets to total assets, foreign sales to total sales, and foreign employment to total employment.

telecom and communication technology company (Vodaphone Group plc) also make the list. Out of the top 100 multinational industrial corporations, 12 of them not only originated from emerging market countries, but also operate and are registered in their respective EMCs. At the top of the list is a Taiwanese technology group, four companies from China (including one from Hong Kong), three from Spain, an Israeli pharmaceutical company, and the Korean technology giant Samsung Electronics. The highest TNI index among corporations from GEM countries is still the South African corporation SAB-Miller plc. Although they are not among the top companies on this list, the dynamics of internationalization will surely raise the rankings of corporations from the GEM and increase their numbers on these types of evaluations. The strategic significance of globalized companies from EMCs will continue to grow.

The rise of globalized companies has created new strategically significant implications for human resource executives and search companies. Human integration has become a major trend for these global companies' human resource departments, which have to coordinate the integration of thousands of employees from a multitude of countries, cultures, ethnicities, religions, etc., toward shared goals and ethics. This has created a new global business culture, an important quality of the emerging global business order. The most successful globalized companies have become integrated within the business systems of the foreign countries in which they operate, to the point that they are essentially *multi-domestic organizations*. Local people, who use their products and services and even work for them, do not see these corporations as foreign entities. Multi-domestic organizations often name their local subsidiaries in the language and according to the preferences of the local culture. In some cases people are not even aware that these companies are foreign entities. Globalized companies can also be seen as an important factor for the prevention of international conflict because they are typically very influential, combining the interests of nations, companies, and individuals throughout the world. Countries in business with one another usually engage in open conflict only as a last resort. These are just a few of the important qualities of globalized companies that strategists should take into account.

Increased internationalization of businesses complicated the strategizing of this process due to the absence of appropriate global regulations to optimize this process. The need for new global institutions to cooperate in real time to regulate international financial, currency, and inter-banking transactions has became obvious. The Bretton Woods multilateral institutions (especially the IMF) were overwhelmed by these unanticipated economic and business needs. Instead of adapting to the new reality, they continued to use traditional outdated methods that were mostly oriented for relationships with governmental institutions and did not reflect in their functions the full capacity of modern technologies and opportunities of the global marketplace. According to Professor Steven Bernstein of the University of Toronto, during this period, "global institutions simultaneously face challenges to their legitimacy and increasing demands to widen their scope and authority in response to material and social forces associated with globalization."[50]

Two mainly related international spheres emerged—the global business world and the world of intergovernmental and multilateral organizations. Due to the Bretton Woods institutions' inability to adapt to these developments, the practical need for new and differently functioning global institutions became clear. The practical needs of businesses acted as a strategic trigger for the accelerated development of three new phenomena—the global emerging market, the global workplace, and the global marketplace, which unified the global emerging market and the global workplace. None of these phenomena

Table 8.2 Top Non-Financial Multinational Corporations from EMCs from the List of Top Non-Financial Multinational Corporations Ranked by Transnationality Index, January 2015

Rank	*Corporation*	*Home Economy*	*TNI*
13	Hon Hai Precision Industries	Taiwan Province of China	84.39
16	Hutchison Whampoa Limited	Hong Kong, China	82.95
22	Teva Pharmaceutical Industries Limited	Israel	79.13
46	Iberdrola SA	Spain	66.58
51	Repsol YPF SA	Spain	63.99
53	Telefonica SA	Spain	63.62
70	Samsung Electronics Co., Ltd.	Korea, Republic of	58.35
80	China Ocean Shipping (Group) Company	China	48.86
83	Vale SA	Brazil	46.43
95	Petronas—Petroliam Nasional Bhd	Malaysia	39.17
99	China National Offshore Oil Corp	China	18.63
100	CITIC Group	China	17.11

Based on data from the *UNCTAD World Investment Report* (2014). Annex. Table 28. Retrieved from www.unctad.org/Sections/dite_dir/docs/WIR2014/WIR14_tab28.xls

Note: TNI, the Transnationality Index, is calculated as the average of the following three ratios: foreign assets to total assets, foreign sales to total sales, and foreign employment to total employment.

would exist without the technological advancements achieved in response to the interests of international business. Some authors evaluate the role of technology in the reengineering of the global business order to such an extent that they refer to the new "techno-economic paradigm," the major features of which are:

- New forms of organizational "best practices"
- New skill profiles affecting worker quality/quantity
- New "product mix" through new technology
- New innovation trends (radical and incremental) to use new low-cost technology
- New patterns in investment locations—changing comparative advantage
- Growth of small innovative firms in rapidly growing technology sectors
- Concentration by large firms in new sectors—growth, diversification
- New patterns of consumer behavior, consumption, and economic distribution.[51]

Technologies like the Internet, the concentrated result of many scientific, knowledge-based developments which were almost unknown, became essential tools for global businesses, especially in the processes of globalization of financial markets of derivatives and futures and options operating in real time. The delayed reaction of Bretton Woods institutions and the increasing need for cross-border cooperation among businesses without appropriate regulations by global institutions accelerated the creation of regional economic organizations. The internationalization of national economies, initiated by national governments of developed and emerging market countries as a means of increasing national economic efficiency, accelerated this process. These organizations were primarily business oriented. By the middle of the 1990s, regional organizations became substantially more efficient for many economic, business, and financial functions than global Bretton Woods institutions. This triggered all parties to initiate a new strategic framework for the development of a more effective global business order, which then became an unrecognized reality.

Another triggering event was the realization by the business community of its social responsibilities. This understanding developed rapidly and became a globally visible issue as multinational corporations were forced to come to terms with widespread public backlashes in countries and communities in which they operated irresponsibly. The birth of the global marketplace and the development of global business triggered a more intense level of competition, forcing businesses to seek new, untapped markets. This led to the development of strategies to exploit the purchasing power of the so-called bottom of the pyramid (BOP). While the individuals of this market may have very limited purchasing power, as an aggregate it is no fewer than 2 billion people, who represent a huge potential market. The emergence of bottom-of-the-pyramid strategies is another trigger for the development of a global business order that will make this market more conducive to international business and protect individuals from exploitation as a result of BOP-oriented strategies. Corporate social responsibility has already become a major characteristic of the emerging global business order.

Another major triggering event for all existing and developing strategies occurred in 1997, with the so-called Asian financial crisis, the global impact of which the Bretton Woods system did not forecast, prevent, or manage. The Bretton Woods institutions, especially the IMF, failed largely because they incorrectly classified the crisis as a regional (Asian) one. In fact, the "Asian" crisis was just the beginning of a global financial crisis that finally ended in December 2001, in Argentina. The IMF also failed due to its emphasis on working primarily with national governments. It almost entirely ignored the private sector, even powerful, privately held equity and multicurrency funds, like MERK, HARD currency fund, and George Soros's Quantum Fund, among others, ignoring the importance of the role of illiquid investment strategies, which help to prevent crisis, even on a global scale. The global emerging market, which, at that time, was still in its infancy, experienced tremendous damage as a result of the global order's traditional institutions' inability to prevent this crisis. The global emerging market was not even acknowledged by multilateral institutions. As of 2015, about 15 years later, its existence still has not been adequately presented in the country classification of these agencies, which is another trigger of the need for reform of Bretton Woods institutions. It is also an obvious reason for the necessity of a new multilateral organizational structure that focuses specifically on sustainability and improvement of the global business order. Such an organizational structure could be known as the Global Business Coordinating Council (GBCC).

As a result of all of these events, there is a burgeoning need of businesses for professionals—especially strategists, economists, and strategic financiers—who can understand and anticipate new trends in the global marketplace and the upcoming global business order. These professionals must be trained to strategize and analyze in this new global business environment. As a result, the requirements for business and financial education have changed. Companies need universities and business schools to produce graduates specially trained to strategize and operate with and within the global marketplace, the global emerging market, and the global financial market during their continuing internationalization and globalization. The global business order has already begun to emerge in response to these strategic triggering events.

The Changing Strategic Roles of Multilateral Institutions in the Global Marketplace

Many events and power shifts among countries and regional organizations of the GMP have not been reflected in the functions, structure, and relationships of multilateral institutions with one another and with national governments and corporations due to the absence of strategies and/or their effective coordination. Representation of emerging superpowers like China, India, Russia, and Brazil has not duly increased, and the growing importance of REOs is totally unrepresented in the activities and structures of Bretton Woods institutions. As of 2015, the minor changes proposed by the managerial bodies of the World Bank and the IMF do not adequately reflect the new reality of the GMP. These changes, which mostly evince a reshuffling of voting shares in favor of emerging market countries, ignore the role of REOs in the global workplace and marketplace. Even the implementation of these moderate changes proposed by the president and executive directors of the World Bank can be done only by decision of the board of governors. However, the members of this board at any particular time will not be very enthusiastic about giving more power and voting authority to representatives of other member countries from the GEM. No one on the board of governors wants to lose influence. Nevertheless, this change is inevitable and will most likely begin by the end of the first decade of the twenty-first century. More than that, no multilateral institution yet takes into account the existence of the GMP and the GEM (see Chapter 6).

The emerging global business order should reflect the changing strategic balance of power in the world; a fundamental shift in the focus of these institutions is necessary. For example, rather than cooperating with the governments of EMCs, these institutions should cooperate primarily with the private sector, the GEM as a whole, and REOs. Their main role is to provide inexpensive, below-market-rate loans and advice and expertise to the governments of non-developed countries. In some EMCs, the IMF helped to stabilize financial conditions, reduce inflation, establish financial market institutions, and bring national currencies closer to convertibility. However, most often, IMF loans, issued without the backing of a deep strategy, did more to pad the pockets of corrupt bureaucrats and officials than to improve the lives of ordinary people. Loans that were not illegally appropriated by bureaucrats were used to artificially balance current accounts and new multimillionaires appeared in EMCs without strong enforcement of law and corrupt government structures on central and, even more, on regional levels. This was done at the expense of future generations, who will have to repay the debt service of the increased foreign sovereign debt for years and decades to come. As stabilizing instruments of the IMF, currency board arrangements (CBA) were also ineffectual. A currency board is

> a monetary regime based on an explicit legislative commitment to exchange domestic currency for a specified foreign currency at a fixed exchanged rate, combined with restrictions on the issuing authority—the currency board—to ensure the fulfillment of its legal obligation. This structure implies that domestic currency be issued only against foreign exchange and that it remain fully backed by foreign assets. Thus, it eliminates traditional central bank functions like monetary regulation and the lender of last resort.[52]

In most cases, attempts by the IMF to overrule domestic banking and financial institutions of emerging market countries ended in painful failure. For example, despite the IMF's establishment of a currency board in Argentina, the Asian financial crisis eventually spread to this country in 2001. Although it originated in Thailand in 1997, went through Turkey and Russia in 1998, and was observable four years before it affected

Argentina, the currency board did not anticipate it and did little to prevent its contagion in Latin America. As a result, inflation skyrocketed and the peg of the Argentinean peso to the dollar disappeared. Many experts were strongly against the creation of a currency board in Indonesia in 1998 because it was widely believed that the Indonesian dictator General Suharto (1921–2008) would not be in office for much longer,[53] and the deficit of US dollars in the national reserves was not sufficient to support currency board functioning. Under these conditions, a stable exchange rate could not be sustained. Besides that, the transparency of currency emission in Indonesia could not be guaranteed. As a result, the number of currency bills in circulation would not be related to hard currency reserves. Only a couple of months after the establishment of the Indonesian currency board, the Suharto dictatorship collapsed, along with its currency board.

The IMF currency board in Bulgaria was more effective, perhaps because it was established after the country was already relatively financially stable and Bulgarian currency board arrangements already had the opportunity to use the experience of Argentina, Estonia, and Lithuania, where CBAs were established in the early 1990s. After a mild financial crisis, the currency board successfully restricted the activity of inexperienced government financiers. It was also helpful in attracting FDI, which increased largely as a result of its existence. It continues to function, even after Bulgaria joined the European Union in 2007, and will continue until it joins the European Economic and Monetary Union. Despite the Bulgarian example, currency boards are not necessary for a country to improve its financial and monetary situation. Ireland and Turkmenistan are great illustrations of this, as their financial and monetary situations vastly improved without their accepting a single dollar from the IMF. They were able to establish financial stability, a strong banking system, and hard currency reserves. This state strategy resulted in improvements in the standard of living of their people. Ireland became one of the most efficient emerging markets of the world.

According to Dr. Kurt Schuler, "IMF-supported currency-board arrangements have been implemented in Argentina (est. 1 April 1991, abandoned 6 January 2002), Djibouti (est. 1949), Estonia (est. 20 June 1992), Lithuania (est. 1 April 1994), Bosnia (est. 1 August 1997), and Bulgaria (est. 1 July 1997).

There are several non-IMF-supported currency boards—mostly in former British colonies, such as Hong Kong, Bermuda, the Cayman Islands, the Falkland Islands, Gibraltar, and the Faroe Islands (part of Denmark). ...

The main characteristics of a currency board are as follows:

Anchor currency: The anchor currency is a currency chosen for its expected stability and international acceptability. For most currency boards the British pound or the US dollar has been the anchor currency, though for some of the recent currency-board-like systems, the anchor currency is the euro. The anchor currency need not be issued by a central bank; a few currency boards have used gold as the anchor currency.

Convertibility: A currency board maintains full, unlimited convertibility between its notes and coins and the anchor currency at a fixed rate of exchange. Though an orthodox currency board typically does not convert local deposits denominated in its currency into the anchor currency, banks will offer to do so for a small fee.

A currency board has no responsibility for ensuring that bank deposits are convertible into currency-board notes. That is the sole responsibility of banks. The currency board concerns itself only with the notes and coins that it issues. Unlimited convertibility into the anchor currency means that in an orthodox currency board system, no restrictions exist on current-account transactions (buying and selling goods and services) or capital-account transactions (buying and selling financial assets, such as foreign bonds).

Reserves: A currency board's reserves are adequate to ensure that all holders of its notes and coins can convert them into the reserve currency or commodity. Currency boards often hold reserves of 105 or 110 percent of their liabilities, rather than just 100 percent, to have a margin of protection should the bonds they hold lose value.

Profits: Unlike bonds or most bank deposits, notes and coins do not pay interest; they are like an interest-free loan from the people who hold them to the issuer. The issuer's profit equals the interest earned on reserves minus the expense of putting the notes and coins into circulation. These expenses are typically less than 1 percent of assets per year. In addition, if the notes and coins are destroyed, the issuer's net worth increases, because liabilities are reduced but assets are not. Typically, the profits from a currency board left after paying all the board's expenses are roughly 1 percent of gross domestic product (GDP) a year.

Using currency issued by a currency board rather than using foreign currency, such as US dollars, directly captures seigniorage [the net revenue derived from issuing currency] for the domestic government. Also, use of a domestic currency board issue rather than a foreign currency satisfies nationalistic sentiment. …

Relation to banks: Just as a currency board has no share in the profits of banks, it has no responsibility for acting as a lender of last resort to protect them from losses. Bank failures have been rare in orthodox currency-board systems. They have, however, been common in the recent currency-board-like systems, which have inherited many banking problems from the central banking systems that preceded them. Historical experience suggests that lenders of last resort usually create more problems than they solve, because their existence encourages banks to be less prudent than they would otherwise be. Accordingly, the best policy is to let troubled banks fail.

Though a currency board holds 100 percent or slightly greater foreign reserves, banks in a currency-board system are not required to imitate the currency board. Like banks in a central banking system, their reserves in excess of legal minimum requirements typically equal only a few percent of their liabilities. Another way to say this is that in a currency-board system, the monetary base (M0) has 100 percent foreign reserves, but broader measures of the money supply such as M1 (currency in circulation plus demand deposits) or M2 (currency in circulation plus demand deposits plus time deposits) do not have 100 percent reserves."[54]

The IMF practice of allocating quotas is also obsolete, unfair, and ineffectual. The Bretton Woods Formula, which the IMF still uses to determine voting share, does not reflect today's global marketplace. Many countries have fewer votes than they should. For example, as of 2015 China accounts for only 3.81 percent of IMF's 2,519,762 votes, despite the size and influence of its economy. Its shares in total number of votes since the beginning of the IMF "2008 Amendment of Voice" increased by 0.15 only (!). But during this period, nonetheless, the shares of votes of other BRICS countries decreased, and, as of 2015, similar discrepancies exist in the percentage of votes of Brazil (1.72), India (2.34), Russia (2.39), and South Africa (0.7).[55] Bretton Woods institutions and leaders of its member-countries already recognized the potential danger of this and have been seriously discussing this issue since 2006. According to award-winning journalist Emad Mekay:

> Officials of global organisations and rich nations rarely admit it but civil society groups and developing countries say the sad fact has not changed: multilateral bodies meant to help create a global community are in fact undemocratic. From the World Trade Organization (WTO), the International Monetary Fund (IMF), the World Bank and the United Nations, to Interpol and the World Health Organization (WHO), dozens of international agencies now work to regulate world trade, telecommunications, transportation, labour, business, health and the environment, among other issues. In almost all of those bodies, poor and powerless nations, like Somalia and Afghanistan, are under-represented while the rich and powerful, like Britain and the United States, operate with almost unchecked authority and overwhelming power. … Directors from rich countries now control more than 60 percent of the votes at the World Bank and IMF, while the U.S. administration has veto power over any extraordinary vote requiring a super-majority. Even in institutions like the Geneva-based WTO, which theoretically operates under consensus and technically gives each member country veto power, practice is different. Some 28 of the WTO's 146 member nations do not even attend most of the organization's meetings for the simple reason that they lack the resources to set up diplomatic missions in the expensive Swiss city of Geneva. But those countries still figure as part of the consensus when decisions are made.[56]

One of the World Bank Group's strategic problems is related to the unproven allocation of its loans proportionate to the poorest nations, even according to its own classification using income per capita. It considers China, as of 2013, to be an upper-middle-income country with GNI per capita of $11,850 PPP, yet it allocates far more loans to China than it does to the extremely poor countries of sub-Saharan Africa and Southeast Asia (see Table 8.3). One might argue that because of China's huge population and its huge number of poor people, it makes sense for it to receive more attention than other countries. This argument is refuted by the data in Table 8.3, which presents World Bank lending on a per capita basis. The ten underdeveloped countries and one developing country in Table 8.3 receive less lending per capita *combined* than China. Every project that the World Bank finances in China could easily be financed by Chinese national reserves, which are the largest in the world. The World Bank has demonstrated the same questionable use of financial aid to several other countries that are not poor. For example, in 2008 the World Bank decided to finance 10 percent of a public financial education program in Russia. This is not extremely logical due to the fact that Russia not only has the third-largest foreign currency reserves in the world, but it also allocates hundreds of billions of dollars to several other funds, as a

Table 8.3 World Bank Lending (Comparison of China to Selected Underdeveloped and Developing Countries) (US$), 2013

Country	*Total World Bank Lending (US $), 2013*	*World Bank Lending per Capita (US $), 2013*
China	18,847,996,000	13.89
Central African Republic	23,130,000	5.01
Eritrea	481,084,000	75.96
Burundi	173,444,000	17.07
Liberia	58,947,000	13.73
Gambia, The	61,856,000	33.45
Rwanda	472,556,000	40.13
Lao People's Democratic Republic	611,202,000	90.28
Malawi	417,525,000	25.52
Niger	549,653,000	30.83
Guinea	168,047,000	14.31
Bangladesh	11,582,988,000	73.97

World Bank. (n.d.). "Interactive Lending Map." Retrieved from http://geo.worldbank.org/

result of its wealth of cash generated from the export of natural resources. The limited resources of the World Bank should go to the poorest nations of the world, such as Somalia, Sudan, or the Democratic Republic of Congo, which received such insignificant amounts of lending per capita that they were not even included in Table 8.3. It is the same situation with China as a recipient of monetary help from the World Bank. China receives per capita much more money than the poorest nations in the world, like Central African Republic, Liberia, or Congo. The appearance of China on this list is a clear manifestation of the absence of a well-defined poverty-eradication strategy at the World Bank. But in 2014, the World Bank Group developed a new strategy of engagement with member-countries, "The Country Partnership Framework (CPF)."[57] This approach is far from perfect, but is much closer to the strategic rules and on the basis of much better information systems: the "Systematic Country Diagnostic (SCD)." All of these new strategic managerial approaches substantially narrowed the gap between strategic rules and strategic practice of the WBG—including "WBG Guidance."[58] This development of strategy gives hope that more money will go to the poorest countries of the world and much less, or none, to countries with the largest hard currency and gold reserves.

The IMF also does not use its limited resources in a manner appropriate to the needs of the world's poorest people. Its reserves are not even as large as China's. As of 2015, the IMF's total borrowing capacity is about $560 billion[59] and has increased since evaluating, previously six years ago, by almost 65 percent. Nonetheless, this figure is dwarfed by China's foreign currency reserves alone, which are worth over US$3 trillion.[60] This does not take into consideration the almost $200 billion official reserves of Hong Kong[61]—larger than the reserves of the majority of European nations—which is, of course, part of the People's Republic of China. In fact, in addition to China, Taiwan, Russia, and South Korea all have larger reserves than the IMF (see Figure 5.21).

So-called help from the IMF, World Bank, and African Development Bank has caused the external debt of sub-Saharan countries to reach $218.5 billion as of 2008.[62] Most of this money was stolen by kleptocrats, never reaching those who desperately needed it. Without debt relief, future generations will be overwhelmed by these obligations.

In 2005, at the initiative of the G8 and the then prime minister of the United Kingdom, Tony Blair, 100 percent debt relief was granted to 18 countries, mostly in Africa and a few from Central and South American (Bolivia, Guyana, Honduras, and Nicaragua).[63] The United States is by far the largest contributor of official development assistance in absolute numbers; however, several European countries and Japan contribute more as a percentage of GNI.[64] Nonetheless, international attention to this region started to demonstrate positive results and growth of sub-Saharan countries (excluding South Africa) is going at a faster pace than other underdeveloped, developing countries and EMCs (excluding China).[65]

While the World Bank Group does work with the private sector, it is struggling to compete with private banks, despite its below-market interest rates. The majority of companies of the GEM prefer private bank loans because of the World Bank Group's constraining, bureaucratic safeguard policies. There is another strange practice of the World Bank—it penalizes countries for making payments ahead of the agreed-upon schedule, which obviously discourages borrowers from increasing their payments to the World Bank. As a result, money that the Bank could use to help struggling countries remains in the coffers of governments that do not necessarily need it. Changing this regulation should be a first priority, and it can be achieved simply by abolishing a bureaucratic barrier.

Other multilateral organizations monitor and regulate the business infrastructure of the global marketplace. These include the International Telecommunications Union, Air Transport Association, the International Labor Organization (ILO), the World Health Organization, and the United Nations Environment Programme. Some of these organizations are part of the United Nations System of Organizations, while others are independent multilateral organizations or non-governmental global institutions. All of them, despite their business-related nature, work primarily with governments, the United Nations, and, to a much lesser degree, with private businesses. This pattern should be changed according to the emerging global business order.

However, there is one exceptional organization, the International Chamber of Commerce (ICC). "The ICC World Council is the equivalent of the general assembly of a major intergovernmental organization. The big difference is that the delegates are business executives and not government officials."[66] This organization is underestimated and underutilized by the global business community but can be a powerful instrument to promote the global business order.

The new role of the Bretton Woods institutions should be to coordinate, on the strategic level, the activity of private businesses, international and global non-governmental organizations, and national governments to address the needs of the world's poorest people. The projects of highest priority should relate to freshwater access, alternative energy development, the prevention of epidemics, and famine alleviation. Another important objective of the new global business order will be to minimize risk in the GMP. In developing and underdeveloped countries, Bretton Woods institutions will still play a role in helping governments prepare and implement proper economic, financial, and business regulation.

The increasing regionalization of the global marketplace, especially in the global emerging market, requires the World Bank to play a new role: dealing with regional economic organizations. One of the solutions to this issue will be the development of new regional banks that work within the framework of major regional blocs as well as with their territorial subsystems. One of the oldest regional banks in the world is the Inter-American Development Bank, which was established in 1959. Its mission is to "contribute to the acceleration of the process of economic and social development of the regional developing member countries, individually and collectively."[67] An example of a legally independent subsystem of the Inter-American Development Bank is the Andean Development Corp., a regional development bank that has loaned hundreds of millions of dollars to the governments of Colombia, Peru, and Venezuela, mostly to fund infrastructure projects.[68] More regional subsystems are beginning to emerge, such as the Mercosur Development Bank, the creation of which has been a topic of discussion in the meetings of the member-countries of Mercosur.[69] The Caribbean Development Bank is a regional bank that has been operational since 1970.[70] These banks and their regional equivalents throughout the world will be strategically instrumental in the motivation and practice of regional and subregional cooperation between companies of its member-countries. The major customers of these banks are businesses that focus on infrastructure and social development. Issues such as poverty, migration, and mass disease are high on their agenda. Their role has been increasing since the beginning of the twenty-first century, and this trend should continue. Regional banks and other financial, multilateral, credit, and microcredit institutions act as important mechanisms for the prevention of inter-regional crises and conflicts.

As in most institutions, there is a desire within the Bretton Woods system to maintain the status quo. This has been the case with past global orders. However, when global conditions change and the leaders of the current global order fail to adapt, it only expedites its destruction, as the global order becomes less and less relevant. Rather than resisting change, it would behoove the current leaders, while they are still in power, to take an active part in the process of reforming multilateral institutions to meet the requirements of the emerging global order. As the structure of the economic dominance of countries changes, so too does the global order.

Additional Strategic Authorities of the Global Economic and Business Orders

First, current institutions have to change according to the new realities, balance of power, and ethics of international relations. These changes have to be substantial, to the extent that some of these institutions will no longer be required in the global arena, in response to the new, long-term global agenda. One of the most vocal critics of multilateral institutions is Steve Forbes, who argues,

> "if you didn't have the IMF, then lenders and investors would pay more attention" to the riskiness of their loans to developing nations. … Left alone, investors and banks could have sorted out the Asian and Latin American crises better than the IMF did, Forbes said. Forbes also expressed skepticism about the IMF's sister agency, the World Bank, and of the US Agency for International Development.[71]

Second, there are several international organizations and de facto institutions like the G8 meetings, the Bretton Woods Committee, and the World Economic Forum that already play an important role in focusing the opinion of the global community, especially global business leaders, on the major issues facing civilization. These institutions should be formally (de jure) institutionalized. In order for this to occur, mechanisms of practical implementation for the recommendations of these organizations should be developed through multilateral institutions and/or national governments.

The Bretton Woods Committee

For decades multilateral institutions had no agency by which to monitor and report to major donors (member-countries) and offer a second opinion about the activities and plans of these institutions. Bretton Woods institutions were not only without a body to provide criticism, but they also lacked an organization to advocate certain activities and proposals. Finally, in 1983, to address these needs, the Bretton Woods Committee was established, upon the recommendation of two former US Treasury officials—Secretary Henry H. Fowler and Deputy Secretary Charles E. Walker. The mission of the committee is to "increase understanding of the World Bank, IMF, WTO and the regional development banks and their efforts to spur economic growth, alleviate poverty and improve financial stability."[72] The committee consists of economists, financiers, prominent business leaders, and politicians from around the world. Annually, the Bretton Woods Committee meetings always take place the day before the Joint Annual Meeting of the World Bank and IMF in the same location, so that its members do not have to travel just for the meeting. The Joint Annual Meeting is usually in Washington, DC, the headquarters of both these multilateral institutions and the committee. Occasionally, these meetings take place outside of Washington, in different cities around the world.

Every meeting of the Bretton Woods Committee includes the participation of top-level officials from various countries, including the secretary of state and secretary of the treasury of the United States. After reports from the president of the World Bank, the managing director of the IMF, and/or the director-general of the World Trade Organization, there is usually a discussion and Q & A session. Following this, the committee makes its decision based on a consensus of the participants regarding the budgets of the Bretton Woods institutions and contributions of member-countries it will support for the next fiscal year. Two of the most impressive meetings were in July 1994 and July 2004, when the anniversaries of the original Bretton Woods Conference were celebrated. I have participated in all meetings of the Bretton Woods Committee since 1992 but these two particular anniversary meetings were very impressive and thoughtful, not only due to outstanding speeches, but also the collaboration of several participants from the original 1944 conference, who were at both of these meetings.

The Bretton Woods Committee also has as a subsidiary, the International Council, which includes in its membership top financial, business, and political leaders from around the world. The main function of this council, as well as of the committee itself, is to advise and monitor Bretton Woods institutions and political leaders of member-countries regarding these institutions' activity and to suggest alternatives, when warranted. There have been several Bretton Woods Committee annual meetings that took place outside of Washington and beyond the borders of the United States. In 1994 this meeting, as well as the Joint Annual Meeting of the World Bank and IMF, took place in Madrid. In 1998 these meetings occurred in Hong Kong, one year after the United Kingdom handed it over to the People's Republic of China. The reason for this location was to evaluate the functioning of Hong Kong's financial institutions and companies under Chinese authority. Each Annual Meeting of the World Bank and IMF, as well as of the Bretton Woods Committee, that occurs outside of Washington, DC, is used to verify a specific aspect of the global order.

With the increasing importance of the GEM, the Bretton Woods Committee began to give more attention to emerging market countries. On January 25, 2008, the Bretton Woods Committee, in partnership with the Center for Emerging Market Enterprises of the Fletcher School of Tufts University (Massachusetts), held a conference entitled Strengthening Capital Markets in Emerging Market Countries. At this meeting, the lack of definition of an emerging market country and the implications of this for multilateral institutions and the global business community were discussed.[73] As an indication of the openness of this organization, the entirety of this conference, including speakers' PowerPoint presentations, is available online on the Bretton Woods' website.

World Economic Forum

After the first 30 years of the Bretton Woods institutions, it became apparent that their major shortcoming was the absence of cooperation with the business community, scholars, and individual visionaries. The failure of the gold standard system in 1971 made these shortcomings obvious—the missions of Bretton Woods institutions were not in tune with the new objectives of humankind. These objectives were mostly related not to the interest of victorious countries of World War II, but to individuals around the world, through the resolution of issues related to poverty, mass disease, migration, and similar damaging issues (see Figure 8.1). More than that, leaders of these multilateral institutions were not familiar with these objectives, or were at least not focused on their implementation. Several attempts were made to change the situation. One of the first such attempts was the establishment in 1968 of the Club of Rome. Its original agenda focused only on Western European issues, but its mission has evolved to "act as a global catalyst of change that is free of any political, ideological or business interest."[74] The Club of Rome is still operational, but by the beginning of the 1970s it had lost the momentum to establish itself as a permanent organization for global issues. In 1971 the German-born professor Klaus Schwab took and fully implemented the idea of an annual meeting of powerful leaders, strategists, and thinkers when he established the World Economic Forum.

> The World Economic Forum was first conceived in January 1971 when a group of European business leaders met under the patronage of the European Commission and European industrial associations.... Klaus Schwab ... chaired the gathering which took place in Davos, Switzerland. He then founded the European Management Forum as a non-profit organization based in Geneva, Switzerland, and drew European business leaders to Davos for their annual meeting each January. Initially, Professor Schwab focused the meetings on how European firms could catch up with US management practices.
>
> Professor Schwab's vision for what would become the World Economic Forum grew steadily as a result of achieving "milestones." Events in 1973, namely the collapse of the Bretton Woods fixed exchange rate mechanism and the Arab-Israeli War saw the annual meeting expand its focus from management to economic and social issues, and political leaders were invited for the first time to Davos in January 1974. Two years later, the organization introduced a system of membership, which were the 1,000 leading companies of the world.[75]

In addition to its annual meeting, conducted in the Swiss resort town of Davos, in the last week of January and first week of February, the World Economic Forum also conducts region-specific meetings in different parts of the world, throughout the year. The activities of the World Economic Forum now fully live up to its name. However, it is definitely a non-institutional organization, as there is no multilateral institution required to implement its recommendations. Its decisions do not have any executive power. Despite its global importance, it is almost impossible for individuals that are not related to leading corporations or governments of powerful countries to participate in the annual meeting of this organization. Even leading companies are limited to only a few participants. The registration cost alone is thousands of dollars. Nevertheless, governmental officials, corporate leaders, and strategists always try to participate in this event. Through discussions, they can understand or reshape their vision of the future, and it is an ideal place to convene brief and informal meetings with top leaders. Davos is one of the best networking events in the world. Finally, people come to Davos to test their ideas, or to promote them, by influencing key decision-makers. Any strategist or top executive has to pay close attention to this event. At a minimum, it is one of the best ways of developing an understanding of the upcoming global agenda. At the World Economic Forum of 2015, which mostly discussed political risks, including political unrest, and cybersecurity, the structure of professional participants of the event—1,400 business leaders and 40 heads of states and governments—clearly presented the mission of this forum.[76] An example of the impact of the agenda of the World Economic Forum on corporate strategy can be seen in the experience of Marsh & McLennan Companies, a "global professional services firm providing advice and solutions in risk, strategy and human capital."[77] Its president and CEO, Mr. Michael Cherkasky, participated in the 2007 Annual Meeting of the World Economic Forum, which discussed "climate change and the implications on business processes and disclosure."[78] After this meeting, Mr. Cherkasky expressed the following opinion, "As with all risk, management of climate change should not be treated as an 'add-on' to a company's operation. It must be part of an integrated planning that goes into establishing business processes and operations in the first place."[79] This is an example of the correct strategic culture and exemplifies how strategists should react to the agenda of the World Economic Forum and how this agenda influences the strategy of the leading firms of the world.

The World Economic Forum is one the most exclusive and elite organizations of all non-institutional elements of the global order, second only to the Bilderberg Group meetings, which are discussed later in this chapter. Before the advent of the Internet, information about the meeting was barely accessible to the public, and outsiders can still only find a limited amount of information on its website and in media coverage.

Council on Foreign Relations

The Council on Foreign Relations is an independent, non-partisan foreign policy think tank and membership organization established in 1921.[80] Its mission is to be

> a resource for its members, government officials, business executives, journalists, educators and students, civic and religious leaders, and other interested citizens in order to help them better understand the world and the foreign policy choices facing the United States and other countries.[81]

Notable members of its board of directors include former US Secretary of State Madeleine Albright, former US Secretary of State Colin Powell, and former US Secretary of the Treasury Robert Rubin, among others. It is difficult to consider this organization a truly global think tank in light of the fact that membership is restricted to US citizens.

Many conspiracy "theorists" wrongfully characterize the Council on Foreign Relations as a nefarious global authority, arguing:

> if one group is effectively in control of national governments and multinational corporations; promotes world government through control of media, foundation grants, and education; and controls and guides the issues of the day; then they control most options available. The Council on Foreign Relations (CFR) and the financial powers behind it … promote the "New World Order," as they have for over 70 years. The CFR is the promotional arm of the Ruling Elite in the United States of America. Most influential politicians, academics and media personalities are members, and it uses its influence to infiltrate the New World Order into American life.[82]

This quote contradicts itself. People from many strata of society—politicians, academics, and media personalities, who do not have any shared interests—are obviously not promoters of the ruling elite. This unfounded opinion actually makes accusations without any evidence, which is quite typical for conspiracy theorists.

The CFR has several affiliated organizations, such as the World Affairs Council of Oregon, the Cleveland Council on World Affairs, among many others. Participants of the meetings of these councils include regional leaders, scholars, and corporate strategists. All of these organizations have the goal of developing and sharing an understanding of the processes of the global arena based on the opinion of experts with diverse points of view. They do not actually formulate their own opinion. All regional councils and affiliated clubs (like the Channel Club in Santa Barbara) operate as venues for learning and networking. In this sense they are extremely useful, but they do not directly influence the global order or even the national order of the US. However, the Council on Foreign Relations, which has offices in New York and Washington, is different, only because of its very well-known and well-connected members and its powerful board of directors.

One of the council's previous presidents, Leslie Gelb, during an appearance on the popular *Charlie Rose Show* said, "You [Charlie Rose] had me on [before] to talk about the New World Order! I talk about it all the time. It's one world now. The Council [CFR] can find, nurture, and begin to put people in the kinds of jobs this country needs. And that's going to be one of the major enterprises of the Council under me."[83] If conspiracy "theorists" find anything in this quote supporting their ideas, they can find it anywhere.

The Trilateral Commission

The global energy crisis at the beginning of the 1970s and the peak in tension of the bipolar world during the Cold War gave birth to several think tanks that are still operational, such as the Club of Rome and the World Economic Forum. During the same period, in 1973, another organization was founded—the Trilateral Commission. This organization is a think tank with a mission and message similar to that of the Council on Foreign Relations. The major distinction between this commission and the Council on Foreign relations is geopolitical. The Council on Foreign Relations is an overwhelmingly American organization, while the Trilateral Commission is an international group founded by private citizens of "Japan, Europe (European Union countries), and North America (United States and Canada) to foster closer cooperation among these core democratic industrialized areas of the world with shared leadership responsibilities in the wider international system."[84] The influence of this commission is also mostly intellectual, as it promotes certain ideas via their meetings and publications. Both of these institutions are think tanks that do not directly participate in any capacity in the development and operations of the global order. They should not be considered anything other than idea-creating organizations, as they are not institutionalized and no multilateral body implements their recommendations or ideas.

Nonetheless, some connect the Trilateral Commission to the Bilderberg Group, one of the most confidential forums related to the study, monitoring, and evaluation of the global order. This forum has no executive power, but dozens of very important people participate in the club's meetings; several participants are quite active in meetings of both the Bilderberg Group and the Trilateral Commission. Emerging market countries have a disproportionately small presence at Bilderberg events. Participation is by invitation only, and the logic behind the list of invitees from emerging market countries is not totally clear. Of the very few representatives from EMCs that have participated in these meetings, most are not particularly influential. The majority of countries of Latin America, Africa, and the former Soviet bloc have never known representation in the group's annual meeting, although the 2007 meeting did take place in an emerging market country: Turkey. While still in office, the majority of leaders of Bretton Woods institutions have not participated in Bilderberg meetings. Despite the fact that some members of the media participate, publicly available official information about this group is very limited. As a result, any information about the Bilderberg group is almost entirely second hand, and strategists should be cautious regarding its validity.

The Institutionalization of the Global Business Order

None of the organizations previously mentioned (Bretton Woods Committee, the World Economic Forum, the G7 operating de facto after the beginning of Russian-Ukrainian conflict of 2014, the Council on Foreign Relations, and the Trilateral Commission) are institutionalized. However, established multilateral institutions like the World Bank, the IMF, and the WTO do pay attention to the results and recommendations coming from the meetings of these groups. Because the role of these organizations has not been officially acknowledged or institutionalized within the structure of the global order, many worry that the global order is secretly manipulated by these closed organizations of elites. While this is obviously not the case, their influence is significant.

Institutions should be developed to reflect the new realities of the global marketplace, and to present a unified voice and coordinate the activity of emerging market countries. Such an institution could be known as the Global Emerging Market Monitoring and Coordinating Agency. The influence of several regional economic organizations, even outside of the global emerging market, has substantially increased, creating the need for a new multilateral institution to represent their interests and to coordinate their activity and regulations. The Dutch economist who, in 1969, became the first winner of the Nobel Prize in Economics, Jan Tinbergen (1903–1994), argued, "because an effective international order requires institutions at the regional as well as the world level, decision-making bodies at the regional level can be established prior to institutionalizing a decision-making capability at the world level."[85] Tinbergen proposed the establishment of regional institutions to represent certain groups of countries in a world-governing organization. Keeping in mind national interests and democracy, it is difficult to believe that any country would agree to have its global interests represented solely by a super-governing institution.

Tinbergen proposed a regional level of bureaucracy to act as an intermediary between the national interests of a group of countries and the global governing structure. The implementation of such a super-governing bureaucracy does not seem feasible, even in the distant future. However, the existence of regional organizations and their governing, coordinating, or monitoring bodies—depending on the level of regional integration—does suggest the possibility of some type of super-national body. But no regional organization has the ability to rule the national governments of its member-countries. The highest level of integration exists in the European Union, where there is a division of functions between national governments and EU executive and legislative bodies. However, when tighter political integration was proposed in the unified European Constitution, the people of France and the Netherlands roundly rejected it in the referendum of 2005. Later, in December 2007, a looser European law of land replaced the repudiated continental constitution. On December 13, 2007, EU leaders signed the Treaty of Lisbon, thus bringing to an end several years of negotiations about institutional issues. This Treaty "amends the current EU and EC treaties, without replacing them. It will provide the Union with the legal framework and tools necessary to meet future challenges and to respond to citizens' demands."[86] Even this much looser approach to a framework (not even a law) of political-regional integration for some still takes too much power from national governments and their citizens, who have much less influence on supranational bodies than on their national governments. This was proven during the June 2008 rejection by public vote of the Treaty of Lisbon.[87] This example shows that globalization has two major limitations—national interests and national democracies. Beneath these two visible limitations are more powerful basic limitations, especially economic interests, which apply to nations and corporations. While analyzing this conflict of interest, strategists enter the field of geoeconomics and should always consider that the global order is a result of the dialectical relationship between geopolitics and geoeconomics. The upcoming global order will be based more on geoeconomics and the global business order than on geopolitics. At any rate, the global order of the twenty-first century already reflects the growing importance of regions. In the words of Dr. Manoranjan Dutta, a professor of economics at Rutgers University:

> [T]he global order of a free and perfectly competitive market economy certainly remains the ideal, but it continues to elude us. Given the necessary conditions, the global order will foreseeably become real. Until then, the next best option is a marriage between regionalism and globalism, and thus, geo-economics has become the order of the day.[88]

The emerging global business order will have a hierarchy of global institutions with different functions, authorities, and structures. Membership in these organizations will be based on a mixture of representatives from regional executive bodies and national governments. Non-governmental organizations will be represented, as will associations representing corporate interests, like international chambers of commerce, exporters-importers associations, organizations of entrepreneurs, etc.

Another work by Jan Tinbergen, *The Need for an Ambitious Innovation of the World Order*, also promotes the idea that the relevance of national governments is declining in comparison to super-national world-governing bodies. In it, he argues that:

> since business has been much more successful in overcoming narrow national points of view than have governments, most politicians, and the general public, it may be

> useful to look at the world from a *management scientific* viewpoint. This implies that we try to answer the question how the activities necessary to provide humankind with the goods and services needed for maximum welfare have to be organized without the *precondition* of the existence of nation-states.[89]

Unfortunately, world and national leaders experienced the repercussions of the subversion of national governments' authority during the global spread of the "Asian" crisis. Again, it is important to underline that it is more productive to have a partnership between global and regional multilateral institutions, national governments, and corporations than a global super-government. Such a partnership is a keystone of the emerging global order as well as of the global business order.

Strategic Characteristics of the Emerging Global Economic and Business Orders

There is no single organization that dictates or even monitors the current global business order. It is a result of developments of global political, economic, and business systems, most of which are objective. The global business order is also a set of customs that all participants of the global marketplace and global workplace have to agree upon, de facto—obviously not de jure. However, those rules that a country accepts via its membership in multilateral global and regional institutions, like the United Nations and the World Bank, must be respected and obeyed. For example, until the 1990s Switzerland was not a member of the United Nations, and it therefore did not have to accept UN regulations and decisions. The most stable characteristics of the global marketplace and its major global systems have to be monitored and reflected in the activity and functions of global and regional multilateral organizations, national governments, non-governmental organizations, and even popular movements. Does global society need a single, unified organization to monitor and guide the global order? This will be an intensely debated issue for much of the twenty-first century. Modern technology would enable such an organization to communicate efficiently, and the scale of global threats has increased to the point where a unified voice and force may be necessary to protect global civilization. Whether the creation of such an organization is politically feasible is not yet clear. A monitoring agency with the function of making suggestions for global strategy is more likely to come to power than an organization somehow resembling a global government.

The rise of the GEM has created a significant impetus for changes in the global order and its subsystem, the global business order, which greatly influences the global workplace and global supply chains. This influence can be seen in the new industrial and regional structure of the world economy, which mirrors shifts in the production, demand for, and consumption of traditional resources. The high growth rate of several EMCs, especially China, India, and Russia, and increasing standards of living in most countries are causing a shift in energy consumption from developed countries to the GEM. According to Fatih Birol, the chief economist at the International Energy Agency:

> We are entering a new world energy order. Today, demand for oil is dominated by China, India, and even by the Middle East countries themselves. The main actors of the recent past—namely the OECD countries, rich countries, the United States, Europe, Japan—their time is passé. It's over.[90]

A new global energy order, as a subsystem of the emerging global order, is definitely under development; however, Birol's conclusion is a simplification of reality. It does not take into consideration technological achievements and the growing role of alternative energy resources as a substitute for traditional sources. The global order has always been about access to various natural resources, but this pattern may be altered in the twenty-first century due to scientific advancements in nuclear, hydrogen, and bioenergies. In the context of the knowledge-based economy, vital economic needs and substantial investment in science may change this situation.

The role of the US, the lone superpower in the global order, will likely shrink. This will occur as regional superpowers from the GEM, such as China, India, Brazil, Russia, South Africa, and Egypt, rise. The result will be a multipolar world, with the influence of the existing superpower significantly reduced. How will this affect global security? Will it make for a more stable world? History indicates the opposite. Hegemonic periods, dominated by a lone superpower (the hegemon), are typically times of relative peace and prosperity. The rules of engagement are clear, and the authority of the hegemon is unchallenged. This has clearly been the case since the end of the Cold War. It was also the case during the time of the Roman Empire. Bipolar world orders are typically very tense and far less prosperous. History and economic data show that political, economic, and business cooperation between the two powers are kept to a minimum, as was the case between the US and the Soviet Union following World War II. In 1960, at the peak of the Cold War, the US input to gross world product was 38.5 percent,[91] making it without question the dominant economic power. However, the bipolar global order was a poor environment for the internationalization of business, which substantially inhibited its development, due to the existence of the Soviet Union, a superpower of limited economic strength. While the US was unquestionably dominant in economic terms, it was not a hegemon. As of 2015, the input of the US in GWP is much less—22.44 percent[92]—but its dominant role as the hegemon is practically indisputable because the second country, China, still produces substantially less, at 13.34 percent of GWP, which is obviously a colossal achievement for China. The global order in a unipolar system is more clearly defined; a country that accounts for only a quarter of GWP in the unipolar world is more powerful than one that was unchallenged in economic terms in a bipolar world. For corporate strategy, the unipolar global order creates a more predictable and stable business environment in which it is far easier to develop and implement long-term corporate strategy.

Potential conflicts in the new multipolar global order are numerous. The implementation strategy in one country or the emergence of a hostile dictatorship in another nuclear power could lead to a hot or cold war. A new kind of global power, without a formal government or defined territory but unified by terrorist ideology, may also be a major threat to global security in the twenty-first century. This is the type of situation that Professor Peter Drucker described when he wrote:

> [T]he twenty-first century will surely be one of continuing social, economic, and political turmoil and challenge, at least in its early decades. What I have called the age of social transformation is not over yet. And the challenges looming ahead may be more serious and more daunting than those posed by the social transformations that have already come about, the social transformations of the twentieth century.[93]

Some emerging market countries could challenge the existing global order, resulting in a drastic restructuring of it, and subsequently of the global business order. The most economically powerful EMCs or a group of them will likely confront the developed world and direct the creation of a new global order. The power of the GEM will increase significantly at the expense of developed countries; the voice of the GEM in multilateral institutions will grow substantially. Representation of the GEM will increase in the UN Security Council, where it already plays a substantial role but is a minority (Russia and China are the only permanent members from the GEM. The other members are developed countries: the United States, Great Britain, and France). Notably absent from the Security Council are representatives of Latin America, such as Brazil; of the 1 billion people of Africa, such as South Africa; of the Muslim world, such as Egypt; of the 1 billion people of India; and of the most advanced economies of Asia and Europe, Japan and Germany respectively. As they continue to develop, GEM nations and regions will gain an increased representation and voice in the executive bodies of the World Bank, the IMF, and the WTO and its regional subordinates. The new global order will reflect the growing importance and power of the GEM. The various centers of economic power of the GEM will be the regional superpowers of the twenty-first century, each with different levels of democracy and economic and military capacities and goals. These variations will allow the GMP to flourish but will also represent serious challenges to its existence. Global threats such as mass disease, climate change, and global terrorism will likely encourage cooperation among competing regional superpowers.

The role of pre-emerging market countries such as Bolivia, Iraq, and Kyrgyzstan will also increase in certain industries and regions in the new global order. Bolivia is a particularly interesting example because, as of 2015, its orientation is difficult to characterize; it is hard to tell whether it is moving toward the GEM and democracy or toward declining economic and political freedom. Its movement to the left has been influential in Latin America and, as a result, in the global business order. The emerging global order should represent the interests of countries with certain shared characteristics that require special attention in the new conditions of the twenty-first century. For example, the existing Alliance of Small Island States (AOSIS), which is a coalition of 44 states from all oceans, should deepen and expand its role as a lobbying organization to a political, economic, and business bloc of countries without shared borders, but facing common challenges. The mission of such an alliance should be oriented to the development of solutions to the challenges facing these nations, such as the threat of rising sea levels, which will endanger the actual existence of many of these nations. An organization that does not yet exist, but that should be formed, is a formal association of landlocked countries. These states are particularly disadvantaged due to the growing importance of international trade in economic development. As of 2015, there is an informal group of landlocked developing countries within the framework of the UN. These countries need to form an executive body to enhance their coordination and cooperation in order to increase the global community and multilateral institutions' understanding of the issue of not having access to the world ocean, which creates disadvantages in their participation in international trade and in the division of labor. There are a few instances in which countries are separated from the coast by only a few hundred meters of the neighboring countries' territories; this is the case for Moldova, which is blocked by Ukraine. Neighbors of these countries should be appealed to, in order to provide corridors to the coast for nearby landlocked states. This is an example of ethics in international economic relations. When a landlocked country is a member of an REO, it has to be an imperative to provide these member-countries with access to the coast, which will eventually benefit all members of the REO, as well as the global marketplace.

There are still a few nations in the world without statehood, like that of the Kurds, which consists of more than 28 million people.[94] The emerging global business order should develop a way of reflecting the special economic needs of these nations and their businesses, without, of course, ignoring Pareto's principle. The global business order of the twenty-first century and its monitoring and coordinating executive bodies need to have global information and technological structures that optimize business cooperation toward scientific and technological progress for the betterment of humankind. A unified country classification system and terminologies, harmonized national laws, regulations, and standards will be important stabilizing characteristics of the emerging global business order.

Will the new global order and global business order require a world government—a kind of conglomerated union of nations and economic multilateral institutions with greater executive power than their Bretton Woods antecedents? Some authors are strong advocates for such a government. For example, Jean L. Cohen, a professor of political science at Columbia University, writes:

> We have entered a postsovereign, decentered world order … a cosmopolitan legal system regulating global politics actually exists and … it is *already* constitutionalized.… To the systems theorists who elaborate this approach, the key development is the emergence of a world society out of the old international order … The idea is that international society has gone global, shifting from a segmental form of differentiation to a set of relations between many functionally differentiated global systems, of which the political subsystem is only one. Functional differentiation has also occurred within that subsystem, overlaying and undermining the previous order of "international society" composed of sovereign territorial states. … [T]his order is composed not of states but of components of states along with nongovernmental civil actors. From this perspective as well there is a proliferation of law making in world society independent of national governments' consent or control. But here the claim that a constitutional global legal system already exists (which regulates global politics) involves a shift from the external sociological to the internal legal perspective concerned above all with the production of legal validity. Accordingly, the focus is on hard, not soft, law—on the legal system, not on the mere proliferation of regulations. Nevertheless, on this approach too the discourse of sovereignty must be abandoned.[95]

This argument basically promotes a kind of global constitutional governance. The so-called Asian crisis has already demonstrated the danger of a lack of roles for national governments in international business. The financial crisis of 2007–2009, in fact, demonstrated the very positive influence of government's intervention in changing the dynamics of negative processes in cooperation with the corporate world and multilateral institutions. During this crisis, Ben Bernanke, chairman of the US Federal Reserve, characterized it as actually worse than the Great Depression itself.[96] Only the very proactive role of national governments, together with the leadership of the global community, stopped and recuperated this essentially negative and subjective process. This example of two different attitudes of national governments demonstrates even more potential in the new global political, economic, and financial environments of the twenty-first century. The idea of global governance is not desirable for the majority of nations because the implementation of this idea would lead to an unelected super-government unaccountable to the people of its member-countries. The authority of the global order versus that of national governments is a very delicate issue. People are uncomfortable with the idea of ceding the power of their democratically elected national leaders to unelected and relatively unknown global authorities located outside of their borders. It should not have been a surprise when the people of Europe, who have traditionally been the locomotive of international integration and democratic movements, enthusiastically voted against the European constitution. Global government and world governance always draw a great deal of suspicion from people fearful of some kind of international conspiracy that subverts national interests to the nefarious interests of a mysterious group of elites. This fear is one of the explanations of the failure of the European Union to implement its constitution, and even the great difficulties experienced by the EU with the Lisbon Treaty. As of the first quarter of the twenty-first century, the majority of other REOs and political unions based on territorial proximity have not even attempted to implement regional authorities with elements of not only economic but also political power over nations.

Dr. Henry Kissinger (1923–), former secretary of state, and 1973 Nobel Peace Prize Laureate, has stated, "No truly global 'world order' has ever existed."[97] This is an unquestionable truth, but the evidence of new conflicts, which signal the potential development of a new paradigm for the global community, requires a real global order.

The major challenge for multilateral institutions—including the World Bank, the IMF, and the World Trade Organization—is to not merely continue practices of the twentieth century that concentrate their activities on resolving various countries' domestic and international problems. In the twenty-first century, the focus must be on global issues that will not appear on national governments' agendas without the leadership of multilateral institutions in the framework of the new global order and the maturation of the global community.

The global order of the twenty-first century is implementing a new condition, where basic economic factors and the empowering strategic factor of time are changing the qualitative characteristics of the global marketplace and global workplace. Natural finite resources like freshwater and hydrocarbon, an exhausted labor supply already in the phase of staging out, investment capital, the reorientation of traditional economics, the emerging knowledge economy, and new innovations and technologies are already completely revolutionizing the formation of the new global order. In order to answer both the listed and unlisted challenges, leaders need to create a new strategic paradigm.

The basis of this paradigm lies in the strategic development of the knowledge economy. This is the new engine driving the economic train, and it has the potential to utilize innovative ideas and advantages for the achievement of new strategic priorities. Based on this and other chapters, it is possible to conclude that strategic priorities in this new global order will be connected through key positive categories like individual values, ecology, knowledge, prevention, cooperation, stability, tolerance, and enforcement of law, and at the same time through key negative, but traditional, categories like intervention, pollution, weapons, force, and power. Increasing the value of human life and our environment will enhance social morale, establish preventative measures in science and medicine, as well as in politics, increase life expectancy and decrease pollution, prioritize education for both men and women, strengthen the new knowledge-based economy, and draw the world a little closer together in order to help stop bilateral and international military conflicts and global economic crises. These categories and strategic priorities must be the major agenda items for the global community, which will require new and proactive national governments, in cooperation with multinational institutions, private businesses, and non-governmental organizations (NGOs), to support effective market space and global workplaces, all oriented to the acceleration of the knowledge economy in favor of a prosperous global community.

Notes

1 Reagan, R. (1981). Presidential Inaugural Address. January 20.
2 Fulbright, J.W., with Tillman, S.P. (1989). *The Price of Empire*. New York: Pantheon Books, p. 148.
3 Miller, L.H. (1998). *Global Order: Values and Power in International Politics*. New York: Westview Press, p. xi.
4 US Department of Treasury. (n.d.). "Frequently Asked Questions: Currency." Retrieved from www.treas.gov/education/faq/currency/portraits.shtml#q3
5 Barry Brence, S. (2001). *Multiculturalism: The Refusal and Reconstruction of Recognition*. Dissertation presented to the Department of Philosophy Graduate School of the University of Oregon, p. v. Retrieved from https://scholarsbank.uoregon.edu/dspace/bitstream/1794/2038/2/Multiculturalism_the_refusal_and_reconstruction.pdf
6 Kissinger, H. (2014). *World Order*. New York: Penguin Press, p. 363.
7 Pehar, D. (2001). "Use of Ambiguities in Peace Agreements." In Kurbalija, J. and Slavik, H. (Eds.). *Language and Diplomacy*. Malta: Diplo Foundation, p. 177.
8 International Monetary Fund. (n.d.). "Articles of Agreement of the International Monetary Fund." Retrieved from www.imf.org/external/pubs/ft/aa/aa12.htm#2
9 International Monetary Fund. (n.d.). "By-Laws of the International Monetary Fund." Retrieved from www.imf.org/external/pubs/ft/bl/bl10.htm
10 Braithwaite, J. and Drahos, P. (2001). "Bretton Woods: Birth and Breakdown." *Global Policy Forum*. Retrieved from www.globalpolicy.org/socecon/bwi-wto/2001/braithwa.htm
11 Halper, S. and Clarke, J. (2004). *America Alone: The Neo-Conservative and the Global Order*. Cambridge: Cambridge University Press, p. 11.
12 Freyer, T.A. (2006). *Antitrust and Global Capitalism, 1930–2004*. New York: Cambridge University Press, p. 144.
13 Gavin, M. (2000). "Comments." In Fernandez-Arias, E. and Hausmann, R. (Eds.). *Wanted: World Financial Stability*. Washington, DC: Inter-American Development Bank, pp. 228–229.
14 Energy Information Administration. (n.d.). "Non-OPEC Fact Sheet." Retrieved from www.eia.doe.gov/emeu/cabs/nonopec.html
15 OPEC (2013). "OPEC Share of World Crude Oil Reserves." Retrieved from www.opec.org/opec_web/en/data_graphs/330.htm
16 OPEC (n.d.). "Organization of the Petroleum Exporting Countries Functions." Retrieved from www.opec.org/aboutus/functions/functions.htm
17 Stell, J. (2007). "Gas Cartel a Non-starter, Pace Reports." *Oil and Gas Investor This Week*. November 1. Retrieved from www.allbusiness.com/energy-utilities/oil-gas-industry-oil-processing-products/8918900-1.html
18 Goodenough, P. (2008). *Cybercast News Service*. May 1. Retrieved from www.cnsnews.com/ViewForeignBureaus.asp?Page=/ForeignBureaus/archive/200805/FOR20080501c.html
19 Ahuja, A. (2008). "Thailand Pitches Cartel of Rice-producing Nations." Associated Press. May 2. Retrieved from http://abcnews.go.com/Business/wireStory?id=4770402
20 Tabuchi, K. (2008). "Japan Weighs Move to Open Rice Reserves." *The Wall Street Journal.*, May 4. Retrieved from http://online.wsj.com/article/SB121130872443807657.html?mod=googlenews_wsj
21 S&P Dow Jones Indices (n.d.). "S&P BRIC 40." (n.d.). Retrieved from http://us.spindices.com/indices/equity/sp-bric-40-index
22 Dow Jones Indexes. (n.d.) "DJ BRIC 50 Overview." Retrieved from www.djindexes.com/bric50/
23 Hartley, J. (2014). "The BRICS Bank Is Born out of Politics." *Forbes*. July 28. Retrieved from www.forbes.com/sites/jonhartley/2014/07/28/the-brics-bank-is-born-out-of-politics/
24 Association of Southeast Asian Nations (2014). "ASEAN Economic Community." Retrieved from www.asean.org/communities/asean-economic-community
25 Bernstein, S. (2007). *Global Liberalism and Political Order: Toward a New Grand Compromise?* Albany: State University of New York Press, pp. 3–4.
26 United Nations Conference Meetings and Events (2000). "Millennium Summit." September. Retrieved from http://un.org/en/events/pastevents/millennium_summit.shtml
27 "Oxfam Says Richest 1% to Own More than Half of World's Wealth by 2016." (2015). *Japan Today*. January 19. Retrieved from www.japantoday.com/category/world/view/oxfam-says-richest-1-to-own-more-than

28 Held, D., McGrew, A. and Goldblatt, D. (1999). *Global Transformations: Politics, Economics and Culture*. Palo Alto, CA: Stanford University Press, p. 50.
29 International Medical Corps. (n.d.). "About IMC." Retrieved from www.imcworldwide.org/section/about/mission
30 Academy for Educational Development. (n.d.). "About AED." Retrieved from www.aed.org/About/index.cfm
31 Médecins Sans Frontières/Doctors Without Borders. (n.d.). "About Us." Retrieved from www.doctorswithoutborders.org/aboutus/
32 Oxfam International. (n.d.). "Frequently Asked Questions." Retrieved from www.oxfam.org/en/about/faq/
33 NGO Committee on Migration. (n.d.). "Homepage." Retrieved from http://ngocom.blogspot.com/
34 Sayer, P. (2008) "Google Search Share Up, Yahoo and Microsoft Down." *IDG News Service*. March 20. Retrieved from www.netmarketshare.com/search-engine-market-share.aspx?qprid=4qpcustom
35 Singh, I.B. (1995). "Global Network 2000: Emerging Concepts and Strategic Applications." In Hanson, J. and Liebowitz, J. (Eds.), *Advances in Telematics, Volume 3: Emerging Information Technologies*. Norwood, NJ: Ablex, p. 196.
36 Moltke, H. (1995). *Moltke on the Art of War: Selected Writings*. D.J. Hughes and H. Bell (Trans.). New York: Ballantine Books. pp. 93–94.
37 Drucker, P. (1994). "The Age of Social Transformation." *The Atlantic Monthly*, vol. 274. no. 5, p. 80. With all respect to the genius of Peter Drucker, I share Edmund Phelps' point of view that Drucker practically narrowed the phenomenon of innovations only to technological ones, which in reality do play a vital role in societal dynamism.
38 South Korean Ministry of Trade, Industry and Energy. Retrieved from http://mke.go.kr
39 Ministry of Strategy and Finance (2015). "Economic Policy. Government to Boost Investment in Tourism and Innovative Technology." January 19. Retrieved from http://english.mosf.go.kr
40 Pareto, V. (1971). *Manual of Political Economy*. A.S. Scwier (Trans.). New York: Augustus M. Kelley.
41 Wicksell, K. (1959). *Selected Papers on Economic Theory*. E. Lindhahl (Ed.) and R.S. Stedman (Trans.). London: Allen & Unwin.
42 Paquete, L.F. (2006). *Stochastic Local Search Algorithms for Multiobjective Combinatorial Optimization: Methods and Analysis*. Amsterdam: IOS Press, pp. 31–32.
43 Williamson, J. (2002, November 6). Did the Washington Consensus fail? (Speech). Washington DC: Center for Strategic & International Studies. Retrieved from http://petersoninstitute.org/publications/papers/paper.cfm?ResearchID=488
44 Williamson, J. (2002). "Did the Washington Consensus fail?" November 6. Washington, DC: Center for Strategic & International Studies. Retrieved from http://petersoninstitute.org/publications/papers/paper.cfm?ResearchID=488
45 Ramo Cooper, J. (2004). *The Washington Consensus: Notes on the New Physics of Chinese Power*. London: The Foreign Policy Center, p. 3. Retrieved from http://fpc.org.uk/fsblob/244.pdf
46 Ramo Cooper, J. (2004). *The Washington Consensus: Notes on the New Physics of Chinese Power*. London: The Foreign Policy Center, pp. 5–6. Retrieved from http://fpc.org.uk/fsblob/244.pdf
47 Fukuyama, F. (2004). *State-Building: Governance and World Order in the 21st Century*. Ithaca, NY: Cornell University Press, p. 120.
48 Rendall, M. (2006). "Defensive Realism and the Concert of Europe." *Review of International Studies*, vol. 32, no. 3, p. 523.
49 Williett, T.D. and Banian, K. (1988). "Explaining the Great Stagflation: Toward a Political Economy Framework." In T.D. Willett (Ed.), *Political Business Cycles: The Political Economy of Money, Inflation, and Unemployment*. Durham, NC: Duke University Press.
50 Bernstein, S. (2007). *Global Liberalism and Political Order: Toward a New Grand Compromise?* Albany: State University of New York Press, p. 4.
51 University of Sydney, Australia. (n.d.). "New Global Economic Order." Retrieved from www.eng.usyd.edu.au/current-students/InnoManage/ENGG4005/lectures/globalisation.pdf
52 Baliño, T.J.T and Enoch, C. et al. (1997). *Currency Board Arrangements Issues and Experiences*. Washington DC: International Monetary Fund.

53 I remember well the discussion on this issue which took place at the Bretton Woods Committee meeting in Washington, DC when Madeleine Albright, the US secretary of state at that time, supported the recommendations of the majority of members of the Bretton Woods Committee to not install a CBA in Indonesia. Nonetheless, a couple of weeks later, a CBA was created. In another couple of weeks, the dictatorial regime of Suharto failed and the CBA ceased to operate.
54 Currency Boards and Dollarization. Currency Boards. Retrieved from www.dollarization.org.
55 International Monetary Fund (2015). "IMF Members' Quotas and Voting Power and IMF Board of Governors." January 22. Retrieved from www.imf.org/external/np/sec/memdir/members.aspx
56 Mekay, E. (2003). "Rich Nations Continue to Wield Power in Global Bodies." *Inter Press Service*. May 6. Retrieved from www.globalpolicy.org/ngos/int/bwi/2003/0506bodies.htm
57 World Bank. (2014). "Country Strategies." July 1. Retrieved from www.worldbank.org/en/projects-operations/country-strategies
58 World Bank Group Guidance. (2014). "Country Partnership Framework Products." July 14. Retrieved from http://siteresources.worldbank.org/EXTOPMANUAL/Resources/502183 1404156575856/CPFGuidance7-01-14/pdf
59 International Monetary Fund. (2014). "Factsheet—Where the IMF Gets Its Money." October 3. Retrieved from www.imf.org/external/np/exr/facts/finfac.htm
60 International Monetary Fund. (n.d.). "IMF's Financial Resources and Liquidity Position." Retrieved from www.imf.org/external/np/tre/liquid/2008/0208.htm
61 Hong Kong Monetary Authority. (n.d.). "Economic and Financial Data for Hong Kong." Retrieved from www.info.gov.hk/hkma/eng/statistics/index_efdhk.htm
62 International Monetary Fund. (n.d.). "World Economic Outlook Database." Retrieved from www.imf.org/external/pubs/ft/weo/2008/01/weodata/weorept.aspx?sy=2002&ey=2009&scsm=1&ssd=1&sort=country&ds=.&br=1&pr1.x=58&pr1.y=10&c=603&s=D&grp=1&a=1
63 "Cautious Welcome for G8 Debt Deal." (2005). *BBC News*. June 12. Retrieved from http://news.bbc.co.uk/1/hi/business/4084574.stm
64 OECD. (n.d.). "Net Official Development Assistance in 2007." Retrieved from www.oecd.org/dataoecd/27/55/40381862.pdf
65 Mwiti, L. (2015). "The African Economy: What We Learned in 2014, and the Still Sexy Outlook for 2015." *Guardian and Mail Africa*. January 17. Retrieved from http://mgafrica.com/article/2015-01-15-the-african-economy-what-we-learnt-in-2014-and-the-outlook-this-year
66 International Chamber of Commerce. (n.d.). "How ICC Works." Retrieved from www.iccwbo.org/id96/index.html
67 Inter-American Development Bank. (n.d.). "About the IDB." Retrieved from www.iadb.org/en/about-us/
68 Dempsey, M.A. (2002). "The Andean Development Corp., a Regional Development Bank." *Latin Trade*. February. Retrieved from http://findarticles.com/p/articles/mi_m0BEK/is_2_10/ai_82801165
69 BBC News. (n.d.). "Profile: Mercosur—Common Market of the South." Retrieved from http://news.bbc.co.uk/1/hi/world/americas/5195834.stm
70 Caribbean Development Bank. (n.d.). "About the Caribbean Development Bank." Retrieved from www.caribank.org/titanweb/cdb/webcms.nsf/AllDoc/A541525E64242BE7872572BF0 07AECAC?OpenDocument
71 Zitner, A. (1999). "In New Hampshire, Forbes Calls for Eliminating IMF." *Boston Globe*. October 5, p. A14.
72 Bretton Woods Committee (n.d.). "Mission Statement." Retrieved from www.brettonwoods.org/
73 The major thesis of my speech at this event is described in Chapter 6, especially the argument related to analysis, importance, and definition of emerging market countries and the global emerging market as a new phenomenon.
74 Club of Rome. (n.d.). "About." Retrieved from www.clubofrome.org/about/index.php
75 World Economic Forum. (n.d.). "History and Achievements." Retrieved from www.weforum.org/history
76 World Economic Forum. (2015). "World Economic Forum Annual Meeting 2015." Davos, Switzerland, January 21. Retrieved from www.weforum.org/events/world-economic-forum-annual-meeting-2015

77 MMC. (n.d.). "About." Retrieved from www.mmc.com/
78 World Economic Forum Annual Meeting. (2007). "Shaping the Global Agenda: The Shifting Power Equation," p. 25. Retrieved from http://www.weforum.org/pdf/Newsletter/NLenJan07.pdf
79 MMC. (n.d.). "MMC News." Retrieved from www.mmc.com/news/climateChange.php
80 Council on Foreign Relations. (n.d.). "Frequently Asked Questions." Retrieved from www.cfr.org/index.html
81 Council on Foreign relations. (n.d.). "Mission." Retrieved from www.cfr.org/about/mission.html
82 Illuminati Conspiracy Archive. (n.d.). "The Council on Foreign Relations and the New World Order." Retrieved from www.conspiracyarchive.com/NWO/Council_Foreign_Relations.htm
83 The Charlie Rose Show. April 11, 2006.
84 Trilateral Commission. (n.d.). "Homepage." Retrieved from www.trilateral.org/
85 Tinbergen, J., Dolman, A.J. and Ettinger, J. van. (1976). *Reshaping the International Order: A Report to the Club of Rome*. New York: Dutton, p. 104.
86 Europa. (n.d.). "Treaty of Lisbon. The Treaty at a Glance." Retrieved from http://europa.eu/lisbon_treaty/glance/index_en.htm
87 Peterkin, T. (2008). "EU Referendum: Ireland Rejects Lisbon Treaty." *Telegraph*. June 13. Retrieved from www.telegraph.co.uk/news/worldnews/europe/2122654/EU-referendum-Ireland-rejects-Lisbon-Treaty.html
88 Dutta, M. (1999). *Economic Regionalization in the Asia-Pacific: Challenges to Economic Cooperation*. Northampton: Edward Elgar, p. 229.
89 Tinbergen, J. (1977). "The Ambitious Need for an Innovation of the World Order." *Journal of International Affairs*, vol. 31, pp. 305–314.
90 Foreign Policy. (2008). "Seven Questions: The New World Energy Order." June. Retrieved from www.foreignpolicy.com/story/cms.php?story_id=4326
91 Calculated based on data from the World Bank World Development Indicators.
92 Calculated based on data from the World Bank World Development Indicators.
93 Drucker, P. (1994). "The Age of Social Transformation." *The Atlantic*. November. Retrieved from www.theatlantic.com/politics/ecbig/soctrans.htm
94 CIA. (n.d.). *World Factbook*. Retrieved from www.cia.gov/library/publications/the-world-factbook
95 Cohen, J.L. (2008). "Whose Sovereignty: Empire vs. International Law." In C. Barry and T. Pogge (Eds.), *Global Institutions and Responsibilities: Achieving Global Justice*. Malden, MA: Blackwell Publishing, p. 167.
96 Worstall, T. (2014). "Ben Bernanke: The 2008 Financial Crisis Was Worse than the Great Depression." *Forbes*. August 27. Retrieved from www.forbes.com/sites/timworstall/2014/08/27/ben-bernanke-the-2008-financial-crisis-was-worse-than-the-great-depression
97 Kissinger, H. (2014). *World Order*. New York: Penguin Press, p. 2.

9 Investment Strategies for the Global Emerging Market

> Without risk there is no faith. Faith is precisely the contradiction between the infinite passion of the individual's inwardness and the objective uncertainty.[1]
>
> Søren Kierkegaard, Danish philosopher (1813–1855)

> An investment in knowledge pays the best interest.[2]
>
> Benjamin Franklin, (1706–1790)

> Money is like a sixth sense without which you cannot make a complete use of the other five.[3]
>
> W. Somerset Maugham, English author (1874–1965)

Keynote Definitions

Foreign Direct Investment (FDI): The roots of the economic and strategic nature of FDI stem from competitive opportunities abroad: a workforce of appropriate quality, available capital, effective management systems, technology, and know-how—all of which lead to a high level of faster returns, with a manageable level of risk, as outlined by a comprehensive feasibility study and strategy.

Risk of Foreign Direct Investment is an innate characteristic of cross-border business related to the threat of predictable or unpredictable negative changes of the external environment or of a company's internal resources, with manageable and unmanageable consequences leading to potential losses.

Strategic Reasons for Cross-Border Investment

The Strategic Economic Nature of Foreign Direct Investment

In general, strategists, corporate executives, professional strategic investors, and entrepreneurs will not seek foreign investment opportunities when there are equally lucrative prospects in their familiar and stable domestic workplace. It is only natural to invest in what is known rather than venture into the unknown, and to invest in stable domestic, political, economic, and business conditions during times of an economic boom. It is natural to avoid uncertainty and the inevitable risk that comes along with any risky endeavor. Risk of cross-border direct investment from developed countries to the GEM and developing countries always involves higher levels of uncertainty and a limited ability to manage risk according to corporate interests and approved strategy. This obviously can lead to potential threats and losses. In a perfect world, an investor's domestic market would provide ample basic economic factors, including rich and abundant natural resources, inexpensive and highly qualified labor, easily available capital at reasonable rates, well-developed transportation, telecommunication, and free-market infrastructure. National and local authorities would create a friendly investment climate with tax holidays, and competition would not be overly intense. These conditions would almost guarantee a higher and faster return and an absence of investment risk. Unfortunately, these perfect investment conditions do not exist in any country or region. Most regional and national leaders, however, will at least promote the image of having some of these perks in order to motivate investors and entrepreneurs to enter their territories. The reasons for this are obvious. Political leaders know that strategic investment and entrepreneurial activity lead to higher employment, improvements in standards of living, and increased consumption and income tax returns with the subsequent rapid rate of economic growth, which—most important for political leaders—ensures the population's support.

In reality, if a country or region with such an ideal investment climate were to appear, it would be a haven for investors for only a very brief period. Domestic and foreign investors would be drawn to the territory like bears to honey; the surge of investment and business activity would create an extremely competitive environment. Before long many investment projects would fail. This oversimplified scenario illustrates an important point—the sooner a company goes after a strategic opportunity, the more likely it is to succeed. It is always easier for the earlier entrants to a market to obtain concessions, contracts, exclusive agreements, etc. Not all but a few of the first companies to enter emerging markets prospered immensely as a result of the tremendous need in these countries for cutting-edge technology, modern managerial skills, and operational capital. Additionally, the absence of serious competition led national and regional governments to offer lax regulations for incoming foreign investors, liberal tax regimes, and exclusivity, a benefit that later investors did not enjoy. Investors seek certain conditions and are willing to go anywhere in the global marketplace or workplace to find them.

From this basic concept, one can understand the strategic economic nature of foreign direct investment (FDI). The roots of the economic and strategic nature of FDI grow from competitive opportunities abroad that do not exist domestically, a workforce of appropriate quality, available capital, effective management systems and their organizational forms, know-how and technology; all of which lead to a faster level of return under manageable risk, according to a comprehensive feasibility study and strategy. The economics of FDI explain what drives investors into unfamiliar and frontier business environments.

An influx of FDI and its increasing accumulation are very important indicators that a country is becoming an EMC and that its dynamics have a positive vector. Many countries prior to their "emergence" did not receive a single dollar of FDI for a number of reasons. Dictatorships tried to completely control the domestic economy, which allowed them to be above the law and unaccountable when dealing only with domestic investors. In the overwhelming majority of developing countries, conditions are barely or not nearly acceptable for foreign investors, and simply opening the door for them legally is not good enough. FDI requires the existence of free-market or capitalist institutions and a developed legal framework that protects the assets, property rights, and know-how of foreigners. The host developing country needs to create incentives for foreign investors to enter. Multilateral institutions should play a central role in this process.

A very difficult barrier that inhibits FDI in developing countries is the mentality of leaders, potential employees, and society. For many years people in underdeveloped and developing countries have received foreign aid or investments, or nothing, but never both. A major challenge for foreign aid, in any form—food, services, or equipment—is related to its proper distribution. In many cases, unfortunately, governments have not made the efficient management of the distribution of equipment and other types of foreign aid a major priority. The same equipment, when in the form of FDI, requires that users and executives in the host country adopt a new attitude, because FDI is driven by the invisible power of private interests. A business- and efficiency-related mentality cannot appear by decree overnight; it takes time. It is very important for the leadership of country-recipients to understand that foreign investors from developed countries and domestic investors have to deal with issues that they never faced in the developed world. It is a major challenge for leaders of emerging markets and their corporations receiving FDI to recognize that the first priority of foreign investors is to earn a profit. Benefitting the recipient country may also be a motivation of FDI, though usually a secondary one. It is very difficult for members of some EMCs' governments to understand that FDI is not politically motivated, but driven by profits and fast returns. This is the major difference between foreign aid and foreign investment. Countries that are accustomed to receiving foreign aid often struggle to provide the conditions necessary to attract private foreign investment.

Initially, foreign investors from developed countries sought destinations for new strategic opportunities in frontier countries—which later became EMCs—to lower cost production and gain access to less expensive labor (without requirements for social benefits and pensions) and abundant natural resources with lax ecological regulations and a faster return on investments. As developing countries matured and became EMCs, foreign investors began to reevaluate the situation. They realized that the benefits available in these markets involved more than just cheap labor and less restrictive ecological requirements. EMCs also offer less competition, exclusive agreements (for a period of time, which keeps competitors away), and untapped markets with growing consumption power. One of the strongest incentives drawing investors from developed countries to EMCs became the ability to hire more people for less money. The global average number of employees per $1 million of FDI originating from the US is 5.5. In developed countries, for this same amount of investment, a US company is able to hire an average of only 4.7 employees. But in the GEM a US company can hire 7.2 employees for $1 million of FDI. By this indicator, the highest ratio in the GEM is found in the emerging market countries of Southeast Europe and the former Soviet Union (CIS), where US companies can hire 2.72 times more people than in developed countries.

The greater number of employees in the GEM than in developed countries per unit of investment is one of several incentives for strategic investors to go overseas. They are also motivated by the increasing consumption power of people in EMCs, who account for about 68 percent of the global population. In order to cash in on these new potential consumers, employees, and resources, foreign investors flocked to a number of different sectors in the GEM. From 1990 to 2005, the stock of foreign investment in service sectors of the GEM increased by a factor of nine. During the same period, FDI stocks in the production of food, beverages, and tobacco increased in the GEM by a factor of five. In one of the most attractive sectors of the GEM—mining of natural resources and petroleum production—foreign investment stocks increased by a factor of 9.9. The greatest increase of cumulative foreign investment in the GEM occurred in the services of private businesses, which grew by a factor of 38.4.[4] This huge increase of investment can be explained by the virtual nonexistence of private businesses under the reign of dictators in China, the former Soviet bloc, and in many Latin American and Asian countries.

Despite the wealth of opportunities in the GEM, success is not automatic. Even the most efficient strategy-based investment projects will inevitably encounter serious challenges. Strategists should not make the mistake of expecting immediate returns on FDI in the GEM, especially in construction, real estate, and other big projects. Returns can be very high and fast, but the speed at which this occurs is still often not as anticipated. In cases of widespread failure, foreign investors are not the only party harmed. In response to many failed FDI projects in the GEM and the subsequent outflow of FDI and even of domestic investment, Nobel Laureate in Economics Dr. Joseph Stiglitz argued that countries should motivate long-term rather than short-term capital. In his words, "the regulation or taxation of inflows helps to limit outflow surges: if there is less short-term money in the country, there is less that can leave when expectations change and inflows turn into outflows."[5] As the GEM continues to mature and stabilize, and EMC governments intervene less in private business affairs, FDI is flocking to EMCs. As of the first decade of the twenty-first century, EMCs are still competing for foreign investment, but in the future this situation will likely be reversed. The increasing experience and sophistication of domestic investors in the GEM adds to the likelihood of such a situation. The twenty-first century will see the role of the GEM in the global marketplace continue to rise, partially as a result of its increasingly sophisticated domestic investors. Domestic investors of EMCs are already making the investment environment of the GEM more competitive. Nevertheless, strategic investors always compete for the most lucrative projects in the GEM.

Strategic Reasons to Invest in the Global Emerging Market

Prior to the birth of the GEM, there were very few opportunities for large-scale investments with fast and high long-term yields outside of the developed world. During this time there was a shortage of strategic investment opportunities. Investment firms and individual entrepreneurs competed for any projects with the potential for at least moderate levels, as well as speed, of return. Most of these opportunities were found in developed countries like the United States, Canada, and some nations of Western Europe, Japan, Australia, and New Zealand. In the beginning of the 1980s, the situation abruptly changed for most investors. The birth and formation of the GEM and the global marketplace opened up an unprecedented number of strategic opportunities, causing national and regional governments of emerging market countries to compete among themselves for investors. Large losses in developed markets, such as the bursting of the dot-com bubble in 2000 and 2001, directed even more investment to the GEM. Unfortunately, in the case of the dot-com bubble, the GEM was experiencing the tail end of the Asian financial crisis, which ended up affecting Russia, Argentina, and practically the entire GMP. The financial crisis of 2007–2009 again forced a substantial part of FDI out of the GEM. Nevertheless, the trend of increasing investment to EMCs soon recovered and continued. Political leaders of these countries see FDI as a means of converting national resources into socioeconomic prosperity. For the authorities of EMCs, FDI represents an immediate source of employment.

From another perspective, businesses owners in EMCs sought foreign investors as partners to make their production facilities more efficient and to provide access to operational capital and consumers in developed markets. Some owners looked to foreign partners for a legal means to relocate their capital abroad into foreign bank accounts or as FDI in countries with well-established legal protection of private assets. In doing so, these owners created what was essentially a personal hedge fund against any unfavorable changes in the mood of their national governments. As for the people of EMCs, they correctly saw FDI as a ladder out of unemployment, poverty, and, in many cases, starvation. Political leaders and businesses of EMCs began hiring professional consulting firms, usually headquartered in developed countries, in order to create strategies to attract FDI and prepare their businesses for international cooperation.

This initiated the development of various economic mechanisms and organizational forms to lure FDI, such as free economic and technological zones, free-trade zones, tax and custom duties exemptions, tax-free manufacturing zones, special privileges for international joint ventures, territories of accelerated development where foreign strategic investors received privileges and less regulations, which has also decreased any potential racketeering. These strategies were successfully implemented in countries like China, Brazil, Singapore, Taiwan, Korea, and Mexico, as well as in the Balkan and Southern and Eastern European states, such as Croatia, the Czech and Slovak Republics, Hungary, and Poland. These incentives played a very influential role in the great expansion of the traditional marketplace and workplace via the formation of the global emerging market and the global marketplace. The lack of experience of political and business leaders in the GEM, as well as of strategic investors from the developed world in these new markets, caused the failure of a great deal of investment in EMCs (see Figures 4.3, 4.4, and 4.5). Nonetheless, those ventures that were successful provided such a powerful example of high profitability and a faster return on investment that the entire international business community became focused on exploring and comparing strategic opportunities between developed countries and EMCs. From the strategic perspective of companies from the developed world, these markets were wide open. Competition was almost nonexistent. Returns on investment were several times higher and faster than returns in developed countries. The size, scale, and availability of natural resources are radically different in the GEM than in the developed world. In general, natural resources can be exploited for a much longer time in the GEM, as a result of their greater abundance and the initial willingness of EMC governments to attract foreign investors with lax labor and ecological regulations.

To the dismay of their competitors, corporations and individual investors that seized these opportunities began to return to their domestic markets with capital, resources, products, and profits made in EMCs. Businesses that achieved success in the GEM were able to significantly reduce production costs and, subsequently, the prices of their goods and services in traditional markets via economies of scale, cheaper productive labor, and natural resources. This marked the beginning of modern outsourcing to the GEM. The strategic motivation behind this movement is usually to reduce labor and operational costs, increase productivity, and gain access to new technologies. Beginning in the last quarter of the twentieth century, some companies used outsourcing to take strategic advantage of differences in time zones, which allowed them to serve customers around the clock. The typical industries that are outsourced involve these cost and service advantages, such as human resources, real estate and account management, information technology, manufacturing, product design, software and web development, and marketing and advertising. Since the 1990s, India has always led the world as a leader of the strategic trend of outsourcing. According to the 2014 A.T. Kearney Global Services Location

Index™, "financial attractiveness" is India's highest quality and during the last eight years, it has increased its ability to provide better "people skills and availability."[6] Countries on the top of the list, compared to eight years ago, have remained the same: India, China, and Malaysia. Thailand is the only country of the top 10 that declined; declining from fourth to sixth place for the "most attractive outsourcing states." This has happened due to the fact that Indonesia and Mexico, sharing third place on the list, substantially increased their "outsourcing attractiveness," by providing the most inexpensive services and strengthening their "people skills and availability." The best business environment for outsourcing among GEM countries is Singapore, followed by Spain and Ireland. But Mexico, by this indicator, among countries on top of the list, lags only behind Malaysia and is ahead of India and China. In the last eight years, China has demonstrated major progress and is practically India's strongest competitor. Among BRIC countries, only Russia is not among the top 20 countries, and it is very unfortunate because even though Russia has a superior pool of skilled professionals, its place on the index has fallen behind India, China, and even Brazil. Unexpectedly, competition for Russian outsourcing comes from countries like Sri Lanka, Jordan, and the United Arab Emirates, which have already surpassed Russia according to this index. Interestingly, developed countries have also made the list, including the US and Germany, mostly because of a large number of skilled professionals and their ability to provide one of the best business environments in the world, especially in Germany. Outsourcing, unlike other types of services, is a very important site for future innovative development.[7]

A specific form of outsourcing is offshoring to countries or territories with less restrictive regulations. This applies primarily to the banking and insurance sectors. It is important for strategists to be aware of the fact that outsourcing and offshore outsourcing relocate routine operations from the main facilities and headquarters, allowing higher quality and better compensated employees and managers to concentrate on more important strategic issues. FDI established highly efficient production facilities in EMCs, generating cheaper and larger amounts of goods and even services for markets in the developed world. The companies that lost to these brave risk takers had no choice but to reassess their strategies, which were usually oriented to avoiding risky foreign ventures altogether.

The surge in FDI outflows from the developed world created the need for entry strategies specifically crafted for emerging market countries. The overwhelming majority of investors who pursued strategic opportunities in these markets without entry strategies designed for local conditions failed. The simple conversion of strategies that were effective for decades in foreign developed countries consistently crashed and burned in emerging market countries, despite lower competition, cheaper and qualified labor resources, abundant raw materials and production facilities, though they were in need of modernization.

Adapting to the new realities of the global marketplace has been extremely challenging for strategists from North America, Western Europe, Japan, and Australia. The historical experience of American companies in the 1950s and 1960s in Japan—at that time the country of new strategic opportunities with a unique business culture—was not applicable in the diverse cultural and ethical traditions in the GEM. Initially, strategists did not have a term for countries that eventually became known as emerging markets, nor were they aware of the many shared characteristics of these countries regarding FDI, as the concept of the GEM had not yet been developed. Professionals did not have any prepackaged strategies to help their clients in these new markets. The need for strategists specially trained for opportunities in these distant countries with unique cultural, political, economic, business, and technological conditions became apparent. Strategists and consultants with expertise and connections in these countries—which slowly started to become known as emerging markets—were highly valued and compensated by investors, who, to their own surprise, became not only international but also global business players. FDI became a catalyst that jumpstarted EMCs onto the path toward prosperity. Countries that first realized the potential of FDI and actively sought it—like China, Turkey, Brazil, Hungary, and Poland—eventually achieved a cumulative effect. Global investors recognized these countries as poles of strategic investment growth and increased their presence accordingly, developing more and more projects. As a result of this trend, combined with domestic progress in EMCs, by the first 14 years of the twenty-first century, these countries became leaders among national recipients of FDI, surpassing the majority of developed countries.

Data presented in Figure 9.1 suggests that China, including Hong Kong, has maintained unquestionable strategic leadership as a recipient of direct cross-border investment. For this reason, FDI in Hong Kong and mainland China has to be summarized thus: the majority of FDI registered in Hong Kong is, in fact, cross-border investment of production facilities next door in mainland China. In the same way, portfolio investments of companies that registered on the Hong Kong Stock Exchange have in reality based their production in Shenzhen and in other Chinese special economic zones. Ireland, a small country by territory and especially by population, is another salient example of strategic

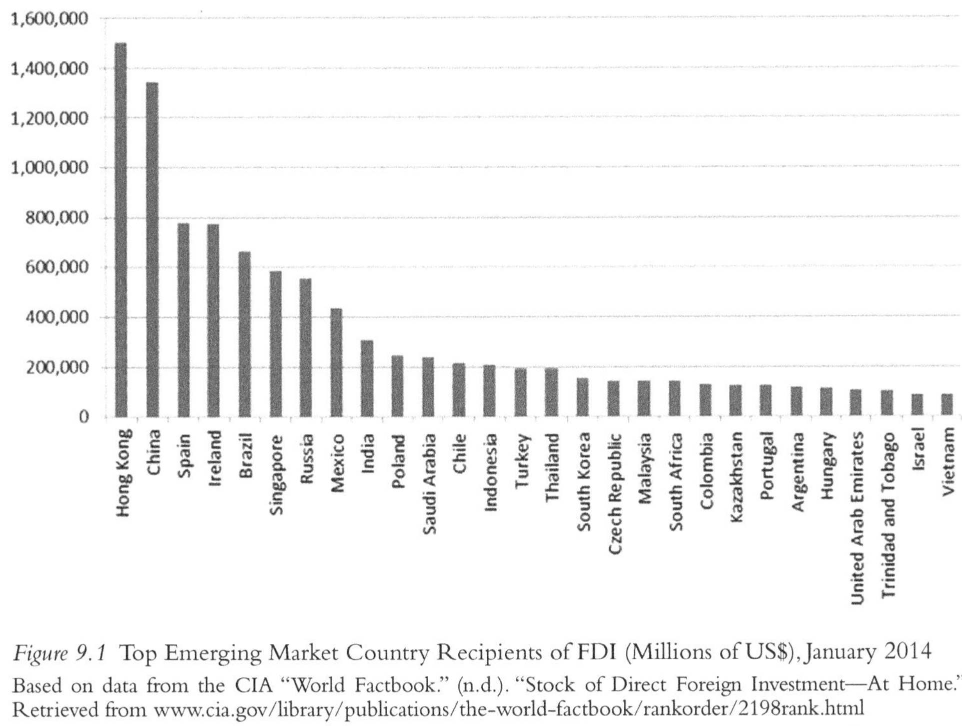

Figure 9.1 Top Emerging Market Country Recipients of FDI (Millions of US$), January 2014

Based on data from the CIA "World Factbook." (n.d.). "Stock of Direct Foreign Investment—At Home." Retrieved from www.cia.gov/library/publications/the-world-factbook/rankorder/2198rank.html

Note: Stock of direct foreign investment at home compares the cumulative US dollar value of all investments in the home country made directly by residents—primarily companies—of other countries as of the end of the time period indicated. Direct investment excludes investment through purchase of shares.

success in attracting and adopting FDI and has surpassed larger countries (e.g. Brazil, India, and Russia) as a recipient. Ireland's success is the direct result of a well-developed national strategy. Neither Brazil nor Russia has a formally developed strategy with the particular aim of encouraging FDI. However, several regions and some corporations of these two countries have developed and implemented sound strategy. St. Petersburg is a great example of territorial strategy, but at the national level Russia has not implemented this kind of strategy. As a result, Russia has lost competition for FDI not only to China, and to Ireland, but as well as to Spain, Brazil, and Singapore. The FDI data in Figure 9.1 was collected at the end of 2013, which does not take into account the tremendous failure of the ruble, Russia's national currency, at the end of 2014, and to any foreign sanctions. Russia's low standing can only be attributed to a lack of national strategy to encourage foreign investment. In 2011 and 2012, to give credit to the country, Russia dedicated substantial FDI inflow, and was at the top of this list, according to this indicator, lagging behind only the US and China. The problem was that Russia was also at the top of the list, only behind the US, Japan, and China, of FDI outflow. This was especially problematic because, as of 2015, Russia was and still is at the top of the list, according to the negative difference between FDI inflow and outflow. For example, in 2013, FDI inflow to Russia was about $79 billion and outflow was $95 billion. By 2015, this situation was further aggravated, mostly by the international relations and declining business climate in Russia.[8] The conventional rule of thumb is that a country rich in natural resources can more easily attract FDI, but comparing the case of Russia, a country rich in natural resources, with Saudi Arabia proves that this is not always the case. Unlike Russia, Saudi Arabia has one of the leading figures of FDI per capita as of 2014. Also, the stabilization of situations in Indonesia, Chile, and Turkey has made these countries a safe harbor for FDI. South Korea, which has an overwhelmingly successful strategy for researching technology, is among the leading recipients of FDI, but only enjoys a paucity of success in the total cumulative number of FDI. For strategic analysis, Figure 9.1 is important because the data is not related to portfolio investments and demonstrates the interests of foreign investors to commit to a long-term presence in these countries, and in particular, the concentration of strategic foreign investors into projects that can lead to a permanent home base in respective country recipients of FDI.

However, in order for FDI to actually work as a significant economic factor of development, as my analysis of many investment projects has shown, it must reach the level of roughly $1,000 (in purchasing power of the early 1990s) per inhabitant in the recipient country or region. This is obviously easier in less populated countries, and extremely difficult to achieve in countries with large populations, such as China, Brazil, India, Indonesia, Russia, and Mexico, where FDI per capita is nowhere near $1,000. In these countries, in order to make FDI a substantial economic factor, governments and national strategists channeled FDI to certain regions and coordinated it with other forms of private, public, and governmental investment in order to create an agglomeration effect. The establishment of special economic and technological zones was one of the most successful means by which to concentrate strategic investment in specific regions. China did not invent this practice—several different zones of economic initiative existed in the US and Mexico prior to the Chinese experience—but China was and is the undisputed leader among EMCs. In terms of using these zones to regionally focus FDI, China's success is unparalleled throughout the world. In its southeast region, China developed several special economic and technological zones, such as the Shenzhen Special Economic Zone, which opened in the spring of 1980. Free economic zones like Shenzhen and the Shenyang Economic and Technological Development Zones account for about 85 percent of Chinese exports. In fact, as of 2015, 85 percent of Chinese territory has actually never received FDI.

Many EMCs and their domestic regions have incorporated the Chinese export-oriented model into their economic development plans. For example, the Indian state Tamil Nadu exports one-third of its $29 billion net state domestic product.[9] By the beginning of the twenty-first century, in the Dominican Republic exports from special economic zones accounted for 80 percent of all exports and for almost all manufactured exports.[10] This situation exists in many other EMCs, including the Czech Republic and Hungary. FDI accounts for "half of China's exports—compared to 45 percent for Malaysia, 38 percent for Singapore, 31 percent for Mexico, and 15 percent for South Korea."[11] National strategists of EMCs should keep in mind that FDI does not have as direct an impact on standards of living as domestic investment because profits from FDI are usually repatriated to their country of origin, while profits from domestic investment typically leave the country at a much lower scale. With or without special economic zones, FDI has become an important factor in the growth of exports from EMCs.

During every year of the twenty-first century, so far surprisingly for many, even for some strategists, Luxembourg had FDI inflows more than three times the value of its GDP. This figure consists mostly of money from abroad deposited in bank accounts in Luxembourg, which qualifies as FDI only in legal and not economic terms. These FDI inflows are mostly "mailbox" investments. Globally, the average of FDI inflows as a percentage of GDP was about 3 percent during the same period. As is clear from Table 9.1, among EMCs the leading role by correlation between FDI and GDP also belongs to Hong Kong and Ireland, closely followed by Singapore. As of 2014, the encouraging example of

Table 9.1 Top 20 Nations by FDI as Percentage of GDP, 2013

Rank	*Country*	*% of GDP*
1	Luxembourg	50.02
2	Mozambique	42.85
3	Liberia	35.89
4	**Hong Kong SAR, China**	**27.97**
5	Mauritania	27.08
6	**Ireland**	**21.53**
7	**Singapore**	**21.40**
8	Djibouti	19.64
9	**Mongolia**	**18.68**
10	St.Vincent and the Grenadines	17.87
11	Congo, Rep.	14.47
12	**St. Kitts and Nevis**	**14.47**
13	Maldives	14.14
14	Seychelles	12.31
15	Equatorial Guinea	12.28
16	**Barbados**	**12.20**
17	Marshall Islands	11.85
18	Panama	11.85
19	Antigua and Barbuda	11.19
20	**Kyrgyz Republic**	**10.48**

Based on data from the World Bank World Development Indicators. Retrieved from http://data.worldbank.org/indicator/BX.KLT.DINV.WD.GD.ZS

Mongolia, where FDI reached almost 90 percent of GDP, is also the clear result of a national strategy that was designed to encourage FDI to industries related to the agriculture, mining, construction, and trade sectors of the national economy. The presence on the list of the top 20 nations of FDI as a percentage of the GDP of small developing and especially underdeveloped countries can be the result of a different correlation. These countries have such a low GDP that even small amounts of FDI can be very significant, and it is therefore strategically important to concentrate these countries in particular areas that can be territories of accelerated development and eventually major poles of national economic and social growth. Countries in which the role of FDI is more than 10 percent of GDP (including mailbox investments like those in Luxembourg, Lichtenstein, and Switzerland) have a national strategy to attract foreign investment. Panama, for example, is a well-known, legitimate offshore bank haven, the result of its successful national strategy. Some countries, like Turkmenistan, attract investment with their natural resources, while others, such as Costa Rica, attract investment both via natural resources and well-established banking institutions. Israel has accumulated substantial foreign investment in its high-tech industry. The Baltic Republic of Estonia has a diversified spectrum of industries that draw FDI from machinery building to the transportation sector. Large EMCs, such as Russia and especially China, despite their huge populations, attract more FDI (as a percentage of GDP) than the global marketplace average. Experts who argue that FDI plays an important role primarily in developing and emerging market countries contradict the statistics (see Figure 9.2). Again I would like to underline that in this UNCTAD statistic most developing economies, as well as transition economies (which is an outdated country classification), are emerging market countries. Strategists should combine data from these two curves into one from which emerges a clear picture of the GEM's importance in attracting cross-border FDI. Among countries of the Eurozone the average role of FDI is about 3.8 percent of GDP, a higher share than in most EMCs. Furthermore, in Iceland and Sweden the percentage of FDI in GDP is 25 and 7, respectively.

When analyzing FDI statistics, strategists should always be aware of the influence of financial factors. The widening gap in the exchange rate between the two most important

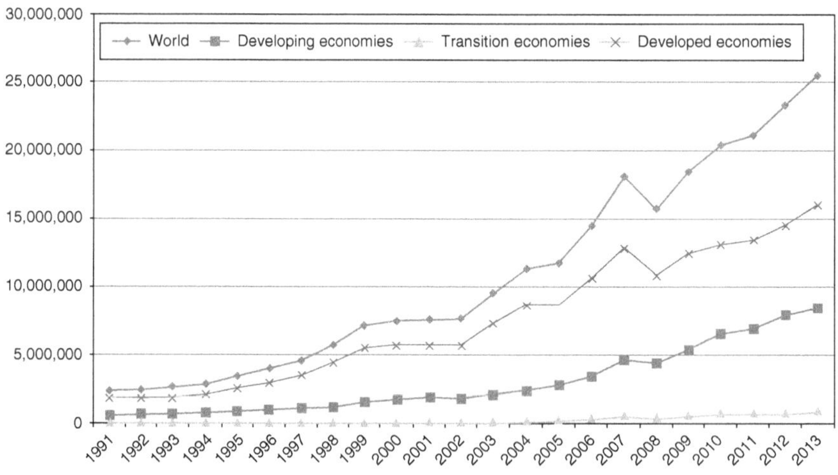

Figure 9.2 Foreign Direct Investment Inflows by Category of Country (Millions of US$), 2013

© Dr. Vladimir Kvint, 2014. Based on data from the United Nations Conference on Trade and Development. Retrieved from http://unctadstat.unctad.org/wds/TableViewer/tableView.aspx?ReportId=89

currencies of the world, the US dollar and the euro, is increasing the role of FDI outflows from the US. For example, US companies' investments in Eastern and Southern European EMCs, as well as in the Baltic states, which adopted the euro as their official currencies or have national currencies pegged to the euro, will yield higher returns than investments outside of the 19 Eurozone countries and countries heavily influenced by the Eurozone. The stronger the euro is, the higher the value of US assets in the Eurozone. A weaker dollar also makes the domestic facilities of US companies more attractive for FDI. In addition to evaluating the role of FDI in GDP, it is useful to analyze the role of FDI in gross national product (GNP). Unlike GDP, GNP takes into account all forms of income and wages, including corporate profit, rent, indirect business taxes, and unincorporated personal income. The most important role of the GNP in relation to the FDI is the inclusion within the indicator of all income made by both the US FDI and US residents abroad during a reporting year. This indicator has both a deep and wide economic meaning. Profits from residents abroad are returned to the home country and reinvested. This indicator cannot possibly represent the entire effect generated by the FDI for a country in a region. Some of the economic effects of FDI, which is not measured by the GDP, will be strategically reflected in the GNP.

The differences between the GNP and GDP are important for strategizing the national and regional economy, employment, and taxation, both in the country within a region and the host country. From the strategic point of view of a host country, the bigger the role of FDI in its national economy, the smaller the GNP in comparison with the GDP. Or, to put it another way, the correct usage of FDI in the host's national economy leads to a bigger percentage of FDI in total inner investment, and results in a wider difference between GDP and GNP. Good strategists take this into consideration during the strategic development of a national and/or regional economy. For corporate strategists, the reflection of a company's FDI in the GNP of a region has a direct influence on employment, turnover, and the volume of corporate taxes. In general, efficient strategizing is required to integrate these national economic indicators into a successful long-term strategy.

Strategic Gauging of Foreign Investment Risk in Emerging Markets

Strategic risks simply cannot be avoided in the GMP of the twenty-first century. *Risk of FDI is an innate characteristic of cross-border business related to the threat of predictable or unpredictable negative changes of the external environment or of a company's internal resources, with manageable and unmanageable consequences leading to potential losses*. Executives and strategists have come to realize that if they are not willing to deal with a certain level of risk, their competitors will be. The need to be able to deal with strategic risk has led to the development of risk management systems. Instead of avoiding risk, executives and strategists use these systems to measure, adjust, and manage it. Strategic risk management is a strategist's everyday work.

These processes began in offices of strategists and only then transferred to the operational managers responsible for FDI in the GEM. Changing national strategies and rising interest rates can negatively influence the inflow of investment to EMCs and their performance. It is especially visible when companies based on FDI go through IPO processes. Leaders of EMCs tend to give more attention to FDI and the activity of foreign banks, mostly ignoring foreign portfolio investment firms and their activities in national stock exchanges, despite the fact that this investment also brings sustainable and strategic capital to the country. A lack of governmental strategy on FDI and related projects of strategic importance for portfolio investment can redirect capital from a net inflow to an outflow. This redirection was described in the analysis of Dr. Frederick S. Mishkin, a member of the board of governors of the US Federal Reserve System: "A dominant phenomenon in emerging market countries is a *sudden stop*, a large negative change in capital inflows, which, as a general rule, appear to contain a large unanticipated component."[12] An example of such a reversal is a serious threat for domestic and banking financial systems of EMCs and does not necessarily benefit developed countries. Investors who sought out foreign markets often could not have efficiently invested this capital domestically. This is especially the case with FDI done by émigrés in developed countries; they tried to use their advantages in terms of native language, experience, and connections to their country of origin.

All strategists, investors, or cross-border entrepreneurs have to develop strategic and operational risk-management systems related to FDI (see Chapter 4). It should be seen as an indivisible part of a strategic management system. The development and implementation of a strategic management system in terms of risk management can be done through the following stages in the concept of strategic management:

- Strategic risk identification;
- Risk measurement;
- Determination of risk aversion;
- Management of unavoidable risk;
- Systematic evaluation and monitoring of strategic risk;
- Adjustment of strategic management system.

Successful strategists classify risk in several different ways in order to evaluate and manage it. The most fundamental classification is based on an entity's ability to change or manage strategic risk. In this regard, risk is typically separated into two categories:

Systematic or *country/region specific*—risk that is usually considered to be non-probabilistic, unpredictable, and unmanageable;

Unsystematic or *company specific*—risk that is probabilistic, and therefore can be predicted, evaluated, and managed strategically and operationally.

Any strategy that is focused on the distant future deals with many uncertainties and unknown factors, yet one must still make a systematic strategy from this unknown chaos. This means that risk is an important component of strategy. When making a strategy based on an unknowable future, the risk involved is always high. As Julius Caesar once claimed, "For such is the weakness of the human mind, that things dark, hidden, and unknown, always produce in us a greater degree of confidence or terror."[13] The level of preparation by strategists and military commanders can help to negate the fears associated with risk, as their past experiences multiplied by theoretical knowledge to prepare a solid strategy factors in unknown risks.

Legendary Biblical leader Moses was always confident about the future of his plan. Outside of religious faith, this confidence of Moses was also derived from belief in his strategic objectives. This made him a credible leader for his followers. His credibility was not just the result of his internal integrity (though that certainly played a role), but because he was dedicated to the strategy received from the "Supreme Commander" of us all. This Supreme Strategy made the unknown future less intimidating and, for Moses, made it almost a reality. The distant objectives and tasks presented to the Israelites generated enthusiasm among the followers of Moses and allowed them to follow him into a dangerous future. On contemplating the unknown, Søren Kierkegaard, on the way from religion and theological studies to philosophy, expressed a similar sentiment:

> I contemplate the order of nature in the hope of finding God, and I see omnipotence and wisdom; but I also see much else that disturbs my mind and excites anxiety. The sum of all this is an objective uncertainty. But it is for this very reason that the inwardness becomes as intense as it is, for it embraces this objective uncertainty with the entire passion of the infinite.[14]

According to Minford, the first century strategic advisor Zhang Yu once gave advice to the usurper Wang Mang to "exploit the disarray and attack."[15] Uncertainty for some can be a great source of power for others, but major power, always in correct understanding and truthful expression of the future, has to be analyzed, predicted, and believed. If truth is subjective, Kierkegaard argues, then truth should be defined as "an objective uncertainty held fast in an appropriation-process of the most passionate inwardness … The truth is precisely the venture which chooses an objective uncertainty with the passion of the infinite."[16] Kierkegaard philosophically summarizes here the phrase that I quoted earlier, the words of Grand Prince Alexander Nevsky, victorious strategist of thirteenth-century Russia, who is attributed with saying "God is not in power, but in truth."

Systematic Risk in the Global Emerging Market

The generally accepted definition of systematic or country/region-specific risk presented above is actually quite problematic. Many risk factors that are usually included in this category, such as investment-related decisions by national governments and regional authorities, can be predicted with reasonable accuracy and thus are probabilistic. However, it is almost impossible to manage country-specific or systematic risk. It is the privilege of the country's citizens, by democratic means, such as state elections, political parties' campaigns, etc., to influence the decision-making process of the national leadership. In most developed countries—including the US—corporations do attempt to promote their interests in governmental structures, via specially registered lobbying organizations, which often hire former government employees and officials. However, this activity generally provokes a negative backlash from society. It is important to understand the distinction between influencing and managing the governmental decision-making process. In the majority of EMCs, the registration of lobbying companies still does not exist. Attempting to manage systematic risk by influencing governments through non-registered unofficial lobbyists is a very risky and publicly controversial maneuver. According to the practice of foreign direct investment strategy, it is possible to conclude that *systematic risk or country/region-specific risk is predictable, though mostly not manageable.*

Systematic Risk of Foreign Direct Investment

Due to the widely accepted paradigm that systematic risk is unpredictable and unmanageable, project and direct investors entering an EMC considered to be of high risk will not be able to obtain full insurance against country-specific/systematic risk. It is a substantially uninsurable risk. However, about three decades of experience in EMCs has led insurers to provide insurance for certain issues related to systematic risk. These issues are usually evaluated by a few specific integrated indicators of political and economic risk. The prism of these indicators can help to partially insure the activity of a company inside a risky country. Corporate strategic management is able to make foreseeing the dynamics of conditions and consequences of their strategic decisions and develop a strategic risk-management system to mitigate different risk factors. Insurers, as well as corporate leaders, mostly deal with company-specific, unsystematic risks. Insurers will not issue policies against changes of government, revolutions, etc. However, by factoring in systematic risk, many will issue policies for certain government actions that are unfriendly to business, like the nationalization or expropriation of properties or profits, changes in credit policy or the convertibility of the national currency, etc. These issues are typically covered by political risk insurance.

ROLE OF RATING AGENCIES IN STRATEGIC MANAGEMENT

When a strategic investor or corporate leader is considering making a foreign investment—especially in countries with unfamiliar political and economic conditions—it usually seeks the opinion of major rating agencies and experts. Several reliable rating institutions have established themselves in the business communities of the GEM. Among the most respected are Standard and Poor's (S&P), Moody's, and, more recently, Fitch Ratings. In addition to the proprietary information and services of these professional companies, which must of course be purchased, there are several public sources of national investment and business climate evaluations, such as the World Bank, the World Trade Organization, and Regional Development Banks (the European Bank for Reconstruction and Development, Inter-American Development Bank, and UNCTAD). Furthermore, there are many nonprofit organizations, publications, think tanks, etc., that provide useful information for investors moving into unfamiliar markets (see Chapter 8). The investment ratings of all of these agencies should not be taken as indisputable fact—there will always be certain characteristics of a particular strategic project that these evaluations do not take into account. Most agencies evaluate different types of risk without rating countries on the specific purposes of an investor.

In addition to regularly updating national investment grades, investment-rating agencies like S&P also evaluate the grades of particular currencies, types of investment instruments, foreign debt, etc. A revision of an investment grade by a major agency is very important news for strategists, investors, and governments. For example:

> [O]n April 30, 2008, Standard & Poor's Ratings Services raised its long-term foreign currency sovereign credit rating on the Federative Republic of Brazil to "BBB-" from "BB+," and its long-term local currency sovereign credit to "BBB+" from "BBB." Brazil is the 14th sovereign whose foreign currency debt has been raised to investment grade. The upgrades reflect the maturation of Brazil's institutions and policy framework, as evidenced by the easing of fiscal and external debt burdens and improved trend growth prospects.[17]

Seven years later, the S&P cut the rating of Vale S.A., one of the largest Brazilian logistic operations and multinational diversified metals and mining companies, to "BBB+."[18] The lower rating raises the question of how strategists can combine and analyze this information together with a practical long-term strategy, not with the same seven-year horizon, but for the years 2015 to 2022. There are substantial differences in the evaluation of particular countries, investment instruments, and corporations even among the major investment rating agencies. How did the vision for the future of Vale S.A. change between the S&P's first and second ratings? Even non-strategists would not have made a correlation between these two ratings. For this reason, investors should always consult the opinion of as many rating agencies as possible. In addition to rating agencies and the previously mentioned sources, investment-banking companies themselves have branches and professionals devoted to evaluating investment-grade levels. According to the Royal Bank of Canada's corporate and investment-banking arm, RBC Capital Markets, as of 2008 roughly 50 percent of EMCs have an investment grade, meaning that they endorse them as destinations for investment.[19] RBC Capital Markets considers countries with a rating of Ba1/BB+ and below to be subinvestment grade. Among countries included in this category are Argentina, Colombia, Venezuela, Egypt, Ukraine, Philippines, and Indonesia. It considers EMCs with at least Baa3/BBB- rating to be of investment grade—Mexico, Chile, Russia, South Africa, Poland, Hungary, and China, among others.[20]

The assignment of an investment grade to an EMC does not mean that there is no serious political, economic, or any other type of risk for incoming FDI. A high return on investment may be a result of an underdeveloped legal framework and/or less environmental regulation than in developed countries. In some cases, systematic risk is high, but there are special laws protecting foreign property, in order to attract FDI. The existence of such specific protection of foreign property and its enforcement is one of the main distinctions between EMCs and developing countries. Foreign companies are very hesitant to invest in countries that do not have enforced legal protection of foreign property and/or ownership rights for the land itself. A lack of transparency in capital markets and the absence of branches or subsidiaries of major global commercial and investment banks, auditing firms, and insurance companies also drive foreign investment away. In these cases companies do not feel comfortable raising capital in the country in which they are investing.

There are several institutions and universities that evaluate national political, economic, and business investment conditions. One of the most useful of these evaluations for foreign investors is the "Doing Business Project," done annually by the World Bank. It evaluates the national climate for almost every facet of conducting business from the moment of registration to closing procedures. Among the ten major indicators evaluated, particular attention should be given to the World Bank's rating of issues related to employment, relationships with banks ("getting credit"), obtaining licenses, and property registration.

By the integrated indicator of this table ("ease of doing business rank"), of the five countries with the best business conditions, three are emerging markets—all of which are economies in bloom. In fact, the country with the best business conditions in the world is the emerging market of Singapore, which has held this position for the last ten years! There is not a single emerging market among the bottom 15 of the ease of doing business rank; they are all underdeveloped and developing countries. This is an illustration of the superior free-market infrastructure available to businesses in the GEM as opposed to that of the developing and underdeveloped world. One of the drawbacks of this index, and practically all comprehensive ratings, is that they are based on data from the previous year. Business conditions in the GEM are far from static. In a relatively short period, countries can make substantial improvements. Many 2015 ratings have not taken into

Table 9.2 Top Nations by Ease of Doing Business, 2014

Country	*Ease of Doing Business Rank*	*Starting a Business*	*Dealing with Construction Permits*	*Getting Electricity*	*Registering Property*	*Getting Credit*	*Protecting Minority Investors*	*Paying Taxes*	*Trading Across Borders*	*Enforcing Contracts*	*Resolving Insolvency*
Singapore	**1**	**6**	**2**	**11**	**24**	**17**	**3**	**5**	**1**	**1**	**19**
New Zealand	2	1	13	48	2	1	1	22	27	9	28
Hong Kong SAR, China	**3**	**8**	**1**	**13**	**96**	**23**	**2**	**4**	**2**	**6**	**25**
Denmark	4	25	5	14	8	23	17	12	7	34	9
Korea, Rep.	**5**	**17**	**12**	**1**	**79**	**36**	**21**	**25**	**3**	**4**	**5**
Norway	6	22	27	25	5	61	12	15	24	8	8
United States	7	46	41	61	29	2	25	47	16	41	4
United Kingdom	8	45	17	70	68	17	4	16	15	36	13

Based on data from the World Bank Doing Business Project. (n.d.). "Economy Rankings." Retrieved from www.doingbusiness.org/rankings

account positive changes in Colombia or Bahrain, for example. Unfortunately, business environments can also worsen, which is happening in countries like Zimbabwe, Venezuela, Bolivia, Russia, and Ukraine. Nevertheless, before making an investment in an unfamiliar country, it is a good idea to consult the World Bank's ease of doing business evaluation.

The International Institute for Management Development (IMD) located in Lausanne, Switzerland, developed an index called the World Competitiveness Scoreboard, which should also be consulted while crafting an investment strategy.[21] This index describes the business environment of a country by evaluating several indicators in four major categories: economic performance, government efficiency, business efficiency, and infrastructure. As of 2015, the US has the highest score as always, followed by Switzerland, and in the third and fourth positions are two EMCs, Singapore and Hong Kong. Among the top 15 positions in other emerging market countries are United Arab Emirates (eighth), Malaysia (twelfth), Taiwan (thirteenth), and Ireland, which is ranked fifteenth, slightly lower than it was in 2008. Of the top 25 countries by this indicator additionally two other EMCs are Qatar and China. Unlike the World Bank index, which evaluates business conditions in 178 countries, the World Competitiveness Scoreboard ranks only 60 economies. As of 2015, the country ranked with the lowest competitiveness is Venezuela (which has held this position for the last eight years).[22] There are a number of questionable evaluations in the IMD's rankings. For example, Croatia is only ranked at fifty-ninth, far below Ukraine (forty-ninth), Romania (forty-seventh), and even Russia (thirty-eighth) and Turkey (fortieth), which is difficult to accept. Surprisingly, the Czech Republic (thirty-third) is ten rankings below China. All of this is impossible to accept, including another example, that Italy is ranked forty-sixth, far below Russia or Turkey. Regardless, a few points of contention are not enough to discredit an index. Good strategists will inevitably find flaws in indices that attempt to comprehensively evaluate countries. As already advised, strategists should always consult several different sources in addition to completing their own detailed analysis, specifically tailored to their potential activity. At this stage of the strategic investment process, strategists should focus on between three and five recipient countries or regions. The final selection of the recipient country or region should be determined primarily by the strategist's own detailed analysis.

SYSTEM OF STRATEGIC INVESTMENT RISK ANALYSIS

Where does a strategic investment risk analysis begin? Many argue that the first issue to evaluate is financial risk, as investment is inevitably tied to finance issues. This is actually false. Imagine a country with the perfect investment climate. Now imagine that the government that supports the current financial regulations is in danger of losing control of the country to an isolationist movement that wants to nationalize the entire national economy and expel foreign entrepreneurs, property owners, or if in power appeared a "party" of aggression. The investment climate of that country is all of a sudden far from perfect. Financial conditions are heavily influenced by politics and a country's international relations. The extensive history of failed and successful strategic investments in developing and emerging market countries clearly indicates that the first evaluation must be the most strategically important—political risk. However, an evaluation of political risk is far from an adequate foundation upon which to base one's final investment decision. The system of investment risk evaluation is predominantly based on four types of risk: *political*, *economic*, *business*, and *technological*. Issues like environmental risk, corruption, and racketeering can be understood as aspects of indicators of the four risk categories. Environmental regulation is obviously a governmental function and therefore an indicator of political risk. Corruption can be considered an indicator of both political, economic, and—to a certain extent—business risk (as a practice).

In business and investment practice, it is difficult to distinguish between these four categories of risk. For this reason, in Figure 9.3, the circles representing the major elements of risk overlap. However, for strategic analysis, they should be divided in order to systematically evaluate risk.

Political risk is a function of a country's political system; on the regional level, it is a function of the strategy and policy of regional authorities. Economic risk is a function of a country's economic system. Business risk is based on the quality of a country's free-market infrastructure. Technological risk is a function of a country or region's education system, its science and technological achievements, and societal attitudes toward education.

STRATEGIC POLITICAL RISK OF INVESTMENT

The GEM revolutionized attitudes toward risk, especially strategic ones. Prior to the appearance of EMCs, executives and strategists would refuse to make a foreign investment in a country where there was even a hint of strategic political risk. However, in the twenty-first century, strategic management of political risk is a fundamental aspect of executive leadership in the GMP. An evaluation of political risk always begins with an analysis of the opinions of the major rating agencies described above. Although they may employ different methodologies, most rating agencies have specific evaluations of political risk, which are often referred to as national credit risk, sovereign risk, political stability indices, or country risk. All of these evaluations focus on a country's political stability and the attitude of its political leadership toward domestic and foreign business. Some of the most well-respected evaluations of strategic political risk include the Economist Intelligence Unit's Country Risk, the Eurasia Group and PricewaterhouseCoopers' evaluation of political stability, and the World Bank's Worldwide Governance Indicators, which are based on voice and accountability, political stability, government effectiveness, regulatory quality, rule of law, and control of corruption—a few of several indicators of political stability.

At this point, the strategist usually returns to the basic question—which country belongs to the GEM, and which does not? An analysis of different points of view on political risk of strategic investment can determine the categorization of a country. If its risk is extremely low, it may indicate that the country already has stability and maturity and is already in the developed category; or perhaps it has left the category of emerging market democracy and is now in the category of an economy in bloom, like the Czech Republic. Alternatively, strategic political risk in a country could increase to such a level that it is no longer an EMC, which is what happened in Venezuela under the presidencies of both Hugo Chavez and Nicolás Maduro.

When any entrepreneur or corporate strategist decides to invest in the GEM, they typically seek an outside source of financing; only a few investors will use their own resources for FDI. In most cases, entrepreneurs or corporations seek financing from investment-banking companies, to whom they present a feasibility study of the project or a strategic business plan. Financing from an investment bank has become an extremely competitive endeavor, especially for greenfield projects. Greenfield investments are

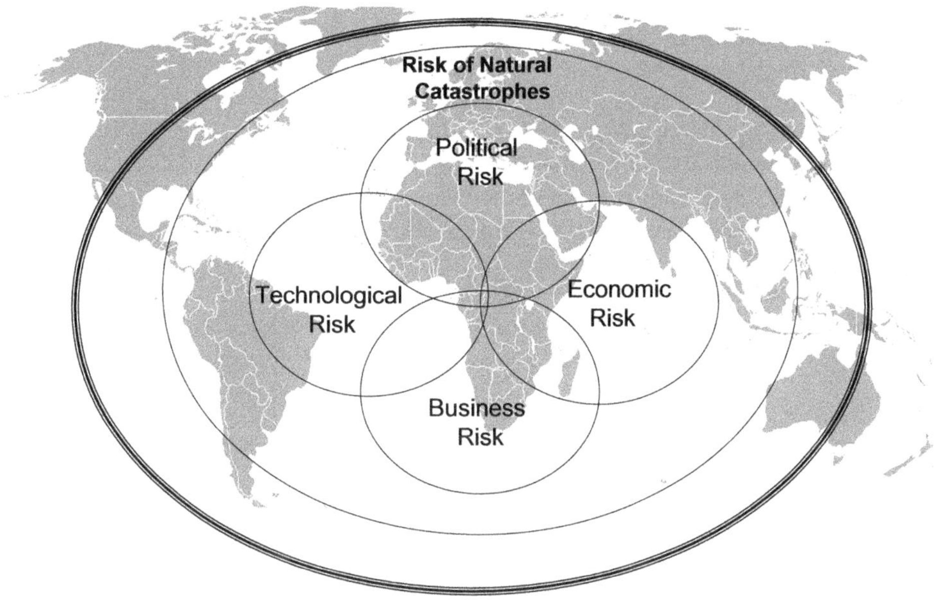

Figure 9.3 Emerging Market Strategic Risk System
© Dr. Vladimir Kvint, 2008

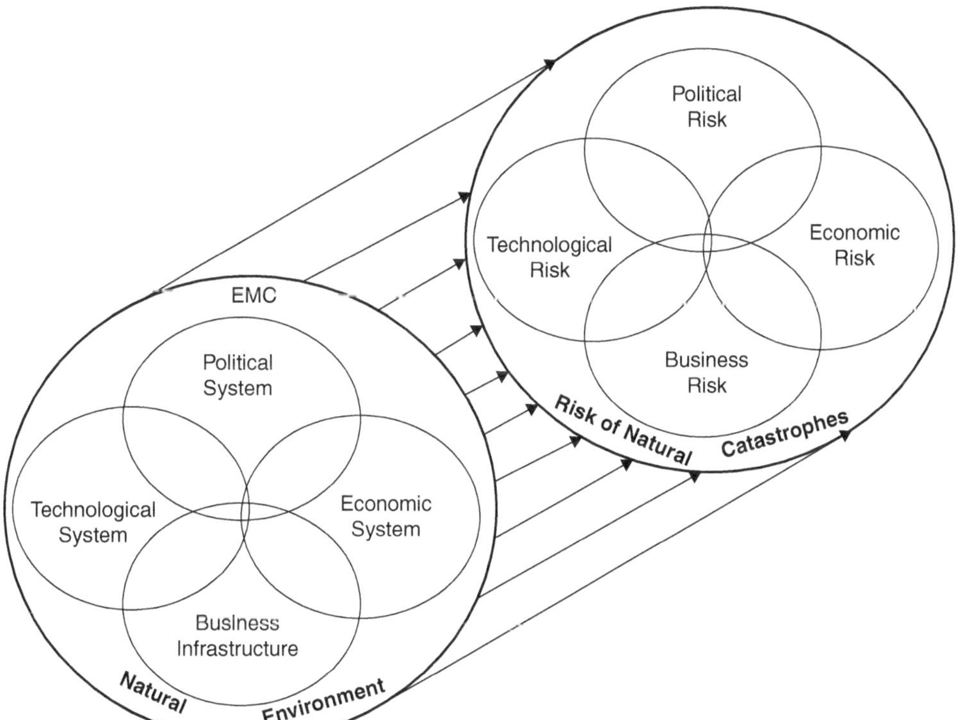

Figure 9.4 Strategic Approach to Systematic EMC Risk Evaluation
© Dr. Vladimir Kvint, 2008

projects that do not involve existing facilities. Not surprisingly, greenfield projects tend to have much higher risk levels than FDI in existing production facilities or mergers and acquisition. Nonetheless, between 2002 and 2006, the number of greenfield projects worldwide more than doubled, according to the United Nations Conference on Trade and Development (UNCTAD). The fastest growing sectors for greenfield FDI projects are related to the development of business services, the number of which more than tripled during this period. A trend that is worth taking note of is the decline in greenfield projects in unhealthy industries like tobacco (see Table 9.3).

Despite the fact that the strategic political risk of greenfield projects in the GEM is obviously higher than that of other forms of FDI, greenfield investments are increasing at a faster rate in the GEM than in the rest of the world. Among the leading EMC

Table 9.3 Number of Greenfield FDI Projects by Sector/Industry, 2003–2013

Sector/industry	*2003*	*2007*	*2010*	*2011*	*2012*	*2013*
Total	9 504	12 974	15 141	16 064	14 215	13 919
Primary	411	141	157	169	94	85
Agriculture, hunting, forestry and fisheries	3	2	1	2	1	3
Mining, quarrying and petroleum	408	139	156	167	93	82
Manufacturing	5 137	6 090	7 666	7 924	6 576	6 585
Food, beverages and tobacco	524	448	540	586	528	476
Textiles, clothing and leather	426	690	1 275	1 157	1 023	1 247
Wood and wood products	183	154	134	136	97	111
Publishing and printing	14	12	20	21	25	12
Coke, petroleum products and nuclear fuel	138	112	117	144	76	61
Chemicals and chemical products	731	715	867	861	695	725
Rubber and plastic products	319	323	436	484	349	408
Non-metallic mineral products	176	239	171	219	126	193
Metals and metal products	247	439	416	497	394	278
Machinery and equipment	358	642	860	1 032	833	817
Electrical and electronic equipment	909	1 008	1 247	1 168	974	868
Precision instruments	96	132	163	179	176	161
Motor vehicles and other transport equipment	878	932	1 082	1 160	956	863
Other manufacturing	138	244	338	280	324	365
Services	3 956	6 743	7 318	7 971	7 545	7 249
Electricity, gas and water	107	351	331	382	273	309
Construction	145	287	176	163	197	171
Trade	717	613	801	801	705	825
Hotels and restaurants	254	264	270	176	130	166
Transport, storage and communications	472	829	957	990	995	1 065
Finance	646	1 233	1 312	1 447	1 201	959
Business services	1 448	2 910	3 121	3 639	3 656	3 460
Education	14	49	99	94	117	60
Health and social services	34	53	64	79	61	39
Community, social and personal service activities	104	132	142	169	184	159
Other services	15	22	45	31	26	36

Based on data from the United Nations Conference on Trade and Development. (2014). "Annex." *World Investment Report 2014*. New York and Geneva: United Nations. Retrieved from http://unctad.org/Sections/dite_dir/docs/WIR2014/WIR14_tab23.xls

recipients of greenfield investment are China, India, Mexico, Singapore, Spain, and Brazil. During this period there have been surprisingly few greenfield FDI projects in other big EMCs like Chile, the Philippines, and South Korea. This is likely a function of these governments not providing incentives for this type of investment. This is especially surprising due to the high quality of the South Korean government, and the establishment at the beginning of 2013 of the Ministry of Strategy and Finance.

During the twenty-first century, EMCs became not only recipients of greenfield FDI projects, but also investors themselves. Among the EMCs that are most aggressively investing in greenfield projects abroad are India, South Korea, Ukraine, Spain, Russia, and China. The role of China during this period would be much higher, but its government limited the outflow of FDI to $10 billion. However, in May 2007 China's State Administration of Foreign Exchange increased the limit of Chinese FDI abroad by three times to $30 billion.[23] Figure 9.5 does not reflect this recent development, but the 2007 outflow of greenfield FDI statistics most certainly will. The government of China made this decision largely in the interest of gaining access to natural resources in emerging market and developing countries as well expanding its winnable investment strategies in the developed world. According to the US-China Economic and Security Review Commission:

> China's government is now adding at least $500b a year to its foreign assets, and perhaps up to $600b. Right now, China's sovereign wealth fund—the China Investment Corporation (CIC)—manages a relatively small share of the total stock of Chinese investment abroad. It is likely to account for a large share going forward.[24]

The underwriter of any investment project seeking public capital in the GEM will almost certainly insist upon obtaining insurance against political risk protection. In one of the

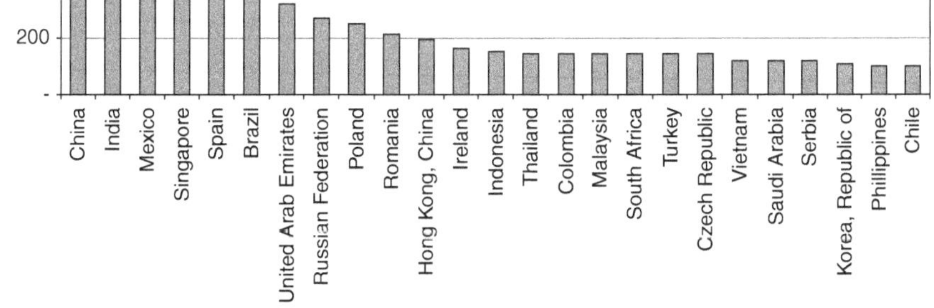

Figure 9.5 Greenfield FDI Projects by Emerging Market Country Recipients, 2013

Based on data from the United Nations Conference on Trade and Development. (2014). "Annex." *World Investment Report 2014.* New York and Geneva: United Nations. Retrieved from http://unctad.org/Sections/dite_dir/docs/WIR2014/WIR14_tab23.xls

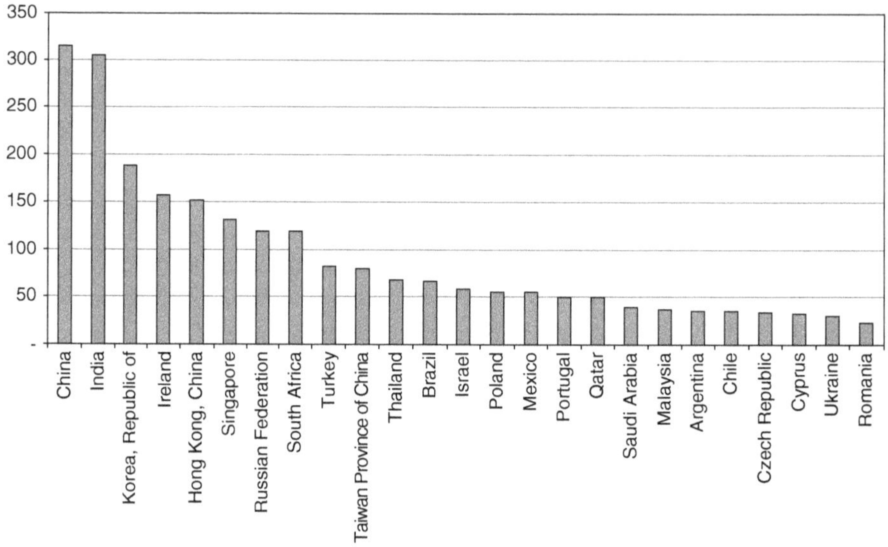

Figure 9.6 Greenfield FDI Projects by Emerging Market Country Investors, 2013

Based on data from the United Nations Conference on Trade and Development. (2014). "Annex." *World Investment Report 2014*. New York and Geneva: United Nations. Retrieved from http://unctad.org/Sections/dite_dir/docs/WIR2014/WIR14_tab23.xls

best-case scenarios, investment banks will issue a letter of preliminary approval contingent upon the acquisition of political risk insurance. How can project leaders obtain such insurance? In the 1980s, at the dawn of the GEM, this was an almost insurmountable challenge. By the end of the twentieth century, it became a regular practice of a few multilateral institutions, governmental agencies, and private insurers. Among multilateral institutions the premier provider of political risk insurance is the Multilateral Investment Guarantee Agency (MIGA). Established in 1988, it is the youngest, but already mature, agency of the World Bank Group. It offers three basic services: political risk insurance, technical assistance, and dispute mediation. MIGA has several limitations for providing political risk insurance. It restricts its guarantees issued annually by total amount, by amount within a particular country, and by amount issued to certain sectors/industries. MIGA—like most insurers—will not issue guarantees for more than 90 percent of total project investment. This means that strategic investors cannot completely rely on the insurance of MIGA and must do their best to adjust and manage risk on their own. MIGA helps investors and lenders deal with political risk by insuring against losses relating to:

- Currency-transfer restrictions
- Expropriation
- War, terrorism, and civil disturbance
- Breach of contract
- Non-honoring of financial obligations.[25]

The first traditional four indicators of strategic political risk are the same as they were when MIGA was established, except for the term "terrorism," which was added after

2008, as well as a fifth indicator, "non-honoring of financial obligations." As of 2015, MIGA issues guarantees for 821 projects in developing countries, according to MIGA classification, for up to 15 to 20 years. "Equity investments can be covered up to 90 percent, and debt up to 95 percent (partial risk guarantees—PRG). MIGA may insure up to $200 million, and if necessary more can be arranged through syndication of insurance."[26] Since 1988, MIGA has issued a total of 885 project guarantees and $17.4 billion in coverage. Forty-one percent of MIGA's gross outstanding portfolio is issued for projects in the poorest developing and underdeveloped countries, although due to its unsystematic country classification, this statistic is an approximation. With a gross exposure of only $5.3 billion,[27] despite the fact that MIGA is a global agency, it has very limited resources even compared with some of its equivalent national agencies. In fact, many of these countries that mistakenly are still classified by MIGA as developing are clearly emerging markets: e.g. Turkey, Mongolia, Hungary, or Brazil. From 1990 to 2013, for all of these countries, MIGA issued guarantees of non-trade projects of about $30 billion.[28]

Long before the establishment of MIGA, several countries created agencies to promote their investments abroad, in order to increase the efficiency of their national economies. The largest national agency providing insurance against political risk for companies investing abroad is a US government agency, the Overseas Private Investment Corporation (OPIC). Congress established it in 1971 to enable US businesses to invest and compete in emerging market countries around the world. As the pioneer of government-backed political risk insurance, direct loans, guaranties, and equity funds, OPIC has helped mobilize and facilitate more than $177 billion in US private capital investment. It has done so at no net expense to the American taxpayer and without the loss of US jobs.[29] OPIC provides insurance against political risk for the following reasons:

- To cover possible damage or loss
  - Tangible assets such as trucks, manufacturing, or drilling equipment
  - Value of investment
  - Earnings or return of the investment
- To obtain or attract financing in the face of risk
- To deter long-term losses through OPIC's advocacy.[30]

In 2007, "OPIC supported 110 projects involving small enterprises, which accounted for 79 percent of the agency's 139 projects."[31] OPIC political risk insurance can cover individual projects up to $250 million with a maturity as long as 20 years.[32] In 2014, OPIC issued $3 billion "in financing and insurance commitments," while they expect that private investors will contribute another $3.2 billion.[33] OPIC is giving special attention to projects related to renewable energy resources, modern agricultural products (e.g. in Senegal), and major projects related to telecom modernization (e.g. in Colombia). "Through its financial and insurance products, OPIC generated $358 million for the U.S. Treasury and produced its 37th consecutive year of reducing the Federal budget deficit. In addition, the Agency's credit portfolio once again performed with lower than 1% write-offs (net of recoveries), an extraordinary accomplishment for a development finance institution taking risks in some of the world's most challenging markets."[33a] It is important to underline that all of these achievements of OPIC, a semi-governmental institution, work without a single dollar from the US taxpayers.

During the 1998 ruble default in Russia, the government of Russia froze all accounts of foreign companies and indefinitely suspended foreign debt payments by banks and enterprises. All foreign investment banks and companies suffered huge losses, except those with guarantees from OPIC or those who had OPIC as an investment partner. The Russian government made sure that all of these companies were reimbursed accordingly. In any case in which a change in government attitude leads to the nationalization or expropriation of foreign properties, OPIC immediately reimburses companies with political risk insurance relative to their insured assets. Furthermore, OPIC negotiates with the government on behalf of the insured investor.

Equivalent agencies to OPIC operate in several countries, including a number of emerging markets like Albania, Bulgaria, and Spain. The rationale behind the establishment of these agencies in the GEM is to help their domestic clients deal with political risk and to provide a competitive edge against foreign companies from the developed world. The Spanish organization CESCE was actually established a year earlier than OPIC, in 1970, "with the primary aim of facilitating the internationalization of Spanish companies."[34]

Quite frequently, American businessmen and companies and foreign leaders are not well informed about OPIC. For example, US companies interested in investing in Bulgaria in the middle of the 1990s were not familiar with OPIC and did not fully utilize its resources and services. They were unaware that OPIC offered political risk insurance for US investors in Bulgaria. Many US and Western European companies were also ignorant of the fact that OPIC provides financing for promising projects abroad. National governments of other EMCs were equally unaware. For this reason OPIC often ends the year with surplus cash.

Besides multilateral and national agencies, political risk insurance can also be obtained from private companies. The largest provider of this service is AIG (American International Group), which operates in more than 130 countries.[35] AIG's menu of political risk insurance protects against

> confiscation, expropriation, nationalization; currency inconvertibility and non-transfer; terrorism, sabotage, war, insurrection, rebellion; government act, law order, or decree; contract frustration, sovereign, non-performance, or payment default, and wrongful calling of contract guarantees and bonds. Coverage can be tailored to the insured's requirements for a broad range of overseas exposures, including equity investments, physical assets, cross-border loans, or contracts for goods and services.[36]

AIG is the leading private provider of strategic political risk insurance but is only one of hundreds of private insurance firms offering this service. Many of them consider this to be a very profitable business, especially when they have branches on the ground in emerging market and developing countries and are very familiar with local conditions.

Any company that seeks political risk insurance from MIGA, OPIC, AIG, or any other national or private insurance agency has to go through an evaluation process. Despite the differences among these agencies and service providers, in the end, all of them evaluate the political risk of a potential project in the GEM by the following major integrated indicators:

Risk of expropriation and nationalization
Risk of civil disobedience and property vandalism

Risk of currency inconvertibility
Risk of terrorism
Risk of governmental breaches of contracts

Each particular provider of strategic political risk insurance uses some different indicators to evaluate integrated risk factors. For certain countries, in addition to the major indicators listed above, agencies and insurance firms will analyze several other issues, such as bilateral relationships with neighboring states or violations of previously signed international documents or treaties like the nuclear non-proliferation agreement. Providers of political risk will also evaluate a country's domestic political system—the existence and enforcement of constitutional law, democratic institutions, and regularly scheduled democratic elections, etc. There are a number of non-governmental international organizations that evaluate political freedom, which can be very useful during this process, such as Freedom House International. The Combined Average Ratings of this organization evaluates political freedom in every country, based on the legitimacy of elections and existence of pluralism, civil liberties, rule of law, and individual human rights.[37] These rankings can be a good indication of the political risk of strategic investment, although they should not be the only source of information when assessing this risk. Some of Freedom House's rankings are questionable. For example, Albania has held legitimate elections since 1998, is politically stable, and is experiencing rapid economic development, and yet in the 2007 evaluation it is ranked in the same category as Bolivia, Nicaragua, Niger, Seychelles, and Papua New Guinea. It is also hard to accept the fact that Estonia is placed in the same category as the US, the UK, Norway, and Switzerland. In Estonia, it is difficult for most native-born, non-ethnic Estonians to get citizenship. Although there is undeniably a high level of economic freedom, political freedom is still below the level that exists in the US, UK, etc. These rankings also do not take into account some of the progress that has been made in Turkmenistan, which is included in the same category as Sudan, Cuba, and North Korea. It is also questionable that Iran is ranked higher than Iraq, a country that has had several legitimate elections. As with any ranking or index, it is important to use one's own experience and opinion to make analyses and strategic conclusions.

It is also very important to keep in mind that the political desires of people of the GEM are often different from those of people in developed countries. In EMCs, substantial segments of populations are frequently willing to concede some elements of political freedom in return for stability and economic freedom. People tend to be resistant to change and the uncertainty that comes along with it. As a result, soft dictatorships such as those in China and Vietnam maintain the support of most people because they provide a stable future and the economic freedom that allows gradual improvements in standards of living. Some dictatorially inclined leaders often use China as a beacon to guide their steps out of democratic transformations. However, one should not make the mistake of overestimating the staying power of "communist" dictatorships. In *Capitalism and Freedom*, the great economist and Nobel Laureate Milton Friedman wrote "communism would destroy all of our freedoms."[38] In fact, Milton Friedman had it backward—freedom destroys communism. The developing free markets in the communist dictatorships of Vietnam, China, and even Cuba are much more likely to destroy the communist political systems than the communist political systems are to destroy free markets. It is only a matter of time before the level of political freedom catches up to the level of economic freedom already established, especially in China, Vietnam, and even Belarus.

In order to minimize political risk, companies should be in direct contact with the national leadership and with any resident professional strategists of the country in which they are considering investing. It is also important to be cognizant of the relationship between the country of origin of the company and the country in which it would like to invest. The best way to establish and improve ties with foreign leaders is through bilateral governmental or semi-governmental cultural and business councils, such as the US-ASEAN Business Council, the US-Taiwan Business Council, etc. The Business Council for International Understanding (BCIU) is another very good vehicle for meeting governmental officials from potential investment-recipient countries. The BCIU was established by the initiative of President Dwight Eisenhower after he saw the many mistakes made by American businessmen as a result of a lack of understanding intergovernmental relations. The BCIU sets up meetings between its members and US ambassadors from abroad while they are visiting the US, and between foreign governmental leaders with the US business community while they are visiting the US. The BCIU also annually presents the Dwight D. Eisenhower Award to a leader of global business. The award ceremony is a major networking event that is useful for business leaders.

In addition to political freedom and stability, another important factor is the quality of law enforcement. Unfortunately, in many EMCs laws look great on paper, but are not enforced. In these cases, law is nothing more than friendly advice. It is very risky to deal with countries that are under UN, NATO, US, or EU embargo. Companies that invest in such countries in violation of restrictions will likely be put on lists compiled by different international and national bodies that monitor dual-use high-tech products. Several companies that invested in projects related to Iranian weapons programs, in spite of UN sanctions, have encountered substantial negative repercussions. However, embargos do offer opportunities (with special legal permission or authorized contracts) for companies that provide certain goods and services, such as health care and baby food, pharmaceutical needs, clothing, etc. This is a legitimate practice that can be very lucrative and socially beneficial.

All integrated indicators of strategic political risk, the practices of political risk insurance agencies/firms, as well as the respect that political risk insurance receives from national governments should be taken into consideration during the stage of strategy formulation. An evaluation of strategic political risk should be done during the entry-strategy development. This will prevent cases in which top executives decide that the level of political risk is too high after already having invested considerable resources in strategy development and implementation.

Of all integrated indicators of strategic political risk, strategists should be most sensitive to the risk of expropriation. If a political leader even mentions this, without making any practical attempts to expropriate foreign property, that country's political risk immediately increases and it will be much more expensive for any strategic investor in that country to obtain political risk insurance. For this reason, as of 2015, the cost of political risk insurance in countries like Venezuela and Bolivia is exorbitant. Any government that, for whatever reason, explores the possibility of nationalizing private assets or renationalizing formerly state-owned companies that have been privatized will instantly increase the political risk of investment in their country. Some inexperienced leaders even publicly announced their inclination to nationalize some privately held companies and properties, a decision that was unquestionably sovereign and national risk increasing. The same applies to national governments that attempt to take control of shares belonging to foreign partners of an international joint venture, a situation that has occurred at some point in China, Russia, Ukraine, Indonesia, Malaysia, Bolivia, and Ecuador, among others. Civil disobedience and widespread violence in the streets can lead to damage of physical assets and properties of foreign investors, even when the unrest has nothing to do with the foreign company's activity. Like the possibility of expropriation, the prospect of civil disobedience immediately increases strategic political risk and the price for insurance against it.

Currency inconvertibility is another major factor of strategic political risk. The overwhelming majority of EMCs have national currencies that are not convertible. In order to avoid this issue as a strategic risk for foreign investors, some countries have strategies (any strategy whether good or bad is better than nothing) to attempt to completely replace or continue to have their national currencies with a convertible foreign currency, like the US dollar or the euro. For example, the US dollar is the currency in El Salvador and Ecuador, as well as the primary currency in Panama. Montenegro, which is not a part of the Eurozone, has accepted the euro as its official currency, as have Kosovo and even the wealthy nation Andorra. As of 2015, the euro is currency for 340 million people. By adopting foreign convertible currencies, the leadership of these countries immediately improved their national strategies and political risk climate. A few EMCs, like the Czech Republic, have reached the level of economic and political maturity whereby its currency is generally accepted as convertible. The national currencies of some EMCs are accepted as convertible by a few other countries, though they are not considered to be convertible currencies worldwide. This is the case for the currencies of South Korea and China—"the Monetary Board of the Bangko Sentral ng Pilipinas (Central Bank of the Philippines) approved the inclusion of the Chinese renminbi (RMB) and the Korean won (KRW) in the list of currencies convertible with the central bank."[39] In order to decrease political risk, some countries are attempting to establish their national currency as a regionally convertible currency. During the St. Petersburg Economic Forums of 2007 and 2008 and the 2008 G8 Summit in Japan, leaders of Russia declared their intent to do so with the ruble. Currency convertibility risk is always a significant factor for FDI in EMCs, especially for companies that generate their revenue from domestic consumers. There are a number of complications that arise when dealing with non-convertible or limitedly convertible currencies, especially regarding the repatriation of profit. This issue is discussed in Chapter 4 (regarding IJVs) and in Chapter 5 (regarding capital as a basic economic factor in the global marketplace).

Tragically, during the twenty-first century another factor of strategic political risk—terrorism and extremism—became a major obstacle for FDI. Emerging market countries are particularly vulnerable to this factor (see Chapter 7). In some parts of the GEM, there is always the danger of financial support for terrorism being disguised as legitimate FDI or other investment transactions. In order to prevent this risk factor, the participants of the 1989 G7 meeting suggested the establishment of the Financial Action Task Force (FATF), "an inter-governmental body whose purpose is the development and promotion of national and international policies to combat money laundering and terrorist financing."[40] As of 2015, there are 34 full member-countries of FATF, including 16 emerging market countries.[41] Additionally, 2 REOs—the European Union and the Gulf Cooperation Council—and about 25 FATF observer organizations are also full members. One other EMC, Malaysia, is an observer. Among the associate members are 8 regional organizations and other financial monitoring agencies, like the Asia/Pacific Group on Money Laundering, and about 25 observer organizations. The FATF publishes an annual list of "Non Cooperative Countries and Territories." The list consists of countries and territories with financial systems that are vulnerable to exploitation by money launderers and terrorist financiers. Before making a foreign investment or engaging in international transactions, it is important to make sure that a potential recipient country is not on this list. In the best case scenario the country is a member or associate member of FATF. As of 2015, after the removal of Nigeria (2005) and Myanmar (2006), there are no countries on this list.[42]

Breach of contract, as a governmental or legal action, is represented by the final integrated indicator of strategic political risk of investment. This is primarily a legal issue. In most cases this risk falls under economic risk of investment. However, when the government is one of the parties of a contract, this issue is an aspect of strategic political risk. In order to reduce potential partners' fears of contract breach, some governments prepare investment agreements or assign conditions to a greenfield FDI project in such a manner as to make it very difficult for future governments to violate contractual obligations. In cases when governments do not take such precautions, agreements are vulnerable to the whims of future governments or even of current superiors. Strategists, together with legal advisors, drafting contracts without the participation of a governmental partner should still prepare long-term preventive measures against governmental meddling. In the GEM it is not unheard of for the government to interfere—for its own reasons—with a contract between two satisfied private parties. Contracts in which one of the parties is a partially state-owned company are particularly vulnerable. This risk factor applies mainly to international joint ventures and companies that are engaged in a *product-sharing agreement*. This type of agreement is typically used by companies developing, producing, and enriching natural resources, like oil, natural gas, coal, non-ferrous and precious metals, fertilizer, etc. When the government is not involved in a breach of contract, this factor should be analyzed as an economic and, in some cases, as a legal risk of investment.

In order to devise strategies to attract FDI, governmental officials of EMCs should evaluate national political risk from the perspective of a foreign company and analyze the practice of political risk insurance agencies and firms. Governments of non-developed countries have to take measures to improve their public image regarding risk. This can be done simply by making governmental or legislative declarations to protect foreign investors from expropriation and nationalization. Such action can even be made illegal. Furthermore, governments can declare that they will not interfere with agreements between domestic or foreign companies, especially if they have certain contracts, like product-sharing agreements. British Petroleum was forced to deal with such interference with a product-sharing agreement in Russia in 2006 to 2008. Governments can develop—and promote internationally—long-term programs to increase the convertibility of the national currency. The same idea applies to a firm, public denouncement of any terrorist attempts against foreign businesses. Due to the fact that only national governments can manage systematic risk, a major priority of non-developed countries should be developing strategy toward FDI with the priority of reducing national political risk according to the practice of major agencies and insurance firms.

STRATEGIZING INVESTMENTS IN WARRING COUNTRIES

The highest levels of strategic political risk and instability are related to countries in a state of war. According to a report by the International Action Network on Small Arms, Saferworld, and Oxfam International, from 1990 to 2005 the cost of wars and civil conflict in 23 African countries alone amounted to $284 billion.[43] Some emerging market countries that are not officially in a state of war devote a substantial part of their national budgets to military purposes. According to the Stockholm International Peace Research Institute (SiPRi), of the top ten countries in terms of military expenditures, five are EMCs: China, Russia, Saudi Arabia, India, and Brazil.[44] These are likely rough approximations, as the exact military expenditures of some countries like China, Russia, and Saudi Arabia are not widely known. However, there are many humane business opportunities in countries that are "under fire," including the delivery of medicine, medical equipment, pharmaceutical products, food, educational materials, construction of social infrastructure, roads, restoration of damaged facilities, etc.[45] In terms of percentage of GDP, a slightly different picture emerges: leaders are South Sudan (10.33%), Oman (8.61%), Saudi Arabia (7.98%), Israel (5.69%), and Russia (4.7%).[46] In some cases, despite the very high risk, investing in countries or regions at war can be very fruitful for strategic investors and the people of the recipient country.

As cynical as it sounds, war is often very profitable for media companies. During the first Persian Gulf War, CNN correctly predicted and strategized that land-based telecommunication infrastructure would be destroyed and invested in a cutting-edge satellite video telecommunication system. Audiences around the globe relied on CNN for up-to-date broadcasts from the battlefield, as it was the only network that could broadcast in real time. Needless to say, this proved to be a very profitable investment for CNN; it also brought to CNN strategic long-term success and made it the primary supplier of first-hand news to people around the world.

The rebuilding process that follows a war is obviously an extremely lucrative time for construction and contracting companies who address vital needs of the surviving population. Many companies have made substantial profits with the strategy of providing much-needed services in Serbia, Bosnia Herzegovina, Albania, Iraq, and later in Libya and Egypt. Post-conflict economies offer great opportunities for young entrepreneurs with a relatively small amount of cash, as governments and people are in desperate need of many services. Small governmental contracts can be very profitable. Some companies are specifically developing strategies oriented toward post-conflict processes of rebirth, such as Kellogg Brown and Root, a subsidiary of Halliburton, which is playing an important role in the reconstruction of Iraq. DynCorp, a subsidiary of CSC, specializes in assisting nascent democracies establish law and order. It has recruited, trained, and deployed more than 5,000 civilian peacekeepers and police trainers to 11 countries, including Haiti, Bosnia Herzegovina, Afghanistan, and Iraq, on behalf of the US Department of State.

Strategic Economic Risk of Investment

Strategic economic risk is a function of the likelihood of governmental intervention in business that reduces economic freedom, especially in times of an economic crisis and heightened uncertainty. It is distinct from strategic political risk, in that political risk is a function of governmental strategy toward private business and does not factor in the economic-crisis issue. For example, when a country cannot pay its foreign debt, causing a default, the long-term economic risk of a country substantially increases. Instances of national default are very dangerous for business. In strategy, economic risk is essentially an intermediary between political risk and business risk. Although these two risks may be difficult to separate, for analytical strategic purposes it is helpful to understand them as distinct categories.

In strategic terms, the higher the level of economic freedom, the lower the economic risk of investment, although this correlation has limits. There is a well-defined role for the government as a regulator of private business activity. Without this limited level of governmental involvement—to prevent monopoly and corruption—the private business arena can become anarchic, with increasing economic risk. The private sector needs governments to establish and enforce rules of the workplace and marketplace. A country whose government is not strong enough to enforce its laws will have a very high strategic economic risk of investment. This is why some companies are often more willing to invest in countries with dictatorships—China, Vietnam, Qatar, Chile during Pinochet's rule, etc.—than in EMCs with nascent democracies that still struggle to enforce the law. But there is always a danger that at any moment a dictator will change his mind.

Economic risk of strategic direct investment or project investment is primarily a systematic or country/region-specific risk. Unlike business risk, economic risk is mostly related to the external economic environment in which a company has to operate, or in which a greenfield FDI project is implemented, such as the quality and availability of industrial infrastructure, like transportation and telecommunication facilities and access to energy, freshwater resources, etc. A substantial part of economic risk is partially self-standing *legal* and *regulatory risk*, i.e., how domestic law protects foreign and individual property rights, know-how, intellectual property, etc. These issues can be evaluated as part of political as well as business risk, but due to the fact that economic and business laws and under-law regulations are a function of the government, they should be evaluated as part of economic risk. Under-law regulation and governmental practices are part of regulatory risk. Economic risk, like political risk, is related to the role of the government in the economic and business realms of a country. Several integrated ratings of economic risk, such as country risk, sovereign risk, and national credit risk are a combination of various indicators of political and economic strategic risk. None of these evaluations provides an adequate explanation as to why certain indicators are taken into consideration while others are ignored. Some strategic country-risk indices include sovereign risk as an element of country risk, but in others the reverse is the case.

In terms of provincial and territorial authorities, regional risk is a mix of indicators of political and economic risk. However, unlike country strategic risk, among the indicators of regional risk are those that describe business and even technological risk. Regional strategies are much denser if they include and correlate with corporate strategies when the region's strategic management systems use a mechanism of technological platforms as a super position and combination of corporate technologies for the implementation of regional strategies. In practice, when companies try to obtain country- and regional-specific risk evaluations from professional firms and consulting companies, they usually, due to lack of strategies, get forecasts containing a mixture of political, macroeconomic, and business indicators and variables. A typical example of this is the product of the Economist Intelligence Unit's (EIU) Country Risk Service. It is a

> two-year forecasting service that monitors risks in 120 key markets. It is designed for commercial bankers, institutional investors and corporate executives who invest in both emerging and developed markets. The service measures political, economic policy and economic structure risks as well as currency, sovereign debt and banking sector risks. In-depth forecasts are provided for up to 180 macroeconomic variables for each country.[47]

Among the indicators included in this evaluation are country, region, currency, and banking-sector risk. According to the opinion of the EIU, as of June 2010, among the least risky European countries (by sovereign risk and overall risk), the best EMC is Slovenia with an A rating (for sovereign risk) and overall rating of BB, followed by Slovakia and the Czech Republic.[48] On the global arena the best rating given by EIU among all EMCs is to Singapore and Hong Kong (both "A" ratings for overall and sovereign categories). In Latin America, Brazil has much higher risk than Argentina. Among BRIC countries, Russia[49] has the same rating as India and Brazil, but the highest rating is China's triple B rating.[50] Some country-risk indices, like *Forbes*' "Best Countries for Business" (formally the Capital Hospitality Index) are mostly a summary of a few selected macroeconomic and financial indicators, which are more of a reflection of economic development than of investment risk.[51] According to the approach of this book, sovereign risk is part of strategic economic risk, not business risk. It is primarily related to the activity of central banks, which to a certain extent function according to state strategy. There are several sources for sovereign risk evaluations, such as Global Insight, a consulting firm specializing in risk forecasting.

The following list covers the most important issues to be examined when evaluating a country's strategic economic risk, especially during initial stages of strategizing:

Strategic economic factors

- Membership in multilateral, international economic organizations (World Bank Group, WTO, IMF, regional economic organizations, like Mercosur, Shanghai Cooperation Organization, GUAM, ASEAN, EBRD, etc.)
- Relations with Paris Club of official creditors
- Laws on the protection of private property, foreign strategic investment, cross-border transactions, etc.
- Cross-border investment and trade barriers (duties, quotas, export-import licenses, non-tariff barriers)
- Existence of Most Favored Nation status or Normal Trade Relations status
- Capital asset pricing regulations
- Tax law and tax code (profit tax, export-import tax, profit-repatriation tax, international and bilateral double taxation agreements)
- Existence of special economic and technological or free-trade zones
- Intensity of competition in the national and regional marketplaces and presence of major competitors
- Patent, trademark, copyright, and know-how protection
- Compliance, confidentiality, and enforcement of regulatory regimes and economic and business laws
- Existence of nepotism, corruption, and rackets
- Hostile takeovers and corporate-raid practices
- Terrorism and extremism and its effect on legal and commercial practice

Strategic economic infrastructure factors

- Adequacy, quality, and cost of telecommunications
    - Local, long distance, and international telecommunications channels
    - Telecommunication penetration

- Access to satellite and mobile communications
- Access to Internet, data communications links; local area network (LAN) capacity
- Access to services of global telecom providers

- Transportation infrastructure
    - Quality and extent of highways and secondary roads
    - Access to air, rail, or water transportation
    - Freight forwarding and customs clearing services
    - Quality and cost of transportation services
- Energy (availability, reliability, and cost of energy for commercial and residential use)

Strategic social-infrastructure factors

- Access to medical services
    - Presence of major medical insurance companies
- Access to hospitality services (hotel availability, quality, and pricing)
- Existence and penetration of restaurants, quality of nutrition for local and foreign personnel
- Cultural infrastructure (movie theaters, theaters, museums, galleries, clubs, etc.)

Strategic industrial structure factors

- Analysis of the maturity and potential dynamics for:
    - Knowledge-based industries
    - Heavy industries (mining, metallurgy, machinery building, etc.)
    - Consumer-oriented industries (textiles, clothing, etc.)
    - Agriculture and food processing
    - Service-related industries

Strategic education and science factors

- Existence of scientific and technological parks, start-ups, and their relations with business and regional leadership
- Availability of quality elementary and high school education
- Availability of quality bachelor's degree and master's degree education

The overwhelming majority of these strategic economic factors are part of country-specific systematic risk evaluation. Corporate strategists and executives cannot develop a system to manage these risks. However, they can make strategic counter-measures by taking into account strategic political risk to make adjustments according to corporate strategy, interests, and capacities. Each strategic factor requires an analysis not only from the point of view of its influence on a company's capabilities, resources, income, and profit, but also its implications on a country's sustainability and predictability. For example, a country's membership in multilateral institutions and international regional economic organizations is relevant from a monetary perspective, as well as for forecasting a company's future in the economic environment of a potential recipient of FDI. If a country is a member of the World Bank or the IMF, it means that the leadership of this country took certain obligations upon itself that have to be followed by all national institutions. This definitely helps corporate strategists and leaders to understand the conditions in which they will operate in the foreseeable future. Some global multilateral or regional organizations are difficult to classify as purely economic or political. From the perspective of corporate and even inner regional strategies, it makes more sense to classify these kinds of organizations as economic ones. Among such organizations are the European Union, Shanghai Cooperation Organization, the African Union, and the Andean Community, among many others.

Special attention should be given to membership in organizations of state-owned or state-controlled banks, creditors, and donors. Quite often, the new leadership of a country would prefer not to recognize debt made by previous governments, according to international agreements with foreign state banks. This is often the case when a newly elected democratic government is forced to deal with foreign debt accumulated by a past dictatorial regime in order to finance its own luxurious lifestyle and pad the pockets of corrupt bureaucrats. Unfortunately, many young democracies have had to deal with this issue. In order to protect themselves, state bank creditors created the Paris Club. The mission of this organization is to "find co-ordinated and sustainable solutions to the payment difficulties experienced by debtor nations." The London Club is a similar organization made up of private donor banks.

In some instances it is difficult to decide under which type of risk a particular factor or indicator should be evaluated. This is especially the case with evaluations of the implications of nepotism, corruption, rackets, as well as nationalism for country risk. It is also important to clarify if foreign entities have rights to invest in any particular elements of this industrial or business infrastructure, which in some EMCs were or still are prohibited. For example, as of 2015, foreign capital is not allowed to be invested in the Indian insurance industry. During the strategizing process, these factors can be classified as both political and economic. Economic crimes often are related to legal risk of FDI, which blurs the line between political and economic risk, and can be classified in either of them, depending on the angle of strategic analysis. In this book, economic crimes are primarily analyzed as an aspect of strategic economic risk of investment. Some factors of legal risk are manageable and have unsystematic characteristics, but most do not.

Raiding is an economic crime that poses a serious threat to businesses in many EMCs. Unlike in developed countries, in the GEM raiding is a practice associated with organized crime. In some EMCs it is not uncommon for organized crime to obtain official ownership documents of a legitimate company by bribing an employee. They then establish a new company, to which they transfer ownership of the legitimate company, using the official ownership documents. Almost immediately, the criminal organization then sells ownership of the legitimate company to another legitimate company. Following this transaction, the company formed by the criminal organization will legally disband and disappear, leaving the two legitimate companies in a very complicated and expensive legal dispute. In the majority of EMCs, the legal code does not yet protect against this type of raiding activity, making it very difficult to prosecute such acts. In many cases, when corruption does not totally inhibit prosecution, raiders are charged with minor civil offenses. Even the vague possibility of such raiding is a major deterrent for foreign investors, and it should be a major priority of governments in EMCs where this activity occurs to develop anti-raiding laws.

Economic, social, and industrial-infrastructure issues are primarily a systematic risk. Regardless of the richness or abundance of a country's resources, foreign companies will not be able to utilize them without the existence of basic industrial infrastructure.

For this reason, prior to deciding on the location of an investment project, an evaluation of the proximity of telecommunication, transportation, and social infrastructure should be done. The same concept applies to the existence of available labor resources, regarding the quality of education and expertise required by a particular project. The proximity of technological parks and special scientific technological zones is particularly important for knowledge-based companies. These types of companies can hire many fewer employees by contracting with technological and scientific companies, which are often concentrated around special scientific and technological zones. For companies involved in the development of industrial infrastructure, the risk of its activity can be both systematic and unsystematic. Even large multinational corporations can fall victim to the governmental bureaucracies of small countries. For example, bureaucratic inertia and a lack of leadership in Albania delayed national progress by threatening a multimillion-dollar investment project of General Electric. In 2006 partisan quarrels embarrassingly led to the suspension of the company's railway infrastructure project between the Durrës seaport and the Albanian capital, Tirana.[52]

Strategists always have to keep in mind when making conclusions about any political or economic risk factors of FDI that they may be generally systematic, but for a particular company in certain situations they are not automatically unmanageable. Unsystematic economic risk is analyzed later in this chapter.

Commercial and Legal Risk: Corruption, Raiding, and Intellectual Property Rights

In the GEM, the most corrupt governmental agencies are those responsible for contracts, tax collection, privatization, real estate development, anti-trust regulators, and law enforcement. The United Nations Office of Drugs and Crime (UNODC) research concluded that in "2009 criminal proceeds amounted to 3.6% of global GDP, with 2.7% (or USD 1.6 trillion) being landed."[53] In EMCs, bribery plays an even larger role. In June 2008 the government of Ukraine published a study of the biggest bribes during the past 12 months. At the top of this list was a bribe of $53.1 million taken by a local authority in the Black Sea Crimea region for transactions related to landownership.[54] It is estimated that companies in heavily corrupt business environments allocate 10 to 20 percent of profit to bribe bureaucrats and officials. These bureaucrats use their positions in government not for the betterment of society, but for their own selfish interests. Corruption is, in effect, a regressive taxation mechanism, with the poorest people taxed the most and the wealthiest paying the smallest proportion of their income.

In 1955, Dr. Simon Kuznets (1901–1985) observed that "with increasing productivity of labor, inequality initially increases, but later decreases."[55] He illustrated this phenomenon with an upside-down symmetric U curve. For his empirical studies and analysis of the influence of economic growth on social dynamics, Dr. Kuznets received the 1971 Nobel Prize in Economics. However, his observation is not fully applicable in EMCs, unless the influence of widespread corruption is factored into the equation. A *corruption coefficient* makes the upside-down U asymmetric, substantially decreasing the rate at which inequality decreases. Corruption and nepotism inhibit the process of reducing income inequality. Corruption negatively influences entrepreneurship from the very beginning when individual investors or executives try to start or register a new business. In the GEM, the coefficient results in balancing of inequality during the continuous increase in the productivity of labor, but at a rate of two to four times slower than inequality increases.

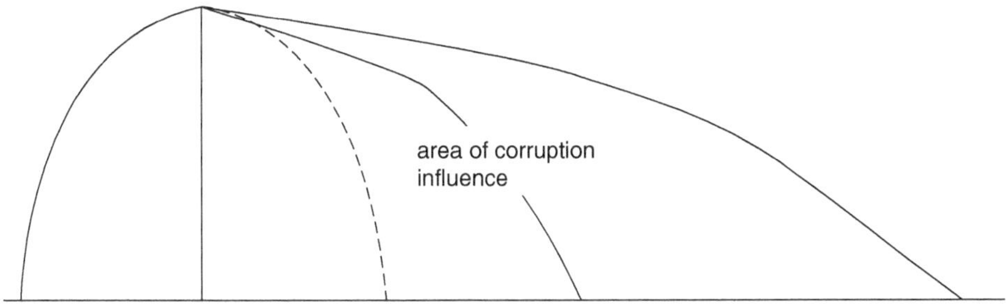

Figure 9.7 Changing Dynamics of the Kuznets Curve Under the Influence of Corruption in the GEM

From an analysis of data provided by Transparency International, a global organization dedicated to monitoring and fighting corruption, it is possible to conclude that the poorer the country and the lower the productivity of its labor, the higher the corruption and the more obstacles there are for FDI. This organization conducted a survey of perceptions of corruption in 180 countries. In African countries, on average more than 55 percent of people surveyed admitted that they paid a bribe in the previous 12 months to the police. High corruption exists in some countries belonging to regions that average lower levels of corruption than Africa. This is the case in countries including Myanmar, Azerbaijan, Russia, Thailand, and Mexico. A high concentration of FDI has an accumulative effect, i.e., as FDI flows and stock increase in a country, corruption also tends to be reduced.

Some governments, such as China and Iran, use the legal system to fight corruption, going as far as to institute capital punishment. China's president Xi Jinping has done everything possible to fight corruption and correctly connects fighting corruption to providing social safeguards and stability and the promotion of social equality and justice.[56] But even a deterrent as strong as death will not end widespread corruption. Ivan the Terrible and Peter the Great both punished bribe taking with death, and yet centuries later Russia is still one of the most corrupt countries in the world. The only way to substantially reduce corruption is through a strategy of economic reform, increasing transparency, and the development of free-market institutions. The more restrictions, regulations, licenses, quotas, permits, etc. in an economy, the greater the need for a governmental bureaucracy connected with business mafia and the more opportunities there are for bureaucrats to exploit the system for their own personal gain. As free-market institutions develop and mature, corruption tends to decline. For example, boards of trade and stock exchanges tend to develop at a faster rate than custodians and trust institutions. As a result, the business mafia satisfies the demand for enforcement agents. As trust institutions and custodians develop and become part of stock transactions, the need for an illegal enforcer disappears.

Fighting corruption has become a very popular area of advocacy during elections in EMCs. However, usually nothing more than empty promises are made—and once the election is over, nothing is done. In some instances, newly elected politicians prosecute a few cases of bribery to make it seem as if fighting corruption is a priority, but they will do little to address the systemic causes. When Vladimir Putin was first elected president of Russia, he declared "war against kleptocrats." A few were exiled or sent to jail. In his second term, he went after a few police, federal security (FSB) officers, federal accounting officials (Schetnaya Palata), mayors, deputy governors, and senators. This did have important implications for foreign investors and companies. Putin has effectively made it difficult for bureaucrats and officials to create artificial barriers to force foreigners to bribe them, i.e., the creation of a racket. However, even at the end of the first decade of the twenty-first century, corruption, which is usually initiated by a businessman, is one of the highest barriers for FDI in Russia. As of 2015, according to the Russian Lawyers' Association's anti-corruption network, Clean Hands without Borders, between 2012 and 2014 the average size of a bribe declined by 27.2 percent during these two years. This association calculated that corruption turnover is about 46 percent of Russia's GDP and it has also declined by 6.6 percent in comparison with 2012. In 2012, the amount of corruption was about 52.6 percent of GDP![57]

There is a method of substantially decreasing corruption and at the same time increasing employment. This can be done through a declaration of fiscal or economic amnesty. Several countries, including Italy, Turkey, Germany, and even the US, achieved substantial success using amnesty strategy. In EMCs, quite frequently, democratic reforms and the development of the free-market economy go at a faster pace than changes in the law. As a result, people who made money in the initial stages of development of a free market unintentionally find themselves on the wrong side of the law. In order to avoid punishment and confiscation, they send their money abroad to tax havens like Luxembourg, Switzerland, Austria, the Cayman Islands, and Panama. Later, when the law is updated accordingly in their native countries, they are usually hesitant to bring their money back home, for fear of being prosecuted for their prior violations of outdated law and regulations. At this point, EMC governments should declare amnesty on gray capital, i.e., capital that was accumulated in the underground economy but is not related to crimes like narcotics or human and weapons trafficking. In most cases, entrepreneurs who return money have to pay very low taxes but must invest most of it for business development and the creation of new jobs. Successful amnesty programs usually last for up to six months. However, countries in which amnesty is initiated with the aim of increasing tax revenue miss out on the opportunity to utilize this capital. This was the cause in the failure of Russia's capital amnesty attempt in 2007 and 2008.

During the strategic consideration of the cross-border investment destination, it is important to evaluate the extent to which the legal system treats citizens and governmental officials equally. A country cannot be considered an emerging market if major disparities in legal treatment exist. EMCs are in the process of transitioning from a society in which rulers are above the law to one in which the government is accountable to society and to the law in the same way as regular citizens. Currently, in most EMCs the legal system treats foreign-owned property and investment differently than domestic-owned property and investment. In most cases, as the domestic economy matures and foreign investment continues to flow, the legal distinctions erode and a unified legal framework on investment and property emerges. However, some EMCs are increasing restrictions on foreign investment as the result of a misguided and backward pursuit of national interests or effective lobbying by domestic executives or oligarchs. This is the case in Venezuela and Zimbabwe—which are no longer considered EMCs—and to a certain extent Russia, where direct or indirect attempts to increase state control over companies with partial foreign ownership have been made since 2007. There is also a non-strategic tendency in EMCs to illegally nationalize companies that were legally purchased by domestic entrepreneurs during the chaotic transitional period of economic liberalization. Whether a government attempts to nationalize domestic or foreign companies, the result is the same: investors lose faith in the government's willingness and ability to protect property rights, causing an outflow of foreign and domestic capital. It also causes domestic companies to register and declare their initial public offerings abroad, in places that they are confident will uphold the law and protect property rights, such as London, Frankfurt, Zurich, or New York. All facilities are located within their own national borders, however, furthering the outflow of capital. Ultimately, the government only undermines its own rule of law and economic freedom.

As strategic investment continues to flow into the GEM and standards of living continue to rise, it is becoming an increasingly important market for luxury goods and services. For example, the Trump Organization, a high-end real estate development company, is active in Mexico, Panama, the Dominican Republic, South Korea, and the United Arab Emirates. Donald Trump has registered trademarks of all of his companies in these countries. In any country the Trump Organization has considered entering, the company has registered trademarks in the areas of real estate development and construction. It has also registered the trademark of the Trump International Hotel & Tower, lengthening the rights of the trademark. In 2003, visitors to Albania would have been surprised to find a Burger King. However, a closer inspection would reveal that despite the almost similar interior design and marquee, they would actually be in a Burger Queen—likely a violation of intellectual property regulations in the developed world. It is not an uncommon occurrence in the GEM for well-known trademarks and brands to be slightly altered and used to promote goods and services below the quality of the original brands. This dilutes the reputation of the brand and misleads consumers.

Failure to enforce intellectual property rights has prevented a great deal of potential investment in the GEM. The WTO has a special branch that oversees and conducts investigations into this issue. In September 2007, the WTO opened a formal investigation into the role of the Chinese government in preventing piracy and counterfeiting. All EMCs should make decisive and forceful action against counterfeiting and piracy in order to illustrate their willingness and ability to protect intellectual property rights to the international business community. The WTO has the right to authorize trade sanctions against any country that does not sufficiently enforce intellectual property rights, trademarks, and copyrights. Unfortunately, red tape and bureaucracy often inhibit punishment for such infractions.

The governments of all developed countries and many EMCs, as well as their regional economic organizations, have developed different institutions and watchdogs to protect intellectual property rights. The US government uses the Office of the US Trade Representative (USTR), which is similar to the ministries of foreign economic relations of many other countries. The office of the USTR annually publishes the "Special 301 Report," which reviews "the global state of intellectual property rights protection and enforcement."[58] This report includes the Priority Foreign Countries list, which was first developed in 1974. President Obama on February 28, 2012 established the Interagency Trade Enforcement Center (ITEC).[59] Placement on this list creates substantial restrictions for international trade and investment. As a result, most countries at least show some effort to obey intellectual property regulations set forth by the WTO. For example, Argentina, which, according to the 2008 USTR's list, was once "the worst expropriator of the intellectual property of the research-based pharmaceutical industry in the Western Hemisphere, and one of the worst in the world,"[60] as of 2015 occupies the fourth position, due to its efforts to address these problems. The 2014 Special 301 Report reviewed 82 trading partners and the Priority Watch List was established with the following order of attention to particular countries: China, India, Russia, Algeria, Argentina, Chile, Indonesia, Pakistan, Thailand, and Venezuela.[61] Regarding China, it is mentioned that "theft of trade secrets remains a significant concern."[62] In 2013, India made some limited progress in improving its weak IPR, legal framework, and enforcement systems.[63] Regarding Russia, "The United States is troubled that IPR enforcement continued to decrease overall in 2013, following a dramatic decline in 2012, and remained plagued by a lack of transparency and effectiveness."[64] Argentina has been on the same list since 1996, but has made a little progress. The problem of Argentina is mostly related to patent issues, especially for pharmaceutical products, etc.[65]

To strategically address legal risk, foreign investors often seek the services of internationally recognized law firms during the process of strategizing. An evaluation of the presence of such firms is crucial when deciding on the location of a potential FDI. Subsidiaries and partnerships with foreign law firms in EMCs are usually employed by investors to file the corporation registration and other key documents with the government. Ideally, these firms have a deep-rooted knowledge of the local law and enforcement regimes, which are crucial during the process of establishing international joint ventures or executing acquisitions. During the twenty-first century, legal fees for real estate transactions have tremendously increased. Registration costs and other legal fees are especially high in South Korea, Greece, Spain, Hungary, and the Czech Republic. In these countries legal expenses for property-transaction costs as a percentage of the total value of the real estate are higher than in the United States, which is well known for its expensive legal costs.[66] Confidentiality of purchase and sale agreements, clean title, trade secrets, technology, and even operational information are all legal issues that should be addressed during the formation of the entry strategy.

Natural Disasters as a Risk of Investment

One of the least manageable but still somewhat predictable and strategizable risk factors of investment is related to the natural environment on a regional, national, and global scale. Improvements and protection of environmental conditions can be achieved. But this requires not only a long-term vision from regional, national, and global leadership, but also a change in the mentality of the global community. Some environmental issues can be solved more efficiently on a regional level, like water or air pollution, especially in the framework of regional strategies. Others, such as the greenhouse effect, rising sea levels, or the development of a system of tsunami and earthquake monitoring and prediction, are mostly beyond regional authorities, requiring national and global attention. There are some global challenges that cannot be solved with the technology of the twentieth century; however, they can at least be anticipated and their consequences should be strategized. For example, experts can forecast which parts of the world will be affected most adversely by rising sea levels. Such issues should be taken care of by national and regional strategies and should be reflected in the strategic considerations of multinational corporations. If possible, companies should adjust their strategies to allocate production facilities and strategic investments to areas that will experience less damage. This is especially related to the health care industries, the production of first-necessity goods, and the preservation of important artefacts and information.

The global workplace has been experiencing growing damage from natural disasters. According to the Johannesburg Declaration on Sustainable Development, "natural disasters are more frequent and more devastating."[67] Furthermore, "the Munich Re Foundation, part of one of the world's leading re-insurance companies, estimated that 2005 had witnessed the largest financial losses ever as a result of weather-related natural disasters, at more than $200 billion."[68] The economic impact of Hurricane Sandy in October 2012 in travel and tourism in one state—New Jersey—was estimated as a $950 million loss in 2013, led to the reduction of total state output by $1.2 billion in the third quarter of 2013 alone, and reduced employment by over 11,000 workers.[69] Construction costs totaled $29.5 billion in repairing and replacing damage. In New York State, construction costs was estimated at $41.9 billion.[70] Managers and executives responsible for corporate operations have a tendency to ignore these potential catastrophes. From a strategic point of view, the correct forecast-following strategy and long-term strategic plan, which inevitably evaluates the influence of natural disasters, not only brings strategic competitive advantages to a corporation, but in some cases can also lead to the protection of human life. This is why an evaluation of the systematic risk of natural disasters is of great strategic importance. Some corporations can be established only for the purpose of operating in times of ecological catastrophes to provide people with assistance, including goods of first necessity, medical supplies, and shelter. Many corporations develop a force majeure strategy for such disasters only as part of the worst-case scenarios of the exit strategy.

Unsystematic Strategic Risk of Investment

Unsystematic Factors of Strategic Economic Risk

Some factors of strategic economic risk of direct investment belong to the category of unsystematic, company-specific risk. These factors are mostly related to the scale and conditions of the economic factors of the external corporate environment. According to a study by Professor Michael R. Walls, of the Colorado School of Mines:

> intuitively one might argue that the degree of risk aversion decreases as wealth increases or, alternatively, the degree of risk tolerance increases with wealth. As we accumulate more and more wealth our willingness to take financial risk, on an absolute basis, increases. Similarly, as the firm grows and accumulates wealth its ability to take on larger, more risky projects also grows.[71]

This basic correlation is supported by studies of several other authors. At the same time, smaller companies, in order to maintain competitiveness, can pursue a more aggressive strategy and be successful, despite a higher ratio of strategic risk to resources. The conclusion of Dr. Walls's study does not contradict this idea. Companies that "reveal a relatively high risk propensity, compared to their competitors, generate significantly higher asset returns."[72] This is a simple example of an unsystematic factor of strategic economic risk of investment.

Another factor of strategic economic risk that can be partially unsystematic and somewhat manageable is the level of competition. In less familiar emerging market countries, companies from the developed world experience specific difficulties in gaining and maintaining market share when confronted by both foreign and domestic competition. The smaller the scale of a region related to the influence of the company's competition, the more this factor is manageable. The lower the intensity of competition, the larger the territory in which competition risk can be adjusted by the company's strategic risk management system. When there are only a few competitors in a market, the economic risk of competition can be managed.

The use of basic economic factors within a corporation is also related to unsystematic strategic economic risk. An obvious example of this is the use of labor resources. Multinational corporations from developed countries are under much less government regulation and oversight in EMCs than in their native countries. Many exploit this to underreport work-related accidents and deaths. In the case of international joint ventures, some corporations delegate responsibility to foreign investors to avoid reporting deaths and accidents. British Petroleum plc did not report the deaths of about 14 people that occurred at the facilities of one of its Russian joint ventures in 2006, despite the fact that it owned 50 percent of the assets. This reflects a lack of respect for human life and projects a terrible image of the company to the public. In order to get an idea of a country's labor regulations, strategists should consult the Index of Economic Security developed by the International Labour Organization. This index is an evaluation of income and representation security, labor market, employment, and job security, and work and skill reproduction security.[73] These major categories are a summary of more specific indicators of strategizing, like incidences of job-related deaths, accidents, sicknesses, etc., which present the characteristics of risk of the use of a country's labor resources. This risk is generally manageable and is another example of an unsystematic factor of economic risk.

INDUSTRIAL INFRASTRUCTURE IN EMCS

Increased competition for FDI has led the governments of EMCs to realize the importance of industrial infrastructure, such as transportation, energy, and telecommunications networks, in attracting foreign investors. The improvement of industrial infrastructure is particularly challenging in large EMCs. Beyond its strategic importance for attracting FDI, the development of infrastructure is extremely beneficial to the hundreds of millions of people who do not live in capital or major regional cities. Poor infrastructure is one of the causes of both the disparities of economic development within EMCs and the tendency of certain regions to be more closely integrated with foreign economies than with other domestic regions within their own borders. In the GMP, international transportation traffic is growing at a faster rate than domestic transportation traffic. The dynamics of this trend indicate that it will continue to grow due to the higher level of integration of EMCs with developed countries in the global marketplace than among themselves in the GEM. In some European EMCs, certain regions will have closer ties with foreign developed countries than with other regions within their own national borders. Attempts to rectify this disparity create a substantial demand for companies that can develop infrastructure, especially high-tech and telecommunication. These companies are usually from the developed world. Most of the expected growth in demand will be for road transportation. By 2025 the world's motor vehicle fleet is expected to be well over 1 billion. The further development of the GEM will intensify this trend due to the poor air-transportation infrastructure in most EMCs. However, aircraft transportation of cargo and people will increase at a higher rate in the more developed EMCs.

The level of development of the transportation sector of the GEM can be seen as both a systematic and an unsystematic strategic risk factor. In general, companies are able to strategize and manage risks related to these factors. They can do so by the strategic allocation of production facilities near existing transportation infrastructure and the development of relationships—including acquisitions—with shipping and delivery companies. Companies from developed countries operating in the GEM have the option of strategy—wisely using existing transportation networks or investing in their own private ones. Strategists also have to balance the tradeoffs between speed and cost. Air delivery is fastest and most expensive, while delivery by sea is the slowest and cheapest. This tradeoff is not only determined by how best to serve consumers and clients. Reducing inventory costs and getting operational capital back often has the most strategic importance. Cargo stuck on a ship is money that a company cannot use as operational capital. Another strategic advantage of air transportation is that it avoids many legal and logistical issues related to ground and sea delivery. For this reason, charter aircraft services have been growing at an exponential rate. Negotiating charter party contracts has become a key service offered by law firms to companies operating in the GEM. In the end, cost advantage is often the most important strategic factor in determining what method of delivery to use.

Products are packaged very differently in the GEM than in developed countries. In developed countries, low cost and waste reduction are key. These issues are of very little importance in the GEM; the most relevant issue there is how well the product is protected. The delivery process is much rougher due to the extreme conditions of many EMCs and the carelessness of package handlers in the GEM. It is also important that instructions be written not only in the language of the country of origin of the product, but also in that of the destination country. Companies should not assume that package handlers in foreign countries will be fluent readers of the company's language, even if it is English. This is especially important for hazardous materials. The relatively common practice of putting advertising on cargo is not a good idea for products going to the GEM, as it will confuse the handlers.

Practically all telecom companies from developed countries are strategizing to capture market share in the GEM, as traditional domestic markets have much lower growth rates, especially in the mobile phone market. Telecommunication infrastructure should be strategized first and foremost in terms of technological development of the environment for FDI (which is why it is evaluated later in this chapter in the section on technological risk of investment). When strategists analyze potential locations, the quality and availability of telecommunication and transportation infrastructure is a top priority.

In developing and pre-emerging market countries, a weak national industrial strategy is a major obstacle for attracting strategic FDI. National governments of these countries have not made the initial investment to make attractive infrastructural conditions for strategic FDI. These issues should also be the focus of multilateral, regional international institutions like the European Bank for Reconstruction and Development, Inter-American Bank, etc.

Strategic Business Risk of Investment

Strategic business risk of FDI is the core of unsystematic risk of strategic investment. This type of risk is typically related to corporate operational activity. Strategists have to analyze and strategize business risk in terms of the prevention and minimization of production risk as well as commercial and financial risk, especially during entry-strategy implementation. Strategic business risk is usually divided into two strategizing categories: *product risk* and *financial risk*. A more accurate name for product risk is *production risk*, because it is related to processes of strategic preparation of production, production itself, the results of these processes—products, goods, and services—and their commercialization through distribution, sales, and post-sales warranties. Among the strategic indicators of production risk are the availability of the necessary resources, product-design issues, and the possibility of injury during the production and usage of the product. Potential technological achievements that would make a company's product obsolete are also among the major dimensions of production risk. Strategic production risk covers the availability and quality of supply (raw materials, parts, energy, etc.)—*raw-material/parts risk*—and the availability, quality, and motivation of labor resources—*human resource risk*. If the company that is analyzing production risk is in the financial services industry, its financial/credit risk is its production strategic risk. The stability of production processes and the required efficiency and production cost control are aspects of *operational risk*. The quality of a company's products, the products' life after sales, and the competitiveness of products on the marketplace are usually covered by product risk. Strategic factors in the product-risk subcategory also include regulatory and even legal risk. However, the logic behind such an inclusion is flawed, as these things are mostly systematic risks, due to the fact that changes in law and regulation are functions exclusively of national government and regional authorities. Processes of sales of final products and post-sales services are usually covered by *commercial risk*. All of these types of risk are aspects of production risk. Some textbooks and source books use the umbrella term "product risk" to refer to all of these risks. In this case, product risk has two meanings—specifically related to products and to all processes of production and commercialization, which is why this book uses the term "production risk."

The other category of business risk—financial risk—is related to all facets of a company's borrowing, usage, and repayment of credit as well as the use of profit. Financial risk is usually divided into four basic categories: *financial instrument risk*, *credit risk*, *operational risk,* and *market risk*. Strategic risk analysis of all of these categories is typically done by an evaluation of the following strategic indicators of financial risk:

- Settlement risk
- Interest rate risk
- Contingent risk
- Direct risk
- Title risk
- Fraud risk
- Relations with the London Club
- Equity risk
- Volatility risk
- Spread risk
- Currency risk
- Derivative risk
- Liquidity risk
- Transactions risk
- Communications risk
- Commodity risk.

In financial institutions and even in industrial companies, strategists together with financial professionals develop strategies to reduce financial risk according to all or some of the above listed indicators, depending on the specific industry and practice of the firm or corporation. The development of a strategy according to these indicators makes it possible to strategically position a company on the market and/or avoid losses by monitoring the market. In other words, such indicators are useful for strategic risk management.

Risk is involved in every strategic decision. Losses related to risk are an inevitable possibility in the GEM, but a carefully crafted strategy brings success. In the words of Jack Welch, "if GE's strategy of investment in China is wrong, it represents a loss of a billion dollars, perhaps a couple of billion dollars. If it is right, it is the future of this company for the next century."[74]

In order to minimize and monitor strategic financial risk in international transactions, several multinational governmental and non-governmental institutions were established beginning in the 1970s. One of the first of these institutions was the Basel Committee on Banking Supervision, which is made up of representatives of developed countries and one formal participant from the GEM—Spain. The enlargement, speed, and frequency of FDI to the GEM now require the same type of authorities to monitor FDI inflows and outflows specifically related to the GEM.

International Business Infrastructure in Emerging Market Countries

What does a company need to be strategically successful or even to operate in a foreign country? From a practical point of view, first of all a company needs to be able to open an account in a reliable commercial bank. Typically, financial executives and entrepreneurs prefer to open accounts in the same banks with which they are accustomed to working in their country of origin. So the presence of subsidiaries and branches of international banks—or at the very least their joint ventures with domestic banks of EMC—is very important. The absence of such banks is an immediate red flag and an indication of a potentially high business risk of investment. In order to obtain capital to finance an investment in a foreign country, companies work with investment banks. The company's relationship with the investment institution will be much better if this institution also has a presence in the country receiving FDI. As mentioned earlier in this chapter, investment institutions will usually insist that any project that they finance in the GEM be insured against political risk—the process of acquiring such insurance is much easier when insurance companies have a presence in the potential recipient country. The same applies to the presence of auditing and accounting firms, especially the Big Four. During strategy implementation, a company engaging in a strategic FDI will be much more confident if it can get counsel from well-known international law firms that have an established branch in the FDI destination. From this perspective, an evaluation of strategic business risk can be done through strategizing of the international business infrastructure of an EMC in the following order:

- Commercial banks
- Investment banks
- Insurers and reinsurers
- Auditing and accounting firms
- Law firms.

For companies with a strategic approach related to public markets of EMCs, the presence of domestic and international capital market infrastructure is vitally important. These companies should evaluate strategic business risk in terms of the existence of the following institutions:

- Stock exchanges
- Currency exchanges
- Trust services
- Trading and brokerage houses
- Settlement organizations
- Custodians
- Clearinghouses.

The presence of these institutions not only attracts strategic FDI, but it also brings a certain level of stability to capital markets of EMCs, as well as to society in general.

Development of Banking Systems in the Financial Conditions of the GEM

CORRELATION BETWEEN CURRENCY EMISSIONS, INFLATION, AND THE DEVELOPMENT OF CONSUMER MARKETS

The development of business and capital market infrastructure both requires and facilitates strategic financial stability in EMCs. In order to be considered an emerging market, a country must have already established a single institution of currency emission, typically a central bank. It is extremely important for the establishment of financial stability and the improvement of a country's standard of living to have a reliable institution to manage the monetary supply and inflation. Figure 9.8 demonstrates that three of the four biggest EMCs—Brazil, Russia, India, and China—the so-called BRIC—have established reliable patterns in the emissions of national currencies. Russia has a less stable domestic monetary policy than India, China, and Brazil. Unfortunately for Russia's people and domestic and foreign investors, the high growth of currency emissions has had political motivations. During parliamentary or presidential election years, Russian authorities usually increase currency emission by as much as 43 percent.

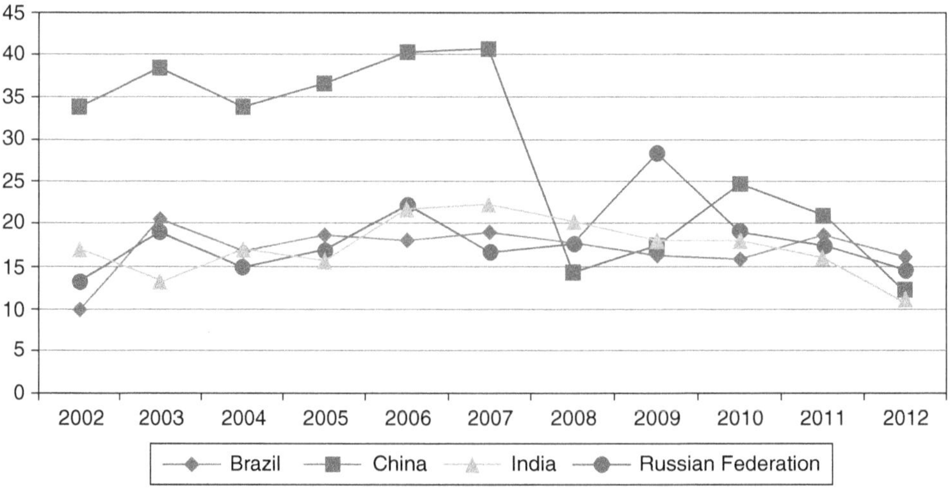

Figure 9.8 M2 Growth Rate in Brazil, China, India, and Russia, 2002–2012

Based on data from the World Bank World Development Indicators. (n.d.). "Money and Quasi Money Growth (Annual %)." Retrieved from http://data.worldbank.org/indicator/FM.LBL.MQMY.ZG/

Several EMCs (as well as some well-developed countries like Norway), mostly producers of natural resources in high demand—oil, natural gas, non-ferrous metals, etc.—have gained tremendous wealth. In order to prevent high inflation, the authorities of these countries created various wealth funds. By investing natural resource–generated revenue into these funds, it is removed from general circulation. However, on the other hand, the quality of life and all kinds of freedoms in these countries are typically far below that of the developed world. By not investing this revenue in service industries like health care, education, and the development of social and industrial infrastructure, they are preventing the use of surplus capital for the improvement of the standard of living of their citizens. This is an inefficient money-management strategy. Among the 14 largest of these funds in the world, 8 were established in emerging markets (Botswana, China, Russia, Saudi Arabia, Chile, South Korea, United Arab Emirates, and Singapore).[75] Strategists should monitor the activity of these funds. Sooner, rather than later, the money in these funds will be available to purchase foreign goods like pharmaceuticals, medical or technological equipment. Transactions such as these do not lead to inflation and increase the quality of life.

A long-term strategy is crucial to successful investment abroad. It is also important to strategize quickening financial and monetary tendencies, especially in EMCs. Local financial and strategic monetary conditions have an important impact on production costs of FDI-based strategic projects. Inflation can severely increase production costs by reducing the purchasing power of the domestic currency. Inflation is essentially excess currency relative to the amount of goods and services produced domestically and imported from abroad. When a central bank emits too much currency (and disproportionate to volume of production and purchasing power of people), the purchasing capacity of the currency—and of the general population—is reduced. This leads not just to tactical consequences but strategic ones. Extra currency creates an excess of demand over supply—a deficit—for certain goods or services, causing prices to rise. While this situation is clearly harmful to the economy as a whole, it can create opportunities for investors if their facilities produce, or are capable of producing, the goods that are in deficit. However, investors that are not capable of producing these goods suffer as a result of rising labor costs. In some cases, production may substantially decrease or freeze as a result of increased costs and a decline in the purchasing power of the general population, which then multiplies by inflation, and in a worst case scenario by stagflation. These incommensurable results of initial economic problems are due to a lack of strategy.

This is why for generations of entrepreneurs, inflation and cost concerns were focused on the specific location of their productive facilities. The integration of markets that were once separated by national borders and different historical and cultural traditions into a single GMP has multiplied the difficulty of anticipating events that trigger inflation with following requirements of strategy adjustment. In the GMP, a shortage of goods caused by natural (a drought, for example) or technogenic (destruction of production facilities) catastrophes in a key country can affect prices throughout the world. Rapid economic growth, increasing standards of living, and an expanding appetite for energy and other raw materials in the GEM has the potential to become a source of global inflation. The strategically uneven economic development in some of the emerging giants, such as India, China, Russia, Egypt, and Ukraine, can actually be harmful to themselves, the GEM, and the GMP.

Unfortunately, governments, especially those of EMCs, do not always fully understand inflation and stagflation. Many governments blame economic and financial instability on globalization and foreign speculators rather than taking responsibility for their own errors, inexperience, and lack of strategy. From the fall of 2007 to 2009, increasing standards of living and unfettered emission of currency in several EMCs caused food prices to rise. A few EMCs that had well-thought-out strategies and national reserves were able to use the proper financial and economic mechanisms to prevent inflation within their borders. Many of the governments that lacked a strategy and the necessary reserves were incapable of doing so, and blamed globalization. Global inflation was 3.7 percent in 2007, which is not very high. In the US, it was even lower at 2.7 percent. However, in some EMCs, inflation was between 11 and 12 percent. Inflation was as much as six to seven times higher than the global rate in parts of the GEM. A well-crafted strategy would have anticipated and reduced the impact of global inflationary pressures.

The governments of many EMCs wrongly blamed their domestic financial problems on China and India, despite the fact that the rate of inflation in these two countries was roughly 4 and 7.5 percent, respectively. The example of the government of the Russian Federation's lack of financial strategy (which is in the best case a matter of tactics) is indicative of the situation in many EMCs. From 2000 to 2006, the Russian consumer price index (CPI), an indicator of inflation, increased by 119 percent, while that of the world, the US, and the EU increased by 21 percent, 17 percent, and 15 percent, respectively. From 2008 to 2013, the same indicators differentiated even faster: CPI of Russia increased by another 65.6 percent, while the world index increased by 29.7 percent, and the indices of the EU and the US increased by only 15.1 percent and 12.4 percent respectively. In the GMP all governments experience influences of the same general financial trends. What differs substantially is the sophistication of the strategies that they use to deal with these trends, which is reflected in the CPI data. Very often, a rise in the prices of certain types of goods can trigger global inflationary pressures. For example, in 2007, the increasing purchasing power of consumers in the GEM led to rising prices for food, a significant inflationary pressure. In China the average price of eggs increased by 20 percent, vegetables by 23 percent, and all other food products by 18.5 percent.

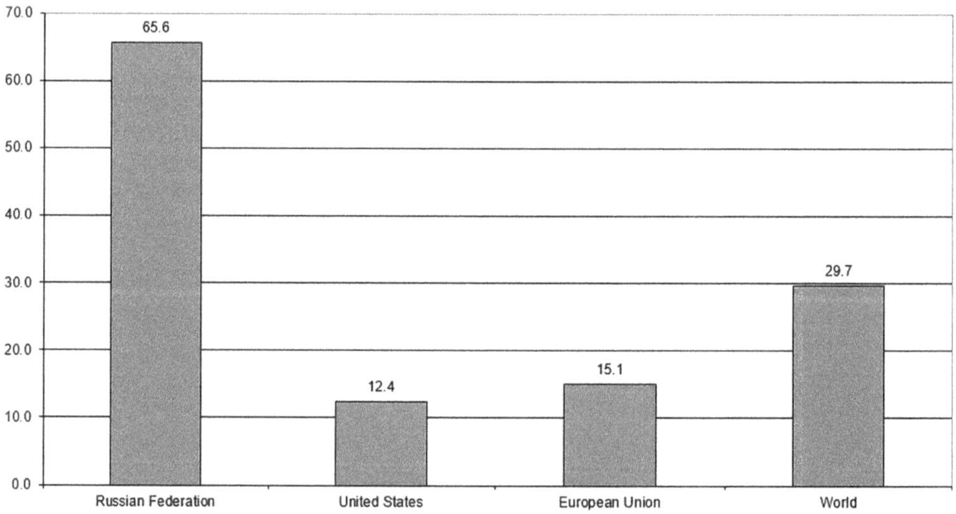

Figure 9.9 Consumer Price Index in Russia, the US, the EU, and the World, Percentage Increase from 2008–2013

Based on data from the World Bank World Development Indicators. Retrieved from http://data.worldbank.org/indicator/FP.CPI.TOTL.ZG

This caused increases in food prices in Japan, India, and even in countries as far away as Chile, which experienced a 15 percent increase in food prices.[76] However, the governments of many other EMCs found mechanisms to keep general inflation under control. It is important for investors to understand the financial strategies (or lack thereof) of national, regional, and local governments of the territories in which they make investments.

Many EMCs were unable to control inflation due to their reliance on imported food. For example, according to the Russian Central Statistical Agency, as of 2014, 41 percent of the Russian daily diet is imported despite the fact that 10 percent of its labor force is employed in the agricultural sector (which produces only 4.1 percent of GDP).[77] In 2013, the same indicator was 36 percent, a proof of Russia's inability to substantially increase domestic production of food.[78] By comparison, only a little over 3 percent of the labor force of the US and the EU is employed in the agricultural sector. Historically, a substantial amount of agricultural goods are imported from developed countries to EMCs despite the fact that far more people in EMCs are engaged in agricultural activity. This is the result of several factors. As previously discussed, private initiative still suffers from the legacy of command management systems, which did not offer normal economic incentives. This is especially the case in the agricultural sector, substantially reducing productivity. Another factor is the superior technology and know-how in developed countries, such as modern agricultural and food-processing machinery, fertilizers, and genetically enhanced livestock. As a result of the lack of advanced farming technology and techniques in much of the GEM, many farmers and entrepreneurs are beginning to take advantage of the very lucrative opportunities for FDI in agriculture in EMCs. Furthermore, many local, regional, and national governments in the GEM have set up incentives to reinvigorate rural areas, which can provide financial support for entrepreneurs and investors from developed countries. FDI from developed countries is bringing sophisticated farming methods, technology, and badly needed capital, rebuilding many villages that were once abandoned. It is not uncommon for farmers to import cows or sheep from Australia, Holland, or the US to improve the productivity of their livestock. In addition, a lack of suitable transportation and telecommunication infrastructure further inhibits productivity. This makes it very difficult for farmers to deliver their goods to major urban markets; a lack of fuel for trucks and cars exacerbates the lack of infrastructure. This issue can be resolved by the production of ethanol, butanol, and other biofuels from agricultural waste and timber byproducts. Unfortunately, the taxation systems of many EMCs essentially prevent the development of these industries. The situation is of course the complete opposite in developed countries, where ethanol production is heavily subsidized. The governments of some EMCs, such as China, India, Kazakhstan, and Spain, have already established national strategic programs to support domestic ethanol production and decrease the dependence of private agriculture and rural areas on the centralized fuel supply. The absolute world leader in ethanol production is Brazil. A substantial part of Brazil's agricultural sector is driven by government initiatives for the production and distribution of ethanol, which removed Brazil from the list of oil-importing countries.

Most EMC governments do not have a strategy to replace imported food with domestic agricultural production and have not been able to motivate domestic producers. Nonetheless, the role of the GEM in the agricultural sector is increasing in the world.[79] In some cases, food crises and inflation can be the result of excessive food exports to developed countries. This was the case with vegetable-oil products and fish products in 2007. Sometimes a local food crisis can be the result of improvements in standards of living. As people become more prosperous, they tend to become more health conscious. Many consumers in EMCs have become aware of the health risks related to trans and saturated fats and have begun to use vegetable oil instead. Some EMC governments have even gone as far as to enact restrictions on trans fat. As a result, the export of vegetable oils and high-quality butter has decreased from many EMCs due to rising domestic consumption.

Agricultural sectors of EMCs still need time to be ready to compete in terms of price and cost production with products from developed countries. This is a major issue of discussion of the Doha Development Agenda of the World Trade Organization. Underdeveloped, developing, and emerging market countries have to temporarily implement a certain amount of protectionist instruments to prevent foreign dominance of their agricultural markets. They need time for domestic agricultural and food-processing companies to stand on their own legs. In the Doha negotiations, western countries, especially the US and member-states of the EU, pushed EMCs to lower import tariffs and quotas by as much as 90 percent in some cases. Leaders of developed countries are afraid to lose their customers, not only in big EMCs like India, China, or Russia, but even in small ones. For this reason, the Doha round of negotiations has been contentious.[80] In most EU countries, subsidies per one cow can reach about 2,000 euros annually, which is several times more than the GDP per head of some countries.

All of the above-mentioned challenges to domestic agricultural production in the GEM have the potential to be multiplied by an unsophisticated monetary strategy. Populist tendencies of national governments are a major cause of inflationary pressures and of financial and production risk for foreign investors. It is not uncommon in the GEM for governments to emit excess currency near parliamentary or presidential elections. Following up on promises to increase salaries and wages (with obvious implications for FDI), pension contributions and military and student stipends can increase the amount of money in circulation at a much faster pace than the rate of food production and first-necessity goods. That is why food shortages are more likely to occur during or immediately following election years in many EMCs. The increases in government expenditures actually end up decreasing people's real purchasing power, as it increases the amount of currency in circulation without increasing the amount of goods and services available, inevitably causing prices to rise. The balance between these two factors is basically what determines the amount of inflation. Governments can prevent and reduce inflation by strategically slowing the currency printing presses and reducing the rise of salaries and wages, significantly reducing the risks for foreign investors. This issue is definitely strategically important for foreign investors in EMCs.

Corporate strategists also have to be aware of the fact that in EMCs with more sophisticated financial systems, inflationary pressures can come from other sources. In order to attract FDI inflows and make their domestic currency more appealing to investors, EMC governments often attempt to make their currency freely convertible as soon as possible. The pursuit of a freely convertible currency often motivates governments with otherwise stable financial and monetary policies to print extra currency notes in order to make them available for foreign currency speculators. If more notes are printed than demanded by the foreign currency markets, the country will have a surplus of currency notes relative to the volume of domestic consumer goods. This causes a decrease in the purchasing power of the domestic currency—the opposite of the desired goal of making the currency freely convertible. This phenomenon played a role in the Asian financial crisis of 1997 and in inflation in Russia in the fall of 2007. In both cases, foreign investors saw their profits decrease as a result. This situation requires governmental intervention in order to create a balance between the money in circulation and the goods and services available. Many instruments used to achieve this balance are not restrictive. Subsidies can create incentives to increase production of certain items like food and first-necessity goods. National government can also increase reserves of these goods, which can be supplied to the poor during times of high inflation. Strategists of foreign companies operating in these markets should take into consideration the fact that, depending on the specific situation, EMC governments may increase or decrease import quotas.

Usually, inflation in the GEM is most harmful to the middle class and poorest parts of society. The prices of first-necessity goods, food, and low-quality products tend to rise at a much higher rate—up to three times faster—than the prices of luxury and high-quality goods. If these prices increase by more than 1 percent per month over several months, the likelihood of galloping inflation is very high. Wise investors pay very close attention to these prices in order to prevent skyrocketing prices and to be prepared to produce goods that are suddenly in higher demand, especially investors that produce agricultural and consumer goods.

Strategists, who often try to use their experience in developed countries when entering the GEM, should keep in mind that the dynamics of prices in developed countries are very different. During times of financial instability, the larger and much wealthier middle and upper classes in developed countries immediately invest in gold and luxury goods. As a result, the prices for these products rise at a much faster pace than the prices of first-necessity goods. This is a major difference between the economic and financial systems of developed countries and the GEM. Regardless, in all types of economies, the government shoulders the responsibility of preventing inflation. Everyone—domestic entrepreneurs, government officials, foreign investors, etc.—should be aware of changes in prices, as they are the most sensitive and painful receptor of an economy.

BANKS AND THE CASH ECONOMY

Without the presence of commercial and investment banks in a country, companies will be hesitant to make an investment. Beginning at the end of the 1980s, internationally recognized banking institutions like Citigroup, Chase Manhattan, HSBC, Barings (acquired by ING in 1995), Merrill Lynch, and Credit Suisse First Boston established their presence throughout the GEM, initially by opening representative offices. Later operational subsidiaries and branches were established, which at first served only foreigners, though they eventually obtained the necessary licenses to provide full service for locals as well. Demand from clients in developed countries to invest in EMCs, combined with EMCs' financial deregulation, growing stability, and increasing economic freedom, were the main factors in the spread of internationally recognized banks in the GEM. *Global Finance* was one of the first publications to realize the importance of the banking sector in the GEM. Since 1994 it has published its annual list of "the Best Emerging Market Banks in the World." Citigroup has occupied the number one spot on this list for many years, a result of its activity in Latin America, Central Europe, and, more recently, Russia, where it is the leading bank. In central Moscow, Citigroup's branches are almost as prevalent as they are in New York City. However, Citigroup's branches abroad do not offer the same services in the GEM. Many branches will work only with businesses or foreigners, and there are often restrictions on transferring money from EMCs. In Moscow, for example, US citizens have different rights from Russian citizens when it comes to transferring money abroad. However, even for US citizens, transferring money abroad is difficult and highly restricted, requiring numerous official documents. ING Barings has been the leading bank in Europe and has also had tremendous success in Africa and the Middle East. *Global Finance* was also one of the first publications to rank the best domestic banks of EMCs.

Foreign companies that choose to work with domestic banks instead of internationally recognized banks, perhaps for cheaper services, should be very cautious. Even the leading domestic banks of the GEM are much more vulnerable to failure than internationally recognized banks and have much smaller amounts of governmentally protected money in the accounts of companies and individuals. Peregrine Bank, once considered the best domestic bank in Asia, impressed several leading international banks when its Hong Kong book of some 45 million shares set a record for oversubscription. Less than a year later, the Peregrine Bank collapsed from the aftermath of the Asian financial crisis in 1997. Foreign banks from developed countries tend to specialize strategically in particular services in the GEM. The risk of specialization is that a crisis in the area of activity can lead to the loss of hundreds of millions of dollars. Focusing on bond trading in Russia caused Credit Suisse First Boston to lose hundreds of millions when the Russian ruble collapsed in 1998. Merrill Lynch and ING, which specialize in several different services in several different regions, profited from a safer strategy. Merrill Lynch equity research activity is concentrated mostly in the Middle East, its debt origination is mostly in Asia, and debt research mostly in Latin America. ING Barings is well known for its corporate finance in Europe, its equity research in Africa and Latin America, and equity sales and trading in Asia. Strategists of international investment banks from developed countries tend to shift banking activity from EMC to EMC, in search of potentially higher profits. Merrill Lynch's $4.5 billion Emerging Europe fund, managed by Alain Bourrier, increased its profits by more than 79 percent by relocating from Poland and Hungary to Russia. It was ranked "no. 1 over the past 12 months [as of March 2006] among 1,000 funds that invest in European stocks and are tracked by Bloomberg with a growth rate over 300 percent from 2003 to 2006."[81]

The transition from command economies to free markets typically starts with the development of free-market institutions to serve growing private businesses and individual customers. During dictatorships, all banking institutions were not only under complete control of the government, but also were owned by the government. There were no privacy laws, and as a result when private companies first began to appear and operate, they were forced to open accounts only in state-owned banks. At that time, it was one of the causes of the rapid development of gray economies in the GEM. Many companies preferred to operate under the state's radar and obviously did not open accounts in state-owned banks. As a result, in the initial stages of a private sector's development, it is typical in EMCs for a substantial part of the economy to be cash based. Companies are usually not officially registered yet, and officially do not have any employees. They pay their unofficial employees in cash, buy raw materials and parts with cash, and even pay the rent for their office and commercial space in cash. Because these companies are not registered and their employees are off the books, the overwhelming majority of their activity is not reported to governments and municipal offices. Subsequently, many companies and their employees do not pay taxes. The accelerating development of the cash economy results in EMCs with huge budget deficits and high unemployment statistics. A substantial part of this unemployment consists of people who work but do not pay taxes, do not even have taxpayer IDs, and are not included in official statistics.

The strategic response to these issues by governments of EMCs usually begins with motivating the development of private commercial banks. If governments of the GEM have a strategic vision for this process, typically at the initial stages they try to protect local financial markets from immediate participation of foreign commercial banks and branches and subsidiaries of international banks, or they limit the licenses granted to a few foreign banks. Otherwise, the small and underdeveloped local banking sector, with a tiny level of capitalization in inexperienced domestic banks, will be totally overwhelmed by foreign banks. Strategists of foreign banks who are interested in cooperating with domestic EMC banks have to be aware of the fact that, in most cases, it takes three to five years of preliminary activity of domestic commercial banks, bankers, executives, and managers to be ready to cooperate with foreign banking institutions. Foreign strategists should also anticipate the fact that domestic banks will be ready to compete with foreign banks within 10 to 15 years. The development of banking regulations, establishment of oversight committees and commissions, the reorientation of the central bank from command economy to a free-market system, and the development of all other banking institutions, such as collection and settlement agencies, brings the local financial market to the point at which private entrepreneurs and individuals start to transition from the gray sector to legitimacy. However, the dominance of the cash economy does not immediately end. During this period, EMCs lack a business culture that is accustomed to using checks to pay suppliers, employee wages, and acquire receivables. In most cases, prior to the widespread use of checks, countries develop interbank wire transactions, followed by the implementation of a debit card system. Companies open debit card accounts for their employees and transfer money through affiliated commercial banks to employees' individual accounts. Employees can then go to banks or cash machines and use their debit card to get cash or pay for goods or services. Lacking experience and faith in the protection of their money in banks, there are often long lines at cash machines, filled with people trying to withdraw their entire wages. Slowly, as they realize that money is not disappearing from their accounts, people leave some of their wages in the bank, and commercial banks have more operational capital. Somewhere during this process, companies, commercial banking institutions, and local populations become ready to develop credit systems. In EMCs, where people have no credit history and the overwhelming majority of them do not have bank accounts, this system develops slowly Strategists of banks that are planning or anticipating the implementation of a credit system should be aware that in many cases more than half of the population has zero savings. At this stage of development, many people begin to prepare to buy durable goods: TV sets, refrigerators, cars, apartments and homes. This is the beginning of the establishment of the middle class, which requires commercial banks to provide credit. The operational activity of several domestic and foreign commercial banks, and the competition between them for customers, finally creates the situation where banks are willing to issue credit. Executives of foreign banks responsible for credit policy have to be aware that, unfortunately, many inexperienced customers take out loans without fully comprehending the difficulty of making monthly payments. During these initial processes in EMCs, credit and mortgage-debt crises are not unusual. Civilian courts are often filled with cases of banks and mortgage institutions filing against their customers, leading to a huge growth in the demand for collection agencies. In most EMCs, the losing side pays all court expenses; the losing side is usually the customer. This is one of the major differences between people in debt in the developed world and in EMCs. As of December 2014, with an average GDP per head of about $54,678, the average US household credit card debt is $15,611.[82] Unlike in developed countries, in the GEM, the most common form of payment is still cash. Nevertheless, the acceptance and use of major credit cards, which first appeared at the end of the 1980s, is spreading rapidly. Initially, they were accepted only in hotels, a few restaurants, and department stores catering to foreigners. Eventually, international commercial banks began issuing credit cards to their most reliable clients in EMCs. Later, international joint ventures between domestic and foreign commercial banks began issuing credit cards, and finally, domestic commercial banks started to issue debit cards (linked to customers' bank accounts), with their own brand names.

Strategists and international credit risk agencies should also strategize financial stability in terms of financial relationships among EMCs. The more international financial transactions that an EMC has with other EMCs and the less with developed countries, the more vulnerable it is to the spread of financial instability from other parts of the GEM. One of the first evaluations of external vulnerability was created by Fitch Ratings in 2007.[83] Rating agencies should explore other methods of measuring external vulnerability and international credit risk. Foreign investors would benefit tremendously from more comprehensive strategic evaluations of these issues.

EMERGING CAPITAL MARKETS AND THE GLOBAL MONETARY SYSTEM

The global and regional trends of currency integration, which began in the European Union, are also underway in the GEM. However, unlike most EMCs, the countries that adopted the euro as an official currency in 2002 already had freely convertible currencies. There is a great deal of variation in the level of maturity and convertibility among currencies of the GEM. Some, like the Czech koruna, are already convertible, while others, like the Argentinean peso, used to be almost freely convertible and were pegged to the US dollar after successful economic restructuring. However, the financial crisis of 2001 ended the period of free convertibility in Argentina. Most EMCs have currencies of limited convertibility. In these countries the exchange rate between national and foreign currencies is established by central banks, not by the market; this is the case with the Russian ruble and the Chinese renminbi. Others, such as the Tunisian domestic dinar, are not convertible at all. Some countries restrict the amount of currency that can be converted by individuals or companies in a given period of time (like the Indian rupee); some restrict the type of currency for which it can be exchanged; and some use a combination of these factors. Many regional blocs of EMCs, such as Mercosur, are trying to increase convertibility among their various currencies. Some European countries that are not members of the EU unilaterally replaced their national currency with the euro. This was the path that Montenegro chose upon achieving its independence. In order to officially adopt the euro and join the Economic and Monetary Union of the EU, a country must give control of currency circulation and interest rates to the European Central Bank, which the Slovak Republic chose to do in 2008. Over time, national central banks gradually regain the right to set interest rates. Strategists should anticipate that the majority of EMCs will have limitedly convertible currencies for the first quarter of the twenty-first century.

The introduction of the euro and its relative stability and increasing number of countries using it has destroyed the dollar's monopoly as the world's banking and reserve currency. As a result, a substantial portion of national reserves that were once in the form of US dollars in central and private banks in EMCs have been diversified into euros, pounds sterling, and Swiss francs. Typically, this substitution is done in proportion to the foreign trade balance of an EMC. Companies from EMCs make profits in their own national currencies. In order to realize their profit in dollars, they have to purchase dollars from banks. Later, when they buy any raw materials, parts, or equipment, or when distribution networks buy consumer-goods products from companies in the 19 countries of the Eurozone, for example, they have to exchange their dollars for euros. Through these currency transactions, companies lose a substantial part of their profits. For this reason, banks and multinational corporations started to diversify their foreign currency reserves, holding euros, pounds, and—for some companies that are active in the GEM—Chinese renminbi or Russian rubles, in addition to US dollars. Under the influence of this trend, during the first decade of the twenty-first century, the dollar slowly depreciated compared with the euro and especially the pound.

The health of the dollar is actually very important for the overwhelming majority of EMCs, and especially for those that rely heavily on the export of raw materials, like oil, natural gas, precious metals, or iron ore, as global commodity markets typically operate in dollars. Furthermore, the reserve funds of countries like China, Russia, South Korea, Saudi Arabia, etc. are primarily held—at least 30 to 60 percent—in dollars. The slow decline of the dollar is manageable for such funds, but the failure of the dollar altogether is not in the strategic interest of these countries. The relationship of natural-resource-exporting countries with the value of the dollar is quite complex. For example, rising oil, gold, and other precious metal prices, as well as those of all other commodities, increase their export revenues. In response, the national financial strategies of EMCs such as Saudi Arabia, Russia, South Africa, Brazil, etc., have become very sophisticated since the beginning of the twenty-first century.

In the same way that EMCs are calling for increased representation in the multilateral institutions of the global business order, they are also asserting themselves in the global monetary system. Decreasing foreign demand for US dollars will eventually reduce foreign interest in US fixed-income securities. Among foreign buyers of US treasury debt and US fixed-income securities there are many EMCs, which was not the case in the twentieth century. While, in terms of political influence, new poles are appearing primarily in the GEM, in the global monetary system, new poles are coming from developed countries of Western Europe. The financial strategies of companies in the GEM have to be more sophisticated to deal with the increasing complexity of the global monetary system. Many companies lost tremendous amounts of money due to overinvestment in telecom and Internet sectors at the turn of the twenty-first century. As a result, capital retreated to the safer waters of its country of origin. However, increased liquidity, as well as an inverted yield curve, have resulted in many companies and banks reorienting themselves toward the riskier and more profitable markets of EMCs. From 2003 to 2004 there was a huge wave of FDI inflow into the GEM. Some of this was capital that fled the US after the tragedy of September 11, 2001. There are several similar strategic challenges of national capital markets in the GEM. As a first priority, national financial strategists of the GEM should consider the following seven steps:

1. Development of a law of protection of minority shareholders' rights
2. Enforcement of legal rights of minority shareholders
3. Improved access of medium-sized and small companies to capital market
4. Continuation of the increasing role of the public sector in the national capital markets
5. Prevention of central and regional governments from breaching contracts
6. Increasing level of convertibility of the national currency
7. World Trade Organization membership and improvement of capital control.

STRATEGIC ROLES OF CURRENCY RATES AND EXCHANGES

Many governments attempt to strengthen their currencies, without a strategic analysis of the implications for the general population and domestic business. The stronger the domestic currency, the more expensive it is for foreigners to buy domestic goods, which obviously has a negative effect on people employed in export-oriented industries. Export-oriented companies' sales will decline, bringing less profit, eventually lowering the wages of their employees. This also reduces profits after they are converted from dollars or euros back to the national currency, causing a reduction in tax revenues from profit taxes and value-added taxes. This decreases funding for state pension funds, health funds, etc. However, there is a benefit to a strong currency; assuming the government does not emit more currency, inflation will decrease. International banks are more likely to invest in a strong currency, and EMC governments, as mentioned earlier in this chapter, increase their money supply in an attempt to increase the convertibility of domestic currency. This makes it easier for foreign banks to buy the domestic currency, and ensures that there is enough currency in circulation to meet demand, preventing deflation. Strategists of foreign companies should anticipate that EMC governments usually increase the money supply by too much and cause inflation. It is important that a strong EMC currency has a strong backing, either in foreign currency or gold reserves. National strategists can also back a strong currency through a positive foreign trade balance. This ensures that there are more opportunities to develop domestic currency convertibility.

The positive impact of a strong currency on the general population is stability and reliability. People are more apt to invest and save domestic currencies, as opposed to hoarding dollars, pounds, euros, etc. Also, foreign goods are more affordable, which is great for consumers but may harm domestic producers. People living and traveling abroad enjoy benefits from a strong currency because it makes foreign currencies and services cheaper. Foreign and domestic investors in real estate profit from less expensive mortgages, which are a result of lower interest rates from the central bank for domestic commercial banks. Affordable mortgages are extremely important for the development of a property-owning middle class, which is what usually makes the transition from a centralized economy to a free-market economy irreversible. Property owners are typically very strong supporters and defenders of economic and political freedom.

The results of a strong currency are mixed in all countries. In the GEM, the positives outweigh the negatives, bringing increased stability, economic maturation, and eventually a fully convertible currency. Convertibility creates many opportunities for domestic markets, which become very attractive to foreign businesses and investors. It makes it much easier for foreign companies to operate, to make and receive international payments, and to repatriate profits.

The growing involvement of the GEM in the GMP required the development of new ways and means of converting profit made in inconvertible currencies. In the majority of countries this was created through the establishment of national and international currency exchanges as a legal entity. In many cases, at the beginning of these entities' operational activities, the government would sell a certain amount of freely convertible currency. Companies that bought seats at the currency exchange could buy the freely convertible currency through open biddings with currency of the country in which they made their profits. The need to have a standard means of evaluating different currencies led to the establishment of currency-risk ranking systems. One of these ranking systems is regularly published by the *Emerging Markets Monitor*, a publication of the Royal Bank of Canada (RBC) Financial Group.

In order to increase demand for their currencies and make them more stable and attractive to currency speculators, EMC governments use a number of strategies. Some EMCs, such as Taiwan, Hong Kong, and Russia, chose to hold a tremendous amount of foreign currency and gold reserves. An alternative strategy used by Argentina, Brazil, Chile, Thailand, and the Czech Republic, among others, is to allow their currency to float freely, with varying limitations. Some of these countries, such as Taiwan and South Korea, also use a hybrid strategy. Countries such as China, India, Singapore, Hungary, Russia, Poland, and Turkey manage the float of their currency within a certain range. Malaysia, as well as Hong Kong, peg their currency to a leading currency, such as the US dollar. Some countries replace their national currency completely with a leading foreign currency—El Salvador, Panama (mostly), and Ecuador with the US dollar, and Montenegro with the euro, as previously mentioned.

Portfolio Investment and Stock Exchanges

With the increasing presence of foreign and domestic investors in EMCs, in order to finance further development, the companies (and investors in the companies) began to look to public markets to raise capital through portfolio investment. They became especially motivated to be listed on foreign and domestic exchanges. In turn, the establishment of stock exchanges in EMCs and the appearance of stocks of GEM companies on foreign exchanges increased the interest of portfolio investors from the developed world in these companies. Portfolio investment primarily falls under the category of systematic risk, which cannot be fully avoided through strategies like diversification. For portfolio investors the world economy, or a particular national economy, represents the same unavoidable and unmanageable systematic risk. The economic and especially business nature of portfolio investment is different from that of direct investment. Foreign direct investment always requires investors to make a choice of where to invest—which country, region, etc.—because direct investment, by definition, needs the investor to play an influential or executive role. Individual portfolio investors, on the other hand, generally do not play a managerial role. It is not necessary for the portfolio investor to make a choice about the particular location of the company's facilities that their money may be financing.

The nature of corporate portfolio investment is also different from FDI. Corporate investors diversify risk by buying shares mostly of corporations with lower profitability from stable markets, making significantly less investments in companies from high-risk countries, such as those of the GEM. However, this is beginning to change. A few portfolio investment funds specialize in the GEM and even in particular EMCs, such as the Vietnam Opportunity Fund Ltd and the Templeton Russia & Eastern European Fund. These funds represent a trend, which first gained momentum in the middle of the 1990s, whereby portfolio managers from developed countries began to invest in companies from the GEM—primarily in economies in bloom and emerging market democracies. Dynamics of the global marketplace do not affect investments in the GEM in the same way that they affect those in developed countries. A slowing growth rate of the global marketplace could lead to more portfolio investment in the GEM from investors seeking higher returns. This can be a risky move for small portfolio investors. The Asian financial crisis (1997–2000) and the failure of the Russian ruble (1998) convinced many small investors to buy high-yielding Argentinean bonds. This proved to be a disastrous investment following the Argentinean debt default in December 2001.

When domestic investors from EMCs observed the considerable interest of individual investors and portfolio investment funds from developed countries in corporate shares of their countries, they started to compete with them. This process initiated the impetus to create stock exchanges in the GEM. In some EMCs, several exchanges were created. By the mid-1990s in Argentina, there were 17 stock exchanges, although the majority of all transactions were done at the Buenos Aires Stock Exchange. As of 2015, several stock exchanges operate in each of the following EMCs: Brazil, India, China, and Russia, among others. In countries of the Caribbean, like Barbados, and in the former communist states of Eastern Europe, stock exchanges appeared during the early stages of privatization. Newly privatized small and medium-size companies in these countries were in need of investment to renovate production facilities and equipment, and even for operational capital. The first private owners of these companies initiated the creation of stock exchanges with the hope of attracting investment from the public. Several of these new Eastern European stock exchanges were modeled after the Vienna Stock Exchange, which only operated half a day, two to three times a week. In many cases newly privatized GEM companies could not procure adequate capital to finance their development on domestic stock exchanges. At the end of the 1990s, but most heavily at the beginning of the twenty-first century, companies from the GEM attained widespread direct representation on the stock exchanges of developed countries. They enjoyed a great deal of interest from portfolio investors on the New York Stock Exchange, American Stock Exchange, NASDAQ, and even on the OTC Bulletin Board (OTCBB) (all of which are in New York City), as well as on the London and Frankfurt stock exchanges. Companies from Pacific Asia often preferred to be listed on the Hong Kong, Shanghai, or Singapore exchanges. These exchanges, despite the fact that they are located in the GEM, have a long and successful history. In some cases, GEM companies went to other emerging market exchanges like India's Bombay Stock Exchange, where the capitalization of companies is not large but there are a great deal of companies listed. As cross-border economic and financial activity continues to increase among EMCs, so too will occurrences of companies raising capital via stock exchanges in other foreign EMCs.

In order to be listed directly on any stock exchange, a company must prove that its accounting system is in compliance with international or US standards. The company must undergo evaluation by one of the Big Four auditing firms or one of their affiliates or subsidiaries for each of the three years prior to its IPO. The company must have no pending legal issues. Ideally, it should have an investment rating from all or several of the major rating agencies, like S&P, Moody's, Fitch Ratings, etc. In most cases, in order to be listed on the NYSE, a company will have to issue at least one million shares and demonstrate dynamics of increasing capitalization and profit over a sustained period. In the US, exchanges like the American Stock Exchange and regional trading floors like the Boston and Philadelphia stock exchanges, among others, are more suited for smaller companies. In terms of minimum number of shares, profitability, and history of success, the requirements for being listed on emerging market stock exchanges are generally much less strenuous than those of the developed world.

NASDAQ is well suited for companies from the GEM because it is capable of monitoring the GMP around the clock. When in 1997 a similar computer system was installed in the London Stock Exchange, NASDAQ, through a joint affiliation, became an international stock exchange. Its members can trade "over the counter" on both coasts of the Atlantic. NASDAQ was the first stock exchange to move toward the technological globalization of capital. By listing their shares on NASDAQ, companies from the GEM gain access to US and even European capital. The OTCBB is pretty similar to NASDAQ and works under its supervision. However, companies listed on the OTCBB have not met NASDAQ requirements in terms of size, capitalization, and profitability. The OTCBB is a good avenue for smaller companies from the GEM to access US capital, however, they cannot be listed on both the NASDAQ and the OTCBB at the same time. Companies from the GEM often experience difficulties when they temporarily transition from the NASDAQ, NYSE, or London Stock Exchange to the OTCBB while they improve their economic and financial indicators. If a company operating in any EMC declares bankruptcy, it cannot be listed on the OTCBB. Regardless of which stock exchange a company chooses, it has to be able to submit quarterly and annual reports to the US Securities and Exchange Commission or an equivalent organization of the country in which it is listed.

Prior to direct listings, GEM companies appeared on these exchanges via American depositary receipts (ADR) and global depositary receipts (GDR). Through these instruments, companies were not directly listed; investment banks from developed countries took responsibility for the shareholding GEM companies. The Bank of New York has a great deal of experience in this practice on the New York Stock Exchange and has represented several companies from the GEM. This allowed investors from the US and other developed countries to buy shares in GEM companies in a manner in which they were more comfortable and experienced.

Regardless, even when relatively big funds invest in a particular EMC by buying shares of companies, they generally do not participate in the management of these companies. Otherwise, their portfolio investment would qualify as a direct investment. There are several new global portfolio investors, like global mutual and equity funds, that allow investors to buy shares from companies throughout the world. According to Mike Thompson, a managing director of Thomson Reuters, "What's changed is the idea that you need to treat U.S. and foreign stocks as distinct assets. In a world where around 65 percent of McDonald's (MCD, Fortune 500) revenue comes from overseas and 35 percent of Toyota's (TM) sales are made in North America, what's the point?"[84] This attitude, however, does not apply to FDI, which always requires a country- and even region-specific analysis. For individuals who make a portfolio investment in McDonald's or Toyota, for example, the risk of investment is practically unchanged when one of these corporations expands its presence in the GEM. However, for the corporate leadership of Toyota or McDonald's, the development of their strategic presence in a new country and even the opening of new facilities in a country in which they already have a presence via direct investment is a serious strategic decision. For this reason, portfolio investment is not a focus of any chapter in this book. Furthermore, the analysis of systematic risk in this book primarily applies to country/region-specific strategic foreign direct investment risk.

The formation of capital markets and the increasing capitalization in EMCs, which occurred during the initial stages of the transition to free-market economies, required development of domestic stock exchanges and the institutions that typically accompany them, like trust companies and settlement organizations, as well as security and exchange commissions and other governmental regulating bodies.

During the initial stages of capital market development in the GEM, experienced foreign branches of investment banks and financial and trading companies with certain quality of entry strategies were the dominant players. Eventually, domestic GEM companies learned from their foreign counterparts and became active participants. The subsequent stage of development will involve domestic companies of the GEM becoming important strategic partners and/or competitors of foreign branches from the developed world. As domestic exchanges mature, governments of EMCs have allowed domestic companies to be listed on foreign stock exchanges and foreign companies to be listed on domestic stock exchanges. This is resulting in a huge increase in the capitalization of companies from the GEM, as they are listed in multiple stock exchanges. Traditionally, companies from the GEM prefer to be listed on the leading stock exchanges of developed countries, such as London, New York, Frankfurt, and even Toronto. In a very interesting development toward the end of the first quarter of the twenty-first century, companies from EMCs are looking to other parts of the GEM, such as stock exchanges in Shanghai, Hong Kong, Singapore, Warsaw, and Moscow. This is greatly increasing the capitalization of GEM countries. Speculators, investment banks, and wealthy individuals are keenly interested in investing in GEM companies that have already demonstrated rapid, steady growth and are internationally recognized. This has led to a huge increase in financial activity in the capital markets of the GEM. A great deal of this activity is handled by leading financial institutions in their offices in London and New York, where emerging market dealer communities are flourishing. In a study on IPOs in the US by GEM companies, Professors Robert Burner, Susan Chaplinsky, and Latha Ramchand compared

> the issue costs of 299 companies from emerging and developed market countries making initial public offerings (IPOs) in the United States between 1991 and 2001. Our results indicate that IPOs from emerging markets experience the same costs on average as IPOs from developed market countries. Although there is a large gap between the country risk ratings of the emerging and developed market countries, IPO issuers from emerging markets appear to bridge that gap by being large issuers in their respective home countries, listing more frequently on the NYSE, and having a greater proportion of activity in manufacture and infrastructure segments, and a lower proportion in high-tech segments. These issues occur following periods of strong U.S. and home market equity performance which helps to alleviate country risk. In comparison to their developed market peers, emerging market issuers are a select group of higher-quality firms.[85]

Emerging Market Securities, Derivatives, and Foreign Debt

The increasing importance of the GEM has led to an explosion in complexity and growth in the global capital market. According to the Bank of International Settlements, the daily turnover of currency trades is worth more than the annual income of economies like Germany and China. Global strategists have to deal with new complications as a result of the increasing scale of international financial transactions under the influence of globalization of the world financial system, which allows risks and uncertainty to be dispersed and absorbed like never before. Bankers and investors from the GEM are becoming more skilled and can compete with their counterparts in developed countries via complex investment instruments like financial derivatives linked to currencies. As a result, trading in foreign exchange markets averaged $5.3 trillion per day in April 2013.[86] In 2013, among emerging market countries involved in foreign exchanges (FX) in the top ten global currencies are two—Mexico and China in eighth and tenth places, respectively. But first place in currency distribution belongs to the US dollar, and following with a far distant second is the euro, followed by the Japanese yen and the British pound.[87] The number of branches and employees of international dealer firms has increased substantially in the GEM. A few EMCs account for most of the trade volume in the GEM, such as Brazil (35 percent), Mexico (15 percent), Russia (more than 14 percent), followed by Venezuela (a developing country), and Turkey. Among EMCs that account for more than 2 percent of GEM trade volume are Colombia, Ecuador, the Philippines, Peru, and Argentina. MarketAxess, a provider of a unified platform for credit dealers, evaluated the trade of 36 EMCs, and found that Brazil had the largest share, and Guatemala and Jamaica each had the lowest share at 0.01 percent.

Countries that once begged for money in the form of aid are now players in international financial markets. They have already become investors in non-developed countries in projects with a high probability of success. High commodity prices (especially those of oil and fertilizer) have filled the coffers of several P-EMCs and EMCs with excess cash. Strategically, if a country can get a higher return on an investment than the interest rate of its debt, then it should be invested. Governments should have companies (international and domestic) compete to come up with projects that address national needs while yielding a high return. However, if the financial strategy of a country is not sophisticated enough to allow efficient investments, it is best to immediately repay the foreign and multilateral debt. The best-case strategic scenario is to earn a large enough return on the investment to gradually repay the debt on the agreed schedule, as loans from multilateral institutions usually have below-market interest rates, but with many restrictions.

First issued in 1994 as a part of Brazil's debt restructuring, its C-bond with a maturity between 20 and 30 years has placed Brazil in the leading position in emerging market securities. According to the Emerging Markets Traders Association (EMTA), Brazilian C-bonds made up 10 percent of all emerging market debt traded.[88] Nigeria, which was once one of the most heavily indebted countries in the world, tapped the international Eurobond markets by launching a bond worth about $1.5 billion. The proceeds of the bond are being used to repay Nigeria's outstanding foreign debt.

In the 1990s, there were very few mutual or public (especially pension) funds in the GEM. Now there is not a single EMC without them. To the surprise of many foreign strategists, pension funds in EMCs grow at double-digit rates annually, unlike their 4 to 5 percent average growth rates in developed countries. According to the IMF, major western pension, mutual, and hedge funds invested 16 percent of their assets in EMCs in 1994, compared with 0.5 percent in 1987.[89] At the beginning of the twenty-first century, all major mutual and pension funds diversified their portfolios with emerging market debt and assets.

> The surge in cross-border capital flows from mature market institutional investors has helped broaden the investor base for emerging market external sovereign debt, leading to the stability and lower volatility of this asset class over the past five years—as reflected in the global spreads of the JPMorgan Chase Emerging Markets Bond index (EMBI). Interest in emerging market assets has undergone a structural upward shift, with institutional investors such as U.S. pension funds adding emerging market external debt to their benchmark portfolio allocation.[90]

All of these movements increased the necessity for strategists to consult with agencies like Fitch Ratings, as well as specialized advisory firms. Strategists should take into consideration that with the dissemination of technology and the consolidation of financial assets in these funds, investing has become less speculative. Derivatives initially originated as instruments to hedge against currencies and interest rate fluctuations, but globalization made them a crucial instrument for strategic investors. Investors often use derivatives in countries with rapidly growing economies, which are often accompanied by current account deficits (though not the case for China and Russia) and relatively low inflation. Without the formation of the GEM, derivatives might never have become a globally accepted financial instrument.

TECHNOLOGICAL RISK OF STRATEGIC FOREIGN DIRECT INVESTMENT

Technological risk of strategic foreign direct investment is a function of the correlation between the technology to be implemented in a cross-border investment project and natural, social, economic, and technological conditions of the country and particular region where the investment will occur. In order to evaluate this risk, strategists must have extensive knowledge of the level of technological advancement of a potential country or region recipient. In the GEM an evaluation of this risk is of great importance because of the substantial variations in technological progress among EMCs. The GEM includes countries that are considered among the global technological leaders of some knowledge-based industries—Taiwan in semiconductors and Russia in nuclear, space, and nanotechnology industries—as well as countries with little to no experience with modern technologies. For this reason, it is important for strategists to get the opinions of rating agencies specializing in evaluations of R&D capabilities. A.T. Kearny, one of the leading global management consultancies, regularly publishes its FDI Confidence Index, which is "constructed using primary data from a proprietary survey administered to senior executives of the world's 1,000 largest corporations."[91] The countries at the top of this list are considered to have a level of technological development sufficient to attract FDI in research and development. According to the 2006 rating, Eastern Europe is "viewed positively as an R&D location, offering both low costs and strong scientific and engineering capabilities. Nearly one-third of global investors are planning R&D-oriented FDI in Eastern Europe over the next three years."[92] Among the leading EMCs in this evaluation are China, India, Poland, Russia, Brazil, Hong Kong, and Hungary.

When strategizing the location of an investment, one of the key aspects of technological risk to consider is the availability of specific natural resources and work power. For example, a large and steady source of water is necessary for chemical production, as it is a very water-intensive process. The production of aluminum is energy intensive; strategically, a reliable source of energy is a major factor. As a result, quite frequently, aluminum production facilities are located not in the country in which the natural resources—bauxite and nefelin—are found, but where energy sources are cheaper and more widely available. Car or machinery assembly plants require a cheap low-skilled workforce, while software and high-tech industries require specifically trained, highly educated professionals. Existing production facilities should also be strategically examined to see if they can be harmonized within the production process of the potential direct investment. If the production process requires highly enriched raw materials, the quality of the products of local enrichment facilities may not be acceptable for companies from developed countries. For example, an EMC may have mines that are much richer sources of metals than in any developed country, but the product of the local enrichment facilities creates raw materials with too much sulfur. This would require additional capital to build an agglomerated factory to remove the sulfur from the raw material, substantially increasing costs.

Indicators of technological development that influence technological risk include (among others): numbers of scientists and scholars per 1,000 people; government and private funding of research and development; access to scientific and technological information; quality of research labs, facilities, and science and technological parks; commercial applications of scientific and technological advancements; and penetration of low and high technologies. Many technological risk indicators are directly related to the quality of the country's education system. Others derive from political risk, such as the interruption of education by civilian disobedience, issues of gender equality, vulnerability to cyber terrorism, fraud, hacking, etc. Many indicators are related to cultural norms and attitudes toward innovative technologies. There are several other factors that determine technological risk, such as regional climates. The climates of EMCs vary much more than those of developed countries in Western Europe and North America. In the GEM, production could occur above the Arctic Circle in Russia, in the tropical conditions of Latin America or Africa, or even extreme desert conditions, in Saudi Arabia, Bahrain, or Mongolia. All of these climates require a strategic regionalization of production processes specifically suited to the local environment. Equipment that is not designed for extreme conditions will not operate efficiently, if at all. Certain metal products that function properly in the moderate conditions of Florida or France would be destroyed after only a few minutes of use in northern Siberia, Inner Mongolia, or the southernmost parts of Argentina in the winter. Cars that are suitable for New York or Moscow are not efficient or safe in desert areas and require substantial mechanical alterations. In order to exploit a huge, rich coal basin in Siberia, for example, special equipment is required, such as excavators or draglines that can move several thousand tons of coal per hour. In moderate areas of the US, Europe, and Asia, this extremely powerful equipment is inefficient. Strategists should be aware that the implementation of equipment of such capacity in any of these regions would nearly bankrupt a company: natural resources are not as large and rich as they are in the extreme climates of parts of the GEM. The process of modernizing equipment according to regional specific conditions is called technological regionalization (see Chapter 7). The most successful FDI in the GEM tailors cutting-edge global technology and strategic management systems to local conditions and opportunities.

Manual labor's share of the total labor force is rapidly decreasing in the GEM. This trend already occurred in developed countries, which are of course more technologically advanced. As the level of technological development continues to improve in the GEM, manual labor's share of the total workforce will continue to decrease, which also decreases technological risk. This is especially the case in EMCs outside of economies in bloom, which are already technologically advanced. Over the last century, manual labor's share of global work power has decreased by more than three times. Companies from technologically advanced EMCs are already competing with their counterparts in developed countries. Increased competition from the GEM forces companies based in developed countries to invest heavily to maintain or regain their technological edge.

Strategically, the GEM is far behind developed countries in terms of technological maturity, which is the cause of its higher levels of technological risk. There are a few exceptions in certain industries, such as Brazil's ethanol industry, Russia's nuclear and space industries, and India's information technology services. However, the national economies of developed countries are much more technologically advanced than any EMC. The level of technological development of a national economy is a major determinant of a country's strategic competitive advantages, priorities, and related technological risk. In order to reduce technological risk for strategic FDI, it is important for emerging market countries that are not technologically advanced to develop national strategies to stimulate investment (domestic and foreign) in high-tech sectors and companies as well as the development of national educational programs. Foreigners investing in high-tech industries should receive special treatment, as should technologically advanced domestic companies. The development of domestic companies and universities specializing in high-tech industries requires preferential treatment by the national government. A certain level of protectionism is needed for countries to jumpstart their technological development.

Despite the fact that technology and other fixed assets in the GEM are nowhere near as modern as those in developed countries, EMCs have demonstrated a much higher speed in the implementation of technological achievements, which has important implications for technological risk. According to the World Bank Report *Technology Diffusion in the Developing World*, during the last decade of the twentieth century, Chile, Hungary, and Poland increased the level of technological achievement by more than 125 percent. In general, lower- and middle-income countries have a higher speed of technological development than high-income countries. Nonetheless, a wide gap in the use of modern technologies is still in place—higher-income countries are far ahead of middle- and lower-income countries. The greatest disparity is related to the use of patents, followed by the use of tractors and rural sanitation, and mobile information technologies. There is also a significant gap between urban and rural areas in EMCs. From 2007 to 2015, India has employed world-class technologies, and as of 2014 has increased rural teledensity to 42.67 percent.[93] By comparison, in 2007, in rural areas India had penetration in less than 10 percent of households.[94] Among EMCs, disparity in the use of basic technologies from developed countries is being reduced at a substantially faster rate than disparities in the use of high-tech, cutting-edge technologies. This has important implications for technological risk of FDI related to high technologies. Access to industrial infrastructure is an important characteristic that determines the extent to which many basic technologies are implemented in the GEM. While transportation infrastructure in Russia and China is far behind countries of Latin America and the Indian subcontinent, Russia is ahead of the overwhelming majority of other EMCs in terms of access to electrical grids. In rural areas of sub-Saharan Africa and some Asian countries, like Myanmar, less than 10 percent of the population has access to electricity. Pre-emerging market countries have much less access to the Internet and personal computers compared with economies in bloom and emerging market democracies. The use of technology, both cutting-edge and basic, is largely correlated to the internationalization of an economy. According to the same World Bank report, "the high-tech business processes, products and services that flow into a country through foreign trade, foreign direct investment (FDI), and contact with migrant populations living abroad offer the critical exposure required to jumpstart technological diffusion."[95]

The World Bank uses the indicator *total factor productivity* (TFP) to demonstrate the role of technological advancement. According to this indicator, since 1990 the most significant technological progress occurred in countries of Southeast Asia, followed by European and Central Asian emerging market countries. The least amount of technological progress during this period occurred in Latin American, the Caribbean, and sub-Saharan countries[96]. Among emerging market countries, the most attractive for technologically oriented FDI are those that are already technological leaders not only within the GEM, but in the global marketplace, like Taiwan, Israel, India, South Korea, and the Czech Republic. According to an evaluation of FDI projects dedicated to R&D as a share of the total number of FDI projects by OCO Consulting Ltd., a leading provider of information on foreign investment, a few EMCs that are quite technologically advanced are not among the leaders. It is especially surprising that Russia, which is technologically advanced in many areas, is not one of the higher ranked EMCs. There are two explanations for this. Some EMCs, like Russia, do not aggressively seek FDI in high technology and even restrict it in sectors of its economy that it considers to be of strategic national importance. Also, other sectors of the economy attract massive FDI inflows, making the share of FDI projects dedicated to R&D less significant. Both of these explanations are relevant to FDI in Brazil, Russia, and Kazakhstan. Brazil is the leading recipient of FDI related to R&D in Latin America. What may also be surprising for strategists evaluating the African market is that technologically intensive FDI projects in Morocco have surpassed those in South Africa. At the beginning of the twenty-first century, tech-related FDI started to play an important role in middle-income countries, where its average role in the GEM is more than 3 percent of GDP. Modern technology is a major vehicle (for example, on the basis of technological platforms) of bringing non-developed countries out of poverty and is one of the most important factors in the process of improving standards of living and economic development.

Information Technology in the GEM

An analysis of telecommunications is usually conducted during the development of the entry strategy. Some preliminary evaluations can be made as early as during the development of strategic scenarios. However, in EMCs, where telecommunication infrastructure is more of a vital issue due to delayed technological development, it is strategically appropriate to analyze telecommunications and information technology during the study of technological risk. In response to a lack of fixed lines and low levels of personal-computer penetration, EMCs are implementing very sophisticated national information technology strategies. The rate of growth of these new technologies is unprecedented. An evaluation of 16 EMCs by the Forrester Research Institute estimated that PC penetration would grow by more than 30 percent annually until 2010 in the GEM.[97] Reality surpassed this projection and as of May 2012 about one billion people in India had access to mobile telephony, and even fourth-generation mobile service is available in the majority of Indian cities, starting with Kolkata as of April 2012.[98] The study cited China, India, Mexico, and Indonesia as the most promising PC markets. Use of mobile phones in the GEM is growing at an even faster pace than that of PCs. In India, the number of cell phones is projected to increase from 93 million (9 percent penetration) in 2006 to 278 million (a little more than 25 percent penetration) in 2010.[99] Technological risk is closely correlated to access to information and telecommunication technology. The consulting firm Ops A La Carte suggests an efficient manner by which to analyze technological risk: "the identification, categorization and prioritization of hardware and software threats to achieving key reliability business objectives."[100] This approach can be used for strategic evaluation of FDI in this industry, but it has to be understood within the context of the specific international financial and economic transactions with the GEM. The changing nature of the use of mobile phones has important implications for technological risk. The conversion of GSM (Global System for Mobile communication) to third generation (3G) networks is facilitating the convergence of PC and mobile phone functions, as is the increasing sophistication of mobile software applications. These developments provide broadband flexibility and increasing connectivity.

In absolute numbers, the GEM recently overcame developed countries in terms of fixed lines and mobile phone usage. China Mobile Communications Corporation is the largest provider of mobile phone services, with more than 350 million subscribers.[101] China also has the most fixed and mobile lines in the world. Initially, telecom companies targeted major capitals of EMCs, but as competition increases, they are beginning to expand into more remote regions. Nokia is expanding its activity from the Pacific coast and southeastern region of China to its least developed provinces. China is Nokia's largest market. They have partnered with Baidu.com, a Chinese-language search engine, to improve the Internet capabilities of its phones. As of 2014, according to the International Telecommunications Union, there are almost 7 billion people with mobile phones and 5.4 billion of them are in emerging market and developing countries![102]

The penetration of mobile telephones, as with all modern technologies, varies to a great extent throughout the GEM, which complicates strategic analyses of technological risk. According to an evaluation made by the OECD, there are four emerging market countries with a higher penetration of mobile phones than the United States: Portugal, Czech Republic, South Korea, and Poland.[103] The leading country by this indicator in Latin America is Mexico. All of these statistics are important not only for strategists from the telecom industry, but also for all businesses that are tech, service, trade, and tourism oriented, as well as for governmental strategists. Between 2000 and 2005, five of the biggest EMCs, BRICS (China, India, Brazil, Russia, and South Africa), annually increased spending on information and communication technologies by 19 percent—reaching $277 billion combined in 2005—compared to a 5.6 percent average for member-countries of the OECD.[104] As of 2014, the lowest level of mobile phone penetration is in Africa (69.3 percent), followed by Pacific Asia (89.2 percent), with the highest level of penetration in CIS countries, including Russia (140.6 percent).[105]

For national strategists, in order to expedite a country's technological and economic progress, it is vital in the twenty-first century to strategize the increase of Internet access for general users and businesses. This requires governments and government-related funds, especially in big EMCs, to allocate substantial capital to develop Internet and telecom infrastructure. Among EMCs, there is a great deal of variation in Internet penetration. Some, like South Korea, United Arab Emirates, Hong Kong, Spain, Argentina, and Singapore, have a higher penetration rate than most developed countries. Most, however, are far behind the developed world. Strategically, Internet usage in total numbers is developing in the world proportionally to the scale of regional populations (see Figure 9.10). This explains why Asia Pacific is the leading region in terms of total Internet users, and the Middle East and Australia have much fewer. The speed at which Asia has surpassed the most developed regions—Europe and North America—in terms of total Internet users is a very surprising dynamic.[106] In terms of penetration, Asia is actually behind the Middle East and Latin America, which is the leading emerging market region by Internet penetration.[107] This was possible to predict as early as 1997–1998, when the Internet received tremendous attention in Argentinean and Brazilian universities and research centers. Among the emerging markets of Europe, the most rapid growth rate of Internet users was demonstrated by Russia, followed by Spain and Ireland, with a growth rate four times faster than the EU average since 2007.[108]

The most practical and important use of information technology innovations is the development of e-commerce. The birth of this new business and economic phenomenon can be traced back to 1984, when the Electronic Data Interchange (EDI) was standardized, allowing companies and consumers to utilize the Internet. But on a practical level,

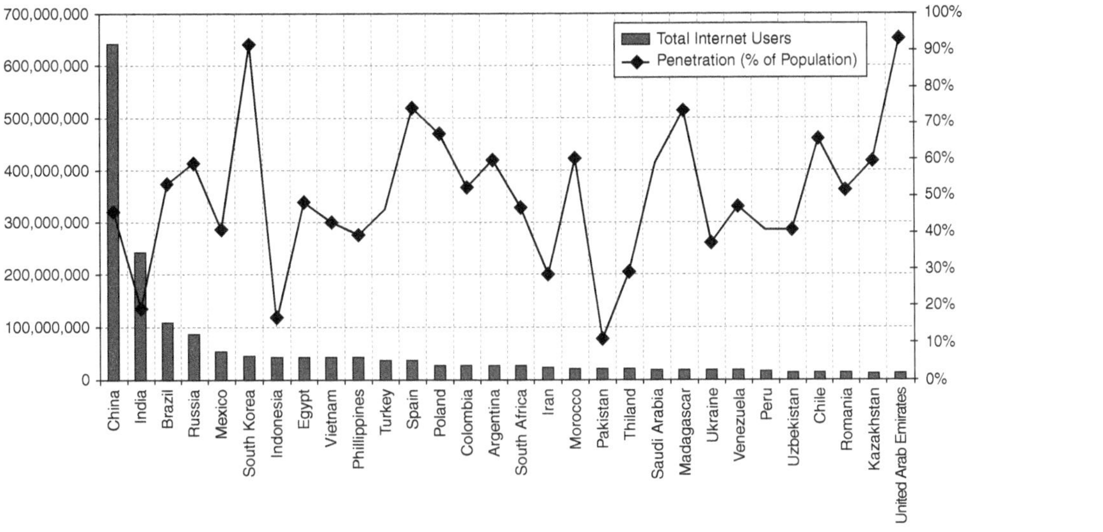

Figure 9.10 Internet Users in the GEM, Total and Penetration (Ordered by Total), 2014
Based on data from Internet Live Stats. Retrieved from www.internetlivestats.com/internet-users-by-country/

e-commerce began in 1995, when two major players in this market—Amazon and eBay—became active. Four years later, global e-commerce sales reached the $20 billion milestone. In 2003, Amazon.com turned an annual profit for the first time. The rapid development of e-commerce is also related to the moratorium of the majority of countries on an Internet sales tax. In emerging market countries, e-business is developing in all directions: business to business, business to consumer, business to government, and even consumer to consumer. The e-commerce market has expanded from $2.6 billion in 1996 to roughly $1 trillion at the beginning of 2008. In the GEM in February 2014, only business to consumer (B2C) e-commerce sales reached $1.5 trillion. EMCs of the Asia Pacific Region, by spending through e-commerce, surpassed North America and reached $525.2 billion, while the North America indicator is equal to $482.6 billion. Leadership of EMCs in the global arena in terms of B2C e-commerce will continue, and in 2017 the Asia Pacific Region will overcome sales of $1 trillion, which is a trifle behind North America and Western Europe combined ($660.4 and $445, respectively). At least to the year 2050 China will continue to hold absolute leadership in spending through e-commerce. Out of ten dollars of spending in the Asia Pacific region, six will be spent in China. In 2016, China, as strategizing shows, will surpass the United States by sales through B2C![109] The lowest level of development of B2C e-commerce by 2017 will be in EMCs of the Middle East, Africa, Central, and Eastern Europe. Among individual leading countries in B2C service will be Argentina, Mexico, Brazil, Russia, Italy, and Canada. These countries will be the locomotives of e-commerce at least until the middle of the twenty-first century, and strategists have to seriously consider this indicator.[110]

Strategists making an investment comparison between different countries through the lens of the expenses versus time ratio have to take into consideration the fact that in the GEM, the process of implementing modern technologies goes much faster. This can also be explained by companies' ability to hire more qualified employees for much lower compensation. For example, the average compensation for information technology managers in EMCs like China, India, and Vietnam as of 2008 reached the median level of $26,000, compared with Switzerland, where the figure is $140,000, and about $105,000 in the United States.[111] The dynamics of technological development in the GEM, as well as increasing education levels and economic integration among EMCs and within the global marketplace, indicate that technological risk of strategic FDI in the GEM will steadily decrease.

Strategic Foreign Direct Investment from the Global Emerging Market to Developed Countries

In the twenty-first century, as the GEM continues to mature, an interesting trend has appeared—an outflow of FDI from EMCs to developed countries. There are four strategic economic reasons for this. The first is related to fluctuations and the instability of FDI in the GEM. The second is the increasing power of domestic companies (with or without FDI) and industries in the GEM whose leaders feel that they are ready to play a more central strategic role in the GMP. The third reason is primarily related to governmental and state-controlled semi-private companies that, for political reasons, are implementing strategies to invest in the developed world. Finally, there is a fourth reason: some EMCs have to deal with reversals of economic maturity, which causes private interests to relocate capital out of the country in order to protect it.

The outflow of FDI from the GEM to the US offers an illustration of these four reasons. In the first three quarters of 2007, Venezuela was the number one Latin American source of FDI in the US. The reason for this was the reversal of progress in the country as a result of President Hugo Chavez's attempt to become the lifetime president and his initiation of the nationalization and expropriation of private domestic and foreign assets. This process in Venezuela has become a major concern not only for businesses from developed countries, but also for those from other EMCs, like Brazil. The Venezuelan government nationalized the assets of several Brazilian companies without any internationally recognized legal basis. In order to protect themselves and their financial well-being, domestic private companies began to sell their assets and convert their profits to FDI in a stable and protected environment like the US, the EU, and other developed countries. At the end of 2007, a long-term process began that has been taking place for the last eight years due to the danger of nationalization and expropriation of private direct investment in Venezuela.

A huge investment in the US economy from Bermuda and in Bermuda from the US is of a different economic nature; this is mostly a reinvestment of US money that left the country for many reasons, including tax evasion. As of 2007, the United States had a negative balance of capital flows with Bermuda. Manufacturing facilities in the US based on FDI from the GEM are often more successful than their US rivals. A strategic analysis indicates that this increases the enthusiasm of other similar EMC companies to invest in the US. At the end of the twentieth century, while the Big Three car manufacturers of the US were struggling to keep their factories open, companies from South Korea and even China successfully opened car-manufacturing facilities in the US. Largely as a result, US market share of the Big Three decreased from 73 percent in 1980 to less than 50 percent in 2008. The main benefactors from this process have been consumers in developed countries. From 1990 to 2003, the overall consumer price index in the US increased by 53 percent, while the average price of a car grew by only 13.4 percent.[112]

Different strategic principles apply to Russia-owned Lukoil gas stations, which are prevalent throughout the East Coast of the United States, especially in New York and Pennsylvania. One may think that this is a result of the increasing importation of Russian oil to the US; however, this is not the case. Lukoil works primarily with oil from the same refinery plants as all other US gas stations. There are three possible strategic reasons for Lukoil's expansion into the US market. One explanation is that its owners desired to decrease risks to their fortune by investing it in one of the most protected and safe parts of the world, where private property ownership is one of the major priorities of the law. The second reason is related to a corporate strategy to position itself as an international player. As of 2008, Lukoil has penetrated the markets of 13 US states with ownership of about 2,000 facilities.[113] The third reason may be explained by Russia's national strategic interest and its strategic leadership's desire to increase its role in the GMP and demonstrate its economic maturity around the world; for this reason, it gave special attention to the global hegemon. These motivations can be found behind the actions of other Russian companies, which are buying oil refineries and electrical distribution systems in Italy and other European countries. An obvious example of this is the state-controlled natural gas monopoly Gazprom. Another interesting fact is that FDI from Russia to Canada is seven times higher than Canadian investment to Russia. An analysis of this investment indicates that it is the result of all four of the factors of FDI outflow from the GEM mentioned above. Chinese companies adopted a similar strategy of purchasing oil facilities in the US; however, US government restrictions prevented them from coming to fruition. One better-documented case of the US blocking a strategic investment from a partially state-owned firm occurred when a company from Dubai with long-term experience managing seaports unsuccessfully tried to acquire seaport facilities in the US. The strategic reasons for the concerns of the US government were discomfort with the idea of a company from the Middle East—the region of the world where most terrorist activity has originated—operating the sea gateway to America. For similar reasons, leaders of several developed countries, and members of the G7, are opposed to sovereign wealth funds of EMCs being used as a major source of investment in strategically important companies. Not surprisingly, leaders from Russia, China, and some other EMCs do not see these as legitimate concerns. In 2007, the Russian Minister of Finance said at the G7 finance meeting, "the investment of sovereign wealth funds should be subject to the general rules of the free movement of capital."[114]

In other cases, this investment is dictated by pure economic factors, such as increasing vertical integration or the development of a distribution network. Other benign motivations also exist. The Russian nuclear atomic state agency Rosatom is one of the largest buyers of uranium from Canada. In November 2007, Sergey Kirienko, the head of Rosatom, and the former prime minister of Russia under President Yeltsin, said, "We have signed an agreement to establish two joint ventures. Diversification of uranium supplies is extremely important for Russia. We want not only to get uranium from Canada, but also we want to have an opportunity to invest in production of uranium in Canada."[115] Strategists have to be cognizant of the fact that political and business leaders from EMCs eventually may succeed in their quest to establish equal treatment of FDI outflows in various forms from their countries to the developed world. For developed countries, FDI from the GEM is often strategically important, especially for those countries with foreign trade and budget deficits. These deficits are partially financed by FDI inflows. Historically, these deficits were balanced by an increase in domestic investment. At the beginning of the twenty-first century, with the growing economic capability of the GEM, businesses from developed countries began to look abroad for financial solutions. The situation in the US is an obvious illustration of this point. Strategic foreign investment from the GEM plays a crucial role in the financing of the current American account and budget deficits.

As of 2008, FDI inflows to developed countries are still higher than inflows to the GEM. Despite subprime-mortgage issues and the slowdown in US real estate, the political and relative economic stability of the United States since 2003 has led investment strategists to recommend channeling FDI to the US. The $237.5 billion worth of FDI inflow to the US in 2007 was an increase of more than 35 percent from the previous year.[116] Since 2000, and especially after 9/11, FDI and domestic investment have fled the US market. The large inflow of FDI that began in 2003 and 2004 was definitely influenced by the absence of any major terrorist attack on US soil since the tragedy of 2001. The situation with FDI in the US signifies general trends in the twenty-first century: *investment goes to stable countries, with low terrorist activity, a lack of breaches of contract by governments, freely or limitedly convertible currencies, and a high level of potential return under moderate risk.*

The importance of direct investment from foreign countries is usually underappreciated. For example, the role of FDI outflows from the United States can be better understood when strategists keep in mind that the return on US investments abroad is larger than all US foreign debt, which means that this investment is quite efficient. US investment abroad outpaces foreign investment in the US. Nonetheless, companies from emerging market countries are playing an increasingly key role as sources of foreign investment in the United States. Among the leading EMCs in terms of acquisition of US targets are Russia, United Arab Emirates, India, Saudi Arabia, Israel, and Brazil. Surprisingly, during some years, such as 2006, the small but wealthy United Arab Emirates invested more in the United States than Hong Kong, Singapore, Mexico, South Korea, or Brazil. However, out of the top ten major acquisitions of US companies by foreign investors, three came from two EMCs: Singapore and Spain.[117] The role of China in terms of FDI in acquisitions in the United States was insignificant as of 2006. However, during 2007 this situation changed. This trend will continue due to the fact that, in 2008, the US and Chinese governments agreed to develop "an investment treaty that would guarantee access for the nations' companies to buy assets in the other country."[118] This agreement will prevent incidents like what occurred in 2005, when China's biggest offshore state-controlled oil company, Cnooc, tried to buy the subsidiary of Unocal Corporation from California for $18.5 billion, but was prevented from doing so by the US Congress.[119] The Chinese government has a long-term strategy to invest in key countries and key industries to gain access to oil and gas, non-ferrous metals, coal, freshwater, and major seaports. Western Europe saw firsthand the growing clout of Russia, as Gazprom so frightened the European leaders with its aggressive acquisition of several gas distribution and oil refinery plants that the EU began to develop regulations to prevent foreign providers of oil and gas from owning distribution infrastructure. Unlike China, India, for decades, did not motivate inflow of FDI. At the same time, during the first years of the twenty-first century, several Indian companies reached power as a global player in their respective industries. For many strategic and economic reasons they started to invest in well-developed states. When Tata Group, an Indian conglomerate, and CSN, a Brazilian company, competed for control of Corus, a British-Dutch steel producer, it was the first time that two companies from the GEM fought over control of a Western European company. Figure 9.11 represents the dynamics of GEM acquisitions of companies in the United States by investor countries of foreign origin.

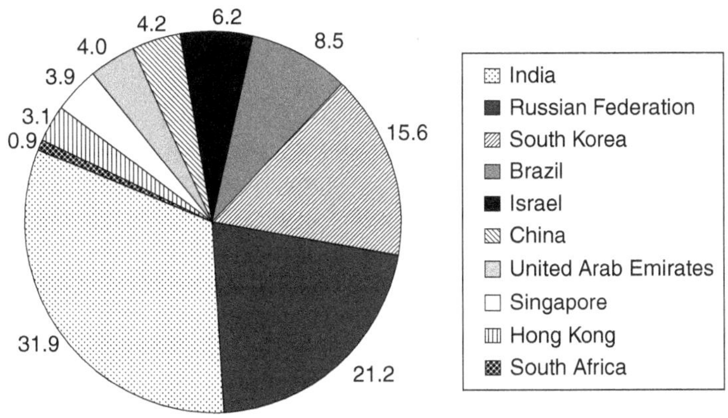

Figure 9.11 Acquisitions of US Targets by Emerging Market Investors (Country Percentage Share)

One of the most profound examples of a fund from the GEM investing in a banking institution from a developed country took place when the biggest bank in the US (in terms of assets), Citigroup Inc., received a $7.5 billion cash infusion from the Abu Dhabi Investment Authority, thus acquiring 4.9 percent of Citigroup stock and becoming its largest shareholder.[120]

The same incentives that led strategic investors of companies from the GEM to the US have led them to target well-developed Western European markets. In 2006, out of $41.5 billion in acquisitions in Western Europe by companies from the GEM, 33.2 percent were from India and almost 13 percent were from the United Arab Emirates. Not far behind these countries were Russia (12.6 percent), Singapore (11 percent), and South Africa (9.5 percent). China was not a leading country in terms of its acquisition of European targets, accounting for only 3.3 percent of Western European targets.[121] But it is strategically possible to expect that Chinese investments in the EU will increase only when EU leaders feel less strategic danger from these investments.

In 2004, EMC acquisitions abroad (not only in developed countries) were worth almost $55 billion, in 2005, almost $120 billion, and in 2006, about $180 billion.[122] Strategists of companies from EMCs have crafted winning strategies for developed markets and have demonstrated that they can indeed compete with well-established investors. Between 1990 and 2005, outflow of FDI from emerging market countries to service sectors aboard increased by a factor of 72. In 1990, FDI outflow stock from the GEM was roughly $11.62 billion to overseas service industries. By 2005, this number reached about $831 billion. During the same period, accumulative foreign investment from emerging market countries to food, beverage, and tobacco production abroad increased by a factor of 5.7 and by a factor of 17 in overseas production of textiles, clothing, and leather. The largest growth in strategic investment from the GEM is related to business services, which increased by a factor of 347 from 1990 to 2005.[123] This surge of FDI outflow is further proof of the maturation of businesses in the GEM. With domestic strategists' and executives' increasing experience, companies from EMCs are investing more and more heavily in developed countries (see Figure 9.12). One often unintended but significant side effect is a loss of potential investment in the GEM. The capital of entrepreneurs and companies from EMCs, which could be used to decrease unemployment, poverty, and migration from GEM countries, is itself migrating, which can also be understood as an indication of the maturation of strategic investors in the GEM.

Corporate and governmental strategists from EMCs have found it very efficient to pursue soft targets in other EMCs and even in developing countries, the conditions of which they are much more accustomed to than their competitors from developed countries. For this reason, investment banks and large companies from the GEM are also acquiring entities in other EMCs and developing countries. The Abu Dhabi Investment Authority (ADIA) established an emerging markets department and invests a significant amount of Abu Dhabi's petrodollars in the GEM. The ADIA has been a strategic investor in privatization in Saudi Arabia, Kuwait, and Tunisia,[124] as well as in all Arab and Maghreb countries, with moderate political regimes and stable economies. ADIA executives clearly have a preference for business climates with which they are already well acquainted. The same applies to the Chinese cross-border investment strategy. Despite the heavy media coverage of the attempted Chinese acquisitions of US companies, the majority of Chinese investment is in the GEM. One of China's biggest investments was the 2005 purchase of PetroKazakhstan by China National Petroleum Corporation for $4.2 billion. Kazakhstan is a very attractive recipient of FDI from other EMCs as well. Several Middle Eastern countries have made significant investments in the banking and service sectors of this Central Asian country.

Nonetheless, many strategic factors and priorities may lead FDI outflows from the GEM to become a slower and lower trend than FDI outflows from the developed world. This trend empowers strategic attraction of the GEM for developed countries' FDI. The strategic cumulative result of this tactic and some other trends will be seen somewhere in 2075–2085, when economic efficiency, the level of business and industrial infrastructure, and quality of life in the GEM will be almost the same as in the developed world. With the birth of the global emerging market, foreign direct investment has become a global phenomenon. FDI not only brings new technologies,

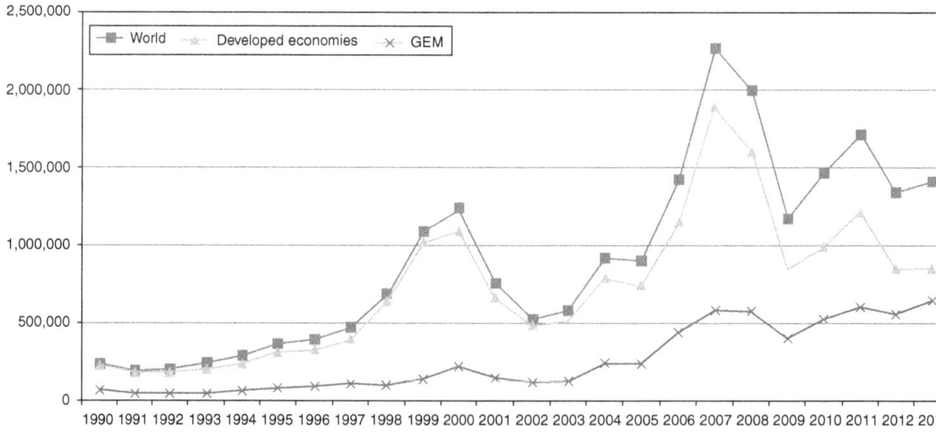

Figure 9.12 FDI Outflow by Category of Country (Millions of $), 1990–2013

Based on data from UNCTAD. (2014.). "World Investment Report: Annex Tables. Annex Table 02: FDI Outflows, by Region and Economy, 1990–2013." Retrieved January 26, 2015 from http://unctad.org/en/pages/DIAE/World%20Investment%20Report/Annex-Tables.aspx

modern managerial skills, employment, and increased development of markets for national products; most importantly, FDI, through its various organizational vehicles, brings peace and stability to new markets. According to Professors Ceyla Pazarbaşıoğlu, Mangal Goswami, and Jack Ree:

> Aside from the institutional money and banking finance, foreign direct investment (FDI) originating from mature market countries has also partially recovered since the bursting of the dot-com bubble. FDI inflows to emerging markets have been increasing but remain largely concentrated, with China accounting for about 50 percent of emerging market flows since 2002. Among the emerging markets, Asia-Pacific and emerging Europe are the leading recipients of FDI, while inflows to Latin America, dominated by Brazil, have fallen since 2000.[125]

When strategic foreign investments are made in volatile parts of the world, they play two key functions: they provide proof that it is possible to cooperate with or within a territory, and they bring international and global cooperation with the territory's people. The success of foreign direct investment in the global marketplace has developed a better environment for multilateral institutions to address truly global issues, a function that they have not yet fulfilled. From the point of view of global strategy, foreign investment builds bridges between nations. *When*, *how fast*, and *where to build*, and *on which technological platform*—and even *whether to build at all*—are the eternal and day-to-day issues found in strategy and in the strategizing process. These questions require not only qualified and efficient strategic answers, but wise and careful reasoning. This is the objective of professional strategists and leaders, whose decisions affect quality of life. If foreign investment—and global economic strategy in general—builds bridges between nations, it is of the utmost importance to carefully strategize ways in which private, regional, national, and multilateral institutions can create economic alliances to address important global issues that will affect the lives of people around the world.

Notes

1 Kierkegaard, S. (1969). "Truth Is Subjectivity." In W.A. Kaufmann (Ed.), *Existentialism: From Dostoevsky to Sartre*. New York: Penguin Books, p. 117.
2 Cited by Kozuskanich, N.R. (2015). *Benjamin Franklin: American Founder, Atlantic Citizen*. New York: Routledge, p. 10.
3 Maugham, W. (1915). *Of Human Bondage*. New York: Garden City Publishing Company, p. 304.
4 UNCTAD. (2007). *World Investment Report 2007: Transnational Corporations, Extractive Industries and Development*. New York and Geneva: United Nations, p. 227. Retrieved from www.unctad.org/en/docs/wir2007_en.pdf
5 Stiglitz, J. (2006). *Stability with Growth: Macroeconomics, Liberalization and Development*. New York: Oxford University Press, p. 206.
6 A.T. Kearney (2014). *Kearney Global Services Index*. Retrieved from www.atkearney.com/research-studies/global-services-location-index/full-report
7 A.T. Kearney. (2007). "Offshoring for Long-Term Advantage." *The 2007 A.T. Kearney Global Services Location Index*. Retrieved from www.atkearney.com/main.taf?p=5,3,1,185
8 World Investment Report. (2014). *Investing in the SDGs: An Action Plan*. New York and Geneva: UNCTAD, pp. xv–xvi. Retrieved from www.unctad.org/en/PublicationsLibrary/wir2014_en.pdf
9 Ramachandran, V. and Cleetus, R. (1999). *Export Processing Zones: The Chinese Experience and Its Lessons for Tamil Nadu*. Retrieved from www.cid.harvard.edu/archive/india/pdfs/china_epz0899.pdf

10 UNCTAD (2002). "Part III: Promoting Export-oriented FDI." In *World Investment Report 2002. Transnational Corporations and Export Competitiveness*. New York and Geneva: United Nations, p. 214. Retrieved from www.unctad.org/en/docs/wir2002p3ch7_en.pdf

11 Hale, D. (2003). "China Takes Off." *Foreign Affairs*. November. Retrieved from http://goliath.ecnext.com/coms2/summary_0199-1184886_ITM

12 Mishkin, F. (2004). *Can Inflation Targeting Work in Emerging Market Countries?* Washington, DC: International Monetary Fund, p. 4. Retrieved from www.imf.org/external/np/res/seminars/2004/calvo/pdf/mishki.pdf

13 Julius Caesar. (1856). *The Commentaries of Caesar*. S. Duncan (Trans.). St. Louis, MO: Edwards and Bushnell. Retrieved from www.www.perseus.tufts.edu/hopper/

14 Kierkegaard, S. (1969). "Truth Is Subjectivity." In W.A. Kaufmann (Ed.), *Existentialism: From Dostoevsky to Sartre*. New York: Penguin Books, p. 117.

15 Sun-tzu. (2006). *The Art of War*. J. Minford (Trans.). New York: Penguin Books, pp. 8, 123.

16 Kierkegaard, S. (1969). "Truth Is Subjectivity." In W.A. Kaufmann (Ed.), *Existentialism: From Dostoevsky to Sartre*. New York: Penguin Books, p. 117

17 Standard & Poor's. (n.d.) "S&P Raises Brazil to Investment Grade." Retrieved from http://www2.standardandpoors.com/portal/site/sp/en/la/page.hottopic/BrazilUP_sp_viewpoint/3,1,1,0,0,0,0,0,0,0,0,0,0,0,0,0.html

18 "S&P Cuts Vale (VALE) to 'BBB+'; Sees Risk Profile Weakening over the Next Few Years." (2015). *Street Insider*. January 23. Retrieved from www.streetinsider.com/

19 Chamie, N. and Biszko, P. (2007). "A Brave New World: Asset Class Views: 07Q4 Update." *Emerging Markets Research*. September 18, RBC Capital Markets, p. 3.

20 Chamie, N. and Biszko, P. (2007). "A Brave New World: Asset Class Views: 07Q4 Update." *Emerging Markets Research*. September 18, RBC Capital Markets, p. 3.

21 IMD. (2014). *World Competitiveness Scoreboard*. Retrieved from http://imd.org/uupload/IMD.WebSite/wcc/WCYResults/1/scoreboard_2014.pdf

22 IMD. (2008). *World Competitiveness Scoreboard*. Retrieved from www.imd.ch/research/publications/wcy/upload/scoreboard.pdf

23 Segal, J. (2007). "Fueling the flow of capital." *Institutional Investor*. July, p. 109.

24 Setser, B. (2007). "Testimony before the U.S.-China Economic and Security Review Commission." February 7. Retrieved from www.uscc.gov/hearings/2008hearings/written_testimonies/08_02_07_wrts/08_02_07_setset_statement.php

25 Multilateral Investment Guarantee Agency. (n.d.). "Guarantees Overview." Retrieved from www.miga.org/guarantees/index_sv.cfm?stid=1509

26 Multilateral Investment Guarantee Agency. (n.d.). "Terms and Conditions." Retrieved from www.miga.org/guarantees/index_sv.cfm?stid=1550

27 Multilateral Investment Guarantee Agency. (n.d.). "Guarantees Projects." Retrieved from www.miga.org/guarantees/index_sv.cfm?stid=1546

28 Humphrey, C. and Prizzon, A. (2014). "Multilateral Investment Guarantee Agency. Guarantees of Development. A Review of Multilateral Development Bank Operations." December. Retrieved from www.odi.org/sites/odi.org.uk/files/odi-assets/publications-opinion-files/9398.pdf

29 Overseas Private Investment Corporation. (2007). *Annual Report 2007*, p. 2. Retrieved from www.opic.gov/pdf/annualreport_2007.pdf

30 Overseas Private Investment Corporation. (n.d.). "Insurance." Retrieved from www.opic.gov/insurance/index.asp

31 Overseas Private Investment Corporation. (2007). *Annual Report 2007*, p. 12. Retrieved from www.opic.gov/pdf/annualreport_2007.pdf

32 Overseas Private Investment Corporation. (n.d.). "Insurance." Retrieved from www.opic.gov/insurance/index.asp

33 Overseas Private Investment Corporation (2014). "OPIC Achieves $3 Billion in Commitments for 2014, Catalyzing Billions More, While Supporting American Business Growth in Developing Countries." December 18. Retrieved from www.opic.gov/press-releases/2014/opic-achieves-3-billion-commitments-2014-catalyzing-billions-more-while-supporting-american-business-growth-

33a Overseas Private Investment Corporation (2014). "OPIC Achieves $3 Billion in Commitments for 2014, Catalyzing Billions More, While Supporting American Business Growth in Developing Countries." December 18. Retrieved from www.opic.gov/press-releases/2014/opic-achieves-3-billion-commitments-2014-catalyzing-billions-more-while-supporting-american-business-growth-

34 Multilateral Investment Guarantee Agency. (n.d.). "Compania Espanola de Seguros de Credito a la Exportacion (Spain)." Retrieved from www.fdi.net/documents/WorldBank/databases/pri-center_mockup/cesce.html
35 AIG. (n.d). "About AIG." Retrieved from www.aig.com/About-aig_20_19308.html
36 AIG. (n.d.). "Political Risk Insurance." Retrieved from www.aig.com/Political-Risk-Insurance_20_27192.html
37 Freedom House. (n.d.). "Freedom in the World: Combined Average Ratings—Independent Countries." Retrieved from www.freedomhouse.org/template.cfm?page=366&year=2007
38 Friedman, M. (2002). *Capitalism and Freedom*. Chicago: University of Chicago Press, p. 20.
39 "Philippines Includes RMB, Won in List of Convertible Currencies." (2006). *AsiaPulse News*. November 10. Retrieved from www.accessmylibrary.com/coms2/summary_0286-25445640_ITM
40 Financial Action Task Force (FATF). (n.d.). "Home." Retrieved from www.fatf-gafi.org/
41 FATF. (n.d.). "Members and Observers." Retrieved from www.fatf-gafi.org/trash/aboutfatf/membersobservers/fatfmembersandobservers.html
42 FATF. (2012). "About the Non-Cooperative Countries and Territories (NCCT) Initiative. August 23. Retrieved from www.fatf-gafi.org/topics/high-riskandnon-cooperativejurisdictions/more/aboutthenon-cooperativecountriesandterritoriesncctinitiative.html
43 Oxfam. (2007). "Africa's Missing Billions: International Arms Flows and the Cost of Conflict. October. Retrieved from www.oxfam.org.uk/resources/policy/conflict_disasters/bp107_africasmissingbillions.html
44 Frohlich, T. and Kent, A. (2014). "10 Countries Spending the Most on the Military." 24/7 Wall St. July 10. Retrieved from http://247wallst.com/special-report/2014/07/10/10-countries-spending-the-most-on-the-military/4/
45 Ackerman, A.R. (Ed.). (2003). *Investing under Fire: Winning Strategies from the Masters for Bulls, Bears, and the Bewildered*. Princeton, NJ: Bloomberg Press, p. 326.
46 Central Intelligence Agency. (2012). "Military Expenditures." In "World Factbook." Retrieved from https://www.cia.gov/library/publications/the-world-factbook/rankorder/2034rank.html
47 Economist Intelligence Unit. (n.d.). "Country Risk Service." *The Economist*. Retrieved from www.eiu.com/default.aspx
48 "Country risk." (n.d.). *The Economist*. Retrieved from http://store.eiu.com/FileHandler.ashx?issue_id=1097293294&mode=pdf
49 According to Alexander Winning, in a January 27, 2015 article from Reuters, the rating agency S&P downgraded Russian sovereign credit rating to "junk" "from BBB- to BB+, citing Russia's weakened economic growth prospects, hit by lower oil prices and western sanctions over the Ukraine crisis."
50 "Country Risk Ratings: European Stability." (2008). *The Economist*. May 27. Retrieved from www.economist.com/markets/rankings/displaystory.cfm?story_id=11435378
51 Gage, J. and Bigman, D. (Eds). (2008). "Special Report: The Best Countries for Business." *Forbes*. June 26. Retrieved from www.forbes.com/2008/06/26/denmark-ireland-finland-biz-cx_db_jg_bizcountries08_0926bizcountries_lander.html
52 SEEurope.net. (n.d.). "Albania: General Electric Says Ready to Negotiate Contract with Albanian Government." Retrieved from www.seeurope.net/?q=node/152
53 FATF. (n.d.). "Money Laundering." Retrieved from www.fatf-gafi.org/pages/faq/moneylaundering/
54 "Ministry of Internal Affairs of Ukraine Publishes Bribery Rating." (2008). *Gazeta*. June 28. Retrieved from www.gazeta.ru/news/lenta/index.shtml
55 Kuznets, S. (1955). "Economic Growth and Income Inequality." *American Economic Review*, vol. 46. no. 1. pp, 1–28.
56 Yi, Z. (2015,). "Anti-graft Watchdog Vows to Net More 'Flies.'" January 21. Retrieved from www.chinadaily.com.cn/china/2015-01/21/content_19362774.htm
57 (2014, September 17). ЧИСТЫЕ РУКИ[Clean Hands] опубликовали ежегодный доклад об уровне коррупции в России 2013-2014гг. Retrieved from www.rusadvocat.com/node/954
58 Office of the United States Trade Representative. (2008). "Special 301 Report," p. 1. Retrieved from www.ustr.gov/assets/Document_Library/Reports_Publications/2008/2008_Special_301_Report/asset_upload_file553_14869.pdf
59 Froman, M.B.D. (2014). "USTR 2014 Special 301 Report." Office of the President, p. 29. Retrieved from https://ustr.gov/sites/default/files/USTR%202014%20Special%20301%20Report%20to%20Congress%20FINAL.pdf

60 Office of the United States Trade Representative. (2001). *PhRMA Special 301 Submission*, p. 4. Retrieved from www.cptech.org/ip/health/phrma/301-01/301-01.pdf
61 Froman, M.B.D. (2014). "USTR 2014 Special 301 Report." Office of the President, p. 29. Retrieved from https://ustr.gov/sites/default/files/USTR%202014%20Special%20301%20Report%20to%20Congress%20FINAL.pdf
62 Froman, M.B.D. (2014). "USTR 2014 Special 301 Report." Office of the President, p. 29. Retrieved from https://ustr.gov/sites/default/files/USTR%202014%20Special%20301%20Report%20to%20Congress%20FINAL.pdf
63 Froman, M.B.D. (2014). "USTR 2014 Special 301 Report." Office of the President, p. 37. Retrieved from https://ustr.gov/sites/default/files/USTR%202014%20Special%20301%20Report%20to%20Congress%20FINAL.pdf
64 Froman, M.B.D. (2014). "USTR 2014 Special 301 Report." Office of the President, p. 43. Retrieved from https://ustr.gov/sites/default/files/USTR%202014%20Special%20301%20Report%20to%20Congress%20FINAL.pdf
65 Froman, M.B.D. (2014). "USTR 2014 Special 301 Report." Office of the President, p. 44. Retrieved from https://ustr.gov/sites/default/files/USTR%202014%20Special%20301%20Report%20to%20Congress%20FINAL.pdf
66 Global Property Guide. (n.d.). "Housing Transaction Costs in the OECD." Retrieved from www.globalpropertyguide.com/investment-analysis/Housing-transaction-costs-in-the-OECD
67 UN Department of Economic and Social Affairs Division for Sustainable Development. (n.d.). "Johannesburg Declaration on Sustainable Development." Retrieved from www.un.org/esa/sustdev/documents/WSSD_POI_PD/English/POI_PD.htm
68 United Nations Environment Programme. (2006). *Global Environment Outlook Yearbook 2006: An Overview of Our Changing Environment*, p. 3. Retrieved from www.unep.org/geo/yearbook/yb2006/PDF/Complete_pdf_GYB_2006.pdf
69 U.S. Department of Commerce: Economics and Statistics Administration, Office of the Chief Economist. (2013). *Economic Impact of Hurricane Sandy*, p. vi. Retrieved from www.esa.gov/sites/default/files/sandyfinal101713.pdf.
70 U.S. Department of Commerce: Economics and Statistics Administration, Office of the Chief Economist. (2013). *Economic Impact of Hurricane Sandy*, p. ix. Retrieved from www.esa.gov/sites/default/files/sandyfinal101713.pdf.
71 Walls, M.R. (2005). "Corporate Risk-taking and Performance: A 20 Year Look at the Petroleum Industry." *Journal of Petroleum Science and Engineering*, vol. 48, nos. 3–4, p. 135.
72 Walls, M.R. (2005). "Corporate Risk-taking and Performance: A 20 Year Look at the Petroleum Industry." *Journal of Petroleum Science and Engineering*, vol. 48, nos. 3–4, p. 139.
73 International Labor Organization. (n.d.). "Socio-Economic Security Programme." Retrieved June 29, 2008 from www.ilo.org/public/english/protection/ses/download/docs/definition.pdf
74 Cited by Vashistha, A. (2010). "Globalization's Strategic Imperative." *HRO Today*. March 18. Retrieved from www.hrotoday.com/contributors/globalizations-strategic-imperative/
75 International Monetary Fund. (n.d.). "Annex 1.2. Sovereign Wealth Funds." *Global Financial Stability Report*, p. 48. Retrieved from www.imf.org/external/pubs/ft/gfsr/2007/02/pdf/annex12.pdf
76 Kvint, V. (2007). "Inflation Rising." *Forbes*. November 28. Retrieved from www.forbes.com/2007/11/27/russia-inflation-rising-oped-cx_vkv_1128kvint.html
77 Aspricio, L. (2013). "¿Has comprado algún producto ruso en tu vida? ¿De qué vive su economía?" Invertia. November 13. Retrieved from www.invertia.com/noticias/has-comprado-producto-ruso-vida-vive-economia-2922047.htm
78 Sabelnikova, M.A. (2014). "Russian State Statistical Agency. Percentage of Imported Food of Food Resource of Retail Trade of Russian Federation." August. Retrieved from www.fedstat.ru/indicator/data.do?id=37164&referrerType=0&referrerId=1293314
79 UN News Centre. (2006). "Developing Countries to Play Growing Role in World Agricultural Trade." *UN Report*. July 5. Retrieved from www.un.org/apps/news/story.asp?NewsID=19102#.VMfZjkJHbGs
80 "Doha Round: 'A global failure of will'?" (2006). *New Economist*. June 26. Retrieved from http://neweconomist.blogs.com/new_economist/2006/06/doha_again.html
81 Clarke, D. (2006). "Funds: Merrill Fund Beats Rivals by Going Further Afield." *The International Herald Tribune*. March 28. Retrieved from www.iht.com/articles/2006/03/27/bloomberg/bxfund.php

82 Chen, T. (2014). "American Household Credit Card Statistics: 2014." Nerdwallet. December. Retrieved from www.nerdwallet.com/blog/credit-card-data/average-credit-card-debt-household/
83 Beadle, S. (2007). "Banking in CEE/CIS Progress, EBRD Role and Involvement in Retail and SME." September 3, p. 5. Retrieved from www.esbg.eu/uploadedFiles/Events/EBRD%20Final.pdf
84 Bigda, C. (2008). "Global Investing: One World, One Fund." *Money Magazine*. June 17. Retrieved from http://money.cnn.com/2008/06/13/pf/funds/global_funds.moneymag/index.htm?postversion=2008061604
85 Burner, R., Chaplinsky, S. and Ramchand, L. (2006). "Coming to America: IPOs from Emerging Market Issuers." *Emerging Markets Review*, vol. 7, issue 3, pp. 191–212.
86 Triennial Central Bank Survey (2013). "Bank for International Settlements. Foreign Exchange Turnover in April 2013: Preliminary Global Results." September, p. 3.
87 Triennial Central Bank Survey (2013). "Bank for International Settlements. Foreign Exchange Turnover in April 2013: Preliminary Global Results." September, p. 10.
88 Guerrero, A. (2005). *Global Finance*. October, p. 1010.
89 Kvint, V. (1995). *The Kvint Newsletter*, vol. 3, no. 1.
90 Pazarbaşıoğlu, C., Goswami, M., and Ree, J. (2007). "The Changing Face of Investors." *Finance & Development*, vol. 44, no. 1. Retrieved from www.imf.org/external/pubs/ft/fandd/2007/03/pazar.htm
91 A.T. Kearney. (2005). "2005 Foreign Direct Investment Confidence Index." Retrieved from www.atkearney.com/main.taf?p=5,3,1,140,14
92 A.T. Kearney. (2005). "2005 Foreign Direct Investment Confidence Index." Retrieved from www.atkearney.com/main.taf?p=5,3,1,140,14
93 Press Release on "Telecom Subscription Data as on 31st December, 2013". Telecom Regulatory Authority of India.
94 World Bank. (2008). *Global Economic Prospects: Technology and Technological Diffusion in the Developing World*. Washington DC: World Bank Publications, p. 91. Retrieved from http://siteresources.worldbank.org/INTPROSPECTS/Resources/334934-1322593305595/8287139-1327608119530/GEP08Chap2.pdf
95 World Bank. (2008). *Global Economics Prospects 2008: Technology Diffusion in a Developing World*. Retrieved from http://siteresources.worldbank.org/INTGEP2008/Resources/GEP08-Brochure.pdf
96 World Bank. (2008). *Global Economics Prospects 2008: Technology Diffusion in a Developing World*. Retrieved from http://siteresources.worldbank.org/INTGEP2008/Resources/GEP08-Brochure.pdf
97 Sharma, D.C. (2004). "Global PC Market to Double by 2010." CNET News. December 14. Retrieved from http://news.cnet.com/Global-PC-market-to-double-by-2010/2100-1042_3-5490500.html
98 "Airtel 4G Launched in Kalcotta." (2012). *The Times of India*. April 11. Retrieved from timesofindia.indiantimes.com/business/india-business/india-business/Airtel-launches-4G-in-Kolkata/articleshow/12617622.cms
99 "'Made in India' Phones Set to Tap Global Markets." (2006). Reuters. Zdnet.com. May 27. Retrieved from www.expressindia.com/news/fullstory.php?newsid=68370
100 OPS A La Carte. (n.d.). "Technology Risk Assessment." Retrieved from www.opsalacarte.com/Pages/reliability/reliability_con_techrisk.htm
101 Jie, L. (2008). "China Mobile Releases Responsibility Report." *China Daily*. March 3. Retrieved from www.chinadaily.net/bizchina/2008-03/03/content_6502654.htm
102 International Telecommunications Union. (2014). "Statistics. Connect 2010: Strategic Goals. Table Key ITC Indicators for Developed and Developing Countries and the World." Retrieved from www.itu.int/en/ITU-D/Statistics/Documents/statistics/2014/ITU_Key_2005-2014_ICT_data.xls
103 OECD. (n.d.). *Information and Communications Technologies: OECD Communications Outlook 2007*. Retrieved from www.oecd.org/dataoecd/3/50/38988835.pdf
104 OECD. (n.d.). *Information and Communications Technologies: OECD Communications Outlook 2007*. Retrieved from www.oecd.org/dataoecd/3/50/38988835.pdf
105 International Telecommunications Union. (2014). "Statistics. Connect 2010: Strategic Goals. Table Key ITC Indicators for Developed and Developing Countries and the World." Retrieved

from www.itu.int/en/ITU-D/Statistics/Documents/statistics/2014/ITU_Key_2005-2014_ICT_data.xls

106 Internet World States. (n.d.). "World Internet Users March 2008." Retrieved from www.internetworldstats.com/stats.htm

107 Internet World States. (n.d.) "World Internet Penetration Rates March 2008." Retrieved from www.internetworldstats.com/stats.htm

108 Comscore. (2007). "European Internet Usage September 2007." Retrieved from www.comscore.com/solutions/technology.asp

109 "Global B2C Ecommerce Sales to Hit $1.5 Trillion This Year Driven by Growth in Emerging Markets." (2013). *E-Marketer.* February 3. Retrieved from www.emarketer.com/Article/Global-B2C-Ecommerce-Sales-Hit-15-Trillion-This-Year-Driven-By-Growth-Emerging markets/1010575

110 "Global B2C Ecommerce Sales to Hit $1.5 Trillion This Year Driven by Growth in Emerging Markets." (2013). *E-Marketer.* February 3. Retrieved from www.emarketer.com/Article/Global-B2C-Ecommerce-Sales-Hit-15-Trillion-This-Year-Driven-By-Growth-Emerging markets/1010575

111 Calculations based on Mercer's 2007 IT Pay around the World survey. Retrieved from www.mercer.com/pressrelease/details.jhtml/dynamic/idContent/1285110

112 Slaughter, M.J. (2007). "Let's Have a Real Debate about Globalization." *Wall Street Journal.* September 26, p. A21.

113 Lukoil. (n.d.). "General Information." Retrieved from www.lukoilamericas.com/geninfo.htm

114 Stewart, C. (2007). "Kudrin Stands Firm on Oil Wealth Spending." *St. Petersburg Times.* October 23. Retrieved from www.sptimes.ru/index.php?action_id=100&story_id=23398

115 "Russian PM Looks for More Trade with Canada." (2007). *Russia Today.* November 30. Retrieved from http://russiatoday.ru/business/news/17808

116 Calculations based on data from U.S. Department of Commerce Bureau of Economic Analysis. Retrieved from www.bea.gov/agency/uguide1.htm#_1_19

117 Goodman, P.S. and Story, L. (2008). "Overseas Investors Buy Aggressively in U.S." *New York Times.* January 20. Retrieved from www.nytimes.com/2008/01/20/business/20invest.html?_r=1&scp=2&sq=414&st=nyt&oref=slogin

118 Delaney, R. and Drajem, M. (2008). "U.S., China to Open Negotiations on Investment Treaty." Bloomberg.com. June 18. Retrieved from www.bloomberg.com/apps/news?pid=20601087&sid=a3EbVuiAoth0&refer=home

119 "China's CNOOC Drops Bid for Unocal." (2005). Associated Press. August 2. Retrieved from www.msnbc.msn.com/id/8795682

120 Candappa, D. and Rao, S. (2007) "Abu Dhabi Blazes Trail with Citi Deal." Reuters. November 27. Retrieved from http://today.reuters.com/news/articlenews.aspx?type=businessNews&storyid=2007-11-27T171201Z_01_L27410094_RTRUKOC_0_US-CITI-ABUDHABI-FUNDS.xml

121 Data provided by Dealogic, quoted in Thal Larsen, P. (2006). "Emerging Markets Bite Back. *Financial Times.* November 29. Retrieved from www.ft.com/intl/cms/s/0/a25f6fe8-7f4e-11db-b193-0000779e2340.html

122 Khalaf, R. (2006). "Abu Dhabi Focus on Investment in Emerging Areas." *Financial Times.* March 23. Retrieved from http://us.ft.com/ftgateway/superpage.ft?news_id=fto032220061913541832

123 UNCTAD. (2007). *World Investment Report 2007: Transnational Corporations, Extractive Industries and Development.* New York and Geneva: United Nations, p. 226. Retrieved from www.unctad.org/en/docs/wir2007_en.pdf

124 Khalaf, R. (2006). "Abu Dhabi Focus on Investment in Emerging Areas." *Financial Times.* March 23. Retrieved from http://us.ft.com/ftgateway/superpage.ft?news_id=fto032220061913541832

125 Pazarbaşıoğlu, C., Goswami, M. and Ree, J. (2007). "The Changing Face of Investors." *Finance & Development*, vol. 44, no. 1. Retrieved from www.imf.org/external/pubs/ft/fandd/2007/03/pazar.htm

Afterword

I dedicate this book to all strategists who have and will improve the world. This is because, when I began my professional career as a strategist, my main obstacle was the absence of an essential roadmap or guideline to aid me in the development of strategy. Several questions needed answers: What is the initial point of strategy development? What kinds of documents contain formal strategy, and without these documents how am I supposed to know if the strategy is completed or not? What is the theoretical basis, if any, for the experience-based recommendations found in some research monographs and textbooks? Unfortunately, I could not find a book that mapped from beginning to end these crucial points of the strategizing process. However, each new project that required the development of strategy was aided and made better by the preparations I had made on previous strategies. I gained leverage not only through these new experiences, but also because I was consciously formulating a theoretical foundation and methodological recommendations for what I was accomplishing during strategizing.

Another problem I faced was related to a lack of explanation of the differences between forecasting and prediction on one side, and planning on the other. Understanding how these three phenomena connected with the fourth phenomenon of strategy itself had never been clearly delineated by any book I had read. In my role as a strategist, attempting to solve these problems of practical necessity motivated me to analyze and develop a theoretical basis for a process of strategizing the futures of corporations and national and regional economies. The farther I travel down this road of development for a theory of strategy, the easier the process of strategizing has become, and the more efficient and powerful are the strategies developed and implemented with my participation and leadership.

When theory is not available, or is still in its infancy, practitioners in any field of activity have to rely on their intuition, multiplied by experience and a hardworking attitude. This is exactly what happened with ancient genius leaders and de facto strategists like Alexander the Great, Hannibal, and Caesar. What historian Theodore Dodge wrote about Hannibal is an apt summation: "[S]trategy, which is still nothing but the highest military expression of the art of deceit, was in that day, as a rule, mere stratagem."[1] Hannibal understood at a gut level the rudimentary concept of strategy even though he did not have the precise knowledge and vocabulary to articulate his strategic perspective. Despite progress in the evolution of strategic theory, raw intuition still gives leaders and strategists incomparable advantages. Even when leaders and strategists are armed with a defined theory, they still have to multiply and use this very powerful weapon through their intuition and hard work. Nonetheless, it is much easier to base strategic conclusions not only on intuition and hard work, but on theory as well, which is none other than a locomotive for all the other elements of strategic genius. When the initial elements of theoretical tools are developed, strategists and leaders derive a plentitude of advantages from competing, even with equally gifted individuals who are without these powerful traits and natural characteristics.

Obviously, my impetus to set forth theory and methodology are still preliminary steps on the stairs of a well-grounded theory of strategy. If I've climbed a few steps leading up to this objective then I would feel proud. I trust and hope that this book will be useful, so that scholars who decide to ascend these stairs can further enrich a true theory of strategy. I also expect that this book will be useful for practitioners of strategizing. What I would like to recommend is that, even with all the theories and methodological recommendations, you should never ignore your intuition and wisdom—they both give you hints on how to use the theory and methodology in any particular practical case and will improve your ability to foresee a strategizing future horizon.

As the main law of strategy—the law of time—states, for strategists it is always important and difficult to recognize the right moment to put the final dot on the development of any strategy. This is why the dot at the end of this sentence is the last dot in this book.

Note

1 Dodge, T. (1891). *Hannibal: A History of the Art of War among the Carthaginians and Romans Down to the Battle of Pydna, 168 B.C., with a Detailed Account of the Second Punic War.* New York: Houghton, Miffin, & Co., p. 246.

Bibliography

Abed, G.T. and Gupta, S. (Eds.) (2002). *Governance, Corruption, and Economic Performance.* International Monetary Fund: Washington, DC.

Ackerman, A. R. (Ed.) (2003). *Investing under Fire: Winning Strategies from the Masters for Bulls, Bears, and the Bewildered.* Princeton, NJ: Bloomberg Press.

Alexander, D. (2002). *Terrorism and Business: The Impact of September 11, 2001.* Ardsley, NY: Transnational Publishers, Inc.

Almaney, A. J. (2001). *Strategic Management: A Framework for Decision Making and Problem Solving.* Salem, WI: Sheffield Publishing Company.

Anderson, T. L. (Ed.) (2004). *You Have to Admit It's Getting Better: From Economic Prosperity to Environmental Quality.* Stanford, CA: Hoover Institution Press.

August, R. (2003). *International Business Law.* Upper Saddle River, NJ: Prentice Hall.

Bagwell, K. and Staiger, R. W. (2002). *The Economics of the World Trading System.* Cambridge, MA and London: MIT Press.

Barnes, I. and Bacon, J. (2010). *The Historical Atlas of Judaism.* Edision, NJ: Chartwell Books.

Barney, J. B. (2006). *Gaining and Sustaining Competitive Advantage.* Upper Saddle River, NJ: Prentice Hall.

BenDaniel, D. J., Rosenbloom, A. H. and Hanks, J. J. (Eds.) (2002). *International M&A, Joint Ventures and Beyond: Doing the Deal.* New York: John Wiley & Sons, Inc.

Booth, K. (2002). *Worlds in Collision: Terror and the Future of Global Order.* New York: Palgrave Macmillan.

Bose, P. (2003). *Alexander the Great's Art of Strategy: Lessons from the Great Empire Builder.* London: Profile.

Bush, G. W. (2010). *Decision Points.* New York: Crown Publishers.

Chia, L. S. (2003). *Southeast Asia Transformed: A Geography of Change.* Singapore: Institute of Southeast Asian Studies.

David, F. R. (2002). *Strategic Management: Concepts and Cases.* Upper Saddle River, NJ: Prentice Hall.

de Kluyver, C. and Pearce, J. (2003). *Strategy: A View from the Top (An Executive Perspective).* Upper Saddle River, NJ: Prentice Hall.

Deresky, H. (2002). *Global Management: Strategic and Interpersonal.* Upper Saddle River, NJ: Prentice Hall.

Emerging Market Investments. (1996). London: World Markets Research Centre, DRI/McGraw-Hill.

Enderwick, P. (2007). *Understanding Emerging Markets: China and India.* New York: Routledge.

Evans, P. and Wurster, T. (1997). "Strategy and the New Economics of Information." *Harvard Business Review*, Sept/Oct. pp. 13–34.

Fatehi, K. (1996). *International Management: A Cross-cultural and Functional Perspective.* Upper Saddle River, NJ: Prentice Hall.

Forbes, S. (1999). *A New Birth of Freedom: Vision for America.* Washington, DC: Regnery Publishing, Inc.

Forrester, J. W. (1977). *World Dynamics.* Cambridge, MA: MIT Press.

Freedman, L. (2013). *Strategy: A History*. Oxford, New York: Oxford University Press.
Freedman, M. and Tregoe, B. B. (2003). *The Art and Discipline of Strategic Leadership*. New York: McGraw-Hill.
Freely, J. (2009). *The Grand Turk: Sultan Mehmet II—Conqueror of Constantinople, Master of an Empire and Lord of Two Seas*. London: I.B.Tauris.
Friedman, M. (1962). *Capitalism and Freedom: A Leading Economist's View of the Proper Role of Competitive Capitalism*. Chicago: University of Chicago Press.
Gabriel, R. (2010). *Phillip II of Macedonia: Greater than Alexander*. Washington, DC: Potomac Books.
Gates, B. (1999). *The Road Ahead*. New York: Viking Penguin.
Gardels, N. (Ed.) (1997). *The Changing Global Order: World Leaders Reflect*. New York: Wiley-Blackwell.
Ghemawat, P. J. (2007). *Redefining Global Strategy: Crossing Borders in a World Where Differences Still Matter*. Watertown, MA: Harvard Business School Press.
Goodstein, L., Nolan, T. and Pfeiffer, J. W. (1993). *Applied Strategic Planning: How to Develop a Plan that Really Works*. New York: McGraw-Hill, Inc.
Grant, R. M. (2007). *Contemporary Strategy Analysis: Concepts, Techniques and Applications*. Oxford, UK: Blackwell Business.
Granberg, A. G. (2000). *Osnovy regional'noĭ ėkonomiki*. Moskva: Gos. universitet Vysshaia shkola ėkonomiki.
Greene, R. (2006). *The 33 Strategies of War*. New York: Viking.
Griset, P. L. and Mahan, S. (2003). *Terrorism in Perspective*. London: SAGE Publications.
Halibozek, E. P., Kovacich, G. L. and Jones, A. (2008). *The Corporate Security Professional's Handbook on Terrorism*. Burlington, MA: Butterworth-Heinemann.
Hanson, V. D. (2010). *Makers of Ancient Strategy: From the Persian Wars to the Fall of Rome*. Princeton, NJ: Princeton University Press.
HBR's 10 Must Reads on Strategy. (2011). Boston: Harvard Business Review Press.
Hill, C.W.L. (2000). *International Business: Competing in the Global Marketplace*. Columbus, OH: McGraw-Hill.
Horváth, G. (2015). *Space and Places in Central and Eastern Europe: Historical Trends and Perspectives of Regional Development*. New York: Routledge.
Janis, I. L. (1989). *Crucial Decisions: Leadership in Policymaking and Crisis Management*. New York: The Free Press.
Jayasuriya, K. (2005). *Asian Regional Governance: Crisis and Change*. London: Routledge.
Johnson, B. and Neledescu, O. (2005). "Impact of Terrorism on Financial Markets." *IMF Working Paper WP/05/60*. March. Washington, DC: International Monetary Fund.
Kahneman, D. (2011). *Thinking, Fast and Slow*. New York: Farrar, Straus and Giroux.
Kierkegaard, S. (1985). *Philosophical Fragments/Johannes Climacus*. Princeton, NJ: Princeton University Press.
Kissinger, H. (2014). *World Order*. New York: Penguin Press.
Kopstein, J. and Lichbach, M. I. (Eds.) (2005). *Comparative Politics: Interests, Identities, and Institutions in a Changing Global Order*. New York: Cambridge University Press.
Kvint, V. L. (Ed. and author) (1998). *Emerging Market of Russia: Sourcebook for Investment and Trade*. New York: John Wiley & Sons, Inc.
Kvint, V. L. (2004). *The Global Emerging Market in Transition: Articles, Forecasts and Studies*. New York: Fordham University Press.
Kvint, V. L. (2009). *The Global Emerging Market: Strategic Management and Economics*. New York: Routledge.
Liddell Hart, B. H. (1991). *Strategy*. 2nd revised edition. New York: Meridian.
Lumpkin, D. (2003). *Strategic Management: Creating Competitive Advantages*. New York: McGraw-Hill Irwin.
Luttwak, E. (1987). *Strategy: The Logic of War and Peace*. Cambridge, MA: Belknap Press of Harvard University Press.
Maskin, E. and Dasgupta, P. (2005). "Uncertainty and Hyperbolic Discounting." *American Economic Review*, Vol. 9, no. 4. pp. 1209-1299.

Maurice (1984). *Maurice's Strategikon: Handbook of Byzantine Military Strategy*. G.T. Dennis (Trans.). Philadelphia: University of Pennsylvania Press.

Mead, R. (2005). *International Management: Cross-cultural Dimensions*. Malden, MA: Blackwell Publishing.

Mintzberg, H., Lampel, J., Quinn, J. B. and Ghoshal, S. (2003). *The Strategy Process: Concepts, Context, Cases*. Upper Saddle River, NJ: Prentice Hall.

Mishkin, F. S. (2004). *Can Inflation Targeting Work in Emerging Market Countries?* Washington, DC: International Monetary Fund.

Mobius, M. (1996). *Mobius on Emerging Markets*. London: Financial Times/Prentice Hall.

McNamara, K. S. (2003). *Information and Communication Technologies, Poverty and Development: Learning from Experience*. Washington, DC: World Bank.

Mucchielli, J. L., Buckley, P. J. and Cordell, V. V. (Eds.). (1996). *Globalization and Regionalization: Strategies, Policies and Economic Environments*. London: Routledge.

Napoleon. (1987). *Military Maxims of Napoleon*. G. D'Aguilar. (Trans.) and D. Changler (Ed.). Boston: Da Capo Press.

North, D. C. (2005). *Understanding the Process of Economic Change*. Princeton, NJ: Princeton University Press.

Nostradamus. (1994). *Nostradamus, the Next Fifty Years: A New Translation*. P. Lemesurier. (Trans.). New York: Berkley Books.

Obstfeld, M. and Taylor, A. M. (2004). *Global Capital Markets: Integration, Crisis and Growth*. New York: Cambridge University Press.

Ohmae, K. (1991). *The Mind of the Strategist: The Art of Japanese Business*. New York: McGraw-Hill, Inc.

Oster, S. M. (1999). *Modern Competitive Analysis*. Oxford: Oxford University Press.

Overholt, W. H. (1993). *The Rise of China: How Economic Reform Is Creating a New Superpower*. New York: W.W. Norton & Company.

Pareto, V. (1984). *The Transformation of Democracy*. R. Girola (Trans.). Piscataway, NJ: Transaction Publishers.

Park, K. H. and Van Agtmael, A. W. (Eds.) (1993). *The World's Emerging Stock Market: Structure, Developments, Regulations and Opportunities*. Chicago: Probus Publishing Company.

Pearce, J. A., II and Robinson, R. B., Jr. (2007). *Strategic Management: Formulation, Implementation and Control*. New York: McGraw-Hill Irwin.

Pelle, S. (2007). *Understanding Emerging Markets: Building Business Brick by Brick*. London: SAGE Publications.

Peng, M. W. (2006). *Global Strategy*. Mason, OH: Thompson South-Western.

Phelps, E. S. (2013). *Mass Flourishing: How Grassroots Innovation Created Jobs, Challenge, and Change*. Princeton, NJ: Princeton University Press.

Pomeranz, K. (2000). *The Great Divergence: China, Europe and the Making of the Modern World Economy*. Princeton, NJ: Princeton University Press.

Porter, M. E. (1980). *Competitive Strategy: Techniques for Analyzing Industries and Competitors*. New York: Free Press.

Porth, S. J. (2003). *Strategic Management: A Cross-Functional Approach*. Upper Saddle River, NJ: Prentice Hall.

Price, M. M. (1993). *Emerging Stock Markets: A Complete Investment Guide to New Markets around the World*. New York: McGraw-Hill, Inc.

Ramo, J. C. (2004). *The Beijing Consensus*. London: The Foreign Policy Center.

Ree, S. (1995). *Strategy, Innovation and Politics: A Process Approach*. Copenhagen: Copenhagen Business School Press.

Rochester, J. M. (2002). *Between Epochs: What's Ahead for America, the World, and Global Politics in the Twenty-first Century?* Upper Saddle River, NJ: Prentice Hall.

Rosenbloom, A. H. (Ed.) (2002). *Due Diligence for Global Deal Making: The Definitive Guide to Cross-border Mergers and Acquisitions, Joint Ventures, Financings, and Strategic Alliances*. Princeton, NJ: Bloomberg Press.

Rumsfeld, D. (2013). *Rumsfeld's Rules: Leadership Lessons in Business, Politics, War, and Life*. New York: Broadside Books.

Sabonis-Helf, T. and Burghart, D. L. (Eds.) (2005). *In the Tracks of Tamerlane: Central Asia's Path to the 21st century*. Honolulu, HI: University Press of the Pacific.

Sharma, K. (2003). *Trade Policy, Growth, and Poverty in Asian Developing Countries*. London: Routledge.

Shiller, R. J. (2012). *Finance and the Good Society*. Princeton, NJ: Princeton University Press.

State of the World 2008: Toward a Sustainable Global Economy. (2008) New York: W.W. Norton.

Stradling, R., Rowe, C. and Council of Europe. (2009). *Handbook on Values for Life in a Democracy*. Strasbourg: Council of Europe Publishing.

Sun-Tzu. (2002). *The Art of War*. J. Minford (Trans.). New York: Penguin.

Suter, K. (2003). *Global Order and Global Disorder: Globalization and the Nation-state*. Westport, CT: Praeger Publishers.

Sweeney, P. (2000). *The Celtic Tiger: Ireland's Continuing Economic Miracle*. Dublin: Oak Tree Press.

Thucydides. (2006). *The History of the Peloponnesian War*. D. Lateiner and R. Crawley. (Trans.). New York: Barnes & Noble Classics.

Truman, H. S. and Rouben Mamoulian Collection (Library of Congress). (1955). *Memoirs*. Garden City, NY: Doubleday. Two Volumes.

Van Agtmael, A. (2007). *The Emerging Markets Century: How a New Breed of World-class Companies Is Overtaking the World*. New York: Free Press.

Weaver, S. C. and Weston, F. (2007). *Strategic Financial Management: Application of Corporate Finance*. Mason, OH: South-Western College Pub.

Westlund, H., Granberg, A. and Snickars, F. (Eds.) (2000). *Regional Development in Russia: Past Policies and Future Prospects*. Northampton, MA: Edward Elgar Publishing.

Wheelen, T. L. and Hunger, J. D. (2007). *Strategic Management and Business Policy*. Upper Saddle River, NJ: Prentice Hall.

Whitehead, L. (2002). *Emerging Market Democracies: East Asia and Latin America*. Baltimore, MD: The Johns Hopkins University Press.

Wright, P., Kroll, M. J. and Parnell, J. (1998). *Strategic Management: Concepts and Cases*. Upper Saddle River, NJ: Prentice Hall.

Yergin, D. and Stanislaw, J. (2002). *The Commanding Heights: The Battle for the World Economy*. New York: Free Press.

Yukl, G. (2001). *Leadership in Organizations*. Englewood Cliffs, NJ: Prentice Hall.

Yunus, M. (1999). *Banker to the Poor: Micro-lending and the Battle against World Poverty*. New York: PublicAffairs.

Index

Page numbers in *italics* refer to figures. Page numbers in **bold** refer to tables.

For Product Safety Concerns and Information please contact our EU representative GPSR@taylorandfrancis.com
Taylor & Francis Verlag GmbH, Kaufingerstraße 24, 80331 München, Germany

www.ingramcontent.com/pod-product-compliance
Lightning Source LLC
LaVergne TN
LVHW080801011026
849160LV00015B/1503
* 9 7 8 1 1 3 8 8 9 2 1 2 5 *